P9-BBV-995

ENTREPRENEURSHIP:
STARTING & OPERATING
A SMALL BUSINESS

ENTREPRENEURSHIP:
STARTING & OPERATING
A SMALL BUSINESS

Fourth Edition

Steve Mariotti • Caroline Glackin

PEARSON

Boston   Columbus   Indianapolis   New York   San Francisco   Amsterdam
Cape Town   Dubai   London   Madrid   Milan   Munich   Paris   Montréal   Toronto
Delhi   Mexico City   São Paulo   Sydney   Hong Kong   Seoul   Singapore   Taipei   Tokyo

Vice President, Business Publishing: Donna Battista
Editor-in-Chief: Stephanie Wall
Acquisitions Editor: Dan Tylman
Program Manager Team Lead: Ashley Santora
Program Manager: Claudia Fernandes
Editorial Assistant: Linda Albelli
Vice President, Product Marketing: Maggie Moylan
Director of Marketing, Digital Services and Products: Jeanette Koskinas
Executive Product Marketing Manager: Anne Fahlgren
Field Marketing Manager: Lenny Ann Raper
Senior Strategic Marketing Manager: Erin Gardner
Project Manager Team Lead: Judy Leale
Project Manager: Ilene Kahn
Operations Specialist: Diane Peirano
Creative Director: Blair Brown

Senior Art Director: Janet Slowik
Interior and Cover Designer: S4Carlisle Publishing Services
Cover Image: venimo/Fotolia
VP, Director of Digital Strategy & Assessment: Paul Gentile
Manager of Learning Applications: Paul Deluca
Digital Editor: Brian Surette
Digital Studio Manager: Diane Lombardo
Digital Studio Project Manager: Robin Lazrus
Digital Studio Project Manager: Alana Coles
Digital Studio Project Manager: Monique Lawrence
Digital Studio Project Manager: Regina DaSilva
Full-Service Project Management and Composition: Christian Holdener, S4Carlisle Publishing Services
Printer/Binder: Courier/Kendallville
Cover Printer: Courier/Kendallville
Text Font: New Aster LT Std

Credits and acknowledgments borrowed from other sources and reproduced, with permission, in this textbook appear on the appropriate page within text.

Microsoft and/or its respective suppliers make no representations about the suitability of the information contained in the documents and related graphics published as part of the services for any purpose. All such documents and related graphics are provided "as is" without warranty of any kind. Microsoft and/or its respective suppliers hereby disclaim all warranties and conditions with regard to this information, including all warranties and conditions of merchantability, whether express, implied or statutory, fitness for a particular purpose, title and non-infringement. In no event shall Microsoft and/or its respective suppliers be liable for any special, indirect or consequential damages or any damages whatsoever resulting from loss of use, data or profits, whether in an action of contract, negligence or other tortious action, arising out of or in connection with the use or performance of information available from the services.

The documents and related graphics contained herein could include technical inaccuracies or typographical errors. Changes are periodically added to the information herein. Microsoft and/or its respective suppliers may make improvements and/or changes in the product(s) and/or the program(s) described herein at any time. Partial screen shots may be viewed in full within the software version specified.

Trademarks

Microsoft® Windows®, and Microsoft Office® are registered trademarks of the Microsoft Corporation in the U.S.A. and other countries. This book is not sponsored or endorsed by or affiliated with the Microsoft Corporation.

Copyright © 2016, 2013, 2010 by Pearson Education, Inc. All rights reserved. Manufactured in the United States of America. This publication is protected by Copyright, and permission should be obtained from the publisher prior to any prohibited reproduction, storage in a retrieval system, or transmission in any form or by any means, electronic, mechanical, photocopying, recording, or likewise. For information regarding permissions, request forms and the appropriate contacts within the Pearson Education Global Rights & Permissions department, please visit www.pearsoned.com/permissions/.

Acknowledgements of third party content appear on the appropriate page within the text, which constitutes an extension of this copyright page.

Unless otherwise indicated herein, any third-party trademarks that may appear in this work are the property of their respective owners and any references to third-party trademarks, logos or other trade dress are for demonstrative or descriptive purposes only. Such references are not intended to imply any sponsorship, endorsement, authorization, or promotion of Pearson's products by the owners of such marks, or any relationship between the owner and Pearson Education, Inc. or its affiliates, authors, licensees or distributors.

Library of Congress Cataloging-in-Publication Data
Mariotti, Steve, 1953-
Entrepreneurship: starting & operating a small business/Steve Mariotti, Caroline Glackin.—Fourth Edition.
 pages cm
 Includes index.
 ISBN 978-0-13-393445-8—ISBN 0-13-393445-4 1. New business enterprises—Management. 2. Entrepreneurship.
I. Glackin, Caroline. II. Title.
 HD62.5.M3567 2015
 658.1'1—dc23

2014032028

10 9 8 7 6 5 4 3 2 1

ISBN 10:   0-13-393445-4
ISBN 13: 978-0-13-393445-8

Special thanks to Shelby Cullom Davis.
Also thanks to Kathryn Davis, Shelby M. C. Davis,
Kimberly La Manna, Abby Moffat,
and Diana Davis Spencer.

—*Steve Mariotti*

To my children, Elise and Spencer, whose support and love
are essential parts of this book.
To my parents, Howard and Maria Wiedenman,
who truly understood the importance
of education. My love and gratitude.

—*Caroline Glackin*

Brief Contents

UNIT 1   **Entrepreneurial Pathways**   **1**

Chapter 1   Entrepreneurs Recognize Opportunities   2

Chapter 2   The Business Plan: Road Map to Success   34

          Honest Tea Business Plan   **65**

Chapter 3   Creating Business from Opportunity   92

Unit 1   **Entrepreneurial Pathways: SPANX—Idea to Entrepreneurial Opportunity**   **123**

UNIT 2   **Integrated Marketing**   **127**

Chapter 4   Exploring Your Market   128

Chapter 5   Developing the Right Marketing Mix and Plan   156

Chapter 6   Smart Selling and Effective Customer Service   196

Unit 2   **Integrated Marketing: Kitchen Arts & Letters, Inc.—An Independent Bookstore Defies Industry Odds**   **219**

UNIT 3   **Show Me the Money: Finding, Securing, and Managing It**   **223**

Chapter 7   Understanding and Managing Start-Up, Fixed, and Variable Costs   224

Chapter 8   Using Financial Statements to Guide a Business   250

Chapter 9   Cash Flow and Taxes   286

Chapter 10   Financing Strategy & Tactics   316

Unit 3   **Show Me the Money: Finding, Securing, and Managing It— Lee's Ice Cream**   **346**

UNIT 4   **Operating a Small Business Effectively**   **351**

Chapter 11   Addressing Legal Issues and Managing Risk   352

Chapter 12   Operating for Success   384

Chapter 13   Management, Leadership, & Ethical Practices   416

Unit 4   **Operating a Small Business Effectively: ONLC Training Centers—Virtual IT Training in a Classroom**   **453**

UNIT 5   **Cashing in the Brand**   **457**

Chapter 14   Franchising, Licensing, and Harvesting: Cashing in Your Brand   458

Unit 5   **Cashing in the Brand: Honest Tea— From Start-Up to Harvest**   **477**

Appendix 1   Sample Student Business Plan   483

Appendix 2   BizBuilder Business Plan   511

Appendix 3   Resources for Entrepreneurs   519

Appendix 4   Useful Formulas and Equations   525

          Glossary   527

          Index   533

Contents

UNIT 1   Entrepreneurial Pathways   1

Chapter 1   Entrepreneurs Recognize Opportunities   2

Entrepreneurship   3

   What Is an Entrepreneur?   3

   The Free-Enterprise System   4

   Voluntary Exchange   5

   Benefits and Challenges of Free Enterprise   5

   What Is a Small Business?   6

   Definitions of Success—Monetary and Other   6

   Taking the Long View   7

Benefits and Costs of Becoming an Entrepreneur   7

   Potential Benefits of Entrepreneurship   8

   Potential Costs of Entrepreneurship   9

   Cost/Benefit Analysis   10

   Opportunity Cost   11

   Seeking Advice and Information to Succeed   11

Entrepreneurial Options   13

How Do Entrepreneurs Find Opportunities to Start New Businesses?   15

   Entrepreneurs Creatively Exploit Changes in Our World   15

   Where Others See Problems, Entrepreneurs Recognize Opportunities   16

   Train Your Mind to Recognize Business Opportunities   16

   Entrepreneurs Use Their Imaginations   17

An Idea Is Not Necessarily an Opportunity   17

   Opportunity Is Situational   18

   The Five Roots of Opportunity in the Marketplace   18

   Integrating Internal and External Opportunities   18

   Establishing Strategies   19

Paths to Small Business Ownership   20

   Securing Franchise Rights   21

   Buying an Existing Business   21

   Licensing Technology   21

   The Many Faces of Entrepreneurship   22

Making the Business Work Personally and Professionally   23

   A Business Must Make a Profit to Stay in Business   23

   Profit Is the Sign That the Entrepreneur Is Adding Value   23

   Profit Results from the Entrepreneur's Choices   23

   Seven Rules for Building a Successful Business   24

   The Team Approach   24

Chapter 2   The Business Plan: Road Map to Success   34

Feasibility Analysis: Does My Idea Work?   36

   Analyzing Product and/or Service Feasibility   36

   Analyzing Market and Industry Feasibility   37

   Analyzing Financial Feasibility   39

Creating a Business Model Canvas   40

What Is a Business Plan?   43

Why Do You Need a Business Plan?   44

   Writing a Business Plan Early Will Save You Time and Money   44

   Your Business Plan Is the Key to Raising Capital   45

   The Business Plan Is an Operations Guide   45

Business Plan Components   45

   Cover Page and Table of Contents   46

   Executive Summary: A Snapshot of Your Business   46

   Mission and Culture: Your Dreams for the Organization   47

   Company Description—Background and Track Record   48

   Opportunity Analysis and Research—Testing Ideas   48

   Marketing Strategy and Plan: Reaching Customers   49

   Management and Operations: Making the Plan Happen   50

   Financial Analysis and Projections: Translating Action into Money   51

   Funding Request and Exit Strategy: The Ask and the Return   55

   Appendices: Making the Case in Greater Detail   56

Business Plan Suggestions   56

Presenting Your Business Plan   57

Business Plan and Venture
Competitions   59

Honest Tea Business Plan   65

Chapter 3   **Creating Business
from Opportunity   92**

Apple and the Personal Computer   93

Business Definition   94

What Sort of Organization Do
You Want?   95

Your Company's Core Values   95

Your Company's Mission Is to Satisfy
Customers   96

Your Company's Vision Is the Broader
Perspective   97

Your Company's Culture Defines the
Work Environment   97

The Decision Process   98

Your Competitive Advantage   99

Find Your Competitive Advantage by
Determining What Consumers Need
and Want   100

You Have Unique Knowledge
of Your Market   100

The Six Factors of Competitive
Advantage   101

Is Your Competitive Advantage Strong
Enough?   101

Checking Out the Competition   102

The Most Chocolate Cake Company   103

Competitive Strategy: Business Definition
and Competitive Advantage   105

Feasibility Revisited: The Economics of One
Unit as a Litmus Test   106

Defining the Unit of Sale   107

Cost of Goods Sold and Gross Profit   107

Your Business and the Economics
of One Unit   108

The Cost of Direct Labor in the EOU—
An Example   110

Hiring Others to Make the Unit of Sale   110

Going for Volume   111

Determining the Value of
a Business   113

Asset Valuation Method   113

Earnings Valuation Method   113

Cash Flow Valuation Method   114

Unit 1   **Entrepreneurial Pathways:
SPANX—Idea to Entrepreneurial
Opportunity   123**

UNIT 2   **Integrated Marketing   127**

Chapter 4   **Exploring Your Market   128**

Markets and Marketing Defined   130

A Business That Markets versus a
Market-Driven Business   130

Research Prepares You for Success   130

Research Your Market *Before* You Open
Your Business   130

Types and Methods of Research   131

Getting Information Directly from the Source:
Primary Research   131

Getting Information Indirectly:
Secondary Research   133

Research Helps You Know Your
Customer   135

Customer Research   135

Industry Research: The 50,000-Foot
Perspective   137

Make Research an Integral Part
of Your Business   138

How Customers Decide to Buy   139

Owning a Perception in the
Customer's Mind   140

Features Create Benefits   140

Home Depot: Teaching Customers
So They Will Return   141

Which Segment of the Market
Will You Target?   141

Successful Segmenting: The Body Shop   142

Applying Market Segmentation Methods   142

The Product Life Cycle   144

Is Your Market Saturated?   146

Market Positioning: Drive Home Your
Competitive Advantage   146

Developing a Marketing Plan   147

Chapter 5   **Developing the Right Marketing
Mix and Plan   156**

The Four Marketing Factors   157

Product: What Are You Selling?   158

Create Your Total Product or Service
Concept   158

Focus Your Brand   159

Ford's Costly Failure: The Edsel   159

Ford's Focus on Success:
The Mustang 160

How to Build Your Brand 160

Price: What It Says about Your
Product 162

Strategies and Tactics for Effective
Pricing 162

Place: Location, Location, Location! 164

Key Factors in Deciding on
a Location 165

Promotion: Advertising + Publicity 165

Use Integrated Marketing Communications
for Success 165

Reinforce the Company's Unique Selling
Proposition 166

Promotional Planning 167

Determine a Promotional Budget 167

The Advertising Advantage 169

Types of Advertising 170

Media Planning and Buying:
Focus on Your Customer 170

Marketing Materials Should Reinforce
Your Competitive Advantage 171

Sales-Promotion Solutions 172

When to Use Promotional Tools 172

Advertising Specialties 172

Trade Show Exhibits 172

Mall Carts or Kiosks 173

Alternative Marketing 174

Other Media Venues 175

E-Active Marketing 175

Publicity Potential 179

Generating Publicity 179

Telling the Story 179

Sample Press Release 180

Follow Up a Press Release 180

Public Relations 180

The Fifth P: Philanthropy 182

Cause-Related Marketing 182

Gaining Goodwill 183

Not-for-Profit Organizations 183

What Entrepreneurs Have Built 184

You Have Something to Contribute 184

Developing a Marketing Plan 184

Marketing Analysis 185

Marketing as a Fixed Cost 185

Calculate Your Breakeven Point 186

Chapter 6 **Smart Selling and Effective
Customer Service 196**

Selling Skills Are Essential to Business
Success 197

Selling Is a Great Source of Market
Research 198

The Essence of Selling Is Teaching 198

The Principles of Selling 198

The Sales Call 200

Electronic Mail, Blogs, and Social
Networks 200

Prequalify Your Sales Calls 201

Focus on the Customer 201

The Eight-Step Sales Call 202

Three Call Behaviors of Successful
Salespeople 203

Analyze Your Sales Calls to Become
a Star Salesperson 204

Turning Objections into Advantages 204

Use Technology to Sell 205

Successful Businesses Need Customers
Who Return 206

Customer Service Is Keeping Customers
Happy 206

The Costs of Losing a Customer 206

Customer Complaints Are Valuable 207

Customer Relationship Management
Systems 208

Why Does CRM Matter? 209

Components of CRM for the Small
Business 210

How Technology Supports CRM 211

Unit 2 **Integrated Marketing:
Kitchen Arts & Letters, Inc.—An
Independent Bookstore Defies
Industry Odds 219**

UNIT 3 **Show Me the Money: Finding,
Securing, and Managing It 223**

Chapter 7 **Understanding and Managing Start-Up,
Fixed, and Variable Costs 224**

What Does It Cost to Operate a
Business? 225

Start-Up Investment 226

Brainstorm to Avoid Start-Up Surprises 226

Keep a Reserve Equal to One-Half the
Start-Up Investment 227

Predict the Payback Period 228

Estimate Value 229

Fixed and Variable Costs: Essential Building Blocks   230

Calculating Critical Costs   230

Calculating Total Gross Profit (Contribution Margin)   231

Calculating EOU When You Sell Multiple Products   231

Fixed Operating Costs   233

Fixed Operating Costs Do Change Over Time   233

Allocate Fixed Operating Costs Where Possible   234

The Dangers of Fixed Costs   235

Using Accounting Records to Track Fixed and Variable Costs   235

Three Reasons to Keep Good Records Every Day   236

Cash versus Accrual Accounting Methods   238

Recognizing Categories of Costs   239

Chapter 8

Using Financial Statements to Guide a Business   250

Scorecards for the Entrepreneur: What Do Financial Statements Show?   251

Income Statements: Showing Profit and Loss Over Time   252

Parts of an Income Statement   252

A Basic Income Statement   253

The Double Bottom Line   253

An Income Statement for a More Complex Business   254

The Balance Sheet: A Snapshot of Assets, Liabilities, and Equity at a Point in Time   256

Short- and Long-Term Assets   257

Current and Long-Term Liabilities   258

The Balance Sheet Equation   258

The Balance Sheet Shows Assets and Liabilities Obtained through Financing   258

The Balance Sheet Shows How a Business Is Financed   259

Analyzing a Balance Sheet   260

Depreciation   262

Financial Ratio Analysis: What Is It and What Does It Mean to You?   262

Income Statement Ratios   262

Balance-Sheet Analysis   265

Chapter 9

Cash Flow and Taxes   286

Cash Flow: The Lifeblood of a Business   287

The Income Statement Does Not Show Available Cash   288

Rules to Keep Cash Flowing   289

Noncash Expenses Can Distort the Financial Picture   289

The Working Capital Cycle   289

The Cyclical and Seasonal Nature of Cash Flow   290

Reading a Cash Flow Statement   292

The Cash Flow Equation   292

Forecasting Cash Flow: The Cash Budget   292

Creating a Healthy Cash Flow   293

Managing Inventory to Manage Cash   295

Managing Receivables to Manage Cash   297

The Cash Effects of Accounts Receivable   297

The Life Cycle of Accounts Receivable   297

The Financing of Accounts Receivable   298

Managing Accounts Payable to Manage Cash   299

Negotiating Payment   299

Timing Payables   299

Capital Budgeting and Cash Flow   300

The Burn Rate   301

The Value of Money Changes Over Time   301

The Future Value of Money   301

The Present Value of Money   303

Taxes   304

Cash Flow and Taxes   304

Filing Tax Returns   304

Collecting Sales Tax   305

Tax Issues for Different Legal Structures   305

Make Tax Time Easier by Keeping Good Records   306

Chapter 10

Financing Strategy & Tactics   316

Going It Alone Versus Securing Financing   317

How Often Do Small Businesses Really Fail?   318

What Is the Best Type of Financing for You and Your Business?   318

Gifts and Grants   319

Debt Financing   320

Debt Financing: Pros and Cons   320

Equity Financing   322

Equity Financing: Pros and Cons   323

Where and How to Find Capital That
Works for You   324
   Having an Excellent Business Plan Goes
   a Long Way   324
   How Capital Sources Read Your Business
   Plan   324
   Family and Friends   324
   Financial Institutions and Dimensions
   of Credit   324
   Community Development Financial
   Institutions (CDFIs)   328
   Venture Capitalists   329
   Angels   330
   Insurance Companies   331
   Vendor Financing   331
   Federally Supported Investment
   Companies   331
   Financing for Rural/Agricultural
   Businesses   332
   Self-Funding: Bootstrap Financing   332
Accessing Sources Through Online
Networking   332
Investors Want Their Money to Grow:
Can You Make It Happen?   333
   How Stocks Work   334
   How Bonds Work   335

**Unit 3   Show Me the Money:
Finding, Securing, and Managing It—
Lee's Ice Cream   346**

**UNIT 4   Operating a Small Business
Effectively   351**

**Chapter 11   Addressing Legal Issues
and Managing Risk   352**

Business Legal Structures   353
   Sole Proprietorship   353
   Partnership   355
   Corporation   356
   Tips for Entrepreneurs Who Want to Start
   a Nonprofit Organization   358
Contracts: The Building Blocks
of Business   361
   Working with an Attorney   361
   Drafting a Contract   362
   Letter of Agreement   363
   Breach of Contract   363
   Small Claims Court   363
   Arbitration   363
   A Contract Is No Substitute for Trust   363

The Uniform Commercial Code (UCC)   364
The Law of Agency   364
Bankruptcy   365
Protecting Intangible Assets:
Intellectual Property   367
   Trademarks and Service Marks   367
   Copyright   369
   Electronic Rights   369
   Patents   370
Protecting Tangible Assets: Risk
Management   371
   Insurance Protects Your Business
   from Disaster   371
   Basic Coverage for Small Business   371
   How Insurance Companies Make
   Money   372
   Protect Your Computer and Data   373
   Disaster Recovery Plans   373
Licenses, Permits, and Certificates   374

Chapter 12   Operating for Success   384

Operations Permit Businesses to Deliver
on Their Promises   386
The Production-Distribution Chain   386
Supply Chain Management   387
   Finding Suppliers   388
   Managing Inventory   388
Facilities, Location and Design   390
Key Factors in Deciding on a Location   391
   Facilities Design and Layout   394
   Special Considerations for Home-Based
   Businesses   398
   Special Considerations for Web-Based
   Businesses   398
Defining Quality: It Is a Matter of Market
Positioning   399
   Profits Follow Quality   399
Organization Wide Quality Initiatives   400
   Benchmarking   400
   ISO 9000   401
   Six Sigma   402
   Total Quality Management   402
   Malcolm Baldrige Award   402
Using Technology to Your Advantage   403
   Computer Access Is Essential   403
   Capture the Potential of the Telephone   404
   Identify Market-Specific Software and
   Technology   404
   Electronic Storefront (Web Site)   405

Chapter 13 **Management, Leadership, & Ethical Practices   416**

The Entrepreneur as Leader   417

Leadership Styles That Work   417

How Entrepreneurs Pay Themselves   418

Manage Your Time Wisely   419

Business Management: Building a Team   420

What Do Managers Do?   421

Adding Employees to Your Business   421

Growing Your Team   427

Creating and Managing Organizational Culture   428

Determining Organizational Structure   428

Getting the Best Out of Your Employees   430

Human Resources Fundamentals   430

Performance Management   432

Firing and Laying Off Employees   434

Ethical Leadership and Ethical Organizations   434

An Ethical Perspective   435

Establishing Ethical Standards   435

Corporate Ethical Scandals   436

Doing the Right Thing in Addition to Doing Things Right   438

Balancing the Needs of Owners, Customers, and Employees   438

Social Responsibility and Ethics   438

Leading with Integrity and Examples   439

Encourage Your Employees to Be Socially Responsible   439

Unit 4   Operating a Small Business Effectively: ONLC Training Centers—Virtual IT Training in a Classroom   453

UNIT 5   Cashing in the Brand   457

Chapter 14 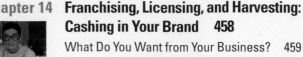 **Franchising, Licensing, and Harvesting: Cashing in Your Brand   458**

What Do You Want from Your Business?   459

Continuing the Business for the Family   460

Growth through Diversification   460

Growth through Licensing and Franchising   461

Focus Your Brand   461

When Licensing Can Be Effective   461

Franchising Revisited from the Franchisor Perspective   462

How a McDonald's Franchise Works   462

Do Your Research before You Franchise   463

Harvesting and Exiting Options   463

When to Harvest Your Business   463

How to Value a Business   464

The Science of Valuation   465

Creating Wealth by Selling a Profitable Business   465

Harvesting Options   466

Exit Strategy Options   468

Investors Will Care about Your Exit Strategy   469

Unit 5   Cashing in the Brand: Honest Tea—From Start-Up to Harvest   477

Appendix 1   Sample Student Business Plan   483

Appendix 2   BizBuilder Business Plan   511

Appendix 3   Resources for Entrepreneurs   519

Appendix 4   Useful Formulas and Equations   525

Glossary   527

Index   533

Preface
Helping Students Own Their Future

Entrepreneurship: Starting and Operating a Small Business (ESOSB), Fourth Edition, is the newest edition in a line of entrepreneurship textbooks written by Steve Mariotti, founder of the Network for Teaching Entrepreneurship (NFTE). Once again, it is written with professor and entrepreneur Caroline Glackin, and it promotes entrepreneurship as a career option for college students.

Business students, as well as those from other disciplines, can benefit from *ESOSB*. For business students, it recasts their prior learning from a typical corporate context and focuses it on small and entrepreneurial enterprises. For students in such fields as hospitality, the arts, engineering, and fashion merchandising, the text introduces key business concepts and provides examples from a broad range of careers. Cases from hospitality, technology, retail, manufacturing, distribution, real estate, finance, and not-for-profit organizations bring a wealth of learning opportunities. Most importantly, *ESOSB 4e* is a balanced mix of the academic and applied components of entrepreneurship education. Students are introduced to the theories, methods, and knowledge and skills required of entrepreneurs and are immediately given practical examples and discussion opportunities. Using the Application Exercises and Exploring Online features at the end of each chapter, they are encouraged to take this new knowledge and apply it in their own lives, so that the course materials are reinforced and internalized.

Highlights of New Content and Changes

Entrepreneurship: Starting and Operating a Small Business, Fourth Edition, contains new content and some changes, including the following:

- Three new Chapter Openers include Mercedes, University Parent, and inDinero.
- Nine new short End-of-Chapter Case Studies: Urban Decay, Gat Creek Furniture, Gentle Rest Slumber, Dr. Farrah Gray, Happy Belly Curbside Kitchen, BNI, Gelato Fiasco, The Bun Company, and Anago Cleaning Systems.
- Seven new longer End-of-Chapter Case Studies: Foursquare, Empact, Amazon.com, Damon White Party Promotions, Airbnb, AYZH, and iContact.
- All new Unit Cases. These are more interesting and relatable for students and include: Spanx, Kitchen Arts & Letters, Inc., Lee's Ice Cream, ONLC Training Centers, and Honest Tea.
- Step into the Shoes, Entrepreneurial Wisdom, BizFacts, and Global Impact Features. These have been updated and expanded with 16 new featured items, including 12 Step into the Shoes and 4 Global Impact Features. Among the newly featured people and organizations are: Indeed.com, In-N-Out Burgers, Sweet dis(Solve), Twitter, ContextMedia, Mental Floss, Zhang Xin, P'Kolino, Jack Threads,

Rent the Runway, Tom's, Vostu, American Public University, and TechWorld These features connect chapter content to business facts and examples to reinforce learning.

■ Honest Tea Featured Business Plan. From its early stage funding search, this example provides students with an interesting start-up plan for a company that is also featured in the Unit 5 case. This bookends the contents of the text.

■ Business Model Canvas. The Osterwalder and Pigneur Business Model Canvas is introduced in Chapter 2 with the example of the University Parent Business Plan that is included in Appendix 1. Students are encouraged to develop a business model and to explore the Lean Startup process.

■ BizBuilder Business Plan Questions. These have been modified to clarify the work and connect the content to student work using the business plan templates.

■ Chapter Learning Objectives. The objectives have been revised to conform more fully to the categories of knowledge acquisition, comprehension, application, analysis, synthesis, and evaluation commonly assessed in higher education.

Combining Street Smarts and Academic Smarts

Entrepreneurship: Starting and Operating a Small Business, Fourth Edition, is an extension of the academic programs developed by Steve Mariotti under the auspices of NFTE. Since 1987, NFTE has reached over 500,000 graduates and trained more than 5,000 teachers in 15 countries to impart its innovative entrepreneurship curriculum through its 17 U.S. sites and 8 international program partners. NFTE is widely viewed as a world leader in promoting entrepreneurial literacy and has a proven track record of helping young people start a great variety of successful ventures.

This textbook unites Steve Mariotti's experience with relevant academic theory and practice, supported by a rich variety of examples and stories. Caroline Glackin brings years of experience in the university classroom, as a lender to small and microbusinesses, and as an entrepreneur and small business owner. Together, these two authors have produced a text that is practical, useful, and academically strong.

Organization

Entrepreneurship: Starting and Operating a Small Business, Fourth Edition, is organized to follow the life cycle of an entrepreneurial venture from concept through implementation into harvesting or replication. It is a comprehensive text written in light of the reality that college students often take only one course in entrepreneurship and the topic is covered in a multitude of ways. For instructors who will teach the course as a "business plan," *ESOSB 4e* offers step-by-step content to build a plan over a semester or a quarter. For those who focus on the management of small and entrepreneurial ventures, there is an abundance of high-quality material on the critical topics of management, human resources, marketing, and operations for such ventures. For those charged with teaching a comprehensive introductory course, all of the components are provided.

Chapter Learning System

Chapter Openers Set the Stage

Each chapter starts with an inspirational quote, an introduction, and Learning Objectives that provide a "road map" so readers know where they are headed. Readers connect with a story of a real business in the opening vignette that sets the stage for upcoming material.

"Step into the Shoes" of the Experts

Step into the Shoes features appear in each chapter and offer insight into the business practices of entrepreneurs and an opportunity to discuss the brief example. It brings the content to life with real-world application.

Step into the Shoes . . .

Russell Simmons Makes Rap Happen

In the late 1980s, Russell Simmons was promoting rap concerts at the City University of New York. At the time, rap was considered a passing fad, but Simmons was passionate about it. Even though most record executives thought rap would be over in a year or two, Simmons believed it was a business opportunity. He formed Def Jam Records with fellow student Rick Rubin for $5,000. Within a year, they produced hit records by Run DMC and LL Cool J, and Simmons went on to become a multimedia mogul.

Simmons took a chance on this opportunity because he felt that, if you personally know 10 people who are eager to buy your product or service, 10 *million* would be willing to buy it if they know about it. He was right about rap's popular potential,

perceived opportunities: You may be passionate about something, but there may not be enough consumer interest to sustain an actual business venture.

Simmons loved rap and hoped other people would, too. That was the internal factor—he had the passion to sustain himself as he worked relentlessly to make his dream come true. As it turned out, music fans at that time were looking for a fresh sound. Rap filled the bill. This was an external opportunity that coincided with Simmons's

BizFacts

BizFacts impart useful information regarding entrepreneurship statistics, company practices, or business applications.

BizFacts

- There are 27.3 million businesses in the United States; approximately 99.9 percent of them are small companies with fewer than 500 employees.
- Small businesses in America employed 49.2 percent of the country's private (nongovernment) workforce, hired 43 percent of high-tech workers, and created 64 percent of net new jobs annually over the last decade.
- Home-based businesses make up 52 percent and franchises 2 percent of all small firms.
- Small businesses represent 99.7 percent of all companies with employees.
- Small firms constituted 98 percent of all identified exporters and produced 33 percent of the country's known export value in fiscal year 2010.

Source: U.S. Small Business Administration, accessed March 9, 2014, http://www.sba.gov.

Entrepreneurial Wisdom

Entrepreneurial Wisdom contains insights or advice that will help students in the preparation of a business plan or management of an enterprise.

Entrepreneurial Wisdom . . .

A useful way to evaluate a business idea is to look at its strengths, weaknesses, opportunities, and threats (SWOT). This is called SWOT analysis.

- **Strengths**—All the capabilities and positive points the company has, from experience to contacts. These are internal to the organization.
- **Weaknesses**—All the negatives the company faces, such as lack of capital or training or failure to set up a

workable accounting system. These are internal to the organization.

- **Opportunities**—Any positive external events or circumstances that can help the entrepreneur get ahead of the competition.
- **Threats**—Any external factors, events, or circumstances that can harm the business, such as competitors, legal issues, or declining economies.

Global Impact

Global Impact, featured in each chapter, provides examples of entrepreneurial ventures around the world or information that can be applied in global trade.

Global Impact . . .

Upcycling Waste Internationally—TerraCycle, Inc.

Wu Kaixiang/Corbis Images

In 2003, John Szaky's TerraCycle won a business plan contest from Carrot Capital for $1 million in seed funding. But the venture capital firm wanted TerraCycle to drop its environmental focus, and Szaky turned down the offer. It was a critical decision that later helped the business achieve its competitive advantage.

TerraCycle converts unrecyclable packaging waste to upcycled products. An early inspiration was implemented when TerraCycle ran out of money to buy bottles in which to sell fertilizer derived from worm waste. It was decided to

a few examples of the more than one hundred TerraCycle products sold in large retail chains, including Home Depot, Whole Foods, Wal-Mart, and Target. The concept has spread to the United Kingdom, Brazil, Mexico, Israel, and Canada, among others. By working with concerned groups in each country, TerraCycle has the potential of becoming an iconic representative of up-

Honest Tea Business Plan

This is the plan developed by founders Seth Goldman and Barry Nalebuff during Honest Tea's first year of operations. It appears following Chapter 2 and includes a comprehensive market analysis and detailed historical financials. The business raised over $1 million at a time when sales were less than $250,000 and the company had operating losses. The Honest Tea plan is an excellent example for students and one that many of them will understand, to some extent, as customers of bottled tea.

Business Plan for 1999
December 1998
4905 Del Ray Avenue, Suite 304
Bethesda, Maryland 20814
Phone: 301-652-3556
Fax: 301-652-3557

E-mail: sethandbarry@honesttea.com

Table of Contents

Mission Statement 70
Executive Summary 71
Company Story 71
The Product 72
   The Taste 72
   Low in Calories 72
   Health Benefits of Brewed Tea 73
   Cultural Experience of Tea 73
   Flagship Line of Flavors 74
Production and Manufacturing 74
Market Opportunity 75
   Beyond Snapple—The Emerging Market for Quality Bottled Tea . . . 75
   Profile of Target Customer 76
   Market Research 77
   Market Response 77
Marketing and Distribution 79
   National Natural/Specialty Foods Channels 80
   Higher End Food Service 80
   Promotion 80
   Packaging and Pricing 81
   International Markets 81
   Product Development and Future Products 81
Management 81
   President & TeaEO 81
   Chairman of the Board 82
   Brewmaster 82
   National Sales Director 82
   Retail Sales Manager 82
   Consultants and Advisors 82
Statement and Aspirations for Social Responsibility . . 83
Financial Statements—Year-to-Date and Projections . . 83
The Investment Opportunity 90
   The Offering 90
   Financing History 90
   Exit Strategies 90
   Investment Risks 90
   Competitive Advantage 90
A Parting Thought 91

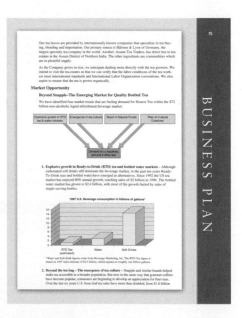

Our tea leaves are provided by internationally known companies that specialize in tea buying, blending and importation. Our primary source is Hälssen & Lyon of Germany, the largest specialty tea company in the world. Another, Assam Tea Traders, has direct ties to tea estates in the Assam District of Northern India. The other ingredients are commodities which are in plentiful supply.

As the Company grows in size, we anticipate dealing more directly with the tea growers. We intend to visit the tea estates so that we can verify that the labor conditions of the tea workers meet international standards and International Labor Organization conventions. We also aspire to ensure that the tea is grown organically.

Market Opportunity

Beyond Snapple–The Emerging Market for Quality Bottled Tea

We have identified four market trends that are fueling demand for Honest Tea within the $72 billion non-alcoholic liquid refreshment beverage market.

1. **Explosive growth in Ready-to-Drink (RTD) tea and bottled water markets** – Although carbonated soft drinks still dominate the beverage market, in the past ten years Ready-To-Drink teas and bottled water have emerged as alternatives. Since 1992 the US tea market has enjoyed 60% annual growth, reaching sales of $2 billion in 1996. The bottled water market has grown to $2.4 billion, with most of the growth fueled by sales of single-serving bottles.

2. **Beyond the tea bag – the emergence of tea culture** – Snapple and similar brands helped make tea accessible to a broader population. But now in the same way that gourmet coffees have become popular, consumers are beginning to develop an appreciation for finer teas. Over the last six years U.S. loose leaf tea sales have more than doubled, from $1.8 billion

75

BUSINESS PLAN

End-of-Chapter Learning Portfolio

End-of-chapter materials help students demonstrate a working understanding of key concepts and develop critical-thinking skills.

All chapters include the following:

- **Key Terms** list.
- **Critical Thinking Exercises** that require students to consider important issues and support thoughtful responses.
- **Key Concept Questions** that review core topics.
- **Application Exercises** that give students a structured opportunity to reinforce chapter topics through experience.
- **Exploring Your Community** and **Exploring Online** assignments that invite students to go into their business communities or search online for information.
- **BizBuilder Business Plan Questions,** which guide students through the development of business plan components as they learn new information throughout the book.
- **Cases for Analysis,** including one short case and one longer case with analytical questions. Cases cover a variety of issues and draw on real business scenarios. Examples of businesses that may be familiar to students include Foursquare, Urban Decay, and Amazon .com. Other organizations that may be less familiar include Happy Belly Curbside Kitchen, Gelato Fiasco, Anago Cleaning Systems, and AYZH. These cases reflect a diverse set of entrepreneurs, industries, and geographic locations.

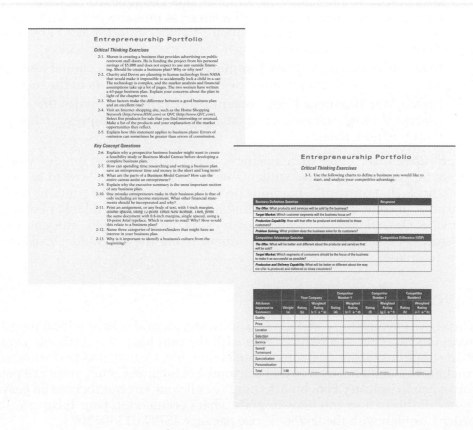

Additional Resources

Instructor Resources

At the Instructor Resource Center, www.pearsonhighered.com/irc, instructors can easily register to gain access to a variety of instructor resources available with this text in downloadable format. If assistance is needed, our dedicated technical support team is ready to help with the media supplements that accompany this text. Visit http://247.pearsoned.com for answers to frequently asked questions and toll-free user support phone numbers.

The following supplements are available with this text:

- Instructor's Resource Manual
- Test Bank
- TestGen® Computerized Test Bank
- PowerPoint Presentations

Student Resources

BizBuilder Business Plan Worksheets and Templates Online

Go to www.pearsonhighered.com/mariotti to download business plan and presentation templates that will help students write a plan and present it.

- **BizBuilder Business Plan Worksheets** provide step-by-step instructions on building a business plan. The MS Word document contains a comprehensive set of questions and tables organized by business plan section. The Excel document includes Start-Up Costs, Sales Projections, Income Statement, Balance Sheet, Cash Flow, and Ratio Analysis worksheets.
- **BizBuilder Business Plan Template** provides a professional-looking format for a business plan that ties in with assignments in the text.
- **BizBuilder Business Plan Presentation Template** guides the student through the process of creating a PowerPoint presentation for a business plan.

Students can build their business plans using the BizBuilder worksheets. Appendix 2 provides students with instructions on how to use the worksheets that mirror the planning process in the book and contains more questions in some areas than are found in commercially available planning software. Once they have created a plan using the worksheets, students can generate a professional-looking document using the BizBuilder Business Plan Template.

LivePlan

Through a partnership with Palo Alto Software, we're able to provide 6-month access to LivePlan at a reduced rate with the purchase of a textbook. LivePlan simplifies business planning, budgeting, forecasting, and performance tracking for small businesses and startups. Set business goals, compare performance to industry benchmarks, and see all your key numbers in an easy-to-use dashboard so you know exactly what's going on in your business. To order LivePlan with the textbook, use package ISBN 0134072073.

About the Authors

STEVE MARIOTTI, founder of the Network for Teaching Entrepreneurship (NFTE), is considered one of today's leading experts in education for at-risk youth. In 1982, he changed career paths when he decided to leave the corporate sector and become a special education teacher in the New York City public school system.

Mariotti's first assignment was in the East New York section of Brooklyn, and his last was in the Fort Apache section of the South Bronx. During his six-and-a-half years teaching, Mariotti discovered he could successfully motivate even his most challenging students by teaching them how to run a business. This experience inspired him to create a new kind of program—the first to bring entrepreneurial education to low-income youth.

In 1987, Mariotti founded The Network for Teaching Entrepreneurship (NFTE). Today, NFTE's mission is to provide entrepreneurship education programs to young people from low-income communities around the world. NFTE's programs have a proven track record of success, and the network is widely viewed as the thought leader in the field. NFTE is an active member of the Council on Foreign Relations. In 2013, Mariotti traveled to Southeast Asia as a guest of the U.S. State Department on a mission to spread entrepreneurial education to youth from emerging economies in the region.

Mariotti was recently nominated for a Pulitzer Prize for his work chronicling the lives of entrepreneurs worldwide for *The Huffington Post* and for a Nobel Peace Prize for his pioneering work in entrepreneurial education. A lifelong advocate for low-income students, Mariotti is the recipient of numerous awards including:

- Ernst & Young Entrepreneur of the Year Award
- Bernard A. Goldhirsh Social Entrepreneur of the Year Award
- National Director's Entrepreneurship Award from the Minority Business Development Agency of the U.S. Department of Commerce
- Association of Education Publishers' Golden Lamp Award
- ACE/Currie Foundation Humanitarian Venture Award
- America's Top High School Business Teacher

In addition, Mariotti has been the subject of many national media profiles on such programs as *ABC Evening News* and *20/20*.

He has authored and coauthored 34 books and workbooks on entrepreneurship, selling over 10 million worldwide and distributing many more copies for free to at-risk communities, including prisons. His popular book *The Young Entrepreneur's Guide to Starting and Running a Small Business* has recently been published in a new edition by Random House and is used to teach entrepreneurship from the United States to China, India, and the Middle East. Mariotti is a regular attendee and speaker at The World Economic Forum.

Raised in Flint, Michigan, Mariotti received his B.B.A. in business economics and his M.B.A. from the University of Michigan, Ann Arbor. He has also studied at Harvard University, Stanford University, and Brooklyn College. He started his professional career as a treasury analyst for Ford Motor Company before founding his own company, Mason Import/Export Services.

 **CAROLINE GLACKIN, Ph.D.**, is a "pracademic" who has successfully worked as a microenterprise and small business owner and manager, as an executive director of a community development financial institution, and as an academic in areas of community development finance, entrepreneurship, and management. She is the Edward L. Snyder Endowed Chair for Business at Shepherd University in West Virginia. She has been assisting entrepreneurs in achieving their dreams for over 30 years.

Glackin earned a doctorate from the University of Delaware, where her research emphasis was on microfinance. She received an M.B.A. from The Wharton School at the University of Pennsylvania and a B.A. from Bryn Mawr College. Her professional career began with the DuPont Company, American Bell, Bell Atlantic, and American Management Systems. She has consulted for businesses and not-for-profit agencies in turnaround and high-growth situations. After exiting a family business, she became the executive director of a community development financial institution serving businesses and not-for-profits.

Dr. Glackin has succeeded in leading change in the practical fields of her research and has received numerous honors and awards. These include the first Gloeckner Business Plan Award at The Wharton School, the Minority Business Advocate of the Year for Delaware from the U.S. Small Business Administration, and the She Knows Where She's Going Award from Girls Inc. Dr. Glackin cochaired the Delaware Governor's Task Force for Financial Independence. She has participated in the Cornell University Emerging Markets Think Tank Series and has presented her research and pedagogy at numerous professional conferences.

Acknowledgments

First, sincere thanks to the team of reviewers and consultants who provided insightful feedback during the development of our books:

Harvey Lon Addams, *Professor Emeritus, Weber State University, Ogden, UT*
Elaine Allen, *CPA, Vice Chair, Not-for-Profit Sector, Mitchell & Titus, LLP (EY Global Limited), New York, NY*
Larry Bennett, *President, Benland Innovations, LLC, New York, NY*
Sunne Brandmeyer, *Retired Lecturer/Advisor, Center for Economic Education, University of South Florida, Tampa, FL*
Stanlee Brimberg, *Teacher, Bank Street School for Children, New York, NY*
Howard W. Buffett, Jr.
John R. Callister, *Cornell University, Ithaca, NY*
John D. Christesen, *Westchester Community College, Valhalla, NY*
Steve Colyer, *Miami Dade College, Miami, FL*
Alan J. Dlugash, *CPA, Partner, Marks Paneth LLP*
Alex Dontoh, *New York University, New York, NY*
Thomas Emrick, *Executive Director, Smithsonian Science Education Center, Washington, DC*
Joyce Ezrow, *Anne Arundel Community College, Arnold, MD*
Rita Friberg, *Pueblo Community College, Pueblo, CO*
George Gannage, Jr., *West Georgia Technical College, Carrollton, GA*
Janet P. Graham, *Coastal Carolina University, Conway, SC*
Vada Grantham, *Des Moines Area Community College, Ankeny, IA*

John Harris, *Eastern High School, Bristol, CT*

Deborah Hoffman, *CPA, Director of Finance, Math for America*

Donald Hoy, *Benedictine College, Atchison, KS*

Samira Hussein, *Johnson County Community College, Overland Park, KS*

Eileen M. Kearney, *Montgomery County Community College, Blue Bell, PA*

Sanford Krieger, Esq., *General Counsel & Managing Director, AEA Investors LP*

Jawanza Kunjufu, D.B.A., *President, African-American Images*

Corey Kupfer, Esq., *Partner, Hamburger Law Firm, Englewood, NJ*

Walter E. Lara, *Florida Community College, Jacksonville, FL*

Emily H. Martin, *Faulkner State College, Bay Minette, AL*

Alaire Mitchell, *Former Assistant Director of Curriculum Research, New York City Board of Education, New York, NY*

Timothy R. Mittan, *Southeast Community College, Lincoln, NE*

Eric Mulkowsky, *Senior Management Consultant, Robin Hood Foundation, New York, NY*

Raffiq Nathoo, *Retired Senior Managing Director, The Blackstone Group, LP, New York, NY*

Ray E. Newton, III, *Senior Managing Director, Evercore Capital Partners, New York, NY*

Arnold Ng, *Pepperdine University, Rancho Palos Verdes, CA*

William H. Painter, *Retired, George Washington University, Washington, DC*

Peter Patch, *President, Patch and Associates, San Francisco, CA*

Alan Patricof, *Founder and Managing Director, Apax Partners and Greycroft LLC, New York, NY*

Carolyn J. Christensen, *CPA, Westchester Community College, Valhalla, NY*

Laura Portolese-Dias, *Shoreline Community College, Seattle, WA*

Christopher P. Puto, *University of St. Thomas, Minneapolis, MN*

Richard Relyea, *President, NY Private Equity Network (NYPEN), New York, NY*

Linda Ross, *Rowan University, Glassboro, NJ*

Ira Sacks, Esq., *Partner, Law Offices of Ira S. Sacks LLP, New York, NY*

William A. Sahlman, *Harvard Business School, Cambridge, MA*

Arnold Scheibel, MD, *University of California at Los Angeles, Los Angeles, CA*

William Searle, *Asnuntuck Community College, Enfield, CT*

LaVerne Tilley, *Gwinnett Technical College, Lawrenceville, GA*

Marsha Timmerman, *LaSalle University, Philadelphia, PA*

Liza Vertinsky, *Emory University, Atlanta, GA*

Peter B. Walker, *Managing Director, McKinsey and Company, Inc., New York, NY*

Donald A. Wells, *University of Arizona, Tucson, AZ*

Dennis R. Williams, *Pennsylvania College of Technology, Williamsport, PA*

I would like to thank my coauthor, Caroline Glackin, without whose talent and expertise this text would not have been possible, and Tony Towle, who from NFTE's inception has helped me organize my thoughts and experiences. I must also single out the help of two outstanding educators: John Harris and Peter Patch. Special thanks as well to Stephanie Wall, Daniel Tylman, Claudia Fernandes, Ilene Kahn, and the rest of the team at Pearson for their professionalism and editorial assistance.

Thanks also to Heather Van Sickle, President and CEO of the National Association of Community College Entrepreneurship (NACCE), and to Tony Mendes, President of the United States Association for Small Business and Entrepreneurship (USASBE), as well as the hundreds of members of these associations that have adopted Mariotti and Glackin texts to teach entrepreneurship to college students.

Additionally, I am grateful to Howard Stevenson, William Bygrave, Bob Pritzker, Stephen Spinelli, and the late Jeffry Timmons for imparting their wisdom; and to Richard Fink of Koch Industries; Carl Schramm, formerly of the Ewing Marion Kauffman Foundation; and Mike Hennessy and John Hughes of the Coleman Foundation. Special thanks to Eddy Bayardelle and Melanie Mortimer of Merrill Lynch Global Philanthropy, and Kim Davis of Teneo Holdings.

Further, I would like to acknowledge Steve Alcock, Harsh and Aruna Bhargava, Lena Bondue, Dawn Bowlus, Shelly Chenoweth, Janet McKinstry Cort, Erik Dauwen, Clara Del Villar, Christine Chambers Gilfillan, Andrew Hahn, Kathleen Kirkwood, Michael Simmons, Sheena Lindahl, Cynthia Miree, Henry To, Carol Tully, Dilia Wood, and Elizabeth Wright, as well as Peter Cowie, Joseph Dominic, Paul DeF. Hicks, Jr., Ann Mahoney, David Roodberg, Phyllis Ross Schless, and Remi Vermeir, who have all provided countless insights into providing entrepreneurial opportunities to young people.

In addition, I would like to thank my brother, Jack, the best CPA I know, and my father, John, for financing much of NFTE's early work, and for their continuing love and guidance. Thanks are due to all the other teachers, students, experts, and friends who were kind enough to look over my work and help me improve it. Finally, I want to thank my mother, Nancy, a wonderful special education instructor who showed me that one great teacher can affect eternity.

Steve Mariotti

To my coauthor Steve Mariotti, who brought hope, opportunity, and change out of adversity to create the Network for Teaching Entrepreneurship and started this journey—many thanks. As Steve noted, the team at Pearson has been wonderful to work with again. Faculty reviewers and faculty members who have contacted me directly regarding earlier materials are always a valued source of insights.

Most importantly, I appreciate the terrific entrepreneurs who shared their stories with me, including the good, the bad, and the downright ugly! Their interest in sharing their experiences with students and willingness to carve out time to tell their tales demonstrates the kind of energy and enthusiasm we associate with successful entrepreneurs. They have made this endeavor interesting and engaging.

On a more personal note, I would like to thank my "family" at Shepherd University for their support and encouragement as I worked on *Entrepreneurship: Starting and Managing a Small Business, 4e*. Special thanks to Jay Azriel, Cynthia deLeon, Gordon DeMeritt, Meg Galligan, Heidi Golding, Terri Hasson, Ann Marie Legreid, Kathy Reid, Cindy Vance, and Hattie Bryant. Finally, to Elise and Spencer Glackin for being the best cheering section a mother could ever have—thanks and love to you both.

Caroline Glackin

ENTREPRENEURIAL PATHWAYS

Chapter 1
ENTREPRENEURS RECOGNIZE OPPORTUNITIES

Chapter 2
THE BUSINESS PLAN: ROAD MAP TO SUCCESS

Chapter 3
CREATING BUSINESS FROM OPPORTUNITY

Kurhan/Fotolia

1 CHAPTER

Entrepreneurs Recognize Opportunities

Learning Objectives

1. Summarize what entrepreneurs do.

2. Examine how free-enterprise economies work and how entrepreneurs fit into them.

3. Identify and evaluate opportunities to start your own business.

4. Explain how profit works as a signal to the entrepreneur.

Tom Szaky, Terracycle.
(Paul Zimmerman/
Getty Images)

"Everyone lives by selling something."

—Robert Louis Stevenson, Scottish author

Tom Szaky was a 20-year-old college student in need of inspiration for a business plan competition, when he happened to visit friends who were using red worms to compost waste that they then used as plant fertilizer. The idea captured his imagination, and he created a business plan for an environmentally friendly company that would convert trash into fertilizer. Although he finished in fifth place in the competition, Szaky moved ahead to make the company a viable venture.[1]

TerraCycle Inc. has expanded its product lines to encompass a wide range of recycling and upcycling, including branded products for Target and Kraft Foods. The company is the producer of the world's first product made from and packed in recycled waste: fertilizer generated from waste. Szaky sells to some of the world's largest retailers, including Wal-Mart, Target, and Home Depot, and oversees programs that involve entire communities in recycling projects. Sales exceed $20 million per year, and the company has collected literally billions of discarded items. TerraCycle plant food was twice named the most eco-friendly product in Home Depot. Tom Szaky and TerraCycle have turned waste into treasure.

Entrepreneurship

Have you ever eaten a Subway sandwich? Used an Apple device? Listened to music with Skullcandy headphones? The entrepreneurs that founded these companies brought these products into your world. Entrepreneurship is all around us.

What Is an Entrepreneur?

Most Americans earn money by working in *business*. They are somehow engaged in the buying and selling of products or services in order to earn money.

product something tangible that exists in nature or is made by people.

- A **product** is something that exists in nature or is made by human beings. It is *tangible*, meaning that it can be physically touched.
- A **service** is labor or expertise exchanged for money. It is *intangible*. It cannot physically be touched.

service intangible work that provides time, skills, or expertise in exchange for money.

Someone who earns a living by working directly for someone else's business is an *employee* of that business. There are many roles for employees. At Ford Motor Company, for instance, some employees build the cars, some sell the cars, and some manage the company. But most employees have one thing in common—they do not *own* the business; they work for others who do. They know how much money they can earn, and that amount is limited to salary or wages, plus bonuses and any stock options they may receive.

entrepreneur a person who recognizes an opportunity and organizes and manages a business, assuming the risk for the sake of potential return.

People who have their own businesses work for themselves and are called small business owners, or **entrepreneurs**. Entrepreneurs are often both owners and employees. For an entrepreneur, the sky is the limit as far as earnings are concerned. Unlike an employee, an entrepreneur owns

---

[1]TerraCycle Inc., accessed March 9, 2014, http://www.terracycle.net.

the profit that his or her business earns, and may choose to reinvest it in the business or take it as payment.

Learning Objective 1

Summarize what entrepreneurs do.

An entrepreneur is someone who recognizes an opportunity to start a business that other people may not have noticed and acts on it. As economist Jeffry A. Timmons wrote in the preface of *New Venture Creation: Entrepreneurship for the 21st Century*, "A skillful entrepreneur can shape and create an opportunity where others see little or nothing—or see it too early or too late."[2]

The French word *entrepreneur* began to take on its present-day meaning in the seventeenth century. It was used to describe someone who undertook any project that entailed risk—military, legal, or political, as well as economic. Eventually, it came to mean someone who started a new business venture—often of a new kind or a new (or improved) way of doing business. French economist Jean-Baptiste Say wrote at the turn of the nineteenth century:

> An entrepreneur is an economic agent who unites all means of production—the land of one, the labor of another and the capital of yet another, and thus produces a product. By selling the product in the market he pays rent on land, wages to labor, interest on capital and what remains is his profit. He shifts economic resources out of an area of lower and into an area of higher productivity and greater yield.[3]

Say argued that entrepreneurs "added value to scarce resources." Coal is a resource because it is used as fuel. Wood is a resource because it can be used to build a house or a table, to make paper, or to burn as fuel. Economists consider *scarce* all resources that are worth money, regardless of their relative availability.

Debbi Fields, founder of Mrs. Fields Cookies, took resources—eggs, butter, flour, sugar, chocolate chips—and turned them into cookies. People liked what she did with those resources so much that they were willing to pay her more for the cookies than it cost her to buy the resources to make them. She *added value* to the resources she purchased by what she did with them and created a multimillion-dollar business in the process.

Entrepreneurs may have different reasons to start and continue their businesses, but they share the common focus of capturing sustained value. Entrepreneurs seek opportunities that they envision as generators of incremental income, or *wealth*. Whether the business is intended to meet short-term household cash needs or to grow into a publicly traded company, viability is critical. Each activity of the firm should be driven by this need.

The Free-Enterprise System

free-enterprise system economic system in which businesses are privately owned and operate relatively free of government interference.

capitalism the free-market system, characterized by individuals and companies competing for economic gains, ownership of private property and wealth, and price determination through free-market forces.

An economy is the wealth and resources of a country or region, including its financial structure. The economy of the United States is a **free-enterprise system** because it is characterized by private (rather than governmental) ownership of capital assets and goods; anyone is free to start a business. Americans do not have to get permission from the government to go into business, although they are expected to obey laws and regulations.

Learning Objective 2

Examine how free-enterprise economies work and how entrepreneurs fit into them.

The free-market system, which is also called **capitalism**, typifies the following attributes:

- Individuals and companies may compete for their own economic gains.

---

[2] Jeffrey A. Timmons, New Venture Creation: Entrepreneurship for the 21st Century. McGraw-Hill

[3] Jean-Baptiste Say, *A treatise on political economy; or the production distribution and consumption of wealth* (*Traité d'économie politique ou simple exposition de la manière dont se forment, se distribuent et se composent les richesse.*), C. R. Prinsep, trans. [slightly modified] and Clement C. Biddle., ed. (Philadelphia: Lippincott, Grambo & Co., 1855). Library of Economics and Liberty, accessed June 26, 2013, http://www.econlib.org/library/Say/sayT.html.

- Private wealth and property ownership are permissible.
- Free-market forces primarily determine prices.

Cash or goods invested to generate income and wealth is called **capital**; in a free-enterprise system anyone who possesses or can raise the necessary capital may start a business.

capital money or property owned or used in business.

Voluntary Exchange

The free-enterprise system is also sometimes referred to as a private enterprise free-trade system because it is based on **voluntary exchange**. Voluntary exchange is a transaction between two parties who agree to trade money for a product or service. Each wishes to take advantage of what the trade offers. The parties agree to the exchange because each will benefit.

voluntary exchange a transaction between two parties who agree to trade money for a product or service.

For example, José has a construction business, and his neighbors hire him to renovate their kitchen. He wants to earn money and is willing to use his skills and time to do so. The neighbors are willing to give him money to get the renovation done. They each have something the other wants, so they are willing to trade. A satisfactory exchange only takes place when both parties believe they will benefit.

Benefits and Challenges of Free Enterprise

The public benefits from living in a free-enterprise system because it discourages entrepreneurs who waste resources by driving them out of business. It encourages entrepreneurs to use resources to satisfy consumer needs efficiently by rewarding them with profit and wealth.

Where entrepreneurs are free to trade voluntarily to as large a market as possible, their ability to find customers to buy their goods or services increases, as well as their overall ability to meet customer needs. Meanwhile, the Internet has made it much easier for businesses to sell to clients all over the world. Shipping, too, has become much faster and less expensive.

Society in general benefits because free enterprise encourages competition between entrepreneurs. Someone who can make cookies that taste as good as Mrs. Fields Original Cookies and sell them at a lower price would eventually attract the company's customers. This would force Mrs. Fields to lower prices to stay competitive, or the company would go out of business. Consumers would benefit because they would get to buy the same-quality cookie at a lower price.

Global Impact . . .

Free Trade

For much of recorded history, international trade was difficult and hazardous. To sell products in another country often required long and dangerous journeys overland or by ship. Many countries were closed to outside trade. Governments also used their power to give their own businesspeople competitive advantages over those from other countries by establishing trade barriers, such as imposing taxes (tariffs) on foreign goods that made them very expensive. Governments could also enforce restrictions on how many imports or exports could cross their borders.

Today, trade barriers have fallen in many parts of the world. The North American Free Trade Agreement (NAFTA) of 1994 eliminated trade barriers between the United States, Mexico, and Canada. This turned the entire continent into a free-trade zone. The General Agreement on Tariffs and Trade (GATT) cut or eliminated tariffs between 117 countries. This evolved into the World Trade Organization, which has 159 members.

On the flip side, free enterprise has some disadvantages. If a company fails, its employees are out of work. Owners who have invested their financial resources in the business lose money. Other companies or individuals that depended on the products and services of the failed business themselves lose customers or suppliers.

What Is a Small Business?

Many people think of business only in terms of "big" businesses—companies such as Apple, Wal-Mart, Microsoft, General Motors, and Berkshire Hathaway. However, the vast majority of businesses are small businesses. A small business is defined by the U.S. Small Business Administration's Office of Advocacy as having fewer than 500 employees and selling less than $5 million worth of products or services annually. A neighborhood restaurant, a mattress manufacturer, a technology research company, and a clothing boutique can all be examples of a small business; even a leading local employer may be classified as "small" under this definition.

The core principles involved in running a large company—like Microsoft—and a corner deli are the same. However, the operations of a small business are not the same as those of a large one. Most multimillion-dollar businesses started out as small, entrepreneurial ventures. This is why entrepreneurship is often called the engine of an economy. It drives economic creativity, giving rise to wealth and jobs and improving the standard of living.

Definitions of Success—Monetary and Other

The Millennial Generation (born between 1977 and 1995) has redefined success. It is more individualized than the traditional concept and based on factors beyond those of income and wealth. Business owners may start an enterprise to create a more environmentally friendly approach to a product or process, to provide jobs for a disadvantaged population, or to improve the mental or physical health of themselves or others. For these entrepreneurs, success might be measured by the ability to have an impact on the population they serve. Or, success may mean working to provide a lifestyle that permits a shortened work week or telecommuting. Recognition from peers and others could also be a goal. Financial success may be just one of many measures of achievement for an entrepreneur.

Starting a business is an opportunity, and like any opportunity, it should be evaluated by taking a careful look at all aspects of it. One thing

---

BizFacts

- There are 27.3 million businesses in the United States; approximately 99.9 percent of them are small companies with fewer than 500 employees.
- Small businesses in America employed 49.2 percent of the country's private (nongovernment) workforce, hired 43 percent of high-tech workers, and created 64 percent of net new jobs annually over the last decade.
- Home-based businesses make up 52 percent and franchises 2 percent of all small firms.
- Small businesses represent 99.7 percent of all companies with employees.
- Small firms constituted 98 percent of all identified exporters and produced 33 percent of the country's known export value in fiscal year 2010.

Source: U.S. Small Business Administration, accessed March 9, 2014, http://www.sba.gov.

is certain, though: *The desire to make money, alone, is not a good enough reason to start one's own business.*

The financial rewards of owning your own business may not occur until you have put in years of hard work. The desire to make money may not be enough to keep you going through the difficult early period. Most successful companies have been founded by an entrepreneur with a powerful and motivating vision and passion, balanced by a strong work ethic and dedication.

Entrepreneurs have declared that they are "not in business for the money" so often that it has become a cliché, but like most clichés, it is based on a degree of truth.

Taking the Long View

Successful entrepreneurs know it is important to begin with the end in mind, so that they can have an idea of where they want the organization to be at their personal exit point, even before they make the first sale. Because the daily tactical decisions they make will be affected by what they hope to create in the short *and* long term, a clear vision is vital. As you consider an entrepreneurial path, consider these questions:

- Are you planning to be active in the business until retirement? At what age will you retire? Who will take over then? A family member? A new owner?

- Do you plan to grow the business to a certain size or level of maturity and then sell it? If so, what is the target level? Are you looking at an initial public offering or a small private sale? Would you stay with the business after it was sold?

- Would you want to stay active for a given number of years? Then what would you do?

Taking the long view also means considering personal satisfaction, including conformance with individual values and ethics. Entrepreneurs make hundreds of choices and decisions every day. These decisions may conform to their values and ethics or violate them to meet a customer need, provide an expedient or cost-effective solution to an immediate problem, or the like. If you find yourself facing such a decision, for your long-term wellness and the benefit of those around you, it will be critical to keep your core values in the forefront. Consider the legacy you want to leave behind for your successors.

Benefits and Costs of Becoming an Entrepreneur

Entrepreneurs put a great deal of time and effort into launching their own businesses. While establishing a business, an entrepreneur may also pour all of his or her money into it. An entrepreneur may not be able to buy new clothes or a fancy car, go on vacation, or spend much time with family—until the business becomes profitable and starts generating cash.

If so much work and sacrifice are involved, why become an entrepreneur? Even if you have a clear vision that you believe will motivate you through the ups and downs of running a business, look closely at the costs and benefits of being an entrepreneur before you decide whether this is the life for you. This examination is fundamental in the decision to become an entrepreneur.

Potential Benefits of Entrepreneurship

The entrepreneur is working for the following potential rewards:

1. *Control over time.* Do you work better at midnight than at 8 A.M.? Are you the kind of person who would rather work really hard for two weeks, nonstop, and then take a break? If you start your own business, you will have control over how you spend your time by the type of business it is. You can structure your schedule to make this possible. You can also choose to hire others to perform tasks you do not like to do or are not good at, so you can stay focused on what you do best. Bill Gates liked to spend his time designing software. He hired people to manage Microsoft's operations and to market and sell its products. Many eBay entrepreneurs have carved out flexible schedules for responding to orders, packaging, and shipping. Brick-and-mortar retail stores, on the other hand, do not often afford such flexibility.

2. *Fulfillment.* Successful entrepreneurs are passionate about their businesses. They are excited and fulfilled by their work. Entrepreneurs who are working to reach their full potential are rarely bored, because there is always plenty to do. If one facet of running the business is uninteresting, and they have the income to support it, they can hire someone else for that task.

   Social entrepreneurs who want to contribute to societal improvement find ways to do this while also earning profits. Founders of not-for-profit organizations create enterprises to address public issues that are personally important. Other entrepreneurs start lifestyle businesses that allow them to earn money while following a passion. For example, avid pilots may operate aviation-oriented businesses in which they can fly often, such as specialty delivery companies or flight instruction. Art lovers may open galleries, create art-rental firms, or operate art tours.

3. *Independence/autonomy.* Because they are not reporting to managers or supervisors, business owners do not have to follow orders or observe working hours set by someone else. They have control over their decisions.

4. *Creation/ownership.* Entrepreneurship is a creative endeavor. Doing what they love to do or turning a skill, hobby, or other interest into a business can be highly satisfying. The words of Confucius, "Choose a job that you love, and you will never have to work a day in your life," are often cited with respect to entrepreneurship.

   Entrepreneurs put time and effort into creating a venture they expect will survive and become profitable. Entrepreneurs own the businesses they create and the profits those businesses earn. *Ownership* is the key to wealth. One goal is to build a business that creates a continuing stream of earnings. Eventually, you may be able to sell that company for a multiple of those earnings. That is how entrepreneurs create wealth. Many entrepreneurs, such as Bill Gore, the inventor of GORE-TEX fabric, start their own business after becoming frustrated or disillusioned in other roles or having ideas rejected by an employer.

5. *Financial reward/control over compensation.* Entrepreneurs can build income and wealth through their endeavors. Although income potential is generally capped for employees, entrepreneurs are limited only by their own imagination and tenacity. Entrepreneurs built most of our country's great fortunes. At the same time,

many part-time, seasonal, and lifestyle entrepreneurs find ways to fund gaps in household income, pay for college, or support extraordinary expenses through their business endeavors.

Entrepreneurs choose how and when they are paid. As owner of your company, when funds permit, you can decide to:

- **Pay yourself a salary**, a fixed payment made at regular intervals, such as every week or every month. Salaries are not applicable to sole proprietorships, where owners may take a "draw" on revenues, or partnerships, where they may "draw down" profits.

- **Pay yourself a wage**, a fixed rate per hour. This is not a common choice, but it is available.

- **Take a share** of the company's profit. As the owner, you can pay yourself a portion of the business's profits. In a corporation this kind of payment is called a **dividend** and must be paid to all shareholders.

- **Take a commission** on every sale you make. A commission is a percentage of the value of a sale. If you decide to pay yourself 10 percent commission, and sell an item for $120, your commission on the sale would be $12.

6. ***Control over working conditions.*** As an entrepreneur, you can create a work environment that reflects your values. If you support recycling, you can make sure your company recycles. You will also evaluate your own performance. As long as you have control of the company, no one else has the power to fire you. If equality is essential, you may have an office with equal working spaces, no special privileges for managers, and few management layers.

7. ***Self-esteem.*** Knowing that they created something valuable can give business owners a strong sense of accomplishment. It can help them feel good about themselves and increase their self-confidence.

8. ***Contribution to society.*** Business owners decide how they can add value to their communities and the wider world. The issues they care about can be "designed-in" when they form their companies.

Some of the greatest entrepreneurs in the world dealt with problems as they were growing up, such as extreme poverty, abuse, or learning disabilities. Sir Richard Branson, for example, had such severe dyslexia that he dropped out of high school. He became a successful entrepreneur, however, creating more than 200 companies—including Virgin Airlines, Virgin Galactic, and Virgin Records. The Virgin Group employs about 50,000 people in 34 countries and has revenues of approximately $21 billion.[4] Branson has a personal net worth of about $4.6 billion, making him number 272 on the Forbes list of billionaires.[5] As an entrepreneur, he was able to create an environment in which he could succeed.

Potential Costs of Entrepreneurship

While there are many potential benefits of entrepreneurship, entrepreneurs also face numerous possible costs.

1. ***Business failure.*** About one in five new businesses fails in the first eight years. Another third close because the entrepreneurs become discouraged and give up. Entrepreneurs risk losing not only their own money but also the financial investments of others.

salary fixed amount of money paid to an employee at regular intervals.

wage fixed payment per hour for work performed.

dividend each stockholder's portion of the profit-per-share paid out by a corporation.

commission a percentage of a sale paid to a salesperson.

---

[4]Virgin Group, accessed June 26, 2013, http://www.virgin.com.

[5]"The World's Billionaires," *Forbes*, March 2013, accessed June 26, 2013, http://www.forbes.com.

Step into the Shoes . . .

Solving a Problem and Founding a Company

When Jennifer Hyman (Jenn) recognized a problem that her sister encountered, she processed the idea into an opportunity with her Harvard Business School section mate, Jennifer Fleiss (Jenny). Jenn's sister wanted a fashionable outfit to wear to a wedding, but such an outfit was beyond the budget for her salary. What if, Jenn thought, the Beckys of this world could have access to their dream closet—a new dress for every occasion? And what if designers were able to get their pieces into the hands of young, fashionable women and build an addiction for designer fashion?[6] Jenn and Jenny tested the concept and created Rent the Runway, where users rent designer clothing for special events.

2. ***Obstacles.*** Entrepreneurs run into problems that they will have to solve, primarily by themselves. In addition, their families and friends may not support their vision and may actively discourage them.

3. ***Loneliness/isolation.*** It can be lonely and even a little frightening to be completely responsible for the success or failure of a business. While owners have control, they also have responsibility and cannot defer to someone else for decisions.

4. ***Financial insecurity.*** Owners are not guaranteed a set salary or benefits. They may not always have enough money to pay themselves, particularly in the first 18 months or so of a new enterprise. They also have to set up and fund their own retirement funds.

5. ***Long hours/hard work.*** Entrepreneurs have to work long hours to get their businesses off the ground. Many entrepreneurs work six or even seven days a week, often for 12 hours or more per day. While they decide when to work, they often end up working or thinking about their businesses many more hours as entrepreneurs than they would as employees.

6. ***Strain on personal relationships.*** Even with the strong support of family and friends, the inherent challenges of a small business can strain relationships to the breaking point.

Not everyone is cut out to be an entrepreneur. Entrepreneurs have to be able to tolerate a higher degree of risk and uncertainty than people who work steady jobs for established employers. With higher risk, however, comes the potential of higher rewards.

Cost/Benefit Analysis

cost/benefit analysis
a decision-making process in which the costs of taking an action are compared to the benefits.

Using a comparison of benefits and costs to make a decision is called **cost/benefit analysis**. It is a helpful tool because people often make decisions based on emotions, not intellect, to evaluate pros and cons. Strong emotions may take over to the point where they see only the benefits and not the costs of an action (or vice versa).

For example, Xavier plans to buy a car. He might be overwhelmed by the idea of making such a large purchase, even if the benefits are greater than the costs. On the other hand, he might decide to buy a car at a cost that outweighs the benefits it will bring, simply because he is temporarily blinded by a desire to own a really impressive vehicle. Making a list that includes the dollars and cents of the costs and benefits of a purchase is a concrete way to take the emotion out of the decision, while also considering nonfinancial factors.

[6]Rent the Runway, accessed March 10, 2014, http://www.renttherunway.com.

To turn an opportunity into a business, entrepreneurs invest both time and money. Before making this kind of investment, think carefully about:

Costs. The money, energy, and time you will have to invest, as well as the opportunities you will be giving up, to operate the business.

Benefits. The wealth you will accrue and the knowledge, skills, self-esteem, and experience you will gain.

Opportunity Cost

Cost/benefit analysis is incomplete without considering opportunity cost. This is the cost of your "next-best investment." Perhaps your goal is to become a composer who writes scores for movies. You get a full-time job at a local music store for $400 a week to support yourself, so you can write and record music in the evenings that you hope to sell to producers, agents, or film companies.

You find, however, that whenever a producer or agent wants to meet with you, you cannot get out of work to go. You realize that, even though you are making $400 a week, you are missing some important opportunities. Perhaps it would be smarter to take a part-time job for $300 a week that would leave your mornings free for meetings. The opportunity cost of the $100 a week you will lose is offset by the potential income from film-scoring jobs you are missing by not being free to see people in the business. If your first film-scoring job pays $5,000, for example, you definitely would have made the right decision to earn $100 a week less for a few months.

People often make decisions without considering the opportunity cost and then wonder why they are not happy with the outcome. Each time you make a decision about what to do with your time, energy, or money, think about the cost of the opportunities you are giving up. **Exhibit 1-1** presents a simple quiz that can help you decide whether you have what it takes to be an entrepreneur.

opportunity cost the value of what must be given up in order to obtain something else.

Seeking Advice and Information to Succeed

While experience is an excellent teacher, using knowledge, skills, and abilities to avoid errors, problems, and delays is much healthier. A savvy entrepreneur learns from the mistakes of others and appreciates the wisdom and experience of trusted advisors and mentors.

Preparation and planning are keys to avoid making mistakes. Thoughtful consideration of the entrepreneurship option is an excellent starting point. Thorough research and taking advantage of training and/or one-on-one consulting to bridge gaps in your preparation can make a world of difference.

Two of the best resources for keeping on track are mentors and advisors. A mentor is a trusted advisor with whom a person forms a developmental partnership through which information, insight, skills, and knowledge are shared to promote personal and/or professional growth. Finding a committed business mentor with industry-specific knowledge and experience, broad general business experience, or both, is a worthwhile endeavor. A successful entrepreneur in your field, perhaps outside of your geographic area, may prove invaluable if he or she will mentor you. Many successful entrepreneurs will carve out time for promising newcomers. Unfortunately, becoming a mentor may be more of a commitment than your identified entrepreneur is willing or able to make. Perhaps he or she will become an advisor instead.

In addition to your paid professional advisors, such as attorneys and accountants, individual advisors or an advisory board may mean the

mentor a trusted advisor with whom a person forms a developmental partnership through which information, insight, skills, and knowledge are shared to promote personal and/or professional growth.

Exhibit 1-1 *"Do You Have What It Takes?" Quiz*

Take the following quiz to learn more about yourself and whether you may have what it takes to be an entrepreneur. Circle the answer that best represents how you feel.

1. You are at a party and a friend tells you that the guy in the expensive-looking suit recently invested in another friend's business. What do you do?

   a. Race over to him, introduce yourself, and tell him every detail of your business idea while asking if he would be interested in investing in it.

   b. Ask your friend to introduce you. Once introduced, you hand the potential investor your business card and politely ask whether you might be able to call on him sometime to present your business plan.

   c. Decide that it is probably not a good idea to bother the man at a party. After all, he is here to relax. Maybe you will run into him again somewhere else.

2. Your boss asks you to take charge of researching office supply stores and choosing the one that you think would be best for the company to use. What is your response?

   a. Yes! Finally, a chance to show the boss what you are made of—plus, you will be able to spirit a few of the supplies away for your own business.

   b. You are terrified; this is more responsibility than you really want. What if you make a mistake and cost the company money? You do not want to look bad.

   c. You are excited. This is a good opportunity to impress your boss and also learn how to compare and negotiate with suppliers . . . something you will need to do for your own business.

3. You are already going to school full time when you are offered a part-time job that is in the same field as the business you want to start when you graduate next year. What do you do?

   a. Take the job, after talking with your student advisor about how to juggle your schedule so it will fit, because you believe the experience and the contacts you will develop will be invaluable when you start your business.

   b. Take the job. In fact, you ask for extra hours so you can finally start making some real money. Who needs sleep?

   c. Turn down the job. School is hard enough without working, too. You do not want your grades to suffer.

4. You are offered a job as a survey-taker for a marketing firm. The job pays really well but will require you to talk to a great many people. What do you do?

   a. Take the job. You like people and this job will be a good way to practice getting to know what consumers want.

   b. Turn down the job. Just the thought of approaching strangers makes you queasy.

   c. Take the job so you can conduct some market research of your own by also asking the people you survey what they think about your business idea.

5. Your last job paid well and was interesting, but it required you to put in long hours and sometimes work on the weekends. What was your response?

   a. You put in the extra hours without complaint, but mainly because you felt that the rewards were worth it.

   b. You went a little overboard and worked yourself into a state of exhaustion; moderation is not your strong suit.

   c. You quit. You are strictly a nine-to-five person. Work is definitely not your life!

6. You are such a good guitar player that friends keep offering to pay for you to give them lessons. What is your response?

   a. You spend some money to run a six-week advertisement in the local paper, announcing that you are now available to teach at the same rate that established teachers in the area charge.

   b. You start teaching a few friends to see how it goes. You ask them what they are willing to pay and what they want to learn.

   c. You give a few friends some lessons but refuse to take any money.

7. Your best friend has started a business designing Web sites. He needs help because the business is really growing. He offers to make you a partner in the business even though you are computer-illiterate. What is your response?

   a. You jump in, figuring that you will learn the ropes soon enough.

   b. You ask your friend to keep the partnership offer open but first to recommend a class you can take to get your skills up to speed.

   c. You pass. You do not see how you can work in a business you know nothing about.

Analysis of the "Do You Have What It Takes?" Quiz
Scoring

1. a = 2	b = 1	c = 0
2. a = 2	b = 0	c = 1
3. a = 1	b = 2	c = 0
4. a = 1	b = 0	c = 2
5. a = 1	b = 2	c = 0
6. a = 2	b = 1	c = 0
7. a = 2	b = 1	c = 0

Exhibit 1-1 *"Do You Have What It Takes?" Quiz*

12 Points or More: You are a natural risk-taker and can handle a lot of stress. These are important characteristics for an entrepreneur to have to be successful. You are willing to work hard but have a tendency to throw caution to the wind a little too easily. Save yourself from that tendency by using cost/benefit analysis to carefully evaluate your business (and personal!) decisions. In your enthusiasm, do not forget to look at the opportunity costs of any decision you make.

6 to 12 Points: You strike an excellent balance between being a risk-taker and someone who carefully evaluates decisions. An entrepreneur needs to be both. You are also not overly motivated by the desire to make money. You understand that a successful business requires hard work and sacrifice before you can reap the rewards. To make sure that you are applying your natural drive and discipline to the best possible business opportunity, use the cost/benefit analysis to evaluate the different businesses you are interested in starting.

6 Points or Fewer: You are a little too cautious for an entrepreneur, but that will probably change as you learn more about how to run a business. You are concerned with financial security and may not be eager to put in the long hours required to get a business off the ground. This does not mean that you cannot succeed as an entrepreneur; just make sure that whatever business you decide to start is the business of your dreams, so that you will be motivated to make it a success. Use cost/benefit analysis to evaluate your business opportunities. Choose a business that you believe has the best shot at providing you with both the financial security and the motivation you require.

---

difference between success and failure. Even if you are forming a venture with a full slate of experienced technical and managerial professionals, the guidance of a carefully composed advisory board can provide valuable counsel and connections. Such a board might meet only once or twice a year to listen to your problems, share experiences, and help you avoid mistakes. During the times between meetings, advisors may also be able to offer substantial assistance.

Of course, taking advantage of available courses in entrepreneurship, whether brief workshops, individual college courses, an entrepreneurial certificate program, or a degree program, can offer considerable benefits. The opportunity to learn from the experiences of others and to systematically explore entrepreneurial options and build skills can be important. There are numerous Internet resources for nascent entrepreneurs, too.

A well-prepared entrepreneur is more likely to get and stay on the path to success.

Entrepreneurial Options

Entrepreneurship extends beyond the fast-growing technology enterprises that are most commonly associated with it. There are many variations on entrepreneurship, and the opportunities are innumerable. For example, entrepreneurship may include for-profit enterprises that support the missions of not-for-profit organizations, businesses designed for social impact, and ventures that are environmentally oriented.

Social entrepreneurship has multiple definitions and forms, but it is commonly thought of as a for-profit enterprise with the dual goals of achieving profitability and attaining beneficial returns for society. Another view is that of taking an entrepreneurial perspective toward social problems. Gregory Dees has created the following definition:[7]

Social entrepreneurs play the role of change agents in the social sector by:

- adopting a mission to create and sustain social value (not just private value),

social entrepreneurship
a for-profit enterprise with the dual goals of achieving profitability and attaining social returns.

---

[7]Gregory Dees, "The Meaning of 'Social Entrepreneurship,'" May 30, 2001, accessed July 9, 2013, http://www.fuqua.duke.edu/centers/case/documents/dees_SE.pdf.

- recognizing and relentlessly pursuing new opportunities to serve that mission,
- engaging in a process of continuous innovation, adaptation, and learning,
- acting boldly without being limited by resources currently in hand, and
- exhibiting heightened accountability to the constituencies served and for the outcomes created.

In this view, social entrepreneurship is less about profit than it is about social impact.

In addition to "social entrepreneurship," there is the more recent concept of the **social business**, "a non-loss, non-dividend company designed to address a social objective within the highly regulated marketplace of today. It is distinct from a non-profit because the business should seek to generate a modest profit but this will be used to expand the company's reach, improve the product or service or in other ways to subsidize the social mission."[8] In his book *Creating a World without Poverty—Social Business and the Future of Capitalism*, Mohammad Yunus suggests two kinds of social business:

- Type I provides a product and/or service with a particular environmental, social, or ethical purpose. Grameen Danone does this by providing food for the poor in Bangladesh.
- Type II is profit-oriented business with ownership consisting of underprivileged people who have the opportunity to benefit directly or indirectly.

In addition, **venture philanthropy** is a subset or segment of social entrepreneurship. Financial and human capital is invested in not-for-profits by individuals and for-profit enterprises with the intention of generating social rather than financial returns. In some cases, venture philanthropy may involve the investment of capital in the for-profit, commercial part of a not-for-profit. In others, it may mean investing in not-for-profits directly, to encourage entrepreneurial approaches to achieve social impact.

Green entrepreneurship is another form of social entrepreneurship and can be defined as: "Enterprise activities that avoid harm to the environment or help to protect the environment in some way."[9] TerraCycle is an excellent example of green entrepreneurship. According to the Corporation for Enterprise Development (CFED), green entrepreneurship can:

- create jobs and offer entrepreneurship opportunities,
- increase energy efficiency, thus conserving natural resources and saving money,
- decrease harm to workers' health,
- enable businesses to tap into new sources of local, state, and federal funding,
- take advantage of consumer preference for environmentally friendly goods, and

---

social business a company created to achieve a social objective while generating a modest profit to expand its reach, improve the product or service, and subsidize the social mission.

venture philanthropy a subset or segment of social entrepreneurship wherein financial and human capital is invested in not-for-profits by individuals and for-profit enterprises, with the intention of generating social rather than financial returns on their investments.

green entrepreneurship business activities that avoid harm to the environment or help to protect it in some way.

Ulrich Willmunder/ Shutterstock

---

[8]Muhammad Yunus, *Creating a World without Poverty: Social Business and the Future of Capitalism,* New York: PublicAffairs, 2009, p. 320.

[9]"Green Entrepreneurship," *Corporation for Enterprise Development: Effective State Policy and Practice,* Volume 5, Number 2, April 2004, http://www.cfed.org.

- preserve limited natural assets on which businesses and communities depend for business and quality of life.

Each of these alternative approaches offers opportunities for innovation and growth for the right entrepreneur.

How Do Entrepreneurs Find Opportunities to Start New Businesses?

In the twentieth century, Joseph Schumpeter expanded on Say's definition of entrepreneurship by adding that entrepreneurs create value "by exploiting an invention or, more generally, an untried technological possibility for producing a new commodity or producing an old one in a new way, by opening up a new source of supply of materials or a new outlet for products, by reorganizing an industry and so on."[10] This view emphasizes innovation as the key to entrepreneurship. Management expert Peter Drucker simplified this view to its essential core of creating a new business, taking on risk, and persevering in light of uncertainty.[11]

Schumpeter's definition describes five basic ways that entrepreneurs find opportunities to create new businesses:

> ◀ **Learning Objective 3**
> Identify and evaluate opportunities to start your own business.

1. Using a new technology to produce a new product
2. Using an existing technology to produce a new product
3. Using an existing technology to produce an old product in a new way
4. Finding a new supply of resources (that might enable the entrepreneur to produce a product more economically)
5. Developing a new market for an existing product

Entrepreneurs Creatively Exploit Changes in Our World

Contemporary economists and business experts have defined entrepreneurship even more specifically. Drucker pointed out that, for a business to be considered entrepreneurial, it should exploit changes in the world. This is in alignment with Schumpeter's definition of entrepreneurship but explicitly takes it a step further—to take advantage of circumstances. These changes can be technological, like the explosion in computer technology that led Bill Gates and Paul Allen to start Microsoft, or cultural, like the collapse of Communism, which led to a great many new business opportunities in Eastern Europe. Babson professor Daniel Isenberg narrows the definition of entrepreneurship to "the contrarian creation and capture of extraordinary value."[12]

Nothing changes faster than technology. Not so many years ago, there were no bar codes and no electronic scanners, hardly anyone used e-mail, and "smart phones" didn't exist. Today, even the smallest of organizations must use current technologies to be competitive. Sharp entrepreneurs increase their efficiency by taking advantage of the latest breakthroughs. To learn about what's new in technology, read current business and trade magazines and visit such Web sites as:

- TechCrunch, *http://www.techcrunch.com*
- Start-up Digest, *http://www.start-updigest.com*

---

[10]Joseph A. Schumpeter, *Capitalism, Socialism and Democracy*, New York: Harper & Row, 1942.

[11]Peter Drucker, *Innovation and Entrepreneurship: Practice and Principles*, New York: Harper Collins, 1985.

[12]Daniel Isenberg, *Worthless, Impossible and Stupid: How Contrarian Entrepreneurs Create and Capture Extraordinary Value*, Cambridge, Massachusetts: Harvard Business Press, 2013.

BizFacts

Entrepreneurship has proven to be an effective way for minorities and women to enter the business world.

- More than 6.1 million businesses were minority-owned in 2007, and they generated $871 billion in revenues.
- There were more than 12.4 million non-farm businesses owned by women (or co-owned equally with men), accounting for 45.4 percent of all U.S. companies.

Source: U.S. Small Business Administration, accessed March 9, 2014, http://www.sba.gov.

Peter Drucker defined an entrepreneur as someone who "always searches for change, responds to it, and exploits it as an opportunity." Entrepreneurs are always on the lookout for ways to create businesses from the opportunity of change.

Where Others See Problems, Entrepreneurs Recognize Opportunities

Here is a simple description of an entrepreneur that captures the essentials: *An entrepreneur recognizes opportunities where other people see only problems or the status quo.*

Many famous companies were started because an entrepreneur turned a problem into a successful business. An entrepreneur recognized that the problem was actually an opportunity. Where there are dissatisfied consumers, there are likely opportunities for entrepreneurs.

Anita Roddick was an excellent example of an entrepreneur who started off as a dissatisfied consumer. She started The Body Shop International because she was tired of paying for unnecessary perfume and fancy packaging when she bought makeup, and she thought other women might feel the same way.

Train Your Mind to Recognize Business Opportunities

An important step in becoming an entrepreneur is to train your mind to recognize business opportunities. A further step is to let your creativity fly. Consider developing your entrepreneurial instincts by asking yourself:

- What frustrates me the most when I try to buy something?
- What product or service would really make my life better?
- What makes me annoyed or angry?
- What product or service would take away my aggravation?

How Do Entrepreneurs Create Business Ideas?

1. *Listen.* By listening to others, entrepreneurs get ideas about improving a business or creating a new one. Create one business idea by listening. Describe how you got the idea.
2. *Observe.* By constantly keeping their eyes and ears open, entrepreneurs get ideas about how to help society, about what kind of businesses they could start, and about what consumers need. Create a business idea by observing. Describe how you got the idea.
3. *Analyze.* When entrepreneurs analyze a problem, they think about what product or service could solve it. Create a business idea by thinking up a solution to a problem. Describe how you arrived at the idea.

Entrepreneurs Use Their Imaginations

Businesses are also formed when entrepreneurs not only fume about products or services that annoy them but fantasize about products or services they would like to have in their lives. Jump-start your imagination by asking yourself such questions as

- What is the one thing I would like to have more than anything else?
- What would it look like? What would its other attributes be like?
- What would it do?
- What innovative product or service idea have I been mulling over in my mind?
- What problem have I encountered in everyday life and thought: "There has to be a better way to do this?"

Consider posing these questions to friends and family members as well. You might hear about an opportunity you had not yet recognized.

An Idea Is Not Necessarily an Opportunity

Not every business idea you have or invention you explore is an opportunity. In fact, the majority of ideas are not viable business possibilities. An *opportunity* has a unique characteristic that distinguishes it from an ordinary idea. An opportunity is *an idea that is based on what consumers need or want and are willing to buy sufficiently often at a high enough price to sustain a business*. A successful business sells what customers need at prices they are willing to pay. Many small businesses fail because entrepreneurs do not understand this.

In addition, according to the late Jeffry Timmons, "An opportunity has the qualities of being attractive, durable, and timely and is anchored in a product or service which creates or adds value for its buyer or end user."[13]

Timmons's definition of a business opportunity includes these four characteristics:

1. It is attractive to customers because it creates or adds value for its customers.
2. It will work in the business environment.
3. It can be executed in a defined window of opportunity.
4. It can be implemented with the right team to make it durable.

The window of opportunity is the length of time available to get the business idea to market before the market either diminishes due to lessening demand or is dominated by a competitor. You might have a great idea, but if other entrepreneurs have it too, and have already brought it to the marketplace, that window of opportunity is potentially closed or closing.

Remember, *not every idea is an opportunity*. For an idea to be a genuine opportunity, it must lead to the development of a product or service that is of value to the customer and is profitable for the business.

Larry Lilac/Alamy

[13]Jeffry Timmons, *New Venture Creation: Entrepreneurship for the 21st Century*, 5th ed., New York: Irwin/McGraw-Hill, 1999, p. 7.

Entrepreneurial Wisdom . . .

A useful way to evaluate a business idea is to look at its strengths, weaknesses, opportunities, and threats (SWOT). This is called SWOT analysis.

- **Strengths**—All the capabilities and positive points the company has, from experience to contacts. These are internal to the organization.
- **Weaknesses**—All the negatives the company faces, such as lack of capital or training or failure to set up a

workable accounting system. These are internal to the organization.

- **Opportunities**—Any positive external events or circumstances that can help the entrepreneur get ahead of the competition.
- **Threats**—Any external factors, events, or circumstances that can harm the business, such as competitors, legal issues, or declining economies.

Opportunity Is Situational

Opportunity is *situational,* meaning it is dependent on variable circumstances. There are no rules about when or where an opportunity might appear. A problem is one example of an opportunity that entrepreneurs need to be able to recognize. A changing situation or a trend is another.

Consider recent changes in computer technology. In the early 1990s, the conventional wisdom was that only the biggest telecommunications companies were in a position to exploit the Internet and all the opportunities it had to offer. How could entrepreneurs compete with established, resource-laden companies? The opposite has been true. Entrepreneurs penetrated and have dominated the market for Internet-based services. Think of Facebook, Google, and Foursquare. Each was an entrepreneurial venture that left industry giants scrambling to catch up.

It can take a huge corporation multiple years to develop and implement a new business strategy, while entrepreneurs can be nimble and enter and exit the market like roadrunners. Successful entrepreneurs can "turn on a dime rather than a dollar bill."

The Five Roots of Opportunity in the Marketplace

Entrepreneurs can exploit "five roots of opportunity."[14] Notice how similar these are to Schumpeter's definition of entrepreneurship.

1. **Problems** your business can solve
2. **Changes** in laws, situations, or trends
3. **Inventions** of new products or services
4. **Competitive advantages** in price, location, quality, reputation, reliability, speed, or other attributes of importance to customers
5. **Technological advances** that entrepreneurs take from the laboratory to the marketplace

Integrating Internal and External Opportunities

It is helpful not only to be aware of the five roots of opportunity in the marketplace but to think also about how we perceive opportunities ourselves. Opportunities fall into two classes: internal and external. An internal opportunity is one that comes from inside you—from a personal hobby, interest, or even a passion—or inside your organization. These can come in

---

[14]Adapted from John Clow (ed.), *Master Curriculum Guide: Economics and Entrepreneurship*, New York: Joint Council on Economic Education, 1991.

Step into the Shoes . . .

Russell Simmons Makes Rap Happen

In the late 1980s, Russell Simmons was promoting rap concerts at the City University of New York. At the time, rap was considered a passing fad, but Simmons was passionate about it. Even though most record executives thought rap would be over in a year or two, Simmons believed it was a business opportunity. He formed Def Jam Records with fellow student Rick Rubin for $5,000. Within a year, they produced hit records by Run DMC and LL Cool J, and Simmons went on to become a multimedia mogul.

Simmons took a chance on this opportunity because he felt that, if you personally know 10 people who are eager to buy your product or service, 10 *million* would be willing to buy it if they knew about it. He was right about rap's popular potential, but he could have been wrong. That can be a problem with

perceived opportunities: You may be passionate about something, but there may not be enough consumer interest to sustain an actual business venture.

Simmons loved rap and hoped other people would, too. That was the internal factor—he had the passion to sustain himself as he worked relentlessly to make his dream come true. As it turned out, music fans at that time were looking for a fresh sound. Rap filled the bill. This was an external opportunity that coincided with Simmons's internal commitment.

© Everett Collection Inc/ Alamy https://rms.pearson .com/Images/WebDataGrid/ ig_checkbox_on.gif

the form of the resolution of a problem, such as creating a viable product from scrap material, or the potential for a new product line.

An external opportunity, in contrast, is generated by an outside circumstance. External opportunities are conditions you notice that make you say to yourself, "Hey! I could start a great business from that!" For example, you see that people in your neighborhood are complaining about the lack of available day care, so you start a day care center after confirming the market need. But what if you find out very quickly that two-year-olds get on your nerves? That can be a major drawback for external opportunities. Your idea may fill a market need, but you may not have the skills or interest to make it a successful business.

The best business opportunities usually combine both internal and external factors. Ideally, a business that you are passionate about fills a sustainable need in the marketplace.

Establishing Strategies

Business success depends on the creation and application of profitable strategies. A **strategy** is a plan for how a business intends to go about its own performance and outdo that of its competition. Michael Porter created a "strategy framework" that delineates cost leadership and differentiation as low-cost and product-uniqueness strategies.[15] It also layers in the concept of focus strategies, which work in narrow market segments rather than broad ones. The illustration in **Figure 1-1** shows how each of Porter's Generic Strategies relates to the other.

A firm using a product-uniqueness strategy bases its competitive advantage on its ability to differentiate the firm's products and/or services from others in its competitive market space. Such factors as quality, availability, customer service, and the like are critical to differentiation, as will be discussed in greater detail in the marketing chapters of this text.

If you choose to emphasize a low-cost approach, you will be using a "cost-leadership" strategy. You are finding ways to reduce the costs of

strategy a plan for how an organization or individual plans to proceed with business operations and outperform that of its competitors.

---

[15]Michael Porter, *Competitive Strategy: Techniques for Analyzing Industries and Competitors*, New York: Free Press, 1998.

Figure 1-1 *Porter's Generic Strategies*

	Strategic Advantage	
Scope of Target Market	**Product Uniqueness**	**Low Cost**
Industry-Wide (Broad)	Differentiation Strategy	Cost Leadership Strategy
Market Segment (Narrow)	Focus Strategy (Differentiation)	Focus Strategy (Low Cost)

Source: Adapted from Michael Porter, *Competitive Strategy: Techniques for Analyzing Industries and Competitors,* Free Press, 1998.

operations and management sufficiently to be able to undercut the pricing of your competition and to sustain that price advantage.

Another component of the Porter framework is a focus strategy. This line of attack narrows in and creates a laserlike focus on a particular market segment or group. Rather than targeting an entire industry, you locate a niche or subset of the customer base and focus your marketing efforts on it. If you can find a sufficiently large niche to sustain your business, you can set the company apart from the competition and maintain the advantage. A focus strategy can work with differentiation and cost leadership.

Paths to Small Business Ownership

Not all business owners start their ventures from the ground up. Although the emphasis of this book is on starting and growing your own enterprise, the paths to business ownership are varied. You could buy an existing company, secure franchise rights, license or purchase critical technology or methods, inherit a company, or be hired as a manager.[16] There are pros and cons to each approach, and it is worthwhile to give thought to each option. Note the possibilities in **Exhibit 1-2**.

Exhibit 1-2 *Selected Business Entry Options*

Business Aspects	Start a Business	Buy an Existing Business	Secure a Franchise or License	Licensing Technology
Customers	None	Established	None—but may have name recognition	None
Location	Needed	In place	Assistance possible	Needed
Management Control	Owner	Owner	Owner within terms of license	Owner within terms of license
Operational Control	Owner	Owner	Owner within terms of license	Owner
Marketing	Needed	In place (+/−)	Assistance possible. Rules absolutely.	Needed
Reputation	None	In place (+/−)	Should exist. If not, why license?	Possible
Royalties/Fees	Not usual	Maybe	Ongoing	Likely
Financing	Needed	Prior owner may provide	Assistance possible	Needed
Disclosures	None	Buyer beware	FDD and contracts	Agreement

[16]Jerome A. Katz and Richard P. Green, *Entrepreneurial Small Business*, New York: McGraw-Hill/Irwin, 2008.

Securing Franchise Rights

"A franchise is a legal and commercial relationship between the owner of a trademark, service mark, trade name or advertising symbol and an individual or group seeking to use that identification in a business."[17] The two primary forms of franchising are product/trade name franchising and business format franchising. Franchisors can provide assistance in marketing, site selection, securing financing, training, product supply, and business systems. McDonald's is an example of a business format franchise. Each company's franchise agreement is different, and while franchises fail less often than fully independent businesses, they cannot guarantee success.

For many people who want to own and operate a business, it is worthwhile to consider franchising as a path to business ownership. Some factors to consider before selecting this option are shown in Exhibit 1-2.

Buying an Existing Business

The purchase of a business, or acquisition, can be a good way to jump-start entry into small business ownership. If you are purchasing a company, you should perform due diligence, which is the process used to learn about its true financial condition (the current owners may have incentives to provide incomplete, misleading, or inaccurate information), its reputation, and its continuing viability. There is both an art and a science to buying an existing business.

The challenge is to do a complete, in-depth analysis of the opportunity, just as you would for a start-up, with the added dimension of taking into account an existing history, whether for better or worse. Be wary of owners whose businesses seem to be too good to be true or who are overly eager to sell. Be thorough, whether you are buying an entire firm, a customer list, or some or all assets and especially if you are taking on some or all debt. Done well, buying a business can be the starting point for success. Done poorly, buying a business can be more challenging and problematic than starting a new venture.

Licensing Technology

One way to potentially shorten the product-development cycle and to access innovative technology is to identify and *license* that technology—that is, to enter into a contract to use it without purchasing the rights to own it. Whether you acquire such rights through a university, economic development office, federal agency such as NASA, or an individual scientist/inventor, you can create a business based on technology transfer. Or, you may find that it makes more sense to purchase the rights outright or over time.

The MBA team of Bruce Black and Matt Ferris, from the University of Georgia, developed a business plan that garnered numerous competitive awards for the KidSmart Vocal Smoke Detector, someone else's invention that they legitimately brought to market. The product is now available in major retail stores and on the Internet as the Signal One Vocal Smoke Alarm.

Before securing franchise rights, purchasing a business, or licensing technology, be certain to do your research thoroughly to understand what you are and are not buying, and what your ongoing obligations—financial, operational, legal, and reporting—will be. Because these transactions are

franchise a business that markets a product or service developed by a franchisor, typically in the manner specified by that franchisor.

acquisition a business purchase.

due diligence the exercise of reasonable care in the evaluation of a business opportunity.

[17]U.S. Small Business Administration Workshop, "Is Franchising for Me?" accessed December 2007, http://www.sba.gov/idc/groups/public/documents/sba_homepage/serv_sbp_isfforme.pdf.

complex and can have significant financial and personal implications, it is important to invest in qualified legal and financial counsel before signing any agreements of this kind.

The Many Faces of Entrepreneurship

Entrepreneurs are as diverse as the composition of the economy. They are of all ethnicities, races, and religions, and come from every socioeconomic status. They enter into self-employment for a wide range of reasons and choose to continue as entrepreneurs or return to outside employment for just as many. There are women and minority entrepreneurs and young entrepreneurs in record numbers. There are also refugee and immigrant entrepreneurs.

This diverse pool of entrepreneurs does not produce a single path to entrepreneurial success. Rather, the types of businesses formed reflect the diversity of the founders. In addition to full-time ventures founded to maximize growth and wealth, some are started as part-time and microenterprises, artisanal and opportunistic businesses, and others.

Gazelles

gazelle a company that achieves an annual growth rate of 20 percent or greater, typically measures by the increase of sales revenue.

A classic entrepreneurial story is that of a pair of inventors who develop a new, innovative technology or product in a garage, basement, or dormitory; lift themselves up by their bootstraps into a wildly successful business venture in virtually no time; take the company public; and become incredibly wealthy in the process. This stereotype describes the founders of a gazelle, a company that achieves an annual growth rate of 20 percent or greater, typically measured by the growth of sales revenue. Gazelles tend to be the exception rather than the rule for entrepreneurial enterprises but are a significant type of firm. Gazelles are financed by a combination of found resources with significant outside assistance. They rely heavily on external financial support and counsel.

Microenterprises

microenterprise a firm with five or fewer employees, initial capitalization requirements of under $50,000, and the regular operational involvement of the owner.

Most businesses are founded as microenterprises, which are defined as businesses with five or fewer employees, initial capitalization requirements of less than $50,000, and the habitual operational involvement of the owner. In fact, more than 60 percent of all U.S. firms have four or fewer employees, according to the U.S. Small Business Administration.[18] The Association for Enterprise Opportunity (AEO) estimates that the more than 25.1 million microenterprises in the United States account for 88.2 percent of all businesses and 22 percent of all private employment.[19]

lifestyle business a microenterprise that permits its owners to follow a desired pattern of living, such as supporting college costs or taking vacations.

Microenterprises are founded for a variety of reasons and are often more fluid than other types of businesses. These firms may be founded to provide only part-time employment for their owners. They may not be intended as long-term enterprises and may not have the goal of growing larger. They may be planned as only temporary ventures to provide income during periods of unemployment or to supplement household finances for a particular purpose. Lifestyle businesses are microenterprises that permit their owners to follow a desired pattern of living, such as supporting college costs or taking vacations. On the other hand, a microenterprise could make the difference between a family living in poverty and achieving economic stability.

---

[18]U.S. Small Business Administration, Office of Advocacy, 2013.

[19]Association for Enterprise Opportunity, accessed June 30, 2013, http://www.microenterpriseworks.org.

Mainstream Small Firms

These constitute the bulk of the small businesses in public perception, in the press, and in community visibility. They provide, or have the potential to provide, substantial profits to their owners. Mainstream small firms can be operated by founder-entrepreneurs, subsequent generations of family members, successor owners, or franchisees. They create many of the jobs included in statistics from the U.S. Small Business Administration and employ the majority of American workers. Unlike many microenterprises, they are established with continuity and permanent wealth building in mind and are more often registered with local, state, and federal agencies.

Making the Business Work Personally and Professionally

What makes a business work is not only profitability and cash flow. Each entrepreneur has his or her own goals and objectives for the business. As an entrepreneur, it will be up to you to determine how you want your business to be and to make it happen.

A Business Must Make a Profit to Stay in Business

No matter how big or small, a business must make a **profit**—that is, show a positive gain from operations after all expenses are subtracted. Most businesses lose money initially because entrepreneurs have to spend money to set up operations and advertise to attract customers. If the business cannot make a profit and generate cash, eventually the entrepreneur will be unable to pay the bills and will have to close.

profit amount of earnings remaining after all costs are deducted from the income of a business.

Closing a business is nothing to be ashamed of, if you operate ethically and learn from the experience. In fact, many successful entrepreneurs open and close more than one business during their lives. If your venture is not making a profit after you have gotten it up and running, that is a signal you may be in the wrong business. Closing it may be the best decision.

An entrepreneur may change businesses many times over a lifetime in response to changing interests, competition, and consumer needs.

Profit Is the Sign That the Entrepreneur Is Adding Value

Profit is the sign that an entrepreneur has added value to the resources he or she is using. Debbi Fields added value to scarce resources by creating something that people were willing to buy for a price that gave her a profit. In contrast, not making a profit is a sign that the entrepreneur is not using resources well and is not adding value to them.

◀ Learning Objective 4
Explain how profit works as a signal to the entrepreneur.

Profit Results from the Entrepreneur's Choices

An entrepreneur's choices directly affect how much profit the business makes. For example, suppose, like Debbi Fields, you have a business selling homemade cookies. You might decide one week to buy margarine instead of butter because it is cheaper and you haven't promised real butter in your advertising, even though the cookies may not taste as good made with margarine. This type of choice is called a **trade-off**. You are giving up one thing (taste) for another (money).

trade-off the act of giving up one thing for another.

If your customers do not notice the change and continue to buy your cookies, you have made a good choice. You have conserved a resource (money) and increased your profit by lowering your costs. The increase in profit confirms that you have made the right choice.

If your customers notice the change and stop buying your cookies, your profit will decrease. The decrease in profit signals that you have made a bad choice. Next week you should probably go back to butter and hope that you can regain the lost customers. The profit signal taught you that your customers were dissatisfied and the trade-off was not worth it. Every choice an entrepreneur makes is a trade-off.

Seven Rules for Building a Successful Business

Russell Simmons and Rick Rubin were successful in creating Def Jam because they instinctively applied the seven basic rules of building a successful business:

1. *Recognize an opportunity.* Simmons observed that rap music was an untapped business opportunity.
2. *Evaluate it with critical thinking.* He tested his idea by promoting concerts and observing consumer reaction.
3. *Build a team.* Simmons formed a partnership with Rubin.
4. *Write.* Simmons and Rubin created a realistic business plan.
5. *Gather resources.* Simmons and Rubin pooled their $5,000 and the skills they needed.
6. *Decide ownership.* Simmons and Rubin formed a legal partnership.
7. *Create wealth.* Def Jam became a source of wealth for themselves and others.

The Team Approach

While most businesses do not hire employees, successful entrepreneurial ventures grow well beyond their initial founder. Some have multiple cofounders while others grow their teams along with their businesses. The team approach can make or break a business. For example, alone, neither Simmons nor Rubin had enough skills or money to launch a record label, but together they were able to do it. Def Jam was also aided by the fact that each knew different artists and had different contacts in the recording industry.

Entrepreneurial Wisdom . . .

Build Your Brain

Becoming a successful entrepreneur is all about making connections, those "Aha!" moments when you realize what your business opportunity is or when you figure out how to do something better than the competition. Research indicates that mental exercise helps the brain become better at making such connections. Even the most erudite scientists recognize the value of activities that encourage brain cells to make new connections. Robotics engineer Hugo de Garis, who has worked on such projects as building an artificial brain for an artificial cat, plays classical piano every day before he sits down at the computer. "This helps to build my own brain," he told *The New York Times*.[20] Arnold Scheibel, head of the University of California–Los Angeles Brain Research Institute, suggests the following brain-builders:

- Solving puzzles
- Playing a musical instrument
- Fixing something, such as learning to repair cars or electrical equipment
- Creating art, writing poetry, painting, or sculpting
- Dancing
- Making friends with people who like to have interesting conversations

[20]Nicholas D. Kristof, "Robokitty," *The New York Times*, August 1, 1999.

Potential team members are all around you. Some might be in your immediate circles of friends and family members who have skills, financial resources, equipment, or contacts that would make them valuable business partners. At the same time, you may reach across the globe to find team members. Perhaps you very much want to start a Web site design business, because you know of companies in your community that want to put up Web sites. You are a graphic artist, but you do not know how to use Web site development programs. If you have a friend who has that knowledge, you might start a business together. Or maybe you would like to start a DJ venture, but you only have some of the necessary equipment. If you form the business with a friend, you can pool equipment. (When forming a business team, organize the enterprise so that everyone involved shares in the ownership and profits. People work better when they are working for themselves.) Just be careful of jumping into business relationships with undue haste.

Now carry this idea a step further. Everyone you meet is a potential contact for your business, just as you may be a valuable contact for theirs. Thinking this way will encourage you to *network*, or exchange valuable information and contacts with other businesspeople. Keep your business cards with you at all times and truly view every individual you encounter as an opportunity for your business. Remember, though, that networking is a two-way street. See how you can help those that you meet first rather than always focusing on how they can help you. The results can be nothing short of amazing.

Chapter Summary

Now that you have studied this chapter, you can do the following:

1. Summarize what entrepreneurs do.
   - Entrepreneurs start their own businesses and work for themselves.
   - Entrepreneurs recognize opportunities to start businesses that other people may not have noticed.
   - Entrepreneurs shift economic resources from an area of lower productivity into an area of higher productivity and greater yield. By doing this, they add value to scarce resources.
2. Examine how free-enterprise economies work and how entrepreneurs fit into them.
   - The free-enterprise system is based on voluntary exchange. Voluntary exchange is a trade between two parties who agree to trade money for a product or service. Both parties agree to the trade because each benefits from the exchange.
   - The free-enterprise system encourages entrepreneurs who use resources efficiently to satisfy consumer needs by rewarding them with profit.
3. Identify and evaluate opportunities to start your own business.
   - The five roots of opportunity are
     i. problems that your business can solve;
     ii. changes in laws, situations, or trends;
     iii. inventions of totally new products or services;
     iv. competition (if you can find a way to beat the competition on price, location, quality, reputation, reliability, or speed, you can create a successful business with an existing product or service); and
     v. technological advances (scientists may invent new technology, but entrepreneurs figure out how to sell it).

4. Explain how profit works as a signal to the entrepreneur.
   - Profit is the sign that an entrepreneur has added value to the scarce resources he or she is using.
   - Not making a profit is a sign that the entrepreneur is not using resources well and is not adding value to them.
5. A business opportunity is an idea plus these three characteristics:
   - It is attractive to customers.
   - It will work in your business environment.
   - It can be executed in the defined window of opportunity.
6. Use cost/benefit analysis to make decisions.
   - Cost/benefit analysis is the process of comparing costs and benefits in order to make a good decision.
   - Cost/benefit analysis can be inaccurate without including opportunity cost. This is the cost of missing your next-best investment.
7. Use SWOT analysis to evaluate a business opportunity.
   - Strengths: all of the capabilities and positive points the entrepreneur has, from experience to contacts. These are internal to the organization.
   - Weaknesses: all of the negatives the entrepreneur faces, such as lack of capital or training or failure to set up a workable accounting system. These are internal to the organization.
   - Opportunities: any positive external events or circumstances (including lucky breaks) that can help the entrepreneur get ahead of the competition.
   - Threats: any external factors, events, or circumstances that can harm the business, such as competitors, legal issues, or declining economies.

Key Terms

acquisition	microenterprise
capital	opportunity cost
capitalism	product
commission	profit
cost/benefit analysis	salary
dividend	service
due diligence	social business
entrepreneur	social entrepreneurship
franchise	strategy
free-enterprise system	trade-off
gazelle	venture philanthropy
green entrepreneurship	voluntary exchange
lifestyle business	wage
mentor	

Entrepreneurship Portfolio

Critical Thinking Exercises

Control - freedom - independence

1-1. What would be the best thing about owning your own business? What would be the worst? Why? *insecurity*

1-2. Choose three nonfinancial benefits of entrepreneurship that might be important to you. Write a paragraph about each.

1-3. If you were to start a business five years from now, what would be your opportunity cost? In other words, what is the next-best use of your time? How much money could you make working at a job, instead? The answer to this last question will give you a rough idea of how to value your time when you start a business and figure out how much to pay yourself.

1-4. Select and describe an idea that you have for a business. Summarize how it could satisfy a consumer need.

1-5. Provide an example of a change that has occurred or is about to occur in your area/neighborhood. Discuss business opportunities this change might create.

1-6. Identify and list five business opportunities in your environment and the need(s) each would satisfy. Indicate whether each opportunity you describe is internal, external, or a mix.

Key Concept Questions

1-7. Define *small business*. How, if at all, does this differ from what you would have expected the definition to be?

1-8. Explain how profit works as a signal to the entrepreneur.

1-9. It will probably take about three months for your business to start earning a profit. Do you agree or disagree? Why? If you disagree, how long do you expect it to take? What are the three most important factors in determining the time frame?

1-10. Summarize three facts about capitalism.

1-11. Compare and contrast the meaning of a business opportunity and a business idea.

1-12. Visit the U.S. Small Business Administration Web site (http://www.sba.gov). Read an article on starting a business and write a brief summary of the key information (200 words or fewer). Remember to create a proper citation for the article.

Application Exercises

1-13. Have a conversation with a friend or relative. Discuss things he or she finds frustrating in his or her area/neighborhood.

   a. Write down these comments.

   b. Generate at least three business opportunities from this conversation.

   c. Use the checklist below to evaluate each of your three business ideas as opportunities.

Business Idea _____	Critical Evaluation	
Would it be attractive to potential customers?	Yes __√__	No _____
Would it work in your business environment?	Yes __√__	No _____
Is there a sufficient window of opportunity?	Yes __√__	No _____
Do you have the skills and resources to create this business?	Yes ____√	No _____
If you do not have the skills and resources to create this business, do you know someone who does and might want to create the business with you? (Consider how you might determine this.)	Yes __√__	No _____

d. Choose the best of the business opportunities and develop a SWOT analysis for it.

e. Create a cost/benefit analysis for starting this business. Use the analysis to explain why you would or would not actually start it.

Exploring Your Community

1-14. Interview an entrepreneur, preferably in person. Entrepreneurs are busy people, but many are willing to spend time speaking with someone who is interested in what they are doing. Meeting over a light meal might be the most efficient use of the entrepreneur's time. Before the interview, brainstorm 10 questions in the following four categories. After the interview, be sure to write a thank-you note.

a. ***Information gathering.*** Open the interview with questions about the entrepreneur's family (any other entrepreneurs in it?) and educational and work background.

b. ***About the business.*** Next, ask questions about how the business was started. How did the entrepreneur recognize an opportunity and develop it?

c. ***Running the business.*** Ask about which challenges arose as the business got underway and how they were solved.

d. ***Reflection.*** Ask the entrepreneur to reflect. What advice would he or she give to an aspiring entrepreneur? Has running a business been rewarding?

e. ***Evaluation.*** Reflect on the interview and what you learned about entrepreneurship and small business. Summarize your thoughts and describe how this new learning may impact you as an entrepreneur.

Exploring Online

1-15. Visit an Internet search engine such as Google, Yahoo, or Bing. Search for one of the following terms: *entrepreneurship ideas*, *businesses for sale*, or *franchise opportunities*. For the search you selected, answer:

a. Which search engine and term were used and

b. What were the number of matches ("hits").

1-16. Find a Web site based on question 1-15 that looks promising and answer these questions:

  a. What is the Web site (URL and name)?

  b. Who is sponsoring the Web site?

  c. Is the Web site selling a product or information (as a primary function, not through banner ads)? If so, what products or information?

  d. Identify three businesses/ideas/opportunities from the site, and state why they might or might not be viable opportunities for you.

Urban Decay: Finding an Entrepreneurial Opportunity

Sandy Lerner cofounded Cisco Systems in 1984 with her former husband, Leonard Bosack. It became a world leader in sales of computer routers. When she was ousted from the company in 1990, Lerner had the time and financial resources to focus on charitable activities and other business opportunities. By 1995, she was ready to start another company that would fill a market void.

Lerner believed that there was an opportunity in the beauty market for quality, nontraditional products. According to the Urban Decay Web site, "Our story opens 15 years ago, when pink, red and beige enslaved the prestige beauty market. Heaven forbid you wanted purple or green nails, because you'd either have to whip out a marker, or risk life and limb with that back alley drugstore junk." Lerner had seen a Chanel polish that was a deep red color, nearly black, but found little else in high-end products that met the need she identified.

Lerner's business manager introduced her to a creative businesswoman and self-described makeup addict, Wende Zomnir, and the business began to take shape. "Over high tea, the two forged a pact that led to renegade nail polish mixing sessions in Wende's Laguna Beach bungalow." Urban Decay launched in 1996 with 12 nail enamels and 10 lipsticks. "Inspired by seedier facets of the urban landscape, they bore groundbreaking names like Roach, Smog, Rust, Oil Slick, and Acid Rain. The first magazine ad queried 'Does Pink Make You Puke?,' fueling the revolution as cosmetics industry executives scrambled to keep up." Today, the company describes itself this way: "Urban Decay is beauty with an edge. It is feminine, dangerous and fun . . . appealing to anyone who relishes her individuality and dares to express it."

Even after the '90s grunge style faded, Urban Decay thrived. The company became a global organization; it is a popular full cosmetic line at major retailers such as Sephora, Macy's, and Ulta and is found on the Internet through Beauty.com. Urban Decay is sold by retailers in the Middle East, the United Kingdom, Italy, Canada, France, Singapore, and Spain. After several transitions, it is currently owned by L'Oreal Cosmetics, and Zomnir continues to work at the company.

Urban Decay notes factors contributing to its success: "And although UD fans around the

Alamy

world might approach our products in wildly different ways, we've noticed they share an independent spirit that unites them. Maybe this hunger for something unique explains the passionate support we've received over the years."

Clearly, Lerner and her cofounders saw opportunity in beauty.

Case Study Analysis

1-17. What unmet needs of the consumer contributed to the success of Urban Decay?

1-18. Was founding Urban Decay an expected next step after leaving Cisco Systems for Sandy Lerner? Why or why not?

1-19. What characteristics made Urban Decay an opportunity rather than simply an idea? Which of the five roots of opportunity apply here?

1-20. Is there a future for Urban Decay? Assess what that future might look like.

Case Sources

"Sandy Lerner," *Encyclopedia of World Biography*, accessed March 10, 2014, http://www .notablebiographies.com/newsmakers2/2005-La-Pr/Lerner-Sandy.html.

Urban Decay, accessed March 10, 2014, http:// www.urbandecay.com.

Foursquare is the ubiquitous location-based social network that creatively incorporates gaming elements and marketing. It is the brainchild of Dennis Crowley and Naveen Selvadurai.

Dennis Crowley and Naveen Selvaduri.
(Scott McDermott/Getty Images)

The Founders

Crowley and Selvadurai met in New York City in 2007. They worked for different technology companies (AreaCode and Socialight, respectively), but in the same office space. Crowley is a graduate of Syracuse University. He has a degree in advertising and holds a master's from New York University's Interactive Telecommunications Program. Selvadurai, a software engineer, holds computer science degrees from King's College (London) and Worcester Polytechnic Institute (Worcester, Massachusetts).

Both founders had prior experience in the technology field. Crowley worked at Jupiter Communications directly out of college, and Vindego after that. He cofounded Dodgeball in 2003 and sold it to Google in 2005; he worked for Google after the acquisition. Then, he joined AreaCode as its director of product development. Selvadurai worked at Sun Microsystems, Lucent, RunTunes, and Sony Music. He later joined Socialight as its Vice President of Engineering.

The companies where the founders worked were related to the business that Foursquare is today. Vindego created mobile applications, including city guides. Dodgeball was based on Crowley's graduate thesis, which he partnered with Alex Rainert (currently head of product at Foursquare) in order to commercialize the

concept. Dodgeball was a location-based social networking option for mobile devices that was available in a number of U.S. cities. Google acquired and operated Dodgeball until 2009, when Dodgeball was shut down and replaced with Google Latitude. AreaCode was a software start-up in the area of game play when Crowley worked there.

RunTunes was a company, started by some friends of Selvadurai, that aimed to bring music to phones. It was bought by Sony Music. Finally, Socialight is a company that creates and promotes local content with social interaction and user-content contributions.

According to Christopher Nomes, "Partnership between Naveen and Dennis was a perfect match. Both young and brilliant, both with already hefty working experience from working in cool and innovative companies, and both with ability to take everything they learned and forge it into something new and special that will overshadow everything they did before."

© NetPhotos/Alamy

Creating at the Kitchen Table

About a year after they met, Crowley and Selvadurai began building the first version of Foursquare at Crowley's kitchen table in the East Village. In March 2009, Foursquare launched at South by Southwest Interactive. Most recent numbers suggest that Foursquare has over 45 million users and is growing at a rate of 25,000 new users per day. Check-ins exceed 5 billion.

The App

Foursquare is widely popular and becomes an even more useful mobile app with its increasing numbers of users. As users check in on their mobile devices at various locations, such as restaurants, retail stores, and museums, they can add recommendations/reviews. This serves three purposes: (1) They can tell friends where they are. (2) They construct a set of places visited to serve as reminders. (3) The recommendations provide additional data for other Foursquare users and thus add value to the app.

To increase usage and improve the user experience, Crowley and Selvadurai built incentives into the app. For example, users become the "mayor" of a particular location based on the number of visits. Users earn virtual badges for the number or variety of check-ins. They also can receive discounts and incentives from advertisers when they check in. A restaurant might provide a 10 percent discount or a free dessert.

Foursquare was designed to generate frequent use. Selvadurai says, "Your app has to have a primary-use case. That brings people back. I think simplicity has a lot to do with it. Simplicity is probably high on that list." In the case of Foursquare, the "check-in" is the primary use case. The app is designed to make the process quick and easy.

zeljkodan/Shutterstock

Financing

A start-up like Foursquare required resources beyond what Crowley and Selvadurai could contribute. They sought venture capital in multiple offerings. The Series A round totaled $1.35 million, which they raised in 2009. The primary investors were Union Square Ventures with O'Reilly AlphaTech Ventures, and the funding was an equity investment. At the time of the investment, Foursquare was valued at $6 million.

The Series B, or second round, totaled $20 million, with Foursquare valued at $95 million

in 2010. The group of venture capitalists was led by Andreessen Horowitz with participation by Union Square Ventures and O'Reilly AlphaTech Ventures. The funds were needed to continue the expansion of the company, including the addition of critical team members and a new office space.

The next round of financing was raised on June 24, 2011, at $50 million in equity from Andreessen Horowitz, with Union Square Ventures, O'Reilly AlphaTech Ventures, and Spark Capital. Interestingly, Sarah Lacy notes, "Some firms said they shied away from the deal, because they felt monetization was only more unclear now. With the local space on fire, Foursquare's target advertisers are already beset with salespeople from Yelp, Living Social, Groupon, Google, and others calling on them. There's going to be a level of retailer fatigue, and business-wise Foursquare is late to the party." For this round, the company was valued at $600 million; again, the funds were needed for expansion.

In the spring of 2013, Foursquare raised an additional $41 million in a loan and convertible debt, rather than equity. The lead on this round was Silver Lake, a private equity firm, which provided a multi-year loan. Both Andreessen Horowitz and Union Square Ventures participated in this round, but with convertible debt. According to Tomio Geron, "The mobile location app was a social media darling after championing the check-in and surviving as others in the space faded away. But it has been struggling to revamp itself as a local search and commerce tool as the check-in becomes more of a commodity available on other apps such as Facebook."

In total, through these four rounds of financing, Foursquare raised $112.35 million in five years to fuel its start-up and growth.

Cofounder Perspective

During a presentation in October 2001, Selvadurai shared his seven formulas for creating and building a successful venture:

1. Keep good company.
2. Make something people want.
3. Build around an "atomic action" (i.e., check-in).
4. Seek mentors early.
5. At first, hunch; then, data.
6. Balance unknowns with knowns.
7. Always be recruiting.

Foursquare is a reflection of the opportunity its founders identified, the team they created, and the resources they garnered.

Case Study Analysis

1-21. Evaluate how Foursquare fits Schumpeter's definition and the five basic ways entrepreneurs find opportunities to create new businesses.

1-22. Compare Selvadurai's seven formulas with the seven rules for building a successful business in this text.

1-23. Apply Porter's generic strategies to the industry in which Foursquare competes, using case information and your own knowledge. Synthesize your analysis. Based on this work, what did you find?

1-24. What prepared the founders to create Foursquare?

1-25. What gaps in the founders' team and resources needed to be filled by outside sources? Name four specific resources they acquired.

1-26. Identify the features and benefits the founders included in the app to ensure its popularity. Why were these selected?

1-27. Is Foursquare the only app of its kind? If not, what other apps are similar?

1-28. What future do you predict for Foursquare?

Case Sources

Spencer E. Ante, "Foursquare locates new funds to expand," *The Wall Street Journal*, June 28, 2010, accessed June 30, 2013, http://online.wsj.com/article/ SB10001424052748704846004575333222375027784 .html.

"Foursquare," *Crunchbase*, accessed June 29, 2013, http://www.crunchbase.com/company/ foursquare.

Dan Frommer, "Foursquare raises $1.35 million, led by Union Square Ventures," BusinessInsider, September 4, 2009, accessed June 30, 2013, http://www.businessinsider.com/foursquare-raises-13-million-from-union-square-ventures-2009-9.

Tomio Geron, "Foursquare gets $41 million, postpones valuation question," April 11, 2013, accessed June 20, 2013, http://www.forbes.com/ sites/tomiogeron/2013/04/11/foursquare-gets-41-million-postpones-valuation-question/.

Antiq Hawk, "Dennis Crowley – Co-Founder and CEO of Foursquare," *Who & Whom*, accessed June 29, 2013, http://www.whoandwhom.com/ dennis-crowley/.

Sarah Lacy, "Foursquare Closes $50M at $600M Valuation," TechCrunch, June 24, 2011, accessed June 20, 2013, http://techcrunch.com/2011/06/24/ foursquare-closes-50m-at-a-600m-valuation/.

Christopher Nomes, "Naveen Selvadurai—Co-Founder of Foursquare," *Who & Whom*, accessed June 29, 2013, http://www.whoandwhom .com/naveen-selvadurai/.

Foursquare, accessed May 7, 2013, http://www .foursquare.com/about/.

Naveen Selvadurai, September 30, 2011, Presentation, Reuters Video, accessed June 29, 2013, http://www.youtube.com/watch?v= AbgcM4QFaH0&feature=player_embedded.

Naveen Selvadurai, October 2, 2011, Presentation, Start-Up Bootcamp, accessed June 29, 2013, http://www.youtube.com/watch?v= hHKdkfUM4Js.

Note: Since this case written, Foursquare has introduced "Swarm" for location-based services.

The Business Plan: Road Map to Success

Learning Objectives

1. Describe what a feasibility analysis is and choose when to create one.

2. Prepare a Business Model Canvas.

3. Identify primary business plan contents.

4. Summarize the various purposes for a business plan and the audiences for one.

5. Differentiate the components of a business plan.

6. Recognize and demonstrate proper development and formatting of a business plan.

Blend Images/Alamy

> *"If you don't know where you are going, any road will get you there."*
>
> —Lewis Carroll, English author

Great business ideas can grow into great businesses, or they can wither away from neglect or unfavorable circumstances. One thing that successful businesses have in common is a sound idea and an entrepreneur who has a plan for turning the idea into reality.

Frank Jao worked as a translator for the American military during the Vietnam War, and when Saigon fell in 1975, he and his wife, Kathy, were flown out of the country to Camp Pendleton, California.[1] They had the clothes on their backs and about $20.

Frank got a job selling vacuum cleaners door to door within 48 hours of arrival. He also met with a community college counselor who discovered that Frank had sold heavy equipment in Vietnam. The counselor suggested that, because such equipment was a big-ticket item with a long sales cycle, perhaps Frank should try real estate—which was also a big-ticket item with a long sales cycle.

He joined a firm that had commercial and residential divisions and was assigned to work in residential sales. Frank observed that the agents working on the commercial side were making more money than those in his group, so he set a goal to earn the right to move to the commercial division. In 1979, he made a sale that brought a commission of $350,000. He and Kathy used those earnings to purchase a parcel of raw land in Westminster, California.

Frank dreamed of building and operating a shopping area that would provide a place for the Vietnamese community to buy and sell the types of products and services they enjoyed in their native land. This dream was realized as the Asian Garden Mall. It is a modern indoor mall that stands at the center of what is known in Orange County as Little Saigon. Frank has done so much for this community that city leaders gave him his own "Exit" on the busy Interstate 405 freeway.

Was it easy to parlay the $350,000 into Asian Garden? No. Remember that Frank put all his cash into the raw land. Next, he had to convince a banker to loan him the $3 million he needed to build on the land. The banker told Frank that to get a loan he must bring back a feasibility study and a loan package. In 1979, there was no Internet on which to find free business-plan and feasibility-analysis templates—and he did not have enough money to pay for a professionally prepared loan package with a business plan.

That night, after Frank met with the loan officer, when the bank was closed and the parking lot dark, he climbed into the bank dumpster, where he found several loan packages (privacy rules were different then). He figured that, because they were in the trash, no one would miss them. Using these as guides, he and Kathy created a plan. Three weeks after his first meeting with a commercial lender, Frank was back with the complete loan package, and that banker made the $3 million loan.

H. Lorren Au Jr/The Orange County Register/ZUMAPRESS/Alamy

---

[1]Original case prepared by Hattie Bryant, creator of *Small Business School*, a television series made for PBS and Voice of America, http://SmallBusinessSchool.org.

Because of Frank and Kathy's creativity, courage, and persistence over the years, their company, Bridgecreek, has developed more than 2 million square feet of retail, condominium, and apartment space. It owns and manages 1.5 million square feet of space in Southern California.

Feasibility Analysis: Does My Idea Work?

Learning Objective 1

Describe a feasibility analysis and choose when to create one.

feasibility analysis a study to assist in making the go/no go decision based on a close examination of product/service, market, industry, and financial data.

The time and energy involved in generating and exploring business ideas can be extensive, with the SBA reporting that, for many entrepreneurs, the process can take years. With that sort of massive investment, it is an advantage to filter out the ideas that are viable from those that are not. A feasibility analysis will assist in making the go/no go decision—based on a close examination of product/service, market, industry, and financial data, in a sufficient degree of detail to ensure confidence in the results. This is an excellent precursor to committing the time and resources to planning the implementation of the business and then presenting it for financing—after the creation of a comprehensive business plan. The feasibility analysis essentially tests a business concept for viability in three areas:

1. product and/or service feasibility,
2. market and industry feasibility, and
3. financial feasibility.

A feasibility study presupposes the business's desirability and your interest in this segment of the industry.

Analyzing Product and/or Service Feasibility

Entrepreneurs are often described as committed to their business idea. They take on an almost religious zeal and essentially fall in love with the concept of the product or service, creating a fantasy of what the business will be. Conducting a product or service feasibility analysis serves the dual purpose of determining whether realization of the product or delivery of the service is possible at a profit and whether customer demand will be sufficient. Without affirmative answers to both these questions, success will be elusive at best.

A product or service is only worthwhile pursuing if it can be produced and delivered at a profit in an ongoing manner. For example, scientists develop innovative technologies in their laboratories that can significantly outperform any technology that is commercially available. Some entrepreneurs may want to introduce products that embody the next big technology and move down the path toward securing financing and establishing marketing strategies only to find out that the production cost would lead to an unreasonable price and the volume of production would be too low to serve the target market. In order to avoid such unwelcome surprises, you can create the production design for your product and create a working model, called a *prototype*, fabricated for testing by laboratories and prospective customers. Services can also be tested for timeliness and cost of delivery.

Determining whether a product appeals to prospective customers and whether the appeal would translate into sales will be vital to assessing feasibility. Subsequent chapters of this text will address specific sources of information that you can use to determine feasibility. These sources can be learned directly from the targeted customer base (primary) or through already existing research (secondary).

It is important to perform this feasibility study in order to avoid wasting valuable resources. An amazing product or innovative service would not necessarily translate into enough sales to sustain your business.

If the results of the feasibility analysis are negative, it is time to seriously rethink the product or service and its potential fit in the marketplace. Inconclusive or positive results on the product or service itself can be considered, with the balance of the feasibility analysis, to decide whether to proceed to the business-plan stage.

Analyzing Market and Industry Feasibility

Patrick Breig/Shutterstock

Evaluating the targeted market and industry is essential to determining the viability of a business idea. Just as a seed will grow in fertile soil and wither away in barren earth, business ideas will take hold or fail based largely on the market and industry environment in which they are launched. This segment of a feasibility analysis examines the attractiveness of the proposed industry and the opportunity to find strategic, defensible niches. Later chapters will provide resources for conducting such analysis in greater detail.

One tool that is frequently used for industry analysis is the "five forces" model created by Michael Porter of Harvard University, which focuses on the competitive intensity of a market. The model is designed to assess the overall industry-competitiveness level in which closely related or similar products and/or services are sold. You would create a separate model for each proposed line of business. **Figure 2-1** provides a visual summary of the model.

The interaction of the forces creates the industry environment, and the attractiveness of participating in it, for a given business.[2] The five industry forces identified by Porter are essentially:

1. existing competitive rivalry,
2. barriers to entry,
3. threat of substitutes,
4. supplier power, and
5. buyer power.

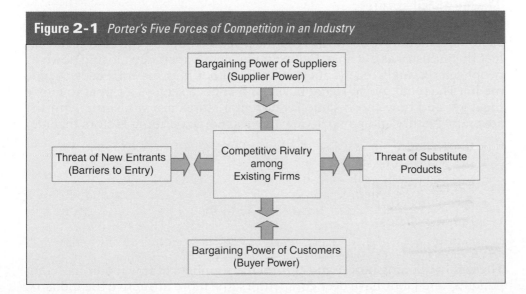

Figure 2-1 *Porter's Five Forces of Competition in an Industry*

Bargaining Power of Suppliers (Supplier Power)

Threat of New Entrants (Barriers to Entry)

Competitive Rivalry among Existing Firms

Threat of Substitute Products

Bargaining Power of Customers (Buyer Power)

---

[2]Adapted from Michael E. Porter, "How Competitive Forces Shape Strategy," *Harvard Business Review*, March/April 1979, pp. 137–145.

Existing Competitive Rivalry

The degree of rivalry among existing competitors is generally the strongest force in an industry and is influenced by all the other forces. Some industries are more aggressive and competitive than others, and you will want to know how your business could fit in the existing environment. For example, look at the number of Chinese restaurants in a large city or the competitive environment for power companies. Key aspects of intense rivalry, according to Porter, include:

- Many firms of approximately the same size
- An industry experiencing slow growth
- Lack of differentiation
- Low switching costs for customers
- High fixed costs
- Perishable products
- The need to create new production capacity in large increments
- High barriers to exiting
- Diverse rivals

Barriers to Entry

In an industry the threat of new entrants is largely defined by the strength of the barriers erected to prevent them. As an entrant, you want the barriers to be low. As an established firm, you want them to be high. For example, it is relatively easy to start a landscaping company, so competitors range from the neighborhood teenager with the family mower to larger companies with more expensive equipment and many employees. According to Porter, sources of barriers to entry include:

- Capital requirements
- Cost advantages
- Economies of scale
- Access to distribution channels
- Product differentiation
- Government policy

Threat of Substitutes

The level of threat posed by alternative products and services to industry customers matters. Substitutes cap the price a company can charge and affect the industry as a whole. For example, newspapers are closing down as people increasingly receive their news and other information via electronic media. The retail movie-rental business had been seen as a threat to movie theaters, and now those same retail rental stores are vanishing with the advent of Netflix and pay-per-view movies. Some defining factors include:

- Convenience
- Price competitiveness
- Supply availability
- Switching costs
- Public policies

Supplier Power

The less bargaining power and control the suppliers of raw materials, components, and labor have over competitors, the more attractive the industry. Where there are a few powerful suppliers, new entrants will have little flexibility or control, both of which they need. Porter suggests that suppliers are more powerful when the following industry factors apply:

- There is domination by a few companies.
- The products are differentiated.
- Switching costs are high.
- Substitutes are not readily available.
- They can threaten to move into the business themselves.
- The industry is not important to the supplier.

Buyer Power

This force is similar to that of suppliers, but on the demand side. The larger and more diverse the customer base, the less dependent competitors in an industry will be on particular customers. Where customers are many, they can exert control to force prices downward, quality upward, and margins to the floor. Generally, the more a company is recognized for being the low-price leader in its industry, the more it applies pressure to its suppliers and will have the power to get what it wants. According to Porter, buyers are more powerful in an industry if:

- They are concentrated.
- They purchase a lot.
- Products are undifferentiated or standard.
- Products are not a big part of the overall cost.
- Profits are low.
- Product quality is not important.
- Products do not save money for the buyer.

As you examine the industry in relation to each business idea, it will become easier to determine the current attractiveness of the industry. To further analyze the information, you can create a table listing each factor and assign a weight to each to develop a quantitative analysis of the competitiveness in each industry.

Once you have selected the industry, it is time to find a defensible target or set of targets that you can claim and protect. You can design a successful focus strategy to foster business success if you have identified a niche of sufficient size to permit profitability. Identifying this niche and the potential growth of the segment will be an excellent precursor to completing financial feasibility analysis.

Analyzing Financial Feasibility

Having completed the product or service feasibility analysis and also conducted one for the market and industry, you can complete the process by assessing the financial viability of your business idea. This analysis does not need to be detailed. At this point, addressing capital requirements, revenues, costs, and earnings should suffice.

The amount of start-up capital required will be a function of the size and type of organization you are starting. For example, a business that is bringing a patented technology to market by assembling components manufactured by other companies will have lower capital costs than one that manufactures and assembles the parts. Some businesses require very little start-up capital (less than $50,000), whereas others might require millions of dollars before making a single sale. A complete financial feasibility analysis will forecast and incorporate such factors.

An entrepreneur can assess feasibility better with a reasonable projection of revenues, based on anticipated pricing and volume. Using industry-comparable data, particularly any growth statistics for similar firms, can help to make such estimates valid. There is often a temptation to be either overly optimistic or overly pessimistic at this stage, so tempering these extremes with solid data can be significant.

Finally, cost factors should be calculated and returns on investment projected. The earlier analysis of the product or service viability feeds directly into this calculation. By understanding projected costs and offsetting them against revenues, profit projections are possible. With these projections in hand, you can evaluate the return on the capital invested to make a go/no go decision.

The outcome of the feasibility analysis will be to show whether the business idea can be a profitable venture with a sufficiently large return on investment. This is a step in the filtering and selection process that narrows and focuses the business idea so that it can be further developed in a business plan or set aside for a stronger concept.

Creating a Business Model Canvas

In recent years, much work and discussion has revolved around what the best way is to assess feasibility and how entrepreneurs should proceed. After the dot.com bubble collapsed, the heady days of creating business models without business plans for investors gave way to a reconsideration of the importance of business plans and viable models. In addition, various methods of getting to a more rapid revenue stream have evolved. It is important to understand that the audiences for your business concept and the industry in which it will compete have a lot to do with what will work best. There is benefit to each of the options, and it is always a good thing to know how to create a full business plan. That said, this text will walk you through the business plan development process and make the value clear. However, beyond the feasibility analysis described earlier, there is a certain value and elegance in creating a "business model canvas" to focus your thinking as you launch the business planning process.

business model a company's plan to generate revenue and make a profit from operations.

Alexander Osterwalder and Yves Pigneur, along with hundreds of online collaborators, have created a tool for generating business models called the Business Model Canvas.[3] A **business model** is a company's plan to generate revenue and make a profit from operations. The Business Model Canvas is a visual representation of the critical components, and creating it well will compel you to think through many facets of the business. The "canvas" is intended to be created on a large scale, so that ideas and information can be posted on it to create a clear representation. A number of variations on the business model canvas have been created and are available online. An illustration of the Osterwalder-Pigneur canvas is included here as **Figure 2-2**.

The canvas includes nine core building blocks that are intended to supply answers to critical questions. These building blocks are meant to be implemented in the company. They are:

Learning Objective 2

Prepare a Business Model Canvas.

1. Customer Segments (CS): the customers for whom the company creates value
   a. Mass market—large, broadly similar group of customers
   b. Niche market—narrow, specialized, specific
   c. Segmented market—groups with slightly different needs and problems

---

[3]Alexander Osterwalder and Yves Pigneur, *Business Model Generation: A Handbook for Visionaries, Game Changers, and Challengers,* Hoboken, NJ: John Wiley & Sons, 2010.

Figure 2-2 *Business Model Canvas*

Key Partners	Key Activities	Value Propositions	Customer Relationships	Customer Segments
Who are our Key Partners? Who are our Key Suppliers? Which Key Resources are we acquiring from partners? Which Key Activities do partners perform? **Motivations for partnerships:** Optimization and economy Reduction of risk and uncertainty Acquisition of particular resources and activities	What Key Activities do our Value Propositions require? Our Distribution Channels? Customer Relationships? Revenue Stream? **Categories:** Production Problem Solving Platform/Network	What value do we deliver to the customer? Which one of our customer's problems are we helping to solve? What bundles of products and services are we offering to each Customer Segment? Which customer needs are we satisfying? **Characteristics:** Newness Performance Customization "Getting the Job Done" Design Brand/Status Price Cost Reduction Risk Reduction Accessibility Convenience/Usability	What type of relationship does each of our Customer Segments expect us to establish and maintain with them? Which ones have we established? How are they integrated with the rest of our business model? How costly are they? **Examples:** Personal Assistance Dedicated Personal Assistance Self-Service Automated Services Communities Co-creation	For whom are we creating value? Who are our most important customers? Mass Market Niche Market Segmented Diversified Multi-sided Platform

Key Resources

What Key Resources do our Value Propositions require? Our Distribution Channels? Customer Relationships? Revenue Streams?

Types of Resources:
Physical
Intellectual (brand patents, copyrights, data)
Human
Financial

Channels

Through which Channels do our Customer Segments want to be reached?
How are we reaching them now?
How are our Channels integrated?
Which ones work best?
Which ones are most cost-efficient?
How are we integrating them with customer routines?

Channel Phases:
1. Awareness
2. Evaluation
3. Purchase
4. Delivery
5. After sales

Cost Structure

What are the most important costs inherent in our business model?
Which Key Resources are most expensive?
Which Key Activities are most expensive?

Is your business more:
Cost Driven?
Value Driven?

Sample Characteristics:
Fixed Costs
Variable Costs
Economies of Scale
Economies of Scope

Revenue Streams

For what value are our customers really willing to pay?
For what do they currently pay?
How are they currently paying?
How would they prefer to pay?
How much does each Revenue Stream contribute to overall revenues?

Types:	Fixed Pricing:	Dynamic Pricing:
Asset sale	List Price	Negotiation (bargaining)
Usage fees	Product-feature dependent	Yield Management
Subscription fees	Customer-segment dependent	Real-time-Market
Lending/Renting/Leasing	Volume dependent	
Licensing		
Brokerage fees		
Advertising		

Designed by: Business Model Foundry AG.
The makers of Business Model Generation and Strategyzer.
This work is licensed under the Creative Commons Attribution-Share Alike 3.0 Unported License. To view a copy of this license, visit:
http://creativecommons.org/licenses/by-sa/3.0/ or send a letter to Creative Commons, 171 Second Street, Suite 300, San Francisco, California, 94105, USA.

    d. Diversified markets—segments that aren't related and have very different needs

    e. Multi-sided markets—generally are composed of supplier and customer segments that are all served

2. Value Proposition (VP): the reason customers select the products/services

    a. Newness

    b. Performance

    c. "Getting the job done"

     d. Design

     e. Brand/status

     f. Price

     g. Cost reduction

     h. Risk reduction

     i. Accessibility

     j. Convenience/usability

3. Channels (CN): how the company reaches and communicates with customer segments

     a. Own channels versus partners

     b. Direct (sales force, Web sales, own stores) versus indirect (partner stores, wholesalers)

4. Customer Relationships (CR): types established through consumer segments reached

     a. Personal assistance

     b. Dedicated personal assistance

     c. Self-service

     d. Automated services

     e. User communities

     f. Co-creation

5. Revenue Streams (R$): how funds are generated

     a. Asset sales

     b. Usage fee

     c. Subscription fees

     d. Lending/renting/leasing

     e. Licensing

     f. Brokerage fees

     g. Advertising fees

6. Key Resources (KR): that which is critical to making the model function

     a. Physical

     b. Financial

     c. Intellectual

     d. Human

7. Key Activities (KA): critical actions for success

     a. Production

     b. Problem solving

     c. Platform/network

8. Key Partnerships (KP): the particular suppliers and partners needed in the network

     a. Strategic alliances between noncompetitors

     b. Cooperation (strategic alliances between competitors)

     c. Joint ventures

     d. Buyer–supplier relationships

9. Cost Structure (C$): all costs of operations

An example of a Business Model Canvas for University Parent (see Appendices) is shown in **Figure 2-3**. It creates a clear visual representation of the critical factors for the success of the company as described in the business plan. A video about the canvas and a printable poster are available on the Business Model Generation site at http://www.businessmodelgeneration.com.

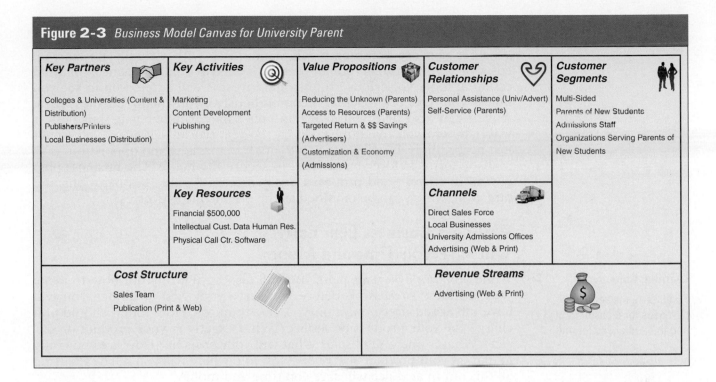

Figure 2-3 *Business Model Canvas for University Parent*

Key Partners	**Key Activities**	**Value Propositions**	**Customer Relationships**	**Customer Segments**
Colleges & Universities (Content & Distribution) Publishers/Printers Local Businesses (Distribution)	Marketing Content Development Publishing	Reducing the Unknown (Parents) Access to Resources (Parents) Targeted Return & $$ Savings (Advertisers) Customization & Economy (Admissions)	Personal Assistance (Univ/Advert) Self-Service (Parents)	Multi-Sided Parents of New Students Admissions Staff Organizations Serving Parents of New Students
	Key Resources Financial $500,000 Intellectual Cust. Data Human Res. Physical Call Ctr. Software		**Channels** Direct Sales Force Local Businesses University Admissions Offices Advertising (Web & Print)	

Cost Structure	**Revenue Streams**
Sales Team Publication (Print & Web)	Advertising (Web & Print)

What Is a Business Plan?

By the time you complete this book, you will have written a **business plan** that you can use to design, start, and operate your own venture. A business plan is a document that thoroughly explains a business idea and how it will be carried out. The plan should include the following:

- the story of what the business is and will be,
- all costs and a marketing plan,
- description of how the business will be financed, and
- an estimate of projected earnings.

The foremost reason to write a business plan is to organize your thoughts *before* starting a business. Many of the entrepreneurs mentioned in this book wrote a business plan before they made a single sale. However, many, if not most, businesses are started based on a concept in the founder's head. Writing a business plan can be a daunting and time-consuming process. Even though creating a plan is a best practice, many entrepreneurs elect not to create one, often to their detriment. In fact, a well-written plan will guide you every step of the way as you develop your business.

Two complete business plans are included in this chapter and the Appendices of this book to assist you in developing your plan. They are both actual plans created by the founders of real businesses. The Honest Tea business plan was created by Seth Goldman and Barry Nalebuff in 1998. The University Parent plan was created by Sara Schupp and some classmates from the University of Colorado in 2004. Both have strengths and weaknesses, but they will show how you might create a plan of your own. In addition, the BizBuilder Business Plan template will lead you through a series of questions to assist in your plan's development.

business plan a document that thoroughly explains a business idea and how it will be carried out.

◀ **Learning Objective 3**
Identify primary business plan contents.

Why Do You Need a Business Plan?

Whether you are planning a microenterprise with virtually no start-up costs or a multimillion-dollar venture, you will find a business plan an essential tool. No serious professional investor will agree even to see you unless you have put together a comprehensive, convincing business plan. A plan can also help you determine on paper whether your business is viable before you make mistakes in the real world—allowing you to adjust accordingly. It will force you to analyze markets and opportunities in realistic terms before you attempt to secure financing. The business plan is vital to current and proposed businesses as a guide to operations and direction, which can be modified as the organization evolves.

Writing a Business Plan Early Will Save You Time and Money

Learning Objective 4

Summarize the various purposes for a business plan and the audiences for one.

While you work on your plan, you will also be figuring out how to make your business successful. Before you serve your first customer, you will have answered every question you can think of. How much should you charge for your product or service? What exactly *is* your product or service? What is one unit of sale? What will your costs be? How are you going to market your product or service? How and where will you sell it? Figuring all this out in advance will save you time and money.

The business plan can be a front line of defense against a poor idea. If your proposed business is weak or marginal, you should see this as you develop the plan and avoid the high cost of failure. It is less costly not to begin a business than it is to fail in one that had fatal flaws from the outset.

If you start your business without a plan, these kinds of questions can overwhelm you. By the time you have completed the exercises in this book, though, you will have answers, and you will be able to chart a road map for your own business. You can use the BizBuilder tools to create a professional plan and a presentation deck (often in PowerPoint) that will emphasize the highlights of your strategy.

Several software packages on the market are designed to help you write a business plan, including:

- Business Plan Pro® (Palo Alto Software, http://www.BusinessPlanPro .com). There is also a Social Enterprise Edition and LivePlan available.
- BizPlan.com (by the Go BIG Network team, http://www.bizplan.com).
- Biz Plan Builder (JIAN, http://www.BizPlanBuilder.com).
- Business PlanMaker Professional (Individual Software, Inc.).
- Ultimate Business Planner (Atlas Business Solutions, http://www .abs-usa.com).

These software packages and their sample business plans will provide guidance in developing your own unique design. Be wary of creating a cookie-cutter plan and falling into the trap of using the data and financial projections of sample plans. In the end, a business plan must be the creation of the individual who will operate the business.

In addition, by using the Web, you can save some time and money by presenting your business plan to several investors at a time, no matter where they are located. With a presentation program like PowerPoint, you can broadcast your presentation in real time over the Web or send it electronically to interested parties. With proper technology, you can also include audio to accompany the presentation. Whereas it is always preferable to make a presentation in person, this can be an effective way to submit your business plan to investors at their convenience. Remember, though, that proper nondisclosure agreements are an absolute necessity, because business plans are the valued property of their developers.

Your Business Plan Is the Key to Raising Capital

As mentioned, bankers and other potential investors will refuse to see an entrepreneur who does not have a business plan (unless the loan or investment you are seeking is very small). You may have a brilliant idea, but if it is not written out, people will be extremely unlikely to invest in your business or loan you money.

Writing a business plan will allow you to address all angles of your business idea.
(George Doyle/Getty Images)

A well-written plan will show investors that you have carefully thought through how you intend to make your business profitable. The more detail you offer investors about how their money will be used, the more willing they will be to invest. The financial projections should be realistic and attainable. Your plan should be so thoughtful and well written that the only question it raises in an investor's mind is: "How much can I invest?"

The Business Plan Is an Operations Guide

Whether or not you need to raise capital, a business plan will be a vital tool for guiding the internal operations of your enterprise. Business owners and managers increase the probability of success by taking the plan in their heads and committing it to paper. The transition may be bumpy, because the process of writing a coherent plan will require answering difficult questions. However, in addition to guiding you as the entrepreneur, developing the plan will generate an increased clarity of vision, mission, and goals for your entire team. With your business plan as your benchmarking tool, you can compare your company's progress to your stated plan. You can also use the business plan as a point of reference when it seems you are going off track or becoming distracted from your goals. The presence of financial and operational goals and measures, as well as mission and vision statements, can feed a drive for success and motivate a team to excellence.

Business Plan Components

As you begin a new enterprise, you can find a seemingly endless variety of problems to address and questions to answer. Such a situation could quickly overwhelm you if you don't have a plan. However, by the time you have worked through all the steps of a business plan, you will have answers. You will develop a love *for* the business, rather than being in love with the *idea* of the business and having unrealistic expectations. The order of the components of a plan can vary somewhat, but there are elements common to all. An outline of one kind of business plan is illustrated in **Exhibit 2-1**.

◀ Learning Objective 5
Differentiate the components of a business plan.

Exhibit 2-1 *Business Plan Outline*

Cover Page
Table of Contents
1.0 **Executive Summary**
2.0 **Mission, Vision, and Culture**
3.0 **Company Description**
4.0 **Opportunity Analysis and Research**
    4.1 Industry Analysis
    4.2 Environmental Analysis
    4.3 Competitive Analysis
5.0 **Marketing Strategy and Plan**
    5.1 Products/Services
    5.2 Pricing
    5.3 Promotion
    5.4 Place
6.0 **Management and Operations**
    6.1 Management Team
    6.2 Research and Development
    6.3 Physical Location
    6.4 Facilities
    6.5 Inventory, Production, and Quality Assurance
7.0 **Financial Analysis and Projections**
    7.1 Sources and Uses of Capital
    7.2 Cash Flow Projections
    7.3 Balance Sheet Projections
    7.4 Income Statement Projections
    7.5 Breakeven Analysis
    7.6 Ratio Analysis
    7.7 Risks and Assumptions
8.0 **Funding Request and Exit Strategy**
    8.1 Amount and Type of Funds Requested
    8.2 Exit Plan
    8.3 Milestones
Appendices
    Resumes
    Sample Promotional Materials
    Product Illustrations/Diagrams
    Detailed Financial Projections

Cover Page and Table of Contents

Begin the plan as you intend to continue it. The cover page should be professional, neat, and attractive. It should provide the name of the business and the principals, the date, contact information, and any confidentiality statement. The table of contents should be sufficiently detailed so an investor or manager can easily find a section, but not so detailed that it takes up pages of the plan.

Executive Summary: A Snapshot of Your Business

The executive summary has to be compelling and comprehensive. It may be the only part that many people will read. It will be the hook that either catches potential investors or loses their attention. If a reader doesn't fully understand the business concept and the purpose of the plan from the executive summary, the rest of the plan is likely to remain unread. The executive summary must encapsulate the story of the business clearly and concisely, propose the funding request, and inspire enthusiasm for the possibility of its success.

This section should be written last and limited to one or two pages. It should answer the *who, what, when, why,* and *how* questions for the business. Who will manage the business? What will it do, and what is the owner asking for in the plan? When will the proposed plan be implemented? How will the business succeed? Done well, the reader will have a "light-bulb" moment and be eager to read the rest of the plan.

Mission and Culture: Your Dreams for the Organization

Each company has the opportunity to create its own unique mission, vision, and culture. The founding team can determine how to strategically use the company's competitive advantage to satisfy customers. Culture that the owners model and support can be shaped according to the environment and the manner of treating employees, customers, and other stakeholders. The **mission** of your business, expressed in a mission statement, is a concise communication of strategy, including your *business definition* and *competitive advantage*. The function of a **mission statement** is to clarify what you are trying to do, and it can provide direction and motivation to those who are involved in the business.

A clearly stated mission statement not only tells your customers and employees what your business is about, but can also be a guide for every decision you make. It should capture your passion for the business and your commitment to satisfying your customers. The mission statement should be clear and concise, no more than 21 to 40 words.

The **vision** for your business will be broader and more comprehensive, painting the big picture of what you want your organization to become. It is built on the core values and belief system of the organization. It is typically shorter than the mission statement, with a loftier perspective.

The **culture** of an organization, whether intentionally or unintentionally created, is largely defined by its leadership. You can build a culture for your company by making beliefs, values, and behavioral norms explicit and intentional. A business's culture has many components, including attitudes toward risk tolerance and innovation and its orientation with respect to people, team formation and outcomes, attention to detail, and communication. Whether you want a free-thinking, aggressive company with informal communications or a structured, formal organization with more "official" interactions, you will set the standards and be the role model for your business's culture.

mission a concise communication of strategy, including a business definition and explanation of competitive advantage.

mission statement a brief, written statement that informs customers and employees what an organization's goal is and describes the strategy and tactics to meet it.

vision a broader and more comprehensive perspective on an organization than its mission; built on the core values and belief systems of the organization.

culture the beliefs, values, and behavioral norms of an organization.

Global Impact . . .

Upcycling Waste Internationally—TerraCycle, Inc.

In 2003, John Szaky's TerraCycle won a business plan contest from Carrot Capital for $1 million in seed funding. But the venture capital firm wanted TerraCycle to drop its environmental focus, and Szaky turned down the offer. It was a critical decision that later helped the business achieve its competitive advantage.

TerraCycle converts unrecyclable packaging waste to upcycled products. An early inspiration was implemented when TerraCycle ran out of money to buy bottles in which to sell fertilizer derived from worm waste. It was decided to pack it in recycled soda bottles. This concept expanded into the production of other green products. Pencil holders made from Kool-Aid packets, tote bags made from Capri Sun-drink pouches, and backpacks made from Clif Bar wrappers are just a few examples of the more than one hundred TerraCycle products sold in large retail chains, including Home Depot, Whole Foods, Wal-Mart, and Target. The concept has spread to the United Kingdom, Brazil, Mexico, Israel, and Canada, among others. By working with concerned groups in each country, TerraCycle has the potential of becoming an iconic representative of upcycled waste. TerraCycle calls this process turning "branded" waste into "sponsored" waste.

Wu Kaixiang/Corbis Images

Source: TerraCycle, Inc., accessed April 6, 2014, http://www.terracycle.com.

Company Description—Background and Track Record

If the company is already established, is a franchise, or is the reincarnation of a previous business, there will be a history to share with the reader of the plan. The business description does not need to be long. It should simply provide the background for understanding the rest of the plan. It should include summary information about the company's founding, its progress, and its financial success.

If this is a start-up venture, this section should describe briefly the background story of the company, explaining what you have done thus far and why you have done it. The legal form of the business (sole proprietorship, corporation, LLC, partnership) should also be noted.

Opportunity Analysis and Research—Testing Ideas

The opportunity-analysis and research section will provide the credible data and information to determine and demonstrate the market viability of your proposed business on paper, and perhaps in the field, before you start. It should be a clear description of why the business presents an excellent opportunity, based on sound research and logic. Entrepreneurs often either put little time and attention into this section or ignore data that contradict their optimistic view of the opportunity. This can prove to be a fatal flaw in business planning. A well-researched opportunity analysis can help to move your business to the head of the line for financing.

industry analysis a critical view of industry definition, industry size and growth (or decline), product and industry life cycle, and any current or anticipated legal or regulatory concerns.

The **industry analysis** will provide the broad context for your business plan. It will deal with such factors as industry definition, industry size and growth (or decline), product and industry life cycle, and any current or anticipated legal or regulatory concerns. Determining industry structure, including geographic distribution, business size of member firms, concentration of power, and rates of failure, is also important. For example, the failure rate of restaurants is notoriously high and should be addressed in a business plan for a dining establishment. This is also the place to discuss how you will track industry developments on an ongoing basis.

environmental analysis a review that addresses the roles of the community, region, nation, or the rest of the world, as they relate to a business.

The **environmental analysis** addresses the roles of the community, region, nation, and/or the rest of the world as they relate to your business. Whether or not demographic and family changes are working in your favor could mean adjustments for the business. Changes in technologies and economic conditions might radically alter your plans. Examples could include the aging of the baby boomer generation or the prevalence of computer technology.

proof of market an investigation that provides evidence of a market opportunity.

The opportunity analysis should include a **proof of market** investigation that will provide evidence of a market opportunity for your organization. This should identify market size, both in terms of dollars and units. There have to be enough customers who will purchase your product or service in sufficient quantity at a high enough price and often enough for your business to be sustainable.

target market groups defined by common factors such as demographics, psychographics, age, or geography that are of primary interest to a business.

Next, this analysis should describe your **target market** segments, which are groups of people defined by common factors, such as demographics, psychographics, age, or geography. For example, your target market segment for a gospel club may be African-American Christians between 18 and 25 years of age living in the Detroit metropolitan area. Discuss the size of your target market and the market share that would be attainable. This is also where you can describe your 10 identified customers (remember Russell Simmons's comment).

competitive analysis research that compares an organization with several direct and indirect competitors by name in a manner that is meaningful to targeted customers.

A **competitive analysis** is the next important component of the opportunity analysis. This should compare your organization with several direct and indirect competitors by name and include comparisons that would be meaningful to customers. The format of a competitive analysis can vary significantly, but it must make clear where your competitive strengths and weaknesses are and where there are holes in the competitors' businesses. Factors to compare may include, but would not be limited to, location, product selection, market share, product or service quality, experience, advertising, pricing, finances, capacity, hours, size and skill of workforce, and reputation. It is often most effective to create a chart or table to show this.

Marketing Strategy and Plan: Reaching Customers

A description of how you will reach your customers and your anticipated sales volume brings the opportunity and research discussion to the bottom line of sales. Your **marketing mix** will be the combination of the four factors (the "Four Ps") that form your competitive advantage—also known as *core competency*—product, price, promotion, and place. As you choose the elements of your **marketing plan**, always keep your vision in mind. What benefit is your product or service providing to customers?

> **marketing mix** the combination of the four factors—product, price, place, and promotion—that communicates a marketing vision.

> **marketing plan** a statement of the marketing goals and objectives for a business and the intended strategies and tactics to attain them.

- *Products/Services.* The product or service should meet or create a customer need. The distinctive features and benefits of the product or service must be clearly stated. Remember, the packaging is also part of the product. Your customer may throw away your packaging but that does not mean it is unimportant. If you are introducing an innovative technology, the value of the innovation to customers warrants explanation here.

- *Pricing.* The product or service has to be priced so that your target customers will buy it and the business will make a profit. Price should reflect your vision, strategy, and policy. It has to be right. For example, if you are marketing a luxury item, a relatively low price might not send the right message to your target customers. Highlight competitive advantages—such as quality, credit terms, warranty type and length, service, and innovativeness—that support the pricing.

- *Promotion.* Promotion consists of advertising, publicity, and other promotional methods, such as discount coupons or giveaways. Publicity is free, whereas advertising is purchased. The description of your promotional plans should be specific with respect to the methods used, the time line for implementation, and the budget. Often this section is further divided into advertising, public relations and publicity, and direct marketing. **Advertising** consists of paid promotion through media outlets, such as broadcast or cable television, the Internet, radio, magazines, and newspapers. **Public relations** consists of community activities that are designed to enhance your organization's image. **Publicity** is free notice in the media presented as news. **Direct marketing** includes telemarketing, direct mail, in-person selling, and other personalized efforts. Remember to include samples of your promotional materials in the appendices of your plan, if possible.

> **advertising** paid promotion through media outlets.

> **public relations** community activities that are designed to enhance an organization's image.

> **publicity** free promotion.

> **direct marketing** includes telemarketing, direct mail, in-person selling, and other personalized promotional efforts.

- *Place.* This is the venue from which you will sell and distribute your product. Your selling location should be where consumers in your target market do their shopping. Where should you go to bring your product or service to the attention of your market? If you are selling a luxury item, you will need to place it in stores or on Web sites that are visited by customers who can afford it. Included in *place* is your selection of a type of sales force (i.e., independent, company, single line, or multiline), any geographic definition of your market, and all channels of distribution. Are you going to sell directly to consumers, work through wholesale distributors, be Web-based, or sell at retail?

Management and Operations: Making the Plan Happen

The people you hire and the processes you plan to implement will be an essential part of your business plan. This is where the rubber meets the road in the planning process.

The management team is often the deciding factor for a potential investor's decision to financially support a business. Moreover, with all other factors being equal, a strong management team will be successful in a business and a weak one will fail. The team must be composed of an effective balance of members with technical expertise (e.g., engineering, marketing, accounting, and operations), experience in the field, and life experience. Briefly discuss the current and proposed management team and reference their resumes in the appendices.

It can also be worthwhile to add an organizational chart representing the company as it is proposed in the near term and with growth. In addition, descriptions of key roles and responsibilities, and the compensation rates and structures for each, will need to be included.

If your business will be involved in research and development, this section should describe it. Include the state of development, such as prototype, testing, or commercialization. Any patents, patents pending, or other intellectual property should be discussed, with the limits or law (not losing protection) and the stage of commercial readiness.

The description of the physical location is similar to the discussion of *place* in the marketing mix but with the emphasis on logistics and workforce readiness. Describe the desired physical location(s) of the organization and the rationale. For example, if you require a concentration of highly skilled scientists, you might want to locate near a university with a strong science orientation or near other firms with similar labor-pool requirements. Local wage rates and community support are other factors to mention. In addition, geographic proximity to customers and/or suppliers or distributors may be a critical site factor. Other aspects to consider are business-friendly laws and courts, tax rates and structures, school systems, overall quality of life, and environment.

The facilities required for the success of your enterprise should be discussed in detail. You should describe the building according to its type and size, and equipment should be specified and "costed out" (details can be included in the appendices). If you know that you require production, warehousing, showroom, or office space, you can describe each. This is where you should discuss your plans to lease or purchase property and equipment and a tipping point for going from lease to purchase. Remember that it isn't financially prudent to buy a building when you only need a small "incubator" space to get started. Often, nascent entrepreneurs immediately want to buy their own facilities and brand-new equipment. In reality, leasing space and equipment reduces required start-up capital and can provide greater flexibility.

The production methods and inventory-control systems that you plan to use will be critical to your success. Even if you are in a service enterprise, you will have supply issues to address in terms of staffing, logistics, and materials. The business plan is an opportunity to set inventory control systems, production processes, and quality-assurance methods. You can highlight any technological innovations that will enhance the company's competitive position. What to include will vary considerably, but the identification of your choices and methods of measurement is essential.

The facilities and equipment for your business should be planned with the management team.
(© Blend Images/Alamy)

Step into the Shoes . . .

JackThreads, Planning for Success

Bloomberg/Getty Images

After Jason Ross graduated from Ohio State University in 2003 with a degree in finance, he and a friend founded a sports marketing company. In 2005, they sold SMI Ventures after realizing they weren't passionate about it and wanted to do something with greater potential for growth.

Jason decided he wanted to start an entrepreneurial venture that he could be passionate about and that had viable prospects for growth. He had a passion for street wear and was a bargain shopper. He identified the opportunity to create a pure-play e-commerce-flash-sale site that met his criteria. This time, he recognized the value of creating a business plan. Jason comments, "Everybody stresses, 'Write a business plan before you start a company!' but we were young and naïve and didn't do it. Now I definitely recommend it. While I wrote the business plan for JackThreads in 2006, I was working at bars, working anywhere I could find part-time money that would allow me to keep pursuing this dream. And I was always bouncing ideas off my friends and local VCs in Columbus."[4]

JackThreads launched in July 2008 as a members-only boutique e-commerce site offering private, limited-time sales events. Products include contemporary fashion apparel for surfing, skating, and street wear, as well as sneakers and accessories. The lines are strictly menswear and are priced 40 to 80 percent off retail. Five to seven new sales are posted daily and run for between 48 and 72 hours.

In 2011, Jason teamed up with Adam Rich and Ben Lerner and became part of Thrillist. The Thrillist.com site provides a digital lifestyle publication for men. As of early 2013, JackThreads had over three million members. The time Jason devoted to researching and planning JackThreads has paid off handsomely.

Sources: Lauren Drell, "JackThreads' Jason Ross: How a Kid from Ohio Took the Fashion World by Storm," *AOL Small Business*, February 8, 2011, accessed May 8, 2013, http://smallbusiness.aol.com. *JackThreads*. Accessed July 9, 2013, https://www.jackthreads.com.

Financial Analysis and Projections: Translating Action into Money

The financial section of the business plan will be the numeric representation of all that you wrote previously. This section should demonstrate organizational viability in financial terms. Commercial lenders in particular will often go directly from the executive summary to the financials before reading anything else. If the numbers make sense, they may look at the rest of the plan. If not, your plan may well land in the trash basket. Your financial estimates should be as realistic as you can make them. Don't pad the numbers. It is not in your best interest to create unrealistic expectations, to delude yourself and your business associates, or to have potential investors or lenders reject your projections as pie-in-the-sky. You are likely to show initial losses, and you should be up front about this. The financials should match both the general market and the other information you provided throughout the business plan. Investors can sense overblown numbers and will react accordingly.

- *Sources and uses of capital.* This section is the numeric representation of the start-up costs plus a verbal description of capital requirements. It states where you expect to obtain your financial support and how you will use the funds. When securing bank or community development financing, your lender may require you to "draw down" (take in incremental amounts) funds in accordance with your list of costs. It is essential to make the list as complete and accurate as possible. It is a sad day for everyone when an entrepreneur's credit and cash are completely exhausted just short of the start-up point. A sample start-up cost list is shown in **Exhibit 2-2**.

[4]Lauren Drell, "JackThreads' Jason Ross: How a Kid from Ohio Took the Fashion World by Storm," *AOL Small Business*, February 8, 2011, accessed May 8, 2013, http://smallbusiness.aol.com.

Exhibit 2-2 *Start-Up Costs*

Energy Mavens LLC
Estimated Start-Up Costs

Start-Up Expenses	Estimate	Notes/Assumptions
Certifications	$ 20,000	Federal certifications for manufacturing
Consulting Fees	$ 5,000	Manufacturing consultants
Expensed Equipment	$ 3,000	Computers, printers, and the like
Financial Institution Fees	$ 5,000	Loan fees at 2%
Identity Set/Stationary	$ 2,000	Letterhead, business cards, envelopes
Insurance	$ 6,000	6 months
Licenses	$ 300	City, State, County
Marketing	$ 19,000	Pre-venture advertising and promotion
Marketing Materials	$ 20,000	Website, brochures, presentations
Owner's Wages	$ 7,500	Pre-opening 3 months
Payroll (with taxes)	$ 40,000	Engineer and manager 3 months
Permits	$ 200	Building permits for leasehold improvements
Professional Fees - Accounting	$ 1,000	Set-up of accounting system
Professional Fees - Legal	$ 3,000	LLC formations, lease review, contracts
Professional Fees - Other	$ 2,000	Professionals involved in leasehold improvements
Rent	$ 15,000	$4.00/sq. foot - 15,000 sq. foot - 3 months
Research & Development	$ 5,000	Technical analysis
Supplies - Office	$ 1,000	General supplies
Telephone/Internet	$ 300	$100 per month for 3 months
Travel/Fuel (.55xMILES)	$ 10,000	Pitching product to companies & investors
Utilities	$ 9,000	Eventually switch over to panels
Web Fees	$ 500	Web - URL and fees
Other	$ 300	Accounting software
Total Start-Up Expenses	$ 175,100	
Start-Up Assets		
Cash on Hand	$ 1,000	Funds for miscellaneous purchases
Building (if purchased)	$	not applicable
Cars, Trucks, and Other Vehicles	$ 60,000	Prius with company logo & local delivery truck
Equipment (including installation)	$ 20,000	Factory equipment
Furniture & Fixtures	$ 20,000	Primarily warehouse fixtures
Inventory - Raw Materials	$ 100,000	Component items
Inventory - Semi-Finished Goods	$ 25,000	Partially produced components
Inventory - Finished Goods	$	not applicable
Land (if purchased)	$	not applicable
Leasehold Improvements	$ 20,000	Custom system and other fit-out
Machinery	$ 3,200,000	Specialized equipment detailed in plan
Rent Deposit (Prepaid Expense)	$ 10,000	First and last month
Signage	$ 10,000	Exterior and interior
Software for Manufacturing	$ 50,000	Specialized software
Utility Deposits (Prepaid Expense)	$ 3,000	All deposits
Total Start-Up Assets	$ 3,519,000	
Total Start-Up Requirements	$ 3,694,100	
Contingency Funds (10%)	$ 369,410	
Start-Up with Contingency	$ 4,063,510	Budgeted Start-up Investment

- *Cash flow projections.* The cash flow statement shows cash receipts less cash disbursements over a period of time. Creating your cash flow projections for three years will bring financial potential and risks into clear focus both for you and your stakeholders. Don't be alarmed to see negative numbers on your first couple of efforts at this. However, if the numbers truly do not work, it might be time to reconsider your business approach, or the basic concept, rather than simply manipulating the figures to achieve satisfactory results on paper.

   In a start-up business, cash flow is likely to be negative at various points, such as the early months or in certain seasons. A business cannot survive long with negative cash flow, so it must increase cash coming in (revenues, loans, equity investments, and the like) and/or reduce the amount of cash going out (expenses, equipment purchases, debt repayment, for example). Remember, be realistic about these projections. Be careful of significantly increasing your revenue projections solely to improve the numbers. If you add debt, account for its interest and principal repayment in future periods. When you have finished your business plan, it should never show a negative cash balance at the end of a period, because negative cash means you are overdrawn in your accounts, and projecting overdrawn accounts in a business plan, or operating that way, is hardly a best practice. You may very well have suffered losses that are reflected on your income statement, but the ending cash balance cannot be negative. **Exhibit 2-3** shows how cash balances are calculated.

- *Balance sheet projections.* Your three years of projected balance sheets will provide snapshots of your business at specific points in time, such as the last day of a month, quarter, or year. Balance sheets show the business's assets (what you own), liabilities (what you owe), and net worth, or owner's equity. These statements provide insights into your financing strategy and overall business health. **Exhibit 2-4** shows a rudimentary balance-sheet format.

Assets = Liabilities + Owner's Equity

- *Income statements for three years.* An income statement (or profit and loss statement—P&L) summarizes income and expense activity over a specified period, such as a month, quarter, or year, and shows *net profit* or *net loss*. Generally, start-up enterprises suffer losses for several months, or even a few years, depending on the

cash flow statement a financial statement showing cash receipts less cash disbursements for a business over a period of time.

balance sheet a financial statement summarizing the assets, liabilities, and net worth of a business.

asset any item of value.

liability a business debt.

net worth the difference between assets and liabilities.

owner's equity net worth.

income statement a financial document that summarizes income and expense activity over a specified period and shows net profit or loss.

profit and loss statement (P&L) an income statement.

Exhibit **2-3** *Cash Flow Calculations*	
Starting Cash	(+)
Cash In from Operations [Sales]	(+)
Cash Out from Operations [Cost of Goods Sold, Expenses, Taxes]	(−)
Cash In from Investing [Equity Infusions, Earnings on Investments]	(+)
Cash Out from Investing [Equipment Purchases, Repaying Investors]	(−)
Cash In from Financing [Loans]	(+)
Cash Out for Financing [Repayment of Debt]	(−)
Ending Cash Balance [Starting Balance for Next Period]	(=)

Exhibit 2-4 *Balance Sheet Summary Format*

Energy Mavens LLC Balance Sheet as of December 31			
	2014	**2015**	**2016**
Assets			
Short-Term Assets	$200,000	$300,000	$450,000
Long-Term Assets	3,500,000	3,200,000	2,800,000
Total Assets	**$3,700,000**	**$3,500,000**	**$3,250,000**
Liabilities			
Short-Term Liabilities	$100,000	$200,000	$200,000
Long-Term Liabilities	1,500,000	1,050,000	800,000
Total Liabilities	**$1,600,000**	**$1,250,000**	**$1,000,000**
Owner's Equity	**$2,100,000**	**$2,250,000**	**$2,250,000**
Total Liabilities & Equity	**$3,700,000**	**$3,500,000**	**$3,250,000**

Exhibit 2-5 *Income Statement Summary Format*

Energy Mavens LLC Income Statement for the Year Ending December 31			
	2014	**2015**	**2016**
Net Sales Revenue	$2,500,000	$3,500,000	$5,500,000
Cost of Goods Sold	1,400,000	1,700,000	3,000,000
Gross Profit	**$1,100,000**	**$1,800,000**	**$2,500,000**
Operating Expenses	300,000	400,000	600,000
Earnings before Interest & Taxes	**$800,000**	**$1,400,000**	**$1,900,000**
Interest Expense	100,000	90,000	80,000
Taxes	0	0	0
Net Income	**$700,000**	**$1,310,000**	**$1,820,000**

type of business. You can show initial losses in your statements, but they must be comparable to industry norms, and you must have cash to cover any shortfalls. The projections you provide should clearly be your best estimate and based on the detailed breakdown of sales, pricing, cost, and other data contained in your plan. It is helpful to show best-case, worst-case, and expected scenarios for income. Be careful to avoid ski-slope projections, which add projections linearly, with profitability occurring suddenly in either year three or five. A simple example of an income statement is shown in **Exhibit 2-5**.

- **Breakeven analysis.** This calculation will determine your organization's **breakeven point**—that is, when the volume of sales exactly covers the fixed costs. Calculating the breakeven point will help demonstrate whether there is a viable market for your business. For example, if there are 1,500 students in a school and you must sell

breakeven point when the volume of sales exactly covers the fixed costs.

2,500 yearbooks to reach breakeven, you know that it is time to reconsider your plan. Breakeven is calculated as

$$\frac{\text{Fixed Cost (\$)}}{\text{Gross Profit per Unit (\$)}} = \text{Breakeven Units}$$

- **Ratio analysis.** To understand your business performance relative to your industry peers, you can use ratio analysis. A business plan should include standard ratios: gross profit, quick, current, debt, collection period, receivable turnover, inventory turnover, net profit on sales, net profit to assets, and net profit to equity. One of the best ways to interpret your calculated ratios is to compare them with others in your industry via the Risk Management Association (RMA) Annual Statement Studies, which you may access at a library or purchase online for specific industries (http://www.rmahq.org). If you use Business Plan Pro, industry ratios will be available when you calculate them for your business plan. By comparing your business from one period to another and looking at the industry norms, you can adjust the way you will operate, or you can explain why you are outperforming your industry through your competitive advantages or underperforming because of specific circumstances.

- **Risks and assumptions.** All businesses take risks and make their projections based on assumptions. To present a realistic plan, you will need to state your assumptions and known risks explicitly. You will have done some of this in your SWOT analysis; this section pertains to the financial projections. For example, you can include the per-unit costs and volume projections, anticipated tax and benefits rates, and other calculated and projected values. You can also articulate the risks of implementation delays, cost overruns, lower-than-expected sales, industry price wars, and so forth. As with the other sections in your plan, this should be balanced and realistic, not overstated or underplayed.

Funding Request and Exit Strategy: The Ask and the Return

Your business plan should explicitly state the amount of funds you will need in accordance with the financial projections you provide. Whether the need is $500 or $50 million, the reasoning for the request will have to be clear and compelling. Then you should identify the type of financing you require or are requesting and include your own financial contribution and that of any partners or co-owners, the amount of debt (loans) you will need to take on, and the percentage of equity (ownership) you want to retain. This is where you state the financing terms you would like, including rates and repayment periods. Recognize that this is part of a negotiation process and that the request should be carefully structured. If you intend to sell shares of stock in a corporation or are forming a business partnership, legal counsel will be essential so that you do not violate federal regulations and laws or create an improper agreement. The importance of your "ask" cannot be overemphasized. Business plan readers need to know what you want.

The exit strategy is the way in which you and/or your investors expect to leave the company someday in a planned and orderly way. For investors, this might mean a buyout plan for their equity, or an **initial public offering (IPO)** when the company goes public—that is, puts itself on the stock exchange.

initial public offering (IPO) first offering of corporate stock to investors on the open (public) market.

Step into the Shoes . . .

Turning Play into Profits

P'Kolino, LLC, 2004 MOOT Corp Competitor

What happens when you pair up two Babson MBA students with an idea and a group of students from the Rhode Island School of Design (RISD)? In 2004, the answer was P'Kolino, a creative company focused on "better" play.

Antonio Turco-Rivas and J. B. Schneider worked together to create a winning business plan that succeeded in being selected for the prestigious international business plan competition called MOOT Corp in 2004. Their initial product was an innovative play table designed by the RISD team.

Since then, Turco-Rivas and Schneider have combined their interests as fathers with a desire to have well-designed products for children to create a successful company. P'Kolino products are sold in such upscale locations in New York as the Metropolitan Museum of Art, the Guggenheim Museum, the Museum of Modern Art, the Strand Book Store, and Saks Fifth Avenue. National mass-market retailers Toys R Us and Buy Buy Baby feature P'Kolino products in selected stores.

For P'Kolino's founders, the business plan was an exercise that let them play in the children's market.

Source: P'Kolino. Accessed July 9, 2013, http://www.pkolino.com.

It could mean the sale of the business when certain benchmarks are met or at a predetermined point in time. It could mean having you give up day-to-day operations according to a succession plan. Lenders and investors will want to know how they will recoup their investment and earn enough profit to warrant the risk they are taking.

Any business plan is only as strong as its implementation schedule. Therefore, the schedule—timetable—of *milestones* (goals) that you include will be important to your business and your stakeholders. By establishing realistic deadlines for the completion of activities, you demonstrate knowledge and understanding of the necessary tasks. You can use PERT or GANTT charts or any structured method that details the starting and ending dates of tasks and enumerates the resources needed and the responsibility of personnel. Using a software tool such as Microsoft Project or Excel can make this process easier to manage.

Appendices: Making the Case in Greater Detail

The appendices will provide you with an opportunity to strengthen your business plan with examples and details that are not critical for inclusion in the main portions. This is the place to add management resumes, sample promotional materials, and illustrations or diagrams of products and packaging. In some cases, the detailed financial projections will appear in the appendices. Each appendix should be numbered and placed in the plan according to the order of reference in the text. The appendices should be listed in your table of contents.

Business Plan Suggestions

As you put together your business plan, a number of guidelines and suggestions can help you get the most value for your time and effort. These will make the plan look more professional, easier to read, and more likely to be thoughtfully considered. In fact, you will find it easier to refer back to your business plan if it is clear, concise, visually appealing, and well organized. With this in mind, you should

Learning Objective 6

Recognize and demonstrate proper development and formatting of a business plan.

- *Write for your audience.* Whether the plan is for an internal (you and your team) or an external (lenders and investors) audience, it will need to address issues and concerns in language your readers will understand. They need to see that this business is something they want to be on board with (if company personnel) or that it satisfies a market need (if potential investors).

- *Show that you have skin in the game.* No matter who the audience is, they will want to know that you are emotionally, intellectually, and financially invested in the business.

- *Be clear and concise.* Simple, direct language written without too many adjectives or unnecessarily complex terminology is best. Even for highly technical sections, the business plan should avoid jargon and repeated references made through acronyms and initials. This includes writing in a pompous (self-important) way. Keep it simple. Readers know that explaining a complex subject in a clear, concise manner requires a thorough understanding of the subject. Depending on your audience and the type of business, your plan should be from 15 to 40 pages long, including appendices.

- *Use current data and reports for your industry.* This is important to validate that you are being realistic and have truly done your research. If you are out of step with current or anticipated conditions, the assumptions you make for your financial and market performance are likely to be inaccurate and unrealistic.

- *Choose a voice and stick with it.* It is best to write your business plan in the third person (not the first person—"I" or "we") to give it an objective tone. Be careful not to switch back and forth between voices.

- *Use a consistent, easy-to-read format.* Choose a format and use it consistently throughout the plan. For example, using 1-inch margins, double spacing, and a serif font (such as Times New Roman) will make the document easy to read.

- *Number and label.* Number pages, figures (drawings, illustrations, photos), and tables, and refer to each in the text by title and number to make it easy for the reader to understand and find sections of the plan. Each figure or table should be numbered sequentially and should be given a heading.

- *Present it professionally.* A professional business plan on high-quality paper with a neat, attractive cover, cover page, and professional binding will go a long way toward impressing the reader. A dirty, dog-eared, or unbound business plan will probably not even be read. An overly fancy, elaborate plan, bound like a book, with four-color glossy illustrations, may cause the reader to wonder why you have gone to such unnecessary expense, suspecting that you are either being wasteful or are perhaps camouflaging an unsound plan with bells and whistles.

It is a good idea to have others look at your business plan before you circulate it to potential investors. If you can get relatively objective friends, colleagues, or family members to read the plan as early as the first draft, you can probably get valuable feedback and ideas for improvement. If you need assistance with spelling and grammar, or any other aspect of the format, this is the time to get it. It is also a good time to use any community resources that may be available to you, such as a Small Business Development Center (SBDC) or Rural Entrepreneurship Center.

Presenting Your Business Plan

A written business plan is only one component of the business-planning process. It may open the door for a presentation to potential investors (stakeholders), or it may be the leave-behind document that is meant to remind the investors of your conversation. In either case, the presentation of the road map for your venture, whether live, Web-based, or in some other form, is your opportunity to convey your business concept to a particular audience and then to have an interactive discussion regarding your proposal.

Business plan presentations may be formal or informal, and you may have anywhere from a few minutes to a couple of hours for the complete presentation and discussion. Presentations to venture capitalists may be limited to as little as 5 to 20 minutes. Regardless of the setting or audience, your presentation should be articulate, well thought out, organized, rehearsed, polished, and professional. As you work on plans for your enterprise, it is a good idea to work on an **elevator pitch** that quickly conveys to the listener in an engaging way what you are proposing and why he or she should be interested. This quick spiel should take 30 seconds to a maximum of 2 minutes (the duration of an elevator ride). It is often more challenging to boil the business plan down to its essentials than to make a full exposition. For a formal presentation, an attractive multimedia presentation, free from errors, excessive animation, and other distractions is advisable. Some venture presentation tips are given in **Exhibit 2-6**.

Business plan and pitch competitions provide advantages and disadvantages. Certainly, the preparation for competition is an excellent opportunity to put a deadline on the creation of a plan, and the presentations are opportunities to hone a variety of skills, as well as strengthen the concept. Also, competitions may provide significant cash prizes and access to venture capital. However, business plan competitions are time consuming and can prove a distraction from making progress on the actual business.

elevator pitch a 30-second to 2-minute presentation that conveys in an engaging way what a business is proposing and why the listener should be interested.

Exhibit **2-6** *Venture Presentation Tips*	
Timing	• Be prompt and ready to start on time. • Use the entire time allocated and use it productively.
Audience	• Know your audience and tailor the presentation accordingly. • Establish rapport with the audience.
Presentation Style	• Dress appropriately and maintain a professional demeanor. • Be enthusiastic, but not artificial or arrogant. • Use proper pronunciation and language.
Presentation Contents	• Create a "hook" to capture the audience quickly. • Hit the highlights without going into excessive detail. • Keep it simple by emphasizing key points and avoiding technical jargon and acronyms that will lose your audience's interest. • Use visual aids, such as slides and sample or prototype products, to reinforce your message without distracting from it. • Emphasize the benefits of the opportunity so that they are absolutely clear to the audience. • Conclude with a "Thank You."
Follow-Up	• Expect and prepare for questions. Be thoughtful and positive in your responses. • Contact each audience member to move toward your goals.

Source: Adapted from Thomas W. Zimmerer and Norman M. Scarborough, *Essentials of Entrepreneurship and Small Business Management,* 5th ed. (Upper Saddle River, NJ: Prentice Hall, 2007).

Some competitions will likely have team guidelines that do not conform to your actual business team, so the competitors on the team will have varying levels of interest and commitment, which may create tension and conflict. Even if you win a competition, you may not want to accept the prize if the terms and conditions are not acceptable. Your time might be better spent elsewhere. Weigh the pros and cons before investing the time and effort.

Business Plan and Venture Competitions

Numerous business plan and venture-funding competitions are held each year for young people, undergraduate students, graduate students (primarily MBAs), and nonstudent professionals. Many business schools and classes hold internal competitions and then advance winners to regional, national, and even international events. Prizes may range from $500 to financing and professional-services packages worth millions. A list of selected regional, national, and international competitions for undergraduate and graduate students can be found in **Exhibit 2-7**.

Exhibit 2-7 *Business Plan and Venture Competitions for Undergraduate and Graduate Students*

Competition	Host/Sponsor	Web Site
Audacia International Business Plan Competition	Great Lakes Institute of Management, Chennai, India	http://greatlakes.edu.in
Camino Real Venture Competition	University of Texas at El Paso	http://caminorealcompetition.org
Cardinal Challenge Business Plan Competition	University of Louisville	http://business.louisville.edu
CEO Best Elevator Pitch Competition	Collegiate Entrepreneurs, Organization	http://www.c-e-o.org
CU Cleantech New Venture Challenge	University of Colorado at Boulder	http://nvc.cucleantech.org
Cornell Venture Challenge	Cornell University	http://www.brventurefund.com
Dell Social Innovation Challenge	Dell/University of Texas at Austin	http://www.dellchallenge.org
Emerging Business Leaders Summit (EBLS) Business Plan Competition	Minority Business Development Agency	http://www.medweek.gov
FLoW Business Plan Competition	California Institute of Technology	http://flow.caltech.edu
Giants Entrepreneurship Challenge	University of North Dakota	http://business.und.edu
Global Social Entrepreneurship Competition	University of Washington	http://www.foster.washington.edu
Global Social Venture Competition	University of California at Berkeley, London Business School, Columbia University, Indian School of Business, Thammasat University	http://www.gsvc.org
Global Venture Labs Investment Competition	University of Texas at Austin	http://www.mccombs.utexas.edu
Harvard New Venture Competition	Harvard Business School	http://www.hbs.edu
HATCH Startup Pitch Competition at SXSW	Houston Technology Center	http://www.hatchpitch.com
IBK Capital Ivey Business Plan Competition	University of Western Ontario	http://www.iveybpc.com
Idea to Product Competition (I2P)	University of Texas at Austin	http://www.ideatoproduct.org

(continued)

Exhibit 2-7 *Business Plan and Venture Competitions for Undergraduate and Graduate Students (continued)*

Competition	Host/Sponsor	Web Site
MIT Clean Energy	MIT, U.S. Department of Energy, NSTAR	http://cep.mit.edu
MIT $100K Entrepreneurship Competition	MIT	http://wordpress.mit100k.org
McGinnis Venture Competition	Carnegie Mellon University	http://www.mcginnisventurecompetition.com
New Venture Championship	University of Oregon	http://www.oregonnvc.com
NYC Next Idea Competition	Columbia University	http://www.nycedc.com
OFC Venture Challenge	Clark Atlanta University	http://www.ofcvc.org
Oh-Penn for Business: College Business Plan Competition	Grove City College	http://gccentrepreneurship.com
Rhode Island Business Plan Competition	University of Rhode Island	http://ri-bizplan.com
Rice Business Plan Competition	Rice University	http://www.alliance.rice.edu
Spirit of Enterprise MBA Business Plan Competition	University of Cincinnati	http://www.uc.edu
Student Venture Open	University of San Diego	http://www.wbtshowcase.com
TiE International Business Plan Competition	The Indus Entrepreneurs	https://www.tie.org
Utah Entrepreneur Challenge	University of Utah	http://www.uec.utah.edu
Wake Forest Elevator Corp.	Wake Forest University	http://www.mba.wfu.edu
West Virginia Statewide Collegiate Business Plan Competition	West Virginia University	http://www.be.wvu.edu

Chapter Summary

Now that you have studied this chapter, you can do the following:

1. Describe what a feasibility analysis is and choose when to create one. The feasibility analysis essentially tests a business concept for viability through:
   - product and/or service feasibility,
   - market and industry feasibility, and
   - financial feasibility.
2. Prepare a Business Model Canvas and make a visual representation of the nine facets:
   - Key partners
   - Key activities
   - Key resources
   - Value propositions
   - Customer relationships

- Channels
- Customer segments
- Cost structure
- Revenue streams

3. Identify primary business plan contents.
   - the story of what the business is and will be,
   - all costs and a marketing plan,
   - a description of how the business will be financed, and
   - an estimate of projected earnings.

4. Summarize the various purposes of a business plan and the audiences for one.
   - A business plan is used by entrepreneurs to organize their thoughts before starting a business and to determine business viability.
   - It can be used to raise money from investors and lenders. Almost always, bankers and other potential investors will refuse to consider funding an entrepreneur who does not have a business plan.
   - It can help guide the operation of the business.

5. Differentiate the components of a business plan.

   The parts of a business plan include a cover page; table of contents; executive summary; mission, vision, and culture; company description; opportunity analysis; marketing strategy and plan; management and operations; financial analysis and projections; funding request; and exit strategy.

6. Recognize and demonstrate proper development and formatting of a business plan.

   A solid, viable business plan that is sloppy and filled with errors may be rejected on that basis alone. The business plan should be well organized, neatly presented, and written in correct English.

Key Terms

advertising	initial public offering (IPO)
asset	liability
balance sheet	marketing mix
breakeven point	marketing plan
business model	mission
business plan	mission statement
cash flow statement	net worth
competitive analysis	owner's equity
culture	profit and loss statement (P&L)
direct marketing	proof of market
elevator pitch	public relations
environmental analysis	publicity
feasibility analysis	target market
income statement	vision
industry analysis	

Entrepreneurship Portfolio

Critical Thinking Exercises

2-1. Shawn is creating a business that provides advertising on public restroom stall doors. He is funding the project from his personal savings of $5,000 and does not expect to use any outside financing. Should he create a business plan? Why or why not?

2-2. Charity and Devon are planning to license technology from NASA that would make it impossible to accidentally lock a child in a car. The technology is complex, and the market analysis and financial assumptions take up a lot of pages. The two women have written a 63-page business plan. Explain your concerns about the plan in light of the chapter text.

2-3. What factors make the difference between a good business plan and an excellent one?

2-4. Visit an Internet shopping site, such as the Home Shopping Network (*http://www.HSN.com*) or QVC (*http://www.QVC.com*). Select five products for sale that you find interesting or unusual. Make a list of the products and your explanation of the market opportunities they reflect.

2-5. Explain how this statement applies to business plans: Errors of omission can sometimes be greater than errors of commission.

Key Concept Questions

2-6. Explain why a prospective business founder might want to create a feasibility study or Business Model Canvas before developing a complete business plan.

2-7. How can spending time researching and writing a business plan save an entrepreneur time and money in the short and long term?

2-8. What are the parts of a Business Model Canvas? How can the entire canvas assist an entrepreneur?

2-9. Explain why the executive summary is the most important section of any business plan.

2-10. One mistake entrepreneurs make in their business plans is that of only including an income statement. What other financial statements should be incorporated and why?

2-11. Print an assignment, or any body of text, with 1-inch margins, double spaced, using 12-point Times New Roman. Then, print the same document with 0.8-inch margins, single spaced, using a 10-point Arial typeface. Which is easier to read? Why? How would this relate to a business plan?

2-12. Name three categories of investors/lenders that might have an interest in your business plan.

2-13. Why is it important to identify a business's culture from the beginning?

Application Exercises

2-14. Prepare a Business Model Canvas for Honest Tea based on the business plan included at the end of this chapter.

2-15. Call and visit an entrepreneur in your community to discuss business plans.

    a. Ask whether he or she wrote a business plan before starting the business. Since then?

    b. If the owner did write a plan, for what has it been used?

    c. If the owner did not write a plan, why not?

    d. Did the owner have any assistance in writing or reviewing the plan?

    e. If so, what was the source of assistance?

Exploring Online

2-16. Find a business plan on the Internet. Examine it to see whether it follows the guidelines provided in this text. Use a highlighter to mark the sections of the plan that are present. Then, make a list of missing or incomplete sections. Indicate how it does/does not follow the rules for formatting and content. Is the plan viable? Why or why not? Would you invest in it? Why or why not?

In Your Opinion

2-17. If an entrepreneur presents a business plan that an investor believes is deliberately vague and has provided inflated financial statements, what should that investor do?

Honest Tea
Business Plan

Honest Tea

Business Plan for 1999
December 1998
4905 Del Ray Avenue, Suite 304
Bethesda, Maryland 20814
Phone: 301-652-3556
Fax: 301-652-3557

E-mail: sethandbarry@honesttea.com

Table of Contents

Mission Statement. 70

Executive Summary 71

Company Story. 71

The Product. 72

    The Taste 72

    Low in Calories 72

    Health Benefits of Brewed Tea 73

    Cultural Experience of Tea 73

    Flagship Line of Flavors 74

Production and Manufacturing 74

Market Opportunity 75

    Beyond Snapple—The Emerging Market for Quality Bottled Tea. 75

    Profile of Target Customer 76

    Market Research 77

    Market Response 77

Marketing and Distribution. 79

    National Natural/Specialty Foods Channels 80

    Higher End Food Service. 80

    Promotion 80

    Packaging and Pricing 80

    International Markets. 81

    Product Development and Future Products 81

Management 81

    President & TeaEO 81

    Chairman of the Board. 82

    Brewmaster 82

    National Sales Director 82

    Retail Sales Manager. 82

    Consultants and Advisors 82

Statement and Aspirations for Social Responsibility 83

Financial Statements—Year-to-Date and Projections 83

The Investment Opportunity. 90

    The Offering 90

    Financing History 90

    Exit Strategies 90

    Investment Risks 90

    Competitive Advantage 90

A Parting Thought. 91

BUSINESS PLAN

Mission Statement

Honest Tea seeks to provide bottled tea that tastes like tea—a world of flavor freshly brewed and barely sweetened. We seek to provide better-tasting, healthier teas the way nature and their cultures of origin intended them to be. We strive for relationships with our customers, employees, suppliers and stakeholders which are as healthy and honest as the tea we brew.

Executive Summary

Honest Tea, a bottled iced tea company, has completed a strong summer of sales in the mid-Atlantic region and is now raising capital to fund the brand's expansion across the United States as well as overseas. Since the all-natural tea first hit the mid-Atlantic market in June of 1998, Honest Tea has developed a loyal following of customers who have made the product the best-selling tea in its largest account, Fresh Fields/Whole Food Markets, significantly outselling Snapple and the Whole Foods 365 brand. In addition to success in retail channels, Honest Tea has also been warmly received in food service channels.

Unlike the sweetened tea drinks made from concentrate or powder which currently dominate the $2 billion bottled tea market, Honest Tea is brewed with loose leaf tea and then barely sweetened with pure cane sugar or honey. The product is poised to take advantage of the rapid growth in the bottled tea, bottled water, and natural food markets, as well as the developing "tea culture" in the United States. It also has potential to tap into the large market of health-conscious diet soda drinkers. The target audience is an emerging subset of the population, which seeks out authentic products and is attuned to global and environmental issues.

Toward the end of the summer and through the fall the company continued to penetrate large supermarket chains and is in the process of finalizing a national network of brokers and distributors for 1999. In September 1998 the company hired two sales managers, each of whom brings more than 15 years of experience and contacts to the business.

Although there was an often painful and occasionally costly product development phase, the company has now perfected the brewing and production process to the point where it can produce several thousand cases in one shift with the desired consistency. In early 1999 the company will add a West Coast site to its current East Coast production site. In addition, the company will be implementing steps to consolidate its packaging operation which will widen the per case profit margin.

The company has demonstrated an ability to gain free media coverage, including stories in the *Washington Post*, the *Wall Street Journal*, and *Fitness Magazine*. It has also cultivated a loyal customer base among some of the country's most influential celebrities which it intends to publicize at the appropriate time. It has just entered into a contract with a well-recognized public relations firm, which has demonstrated its success with several early-stage companies. Finally, the company has finalized a partnership with a Native American tribe that will position Honest Tea to emerge as a leader in the socially responsible business movement.

Honest Tea is looking to raise up to $1.2 million in equity capital to finance the national distribution of the product as well as the introduction of two new flavors and international sales.

Company Story

Honest Tea is a company brewed in the classic entrepreneurial tradition. After a parching run through Central Park in 1997, Seth Goldman teamed up with his Yale School of Management professor, Barry Nalebuff, to reignite their three-year old conversation on the beverage industry. While at Yale Goldman and Nalebuff had converged on the opportunity in the beverage market between the supersweet drinks and the flavorless waters. The energy they share around the idea of a less-sweet beverage leads to several marathon tea-brewing sessions. Their conversation is fueled in part by their extensive travels through tea-drinking cultures such as India, China and Russia. As ideas and investors for the company gather critical mass, Seth takes the dive. He leaves his marketing and sales post at Calvert Group, the nation's largest family of socially and environmentally responsible mutual funds, and launches Honest Tea out of the guest room in his house. Using five large thermoses and label mock-ups, he sells the product to the eighteen Fresh Fields stores of the Whole Foods Market chain. Once the tea has been manufactured, the company moves into a small office and distributes tea out of U-Hauls until other distributors start carrying the product. By the end of the summer, Honest Tea has become the best-selling tea throughout the Fresh Fields chain and has been accepted by several national supermarket chains and distributors.

The Product

The Taste:

Bottled tea that tastes like tea, freshly brewed and barely sweetened.

Somewhere between the pumped-up, sugar-saturated drinks and the tasteless waters, there is a need for a healthier beverage which provides genuine natural taste without the artificially concocted sweeteners and preservatives designed to compensate for lack of taste.

Honest Tea allows people to enjoy the world's second most popular drink the way hundreds of civilizations and nature intended it to be. Tea that tastes like tea—A world of flavor freshly brewed and barely sweetened. The concept of Honest Tea is as direct and clear as the tea we brew—we start with select tea leaves from around the world, then we brew the tea in spring water and add a hint of honey or pure cane sugar. Finally, we filter the tea to produce a pure genuine taste that doesn't need a disguise.

Unlike most of the bottled teas in the marketplace, Honest Tea is not made with bricks of tea dust, tea concentrate, or other artificial sweeteners or acids. The tea has no bitter aftertaste or sugar kick, and does not leave a syrupy film on the drinker's teeth. To make a comparison with wine, today's leading iced teas are like jug wine and Honest Tea is like Robert Mondavi Opus One. But unlike fine wine, premium bottled tea is quite affordable, usually priced under $1.50 for 16 ounces.

Although taste is the primary benefit of drinking Honest Tea, the product has three other benefits which enhance its acceptance and marketability:

Low in calories:

A 12-ounce serving of Honest Tea has 17 calories, dramatically less than other bottled teas or comparable beverages. We have found that the low-calorie profile of Honest Tea makes the drink attractive to three key audiences – 1) Disenchanted bottled tea drinkers who think the drinks are too sweet, 2) Bottled water drinkers who long for taste and variety and 3) diet soda drinkers who are interested in a low-calorie beverage that doesn't contain artificial sweeteners such as Nutrasweet. The following table illustrates the difference between Honest Tea and the rest of the beverage market:

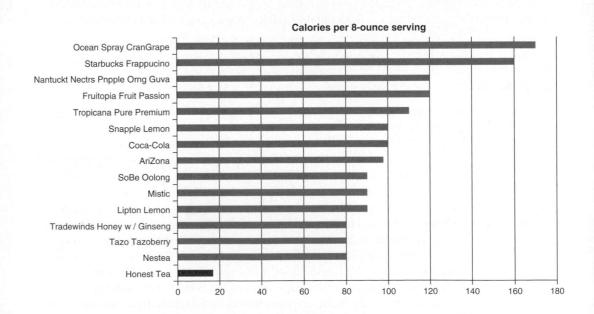

Calories per 8-ounce serving

There are three other players in the less-sweetened bottled tea market that can be considered among the competition for Honest Tea: TeJava, Malibu Teaz and The Republic of Tea. All three brands are currently based and primarily focused on the West Coast. We are heartened by their existence because it confirms our belief that there are untapped opportunities in the beverage market, particularly on the East Coast, where none of the new entrants has any significant presence. TeJava, which is enjoying a warm reception in California, is a mild-tasting, zero-calorie unsweetened tea produced by Crystal Geyser that comes in only one flavor. We believe this product, which has been described by a beverage consultant as "water with a tea aftertaste," would be more flavorful if it were barely sweetened. While TeJava clearly competes with our product, we believe there is room for more than one product in the low-calorie tea marketplace. We also believe that Honest Tea has an edge over TeJava because our drinks are more flavorful and come in a wider variety of flavors.

Malibu Teaz is a company focused on lightly sweetened herbal tea, 35 calories for an 8 ounce serving. The products seem to have limited distribution and the label, which features a topless mermaid, seems designed to cater to a different clientele than Honest Tea.

The Republic of Tea is a well-established producer of loose leaf teas which has recently begun selling unsweetened bottled tea exclusively through its catalogue and premium restaurants. The cost of a four-pack in the catalogue is $15.00, or $3.75 for a 17 ounce bottle. We believe that this price is not viable in retail channels and have spoken with several disillusioned distributors whose experience confirms that assumption. Even if the Republic of Tea changed its sales strategy, we still see room for more than one player in the low-calorie tea market. We also think the modest amount of natural sweetener in Honest Tea helps create a superior flavor.

One other brand that can be considered competition is Tazo, which presents itself as "The reincarnation of Tea." While Tazo is enjoying some success in natural foods channels, we feel that Honest Tea is different from Tazo in three important ways: first Honest Tea is genuine tea whereas Tazo is usually tea mixed with juice or other sweeteners, (usually 80 calories for an 8-ounce serving). Secondly, Tazo's packaging, with its mysterious symbols and discussion of "the mumbled chantings of a certified tea shaman" is designed to reach a New Age audience. In contrast, the colorful art on the Honest Tea labels are accessible to a wider audience, offering a more genuine tea experience. Finally, Tazo's price point is significantly higher than Honest Tea in supermarket channels, selling for $1.69 versus Honest Tea's price of $1.19. Where the two brands have competed head-to-head, Honest Tea has significantly outsold, and in many cases, eliminated Tazo from the shelf. Our response to Tazo's "reincarnation of tea" is that tea doesn't need to be reincarnated if it is made right the first time.

Health benefits of brewed tea:

The curative properties of tea have been known for thousands of years. Because Honest Tea is brewed from genuine tea leaves it imparts many health benefits not found in tea-flavored drinks. In addition to serving as a digestive aid, tea has powerful antioxidants, which impair the development of free radicals which contribute to cancer and heart disease. The antioxidants in green tea are believed to be at least 100 times more effective than Vitamin C and twenty-five times better than Vitamin E at protecting cells and DNA from damage believed to be linked to cancer, heart disease and other potentially life-threatening illnesses.

Cultural experience of tea:

Each Honest Tea flavor is brewed based on a recipe perfected over generations in a specific region of the world. As a result, drinking Honest Tea becomes a cultural experience, from the genuine tastes to the distinctive international art and information on the label. While some bottled teas seek to cloak themselves in a cosmopolitan mantle by including exotic-looking drawings on the label, the front of each Honest Tea label features authentic art from the culture of origin.

Flagship line of flavors

Our flagship line of teas come from four different continents:

Kashmiri Chai – The people of Kashmir have mixed spices into their chai for generations. Our recipe is made with spring water, premium tea leaves, crushed cardamom, cinnamon, orange peel, cloves, pepper, ginger, malic acid and a touch of sucanat evaporated sugar cane juice. Approximately one third the caffeine of coffee.

Black Forest Berry – Our Black Forest Berry tea is a fruit infusion made with spring water, hibiscus, currants, strawberries, raspberries, brambleberries, elderberries, and a touch of unrefined organic cane sugar. Caffeine-free.

Moroccan Mint – Our Moroccan Mint is a tightly rolled green tea from China blended with a generous amount of peppermint, brewed in spring water with citric acid and a touch of white clover honey. Approximately one fourth the caffeine of coffee.

Gold Rush – Our Gold Rush tea is an herbal infusion made with spring water, rooibush, rose-hips, chamomile, cinnamon, peppermint, ginger, orange peel, malic acid, and a touch of raw cane sugar, and natural flavors. Caffeine-free.

Assam – These golden-tipped flowery leaves from the Sonarie Estate gain their distinctive taste from being picked as tender leaf buds at the height of the season. Brewed in spring water with Vitamin C, malic acid, unrefined organic cane sugar, and a hint of maple syrup. Approximately one half the caffeine of coffee.

In early 1999 we will be introducing two new teas:

Decaf Ceylon – In response to feedback from more than 500 sampling events where we continually heard requests for a decaffeinated black tea, we will be introducing a Decaf Ceylon with lemon grass. The label for this tea features original art which captures the cultural and relaxing attributes of the tea.

First Nation's Peppermint – After months of negotiation and a consultation with the tribal elders, we have developed an organic herbal tea in conjunction with a woman-owned company based on the Crow Reservation in Montana. This tea is exciting not only for its flavor but also for the partnership we have developed with the tribe. In addition to licensing the flavor and artwork from the tribe, we are also buying the tea from our partner on the reservation with the understanding that over time the community will develop the capacity to grow all the ingredients on the reservation. This unprecedented relationship should prove to be a valuable public relations tool.

Production and Manufacturing

Though we had our share of "learning experiences" along the way, we have developed several proprietary brewing tools and techniques which enable us to manufacture several thousand cases of tea a day on both coasts with the desired consistency. In addition, since we have a full-time brewmaster on staff, the company retains the knowledge of manufacturing the product, instead of relying on a co-packer for that information.

The tea is brewed at a brewing and bottling facility located within driving range of the target market. The site was selected based on numerous criteria including capacity, reputation, quality control, production efficiency and willingness to invest in a long-term partnership with Honest Tea. All partners involved in the production process meet United States Department of Agriculture Hazard Analysis Critical Control Plant (HACCP) standards. We are in the process of obtaining Kosher certification from the Orthodox Union ("Circle U").

In early 1999 we will be making a change in our manufacturing process that will not affect the quality of the product but will have important ramifications for our profitability. Instead of a two-step packaging process, we will consolidate the brewing and labeling under one roof. This consolidation will save Honest Tea more than two dollars a case.

Our tea leaves are provided by internationally known companies that specialize in tea buying, blending and importation. Our primary source is Hälssen & Lyon of Germany, the largest specialty tea company in the world. Another, Assam Tea Traders, has direct ties to tea estates in the Assam District of Northern India. The other ingredients are commodities which are in plentiful supply.

As the Company grows in size, we anticipate dealing more directly with the tea growers. We intend to visit the tea estates so that we can verify that the labor conditions of the tea workers meet international standards and International Labor Organization conventions. We also aspire to ensure that the tea is grown organically.

Market Opportunity

Beyond Snapple–The Emerging Market for Quality Bottled Tea

We have identified four market trends that are fueling demand for Honest Tea within the $72 billion non-alcoholic liquid refreshment beverage market.

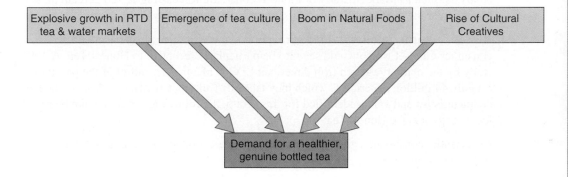

1. **Explosive growth in Ready-to-Drink (RTD) tea and bottled water markets** – Although carbonated soft drinks still dominate the beverage market, in the past ten years Ready-To-Drink teas and bottled water have emerged as alternatives. Since 1992 the US tea market has enjoyed 60% annual growth, reaching sales of $2 billion in 1996. The bottled water market has grown to $2.4 billion, with most of the growth fueled by sales of single-serving bottles.

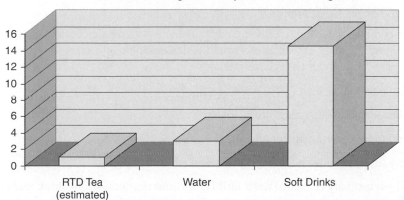

1997 U.S. Beverage consumption in billions of gallons*

*Water and Soft drink figures come from Beverage Marketing, Inc. The RTD Tea figure is based on 1997 sales estimate of $2.5 billion, which equates to roughly one billion gallons.

2. **Beyond the tea bag – The emergence of tea culture** – Snapple and similar brands helped make tea accessible to a broader population. But now in the same way that gourmet coffees have become popular, consumers are beginning to develop an appreciation for finer teas. Over the last six years U.S. loose leaf tea sales have more than doubled, from $1.8 billion

BUSINESS PLAN

in 1990 to $4.2 billion in 1996[1] According to the Tea Council, there are over a thousand tea houses or tea parlors in the country, mostly opened within the last two or three years. These parlors focus almost exclusively on tea, products that go with tea as well as tea hardware. They carry names such as Teaism, TeaLuxe, Elixir Tonics and Teas, and Tea & Company. Even Lipton is opening a flagship tea bar in Pasadena, California. In addition to the burgeoning of tea cafes, tea culture is spreading in the form of tea magazines, tea-flavored ice cream, frozen tea ice bars, tea-scented perfume and bubble bath, tea jelly, tea calendars and even books about tea. The paperback Loving Tea was recently spotted as a "cash register book" at the bookstore, commanding prime space next to Dilbert and Chicken Soup for the Soul.

3. **The natural foods boom** – The natural product category has also exploded in the past 6 years. Fueled by an increase in health consciousness and rising environmental awareness, demand has grown for foods and products which are best when eaten or used as close to their original state in nature. According to Natural Foods Merchandiser, the natural products industry has nearly tripled in size since 1990 from $4.2 billion to $11.5 billion in 1996. And the boom is expected to continue well into the next decade. Analysts, such as Mark Hanratty of Paine Webber, are forecasting 15–20 percent annual growth over the next three to five years, reaching $50 billion by 2003.

4. **Rise of Cultural Creatives** – Market research in the past three years has identified a consumer mindset which would seem to be particularly receptive to Honest Tea. A 1996 study by the market research firm American LIVES identified a subset of the population, roughly 44 million Americans, which they labeled "Cultural Creatives."[2] Among the key characteristics and values identified for this group, the following seem to make them ideal customers for Honest Tea:

- Experiential consumers – they want to know where a product came from, how it was made, and who made it

- Holistic – they view nature as sacred; they form the core market for alternative health care and natural foods

- Aggressive consumers of cultural products, love of things foreign and exotic

- Desire for authenticity – favoring high integrity over high fashion

- Disdainful of mainstream media and consumerist culture which, in their view, is too superficial, not enough attention to the full story

- Attuned to global issues and whole systems, have a sense of belonging to a global village

Profile of Target Customer

When we combine these four trends and compare them with the demographics of the Cultural Creatives study as well as other market demographic information[3], we are able to develop a profile of our target customers:

- 60% women, 40% men

- Median age 42, with a range from 30–65

- Likely to live near a concentrated urban area

- Likely to have graduated college or have an advanced degree

- Likely to currently be bottled water or RTD tea drinkers, occasionally drink iced cappuccino

- Interested in running, hiking and outdoor healthy activities

- Average family income $52,000

---

[1] Investor's Business Daily, "Tea: Are you Prepared to Join the Party?", January 30, 1998, p. 1.

[2] American Demographics, February 1997, Dr. Paul H. Ray.

[3] 1997 MRI Spring data, population weighted.

Market Research

To test the receptivity of this audience to Honest Tea, we held two focus groups in New York. The sessions, facilitated by an independent market research firm, provided encouraging results and helpful guidance in terms of product line and label presentation. The first focus group consisted of health-conscious women between the ages of 30 and 60, all of whom occasionally drink bottled tea or bottled water. The second group was a mix of men and women who were selected based on their responses to questions which identified them as fitting the Cultural Creatives profile. The sessions began with a discussion of what was missing in the beverage market. Within 5 minutes, unprompted by the moderator, both groups agreed that they wanted something that was not as boring as water but didn't have all the "junk" in commercial bottled tea.

One important lesson from the focus groups was that most consumers have a limited understanding about the differences between tea varieties. The situation may be comparable to the way many consumers thought about wine several decades ago. At first people distinguished wines in terms of red and white wine, then in terms of rose and chablis, then in terms of California wines versus French wines, later by the kind of grape, and today some people select wines based on the estate. The focus groups suggested that the American tea market is still in the red versus white stage. One implication of this finding was that our labels and other communications needed to include some educational information about each tea, including health benefits, history and country of origin.

Market Response

More important than our pre-market focus group is the market response to Honest Tea, i.e., sales. In the eighteen Fresh Fields/Whole Foods Markets of the mid-Atlantic region Honest Tea has become the best-selling bottled tea, outselling Snapple and the house brand. During the month of August, when Honest Tea was promotionally priced at 99 cents, 22,417 bottles of teas were sold, with several stores averaging more than 100 bottles per day.

Perhaps more important than the numbers from one region are the thousands of responses we have gotten from our customers via unsolicited emails, letters, phone calls, and conversations at hundreds of sampling events. The feedback we have received make it clear that we have created something that was missing in the marketplace. Every week we receive several unsolicited emails and letters from customers. Typical comments include the following (see Exhibit A for more tea-mail – Excluded in the interest of space):

```
Subject: BEST TEA EVER!

Dear Honest Tea,

I have never bought a product that I thought was so fantastic that I felt
the need to write about it. I love tea, but I always would brew it myself
and cart it around because I can't stand the syrupy-sweet "tea" that is
sold most places.

I saw your tea at Fresh Fields in Annapolis, MD. At first I was hesitant
because I have it in my mind that all bottled iced teas = yucky sweet.
But I was intrigued by the flavor choices and yes, the pretty bottles
and bought one of each. Well, I went to my car and proceeded to drink all
of them right then and there. The first one was so good and so different
that I couldn't help myself and had to try the rest. It actually tasted
like tea! THEN... when I turned the bottle over and saw how few calories
were in it I flipped! There is no reason not to drink this tea! You guys
have truly done it, this is quality stuff! So keep it up and get this tea
out there! I wish you success and happy brewing!

-Cindy W., Annapolis, MD
```

RE: Help! I need Honest Tea!

I just returned from a trip to Wash, DC (I live in Pittsburgh) and found that your tea is not available here. I love it and must have more. Can you ship it to me? Price is no object (to some degree).

If you cannot ship it to me please advise me of any support groups or counseling that I may seek in order to recover from this lack of Honest Tea. I must warn you that I may get desperate, causing me to highjack an Honest Tea truck in the Washington area and bring it back to Pittsburgh. I am becoming a heartless, Honest Tea junkie. I hope that you can help.

Thanks, EEOber

Subject: Chai tea was great!

I just came from my local Fresh Fields Market in Reston, VA after trying a bottle of your Kashmiri Chai tea. Fantastic! Imagine my surprise to learn the entire bottle was only 34 calories and 1/3 the caffeine of coffee!

This is great stuff folks - my only complaint is that I can't seem to find anywhere that sells it by the case. I don't mind buying a couple bottles at a time for occasional consumption, but I would appreciate being able to purchase a case to bring to work and a case to keep at home. It would be a great way to replace soda and other sugary, high calorie drinks in my diet. Unfortunately, I cannot spare the time to stop at the store every day to pick up a couple bottles. Any plans to sell by the case (hopefully at a slight discount)??

Colin C. Reston, VA

Re: Honest Tea!

Your tea is fabulous! I have never written a letter in support of a food product before, but ever since I stumbled across your Honest Tea last week at Fairway, I've been raving about it! At last, someone intelligent enough to realize that not all people like that syrupy junk that is on the market, and that nutri-sweet and artificial sweeteners taste like crap. I've grown so tired of "well, it's what the consumers are demanding." Not. The rest of us have spent the last decade or so brewing tea at home and keeping it in our refrigerators since traditional marketing researchers have been incapable of using their research to produce anything innovative. Bravo, bravo, bravo. Nice labels, too.

Lisa P., New York City

The response from grocery buyers at the corporate level has been equally as exciting.

The new products buyer for Wild Oats/Alfalfa Community Market approved Honest Tea for sale in all of the chain's 60+ stores. Here is her comment to the grocery buyers which she sent out on the Product Approval Form (see Exhibit B – Excluded in the interest of space):

> Mark My Words: Honest Tea will be a success. The *only* bottled tea that is not loaded with sugars and tastes great. This is what people (like me) have been seeking for years. Too good to be true? No! I mean it now – BRING THESE IN!

The natural foods buyer for Harris Teeter chose to carry the product in all 140 stores. Her buying committee told her this was the first innovation in the iced tea market they'd seen in about five years. Some even said that Honest Tea represents a new beverage category.

In addition to this feedback, Honest Tea has been presented with several promising opportunities to be plugged into several large supermarket chains. The status of these opportunities is as follows:

Store	# of Outlets	Region	Status	Penetration
Albertson's	96	Florida	December decision	
Food Emporium	40	NY/NJ	December decision	
Genuardi's	32	NJ/PA/DE	Approved for all stores	Will go on sale in December '98
Giant	179	C/MD/VA/DENJ/PA	Approved	On sale in flagship store
Harris Teeter	140	NC/SC/GA/VA/KY/TN	Approved for all stores	On sale in all stores
Shaw's	127	New England	Approved	On sale in test market store
Superfresh	78	NJ/PA	Approved for all stores	On sale in some stores
Ukrop's	40	VA	Approved for all stores	On sale in some stores
Whole Foods	117	Nationwide	Approved for mid-Atlantic and SE	On sale in 20 stores
Wild Oats/Alfalfa's	60	Nationwide	Approved for all stores	On sale in 12 stores

In addition to success in the supermarket channel, Honest Tea is also being warmly received in food service and retail accounts. We have experienced strong repeat sales in cafeterias such as Bear Stearns, Lazard Freres and have just been approved for sale in the NFL corporate cafeteria. Honest Tea is the best-selling beverage at the Mangia gourmet eatery in Manhattan where it is priced at $2.50 a bottle. Honest Tea is also sold in well-known restaurants such as Legal Sea Foods. Finally, we have also had strong repeat sales from food outlets on the campuses of Boston University, Harvard University, Yale University and Wellesley College.

As with Snapple and other bottled iced teas, there does seem to be a seasonality affect to the sales of Honest Tea, particularly in the supermarket channel. However, as we expand our distribution to the Southern states and to more upscale cafeterias, we expect to see less of a dip in sales during the winter months.

Marketing & Distribution

Given the above market trends, target customer profile and record of success in the mid-Atlantic natural and specialty foods market, Honest Tea's marketing and distribution strategy for 1999 is as follows:

1. National natural/specialty foods channels, working with brokers and distributors to achieve full distribution throughout the Whole Foods and Wild Oats chains as well as natural foods buyers in mainstream supermarkets.

2. Higher end food service – working with large national food distributors such as Sysco, Aramark and Marriott to penetrate restaurants and institutional eateries.

3. Opportunistic public relations and extensive sampling in health and natural food settings to build the brand name as well as facilitate trial.

BUSINESS PLAN

National natural/specialty foods channels

We are in the process of finalizing national distribution and brokerage arrangements. We are currently working with Haddon House, the largest retail distributor of gourmet foods on the East Coast. In addition, we have recently contracted with numerous natural food brokers to represent our product for the East Coast, Midwest, West Coast and the South.

Higher end food service

We are working food management companies to expand our presence in business and institutional cafeterias. and has been approved for sale in Restaurant Associates and Marriott International. We are currently in discussions with Aramark and Sysco. We are also in conversation with several large restaurant chains and sports arenas.

Promotion

We recognize that because we are not as well-financed or as well-established as much of our competition, whenever we play by their marketing rules, we are at a disadvantage. Therefore, instead of spending a lot of money on advertising, Honest Tea relies instead on opportunistic ways to gain public attention and promote trial of the product.

We have proven our ability to gain positive free media coverage in *The Washington Post, The Wall Street Journal, Christian Science Monitor* and *Fortune* magazine. (See Exhibit C). In addition to what has already been printed, several articles are in the pipeline, including upcoming articles in magazines such as *Shape, Self, Fitness, Start-Ups*, and *Seventeen*. We are currently finalizing a contract with a highly-regarded public relations firm, which has a proven track record of gaining extensive exposure for early-stage companies. Just as we have paid a portion of our label designer's expenses in the form of equity, we intend to pay a portion of the PR firm's retainer in stock to encourage their investment in our business. We also have developed a web page at www.honesttea.com which has regularly attracts 50 visitors a day and has helped attract several new accounts.

In addition we have been very aggressive with sampling. Because Honest Tea started the summer as an unknown product and is unlike any product currently on the market, we took great pains to introduce as many people to the product as we could. During the month of August we organized demos as often as eight times a month per Fresh Fields/Whole Foods Market (See Exhibit D – Excluded in the interest of space).

Finally, we have developed a loyal following among several nationally-known celebrities which we hope to use to our advantage this coming Spring. For example, we recently rushed the delivery of ten cases to Oprah Winfrey's studios at her personal request.

Packaging and Pricing

Honest Tea's flagship line of products is sold in 16 ounce glass bottles. All of our labels feature culturally authentic artwork from the tea's country of origin. All of our caps have a distinctive black matte finish which complements the black border on the front of the label. In 1999 our caps will have the "pop-button" seal. Our packaging communicates the attributes of the tea inside in four ways:

1. High quality – By using colorful and artistically sophisticated artwork presented with spot labels, (i.e., front and back instead of wraparound) our bottles evoke comparisons with a bottle of fine wine or other gourmet food.

2. Culturally authentic – By using artwork directly from the culture where the tea comes from, we are presenting the tea as is, without any "spin" or Westernized interpretation of what an Indian painting might look like.

3. Honest – By using the spot labels, there is more space for the consumer to see the tea. Since we use real tea leaves, we have nothing to hide inside.

4. Simplicity – The essence of this millenia-old drink of water and leaves is its simplicity. Our packaging has no flashy slogans, advertising call-outs or marketing hype. The package helps condition the consumer for what they are about to experience, an honest taste of tea.

In 1999 we plan to introduce a "Varietea" pack which will contain a selection of flavors, and will help introduce consumers to our product. The Varietea pack will be sold at a modest discount to encourage first-time trial.

The retail price for a 16 ounce Honest Tea varies between $1.19 and $2.00, slightly more expensive than Snapple, which usually sells for $.99. In food service accounts we have seen the price range from $1.29 to $2.50.

International Markets

Since tea is the world's second most popular beverage, there is an intrinsic international appeal for Honest Tea's world of flavor freshly brewed and barely sweetened. Although our primary energies are directed toward the US market, we have recently entered into a contract with a firm that has extensive international marketing expertise. They will be showing our product in the UK early next year with the intent to sell the bottled tea in the Spring of 1999.

Product Development and Future Products

In 1999 we will be introducing at least two new flavors in direct response to feedback from our customers. Our Decaf Ceylon will be the only decaffeinated black tea served in a Ready-to-Drink bottle. The decaf tea has a great taste and a captivating label.

In addition to being our first organic tea, our First Nation Peppermint has a smooth taste and a compelling label featuring an intense photo of a Crow warrior. This product should also attract free media coverage for the innovative partnership we have forged with the Crow Nation.

Despite the thousands of tea flavors that exist, we have taken a relatively conservative approach by identifying accessible flavors from different continents. In addition to Decaf Ceylon and First Nation's Peppermint, several more flavors have been identified which will be introduced within the next twelve months. Some are as accessible as the flagship products, others may be more appealing to certain segments of the population. For example, Japanese green tea has a strong taste which can repel untrained Western tastebuds, but we believe this product has commercial viability provided it is strategically marketed and distributed.

In addition to other bottled tea flavors, we are exploring related products such as "Tea"-shirts featuring art from our labels, tea bags sold under the Honest Tea name and other tea-related products such as tea marinade and even "tea bags" for the bathtub.

Management

The management team of Honest Tea has a proven record of entrepreneurial success and innovative business strategy and has recently added two senior sales managers with extensive experience in the specialty foods and beverage industries. They are, in order of seniority:

President & TeaEO

Seth Goldman launched Honest Tea after leaving the Calvert Group where he was Vice President of Calvert Social Investment Fund, the nation's largest family of mutual funds that invest in socially and environmentally responsible companies. In this role, Seth managed the marketing and sales efforts, including a ground-breaking public awareness campaign that increased website traffic eightfold and doubled sales in the company's flagship equity fund. His other work at Calvert Group includes active involvement in the company's private equity portfolio and managing a corporate child labor initiative for the Calvert Foundation.

His previous work includes directing a nationally-recognized demonstration project for Americorps, the president's national service program, and serving as Senator Lloyd Bentsen's Deputy Press Secretary for two and a half years. Before that he worked for a year in China (1987-1988) and a year and a half in the former Soviet Union (1989-1990), where he developed, among other things, an appreciation for the role tea plays in bringing people together.

Seth graduated from the Yale School of Management in 1995. While at Yale, he and a classmate were winners of the inaugural Connecticut Future Fund New Enterprise Competition for a business plan they developed based on a diagnostic invented at the Yale School of Medicine. Seth is a graduate of Harvard College, where he was elected Class Marshal and was a member of the Varsity Track team. He serves as Chair of the Yale School of Management Annual Fund and the Montgomery Public Schools Educational Foundation. He is a former board member of Students for Responsible Business.

Seth's experience at Calvert Group has enhanced his contribution to Honest Tea in two important ways. As Calvert's most visible presence within the community of socially responsible businesses, Seth's contacts and connections help give Honest Tea a mark of credibility which is essential for the brand identity the Company is trying to create. In addition, the target customer for Calvert's equity funds is very much in line with the Cultural Creative profile discussed earlier. Seth's record of success in communicating with this audience while at Calvert Group has conveyed well to Honest Tea.

Chairman of the Board

Barry Nalebuff is the Milton Steinbach Professor of Economics and Management at Yale School of Management. He taught at Harvard and Princeton before coming to Yale. He teaches competitive strategy, mergers and acquisition, political marketing, and decision-making and game theory at the management school negotiation at Yale law school, and social choice, political theory, and welfare economics to undergraduates. An expert on Game Theory, he has written extensively on its applications for managers. Barry is co-author of *Thinking Strategically: The Competitive Edge in Business, Politics, and Everyday Life.* His new book on business strategy, *Co-opetition*, co-authored with Adam Brandenburger, was a *Business Week* bestseller. He has applied the use of game theory in consulting to companies in banking, consumer products, healthcare, high-tech manufacturing, insurance, oil, pharmaceuticals software, and telecommunications. A graduate of M.I.T. and a Rhodes Scholar, he earned his doctorate in economics at Oxford University.

Brewmaster

George Scalf joined Honest Tea in March of 1998 to manage the production of the tea. As the founder of numerous natural beverage enterprises including Blue Range Natural Foods and New Dawn Natural Foods, George brings more than 20 years of expertise and contacts in beverage manufacturing. He also has numerous contacts in the natural foods marketplace.

National Sales Director

Jim Lambert joined Honest Tea in September from Stanley Foods where he was the Vice President of Sales for the DC/ Baltimore area's premier specialty food distributor. Jim is a 15 year veteran of the food industry. His previous positions include Chain Accounts Manager at US Foodservice Baltimore and with Atlantic Foodservices. In his role as National Sales Director, Jim is responsible for overseeing all sales and distribution relationships, with particular focus on food service and mainstream supermarket accounts.

Retail Sales Manager

Melanie Knitzer came to Honest Tea in October from her post as Director of Corporate Sales with Gourm-E-Co Imports, a mid-Atlantic specialty food distributor. Melanie also brings 15 years of experience to Honest Tea, including roles as General Manager with Dolce Europa and Gourmand. In her role as Retail Sales Manager, Melanie is responsible for managing all natural foods and gourmet foods retail accounts.

Consultants and Advisors

Throughout the development of the Honest Tea business planning process, we have been fortunate to tap into a wealth of tea, beverage, natural foods, and entrepreneurial expertise. The people listed below have served as resources for us. Several of them may continue to play a role in the company in the future.

Joe Dobrow – Director of Marketing Programs, Fresh Fields/Whole Foods Markets

John May – Managing director, New Century Partners, social venture capital investment advisor

Lawrence Omene – Quality Assurance Manager, Mid-Atlantic Coca-Cola Bottling Company

Karin Schryver – Natural foods buyer for Harris Teeter, chain of 140 upscale supermarkets in the Southeastern United States

Statement and Aspirations for Social Responsibility

Although a statement of social and environmental responsibility is not usually found in most business plans, these issues are central to Honest Tea's identity and purpose. Not only is the value of our brand based on authenticity, integrity and purity, but our management team is committed to these values as well. We will never claim to be a perfect company, but we will address difficult issues and strive to be honest about our ability or inability to resolve them. For example, we recognize that the labor and environmental conditions on many tea estates are below internationally accepted standards. We will strive to work with our suppliers to promote higher standards while recognizing the limited influence we have as a small company. We value diversity in the workplace and we intend to become a visible presence in the communities where our products are sold. When presented with a purchasing decision between two financially comparable alternatives, we will attempt to choose the option which better addresses the needs of economically disadvantaged communities.

We have taken our first substantive step in that direction with the development of our newest tea flavor, First Nation's Peppermint. After much negotiation with Itchik, a woman-owned company based on the Crow reservation, we have created a partnership that allows the Crow community to be economically involved in the production and sale of the tea. Itchik is serving as Honest Tea's buyer for the ingredients, charging a modest administrative fee per kilo of tea with the understanding that over time Itchik will develop the capacity to harvest the tea on the reservation. In addition Itchik is licensing the recipe and artwork to Honest Tea in a royalty arrangement. A portion of the royalties will be directed to the Pretty Shield Foundation, a non-profit created to address the needs of foster Native American children.

Financial Statements–Year-to-Date and Projections

Exhibit E presents the monthly income statement and balance sheet for Honest Tea from January 1998 through November 30, 1998. Exhibit F presents the 1999 projected income and cash flow statement, with assumptions included at the bottom.

Exhibit E
Honest Tea Balance Sheet 1998

	February 28	March 31	April 30	May 31	June 30	July 31	August 31	September 30	October 31	November 30
ASSETS										
Current Assets										
Checking/Savings										
Chevy Chase Bank Checking	$ 16,875	$ 264,699	$ 364,259	$ 90,394	$ 48,470	$ 13,740	$ -	$ -	$ -	$ -
FCNB Checking Account			$ 1,000	$ 19,759	$ 11,281	$ (2,616)	$ (27,575)	$ 13,063	$ (7,896)	$ 23,493
FCNB Repo Account	$ -	$ -	$ -	$ 228,029	$ 230,028	$ 252,031	$ 232,084	$ 135,015	$ 67,006	$ 17,187
Total Checking/Savings	$ 16,875	$ 264,699	$ 365,259	$ 338,181	$ 289,779	$ 263,155	$ 204,509	$ 148,078	$ 59,110	$ 40,680
Accounts Receivable	$ -	$ -	$ -	$ 12,866	$ 21,047	$ 23,512	$ 67,252	$ 78,081	$ 64,774	$ 59,201
Other Current Assets										
Cert. of Deposit/Capital Bank			$ 24,000	$ 24,000	$ 24,000	$ 24,300	$ 24,300	$ 24,300	$ 24,300	$ 24,300
Inventory										
Raw Materials						$ 2,976	$ 2,976	$ 2,976	$ 2,976	$ 2,976
Total Inventory	$ -	$ -				$ 2,976	$ 2,976	$ 2,976	$ 2,976	$ 2,976
Total Other Current Assets	$ -	$ -	$ 24,000	$ 24,000	$ 24,000	$ 27,276	$ 27,276	$ 27,276	$ 27,276	$ 27,276
Total Current Assets	$ 16,875	$ 264,699	$ 389,259	$ 375,047	$ 334,826	$ 313,943	$ 299,038	$ 253,436	$ 151,160	$ 127,157
Fixed Assets										
Computer Equipment		$ 635	$ 635	$ 635	$ 2,687	$ 2,687	$ 2,687	$ 2,687	$ 6,277	$ 6,277
Office Furniture & Equipment				$ 3,500	$ 3,709	$ 3,709	$ 3,709	$ 3,709	$ 3,709	$ 3,709
Coolers/Glide Racks						$ 352	$ 352	$ 9,582	$ 9,582	$ 9,582
Tea Brewing Equipment						$ -	$ -	$ -	$ 3,000	$ 3,000
Total Fixed Assets	$ -	$ 635	$ 635	$ 4,135	$ 6,396	$ 6,748	$ 6,748	$ 15,978	$ 22,568	$ 22,568
TOTAL ASSETS	$ 16,875	$ 265,334	$ 389,893	$ 379,182	$ 341,222	$ 320,691	$ 305,786	$ 269,413	$ 173,728	$ 149,725

	February 28	March 31	April 30	May 31	June 30	July 31	August 31	September 30	October 31	November 30
LIABILITIES & EQUITY										
Liabilities										
Current Liabilities										
Accounts Payable	$ -	$ -	$ -	$ -	$ -	$ -	$ (16)	$ -	$ -	$ -
Total Accounts Payable	$ -	$ -	$ -	$ -	$ -	$ -	$ (16)	$ -	$ -	$ -
Credit Cards										
First USA		$ 231	$ 826	$ 968	$ 604	$ 2,694	$ 188	$ 1,679	$ 5,239	$ 1,471
Halssen and Lyon		$ (5,000)	$ (2,560)	$ (2,560)	$ (2,438)	$ 538	$ -	-	-	$ -
Mayer Bros.		$ (5,000)	$ (5,000)	$ (500)	$ 7,585	$ 7,295	$ 6,298	-	-	-
Slate Packaging			$ (30,800)	$ (12,914)	$ 435	$ 7,295	$ 14,000	-	-	$ -
Staples					$ 170	$ 181	$ -	$ 66	$ 219	$ -
Strasburger and Siegel, Inc.		$ (1,000)	$ 356	$356	$ 355	$ -	$ -	$ -	$ -	$ -
Total Credit Cards	$ -	$ (10,770)	$ (37,179)	$ (14,651)	$ 6,713	$ 18,003	$ 20,486	$ 1,745	$ 5,458	$ 1,471
Total Current Liabilities	$ -	$ (10,770)	$ (37,179)	$ (14,651)	$ 6,713	$ 18,003	$ 20,471	$ 1,745	$ 5,458	$ 1,471
Total Liabilities	$ -	$ (10,770)	$ (37,179)	$ (14,651)	$ 6,713	$ 18,003	$ 20,471	$ 1,745	$ 5,458	$ 1,471
Equity										
Capital Investment @ 0.01 PAR	$ 20,000	$ 300,001	$ 505,001	$ 507,501	$ 517,501	$ 517,501	$ 517,501	$ 517,501	$ 517,501	$ 517,501
Net Income	$ (3,125)	$ (23,898)	$ (77,929)	$ (113,668)	$ (182,992)	$ (214,813)	$ (232,186)	$ (249,833)	$ (349,231)	$ (369,248)
Total Equity	$ 16,875	$ 276,103	$ 427,072	$ 393,833	$ 334,509	$ 302,688	$ 285,315	$ 267,658	$ 168,270	$ 148,253
TOTAL LIABILITIES & EQUITY	$ 16,875	$ 265,334	$ 389,893	$ 379,182	$ 341,222	$ 320,691	$ 305,786	$ 269,413	$ 173,728	$ 149,725

Exhibit E Honest Tea Income Statement 1998

	Feb	Mar	Apr	May	June	Jul	Aug	Sep	Oct	Nov
Ordinary Income/Expense										
Income										
Sales - Glass Bottles				14,035	9,396	26,806	55,988	49,221	31,633	31,003
Sales Discounts Off Invoice Glass Bottles				(21)	(22)	(101)	(2,878)	(1,985)	-	(181)
Total Income	-	-	-	14,014	9,374	26,705	53,109	47,236	31,633	30,822
Cost of Goods Sold										
Contract Labeling				5,461	3,169	6,859	6,277	-	12,901	8,420
Bottles & Caps			23,831	-	19,656	8,017	6,552	15,121	17,633	-
Label Printing		5,000	(5,000)	12,425	10,182	-	-	-	6,485	-
Spring Water			33	1,250	2,025	675	1,660	1,350	1,104	675
Sweeteners				2,694	-	2,784	-	3,346	-	-
Tea			7,480	2,700	445	1,877	2,520	5,155	3,180	3,594
Freight - Glass Bottles				1,891	2,833	1,480	3,033	6,741	5,953	2,400
Brewmaster Fees - Glass				4,500	10,962	4,710	6,775	5,214	15,146	2,415
Broker Fees				-	144	-	-	-	-	-
Tea Supplies		381	112	13	-	-	-	-	-	23
Total Cost of Goods Sold	-	5,381	26,456	30,934	49,415	26,402	26,817	36,927	62,403	17,527
Gross Profit	-	(5,381)	(26,456)	(16,920)	(40,041)	302	26,293	10,308	(30,769)	13,295
Expense										
Broker Commissions								100	1,638	-
Consultants & Interns										
Consultants	1,323	13,000	3,000	7,244	6,000	6,600	3,915	7,290	11,337	6,390
Total Consultants & Interns	1,323	13,000	3,000	7,244	6,000	6,600	3,915	7,290	11,337	6,390
G & A Expenses										
Bank Fee		15	10	120	-	-	44	-	9	60
Payroll Fee			86	46	49	47	91	49	137	94
Other Licensing		20	-							-
Legal							490	-	18,991	-
Miscellaneous										(178)
Computer Supplies/Software	50	236	486	-	110	400	-	-	(10)	45
G & A Expenses - Other					30	241	-	-	-	-
Insurance - Business						1,751	-	-	-	(5)
Memberships		300	-	-	-	290	300	-	30	-
Office Supplies		252	106	3	642	513	971	73	367	-
Photocopies			30	3	-	-	61	1,185	-	-
Recruitment						26	362	292	-	-
Rent				1,833	-	-	3,666	917	917	917
Postage and Delivery		65	330	263	234	1,377	687	552	813	943
Telephone	90	149	166	161	505	756	665	623	626	520
Total G & A Expenses	140	1,036	1,214	2,428	1,568	5,891	6,848	3,691	21,880	2,395

	Feb	Mar	Apr	May	June	Jul	Aug	Sep	Oct	Nov
Marketing Expenses										
Marketing & Promotions					$ 14	$ -	$ -	$ -		$ 84
Wearables				$ 1,550	$ 1,394	$ 2,544	$ 3,257	$ 4,640	$ 4,096	$ 2,126
Corp. Samplers, Demos						$ 675	$ -	$ -	$ 7,571	$ -
Independent Samplers, Demos						$ 831	$ 1,641	$ 344	$ 486	$ -
Packaging Supplies for Samples				$ 105	$ -	$ 164	$ -	$ -	$ 140	$ 213
Public Relations							$ 10,000	$ 377	$ 5,586	
Donations				$ 30	$ -	$ -	$ -	$ -	$ -	$ -
Sampling Wages						$ 115	$ -	$ -	$ -	$ -
Trade Show Fees & Other Exp.					$ 45	$ 64	$ 521	$ 555	$ 500	$ 300
Website Fees			$ 35	$ 35	$ 35	$ 135	$ 35	$ 35	$ 35	$ 35
Total Marketing Expenses	$ -	$ -	$ 35	$ 1,720	$ 1,488	$ 4,528	$ 15,454	$ 5,950	$ 18,414	$ 2,758
Payroll Taxes & Benefits										
Medical Insurance										$ 796
Payroll Taxes			$ 1,208	$ 493	$ 1,188	$ 1,184	$ 1,405	$ 843	$ 1,251	$ 1,532
Total Payroll Taxes & Benefits	$ -	$ -	$ 1,208	$ 493	$ 1,188	$ 1,184	$ 1,405	$ 843	$ 1,251	$ 2,328
R&D										
Product Development			$ 4,461	$ 1,161	$ -	$ 410	$ -	$ -	$ 146	$ -
Market Research					$ 6,398	$ -	$ -	$ -	$ -	$ -
Graphic Development	$ 100	$ 112	$ 5,000	$ -	$ -	$ -	$ -	$ -	$ -	$ -
Total R&D	$ 100	$ 112	$ 9,461	$ 1,161	$ 6,398	$ 410	$ -	$ -	$ 146	$ -
Payroll Wages										
Salaries and Wages			$ 12,500	$ 5,792	$ 12,250	$ 12,250	$ 14,917	$ 10,040	$ 11,566	$ 17,066
Total Payroll Wages	$ -	$ -	$ 12,500	$ 5,792	$ 12,250	$ 12,250	$ 14,917	$ 10,040	$ 11,566	$ 17,066
State/Federal Taxes										
State Franchise Tax	$ 50	$ -	$ -	$ -	$ -	$ -	$ -	$ -	$ -	$ -
Licenses & Fees	$ -	$ 970	$ 79	$ -	$ -	$ -	$ -	$ -	$ 245	$ 250
Total State/Federal Taxes	$ 50	$ 970	$ 79	$ -	$ -	$ -	$ -	$ -	$ 245	$ 250
Travel & Entertainment										
Travel and Lodging			$ 55	$ 375	$ 446	$ 918	$ 1,336	$ 642	$ 2,127	$ 214
Mileage		$ 252	$ -	$ 62	$ 724	$ 1,462	$ 330	$ 30	$ 164	$ 1,925
Meals		$ 22	$ 23	$ 63	$ 134	$ 73	$ 370	$ 12	$ 195	$ 102
Total Travel & Entertainment	$ -	$ 274	$ 78	$ 500	$ 1,303	$ 2,453	$ 2,036	$ 683	$ 2,485	$ 2,241
Total Expense	$ 1,612	$ 15,392	$ 27,575	$ 19,340	$ 30,196	$ 33,316	$ 44,574	$ 28,598	$ 68,960	$ 33,427
Net Ordinary Income	$ (1,612)	$ (20,773)	$ (54,032)	$ (36,259)	$ (70,237)	$ (33,014)	$ (18,282)	$ (18,289)	$ (99,729)	$ (20,133)
Other Income/Expense										
Other Expense										
Interest/Dividend Income										
Interest Income	$ -	$ -	$ -	$ (520)	$ (914)	$ (1,193)	$ (909)	$ (642)	$ (331)	$ (116)
Total Interest/Dividend Income	$ -	$ -	$ -	$ (520)	$ (914)	$ (1,193)	$ (909)	$ (642)	$ (331)	$ (116)
Total Other Expense	$ -	$ -	$ -	$ (520)	$ (914)	$ (1,193)	$ (909)	$ (642)	$ (331)	$ (116)
Net Other Income	$ -	$ -	$ -	$ 520	$ 914	$ 1,193	$ 909	$ 642	$ 331	$ 116
Net Income	$ (1,612)	$(20,773)	$ (54,032)	$ (35,739)	$ (69,324)	$ (31,821)	$ (17,373)	$ (17,647)	$ (99,398)	$ (20,017)

Exhibit F
Honest Tea Cash Flow Projections 1999

	Jan	Feb	Mar	Apr	May	Jun	Jul	Aug	Sep	Oct	Nov	Dec	1999
Starting Cash	$ 100,000	$ 1,046,136	$ 941,078	$ 863,133	$ 848,706	$ 908,967	$ 971,072	$ 1,047,802	$ 1,346,907	$ 1,488,037	$ 1,635,398	$ 1,776,446	$ 100,000
Cash in from Operations (Sales)	$ 80,219	$ 96,525	$ 162,338	$ 266,906	$ 347,344	$ 363,188	$ 377,813	$ 402,188	$ 377,813	$ 337,594	$ 281,531	$ 201,094	$ 3,294,553
Cash out from Operations (COGS, Expenses, Taxes)	$ 134,083	$ 201,583	$ 240,283	$ 281,333	$ 287,083	$ 301,083	$ 301,083	$ 303,083	$ 236,683	$ 190,233	$ 140,483	$ 137,233	$ 2,754,246
Cash in from Investing (equity infusions, earnings on investments)	$ 1,000,000	$ -	$ -	$ -	$ -	$ -	$ -	$ 200,000	$ -	$ -	$ -	$ -	$ 1,200,000
Cash out from Investing (equipment purchases, repaying investors)	$ -	$ -	$ -	$ -	$ -	$ -	$ -	$ -	$ -	$ -	$ -	$ -	$ -
Cash in from Financing (loans)	$ -	$ -	$ -	$ -	$ -	$ -	$ -	$ -	$ -	$ -	$ -	$ -	$ -
Cash out for Financing (repayment of debt)	$ -	$ -	$ -	$ -	$ -	$ -	$ -	$ -	$ -	$ -	$ -	$ -	$ -
Ending Cash Balance (= starting balance for next period)	$ 1,046,136	$ 941,078	$ 863,133	$ 848,706	$ 908,967	$ 971,072	$ 1,047,802	$ 1,346,907	$ 1,488,037	$ 1,635,398	$ 1,776,446	$ 1,840,307	$ 1,840,307

ASSUMPTIONS

Collections = Net 45 day

Purchases = Prepaid 30 days

Equity raised in January and August totaling $1.2 million

Debt not required for financing

Other assumptions per Profit and Loss Projection for 1999

Exhibit F Honest Tea Income Statement Projections 1999

	Jan	Feb	Mar	Apr	May	Jun	Jul	Aug	Sep	Oct	Nov	Dec	Total
Ordinary Income/Expense													
Income													
Sales	$ 80,000	$ 112,000	$ 240,000	$ 320,000	$ 400,000	$ 400,000	$ 400,000	$ 400,000	$ 400,000	$ 320,000	$ 240,000	$ 160,000	$ 3,472,000
Sales Discounts and Damage	$ 800	$ 1,120	$ 31,200	$ 3,200	$ 4,000	$ 52,000	$ 4,000	$4,000	$52,000	$3,200	$2,400	$1,600	$159,520
Total Income	$ 79,200	$ 110,880	$ 208,800	$ 316,800	$ 396,000	$ 348,000	$ 396,000	$ 396,000	$ 348,000	$ 316,800	$ 237,600	$ 158,400	$ 3,312,480
Cost of Goods Sold													
Total Cost of Goods Sold	$ 72,800	$ 156,000	$ 160,000	$ 200,000	$ 200,000	$ 200,000	$ 200,000	$ 200,000	$ 160,000	$ 120,000	$ 125,000	$ 80,000	$ 1,873,800
Gross Profit	$ 6,400	$ (45,120)	$ 48,800	$ 116,800	$ 196,000	$ 148,000	$ 196,000	$ 196,000	$ 188,000	$ 196,800	$ 112,600	$ 78,400	$ 1,438,680
Expense													
Broker Commissions	$ 3,200	$ 4,480	$ 9,600	$ 12,800	$ 16,000	$ 16,000	$ 16,000	$ 16,000	$ 16,000	$ 12,800	$ 9,600	$ 6,400	$ 138,880
Consultants & Interns	$ -	$ -	$ -	$ -	$ 4,500	$ 4,500	$ 4,500	$ 7,500	$ -	$ -	$ -	$ -	$ 21,000
G & A Expenses	$ 31,420	$ 31,420	$ 31,420	$ 31,420	$ 31,420	$ 31,420	$ 31,420	$ 31,420	$ 31,420	$ 31,420	$ 31,420	$ 31,420	$ 377,040
International					$ 875	$ 875	$ 875	$ 875	$ 875	$ 875	$ 875	$ 875	$ 7,000
Marketing & Promotion	$ 7,000	$ 8,000	$ 12,500	$ 15,300	$ 16,300	$ 30,300	$ 30,300	$ 29,300	$ 15,400	$ 12,200	$ 5,700	$ 5,700	$ 188,000
Miscellaneous	$ 1,736	$ 1,736	$ 1,736	$ 1,736	$ 1,736	$ 1,736	$ 1,736	$ 1,736	$ 1,736	$ 1,736	$ 1,736	$ 1,736	$ 20,832
Research & Development	$ 15,000	$ 3,000	$ 2,000	$ 2,000	$ -	$ -	$ -	$ -	$ -	$ -	$ -	$ -	$ 22,000
Sales Support	$ 8,750	$ 8,750	$ 8,750	$ 8,750	$ 8,750	$ 8,750	$ 8,750	$ 8,750	$ 8,750	$ 8,750	$ 8,750	$ 8,750	$ 105,000
Total Expense	$ 67,106	$ 57,386	$ 66,006	$ 72,006	$ 79,581	$ 93,581	$ 93,581	$ 95,581	$ 74,181	$ 67,781	$ 58,081	$ 54,881	$ 879,752
Net Ordinary Income	$ (60,706)	$ (102,506)	$ (17,206)	$ 44,794	$ 116,419	$ 54,419	$ 102,419	$ 100,419	$ 113,819	$ 129,019	$ 54,519	$ 23,519	$ 558,928
Other Income/Expense													
Other Expense													
Interest/Dividend Income													
Interest Income	$ 200	$ 941	$ 863	$ 848	$ 908	$ 971	$ 1,047	$ 1,146	$ 1,288	$ 1,435	$ 1,576	$ 1,640	$ 12,863
Total Interest/Div. Inc.	$ 200	$ 941	$ 863	$ 848	$ 908	$ 971	$ 1,047	$ 1,146	$ 1,288	$ 1,435	$ 1,576	$ 1,640	$ 12,863
Total Other Expense													
Net Other Income	$ 200	$ 941	$ 863	$ 848	$ 908	$ 971	$ 1,047	$ 1,146	$ 1,288	$ 1,435	$ 1,576	$ 1,640	$ 12,863
Net Income	$ (60,506)	$ (101,565)	$ (16,343)	$ 45,642	$ 117,327	$ 55,390	$ 103,466	$ 101,565	$ 115,107	$ 130,454	$ 56,095	$ 25,159	$ 571,791

ASSUMPTIONS

Effective invoice price (case)	$	16.00
Cost per case on 4/99	$	8.00
Cost per case until 4/99	$	10.40
Percent of brokered sales		80%

International Marketing

R&D	$	7,000
Total	$	7,000

Overhead & GNA Monthly

Salaries	$	24,000
Insurance	$	220
Office rent	$	2,300
Legal expenses	$	1,000
Accounting	$	400
Benefits/staff support	$	1,500
Phone/computer	$	1,000
Travel	$	1,000
Total	$	31,420

Marketing & Promotion

Trade shows	$	10,000
PR agency & ex	$	50,000
Sales sheets &	$	8,000
Sampling	$	70,000
Shirts & promo	$	12,000
Postage/shipping	$	6,000
Reg. radio ads	$	30,000
Website	$	2,000
Total	$	188,000

Sales Support

Slotting/intros	$	80,000
Coolers	$	25,000
Total	$	105,000

Finished Inventory

12/31/98 inventory	$	120,000
12/31/99 inventory	$	125,000

1999 Totals

Gross income	$ 3,312,480
Total COGS	$ 1,873,800
Gross profit	$ 1,438,680
Gross Profit Margin	43.4%
Expenses	$ 879,752
Pretax net	$ 571,791
Profit Margin	17.3%

BUSINESS PLAN

The Investment Opportunity[4]

Honest Tea is seeking equity investments totaling $1.2 million in equity capital to finance the national distribution of the product as well as the introduction of two new flavors and international sales.

The Offering

(Excluded from the Plan)

Financing History

Initial financing for Honest Tea came from the founders, Seth Goldman and Barry Nalebuff, and their friends and family. This equity funding of approximately $500,000 was used to start the business and to generate the first production run.

Exit Strategies

Investors in Honest Tea would be able to realize a return on the appreciation of their investments under any of the following scenarios:

Investment by a strategic partner—As Ocean Spray's recent purchase of a significant share of Nantucket Nectars demonstrates, there may be opportunities for investors to realize their gains through the sale of their Honest Tea shares to a strategic investor who can help the company expand its production and distribution.

Acquisition—There are numerous precedents of companies that might be interested in leveraging the integrity and purity of Honest Tea's brand. Some recent examples are the acquisition of Mistic and Snapple by Triarc. Honest Tea has already been approached by some well-known beverage companies to discuss possible acquisition opportunities.

Initial Public Offering—If Honest Tea meets our expectations for growth, the Company might consider some form of public offering to raise capital for expansion in the future.

Investment Risks

In addition to the economic and business factors which pose risks for most early-stage companies, an investment in Honest Tea carries several other risks:

Product Risk—Although we are insured for product liability, a health-related incident such as the one Odwalla experienced several years ago could do significant damage to the Honest Tea brand name. Of course, since our product is pasteurized twice, there is less of a risk that the same types of bacteria could emerge.

Competitive Risk—Republic of Tea, a company that has a well-established brand name among tea lovers, might decide to enter the retail market with a more competitively priced product. Such a move could dampen the uniqueness of our message. Crystal Geyser, a company which has deep pockets and preexisting distribution relationships, might decide to introduce additional products beyond TeJava and spread its distribution more aggressively beyond the West Coast.

Management Risk—At this point, the development of the company has been concentrated largely in the hands of Seth Goldman and Barry Nalebuff. If either of them were unable to continue to play a role in the Company's progress, the growth of Honest Tea might be impaired.

Competitive Advantage

The results of this past summer clearly indicate that Honest Tea has tapped into a market opportunity. When we were planning the company's strategy last year we entertained the idea

---

[4]The Investment Opportunity section, including the offering and financing history is not included in the business plan as available on the Honest Tea Web site. The comments included here are based upon multiple sources and are meant to be a fair representation of the original information.

of spending several years building up a strong presence in a local market before expanding nationally. We have chosen to grow in a more aggressive manner for several reasons:

Market Niche—We have created a new beverage category and are currently the only company filling that category. If we hesitate, other companies are likely to move in.

Compelling brand image and story—The packaging, presentation and profile of the Honest Tea brand fit together extremely well with the product. Although we may improve on the bottle design in the future, this is a package that comes close to selling itself. It is also a brand and a story, which has successfully gained free media coverage, and should continue to do so.

Management Team—We have developed a team with the right combination of sales experience and market creativity that is capable of growing the company on a national, and even international, scale.

A Parting Thought

Prospective investors in Honest Tea are advised to keep in mind the words of Sung Dynasty poet Li Chi Lai who cited the three great evils that might beset the land:

> the spoiling of gallant youths through bad education; the degradation of good art through incompetent criticism; and the waste of fine tea through careless making.

While we may not be able to have much direct influence over education and the arts, Honest Tea stands poised to restore integrity to a beverage that has brought people together for hundreds of generations and throughout dozens of civilizations. There has never been a time when consumers have been so overwhelmed with choices. And yet there has never been a time when integrity and authenticity are as cherished as they are scarce. There has never been a better time for Honest Tea.

3

CHAPTER

Creating Business from Opportunity

Learning Objectives

1. Define your business.
2. Articulate your core beliefs, mission, and vision.
3. Analyze your competitive advantage.
4. Prepare viability tests using "the economics of one unit."
5. Calculate the value of a business.

Tony Hsieh, Zappos.com
(Getty Images)

> ***"Problems are only opportunities in work clothes."***
>
> —Henry J. Kaiser, American industrialist

Entrepreneurs find and take advantage of opportunities that others don't recognize or cannot access the resources to exploit. When Zappos.com founder Nick Swinmurn became frustrated by looking for shoes in a San Francisco mall and online, he saw an opportunity to create an online pure-play e-commerce megastore that would carry a multitude of sizes, styles, and colors. Swinmurn was three years out of college when he launched ShoeSite.com, with $150,000, in 1999. Within a month, he relaunched as Zappos.com. In 2000, Tony Hsieh of Venture Frog Incubators saw the opportunity in Zappos, investing $1.1 million and joining Swinmurn. The company has thrived on providing the best selection and service, with a focus on the "wow" factor and delivering happiness. Zappos.com carries more than 1,000 brands, employs 3,800 people, and has annual revenues in excess of $1 billion.[1] In November 2009, Amazon.com acquired Zappos.com Inc. in a deal valued at $1.2 billion. Zappos.com has since expanded its product offerings to include handbags, clothing, and other items and was restructured into 10 separate companies.

Apple and the Personal Computer

market a group of people or organizations that may be interested in buying a given product or service, has the resources to purchase it, and is permitted by law and regulation to do so.

In 1943, IBM's founder Thomas Watson commented, "I think there is a world market for about five computers." A **market** is a group of people or organizations that may be interested in buying a given product or service, has the resources to purchase it, and is permitted by law and regulation to do so. When Watson made his statement, computers were forbiddingly large and expensive machines that only the government, universities, and a few giant corporations could afford. That was the perceived *market* for computers at the time.

By the 1970s, however, a few people were talking about creating "personal" computers. These enthusiasts were outside of mainstream thinking. One such visionary was Steve Wozniak, who had landed his first job at Hewlett-Packard, then as now a major company. He was also attending meetings of the Homebrew Club, a Palo Alto-based group of electronics hobbyists. Wozniak was determined to build a small personal computer to show the club members, using existing technology. He believed there was a much larger market for hobbyist computers than IBM and Hewlett-Packard thought. Hewlett-Packard, IBM, and Tandy all had personal computers on the market, but not of the sort Wozniak envisioned.

Wozniak offered Hewlett-Packard a chance to codevelop his small computer. The company was not focused on desktop computing, and the technology did not fit within its computer or calculator strategies, so it turned him down. Wozniak's friend Steve Jobs also was interested in the technology

Apple cofounder Stephen Wozniak
(Getty Images)

---

[1]Zappos.com Inc., accessed July 21, 2013, http://www.zappos.com.

and set out to sell some hobbyist computers. After some time and considerable effort, Jobs sold 100 circuit boards to a local start-up computer shop, and then Wozniak, Jobs, and three helpers soldered together the components in the garage of Jobs's home in Cupertino, California.

Wozniak worked on his design concepts until he created the Apple II, which could display pictures and text. It is now considered one of the great achievements in computer history. Jobs, meanwhile, searched for an investor. Finally, after being turned down by friends and family, he found Mike Markkula, who also saw the possibilities of Apple. Markkula agreed to invest $80,000 in the company in return for a significant share of equity. He also put together Apple's business plan and worked to secure additional investors. This is a classic demonstration of entrepreneurs recognizing opportunities others do not see.

By 1984, Apple had sales of $1.5 billion, and sales topped $170 billion in fiscal year 2013. Wozniak and Jobs recognized an opportunity that led to a product that satisfied the needs of an enormous market the giants of the industry did not recognize.

Business Definition

Learning Objective 1

Define your business.

Before you can start a business, you should define it along several dimensions. This *business definition* includes the offer, target market, and product and delivery capability—answering the questions of who, what, and how. A solid business definition has three elements:

1. ***The offer.*** What will you sell to your customers? That is called your *offer* and includes the complete bundle of products and services you will be bringing to the marketplace. This should address not only the tangible product or intangible service but its benefits. For example, you will provide online and telephone fitness-consulting service for an initial four-week period at $25 per week, or eight weeks at $20 per week.

2. ***Target market.*** Which segment of the market are you aiming to serve? As discussed in Chapter 2, this will be your *target market*. Defining your target market in a way that will help you identify qualified potential customers is an important factor in achieving success. This definition must be precise enough so that you can identify a viable market for the business and focus your marketing efforts. A target market of every adult in the United States is clearly too broad and unfocused. A market of every member of Congress from the state of Rhode Island (three individuals) would be too narrow. Customers may not currently recognize a need for *your* product or service, but they are in the market for the products or services of your direct or indirect competition.

3. ***Production and delivery capability.*** How will you provide your offer to your targeted customers? This includes how to perform the key activities required to produce the product or service, deliver it to your customers, and ensure they are satisfied. This part of the business definition includes the primary activities of
   - buying, developing, or manufacturing the product;
   - identifying its potential qualified customers and selling the product to them;
   - producing and delivering the product or service; and
   - receiving payment.

Step into the Shoes . . .

Zhang Xin—Building a Real Estate Empire from Opportunity

Real estate developer Zhang Xin has built a fortune by identifying economic opportunities in China. She is the cofounder and CEO of SOHO China. As of April 2014, she and her family had an estimated net worth of $3.8 billion.[2]

This is a very different life from her early days of living in poverty in Henan province and in Hong Kong. She left China for an education in England at the University of Sussex and then Cambridge. Her work history includes investment banking in New York and Hong Kong. Yet, she always maintained ties to the land of her birth.

Zhang and her husband, Pan Shiyi, created Beijing Redstone Industries Co. Ltd., a property development firm they later renamed SOHO China, in 1995. SOHO China is the nation's largest commercial real estate developer, with 56 million square feet of developments, and is a public company trading on the Stock Exchange of Hong Kong. Zhang and Pan saw opportunities for modern, high-style properties in Beijing and Shanghai when others did not.

Zhang is a prominent woman in China, with over 5.9 million Sina Weibo (similar to Twitter) followers. She is recognized for her business acumen, her role in urbanizing China, and the staunch belief that democracy will come to China.

Source: Kerry A. Dolan and Luisa Kroll, "The Richest People on the Planet Now, Zhang Xin & family (#420)," *Forbes*, April 13, 2014, accessed on April 13, 2014, http://www.forbes.com. "Company Profile," SOHO China, accessed July 19, 2013, http://www.sohochina.com.

Zhang Xin, SOHO China
(Bloomberg/Getty Images)

What Sort of Organization Do You Want?

Each organization has the opportunity to create a unique mission, vision, and culture that will be supported by its core values. The management team can determine how to use the company's competitive advantage to satisfy customers. The organization's culture can be shaped according to the business environment and by the way employees, customers, and other stakeholders are treated—an example that is set by the founding entrepreneur (owner).

Your Company's Core Values

When you start your own company, what beliefs will you use to guide it? These are the **core values** of your business. Core values include the fundamental ethical and moral philosophy and beliefs that form the foundation of the organization and provide broad guidance for all decision making. Examples of the core values of a business might be:

- "At Superior Printing, we engage in business practices that affect the environment as little as possible."
- "At Sheila's Restaurant, we believe in supporting local organic farmers."

Core values will affect business decisions. The owner of Superior Printing, for example, will choose ink that is less harmful to the environment over a cheaper ink that is more harmful. Superior Printing may also have a paper-recycling program to minimize its paper consumption. The owner of Sheila's Restaurant will buy fruits and vegetables from local organic farmers. Your core beliefs will affect everything, from the cost of materials to the prices you charge and how you treat customers. For additional examples of core values, see **Exhibit 3-1**.

◀ Learning Objective 2

Articulate your core beliefs, mission, and vision.

core values the fundamental ethical and moral philosophy and beliefs that form the foundation of the organization and provide broad guidance for all decision making.

---

[2]Kerry A. Dolan and Luisa Kroll, "The Richest People on the Planet Now, Zhang Xin & family (#420)," *Forbes*, April 13, 2014, accessed on April 13, 2014, http://www.forbes.com.

Exhibit 3-1 *Core Values*

Zappos.com

1. *Deliver WOW through service*
2. *Embrace and drive change*
3. *Create fun and a little weirdness*
4. *Be adventurous, creative, and open-minded*
5. *Pursue growth and learning*
6. *Build open and honest relationships with communications*
7. *Build a positive team and family spirit*
8. *Do more with less*
9. *Be passionate and determined*
10. *Be humble*

Dow AgroSciences

To ensure the prosperity and well-being of Dow AgroSciences employees, customers, and shareholders, cumulative long-term profit growth is essential. How we achieve this objective is as important as the objective itself. Fundamental to our success are the core values we believe in and practice.

- *Employees are the source of Dow AgroSciences success. We communicate openly, treat each other with respect, promote teamwork, and encourage personal initiative and growth. Excellence in performance is rewarded.*
- *Customers receive our strongest commitment to meet their needs with high quality products and superior service.*
- *Products are based on innovative technology, continuous improvement, and added value for our customers and end users.*
- *Our conduct demonstrates a deep concern for human safety and environmental stewardship, while embracing the highest standards of ethics and citizenship.*

DuPont Company

Safety, concern, and care for people, protection of the environment, and personal and corporate integrity, are this company's highest values, and we will not compromise them.

Your Company's Mission Is to Satisfy Customers

The mission of your business, expressed in a *mission statement*, is a concise communication of your purpose, business definition, and values. The function of a mission statement is to clarify what the business is trying to do in the present, but it can provide direction and motivation for future action through a clear and compelling message.

As noted in Chapter 2, a well-crafted mission statement will not only tell your customers and employees what your business is about, but can (and should) be a guide for every decision you make. It should capture your passion for the business and your commitment to satisfying your customers. A mission statement should be limited to 21 to 40 words to induce clarity in concept and expression. The mission statement should address the following topics: target customers; products and services; markets served; use of technology; importance of public issues and employees; and focus on survival, profitability, and growth.

Here is an example of a mission statement for the Most Chocolate Cake Company:

> To create the richest, tastiest, most chocolaty cakes made from the finest, freshest ingredients according to our secret recipes and decorated with our extraordinary frostings and fillings.

Exhibit 3-2 *Mission Statements*

The Dow Chemical Company—To constantly improve what is essential to human progress by mastering sciences and technology.
Google—To organize the world's information and make it universally accessible and useful.
The Hershey Company—Undisputed Market Leadership.
Krispy Kreme Doughnuts—To touch and enhance lives through the joy that is Krispy Kreme.
Nike—To bring inspiration and innovation to every athlete in the world.
Teach for America—is growing the movement of leaders who work to ensure that kids growing up in poverty get an excellent education.
Walt Disney Company—To be one of the world's leading producers and providers of entertainment and information, using its portfolio of brands to differentiate its content, services and consumer products.
Wounded Warrior Project—To honor and empower wounded warriors.

The Most Chocolate Cake Company's mission statement defines the business and its competitive advantage, the core of its strategy. Examples of mission statements from a range of organizations appear in **Exhibit 3-2**.

Your Company's Vision Is the Broader Perspective

The *vision* for your business is broader and more comprehensive than its mission, painting a picture of the overall view of what you want your organization to become in the future, not what it is at the moment. It is built on the core values of the organization. It should energize your people, and they should embrace it with enthusiasm and passion. This means the vision has to be compelling across the organization. It has to matter. Employees need to be empowered to fulfill the vision. Examples of vision statements for various organizations appear in **Exhibit 3-3**.

Your Company's Culture Defines the Work Environment

The culture of an organization is largely shaped by its leadership. *Culture* is composed of the core values in action. Leaders of a company build a particular culture by making the beliefs, values, and behavioral norms explicit and intentional. Culture includes factors such as risk tolerance and innovation; orientation with respect to people, teams, and outcomes; attention to detail; and communications norms. Organizational culture is learned by members of the team in a number of ways, including anecdotes, ceremonies and events, material symbols, and particular use of language. For example, at General Electric, stories of Jack Welch are legendary. At Hewlett-Packard there was the "Hewlett-Packard Way," based on anecdotes

---

Exhibit 3-3 *Vision Statements*

Amazon—Our vision is to be earth's most customer centric company; to build a place where people can come to find and discover anything they might want to buy online.
Bimbo Bakeries USA—We strive to be a highly productive and deeply humane company.
DuPont Company—Our vision is to be the world's most dynamic science company, creating sustainable solutions essential to a better, safer, healthier life for people everywhere.
General Motors—To design, build and sell the world's best vehicles.
Kiva—We envision a world where all people – even in the most remote areas of the globe— hold the power to create opportunities for themselves and others.
Krispy Kreme Doughnuts—To be the worldwide leader in sharing delicious taste and creating joyful memories.

passed down from one generation of employees to the next. Those who work in small enterprises often see the top management daily and take their cues directly, because there are very few or no layers between them. As enterprises become larger, the firm's leaders may not often be on view to most employees and frequently take on larger-than-life roles through stories.

Ceremonies can make a significant difference in a company's culture. Are there periodic recognition events for innovation? Does the company invite family members to appropriate occasions throughout the year? Is there a birthday celebration for each employee? Are years of service recognized? Material symbols come in many shapes and forms. At the Wilmington, Delaware, headquarters of Legacy MBNA America, the values of the company appear on every archway, and handprints of the employees make colorful wall art in some buildings. At any business, reserved parking spots and special privileges for certain employees send a message to everyone. Are these spaces for top executives? Expectant mothers? Are office sizes determined by pay grade? Finally, language tells a lot about the culture. Is everyone on a first-name basis with everyone else? Are some people addressed formally and others not? Is the language around the company in general formal or informal? Is communication respectful?

These and many other factors are all part of the culture of an organization. Culture should be crafted to follow core beliefs and support the mission and vision of the business.

The Decision Process

Translating opportunity into success can and has happened in literally millions of different ways. Each business has a different story. However, there are three primary routes in the deliberate-search process to identify opportunities:

- The entrepreneur looks for business opportunities through a process of identification and selection, beginning with self-developed (or group-developed) ideas.
- The entrepreneur uses essentially the same process but starts with research on hot businesses, trends, or growth areas.
- The entrepreneur has an idea for a product or service and searches for a market.

These processes are illustrated in **Figure 3-1**.

In each case, a decision is made based on personal values and thinking. Whereas each ultimately funnels the procedure down to a business concept, the processes are repeated—often with many ideas being considered—before a viable picture emerges. The first two options are market driven; the third is product driven. Entrepreneurs do better looking to the market(s) of interest, rather than creating a product and then trying to find a customer base. You can do all this alone, but it is best to work with others who will provide honest, constructive feedback.

Critical to this process is continuous feedback and development with an emphasis on getting prototypes into the hands of prospective customers early and often. By getting market feedback early in the process, you create products that are meaningful to your target market. This process of creating minimum viable products (MVP) is part of the Lean Start Up process described in the work of Eric Ries.[3]

---

[3]Eric Ries, *The Lean Startup: How Today's Entrepreneurs Use Continuous Innovation to Create Radically Successful Businesses*, New York: Crown Business, 2011.

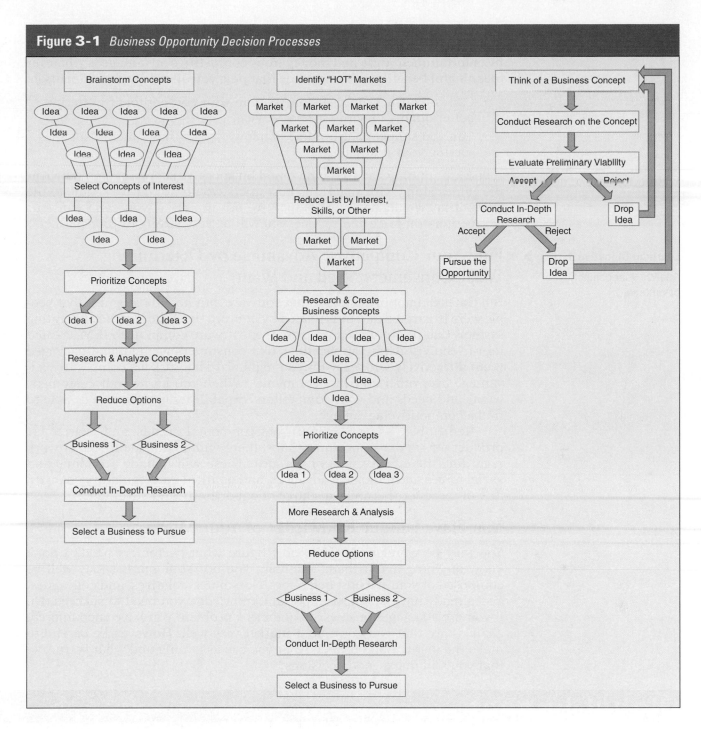

Figure 3-1 *Business Opportunity Decision Processes*

Your Competitive Advantage

For your business to be successful and to fulfill your mission and vision, you will need a strategy for beating the competition. This will be your *competitive advantage,* or core competency. It is whatever you can do better than the competition that will attract a sufficient number of customers to your business so it can succeed. The competitive advantage must be *sustainable* in order to create long-term viability. Your competition is defined by your target market and can be *direct* (selling the same or similar products to the same market) or *indirect* (selling different products that compete for the same share of customer spending). For example, a children's museum will indirectly compete with rental movies/movie theaters, indoor/outdoor play areas, sports and recreation, and other leisure-time activities for family entertainment time and money. Your competitive advantage is whatever meaningful benefit you can provide that puts you ahead of the competition.

- Can you attract more customers than your competitors by offering better quality or some special service?
- Can you supply your product at a lower price than other businesses serving your market?

If you are running a video game rental business, perhaps you could deliver the games along with snacks, so customers would not have to come to the store. That would be your competitive advantage. If you can beat your competitors on price *and* service, you will be very strong in your market.

Learning Objective 3

Analyze your competitive advantage.

Find Your Competitive Advantage by Determining What Consumers Need and Want

Bill Gates did not invent computer software, but he did recognize that people were frustrated and intimidated by it. From there, he supplied operating systems that he purchased from another software company to IBM, created user-friendly software applications that consumers wanted, and packaged them attractively with easy-to-read manuals. That was his competitive advantage over other software companies. When you know your customers' wants and needs and your competitors' capabilities, you should be able to find a competitive advantage.

Remember, as you identify environmental trends and search for product- or service-opportunity gaps, there will be outside forces at work regarding the effectiveness of the idea. These will include economic and social forces, technological advances, and political and regulatory changes. Any of these forces can be a source of opportunity and advantage.

You Have Unique Knowledge of Your Market

You may be wondering: "How do I figure what customers need? I don't know anything about them." Actually, you do. Your market may well be composed of your friends, neighbors, classmates, relatives, and colleagues. You already have the most important knowledge you need to succeed. Or, if you are starting a business to address a problem you have encountered, chances are that you know your market very well. However, be careful to make the distinction between what you are assuming and what is true, so that you will make good decisions.

Global Impact . . .

SOFTtribe Founders See Tropical Tolerance Needed for Software in Ghana

Herman Kojo Chinery-Hesse and Joe Jackson saw an opportunity in the need for adapting software for tropical climates when they founded SOFTtribe in 1991. Their company develops software, taking into consideration the unique requirements of the West African social and business environment. According to their partner, Microsoft, "The SOFTtribe software is practical and resilient, functional under conditions of intermittent connectivity, power fluctuations, low bandwidth, and operators who, as a rule, are less familiar with computing than in some other parts of the world."[4]

Chinery-Hesse has been called the Bill Gates of Ghana for his success in building SOFTtribe. It is the largest software company in Ghana and is a Microsoft partner to permit its expansion.

---

[4]"Taking African Business Global," Microsoft Unlimited Potential, May 27, 2009, accessed January 13, 2010, http://www.microsoft.com/unlimitedpotential/.

Sir Richard Branson, the CEO of Virgin Corporation, chose "Virgin" because it reflected his total inexperience in business. His empire, which includes Virgin Megastores, Virgin Atlantic Airways, and Virgin Mobile, began as a tiny discount mail-order record company, which he started at age 19 after he had dropped out of high school. Branson knew his market—other young people who were into music—very well. Then, he learned about the other markets before he entered them.

How will you know if a business idea is going to be successful? You cannot have a guarantee, but your market will tell you a lot about your chances. The answer will come in the form of the signal called *profit*. You can learn a lot about the potential for success well ahead of starting your enterprise, through customer and market research, in addition to competitive analysis.

The Six Factors of Competitive Advantage

Competitive advantage comes from one (or a combination) of six factors:

1. *Quality.* Can you provide higher quality than competing businesses?
2. *Price.* Can you offer a lower price on a sustained basis than your competition, or does your higher price reflect quality and/or uniqueness?
3. *Location.* Can you find a more convenient location for customers?
4. *Selection.* Can you provide a wider range of choices than your competitors can?
5. *Service.* Can you provide better, more personalized customer service?
6. *Speed/turnaround.* Can you deliver your product/service more quickly than the competition?

The importance of each factor will depend on the wants and needs of target customers. More isn't always better, if customers aren't interested.

Is Your Competitive Advantage Strong Enough?

When deciding whether your business concept is viable, it will be essential to determine your competitive advantage and whether it is strong enough. According to Jeffry Timmons's *New Venture Creation*, a successful company needs to do one of the following.

- *Sell to a market that is large and growing.* The market for smart phones is a good example. New products are being marketed to meet the demand, such as printers that turn digital photos into prints with digital-photo frames.
- *Sell to a market where the competition is able to make a profit.* It will be interesting to observe what happens in the market for hybrid cars. The jury is out as to whether the companies manufacturing them can make a profit, so most automakers are not yet entering the field. There still may not be a sufficiently large market to make entry worthwhile.
- *Sell to a market where the competition is succeeding but is not so powerful as to make it impossible for a new entrepreneur to enter.* Microsoft has been taken to court several times by competitors who argue that it is so big that new software companies cannot enter the market. **Barriers to entry** are the factors that contribute to the ease or difficulty of a new competitor joining an established market, and they cannot be so high that market entry and success are not possible.

barriers to entry the factors that contribute to the ease or difficulty of a new competitor joining an established market.

Entrepreneurial Wisdom . . .

A new business usually will require time before it can turn a profit. Federal Express, in fact, suffered initial losses of a million dollars a month! But if you are not making enough money to stay in business, that is the market speaking. It is telling you that your business is not satisfying consumer needs well enough. Do not take it personally. Many famous entrepreneurs opened and closed a number of businesses during their lifetime.

Henry Ford failed in business twice before the Ford Motor Company was a success. If you want to be a successful entrepreneur, start growing a thick skin and decide right now that you intend to learn from failures and disappointments. Do not let them get you down. Learn, so that you do not make the same mistakes again.

- *Sell a product or service that solves problems consumers may have with the competition.* Problems can include poor quality or slow delivery. FedEx beat its competition—the Flying Tigers, the U.S. Postal Service, and United Parcel Service (UPS)—when it entered the package-delivery market with guaranteed overnight service.
- *Sell a product or service at a competitive price that will attract customers.* UPS fought back by offering a less-expensive overnight delivery service than FedEx's.

In addition to the above, it is also necessary to

- understand the needs of your customers;
- have a sustainable competitive advantage or multiple, evolving advantages; and
- deliver a product or service that meets your customers' needs at the right price.

Checking Out the Competition

One useful exercise is to learn everything you can about particular competitors, especially those that have earned the respect of the marketplace. Try to identify the sources of their competitive advantage. Examine their Web sites. Conduct Internet searches. Track their advertising and promotion, including print, broadcast, Internet, and sponsorships. If they are retailers, shop their stores or have your friends and family do so. Get to know them (but do not do anything unethical or illegal to obtain information). You will also need to keep an eye on your competition after you have started your business, because new factors might undermine your competitive advantage.

Today's entrepreneurs, even those starting microenterprises and lifestyle businesses, may face competition from far beyond their neighborhoods, because customers can go shopping on the Web. Optimism is a trait that frequently goes with entrepreneurship, so beginning entrepreneurs tend to get excited about the Web's huge customer base. What they often do not consider is that the competition is already selling to their potential customers through the Web. Therefore, get online and conduct a thorough search of your industry. You may find that there is literally a world of opportunity or, conversely, that the world is full of competitors.

To determine whether you have a competitive advantage that will enable you to outperform your closest and strongest competitors, ask these questions:

unique selling proposition (USP) the distinctive feature and benefit that set a company apart from its competition.

- *Competitive offers.* How does your offer compare with those of your leading competitors? What are the key features of each?
- *Unique selling proposition.* Based on that comparison, what is your **unique selling proposition (USP)**, the distinctive feature and benefit

that sets you apart from your competition? This will require a comparison of offers and identifying what is unique about yours. What is it about your offer that your competitors cannot or will not match?

- *Cost structure.* What is different about your business activities and the cost of doing business, compared to the competition? Overall, are you at a cost advantage or disadvantage?

To be successful, you must have a USP that will attract customers to buy from you. Second, you must have a cost structure that is sufficiently advantageous so that, when all of your costs are deducted from your revenue, you will have sufficient profit left over. If you can achieve a cost advantage or at least minimize any cost disadvantage, this will help you achieve a profit. This profit is your reward for operating a successful business.

The Most Chocolate Cake Company

There are a number of ways to highlight your competitive advantage and to identify opportunities. In this example, Amy makes and sells specialty chocolate cakes. She chose this product because she loves chocolate and she enjoys baking cakes. She decided to make the *most chocolate* cakes possible. From this decision, she developed the concept for her product and the name of her business, The Most Chocolate Cake Company, LLC.

Sergio 33/Shutterstock

Amy's target market was the segment of the public in Springfield that loved chocolate cakes but did not have the time or interest in baking them. Because cakes are usually purchased for special occasions, Amy believed she could charge a premium price, at least as much as a bakery store cake.

She decided she would make the cakes special by

- using the finest ingredients and a secret recipe (quality);
- personalizing each cake through expert custom-decorating (selection); and
- baking the cakes to order, so they would be fresh for the event (quality).

Amy bakes her cakes at home in her specially designed commercial kitchen, which makes them literally homemade, and thus reduces the cost of producing them—she is not renting commercial space or paying a staff. Of course, the flip side of baking at home is that her production is relatively limited. Also, she may have to take time to deliver each cake, depending on local zoning regulations regarding retail trade. **Exhibit 3-4** shows her business definition in tabular form.

Amy expects, after careful analysis, that her more chocolaty cake with its special frosting and decoration, as well as its freshly homemade quality, will be successful in the marketplace. This is her USP. She intends for it to be a source of competitive advantage, along with the cost advantage of baking the cakes at home. Based on this analysis, she has determined how she wants to make her offering better and different from those of her competitors.

Competitive Analysis

Another approach to the analysis is to compare your business concept with the competitors that you have identified through your research. A simple

Exhibit 3-4 *Business Definition*

Business Definition Question	The Most Chocolate Cake Company
1. *The Offer.* What products and services will be sold?	Chocolate cakes with various fillings and decorations for special events at premium prices.
2. *Target Market.* Which consumer segment will the business focus on?	People who love chocolate and want a special cake for a special event. Dual income households with greater than median income.
3. *Production Capability.* How will that offer be produced and delivered to those customers?	Homemade and baked to order to ensure freshness, using high-quality ingredients and a secret recipe.
4. *Problem Solving.* What problem does the business solve for its customers?	Great appearance and flavor without the work or mess for special occasions.

Exhibit 3-5 *Comparative Analysis—Qualitative—The Most Chocolate Cake Company*

	Most Chocolate Cake Company	Mega Super Market, Inc.	Average Bakery Co.	Fancy Bakery, LLC
Quality	Excellent	Fair	Fair	Excellent
Price	Fair	Good	Moderate	Poor
Location	Moderate	Excellent	Moderate	Good
Selection	Fair	Moderate	Good	Moderate
Service	Excellent	Fair	Moderate	Fair
Speed/Turnaround	Good	Excellent	Moderate	Fair
Specialization	Excellent	Poor	Fair	Moderate
Personalization	Excellent	Moderate	Good	Excellent

comparative table is a good way to display this. The table should include each of the six factors of competitive advantage. Plus, if there are particular features you want to highlight, or specific aspects of the six factors, adding them to the table will make them more prominent. These ratings can be done solely by you—your team—through market research techniques, or however you think you can get the most unbiased responses.

There are many ways to construct this type of competitive analysis table. **Exhibit 3-5** includes a simple qualitative competitive analysis which shows ratings of excellent, good, moderate, fair, and poor for each factor with each competitor. The entrepreneur (or prospective customers) can establish this information by using their knowledge of each competitor. It should take into account those factors that are of greatest importance to the target market. Such a table will make competitive advantages and weaknesses readily apparent.

The chart in **Exhibit 3-6** is an example of a more quantitative approach to competitive analysis. First, based on industry data or quality customer research, each factor is assigned a weight according to its importance to the company's target customers, with the total of all factors equaling 1.00 (or 100%). For example, *quality* could be weighted 0.20, *location* weighted 0.10, with other factors adding up to 0.70, if customers are very concerned about the quality of the product and whether they can buy it on the Internet. Second, each competitor should be rated on an odd-numbered scale, such as 1 to 5, with 1 being lowest and 5 being highest, on each factor.

Exhibit **3-6** _Comparative Analysis—Quantitative—The Most Chocolate Cake Company_								
		Most Chocolate Cake Company		Mega Super Market		Average Bakery Co.		Fancy Bakery, LLC	
Attributes Important to Customers	Weight (a)	Rating (b)	Weighted Rating (c = a * b)	Rating (d)	Weighted Rating (e = a * d)	Rating (f)	Weighted Rating (g = a * f)	Rating (h)	Weighted Rating (i = a * h)
Quality	0.20	5	1.00	2	0.40	2	0.40	5	1.00
Price	0.10	2	0.20	4	0.40	3	0.30	1	0.10
Location	0.10	3	0.30	5	0.50	3	0.30	4	0.40
Selection	0.15	2	0.30	3	0.45	4	0.60	3	0.45
Service	0.10	5	0.50	2	0.20	3	0.30	2	0.20
Speed/Turnaround	0.05	4	0.20	5	0.25	3	0.15	2	0.10
Specialization	0.20	5	1.00	1	0.20	2	0.40	3	0.60
Personalization	0.10	5	0.50	3	0.30	4	0.40	5	0.50
Total	1.00		**4.00**		**2.70**		**2.85**		**3.35**

For example, the Most Chocolate Cake Company could rate a 5 on quality and 2 on selection, whereas the supermarket could rate 2 on quality and 5 on location. Third, to calculate a weighted score, each rating should be _multiplied_ by the associated weight to obtain a total. For example, if quality is rated 0.20 and Most Chocolate's quality is rated 5, the weighted value is 1.00. Looking across the competitors' scores on individual factors can yield insights into areas of strength or vulnerability. Finally, all the weighted values for each company should be totaled and an overall rating calculated. By looking at the ratings, it becomes apparent who the strongest and weakest competitors are, and a company can address the results of the analysis.

Competitive Strategy: Business Definition and Competitive Advantage

Your business will only succeed if you can offer the customers in your market something more, better, and/or different from what the competition is doing. Your competitive advantage (core competency) is essential, and once you establish it, your business decisions will start to fall into place. Every advertisement, every promotion, even the price of your product and the location of your business should be designed to get customers excited about your competitive advantage.

Your **competitive strategy** combines your business definition with your competitive advantage. A competitive advantage must be _sustainable_, meaning that you can keep it going. If you decide to beat the competition by selling your product at a lower price, your advantage will not last long if you cannot afford to continue at that price. Small business owners should realize that price alone is not likely to work as an advantage in the long run. A larger business can almost always beat you on price, because it can buy larger quantities than you can and therefore receive a greater discount from suppliers.

Being able to temporarily undercut the competition's prices is not a competitive advantage. Being able to _permanently_ sell at a lower price because you have discovered a cheaper supplier _is_ a competitive advantage. Being able to develop and maintain proprietary product or service features and benefits is another approach to finding a sustainable advantage.

competitive strategy the combination of the business definition with its competitive advantage.

strategy a plan for how an organization or individual intends to outdo competitors.

tactics the specific ways in which a business carries out its strategy.

Strategy versus Tactics

Your **strategy** is the plan for outperforming the competition. Your **tactics** are the ways in which you will carry out your strategy.

If you plan to open a bookstore, how will you compete with the chain outlet in the neighborhood? This competitor buys many more books than you do and will receive higher discounts from wholesalers, so you will not be able to compete on price. How else could you attract customers? Perhaps you could make your bookstore a kind of community center, so people will want to gather there. What tactics could you use to carry out this strategy?

- Hold poetry readings and one-performer concerts to promote local poets and musicians.
- Create special-interest book-discussion groups.
- Offer free tea and coffee.
- Provide comfortable seating areas for conversation and reading, to encourage customers to spend time in your store.
- Set up a binder of personal ads as a dating service.

If your tactics attract enough customers to make a profit, you will have found a strategy for achieving a competitive advantage. Remember, you will also have to create a strategy that considers online bookstores and e-books.

To find a competitive advantage, think about everything your business will offer. Examine your location, product/service, design, and price. What can you do to be different—and better in some way that matters significantly to your customer base—from the competition?

Feasibility Revisited: The Economics of One Unit as a Litmus Test

Once you have chosen a business idea and determined your competitive advantage, you should make a preliminary analysis to determine whether the idea would be financially viable. In other words, can you provide your product or service at a price that will cover your costs and provide you with a profit? Wozniak and Jobs were able to set up business in an office

Step into the Shoes . . .

Mental Floss, LLC—Cooler Conversations

Logan Mock-Bunting/Getty Images

Will Pearson and Mangesh Hattikudur, students at Duke University, were interested in learning and in trivia and started an educational campus newsletter in 2000. By the following year, it had been named *Mental Floss* and, with funding, soon had a national following. These former history and anthropology majors, respectively, created a company that now has a print publication, online materials, books, games, and retail products—based on the opportunity they identified and pursued.

Mental Floss magazine has sections such as Right Brain, Left Brain, Scatter Brain, and Spin the Globe. The company sends daily e-mails, called "Water Cooler Ammo," for unpaid subscribers. They also sell products such as "MBA in a Box" and creative T-shirts via the Web site.

Mental Floss was purchased by Dennis Publishing in 2011, but Will and Mangesh continue to be active in the business.

Source: Mental Floss, LLC, accessed July 18, 2013, http://www.mentalfloss.com.

once they secured Markkula's investment in Apple. This gave them a better environment in which to develop and introduce the Apple II, and that gave them operating profits. Before investing a great deal of time, effort, and money on your business concept, you can use what you learned from your competitive analysis to make a preliminary assessment of the financial opportunity. Considerably more financial analysis will be done before opening your doors, but this is a good point at which to do a preliminary evaluation.

Entrepreneurs use profits to pay themselves, to expand their businesses, and to start or invest in other businesses. Therefore, every entrepreneur needs to know how much **gross profit** (price minus cost of goods sold) the business will earn on each item it sells. To do this, entrepreneurs can calculate the **economics of one unit of sale (EOU)**, which will reveal how much gross profit is being earned on each unit of the product or service that is sold.

Defining the Unit of Sale

Begin with the **unit of sale**, which is the basic unit of the product or service sold by the business. Entrepreneurs usually define their unit of sale according to the type of business. For example,

Manufacturing. One order (any quantity; e.g., 100 watches).
Wholesale. A dozen of an item (e.g., 12 watches).
Retail. One item (e.g., 1 watch).
Service. One hour of service time (e.g., one hour of lawn-mowing service) or a standard block of time devoted to a task (e.g., one mowed lawn).

If the business sells a combination of differently priced items (such as in a restaurant), the unit of sale is more complicated. The entrepreneur can use the average sale per customer minus the average cost of goods sold per customer to find the economics of one unit of sale. The formula would be as follows:

Average Sale per Customer − Average Cost of Sale per Customer = Average Gross Profit per Customer

A business that sells a variety of items may choose to express one unit of sale as an average sale per customer (see **Exhibit 3-7**).

Cost of Goods Sold and Gross Profit

To get a closer look at one unit of sale, entrepreneurs analyze the **cost of goods sold (COGS)** of one unit. These are:

- the cost of materials used to make the product (or deliver the service) and
- the cost of labor directly used to make the product (or deliver the service).

For a product, the cost of direct labor used to make the product plus the cost of materials used are the COGS. The equivalent for a service business, the **cost of services sold (COSS)**, are the cost of the direct labor used to produce the service plus the cost of the delivery of the service.

The cost of goods sold per unit can be thought of as the cost of selling an additional unit. If you buy watches and then resell them, your COGS per unit is the price you paid for one watch. Once you know your COGS, you can calculate gross profit by subtracting COGS from revenue (see **Exhibit 3-8**).

◀ **Learning Objective 4**
Prepare viability tests using "the economics of one unit."

gross profit total sales revenue minus total cost of goods sold.

economics of one unit of sale (EOU) the amount of gross profit that is earned on each unit of the product or service a business sells.

unit of sale the basic unit of the product or service sold by the business.

cost of goods sold (COGS) the cost of producing tangible item.

cost of services sold (COSS) the cost of delivering a service.

Exhibit 3-7 *Unit of Sale as a Combination of Different Items*

UNIT OF SALE AND ECONOMICS OF ONE UNIT OF SALE

Type of Business	Unit of Sale	Economics of One Unit of Sale	Gross Profit per Unit
1. Retail & Manufacturing	One item (e.g., one tie)	$7 − $3 = $4	$4
2. Service	One hour (e.g., one hour of mowing a lawn)	$20 − $10 = $10	$10
3. Wholesale	Multiple of same item (e.g., one dozen roses)	$240 − $120 = $120	$120
4. Combination	Average sale per customer minus average cost of goods sold per customer (e.g., restaurant meals)	$20 − $10 = $10	$10 average gross profit

Exhibit 3-8 *Economics of One Unit of Sale versus Total Gross Profit*

	Economics of One Unit (EOU)	Total Gross Profit for 12 Units (@ $10 per Unit Sold)
Price Sold/Revenue	$20	$240 (12 × $20)
−Cost of Goods Sold	−$12	−$144 (12 × $12)
Gross Profit	$8	$96 (12 × $8)

Your Business and the Economics of One Unit

The economics of one unit of sale is a method for seeing whether your business idea could be profitable. If one unit of sale is profitable, the whole business may be. On the other hand, if one unit of sale is *not* profitable, then no matter how many units you sell, the business will never be successful. The EOU is best for determining what will not be profitable, because the total opportunity analysis will consider all the other costs of doing business. The EOU is a quick and easy method to determine whether profitability is unlikely. Let's use **Exhibit 3-8** as an example.

Say you have a business selling decorative hand-blown wineglasses that you buy from a local artist wholesale for $12 each and resell to friends for $20 each. The cost of goods sold for each wineglass is the wholesale price of $12; gross profit = $8.

You buy a dozen glasses for $12 each wholesale. Your unit of sale is one glass. Your cost of goods sold is $12 per unit, assuming you have no direct labor cost.

You sell all the glasses at $20 each. Here is how you would calculate your gross profit.

Total revenue = 12 glasses × $20 selling price = $240
Total cost of goods sold = 12 glasses × $12 purchase price = $144
Total gross profit (contribution margin) = $96
$240 revenue − $144 COGS = $96

Total Revenue − Total Cost of Goods Sold = Total Gross Profit

You made a gross profit of $96.

For a manufacturing business, one unit might be one pair of sneakers. The costs would include **direct labor**, the money paid to the people who made the product (sneakers, in this example), and the supplies, such as fabric, rubber, and leather (see **Exhibit 3-9**).

The manufacturer makes a gross profit of $3 for every pair of sneakers sold. That may not seem like much, but manufacturers sell in *bulk*. In other words, a manufacturer might sell several million pairs of sneakers per year.

direct labor Employees that actively produce or deliver a product or service.

Exhibit 3-9 *Economics of One Unit, Manufacturing*

ECONOMICS OF ONE UNIT (EOU)			
Manufacturing Business: Unit = 1 Pair of Sneakers			
Selling Price per Unit:			$15.00
Labor Cost per Hour:	$4.00		
No. of Hours per Unit:	2 hours	$ 8.00	
Materials per Unit.		4.00	
Cost of Goods Sold per Unit:		$12.00	12.00
Gross Profit per Unit:			$ 3.00

Exhibit 3-10 *Economics of One Unit, Wholesale*

ECONOMICS OF ONE UNIT (EOU)	
Wholesale Business: Unit = 1 Dozen Pairs of Sneakers	
Selling Price per Unit:	$240.00
Cost of Goods Sold per Unit:	180.00
Gross Profit per Unit:	$ 60.00

Exhibit 3-11 *Economics of One Unit, Retail*

ECONOMICS OF ONE UNIT (EOU)	
Retail Business: Unit = 1 Pair of Sneakers	
Selling Price per Unit:	$60.00
Cost of Goods Sold per Unit:	20.00
Gross Profit per Unit:	$40.00

Exhibit 3-12 *Economics of One Unit, Service*

ECONOMICS OF ONE UNIT (EOU)		
Service Business: Unit = 1 Hour		
Selling Price per Unit:		$50.00
Supplies per Unit (hair gel, etc.):	$ 2.00	
Labor Costs per Hour:	25.00	
Cost of Goods Sold per Unit:	$27.00	27.00
Gross Profit per Unit:		$23.00

The economics of one unit also applies to wholesale, retail, and service businesses. Assume the wholesaler buys a set of one dozen pairs of sneakers from the manufacturer for $180 and sells them to a retailer for $240 (see **Exhibit 3-10**).

The retailer pays the wholesaler $240 for one dozen pairs of sneakers. The retailer's COGS, therefore, is $20 ($240/12 for the shoes only; the retailer does not add direct labor). The store sells one pair at a time to customers for $35 (see **Exhibit 3-11**).

Here is the economics of one unit for a hair stylist who charges $50 per cut (see **Exhibit 3-12**).

The Cost of Direct Labor in the EOU—An Example

Janet has a business designing handmade bookmarkers. Her unit of sale is one bookmarker. Below is additional information about Janet's business:

- She sells 40 bookmarkers per week to a bookstore in her neighborhood.
- Her selling price is $4.50 each, including an envelope.
- Her costs are 80¢ per card for materials (construction paper, glue, and paint) and 20¢ each for the envelopes, for a total of $1.00 each.
- On average, it takes her one hour to make six bookmarkers.
- Janet pays herself $9 an hour.

The direct labor for each bookmarker is $1.50 ($9/6). Janet wisely realizes that she must include the cost of her labor in the EOU. See how she did this in **Exhibit 3-13**.

Janet's gross profit is $2 per bookmarker sold. Assuming no other expenses, such as taxes, she will keep this as owner of the business. She also earns $1.50 per bookmarker by supplying the labor, thus ending up with a profit of $3.50 per bookmarker.

Now, think back to Amy of the Most Chocolate Cake Company and perform a similar analysis.

- Amy takes an average of two hours to bake a cake.
- It costs $5 for the ingredients for an average cake.
- Amy pays herself $15 an hour.
- The price of an average cake is $40.

This cost structure ($5 materials and $30 direct labor) yields a gross profit of $5 per cake on a $40 cake. With the gross profit of $5 and the $30 she paid herself, Amy ends up with $35 per cake. Assuming she does not have to deliver the cakes, this may be sufficient for her. If she needs to earn more, she will have to charge more, work faster, work more hours, or decrease the costs. These may or may not be realistic options.

Hiring Others to Make the Unit of Sale

Janet realizes that if the bookstore wants to order more bookmarkers, or if she can sell them to additional bookstores, she will not have enough time to make them all herself. To solve this issue, she hires a friend to make the bookmarkers for $9 per hour. Although the EOU will stay the same, Janet will have more time to look for new opportunities for her business. Her income from the business will now come solely from the gross profit, which is currently $2 per unit.

Exhibit 3-13 *EOU Example, Janet's Company*

ECONOMICS OF ONE UNIT (EOU)		
Manufacturing Business: Unit = 1 Bookmarker		
Selling Price per Unit:		$4.50
Materials:	$1.00	
Labor:	1.50	
Cost of Goods Sold per Unit:	$2.50	2.50
Gross Profit per Unit:		$2.00

Amy from the Most Chocolate Cake Company can produce about 20 cakes during a 40-hour workweek and 30 cakes in 60 hours. That means she can earn $600 to $750 per week, or between $31,200 and $39,000 per year before taxes, without allowing for vacation or sick days. There would be an additional $100 to $150 in gross profit per week before other expenses are figured. Assuming Amy can sell 20 to 30 cakes per week at $40 each, she will have a maximum income of about $46,800.

Amy knows she will have other expenses, so $40,000 is more realistic. Like Janet, Amy would like to earn more than that per year, so she too could add employees if the market would support greater volume. If she paid her employees $15 per hour (assumed for this example as the minimum living wage), she would need to sell 8,000 cakes per year to make her $40,000. That is 154 cakes per week, requiring perhaps seven full-time bakers. This would not be possible in her home kitchen. The EOU analysis helps to identify this challenge.

However, we have to be sure that Amy is not comparing apples to oranges when making the analysis. With more people, the tasks could be delegated, so that it takes only one hour per cake, bringing the gross profit to $20 each. If Amy could also get better pricing on ingredients because of increased volume, the gross profit would be even higher. At $20 per unit gross profit, Amy would need to sell only 2,000 cakes per year, or 39 per week. That could be accomplished with two full-time bakers. As a home-based business, that would be more realistic.

Amy, like any entrepreneur, has to decide what is achievable and what her goals are.

Going for Volume

Janet meets a bookstore-supply wholesaler. He offers to buy 2,000 bookmarkers if Janet can deliver them in one month and sell them for $3.50 each, $1 less than she had been getting. This would reduce her gross profit but offer higher revenue. Three questions immediately came to her mind:

1. *Can I produce the 2,000-unit order in the required time frame?* After doing some calculations, Janet realizes that if she hires 10 people each to work 35 hours a month, she could deliver the order in time. Janet convinces 10 people to take on the one-month commitment by offering $12 per hour.

2. *If I lower the price to $3.50 for each bookmarker (instead of $4.50), will I still make an acceptable gross profit per unit?* To answer this question, Janet creates a chart (see **Exhibit 3-14**) and realizes that her new gross profit per unit would be $1. Let us look at the EOU if she factors in her labor at $12 per hour, or $2 per bookmarker.

3. *How much in total gross profit will I make from the order?* To answer this question, Janet creates another chart (see **Exhibit 3-15**) and realizes that her total gross profit would be $1,000.

Janet concludes that $1,000 in gross profit is much better than earning $80 a week in gross profit, plus $60 a week for her labor (what she earned making the bookmarkers herself each week at a selling price of $4.50). Even though the wholesaler is asking for a lower selling price, her total revenue, and therefore her total gross profit, would be much higher. When Janet realizes that she could deliver the order in the required time and make $1,000, she accepts the offer.

Exhibit **3-14** EOU Example, Janet's Company with Employees		
ECONOMICS OF ONE UNIT (EOU)		
Manufacturing Business: Unit = 1 Bookmarker		
Selling Price per Unit:		$3.50
Materials:	$1.00	
Labor:	1.50	
Cost of Goods Sold per Unit:	$2.50	2.50
Gross Profit per Unit:		$1.00

Exhibit **3-15** Gross Profit Projection, Janet's Company with Employees		
GROSS PROFIT PROJECTION (BASED ON EOU)		
Janet's Total Gross Profit		
Revenue ($3.50 × 2,000 bookmarkers):		$7,000.00
Materials ($1 × 2,000):	$2,000.00	
Labor ($2.00 × 2,000):	4,000.00	
Cost of Goods Sold:	$6,000.00	6,000.00
Gross Profit:		$1,000.00

Five breakthrough steps entrepreneurs can take to understand preliminary feasibility are:

1. calculating the unit of sale,
2. determining the economics of one unit of sale,
3. substituting someone else's labor,
4. selling in volume, and
5. creating jobs and operating at a profit.

At first, an entrepreneur can be part of his own economics of one unit. If you start making (manufacturing) computers in your garage, like Steve Jobs and Stephen Wozniak did when they started Apple, you should include your labor on the EOU worksheet.

Over time, though, Jobs and Wozniak made enough profit to hire others to manufacture the computers. Jobs and Wozniak took themselves out of the economics of one unit so they could be the creative leaders of the company. And, by lowering prices, they were able to sell millions of units.

currency a term for money when it is exchanged internationally.

foreign exchange (FX) rate the relative value of one currency to another.

Global Impact . . .

Selling Your Product around the World

Through the Internet, even a very small business run by one person can reach customers internationally. What if a customer from Germany contacts you through your Web site and wants to pay for your product in euros, the currency of much of Europe? **Currency** is a term for money when it is exchanged internationally. In the United States, the currency is the dollar. In Japan, it is the yen. In Mexico, it is the peso.

The **foreign exchange (FX) rate** is the relative value of one currency to another. It describes the buying power of a currency. The FX rate is expressed as a ratio. If one dollar is worth 1.25 euros, to calculate how many euros a certain number of dollars is worth, multiply that number by 1.25.

$$\$5 = \$5 \times €1.25 = €6.25$$

How would you figure out how many dollars €6.25 is worth? Simply divide €6.25 by 1.25 to get $5.

Tip: There are currency converters available online, such as at http://finance.yahoo.com/currency?u.

Determining the Value of a Business

The valuation of a business is a combination of art and science, and ultimately a matter of arriving at a price and set of terms that both the buyer and seller find acceptable. For a public company, valuation is the worth of the stockholders' equity. For a going concern with audited financials, the determination can be based on projected earnings and cash flows. For other going concerns, the process is more complex because the quality and reliability of the financial information is less certain. The primary methods of valuation are asset valuation, earnings valuation, and cash flow valuation.

◀ **Learning Objective 5**
Calculate the value of a business.

Asset Valuation Method

Asset valuation is a method that analyzes the underlying value of the firm's assets as a basis for negotiating the price. The four most common standards are

asset valuation a method that analyzes the underlying value of a business's assets as a basis for negotiating a price.

1. **Book value.** Starting with the value of assets reported in the books and records of the firm as a reference point, the actual value will depend on its accounting practices, such as allowances for losses and depreciation.
2. **Adjusted book value.** This takes into account any of the discrepancies identified in the calculation of book value and looks at the actual market value versus the stated book value. Intangible assets are often excluded in this method.
3. **Liquidation value.** This is a determination of the net cash that could be obtained through disposing of assets via a quick sale, with liabilities either paid off or negotiated away. It also includes the cost of liquidating. Neither buyers nor sellers are particularly interested in establishing a price based on liquidation, but it does establish a "floor," or minimum value, for the firm.
4. **Replacement value.** This is the determination of the cost of newly purchasing the assets, as would be required to start up the firm. This is also used more as a point of reference than as a pricing option.

Earnings Valuation Method

Earnings valuation is a method that assesses the value of the firm based on a stream of earnings that is multiplied either by an agreed-upon factor (the capitalization factor) or by the Price/Earnings ratio (for a publicly traded company). As with any methodology of this nature, the challenge is how to determine the variables. Three ways of looking at earnings are

earnings valuation a method that assesses the value of a business based on a stream of earning that is multiplied either by an agreed-upon factor (the capitalization factor) or by the price/earnings ratio (for a publicly traded company).

1. **Historical earnings.** Start with the value of earnings reported in the books and records of the firm over multiple years. This can then be adjusted for items that will distort earnings, such as salaries of family members, or depreciation. Historical earnings can be valid if future earnings can be reasonably projected as a result.
2. **Future earnings under current ownership.** This considers additional information that is available above and beyond historical earnings, such as economic changes, the competitive environment, and new products and services that have been introduced.
3. **Future earnings under new ownership.** This is a determination of the projections that you make according to the changes you plan to implement. This may be the upper limit of what you are willing to consider.

In addition to determining which type of earnings to use, valuation will depend on which measure of earnings is selected. Will it be before or after taxes? Will it be earnings before interest and taxes (EBIT) or operating income? Which one is selected may make a significant difference in the valuation. It is traditional to use the after-tax earnings value without extraordinary items. However, if the new owner will have a different financing structure, using EBIT may be best. Ultimately, a price must be negotiated to the satisfaction of both the buyer and seller.

Cash Flow Valuation Method

cash flow valuation
a method of calculating the worth of a business by using projected future cash flows and the time value of money.

Another method of arriving at the worth of a business is to calculate the **cash flow valuation**, using projected future cash flows and the time value of money to arrive at a figure. This requires assessing the future expectations of cash flows from the business and applying financial calculations to arrive at the current value. It is less likely to be used for an entrepreneurial venture, but may be considered as an option.

Whatever value is calculated through the quantitative methods above, the final price should also reflect nonfinancial variables. While performing due diligence, you gathered information regarding the market space; the competitive environment; the legal and regulatory status of the firm; and any pending changes in the physical environment or labor situation or need for investment in plant, property, or equipment. The value of customer goodwill must also be factored into the price, and the competitive and legal environments also have a role in the pricing. The offer price and the maximum amount you are willing to pay should encompass all of the factors you have identified. This price will have to be tempered by what you can afford.

Chapter Summary

Now that you have studied this chapter, you can do the following:

1. Define your business.
   - Identify the three basic types of "product" businesses.
     - Manufacturing is the making of a tangible product.
     - Wholesale is the buying in quantity from a manufacturer and selling to a retailer.
     - Retail is selling to individual consumers.
2. Articulate your core beliefs, your mission, and your vision.
3. Analyze your competitive advantage.
   - Your competitive advantage is whatever you can do better than the competition that will attract customers to your business.
   - Find your competitive advantage by analyzing what consumers in your market need.

4. Prepare viability tests by calculating the economics of one unit of sale.
   - The EOU is the basis of business profit.
   - Entrepreneurs use profits to pay themselves, expand the business, and start or invest in new businesses.
   - The entrepreneur chooses how the unit is defined:
     - One item (unit)
     - One hour of service time (if the business is a service business)
     - For businesses that sell differently priced items, the average sale per customer, or total sales divided by the number of customers:

     Total Sales/Number of Customers = Average Unit of Sale

   - To get a closer look at the costs involved in figuring one unit, entrepreneurs analyze the cost of goods or services sold (COGS or COSS) of a unit.
     - The cost of materials used to make the product (or deliver the service)
     - The cost of labor used to make the product (or deliver the service)
   - Once you know your cost of goods sold, you can calculate gross profit. Subtract total COGS from your total revenue to get your gross profit.

     Revenue − COGS = Gross Profit

5. Calculate the value of a business.
   - Use asset, earning, and/or cash flow valuation methodologies to arrive at a range of potential prices.
   - Consider the spectrum of nonfinancial factors in the price.
   - Arrive at an offer and maximum price before entering the negotiations.

Key Terms

asset valuation
barriers to entry
cash flow valuation
competitive strategy
core values
cost of goods sold (COGS)
cost of services sold (COSS)
currency
direct labor
earnings valuation

economics of one unit of sale
 (EOU)
foreign exchange (FX) rate
gross profit
market
strategy
tactics
unique selling proposition (USP)
unit of sale

Entrepreneurship Portfolio

Critical Thinking Exercises

3-1. Use the following charts to define a business you would like to start, and analyze your competitive advantage.

Business Definition Question	Response
The Offer. What products and services will be sold by the business?	
Target Market. Which customer segments will the business focus on?	
Production Capability. How will that offer be produced and delivered to those customers?	
Problem Solving. What problem does the business solve for its customers?	
Competitive Advantage Question	Competitive Difference (USP)
The Offer. What will be better and different about the products and services that will be sold?	
Target Market. Which segments of consumers should be the focus of the business to make it as successful as possible?	
Production and Delivery Capability. What will be better or different about the way the offer is produced and delivered to those customers?	

Attributes Important to Customers	Weight (a)	Your Company Rating (b)	Your Company Weighted Rating (c = a * b)	Competitor Number 1 Rating (d)	Competitor Number 1 Weighted Rating (e = a * d)	Competitor Number 2 Rating (f)	Competitor Number 2 Weighted Rating (g = a * f)	Competitor Number3 Rating (h)	Competitor Number3 Weighted Rating (i = a * h)
Quality									
Price									
Location									
Selection									
Service									
Speed/ Turnaround									
Specialization									
Personalization									
Total	1.00		_____		_____		_____		_____

3-2. Are there customers for your business in other countries? How would you plan to reach them?

3-3. Describe any international competitors you have found who may be able to access the same customers. How would you compete?

3-4. Describe three core values you will use to run your own company.

3-5. What are three of the concepts that a mission statement should contain and why?

3-6. Write a mission statement for your planned or envisioned business.

Key Concept Questions

3-7. Gross profit is the profit of a business before which other costs are subtracted?

What is the average unit of sale for the following businesses? (3-8, 3-9)

3-8. A restaurant that serves $2,100 in meals to 115 customers per day.

3-9. A record store that sells $1,500 worth of CDs to 75 customers per day.

3-10. Sue, of Sue's Sandwiches, sells sandwiches and soda from a sidewalk cart in a popular park near her house. She sets up her cart in the summers to earn money for college tuition. Last month she sold $1,240 worth of product (sandwiches and sodas) to 100 customers. She spent $210 on the sandwich ingredients and buying the sodas wholesale. Her unit is one sandwich ($4) plus one soda ($1). Define the unit of sale and calculate the economics of one unit for Sue's Sandwiches.

3-11. When Steve Wozniak and Steve Jobs envisioned a computer in every home, computers were large, expensive machines owned only by the government, universities, and large companies. What technology currently available today to only a few people can you envision meeting a need for many consumers in the future?

3-12. Is there a service presently available to only a few consumers, or one that is not available yet? Write about a service that you can imagine eventually becoming very popular and the need(s) it will meet.

3-13. If the FX rate between the U.S. dollar and the Japanese yen is 1:119, how many yen will it take to equal $20?

3-14. If the FX rate between the Japanese yen and the euro is 189.35:1, how many yen will equal 10 euros?

3-15. Explain three ways businesses can be valued.

Application Exercises

3-16. You own a small record label. You sell CDs through your Web site for $15, including shipping and handling. You get an offer from someone who owns a record store in Germany who wants to buy your CDs at $10 each and sell them for €30. He says his profit from each sale would be €12 and he will split it with you. Assuming the exchange rate between the dollar and the euro is $1 = €2:

a. How much profit would you get from the sale of each CD in the German store?

b. How much is that profit in dollars?

c. Is this a good business opportunity for you? Why or why not?

d. If the FX rate between the dollar and the euro falls to $1 = €1, would this still be a good business idea for you? Why or why not?

Exploring Online

3-17. Use the Internet to research suppliers for a business you would like to start or can envision. Describe the business and list the URL, e-mail, phone and fax, and street address for five suppliers you located via the Internet.

3-18. Visit *http://www.download.cnet.com/windows* and find three shareware programs that would be of value to you as an entrepreneur. List them.

BizBuilder Business Plan Questions

1.0 Executive Summary

A. Note full legal name of your organization.

B. Describe your business idea and the nature of the target market.

2.0 Mission, Vision, and Culture

A. Write a mission statement for your organization in 21 to 40 words that clearly states your competitive advantage, strategy, and tactics.

B. Create a vision statement for your organization.

C. Describe the core beliefs you will use to run your organization and how they will be reflected in its culture.

D. Identify the ways you plan to run a socially responsible organization.

Happy Belly Curbside Kitchen—Finding Opportunity in Healthy Food

Founders Terry and Dawn Hall created Happy Belly Curbside Kitchen out of their experiences, knowledge, skills, and interests. The founders had 30 years of experience in the hospitality business. They traveled extensively across the United States to meet the requirements of their careers in hospitality. They were the children of small business owners and had restaurant experience combined with formal hospitality education.

Terry and Dawn recognized several patterns in their travels:

1. The availability of fresh, natural food was far less than the need for it.
2. The decline in small-business viability.
3. The inverse relationship between the availability of healthy food and the level of obesity.

When their daughter, Mayer, was born, Terry and Dawn decided they wanted her to eat only healthy, fresh foods. They were frustrated by how difficult it was to find the food they wanted when they ate in restaurants. And, they wanted flexibility in work schedules and the opportunity to support their community. This led to the idea of creating a mobile restaurant serving the fresh, healthy foods they desired.

After the initial frustration of being turned down repeatedly by mainstream banks, even though they had related work experience, savings, excellent credit, and no debt, the Halls learned of a financing resource in their community that had different parameters. They secured their initial financing from Access to Capital for Entrepreneurs (ACE Capital), a Cleveland, Georgia-based community development financial institution. ACE had a combination of its own resources and funds from Create Jobs for USA available and was looking for borrowers like the Halls. The loan process took seven days for approval. With the funding from ACE, Happy Belly was able to get rolling. The Halls remodeled their commercial kitchen, purchased a food truck, and hired some dozen people.

Happy Belly Curbside Kitchen was part of the highly competitive Atlanta food-truck market but had some distinctive twists. The Halls didn't call their business a food truck, rather a "curbside kitchen." They had a corporate sponsor, the Big Green Egg, producers of the high-end grill that was pictured on the vehicles. The menu changed frequently, depending on what was fresh and local. Orders were taken on iPads by staff in front of the kitchens, rather than from windows in the truck itself. Also, the Halls had a full commercial kitchen in nearby Smyrna, Georgia, that they used for catering. These factors combined to permit them to provide a great variety of fresh, healthy food.

It was the Halls' intention to keep the money earned in the local community. They donated five percent of profits to the local Boys and Girls Club and purchased locally whenever possible.

Happy Belly targeted customers in Fulton and Cobb Counties and focused on its core value of healthy eating. The Halls partnered with Adam Verner, a local farmer. This was part of what they termed "farm to street," a play on the farm-to-table movement. They were named one of the 10 Healthiest Food Trucks in America in *Shape* magazine and expanded to two trucks serving the Atlanta area, along with their increasingly successful catering business.

Happy Belly Curbside Kitchen was locally based with a global view and was founded out of frustration with food choices.

Case Study Analysis

3-19. How did Terry and Dawn Hall identify the market for Happy Belly Curbside Kitchen? What process did they follow to analyze opportunities?

3-20. What knowledge, skills, and abilities did the Halls have before starting their company?

3-21. Why might *Shape* magazine have named Happy Belly Curbside Kitchen as one of the 10 Healthiest Food Trucks in America? How would they be healthier than most food trucks?

3-22. How was this business tied to a social mission? What did the owners do to demonstrate their commitment?

3-23. Identify four critical resources for Happy Belly and how the owners secured them.

Case Sources

Happy Belly Curbside Kitchen, accessed July 18, 2013, http://www.happybellytruck.com.

Nicole McDermott, "The 10 Healthiest Food Trucks in America," *Shape*, accessed July 22, 2013, http://www.shape.com.

Terry Hall, "Cooking Up Healthy Food and Job Creation in Atlanta," *Huffington Post*, January 28, 2013, accessed July 22, 2013, http://www.huffingtonpost.com.

Case Study | Empact: Making an Impact for Entrepreneurs

Michael Simmons and Sheena Lindahl founded Extreme Entrepreneurship Education LLC (now Empact) after graduating from New York University. The company was started as a for-profit organization, although it centers on a social mission: to facilitate a culture of entrepreneurship in communities around the world through exposure and celebration of young entrepreneur stories.

Michael Simmons and Sheena Lindahl
(Extreme Entrepreneurship Education Corporation)

Making a Strategic Pivot

Michael and Sheena originally intended to be publishers of entrepreneurial content. They launched the company by publishing a book about the entrepreneurial mindset written by Michael, *The Student Success Manifesto*. The profit per book unit was good, but they needed to sell a lot of units in order to make publishing profitable enough to support them.

To sell more books, Michael and Sheena began seeking bulk purchases from schools and other youth organizations. One marketing strategy included talking to groups of students when the schools purchased books. This tactic helped Michael and Sheena to realize that people would pay them to speak, whether books were purchased or not, and their impact as speakers was strong. They started charging for their speaking services.

One thing led to another. They explored ways to include the stories of other young, successful entrepreneurs and the Extreme Entrepreneurship Tour (EET) was launched in 2006.

The EET is the first national entrepreneurship tour in which community members and students from all academic disciplines participate in half-day events featuring young entrepreneurs who share the ups and downs of their experiences in entrepreneurship. The high-energy events are designed to get attendees excited about entrepreneurship and ready to take action and then connect and feed them into the programs and resources available on their campus and in their community that can help them. In addition to delivering great amounts of inspiration to participants, tour events have boosted the number of students taking part in entrepreneurship courses and participating in business plan competitions, and these events have also helped to gain awareness for new offerings. Tour events are customized depending on the audience and goals of a host institution.

The standard four-hour tour event includes two successful young entrepreneurs who serve as keynote speakers and panelists; a moderator who facilitates the day's events and delivers a workshop; exhibits; speed networking; and a panel discussion with local entrepreneurs. Empact also has shorter two- and three-hour tour events for hosts with smaller budgets and will even simply connect organizations with vetted, high-energy, successful entrepreneurs to speak apart from the tour event.

Marketing for the Tour

Extreme Entrepreneurship event organizers can visit a resource Web site to find templates for promotional posters and flyers, marketing best practice reports and checklists, and logistical checklists. An Empact Director of Events supports hosts with marketing and logistics, and Empact offers the complimentary services of a public relations firm to help get local media coverage of the event. The host is responsible for the promotion, event venue, refreshments, and audio-visual. On the day of the event, two Empact staff facilitate registration, hand out materials (including an event program/workbook, a copy of *Inc.* magazine, and other giveaways), and make sure all runs smoothly.

Since the EET was started in 2006, more than 500 events have been held, and that number keeps growing. The core team consists of Michael and Sheena, Chief Operating Officer Sarah Green, and a Director of Events. A key element of delivering successful events is having a large network of quality entrepreneur speakers to choose from. In fact, Empact has found that this focus on building networks based on authentic relationships and connecting individuals from within those networks has led to its success.

120

Extreme Entrepreneurship Tour Bus
(Extreme Entrepreneurship Education
Corporation)

Empact Showcases: Building Recognition, Market, and a Supply of Speakers

Empact achieves its mission to celebrate the many faces of entrepreneurship (and keeps its network of young entrepreneurs fresh) by facilitating a nationwide showcase and annual celebration of young entrepreneurs called the Empact Showcase. Since the Empact Showcase launched in 2011, celebration events have taken place at the White House, U.S. Chamber of Commerce, and the United Nations headquarters. Empact then sources its speakers for the Extreme Entrepreneurship Tour and other events through those the company comes to know from these recognition events.

In order to qualify for the Showcase, entrepreneurs must be age 35 or under and have made at least $100,000 in annual revenue. The average revenue of a Showcase company is $3.2 million; in combination, the 2013 Showcase companies employed more than 8,000 individuals.

Each year at the celebration event, special honor is given to the Empact100 (top 100 companies in the Showcase) as well as category honorees in categories such as most disruptive, largest potential, best social company, best female company, and more. The Empact100 and category honorees are selected by an Academy of high-level entrepreneurs, including folks like Tony Hsieh (President of Zappos), Gene Landrum (founder of Chuck E Cheese), and Kay Koplovitz (founder of USA Networks).

Empact Summits

Another network that Empact has rooted itself in is the entrepreneurship ecosystem at large. Also in 2011, Empact launched the first Empact Summit on the Future of Entrepreneurship Education, created to bring together high-level thought leaders from all parts of the entrepreneurship ecosystem. With a carefully curated invitation-only guest list, the Summit bridged connections between the various elements of the entrepreneurship ecosystem in the United States that don't often communicate with each other, including sectors such as government, investors, foundations, education, corporations, media, entrepreneur support organizations, and entrepreneurs.

The mission of the Summit is to spark conversations that facilitate relationship building to forge and strengthen bonds in both local and global entrepreneurship ecosystems, thus making entrepreneurship a viable career option. The Summit provides a forum for the most influential leaders to share ideas, highlights influential leaders and innovative programs in the "entrepreneurship ecosystem," and demonstrate the importance of the entrepreneurship ecosystem to major societal leaders.

In addition to helping Empact further its social mission, the Summit contributes to Empact's thought leadership, builds goodwill, and helps programs gain financial support that could allow them to host events.

Guest Author: Building Credibility and Broadening Reach

In 2013, Michael began writing a guest column for *Forbes* magazine, and Sheena began writing one for *Entrepreneur* magazine. Their articles focus on building networks and connections and work life balance—key concepts they've come to master in growing their company. The columns provide a forum to share insights and build thought leadership on topic areas the duo find interesting, as well as a way to maintain credibility and offer resources to their markets.

Social Media

Through its social media, Empact has focused on finding a voice that reflects its internal culture and values to deliver wow, pursue growth and learning, and be positive and authentic. All communications are intended to deliver a message that fits these characteristics.

Recognition

The Extreme Entrepreneurship Tour has won recognition for its excellence by receiving Northern Michigan University's 2007–2008 Program of the Year Award and the 2008 Innovation Award from the National Association of Development Organizations. Michael and Sheena have been named to *Inc.* Magazine's 30 under 30 list and *Business-Week's* 25 under 25; they have been recognized on AOL's homepage and featured in many other media outlets.

Case Study Analysis

3-24. Explain how Michael Simmons and Sheena Lindahl incorporate the Four Ps into a creative, effective, integrated marketing effort.

3-25. What product mix have Empact's enterprises developed?

3-26. How are its services delivered (through what channels)?

3-27. Discuss the company's global marketing (check its Web sites, if necessary).

3-28. What was Empact's first marketing effort?

3-29. What was the result of this effort?

3-30. How does Empact extend its brand?

Case Sources

Empact, http://www.iempact.com

Empact Showcase, http://www.empactshowcase.com

Empact Summit, http://www.empactsummit.com

Extreme Entrepreneurship Tour, accessed August 4, 2010, http://www.extremetour.org

Used by permission of Extreme Entrepreneurship Education LLC.

SPANX—Idea to Entrepreneurial Opportunity

White pants. Pantyhose. Scissors. How do these become the opportunity for a highly successful business? When you add Sara Blakely to the equation. She was a woman facing the problem of panty lines showing under white pants, so she took a pair of scissors and cut the feet off the pantyhose. Certainly, Blakely wasn't the first woman to do so. However, she was the first to see an entrepreneurial opportunity and create a successful venture as a result. Spanx was born out of this "ah-hah!" moment for Blakely.

Seeing Opportunity in a Problem

Blakely recognized that women (and men, too) are often bothered by underwear lines and lumps and bumps in their body shapes. She looked at the types of body-shaping garments on the market in the late 1990s and was not satisfied, finding them uncomfortable and ugly. She wanted to make products that were more comfortable and attractive.

Getty Images

Since the introduction of the original Spanx line, Blakely has spotted other opportunities. Her desire for a bra that doesn't show "back fat" resulted in the creation of "Bra-llelujah." Her identification of an opportunity for control-top fishnet tights yielded "Tight-end Tights." In 2010, Spanx added a product line for men, recognizing that many men also had problems that could be solved by shape wear.

Going from idea to product is not always easy. For Blakely and her team, the manufacturer is frequently the naysayer.[5] She has to push the boundaries as a contrarian who creates value.

The Woman Behind the Brand

Sara Blakely was recognized as the world's youngest self-made billionaire (at the age of 41) by *Forbes* in 2012. She was also selected as one of *Time's* 100 Most Influential People. And, in 2013, she pledged one-half of her fortune to charity through the Giving Challenge. The success of her entrepreneurial venture has enabled her to be a major philanthropist.

Blakely was raised in an upper-middle-income household where her father, an attorney, routinely challenged the children with the question, "What did you fail at today?"[6] This suggested that the kids should have tried to accomplish something, for without trying there is no failure—or success. After college, Blakely sold fax machines door-to-door for seven years. She developed sales and organizational skills during this time.

Sara Blakely
(Evan Agostini/AP Images)

[5]David S. Kidder, *The Startup Playbook*, San Francisco: Chronicle Books, 2012, p. 37.
[6]Ibid., p 32.

At a particularly difficult time in her life, Blakely's father gave her Dr. Wayne Dyer's *How to Be a No-Limits Person,* which she credits as a life-changing influence. She learned to see opportunity in adversity and impediments. Blakely became very clear about spending time thinking, to create new ideas. When she cut the feet off the pantyhose, she was poised to spot an opportunity and move forward with it.

Resources

Spanx emerged through a lot of ingenuity, hard work, and limited financial resources. Blakely kept her sales job for a year while she pursued her goal. She didn't share what she was doing with anyone, wanting to establish her plan first. She shared it with hosiery mills and potential investors, but not with her family and friends. She used her time and the $5,000 she had saved to create a prototype and promote it. In fact, she did much of the initial patent filing, hiring a patent attorney to do only a minimal portion. She understood that the patent was more for marketing purposes than as protection from competition.

Blakely used "guerilla" marketing techniques to introduce Spanx to the market. She stood in stores with a laminated set of photos showing a woman (herself) wearing white pants with and without Spanx. She exemplified and articulated the value proposition—thinner appearance, no lines, no restriction on style of shoe.

She also gave considerable thought to naming and packaging. For example, from her work as a stand-up comic, she knew that words with the "k" sound can elicit laughs. However, for a brand name, the letter X gives the impression of strength. Blakely wanted her product names to be memorable. Hence, the originality of Spanx, and subsequent names of Assets, Red Hot Label by Spanx, and Eur-sleek-A were created. Her packaging was inspired by looking at what was on high-end store displays and making the Spanx packaging more attractive and eye-catching.

In addition to acting as chief salesperson when she started out, Blakely did her own publicity. She also engaged friends who were passionate about the product to assist her. These shoestring efforts yielded fantastic results in 2000, when Oprah Winfrey named Spanx one of her "favorite things." This publicity catapulted Spanx into the marketplace.

Team

At the beginning, Blakely had to fulfill all of the company roles herself, rely on friends, or hire contractors to complete tasks. She had a product concept, but it needed to be produced, tested, marketed, and delivered, in return for payment. She realized that the product's technical specifications and production were best left to manufacturers of pantyhose, for whom this would be a use of excess capacity. Blakely relied on their feedback.

Getting the sort of team that she needed was often challenging. For example, hosiery mills repeatedly turned her away, often rudely. Her eventual manufacturer initially turned her down. However, after he discussed the idea of footless pantyhose with his daughters, he understood the opportunity and worked with Sara.

Two years after starting Spanx, Blakely was able to begin hiring employees. She focused on

Laurie Ann Goldman
(Ben Rose/Getty Images)

finding people who had strengths in her areas of weakness. She recognized that she was more creative than consistent and not well suited for day-to-day management. She hired a CEO, Laurie Ann Goldman, who has been with Spanx since 2000. Goldman created Spanx's first business plan. Blakely also worked to move from tasks she did not enjoy to those she did.

Spanx Expands into Shape Wear, Swimwear, and Hosiery

Since its launch in 2000, Spanx has experienced phenomenal growth. Its product line has grown from a single style of footless tights to over 200 products, including shape wear, swimwear, and hosiery. The original Spanx line continues to be sold at many high-end retailers, such as Nordstrom's, Neiman Marcus, and Saks Fifth Avenue. A line of products for Target has been introduced under the ASSETS by Sara Blakely brand, and for Kohl's as ASSETS Red Hot Label by Spanx. In addition, the SPANX for Men line was introduced in 2010.

Spanx products are mentioned in a variety of media on a frequent basis. Just about any guide to looking good will suggest Spanx shape wear. Stars such as Joan Rivers and Kelly Osborne have mentioned Spanx when critiquing runway fashions. Blakely herself has graced the cover of *Forbes* magazine.

As of 2012, Spanx, based in Atlanta, Georgia, was estimated to generate $250 million per year in revenue with a 20-percent return. Because Sara Blakely continues to be the 100-percent owner, this private company does not have to disclose its financial information to the public. Spanx has customers in more than 50 nations and is opening retail stores and in-store boutiques across the United States. With all of this success, the mission of Spanx remains, "To help women feel great about themselves and their potential."

Turning Profits into Philanthropy

From the start, Blakely has always been a staunch supporter of empowering women, a focus that was built into the Spanx mission. Her parents recall that she was always concerned about constraints on opportunities for women, both in the United States and abroad.[7] As the company grew, so did her opportunities to make an impact in this area.

In 2004, Blakely was a competitor on the Fox TV reality show *The Rebel Billionaire: Richard Branson's Quest for the Best.* She took three months away from Spanx and traveled with Sir Richard and her fellow competitors, accomplishing various business-related tasks along the way. Sir Richard surprised Blakely by giving her the $750,000 that he had earned from the show so that she could start her own charitable foundation. In 2006, he was part of the launch of the Sara Blakely Foundation. The foundation focuses on education and entrepreneurship for women around the globe.

The Sara Blakely Foundation's mission is: "Dedicated to changing women's lives through support of awareness education in four primary areas: Self, Social, Entrepreneurial/Financial and Environmental."[8] Oprah Winfrey was a key to Blakely's early success with Spanx and in 2007 the Sara Blakely Foundation made a $1 million contribution to the Oprah Winfrey Leadership Academy Foundation in South Africa.

---

[7]Ibid., p. 37.
[8]"Spanx Gives Back," Spanx, Inc., accessed July 9, 2013, http://pages.email.spanx.com/sarablakelyfoundation/.

Sara Blakely has created value for men and women worldwide, captured value for her, and been able to share her wealth—all by recognizing an opportunity and realizing its worth.

Case Study Analysis

U1-1. What benefits of entrepreneurship does Sara Blakely appear to have attained?

U1-2. Is the desire to earn an income a key motivator for Blakely? Explain your answer.

U1-3. What was Blakely's opportunity cost when she started Spanx?

U1-4. Which of Schumpeter's five basic ways to find opportunity applies to Spanx, both at its start and today? What was the opportunity?

U1-5. Which of Porter's generic strategies best fits Spanx?

U1-6. If Blakely had wanted to buy an existing business to create Spanx, what sort of company would have been logical? Why? Would an acquisition have been feasible? Why or why not?

U1-7. If you were writing a business plan for the Spanx start-up, what knowledge, skills, and abilities would you attribute to Blakely? What expertise would you suggest was needed?

U1-8. Create a business model canvas for Spanx at its start-up in 2000. How would it differ today?

Case Sources

David S. Kidder, *The Startup Playbook,* San Francisco: Chronicle Books, 2012.

Clare O'Connor, "Undercover Billionaire: Sara Blakely Joins the Rich List Thanks to Spanx," *Forbes*, March 7, 2012. Accessed July 7, 2013, http://www.forbes.com/sites/clareoconnor/2012/03/07/undercover-billionaire-sara-blakely-joins-the-rich-list-thanks-to-spanx/4/.

Clare O'Connor, "How Sara Blakely of Spanx Turned $5,000 into $1 billion," *Forbes*, March 14, 2012. Accessed July 7, 2013, http://www.forbes.com/global/2012/0326/billionaires-12-feature-united-states-spanx-sara-blakely-american-booty.html.

Spanx, Inc. Accessed July 10, 2013, http://www.spanx.com.

INTEGRATED MARKETING

Chapter 4
EXPLORING YOUR MARKET

Chapter 5
DEVELOPING THE RIGHT MARKETING MIX AND PLAN

Chapter 6
SMART SELLING AND EFFECTIVE CUSTOMER SERVICE

Apops/Fotolia

Exploring Your Market

Learning Objectives

1. Discriminate between marketing and selling.

2. Summarize how market research prepares you for success.

3. Choose your market segment and research it.

4. Position your product or service within your market.

Thinkstock

"In my factory we make cosmetics, but in my stores we sell hope."

—Charles Revson, founder of Revlon cosmetics

The original McDonald's was a modest burger restaurant in San Bernardino, California, owned by brothers Maurice and Richard McDonald. Ray Kroc was a 52-year-old salesman of Multimixer milkshake machines, and the McDonald brothers' restaurant was his best customer. When Kroc received an order from the McDonald brothers for eight Multimixers, enough to make 40 milkshakes at once, he had to learn more about their operation and its market.

What Kroc found was that the McDonald brothers had hit upon a unique value proposition that drew customers from miles around. The restaurant combined three factors:

1. fast, friendly service;
2. consistent quality in its burgers, shakes, and fries; and
3. low prices.

The McDonalds had found the magic formula for fast-food success. They knew they could expand their business beyond the several outlets they had, but they both hated to fly and wanted to stay locally focused. In 1955, Kroc and the McDonalds formed a partnership to create identical McDonald's restaurants around the country. In 1961, Kroc bought out the brothers for $2.7 million, but he strictly adhered to their original recipes and value proposition. Kroc wanted every McDonald's customer, from Anchorage to Miami, to eat an identical product. Today, there are more than 34,000 McDonald's outlets in more than 100 countries serving some 69 million people per day.

McDonald's has a formula for success.
(© Doug Steley A/Alamy)

Markets and Marketing Defined

Learning Objective 1

Discriminate between marketing and selling.

marketing the development and use of strategies for getting a product or service to customers and generating interest in it.

brand that which distinguishes goods or services through a design, symbol, name, term, or other features.

A *market* is a group of people or organizations that may be interested in buying a given product or service, can afford it, and can do so legally. A market is identified by attitudinal, behavioral, demographic, and other characteristics.

Marketing is the development and use of strategies for getting a product or service to customers and generating interest in it. Marketing is the business function that identifies customers and their needs and wants. Through marketing, the name of your business will become a brand and come to mean something clear and concrete in the customer's mind. A **brand** identifies distinctively the goods or services of one organization from others through a design, symbol, name, term, or other distinguishing features.

As an entrepreneur, your current and future customers should always be your top priority. Above all, marketing is the way a business tells its customers that it is committed to meeting their needs. Marketing should constantly reinforce your competitive advantage.

Nike sells athletic shoes. It puts them in stores where consumers can buy them. But Nike also *markets* athletic shoes. Nike creates advertisements and promotions designed to convince customers that Nike shoes will inspire them to *Just Do It*. You can choose athletic shoes from many companies, but Nike hopes you will feel inspired by its marketing to seek out and buy its brand.

A Business That Markets versus a Market-Driven Business

Do not make the mistake of treating marketing as an isolated business function rather than the engine that drives all business decisions. Most experts agree that, to be successful, a business must develop its marketing vision first, with a consistent customer focus, and then use it as the basis for all subsequent judgments.

Learning Objective 2

Summarize how market research prepares you for success.

Research Prepares You for Success

Whether you have a product or service you want to market, or are searching for a market opportunity with the aim of creating a product or service to fill that need, research can help you succeed. Your research can be conducted at the level of the industry, the market segment, or the individual consumer. Whereas the questions you ask will be different at each level, the methods of conducting the research are similar.

Research Your Market *Before* You Open Your Business

Large corporations spend a great deal of money on marketing and marketing research before they introduce a product or service. They need to get it just right. Take a lesson from the big companies: research your market. Introduce your product to potential customers.

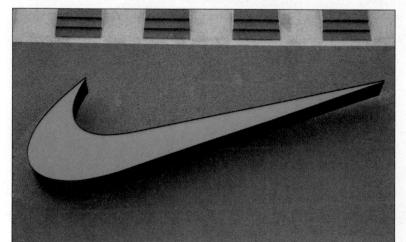

The Nike "swoosh"—a logo recognized worldwide. (Alamy)

Be open to honest criticism. It is not always pleasant to hear, but it can be valuable. Criticism can help you fine-tune your business. Use the information you receive to create a product or service that meets the needs of your customers.

Today, there is an added focus on getting products and services to customers earlier in the development process, to get their feedback sooner and bring in revenues more rapidly. The leading information on lean launches is from Eric Ries in his 2011 book, *The Lean Startup*, as noted in Chapter 3. The Lean Launch Pad and other "lean" start-up methods involve the research methods described here with accelerated and iterative primary research. For additional information, visit Steve Blank's Web site at http://steveblank.com, which offers considerable information about the process and "minimum viable products," or see *The Startup Owner's Manual*, by Steve Blank and Bob Dorf. This is frequently paired with the Business Model Canvas described in Chapter 2.

Types and Methods of Research

How you conduct your research will help determine whether it is reliable and valid. Clearly, you do not want to make business decisions based on incorrect information, although it will be incomplete information. The quality of your research will define the value of the answers to your research questions. If you do not already know how to perform the research, be certain to learn how to generate reliable and valid data before embarking upon a research project. Using incorrect or invalid research can lead to dangerously wrong answers to research questions, resulting in wasted resources, poor performance, and even business failure.

There are two types of research. **Primary research** is conducted directly on a subject or subjects. **Secondary research** is carried out indirectly, through existing resources. For example, if you conducted 100 interviews with students on a campus, it would be considered primary research. If you examined a study on those students conducted by someone else, it would be secondary. Often, primary research is expensive and time-consuming. However, if you want to test a product or idea, it is the best option.

primary research conducted directly on a subject or subjects.

secondary research carried out indirectly through existing resources.

Bear in mind that when you design research, the method you use will affect the answers you get. A combination of primary and secondary research will generally be best, and for each type of research there is a well-established set of methods in which to fit your needs. These tools can aid you in determining the viability of your business concept and/or product. The number of options is seemingly endless. Which methods to use will depend on your level of analysis (individual, market, industry, and so forth), your research questions, and the time and money you can devote. Remember, it is better to do your research and discover that you should revamp your plans than to skip this step or ignore the results and end up with an expensive failure in the marketplace.

Getting Information Directly from the Source: Primary Research

When you need to ask questions specific to your product or service or would like to observe how people act or react, it is best to conduct primary research. Primary research methods include:

- *Personal interviews.* Interview individuals face to face, using either flexible question guides or structured, step-by-step surveys.

Step into the Shoes . . .

Robin Sydney—Zorbitz, Inc.: A Line of Products Worn by A-List Stars

Robin Sydney
(Zorbitz, Inc.)

Could a 19-year-old take $100 in cash and a $5 pile of rocks and create a multi-million-dollar business? Robin Sydney and her mother, Marian, did just that when they created SunRocks, which later became Zorbitz, Inc. Sydney sought out a mentor and found the marketing genius behind VISA and Reebok. The women also learned about retailing and wholesaling from the owner of one of the largest gift stores in Los Angeles. Sydney was conducting research for another idea when she stumbled upon Chinese feng shui jade good-luck charms. This led to selling bead bracelets to Whole Food Markets, which became the top-selling gift product in that company's Southern Pacific region. Zorbitz has since added Karmology Bead Bracelets—combining lucky karma beads with powerful gemstones to bring good luck and good karma.

Zorbitz emphasizes the "healing" qualities of its products (e.g., love, health, wealth, and miracles), the stars that wear them (e.g., Ashlee Simpson, Halle Berry, Paris Hilton, and Freddie Prinze, Jr., among others), and the charitable contributions it makes worldwide. In this case, $100 in cash and $5 in rocks—plus considerable creativity and promotional savvy—added up to more than $2 million in annual sales.

Source: Zorbitz, accessed November 16, 2013, http://www.zorbitz.net; "California Teen Creates Million Dollar Idea and Zorbitz Takes Off," *Los Angeles Cityzine*, December 20, 2007, accessed May 20, 2009, http://www.la.cityzine.com/2007/12/20.

For example, you could interview students in your school or consumers in a local shopping area (mall-intercepts).

- *Telephone surveys.* These are personal interviews conducted via telephone. When your customer base will not be strictly local or readily accessible, you can reach more people this way. However, in the United States, telephone surveys are regulated, so you have to be careful to comply with the law. Also, with the increasing usage of mobile devices, land lines are decreasing in popularity, and samples may be skewed because older populations have the majority of the remaining land lines. These interviews can be conducted by people or computers and can use computer guided questions.

- *Written surveys.* These can be administered through the postal service or by e-mail or on special Web sites. Numerous survey programs available on the Internet can simplify this process. Survey Monkey (http://www.surveymonkey.com) and Qualtrics (http://www.qualtrics.com) create efficient, written surveys online. The survey questions should be clearly stated, easy to understand, and relatively short.

- *Focus groups.* If you want to get information that is generated through guided group discussion, you can use focus groups. There are facilities designed specifically for conducting focus groups, or you can simply find an appropriate quiet space. Focus groups should have a skilled leader who guides the participants through a discussion to arrive at the information you need.

- *Observation.* By watching, you can observe patterns of interaction, traffic patterns, and volume of purchases that will help you understand your prospective customers and your competition. Secret shoppers (people who are hired to shop at and evaluate particular stores) fall into this category. Also, attending an event, such as a trade show or professional meeting, is an opportunity to observe and learn. Make certain, however, that you do this ethically and legally.

- *Tracking.* It can be useful to track advertisements, prices, and other information through the media. You can compile this data to see pricing and promotion patterns, as well as the marketing strategies, of your competitors.

Getting Information Indirectly: Secondary Research

When you want to learn about your industry, competition, or markets, secondary research may be your best option. Some of these methods are:

- *Online searches.* By using search engines—such as Google, Bing, Yahoo!, Dogpile, Ask.com, info.com, and Excite—you can find stories, historical records, biographical information, and statistics. Be wary of sources when using Internet data, such as Wikipedia, that has been contributed by users and may be unreliable.

- *Database searches.* Public databases such as the U.S. Census (http://www.census.gov) are available via the Internet. Such sources can provide extensive consumer and business information and some industry reports. **Exhibit 4-1** is a screen shot of a Census page. You can visit the U.S. Securities and Exchange Commission's EDGAR database to find publicly traded companies in your industry.

    Proprietary databases at universities and public libraries are searchable for articles and books about potential markets. Interestingly, much of the information available on businesses, populations, markets, and the like is not available through free, public search engines. Libraries sign up for databases that are available only through (relatively costly) paid subscriptions. They also have services to provide certain journal and magazine articles for downloading or printing. For example, you can secure financial data through Hoover's subscription information services, articles from JSTOR or ABI/INFORM databases, and industry comparables from Risk Management Associates on a fee basis. Even viewing articles from *The Wall Street Journal* can require a paid subscription.

    Also, reference librarians can assist you in your research, which will help you use your research time more effectively.

- *Industry associations, chambers of commerce, and public agencies.* These types of organizations frequently collect demographic and statistical data on and for their members. They issue publications that contain valuable data in such areas as pricing trends, productivity, cost structures, legal matters, economic and environmental topics, and statistics. This kind of information is sometimes extremely expensive to gather, but can be of great value to a start-up enterprise.

- *Review of books and records.* Although you may not get access to other companies' records or those of a company you are thinking of buying, if you can examine records (or even journals or research notes) that are pertinent to your business, you may gain valuable insights. This is particularly true if you are practicing due diligence with a view to buying a business.

- *Competitor Web sites.* Look for annual reports for public companies, which are required by the Securities and Exchange Commission (SEC) to be available and which reveal marketing and other information about a company. Annual reports provide information for benchmarking and include industry insights. In addition, check out company blogs and newsletters. It is amazing what you can find if you just look.

Exhibit 4-1 *Census Data*

U.S. Census Bureau
American FactFinder

Main   Search   Feedback   FAQs   Glossary   Site Map   Help

Home health care services
NAICS: 621610
Table 1. Selected Industry Statistics for the U.S. and States: 2007

[NOTE. Data based on the 2007 Economic Census and the 2007 Nonemployer Statistics. For information on confidentiality protection, sampling error, nonsampling error, and definitions, see Survey Methodology. Data in this table represent those available when this report was created; employer and nonemployer data may not be available for all NAICS industries or geographies. Data in this table are subject to employment- and/or sales-size minimums that vary by industry.]

Geography	Number of establishments	Number of employees	Annual payroll ($1,000)	Sales, shipments, receipts, or revenue ($1,000)	Nonemployer Number of establishments	Nonemployer Sales, shipments, receipts, or revenue ($1,000)	2007 population estimate
United States	(r)22,975	(r)972,791	(r)23,373,475	(r)46,174,331	N	N	301,621,157
Alabama	423	13,011	355,117	756,080	N	N	4,627,851
Alaska	41	1,732	35,606	50,138	N	N	683,478
California	2,341	56,251	1,724,312	3,575,223	N	N	36,553,215
Colorado	282	13,530	321,077	594,989	N	N	4,861,515
Connecticut	235	15,305	451,262	807,103	N	N	3,502,309
Delaware	44	2,126	68,047	137,058	N	N	864,764
District of Columbia	27	1,835	39,559	67,455	N	N	588,292
Georgia	543	16,554	454,692	960,141	N	N	9,544,750
Hawaii	65	2,872	68,463	120,117	N	N	1,283,388
Idaho	131	3,155	70,309	136,468	N	N	1,499,402
Kentucky	224	6,755	232,449	569,028	N	N	4,241,474
Louisiana	575	15,995	418,448	870,415	N	N	4,293,204
Maine	126	5,308	125,346	239,455	N	N	1,317,207
Maryland	292	8,548	260,959	516,607	N	N	5,618,344
Massachusetts	477	21,321	659,614	1,283,325	N	N	6,449,755
Mississippi	256	7,196	208,528	497,109	N	N	2,918,785
Montana	70	2,019	36,258	73,299	N	N	957,861
Nevada	170	4,646	124,500	247,911	N	N	2,565,382
New Hampshire	96	4,206	106,488	198,819	N	N	1,315,828
New Jersey	537	34,883	848,764	1,494,002	N	N	8,685,920
New Mexico	138	6,466	135,201	243,558	N	N	1,969,915
New York	944	144,246	3,444,280	6,432,091	N	N	19,297,729
North Carolina	1,067	43,154	808,238	1,559,896	N	N	9,061,032
Ohio	993	46,744	1,051,297	2,065,541	N	N	11,466,917
Oregon	178	4,574	143,902	377,065	N	N	3,747,455
Pennsylvania	774	33,622	963,647	1,875,883	N	N	12,432,792
Rhode Island	67	4,571	114,136	209,787	N	N	1,057,832
South Carolina	237	10,025	226,321	478,973	N	N	4,407,709
Tennessee	465	14,404	435,930	1,031,242	N	N	6,156,719
Utah	153	5,110	155,271	376,066	N	N	2,645,330
Vermont	42	2,345	57,662	99,920	N	N	621,254
Virginia	523	18,633	441,868	825,367	N	N	7,712,091
Washington	300	11,136	294,518	566,998	N	N	6,468,424
West Virginia	104	3,061	80,304	163,178	N	N	1,812,035
Wyoming	42	442	10,933	26,197	N	N	522,830

Source: U.S. Bureau of the Census, 2007 Economic Census

D: Withheld to avoid disclosing data for individual companies; data are included in higher level totals.
N: Not available or not comparable.
Q: Revenue not collected at this level.
r: Revised.
S: Withheld because estimate did not meet publication standards.
s: Sampling error exceeds 40 percent.
X: Not applicable.
Z: Less than half the unit shown.
Additional symbols

Research Helps You Know Your Customer

Before you can put a marketing plan in place and deliver a competitive advantage to your customers, you will need to find out who your customers *are* or *can be*. **Market research** is the process of finding out

- who your potential customers are,
- where you can reach them,
- what they want and need,
- how they behave, and
- what the size of your potential market is.

Learning Objective 3
Choose your market segment and research it.

market research the collection and analysis of data regarding target markets, industries, and competitors.

Through marketing research, business owners and/or researchers ask prospective customers questions. You can learn a lot if you actively listen to what your customers are telling you and engage them in discussion. Whether your customers are individual consumers or other businesses, you will want to get into their minds and find out what they really think about such subjects as

- your product or service,
- the name of your business,
- your location,
- your logo and branding materials,
- your proposed prices, and
- your promotional efforts.

If you listen to your customers and talk to them, you can only benefit.

Marketing research helps you get a fix on who your customers are by answering these kinds of questions:

- How old are they?
- What kind of income do they earn?
- What are their hobbies and interests?
- What is their family structure?
- What is their occupation?
- What is the benefit your product or service offers that would best attract them? What problem are you solving with it?

The ideal customer should be at the center of your marketing plan. This profile will guide every marketing decision you make. If your target customer is affluent, for example, you might decide to price your product fairly high to reflect its quality. If your target market is from low to moderate income households, you might choose a strategy of lower prices.

What if you conduct your research and learn that you do not have a winner? Is your business concept dead? Only the one you thought of first! Think positively. This is a chance to develop an even better idea. Developing a winning opportunity is an iterative process, and it is not a straight line from idea to success, so revising your plan based on realistic feedback should strengthen your end product.

Customer Research

You will want to find out everything you can about your ideal customers. What do those individuals eat, drink, listen to, and watch on TV? How much do they sleep? Where do they shop? What movies do they like? How much do they earn? How much do they spend? If they are businesses, questions may revolve around their products, employees, or customers.

A large corporation might hire a consulting firm or advertising agency to conduct marketing research or may have its own marketing division. Small business owners can and should conduct research, too. This can vary from a simple survey that can be carried out in a day to detailed statistical studies of a large population.

Several of the methods described previously are well suited to learning about your prospective customers. If you already have a customer base, you should be learning from it, too. A few examples follow.

- **Surveys.** Well-designed marketing surveys ask people directly, in interviews or through questionnaires, what they would think about a product or service if it were available. Your marketing survey should ask about
  - product or service use and frequency of purchase;
  - places where the product is purchased (the competition!) and why consumers like to purchase from these businesses; and
  - business names, logos, letterheads—everything that will represent your business in a customer's or potential customer's mind.

  Make sure your marketing surveys also gather specific information about customers that will help you understand them better. They should include
  - interests and hobbies,
  - reading, television-watching, Internet, and social-media habits,
  - educational background,
  - age,
  - occupation,
  - annual household income,
  - gender, and
  - family size and structure.

- **Focus groups.** Another way to survey people about a product or service in development is to hold focus-group discussions. A focus group is typically composed of 10 to 12 people who meet screening criteria, such as being users or prospective users of a particular product. The group is led by a facilitator who is trained in market research to ask questions about the product or service. The resulting discussion is usually videotaped or audio taped for later analysis. Competing communications companies, such as AT&T and Verizon, regularly hold focus groups to stay current with how consumers feel about their respective services or to determine how they will react to new calling plans or promotions.

Conducting survey research.
(© Chris Rout/Alamy)

- **Research reports.** Market research firms are paid by other companies to gather information. Researchers study consumers and their purchasing and consumption patterns. The federal government can also provide statistics on consumers, such as from the U.S. Census and the U.S. Department of Labor. These sources can provide statistics on the following:
  - age;
  - annual income;

- ethnic or religious background;
- gender;
- marital status;
- geographic location (zip code, census tract, electoral district);
- interests;
- occupation;
- type of dwelling—single-family home, condominium, townhouse, or apartment (rental or owned); and
- spending and savings patterns.

These research companies keep records of the typical consumer in a given area. They can then provide statistics based on age, occupation, geographic location, income, or ethnic/religious background. Such researchers also delve into consumers' hobbies and interests and home ownership or rental status. Statistics dealing with population data are called **demographics**.

Many kinds of statistics are available from the U.S. Government Printing Office. The latest edition of *The Statistical Abstract of the United States* is available online and provides 1,400 statistical tables.

demographics population statistics.

Industry Research: The 50,000-Foot Perspective

Industry research focuses on a segment of business as a whole rather than on individual consumers. It provides a broader perspective and shows trends, new and emerging opportunities, and industry norms. If you want to start a record label, you will need to know how the recording industry is doing. Is it growing? Are people buying more music this year or less? Who are the major purchasers of music? Which age group buys the most recordings? What kind of music is selling?

To make the best use of industry data, you will have to identify your industry correctly and examine it. The codes of the North American Industry Classification System (NAICS) are generally used as industry identifiers. Once you have the NAICS code (six digits), you can readily search many sources of data. You can find NAICS codes at in the *North American Industrial Classification System: United States, 2007*, or online at the U.S. Census Web site in which you will enter a keyword and then narrow your selections until you find the best fit for your organization.

Once you have identified your industry, you can perform data searches to find relevant statistics and reports. Some places to look include the Standard and Poor's *Industry Surveys*, the U.S. Census Web site, Wetfeet.com, and BizMiner. A local college or university may subscribe to services such as IBISWorld or Dun and Bradstreet, which offer an abundance of information. The Census data will include the number of firms, revenues, number of paid employees, and more. In many cases, industry reports are available on the Census site. There are numerous other sources as well. Once you identify them, you can answer such questions as

- What is the scale (size) of the industry, in units and dollars?
- What is the scope (geographic range) of the industry? Is it local (city or neighborhood only), regional (covering a metropolitan area or state), national, international (present in two or more countries), or global (everywhere)?
- Is it a niche industry or does it reach a mass market?
- What does industry and individual company profitability look like?

- What trends are occurring in the industry? Is it growing? Declining? Stagnating?
- What is the structure of the industry? Is it highly concentrated, with a few companies in control? Is it highly fragmented, with a lot of competition?
- What competition is in the market space, and what are they doing? Perform an industry SWOT analysis to visualize this.

The methods to use for industry research overlap with those for customer research to some extent, but they reach further. Some methods to try include:

- *Interviews.* Perhaps you can find people in the industry (staff) or who study the industry (stock analysts, professors, economic-development professionals) who will share insights and data.
- *Observation.* This might include taking public tours of industry facilities, visiting trade meetings, and so forth.
- *Tracking.* Keeping track of industry advertisements and reports could help. For example, you may want to start a financial services company, so tracking interest rates will be vital.
- *Written sources for statistical data.* A variety of written sources were suggested previously in this chapter. Check out the Internet Public Library at http://www.ipl.org/. For industry and firm profitability, try online services for a fee, such as Risk Management Association (RMA) or BizMiner. Or use free library resources, such as *RMA Annual Statement Studies: Financial Ratio Benchmarks*.
- *Books and articles.* Books and articles are available about almost any business topic you can imagine. If your library doesn't have what you need, you might be able to acquire it for free through interlibrary loan. There is excellent information available only in books.
- *Competitor Web sites.* As noted previously, annual reports often include excellent descriptions of companies within an industry and their respective operating environments.
- *Trade associations and chambers of commerce.* Virtually every industry has at least one professional or trade association. You can search online by industry plus the word *association* to find them. Or, you can look in Gale Publishing's *Directory of Associations* at a library. The American Society of Association Executives gateway (http://www.asaecenter.org) has an online list of members, and you can find association magazines and journals (http://www .mediafinder.com).

By taking the time to research and understand your industry, you can be more successful in your own business. Plus, you will learn a lot more about your field.

Ford and Chrysler each spent millions on market research before producing, respectively, the Mustang and the minivan. It was worth millions of dollars to these companies to determine if the public wanted these automobiles because it was going to cost tens of millions to produce them.

Make Research an Integral Part of Your Business

Research is not something you only do once. Make it an ongoing part of your operations. Just as your tastes and desires change as you learn about new ideas and products, so do those of your customers. By continuing to

Global Impact . . .

College Degrees for the Military

Active-duty members of the U.S. military and their families tend to relocate frequently, often internationally. This job-related relocation makes completing a college degree at a single traditional brick-and-mortar, four-year college difficult at best.

American Military University is a wholly online, private, for-profit, degree-granting program with students across the United States and in more than 100 other countries. Established by a retired Marine Corps officer, James P. Etter, the university has a well-defined target market: military members and their families.

Course delivery, subjects, and content are designed with the military in mind. As long as they have Internet access, military students can enroll and take courses. Also, military personnel earn education benefits from the government and can use them at American Military University.

American Military University has served its global target market profitably for over 20 years.

Source: American Military University website, accessed July 24, 2013, http://www.apus.edu.

---

survey your customers as your business develops, you will stay current with their needs and their feelings about your product. You can provide customers with prepaid response cards and conduct in-store or telephone surveys, depending on your business. By carefully reviewing your customer purchasing and contact history, you can target your surveys for maximum effectiveness. Keeping up with trade journals and business news is also critical.

How Customers Decide to Buy

How will you figure out who the potential customers are for *your* business? It is critical to understand not only which customers are in your target market, but how they will purchase your product (or service).

Step 1. If you have developed a product or service, ask yourself what consumer need it will serve. Arm & Hammer turned this marketing question into a gold mine by developing its simple baking-soda powder into toothpaste, laundry detergent, air and carpet fresheners, and deodorants.

Step 2. Think about who might actually buy your product. Remember that the people who use a product are not always the purchasers. Mothers generally buy children's clothes; if you are making children's playsuits, they should offer features/benefits that appeal to mothers. They could be marketed as easy to clean, for example.

Step 3. Analyze the buying process that will lead customers to your product.

- *Awareness.* The customer realizes a need. Advertising is designed to make consumers and business customers aware of potential needs, for everything from dandruff shampoo to office supplies to automobiles.
- *Information search.* The customer seeks information about products that could fulfill a need. Someone looking for a multivitamin might pick up a brochure on the counter of the local health food store or simply look on the shelves of a supermarket or drug store. A retailer might search online for sign companies.

- *Evaluate alternatives.* Once information is gathered on a single product, the customer may want to examine alternatives before making a purchasing decision. The individual looking for a multivitamin might check out what's available in the health food store, and compare the price and content with the more commercial brands found in the local supermarket or drug store. The business owner might get several quotations on the needed business signs.
- *Decide to purchase.* The first purchase is really a test; the customer is trying a product to see how well it performs (or testing the quality of the service).
- *Evaluate the purchase.* If your product or service is satisfactory, the customer may begin to develop loyalty to your business and tell others about it as well. Now, how can you keep that customer for life?

Owning a Perception in the Customer's Mind

More valuable to McDonald's than all the Big Macs it sells every year is the perception it owns in the minds of its customers—that every time they patronize a McDonald's, they will eat food that tastes exactly the same as at every other McDonald's, that the prices will be reasonable, and that the service will be friendly and fast.

For Burger King to compete with McDonald's, it had to fight for a mind share of the fast-food customer. Burger King opened its attack with "Have It Your Way," which targeted McDonald's mass-manufacturing approach to making hamburgers. It followed up with "Broiled, not Fried" and "The Whopper Beats the Big Mac."

It is almost impossible to topple an established leading brand in a market. Burger King's executives wisely decided that their goal was to be a strong number two. As number two, you try to create a new category (broiled instead of fried hamburgers, for instance) rather than attempting to take over the competitive advantage of the number one company in the market. Avis lost money for 15 years while trying to overtake Hertz. The company finally accepted its number two position and turned it into a competitive and profitable advantage through its "We Try Harder!" advertising campaign.

You do not have to be number one to be successful. Discover a competitive advantage and attack the market by creating a new category in the customer's mind. Domino's Pizza found a competitive advantage by delivering orders in less than 30 minutes. That one marketing insight helped create a hugely successful company.

Features Create Benefits

There is a subtle, but important, difference between the benefits and the features of a product. The features are facts. The features of a drill might include its hardness and sharpness, but the benefit is that it makes a hole. The feature of a Teflon coating on a pan creates the benefit of easy cleaning. The essence of selling is showing how and why the outstanding features of a product or service will benefit customers. Smart marketers always emphasize benefits, not features, because consumers will buy what solves their problems or makes their lives more pleasant.

BizFacts

Minority business owners (often defined to include women) should contact local corporate offices and ask about minority purchasing programs or find the local office of the National Minority Supplier Development Council (http://www.nmsdcus.org) or government diversity agency. Many companies and most government agencies are committed to buying up to 25 percent of their supplies and services from minority-owned businesses.

Home Depot: Teaching Customers So They Will Return

Home Depot's marketing vision is not just to sell tools and materials but to teach people how to use them to improve their homes and lives. The company's marketing vision focuses on what its customers need Home Depot products to do.

Successful companies are not built on one-time sales but on repeat business. The owners of Home Depot have calculated that a satisfied customer is worth more than $35,000 in sales over the customer's lifetime. They found that the slogan "More saving. More doing." works for their customer base.

Home Depot's multimillion-dollar insight was that its customers not only needed the products it sold but also help in using them.

The most successful companies pay close attention to customer demands. They constantly observe their customers, survey them, and analyze their wants and needs. They hire people to look for customer needs that might be going unfulfilled. This is all part of customer analysis, one step in developing a marketing plan.

Which Segment of the Market Will You Target?

Marketing strategies are focused on the customer, and a business has to choose which customers to target. Your product will not be needed by everyone. You will have to figure out which segments of the market to pursue.

There is a huge market for home repair, including professional carpenters and builders. Home Depot's competitive advantage would not be strong in the market segment composed of professionals, in which the distribution channels are strong and well established. A **market segment** is composed of customers who have a similar response to a certain type of marketing. Home Depot chose to market primarily to the nonprofessional, private individual.

market segment a group of consumers or businesses that have a similar response to a particular type of product or service.

In the cosmetics industry, one segment reacts positively to luxuriously packaged, expensive brands. Another is most responsive to products that claim to reduce signs of aging. Another's primary concern is (reasonable) price. A company that recognizes these market segments and chooses one to concentrate on will do better than a business that tries to sell its cosmetics to every adult female in the country.

It is difficult to target very different segments of a market simultaneously. Volvo, for example, has established a reputation as a safe, family car. It targets parents with young children. Volvo would have a difficult time also trying to market a two-seat convertible sports car to young adults who are concerned more with style and speed than safety.

Successful Segmenting: The Body Shop

The Body Shop is a good example of the success that can result from choosing the right market segment. Founder Anita Roddick disliked paying for expensive packaging and perfuming when she bought cosmetics. She was also annoyed by the extravagant claims made by many cosmetics companies and by the high prices of their perfumes and lotions. Price became an integral part of the image for many products. A brand called Joy, for example, was marketed as the most expensive perfume in the world.

Roddick saw an opportunity to create a different line of cosmetics. She would use natural products that would be packaged inexpensively and marketed without extravagant claims. As she wrote in her book, "It is immoral to deceive a customer by making miracle claims for a product. It is immoral to use a photograph of a glowing sixteen-year-old to sell a cream aimed at preventing wrinkles in a forty-year-old."[1]

Roddick tapped into a segment of the cosmetics market that had been neglected, and her business grew explosively as a result. Her success proves that selling an honest product honestly can be the best marketing strategy of all.

But what if Roddick had found that there were very few women interested in natural cosmetics? If she had determined this before starting, then she could have changed her segmentation strategy. If not, her business would not have survived, because even though the cosmetics market is large, her segment would have been too small to support her venture. It is possible to go after a small, niche segment, but then your price would have to be high enough to make a profit, and the customers would have to buy often enough to keep your business going. Jaguar and Rolls-Royce each sell far fewer cars than Honda or Ford, but at much higher prices. Jaguar and Rolls target the luxury segment of the car market.

Applying Market Segmentation Methods

Marketers have developed four basic ways to segment:

- *Geographic.* Dividing a population by location.
- *Demographic.* Dividing a population based on a variable such as age, gender, income, or education. For business customers, variables such as sales volume and number of employees could matter.
- *Psychographic.* Dividing a population by psychological differences, such as values (conservative, liberal, open-minded, traditional), lifestyle (sedentary, active), personality traits (worrier, Type A, shy, extroverted), and social group (white collar, blue collar).
- *Behavioral.* Dividing the market by purchase behaviors that have been observed, such as brand loyalty or responsiveness to price.

Say you want to make and sell hacky sacks on your college campus. Twenty thousand students attend the college. If 50 of the 200 students surveyed are interested in buying your hacky sack, you might expect that approximately 5,000 students of the 20,000 would represent your total potential market. Which segments of that market should you target?

If your company has limited resources, you might choose to target only one segment. A large company might decide to appeal to the entire market by designing a product tailored for each segment. Gap Inc., for example, has three product lines—Old Navy, Gap, and Banana Republic—each priced for and tailored to a segment of the sportswear market.

---

[1]Anita Roddick, *Body & Soul, Anita Roddick Tells the Story of the Body Shop, Inc.,* New York: Crown Publishers, 1991.

Step into the Shoes . . .

How Thomas Burrell Became a Leader in Marketing to African Americans

To market a product or service to a specific market segment, you must research what the people who comprise it want. In the late 1960s, major corporations became more conscious of the potential clout of African-American consumers but were unsure how to market to them.

In 1971, Thomas Burrell and Emmett McBain opened one of the first black-owned advertising agencies in the United States. By the following year, Burrell had convinced McDonald's that Burrell Advertising could help the huge company expand into the African-American market. Burrell came to be the fastest-growing and largest black-owned advertising agency in the country and continues to be one of the largest multicultural global marketing firms.

Burrell Advertising has created more than 100 commercials for McDonald's. Other Burrell clients have included Coca-Cola, Ford Motor, Johnson Products, Schlitz Brewing, Blockbuster Entertainment, Procter & Gamble, Jack Daniels Distillery, Polaroid, Stroh Brewing, and First National Bank of Chicago.

While no longer involved in the marketing firm, Burrell himself could probably quote the demographics of the African-American market off the top of his head. He has combined his company's thorough market research with his own personal experience as an African-American male to create powerful appeals to the targeted market.

Thomas Burrell, founder of Burrell Advertising. (Michael L. Abramson/ Getty Images)

You could use any of the four segmentation methods listed previously for your hacky sack business, as shown in **Exhibit 4-2**.

One way to gauge your market would be to interview a sample of 200 students with a survey while showing them the product and asking such questions as:

- Do you play a sport, whether competitive or not? (Yes/No)
- If so, on average, how often do you play per month? (Numeric response)
  - What, if any cocurricular activities do you participate in? (Open-ended)
- Do you own a hacky sack? (Yes/No)
  - If so, how much did you pay for it? ($ amount)
  - Where did you buy it? (Open-ended or provide a list)
  - Approximately how many months have you had it? (Numeric response)
  - How often do you use it? (Open ended—could create categories)

Exhibit 4-2 *Hacky Sack Segmentation* *		
Segmentation Method	**Description**	**Estimated Size of Segment**
Geographic	Residents within 2 miles of mid-size university	600,000
Demographic	Age 18–24 Full-time students	60,000 45,000
Psychographic	Active lifestyle	15,000
Behavioral	Extroverted Fun-loving Play hacky sack	10,000 18,000 500

*Research would be needed to identify these values.

- How interested would you be in purchasing this hacky sack, if it were available? (Scale of 1 to 5 with 1 being "not at all" and 5 being "extremely")
- How much would you pay for this hacky sack? (Numeric response)
- How many of these hacky sacks would you buy per year? (Numeric response—Could ask the question at a few price points to see what makes the difference)
- What suggestions do you have to improve this hacky sack? (Open ended)
- How old are you? (Numeric response)
- What is your occupation? (Open ended or could create a categorized list)
- What is your annual income? (Best if in categories)

Once you have chosen your market segment, you can really fine-tune your market research, because you now have to focus only on these customers—not on every potential customer in your market. Collecting data from the people in your market segment can be fun as well as financially rewarding. Here are a few questions you can adapt to your own product or service:

1. Do you currently use this type of product?
2. What brand of this product do you currently use?
3. Where do you buy it? Please be specific about the source, such as the name and location of the store, the direct-marketing representative, or Web site.
4. How much do you pay for it? (Probe for size and price, if appropriate.)
5. How often do you buy it?
6. Would you buy our product/service?
7. How much would you be willing to pay for it?
8. Where would you shop for it?
9. How would you improve it?
10. Now that you have seen/tasted/felt/smelled this product, what do you consider to be its closest competitor?
11. Is our product/service worse or better than those of our competitors? Please explain.

To learn more about creating questionnaires and administering survey research, visit your library for books on the topic. The creation and administration of surveys takes considerable thought and preparation including pretesting. You can use standard or common survey instruments to build yours.

The Product Life Cycle

product life cycle (PLC) the four stages that a product or service goes through as it matures in the market—introduction, growth, maturity, and decline.

You will also need to analyze where your market is in its **product life cycle (PLC)**. The PLC is the set of four stages that a product or market goes through from its beginning until its end. **Figure 4-1** illustrates two product life cycles.

1. *Introduction.* Your product or service is in the invention and initial-development stages. It is new to the market and is essentially unknown, so you will need to introduce it to potential customers who may be curious about your product but not familiar with it. Marketing at this stage will require education and testing with price and presentation. Modification of the design or technology may be

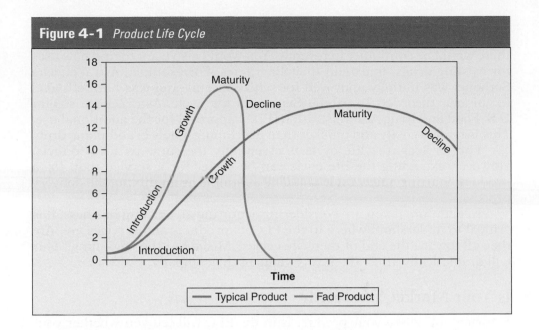

Figure 4-1 *Product Life Cycle*

required. When the personal home computer was first introduced, Apple's marketing was focused on convincing consumers how easy it would be to use. Apple used the same strategy in the introduction of subsequent products.

2. *Growth.* Once you achieve success in introducing your product or service to the marketplace, your organization will grow and inevitably invite attention from competition, as well as perhaps attract new entrants in the field. Perceiving your growth in sales, competitors now start entering your market, or more strongly defend their own market spaces, so efforts at this stage will have to focus on communicating your competitive advantage to consumers. Customer purchases increase dramatically; you have reached the limits of your current market.

3. *Maturity.* At this stage, consumers have become knowledgeable about both you and your competitors. The market has become relatively crowded, and there is no more growth as your product or service is currently offered. Marketing will need to focus on promoting brand loyalty. Stability of profits now depends more on cost strategies as demand has become relatively flat.

4. *Decline.* At this point, your competitive advantage has eroded, and sales and profits are declining. New developments will be necessary to revive the market's interest.

Product life cycles are applicable in different ways. For example, the Pet Rock, essentially a small stone that people were to pretend was a pet, had a very short life cycle. Such fad items attain popularity quickly and mature and decline equally rapidly. Other products, such as prescription drugs, will have longer life cycles because of patent protection, high market-entry costs, and their medical necessity for certain population groups. Ideally, you will look at the overall life cycle of a market to determine where your product or service will fit.

It is important for you to understand where each product or service is in the PLC. See **Figure 4-1** for an illustration of the PLC of a typical product and for a fad item. It is important to have a continuous flow of new products, so that your organization as a whole is sustainable. For example, if you owned a pharmaceutical company, you would want to introduce new medicines well before the existing ones reached maturity/decline, so that there would be continuity in revenue. You would also want to find new uses for existing drugs, to extend their life cycles. For example, AstraZeneca's Seroquel was initially approved for schizophrenia and was used off-label for bipolar disorder. To extend Seroquel's life cycle, AstraZeneca sought U.S. Food and Drug Administration (FDA) approval for the additional use. This is far less costly and quicker than developing a new brand-name drug.

For services, the life cycle is essentially the same as for products. However, extending the life cycle can be easier for a service than for a product. Starting a new cycle could be as simple as modifying the delivery process.

In addition, if you are considering acquiring an existing business, it is critical to understand where in the PLC its products and services are. Are they all toward the end of their life cycles? Mixed? At the beginning? This will dramatically affect the future value of the company.

Is Your Market Saturated?

Figuring out where your product is in the PLC will tell you whether your market is close to saturation. In other words, have all 3 million people in your market already bought a competitor's product? Nokia, for example, had a 39 percent share of the global market of $1.1 billion in mobile phones.[2] But that market was nowhere near saturation. Meanwhile, Nokia introduced its Short Message Service (SMS), which allows e-mail messages to be sent between mobile phones in Finland. SMS quickly became Finnish teenagers' favorite way to communicate. Observing how quickly the technology spread among Finnish teenagers gave the Nokia management ideas about how they would market SMS in the 140 countries where they sold cell phones.

Market Positioning: Drive Home Your Competitive Advantage

Learning Objective 4

Position your product or service within your market.

positioning distinguishing a product or service from similar products or services being offered to the same market.

After deciding which market segments to target, an entrepreneur will need to figure out what position the company should try to occupy in those segments. The *position* of a product is its relative place in the customer's mind compared with its competitors. The goal of market **positioning**, therefore, is to distinguish your product or service from others being offered to the market segments you have targeted. You can do that by focusing on your competitive advantage. "Have It Your Way," Burger King promised, driving home its competitive advantage—that at Burger King you can specify exactly how you want your hamburger prepared and garnished.

As you can see from the Burger King example, positioning involves clearly communicating your competitive advantage to the consumer and demonstrating how your product/service is different. Your goal is to position your product/service clearly in the mind of your target market as the brand that provides that difference. Use the following format to develop a positioning statement for your business:

(Your business name/brand) is the *(competitive industry/category)* that *(provides these benefits, or points of difference)* to *(audience/target market)*.

---

[2]Mark Landler, "Nokia Pushes to Regain U.S. Sales in Spite of Apple and Google," *The New York Times*, December 10, 2007.

Here is an example: *Microsoft is the leading global software producer that provides affordable computer solutions to businesses.*

By the time you have completed the four steps of your marketing plan, you will know your potential customers, your competitors, and your market intimately. It is a lot of work but well worth it. Make a commitment to let marketing drive your business decisions, and you will greatly increase the odds that your business will be successful.

Developing a Marketing Plan

After you understand how customer-focused marketing should permeate your business, you will be ready to develop a plan for introducing your product to your market. The marketing plan can serve as a stand-alone document or be part of an overall business plan. Either way, it should be a functioning, evolving part of your business. We began with customer analysis because before you can develop a marketing vision, you will need to know who your customers are and what they want.

Q: Why does a customer go to a hardware store to buy a drill?

A: Because she needs to make a hole.

The *hole* is what the customer needs, not the drill. If the hole could be purchased at the store, the customer would not bother with the drill. If you are marketing drills, therefore, you should explain to the customer what good holes they make. If someone invents a better hole-maker, drill manufacturers will soon be out of business.

Your marketing plan must include an understanding of prospective customers and their wants, needs, and demands. It should also identify and analyze market segments. The plan should incorporate industry research and trend analysis. It will state your market-positioning approach. In short, a marketing plan looks at all aspects of the market space for your enterprise, from the broadest perspective to the narrowest.

Chapter Summary

Now that you have studied this chapter you can do the following:

1. Discriminate between marketing and selling.
   - Marketing is the business function that identifies your customers and their needs and wants.
   - Through marketing, your business will come to mean something clear and concrete in the customer's mind. Above all, marketing is the way a business communicates its competitive advantage to its market.
2. Summarize how market research prepares you for success. It is the process of finding out who your potential customers are, where you can reach them, and what they want and need.
   - Getting the information directly from the subject: primary research.
     - Personal interviews
     - Telephone surveys
     - Written surveys
     - Focus groups
     - Observation
     - Tracking

- Getting information indirectly: secondary research.
  - Online searches
  - Books and articles
  - Trade associations, chambers of commerce, public agencies
  - Review of books and records
  - Researching customers and industries
3. Choose your market segment and research it.
   - Before you can develop a marketing vision for your business, you will need to know who your customers are and what they want.
     1. A market segment is composed of consumers who have a similar response to a certain type of marketing.
     2. Segmentation methods:
        a. *Geographic.* Dividing a population by location.
        b. *Demographic.* Dividing a population based on a variable like age, gender, income, or education.
        c. *Psychographic.* Dividing a population by psychological differences such as political opinion (conservative, liberal) or lifestyle.
        d. *Behavioral.* Dividing the market by observable purchase behaviors such as brand loyalty or responsiveness to price.
4. Position your product or service within your market.
   - The goal of market positioning is to distinguish your product or service from others being offered to the same market segments. You can do that by focusing on your competitive advantage.
   - Use the following format to develop a positioning statement for your business: (Your business name/brand) is the (competitive industry/category) that (provides these benefits, or points of difference) to (audience/target market).

Key Terms

brand	positioning
demographics	primary research
market research	product life cycle (PLC)
market segment	secondary research
marketing	

Entrepreneurship Portfolio

Critical Thinking Exercises

4-1. Step One: Customer Analysis
Describe the typical consumer your business plans to target.

Segment/Attribute	My Customer
Geographic 1. 2. 3.	
Demographic 1. 2. 3.	
Psychographic 1. 2. 3.	
Behavioral 1. 2. 3.	

What need(s) do you plan to satisfy for this customer?

4-2. Step Two: Market Analysis
- How large is the total market for your product or service? How did you arrive at this figure?
- Which segment of this market do you intend to target? Why? How large is the segment?
- Describe your segmentation method. Why did you choose this method?

4-3. Research can give you a great deal of information, but you will have to use your math skills to make it more useful. For example, imagine you are interested in opening a dog-care service and you have gathered the following facts:
- In 2000, the U.S. Census Bureau estimated that there were 2.67 people per household.
- According to your city's public records, the population of your community is 80,000.

- The *U.S. Pet Ownership & Demographics Sourcebook*[3] estimates that the number of dog-owning households in a community equals 0.361 multiplied by the total number of households.
- The *Sourcebook*[4] also estimates that the number of dogs in a community equals 0.578 multiplied by the total number of households—or 1.6 multiplied by the number of dog-owning households.

Calculate:

  a. The number of dog-owning households in your community.

  b. The number of dogs in your community. Round your answers off to the nearest whole number.

4-4. Analyze and describe what you would expect the target market to be for a single seat hybrid automobile that gets 120 miles per gallon according to the demographic, psychographic, and behavioral segments. Consider such factors as gender, age, marital status, occupation, household size, household income, interests, and beliefs about global warming, gasoline prices, and the like. How might you determine this?

4-5. Choose five people from your market segment to research with a survey. Write 10 questions in a scaled format and ask the survey participants to frame their responses on a scale of 1 to 5, or design your own range. Also ask five open-ended questions (questions that cannot be answered with a yes or no, or scaled response).

Key Concept Questions

4-6. Which four factors should market research include and why?

4-7. Write a positioning statement for your business, or one that you can envision, using the format provided.

4-8. Assess where you think your product or service is in the product life cycle. Where is it and why did you reach this conclusion?

4-9. Read and interpret the chart in **Figure 4-2**.

  a. Which single provider has the largest market share? What is the percentage?

  b. What share do the two largest suppliers enjoy together?

  c. How much bigger is IBM's share than Apple's?

  d. If there are approximately 100 other smaller makers of personal computers, about how much market share would each have on average?

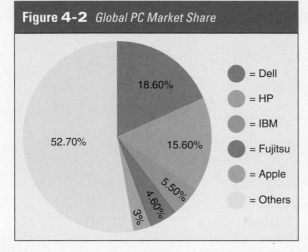

Figure 4-2 *Global PC Market Share*

18.60% = Dell
15.60% = HP
= IBM
= Fujitsu
= Apple
= Others
52.70%
5.50%
4.60%
3%

[3]2007 American Veterinary Medical Association, Schaumburg, IL.
[4]Ibid.

Application Exercises

Order food at three different restaurants/vendors; then answer the following:

4-10. Did you observe any differences in how the employees handled your order? Compare and contrast them.

4-11. Relate what you believe to be the marketing vision of each restaurant based on what you observed. Write a positioning statement for each restaurant.

4-12. Examine the market for each restaurant, using the four methods of market-segmentation analysis: geographic, demographic, psychographic, and behavioral.

4-13. Where do you conclude each restaurant is in the product life cycle?

Exploring Online

4-14. Go online and conduct an industry-wide search for competition for your business or one that interests you. Illustrate a profile of the competition (this may be written using a word-processing program or shown as a table using Excel). It should include minimum and maximum prices, minimum and maximum ordering times, and any other information you feel is pertinent.

BizBuilder Business Plan Questions

4.0 Opportunity Analysis and Research

A. Describe your target customers along as many dimensions as you have defined (demographic, geographic, needs, trends and decision-making processes).

B. Describe the research methods you used to develop this section (surveys, focus groups, general research, and statistical research).

4.1 Industry Analysis (Remember to Correctly Cite Sources)

A. What is the industry or set of industries within which your organization operates (include any applicable NAICS codes and/or SIC codes)?

B. What factors influence the demand for your product or service?

C. What factors influence the supply of your product or service?

D. How large is your total industry (historic, current, projected size)?

E. What are the current and anticipated characteristics and trends in the industry?

F. What are the major customer groups for the industry (consumers, governments, businesses)? Describe them in detail.

G. How large is your target market (number of customers, size of purchases, frequency of purchases, trends)? Quantify it. Describe the entire potential market and the portion that you will address or target.

4.2 Environmental Analysis

A. Perform a SWOT (strengths, weaknesses, opportunities, and threats) analysis of your organization. Remember that strengths and weaknesses are internal to your organization and opportunities and threats are external.

B. What external/environmental factors are likely to impact your business? How likely are they?

C. Are there customers for your business in other countries? How do you plan to reach them?

4.3 Competitive Analysis

A. How do you define/describe your competition, both direct and indirect?

B. Describe your competitive advantage(s) along the dimensions of quality, price, location, selection, service, and speed/turnaround as they apply.

C. Find three competitors and describe them. Use the comparative analysis tables in Chapter 3 to perform a qualitative assessment and/or quantitative analysis.

D. Describe any international competitors who may be able to access your customers. How do you intend to compete against them?

E. Describe your strategy for outperforming the competition.

F. What tactics will you use to carry out this strategy?

G. What barriers to entry can you create to block out competitors? How will you do so?

American Electrical: Understanding the Market Sparks a New Venture

Tom McCormick
(American Electrical, Inc.)

Entrepreneur Tom McCormick was the vice president of sales for an $800-million global manufacturer of electrical components when he proposed an idea for expansion to his boss. By creating another company to sell accessory items to the 50 percent of the market not being supplied through their existing company because of distribution restrictions, the business could generate considerable additional profits. McCormick led the skunkworks project (small, loosely organized group working outside of the mainstream processes) that created a business plan and proposals. The projections were extremely favorable, but due to other pressing issues within the organization, it was ultimately decided that the concept did not fit the company's strategy.

McCormick always wanted to have his own business: "I talked about it constantly to the point where some close friends made fun of me!" In college, he had sold T-shirts, met with business brokers, and networked. When his present employer rejected his expansion proposal, McCormick decided it was time to take the business plan and run with it. "I knew where my first 100 sales were going to be and I had already researched who and how." He found suppliers, starting with one in Germany, and hired a graphic designer to produce two short product catalogs. In July 1997, he took $60,000 from his retirement fund and founded American Electrical, Inc. It wasn't an easy start, even knowing who to talk to and how to sell; it was still an uphill battle to get people to change. Offering a 20 percent discount to market pricing was one good reason for the potential customer to take a look. In the end, it was persistence that prevailed—never giving up—as well as making it as easy as possible for the customer to make a seamless change in the specifications, while improving margins.

Today, McCormick's company generates approximately $4 million per year in sales and has five full-time employees. It operates out of a 5,000-square-foot office/warehouse in Richmond, Virginia. American Electrical imports electrical and electronic-control components from 12 companies, primarily in Europe, for the industrial-controls marketplace in the United States. Tom McCormick took his business plan and turned it into a successful venture.

Courtesy of American Electrical, Inc.

Case Study Analysis

4-15. In what areas of the market did McCormick do research before starting his business?

4-16. What research methods would you recommend for American Electrical today? Name three specific sources of information.

4-17. How did McCormick identify American Electrical's market? Name the segmentation method and the segment he chose.

4-18. What is the role of marketing in McCormick's business?

Russell Simmons, Hip-Hop Entrepreneur

Russell Simmons turned off his cell phone and took a rare moment to admire the view from his fourteenth-floor office in midtown Manhattan. At 47, Simmons knew he had a lot going for him. As the president of Rush Communications, he sat at the helm of a constellation of successful enterprises, including a record label, a clothing line, a philanthropic arts foundation, and a multimedia production company. Lately, he had been thinking about how to leverage his influence as a hip-hop mogul to inspire young people to get involved in social issues, such as voter registration and education reform. Yet, when he was growing up in Hollis, Queens, in the 1960s and 1970s, Simmons never could have imagined that his life would have turned out like this.

Window of Opportunity

Early on, Simmons decided that he wanted to make his own way in the world. His father had been a teacher, and his mother worked as a recreation coordinator. Both enjoyed stable jobs, but Simmons was not driven by a need for security. He wanted to live a fast-paced life and call his own shots. In 1977, Simmons, who never liked school very much, enrolled at the City College of New York as a sociology major. That year, something happened that permanently changed the course of his life. He went to hear a rap artist named Eddie Cheeba perform and was amazed to see how the rapper had cast a spell over the audience with his freestyle rhymes. In Simmons's own words:

> Just like that, I saw how I could turn my life in another, better way. . . . All the street entrepreneurship I'd learned, I decided to put into promoting music.[5]

At that time, rap and hip-hop were underground musical styles, but Simmons set out to change this. He believed that rap music had the potential to reach a larger audience, and so he teamed up with another aspiring rap producer, Rick Rubin. Rubin had built a recording studio for rap artists in his New York University dorm room. Together, they decided to transform Rick's studio into a viable record label. By 1985, Def Jam Records was officially underway.

Def Jam experienced its first surge of success when it scored a hit with Run DMC's remake

Russell Simmons, media mogul.
(Ray Tamarra/Getty Images)

of the Aerosmith classic, "Walk This Way." Bridging the worlds of rock and rap music turned out to be a stroke of genius. Simmons and Rubin single-handedly introduced a whole new market of mostly white, suburban, heavy-metal music fans to hip-hop. Suddenly, Run DMC was being featured on MTV, and rap was no longer an underground fad.

Marketing Insight: Authenticity Matters

Simmons learned an important lesson from Run DMC's success. He realized that these artists had gone to the top of the charts because they had remained true to their street style and musical origins. Whereas Run DMC may have popularized wearing gold chains, branded sneakers, and nameplate belts among suburban teenagers, these were the fashions that its core audience of urban youth had already embraced. Simmons understood that

[5]Russell Simmons, *Life and Def: Sex, Drugs, Money + God,* New York: Crown Publishing, 2002.

being perceived as *authentic* was key to making it in his segment of the music industry.

> You have to tell the truth. It endears you to the community. The [people] can smell the truth, and they're a lot smarter than the people who put the records out.[6]

Simmons knew how to market his product, and his ability to promote rap music and the hip-hop lifestyle was influenced by how close he was to it.

Simmons has maintained this philosophy of "keeping it real" throughout his business career. It permeates everything he does and is even reflected in his preference for wearing Phat Farm sweatshirts instead of Brooks Brothers suits. Since those early days, Simmons has gone on to launch many other business ventures, which are all geared toward the same target market: urban teens and young adults. This market has the power to influence the tastes and preferences of other consumers.

Simmons's Empire Grows

In 1999, Simmons sold his stake in Def Jam records to Polygram Records for over $100 million. He has since focused his energies on developing the various entertainment, fashion, and multimedia companies that make up Rush Communications. Simmons's business goals have evolved from promoting hip-hop music to developing new products and services for the urban youth market.

Simmons also began using his status as a taste-maker and hip-hop entrepreneur to influence public debate about political issues. In 2002, he organized a "youth summit" in New York, featuring hip-hop artists such as Jay-Z and Alicia Keyes. When Simmons put out a call for political action over the airwaves, some 20,000 students showed up at New York's City Hall to protest the mayor's proposed cuts to the education budget. Simmons has demonstrated that he has the skill and sophistication to market ideas as well as products and services. He continues to sit at the helm of Rush Communications, where he keeps his radar attuned to new opportunities in the marketplace.

Case Study Analysis

4-19. Why do you think Russell Simmons has been successful?

4-20. Describe the target market that Simmons is trying to appeal to in all of his business ventures (demographic, geographic, psychographic, and behavioral). What does this target market value?

4-21. Simmons grew up surrounded by hip-hop music and culture. In what ways did this give him an advantage in the marketplace? How might his insider's knowledge also function as a limitation?

4-22. Brainstorm a business idea that you could pitch to Russell Simmons that would be appropriate for his brands and interests. What market research would you need to conduct in advance to assess whether your idea has the potential to be successful?

4-23. Russell Simmons invested $5,000 to start Def Jam and then later sold his business to Polygram Records for $100 million. Calculate Simmons's return on investment (ROI).

Case Sources

Jennifer Reingold, "Rush Hour," *Fast Company* magazine, no. 76, November 2003.

Russell Simmons, *Life and Def: Sex, Drugs, Money + God,* New York: Crown Publishing, 2002.

---

[6]Jennifer Reingold, "Rush Hour," *Fast Company* magazine, no. 76, November 2003.

Developing the Right Marketing Mix and Plan

Learning Objectives

1. Combine the four Ps—product, price, place, and promotion—into a marketing mix.

2. Choose the attributes of your product or service.

3. Price your products for success.

4. Find the best location for maximum efficiency and effective distribution.

5. Select the mix of promotion to use for your business.

6. Add the fifth P, philanthropy, to your business.

7. Recognize the importance of a marketing plan.

8. Apply breakeven analysis to evaluate your marketing plan.

© amana images inc./
Alamy

"I found that if you give the consumer a snapshot where he could see himself as he really is and the way he wants to be portrayed, people really respond to it."

—Thomas Burrell, founder, the Burrell Communications Group

All Mercedes-Benz marketing, from the price of the cars to the advertisements in magazines that cater to people who buy expensive things, is designed to remind customers that it makes luxury automobiles. If Mercedes lowered the price of a sedan, would that damage the customer's belief in its market position as a provider of luxury cars? This is the question that working through the next step of the marketing process will help answer. Mercedes illustrates the importance of getting the marketing mix—product, price, place, and promotion—right. Without an effective combination of these elements, any business is likely to fail.

Mercedes positions its products as luxury purchases.
(© Tim Scrivener/Alamy)

The Four Marketing Factors

Learning Objective 1

Combine the four Ps—product, price, place, and promotion—into a marketing mix.

promotion the use of advertising and publicity to get a marketing message to customers.

The four Ps—product, price, place, and **promotion**—together will communicate your marketing vision and competitive advantage to your customer. If you tweak one P, you will have to pay attention to how it affects the others. If you raise your price, for example, are you now still selling the product in the right place? Or will you need to move to a location that will put you in contact with consumers willing to pay the higher price? Where will you promote your product now? Will you have to take out ads in different magazines or newspapers to reach these new consumers?

As you choose the elements of your marketing plan, always keep your vision in mind. What is the benefit your product or service in providing to customers?

- **Product.** The product or service should meet or create a customer need. The product is the entire bundle, including the packaging. Your customer might not be consciously aware of your packaging, but that does not mean it is unimportant. Starbucks revolutionized the American coffee shop in part by introducing Italian names for the different serving sizes.

- *Price.* A product has to be priced low enough so customers will buy it and high enough for the business to make a profit. Price should also reflect your marketing vision. If you are marketing a luxury item, a relatively low price might confuse the consumer, who will be led to wonder about its quality.

- *Place.* The location where you choose to market your product—whether in a retail storefront, in a customer's home, on an online store, or from a cart on the street—must be where customers who will want or need it shop. Selling bathing suits on a beach in Alaska in February is not going to fill a customer need. Where should you go to bring your product or service to the attention of your market? If you are selling luxury items, you will need to place them in stores that are visited by consumers who can afford them.

- *Promotion.* Promotion is the development of the popularity and sales of a product or service through advertising, publicity, or other promotional devices, such as discount coupons or giveaways. Publicity is notice that is free; advertising is purchased. If a newspaper writes an article about your business, it is publicity. If you buy an ad in that newspaper, you are advertising.

Product: What Are You Selling?

Steve Jobs and Steve Wozniak were in their early twenties in California when Jobs sold his Volkswagen minibus and Wozniak sold his Hewlett-Packard calculator to raise the $1,300 that started Apple. They soldered together circuit boards with three other friends to fill their first substantial order.

Jobs made sales calls to every computer store in the area with their one sample machine and finally convinced a small start-up store in Mountain View to order 50 circuit boards. The owner agreed to pay Apple $548 for each and then had to add the remaining components.

Jobs and Wozniak had one month to build the 50 circuit boards, but they did not have the money to buy the necessary parts. Using the order from the store, though, the partners found a supplier that was willing to give them $25,000 worth of parts on 30-day credit. They started building the circuit boards. By the end of the month, they had built 100 and delivered 50 to the store in Mountain View. They paid the supplier on the 29th day. Apple has come a long way since then.

Your business, no matter how humble its beginnings, may have the potential to grow into a multimillion-dollar company, so it is important that you think through every step of its development. How you define and refine your product or service will have a tremendous impact on your ability to grow.

Create Your Total Product or Service Concept

Learning Objective 2

Choose the attributes of your product or service.

A *product* is something that exists in nature or is made by human industry, usually to be sold, whereas a service is *intangible*—work, skills, or expertise provided in exchange for a fee. Your product will be defined by its physical attributes (e.g., size, color, weight, shape), its performance characteristics (e.g., speed, strength, efficiency, durability), and its pricing, branding, and delivery. It is the total package that people are buying. A dirty stone glued onto a piece of cardboard with a scrawled, handwritten price and sold by a kid on the street would be a much different product from a Pet Rock (a real fad product in 1975) that has been cleaned, polished, placed in a nest of attractive packing material in a box, and displayed in an upscale retail store.

A parallel exists for services. Think about a one-person cleaning business in which the individual looking tired and unkempt arrives in an old, battered van. Compare that image with neatly dressed, uniformed personnel who arrive in a new vehicle (with the name of the company on the side of the truck) to work as a team. Retail service businesses sell directly to the end consumer, but there are also service companies that have only wholesalers or manufacturers as customers.

The selection of your product or service and its branding will be a critical part of your marketing mix.

Focus Your Brand

The key to building a successful brand is to focus tightly on the primary benefit you want customers to associate with your business. Marketing expert Al Ries explains that the most successful businesses *focus* their marketing, so that they come to own a category in the customer's mind.[1] You want to own a benefit the way Volvo owns safety or Federal Express owns guaranteed overnight delivery.

Oprah Winfrey, philanthropist and media mogul.
(Mark J. Terrill/AP Images)

Even entertainers can become a brand. Oprah Winfrey is among the most recognized and wealthiest celebrities in the world today. She is the head of a global media empire and a philanthropist.[2] From her roots in Nashville radio, Winfrey became a media mogul, with such well-recognized names as *The Oprah Winfrey Show*; *O, The Oprah Magazine*; *O at Home*; *OWN—the Oprah Winfrey Network*; *Oprah & Friends Radio*; Harpo Films; and Oprah.com.[3]

Ford's Costly Failure: The Edsel

One of the most notorious examples of a product whose failure was caused by lack of focus is the car Ford introduced in 1958, the Edsel.

Ford tried to include every kind of gadget and design element the company thought consumers might possibly want in a car. They also manufactured multiple models at varying prices that overlapped some Mercury models, thus confusing the public as to which brand was a step up from which. The goal seemed to be to try to appeal to everyone, but Ford soon learned that trying to appeal to everyone resulted in appealing to almost no one. The Edsel had no outstanding benefit that could be clearly marketed. In addition, consumers didn't really like the way the car looked. In the first year, some 63,000 Edsels were produced when sales had been estimated at 200,000 cars.

Even millions of dollars of promotion will not make consumers buy a product they do not want. Ford spent more money on advertising the Edsel

[1] Al Ries, *Focus: The Future of Your Company Depends on It*, New York: HarperCollins, 2005.

[2] Oprah.com, accessed July 9, 2009, *http://www.oprah.com*.

[3] *The Oprah Winfrey Show* and *Oprah & Friends* are registered trademarks of Harpo, Inc. *O, The Oprah Magazine* and *O at Home* are registered trademarks of Harpo Print LLC.

Global Impact . . .

One for One

Blake Mycoskie, TOMS
Shoes founder.
(Kennell Krista/AP Images)

Blake Mycoskie, Founder and Chief Shoe Giver of TOMS Shoes, conceived of his global for-profit enterprise using cause-related marketing while taking a vacation from another entrepreneurial venture. He was in Argentina when he happened to connect with an American woman who was involved in a shoe drive. She told him about the need for shoes on a consistent and reliable basis. He saw the traditional *alparagata*, a ubiquitous casual canvas shoe, as an opportunity, and developed the concept of "one for one"—or donating one pair of shoes for every pair sold.

Blake worked with his polo instructor, Alejo Nitti, to modify the traditional designs of the alparagata for the U.S. market.

During the first year of sales, Blake, his family, and friends personally distributed 10,000 pairs of shoes in Argentina. By September 2010 TOMS had given its one millionth pair. Today, TOMS Shoes are distributed in over 60 countries through some 100 Giving Partners.

TOMS Shoes are made in Argentina, China, and Ethiopia with expansion into India, Kenya, and Haiti planned. The company is working to ensure that by 2015 one-third of its Giving shoes will be produced in the same regions where they will be distributed.

Source: TOMS Shoes, accessed July 30, 2013, http://www.TOMS.com. Blake Mycoskie, *Start Something That Matters,* New York: Spiegel & Grau, 2011.

---

than had ever been spent on one line of cars. Three years and $350 million later, Ford pulled the plug on the Edsel.

Ford's Focus on Success: The Mustang

Ford learned from the Edsel mistake, however. When it introduced the Mustang in 1964, it focused very clearly on a target market of people from 20 to 30 years old who wanted a powerful car. Everything about the Mustang, from its design to the colors it came in, was focused on appealing to young drivers. The marketing described the Mustang as "For the young at heart." Only one model was offered. The Mustang was a huge success.

Interestingly, Ford tried to offer some luxury and four-door versions of the Mustang a few years later. Sales dropped, probably because the brand had started to lose focus. The Mustang remains one of Ford's stronger sellers.

How to Build Your Brand

You can build your own brand by following these steps:

logo short for logotype, a company trademark or sign.

- *Choose a business name that is easy to remember, describes your business, and helps establish mindshare,* which refers to the degree to which your business will come to mind when a consumer needs something your product or service could provide.
- *Create a logo that symbolizes your business to the customer.* A **logo** (short for *logotype*) is an identifying symbol for a product or business. A logo is printed on the business's stationery, business cards, and flyers. When a logo has been registered with the U.S. Patent and Trademark Office to protect it from being used by others, it is called a **trademark**—defined as any word, name, symbol, or device used by a manufacturer or merchant to distinguish a product. The Nike "swoosh" is an example of a logo. So are McDonald's "golden arches."

trademark any word, name, symbol, or device used by an organization to distinguish its product.

Some of the world's best known trademarks.
(© Anatolii Babii/Alamy)

A company uses a trademark so that people will recognize its product instantly, without having to read the company name or even having to think about it. Rights to a trademark are reserved exclusively for its owner. To infringe on a trademark is illegal.

- ***Develop a good reputation.*** Make sure your product or service is of the quality you promise. Always treat your customers well. You want people to feel good when they think of your brand or hear it mentioned.
- ***Create a brand personality.*** Is your brand's personality youthful and casual, like the Gap's? Safe and serious, like Volvo's? Customers will respond to brand personality and develop a relationship with it. Personality will reinforce your name and logo.
- ***Communicate your brand personality to your target market.*** What type of advertising will best reach your target market? Where should you put flyers? Which newspapers, magazines, or blogs does your target market read?

Always present yourself and your business in such a way that people will have confidence in your product or service. Anything that harms your reputation will damage your sales and profits. Anything that boosts your reputation, on the other hand, will have a positive impact on your business. Toward that end:

- Provide a high-quality product or service.
- Maintain the highest ethical standards.
- Define your product or service clearly. *Focus.*
- Treat your employees well.
- Make all your advertisements positive and informative.
- Associate your company with a charity.
- Become actively involved in your community.

Rishi Shah
(ContextMedia Inc.)

Shrada Agarwal

Step into the Shoes . . .

Context Media: Health

Shradha Agarwal and Rishi Shah were undergraduate students and entrepreneurs at Northwestern University when a late-night discussion led to the idea for "hyper-local health content delivery." In 2006, they cofounded ContextMedia, Inc., in Chicago.

Shradha describes the company's role as follows: "We empower the doctor to educate and inspire patients to live healthier. Everything we do, we measure up to that mission."[4] In fact, the firm brands itself as a "for-benefit" company, meaning that is a for-profit enterprise that exists for social benefit.

ContextMedia owns and manages digital healthcare networks that deliver programming at the point of care. The content is developed by experts in their fields and vetted by medical advisors. Context Media: Health places complimentary television systems in the patient waiting rooms of medical professionals

that provide programming on diabetes, cardiovascular health, and rheumatology. The patient-education playlist is dynamic and targets videos most suitable to each demographic and practice by means of adaptive learning algorithms (similar to that of Pandora, for music). Physicians can customize the content of the playlists and add their own; they do not need to worry about maintenance. The more than 20,000 participating healthcare providers agree to play the programming during office hours.

Revenue comes from commercials placed between patient-education segments. There are no infomercials or advertorials, and health care providers can have specific commercials removed from their video. Advertisers include firms such as nutrition and fitness companies, pharmaceutical firms, and medical-device manufacturers. Advertising rates are based on a complex formula determined by the time of ad exposure, quality of ad exposure, and strength of call-to-action follow-on from patients.

ContextMedia has found a way to deliver targeted advertising for its clients while offering important health information where it is likely to have impact.

Price: What It Says about Your Product

Learning Objective 3

Price your products for success.

As reported by author Jay Conrad Levinson, a study of consumers in the furniture industry found that price came ninth when they were asked to list factors affecting their decision to make a purchase.[5] Confidence in the product was the number one influence on buying patterns, and quality was number two. Service was third.

Although your customers may not think exactly like those who buy furniture, the lesson here is that simply undercutting your competitors' prices will not necessarily win you the largest market share. For one thing, consumers tend to infer things about the quality or specialness of a product or service based on its price. Therefore, entrepreneurs should consider not only the economics but also the psychology of pricing. Studying the pricing strategies of your competitors will tell you a lot about the importance of psychological pricing in your market.

Strategies and Tactics for Effective Pricing

Pricing strategy is not a one-size-fits-all proposition. As you define the marketing strategy for your company, including your target market(s), competitive advantages, and overall marketing mix, the range of appropriate pricing strategies emerges. For example, an exclusive, highly specialized product targeted toward upscale consumers would logically be priced at a premium. However, at its point of introduction, it may have to be priced in

---

[4]ContextMedia, "Team – Shradha Agarwal," accessed July 30, 2013, http://www.contextmediainc.com.

[5]Jay Conrad Levinson, *Guerrilla Marketing Attack*, Boston: Houghton Mifflin, 1989.

line with the competition until it is established as the market leader. At the same time, mass-market products may be priced at a lower level.

Common pricing strategies include the following:

Value Pricing Strategy

One popular strategy is **value pricing**, which is offering "more for less" by underscoring a product's quality, while at the same time featuring its price. Value pricing is not just price cutting. It means finding the balance between quality and price that will give target customers the value they seek. Value pricing began in the 1990s as a reaction to the glitzy eighties, when marketers used high prices to pitch luxury and extravagance. Companies like Wal-Mart and Procter & Gamble have effectively used value pricing. This strategy requires a delicate balance, to avoid customer confusion by sending mixed marketing signals.

value pricing "more for less" strategy that balances quality and price.

Prestige Pricing Strategy

When a firm sets high prices on its products or services to send a message of uniqueness or premium quality, it is using a **prestige pricing** strategy. For this to be effective in the long run, the product must fulfill the image and sustain it.

prestige pricing the pricing strategy in which a firm sets high prices on its products or services to send a message of uniqueness or premium quality.

Cost-Plus Pricing Strategy

The **cost-plus pricing** method is one of the most commonly used; you add a desired profit margin to your cost. It is the simplest cost to calculate, once your complete costs are known and your desired rate of return is established. However, it fails to take marketing vision and market conditions into consideration. For example, the competitive environment is neglected, as is the value of the product or service to your targeted customers. **Markup pricing** is a cost-plus pricing strategy in which you apply a predetermined percentage to a product's cost to obtain its selling price. Markup pricing is described in greater detail later in this chapter.

cost-plus pricing takes the organization's product cost and adds a desired markup.

markup pricing a cost-plus pricing strategy in which a predetermined percentage is applied to a product's cost to obtain its selling price.

Penetration Pricing Strategy

Penetration pricing offers a low price during the early stages of a product's life cycle to gain market share. Japanese companies employed this method to dominate consumer electronics markets. Toyota deliberately priced the Prius at about $3,000 below cost to secure a leadership position in the emerging market for hybrid automobiles in the United States. The risk with penetration pricing is that, once you start at a low price, it is often difficult to increase it or to depend on cost savings to increase profitability. "Freemium" pricing is an example of this strategy—commonly used by app developers in which one aspect of a service is offered for free, but customers will have to pay to enjoy the full range (or premium benefits) of the service.

penetration pricing a pricing strategy that uses a low price during the early stages of a product's life cycle to gain market share.

Skimming Price Strategy

The **skimming** strategy is the opposite of penetration strategy because it seeks to charge high prices during the introductory stage when the product is novel and has few competitors, to take early profits, and then to reduce prices to more competitive levels. This strategy recognizes that competition and product maturity may erode the firm's capacity to maintain the pricing. RCA used this strategy when it introduced color television in the 1960s.

skimming pricing strategy seeks to charge high prices during a product's introductory stage, to take early profits when the product is novel and has few competitors, and then to reduce prices to more competitive levels.

Meet-or-Beat-the-Competition Pricing Strategy

It is common for service businesses to use **meet-or-beat-the-competition pricing**, which entails constantly matching or undercutting the prices of

meet-or-beat-the-competition pricing constantly matching or undercutting the prices of the competition.

your competition. Airlines tend to compete intensely by lowering their ticket prices. The more you can show that your business is different from your competition, however, the less you will have to compete with your price. When Sir Richard Branson started Virgin Atlantic Airways, he offered massages and individual videos at each seat. His marketing emphasized how much fun it was to fly on Virgin. This strategy was successful, even though Virgin did not always offer the lowest fares.

Follow-the-Leader Pricing Strategy

follow-the-leader pricing
a pricing strategy that is similar to a meet-or-beat-the competition method, but uses a particular competitor as the model for pricing.

A **follow-the-leader** strategy is similar to a meet-or-beat-the-competition tactic but with a particular competitor as the model for pricing. Typically, the leader is a dominant firm in the industry and controls a substantial portion of market share.

Personalized Pricing Strategy

personalized pricing
a dynamic pricing strategy in which the company charges a premium above the standard price for a product or service to certain customers, who will pay the extra cost.

Personalized (dynamic) pricing charges a premium above the standard price for a product or service to certain customers, who will pay the extra cost. Personalized pricing is particularly applicable when the product or service is highly valued by certain customers—perhaps on the basis of performance or uniqueness or for outstanding delivery or service aspects. Such pricing works only when products are not easily compared and customers are not likely to communicate with one another.

Variable Pricing Strategy

variable pricing strategy
provides different prices for a single product or service.

Many businesses use this type of method, often without conscious recognition of it. They offer discounts, credit terms, and price concessions to their customers, setting different prices for the same product or service and thus **variable pricing**.

Price Lining Strategy

price lining the process of creating distinctive pricing levels.

In addition to selecting among the specific pricing strategies described previously, you may want to create distinctive price levels for your merchandise. **Price lining** is the process of creating graded pricing levels. For example, Sears carries "good, better, best" product lines in its paint products and prices them accordingly.

Place: Location, Location, Location!

Learning Objective 4
Find the best location for maximum efficiency and effective distribution.

Regarding place, the type of business you are running will influence your choice of location and your distribution system for reaching out from that place to your customers. For a retail business, site location is the key to attracting customers. Ideally, you will want your store or business to be where your target market is. This is why you did the work of consumer and market analysis to figure out who your customers are. You should know where they shop. Your goal is to find a location you can afford that is also convenient for your potential customers.

Wal-Mart has done an efficient job of choosing locations that are ideal for attracting potential customers who are underserved by similar retailers. Wal-Mart was the first mass-merchandise store to choose locations in rural and semirural markets. This strategy has been so successful that other stores now seek to be located near a Wal-Mart.

Of course, the Internet has made it possible for an entrepreneur to start a retail business out of her home and reach customers all over the world. This has led to the belief that online stores can forgo the expense of renting a location that caters to foot traffic. As the old saying goes, however, you can lead a horse to water, but you can't make him drink. How do you get your customers to your site and then induce them to buy? If you are planning to start a retail business online, you must figure out how you will attract customers to your Web site—that is, how you will *market* the site.

For nonretail businesses, the key to location might be cost or convenience rather than proximity to the market. Wholesale businesses that require a great deal of storage space do best in areas where rent or property costs are low, where there is space for large commercial buildings, and where their trucks and vans have easy access to roads and highways.

The Internet is making it easier for people who provide services—such as graphic or Web-site design, writing/editing, or accounting—to start businesses at home. Communication with clients is easy via e-mail, and the overhead costs are certainly minimal. On the other hand, working at home requires discipline and a tolerance for isolation. If you are the sort of person who would not be happy spending your workdays by yourself, it is probably not for you.

Key Factors in Deciding on a Location

The key factors in deciding on a location are dependent upon the nature of the business and its customers. Considerations include the following:

- access for customers
- access to suppliers
- climate and geography
- convenience
- cost of facilities (rent, construction, and the like)
- demographics
- economic conditions and business incentives
- governmental regulations and laws, including environmental impact
- labor pool
- proximity to competitors
- visibility

Figure 5-1 shows the factors affecting location decisions at the country, regional/community, and site levels.

Promotion: Advertising + Publicity

Promotion is the use of advertising and publicity to get your marketing message out to your customers. Advertising, as discussed in Chapters 2 and 4, is paid promotion that is intended to generate increased sales of your product or service. Examples of advertising include television commercials, billboards, and magazine ads. Publicity is free mention of a company, person, event, product, or service in media outlets, such as newspapers and magazines or on radio or television.

◀ **Leaning Objective 5**

Select the mix of promotion to use for your business.

Use Integrated Marketing Communications for Success

Marketing communications promotes your business to your current and prospective customers and to those who influence purchasing and sales decisions. All communications include an originator (source), a specific message (overt and/or subliminal), a channel for dissemination, and a target

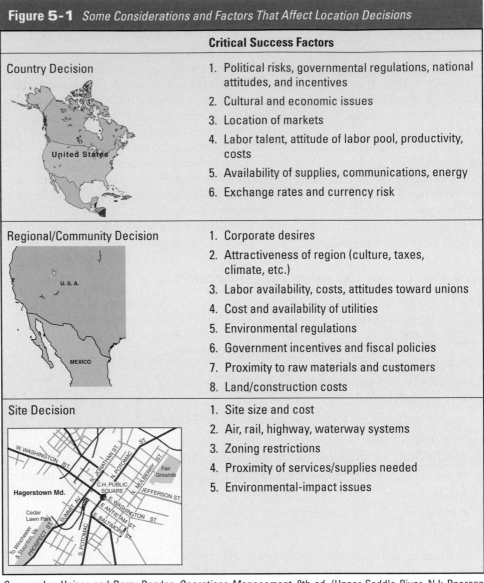

Figure 5-1 *Some Considerations and Factors That Affect Location Decisions*

	Critical Success Factors
Country Decision	1. Political risks, governmental regulations, national attitudes, and incentives 2. Cultural and economic issues 3. Location of markets 4. Labor talent, attitude of labor pool, productivity, costs 5. Availability of supplies, communications, energy 6. Exchange rates and currency risk
Regional/Community Decision	1. Corporate desires 2. Attractiveness of region (culture, taxes, climate, etc.) 3. Labor availability, costs, attitudes toward unions 4. Cost and availability of utilities 5. Environmental regulations 6. Government incentives and fiscal policies 7. Proximity to raw materials and customers 8. Land/construction costs
Site Decision	1. Site size and cost 2. Air, rail, highway, waterway systems 3. Zoning restrictions 4. Proximity of services/supplies needed 5. Environmental-impact issues

Source: Jay Heizer and Barry Render, *Operations Management,* 8th ed. (Upper Saddle River, NJ: Pearson Prentice Hall, 2007), p. 249.

(receiver). By integrating your communications across platforms and media, you can maximize the impact of your communications resources, primarily as expended for promotion.

Promotion has expanded beyond advertising, sales promotions, and personal selling to include database marketing, sponsorships, direct marketing, alternative marketing, e-active marketing, and public relations. Promotion should be based on an organization's strategic marketing plan and is meant to create a unified communications program. Promotional tools, applied well, get your marketing message out to your customers.

Reinforce the Company's Unique Selling Proposition

Your unique selling proposition (USP) becomes valuable to your organization when it is successfully communicated to your target customers and motivates initial and repeat purchasing decisions. Integrated marketing

Entrepreneurial Wisdom . . .

Take advantage of resources available to learn more about target markets.

http://www.nielsen.com	Consumer geodemographic information
http://www.adage.com	Advertising statistics, trends, and examples
http://www.strategicbusinessinsights.com	Values and lifestyles (VALS) psychographic segmentation
http://www.iVillage.com	Target information—Web site for women
http://www.targetmarketnews.com	Target information—African Americans
http://www.pode300.com	Target information—Hispanics
http://www.heremedia.com	Target information—gays and lesbians

communications frame the USP in multiple media to reach targeted audiences and communicate the salient information, evoke positive emotional responses, and create effective, favorable impressions. A unique selling proposition that is not successfully communicated is worthless. A unique selling proposition that is successfully communicated can be priceless.

Promotional Planning

Vast quantities of promotional material bombard consumers and businesses daily, frequently creating unwanted clutter and noise. Nonetheless, these efforts represent opportunities for quality customer contact. The challenge for an organization is to determine the best opportunities and to create promotions that effectively cut through that clutter and noise, engage the attention of prospective customers, and generate profitable sales. Successful promotions are the result of solid planning. For promotional planning to be integrated in the operations of your organization, all of the business's components will need to have meaningful roles in the process. There are many types of options available and **Exhibit 5-1** shows several of them.

Determine a Promotional Budget

The creation and careful control of a promotional budget is essential to marketing success. A well-structured budget—based on the promotions

Exhibit 5-1 *Advertising and Promotion Options*		
Promotion Methods		
Advertising specialties	Coupons	Public speaking
Banner ads	Direct mail	Samples or demonstrations
Billboards	Directories	Signs
Blogs	Flyers	Social media
Broadcast media	Networking	Special events
Brochures	Newsletters	Sponsorships
Business cards	Print media	Telemarketing
Catalogs	Promotional clothing	Web sites

Step into the Shoes . . .

Twitter—Tweeting Becomes Ubiquitous

Jack Dorsey, Co-Founder & Chairman, Twitter.
(© ZUMA Press, Inc./Alamy)

Twitter founder Jack Dorsey, joined by Evan Williams and Biz Stone, created Twitter in 2006. This online social networking and blogging service is designed to send and read text-based messages of up to 140 characters. The company experienced a huge jump in users through its marketing at the 2007 South by Southwest Interactive (SXSWi) conference. The founders placed large plasma screens that streamed Twitter messages in high-traffic areas of SXSWi, and it attracted users. Today, the company is internationally recognized by its "blue bird" logo.

Twitter promotes business marketing, suggesting the use of Twitter buttons, promotions, and advertisements. Businesses can use Twitter for up-to-date content and to connect with targeted customers. They can develop devoted bases of Twitter followers for their brands. Companies make use of Twitter contests and sweepstakes, events, direct response, product launches, and integration of both offline and online marketing campaigns.

One use is in making television more interactive. Companies have used Twitter to encourage people to watch live broadcast events, like the MTV Video Music Awards or the Oscars. Viewers are urged to send "tweets," which may be flashed across the television screen during such shows as *The Bachelorette* and *Dancing with the Stars*.

Readers of online articles are often asked to post the articles on social media, such as Facebook, and to tweet links on Twitter.

Twitter has become ubiquitous.

Source: Twitter, accessed August 3, 2013, http://www.twitter.com.

---

opportunity analysis, promotional objectives, and an effective strategy—will encourage measurement and control. These in turn will foster improved performance. There is no single correct way to determine your promotional budget. However, several methods can be used in combination:

- percentage of sales method,
- competitive spending method,
- excess funds approach, and
- objective and task method.

Percentage of Sales

Percentage of sales is a common way of calculating the aggregate budget. It is the simplest to use because the budget will be derived either from the prior year's sales or anticipated sales. The percentage to be used is best taken from a comparable industry.

The percentage of sales method of budgeting is preferable to not establishing a promotional budget at all but has drawbacks. This approach seems counterintuitive to the promotional needs of an organization, because you will spend less when you most need a promotional boost—when sales are low. You only spend more when you are selling more (i.e., doing well). Also, this technique may not take competitive spending into account and does not consider your overall strategy.

Competitive Spending

Competitive spending is another way to set a promotional budget. It entails researching your competitors to determine their level of spending. This may be as simple as investigating financial-statement studies or as complex as attempting to track and cost out all their promotional activities. This meet-the-competition method is often used in highly competitive markets, in which the objective is to prevent market-share loss.

Although knowing what your competitors are doing and spending is a good practice in general, setting your budget based on theirs is not ideal. This benchmarking implies that you can make a complete assessment, that the competition is spending the optimal amount of money, and that this would also be the right amount for you to spend. The competition may be spending according to available funds or percentage of sales, or basing the budget on favored media and advertising salespeople. In other words, competitors may not be optimizing their promotional budgets, so copying what they do could be counterproductive.

Excess Funds

The excess-funds approach to promotional budgeting means determining what is left over after other expenses are calculated, and allocating funds based on the results. This is among the least strategic of the budgeting methods because it is completely internally driven. It may be better than having no budget at all, but using an excess-funds method is not recommended. It is a particularly poor option for start-up companies and businesses in periods of rapid growth, because they will rarely have excess funds to spend at the very times when promotional efforts are most needed.

Objective and Task

The objective and task method is to budget expenditures according to the strategies and tactics developed to reach specific promotional objectives. This entails building a budget based on what you have determined is needed to be successful. To create this type of budget, management enumerates the objectives for the year and the budget required to reach them. The more specific you can be about measurable objectives and the specific media and methods to be used, the stronger the focus of your efforts will be, and the more effective your budget can be as a guide and control.

There is no single perfect method of establishing a promotional budget because there is both art and science involved. As an entrepreneur, using the best aspects of each of the above methods is your best bet. Rather than determining what you can easily afford, estimate what you would ideally spend and then decide how much you could invest to accomplish your goals and objectives. Know where you plan to spend the funds and how you will monitor and control them. This budget should support your strategy and tactics but not control them so tightly that you cannot take advantage of opportunities as they arise.

The Advertising Advantage

The topic of advertising and advertising management has certain glamour about it. The popular media have portrayed advertising as a fast-paced, highly creative, fun, and lucrative career choice. At the same time, advertising itself has often been shown to be false, manipulative, deceitful, and coercive. For some, it is something to be avoided whenever possible. Others embrace it and enjoy wearing branded clothing, promotional T-shirts, caps, and the like; they watch the annual NFL Super Bowl more for the television ads than for the football. It does not matter where you fall personally in this spectrum. It is important to determine the best, most effective method of advertising for your business to reach your prospective and current customers—to run a successful company. This is where advertising management becomes critical.

As with any aspect of your business, advertising has specific objectives that make it an integral component of the marketing mix. Advertising aids the marketing effort by creating brand awareness and reinforcing the purchasing decision. The objectives of advertising and its management should reflect those of a comprehensive promotional plan, and successful advertising will achieve them all:

- building brand and image,
- providing information,
- persuading,
- stimulating action, and
- reinforcing the purchasing decision.

Advertising builds brand recognition and creates a positive image. For example, General Mills' Lucky Charms cereal and Malt-O-Meal's Marshmallow Mateys are essentially the same product, with slightly higher nutritional value in Marshmallow Mateys; however, Lucky Charms have significantly greater advertising and brand recognition and command a higher average price per pound ($3.17 versus $2.20).[6] Advertising can work for your company, too.

Types of Advertising

Advertising is not a one-size-fits-all proposition; rather, it comes in so many forms and options that the types of advertising seem to be limitless. However, there continue to be two primary categories: institutional advertising and product advertising. **Institutional advertising** provides information about an organization rather than a specific product and is intended to create awareness about the firm and enhance its image. This advertising is exemplified by the Bank of America ads that focus on the company as the "bank of opportunity" rather than promoting particular financial products. Such advertising is designed to build general credibility. **Product advertising** is designed to create awareness, interest, purchasing behavior, and post-purchase satisfaction for specific products and services. Typically, small, entrepreneurial companies expend their limited resources on product advertising. For example, they may want to promote a particular item or a storewide sale.

Institutional and product advertising are not mutually exclusive. For example, all advertisements placed by an organization might include a tag line or feature that extols a virtue of the firm—such as local ownership, length of time in business, quality of workmanship—while at the same time promoting a particular product or service. Or, ads that are more "evergreen" (of longer duration), such as those in directories, may be more institutional, while those that are less durable (e.g., daily or weekly newspaper ads) can focus on products. How you decide to promote your organization and products, respectively, should be defined by your strategy, your industry, available options, and your budget.

Media Planning and Buying: Focus on Your Customer

An effective advertisement for a business typically concentrates on the benefit a product or service provides to the customer. This is why it is important that you base marketing decisions on your customer analysis. You will need to know who your customers are and what their lifestyle is in order to know how to reach them. It is crucial to understand the media habits of people in your target market. What are their reading, viewing,

institutional advertising provides information about an organization, rather than a specific product, and is intended to create awareness about a firm and enhance its image.

product advertising is designed to create awareness, interest, purchasing behavior, and post-purchase satisfaction for specific products and services.

---

[6]Pricing and nutritional information, Malt-O-Meal, accessed May 13, 2009, http://www.malt-o-meal.com.

Exhibit 5-2 *Pros and Cons of Selected Advertising Media*

	Pros (Advantages)	Cons (Disadvantages)
Television	Low CPM Highly targeted with cable High intrusion value High reach and frequency potential Message is immediate	High cost for ad campaign Clutter Short life of advertising message High production costs Long lead time
Radio	Relatively low cost Short-term commitment Short lead time Message is immediate Promotes recall Mobility (radios travel with people)	Auditory only Clutter—information overload Short life of advertising message Low attention Local nature
Newspapers	Geographic targeting Short lead time Flexibility and credibility More copy potential Direct response possible	Expense may be high Demographic targeting is limited Short shelf life Declining readership Waste Poor-quality production
Magazines	Targeted reader interest High color/production quality Direct response possible Long shelf life	Lack of immediacy Exposure dispersed over time Longer lead times High cost
Internet	Targeting potential Moderate cost Global reach Relatively short lead time	Not ubiquitous Banner ads feed-click through to full ads
Outdoor Media	Repeat exposures Geographic selectivity Moderate CPM High-impact, dramatic ads possible	Limited message size Limited demographic selectivity Initial design and production costs Short exposure time

and listening patterns? What appeals to them? What doesn't? If you are advertising a snowboarding trip, it would be a waste of money to take out an ad in a magazine featuring tropical vacations. Avoid wasting money in outlets in which the audience won't be interested in your product or service. Combine this common-sense approach with solid research to maximize advertising effectiveness. **Exhibit 5-2** shows the pros and cons of select media options.

Marketing Materials Should Reinforce Your Competitive Advantage

All promotional items for your business should reflect and reinforce your marketing vision, which in turn will reinforce your competitive advantage. They should include the name of your business, your logo, and a slogan, if you have one.

In fact, you will have a much stronger impact if all your business materials are tied together with a strong, coordinated image. This should extend beyond your logo into the format, font style, colors, and look of your materials. As you create your stationery and business cards (identity set), advertisements, publicity pieces, and brochures, the consistency of your image will help to convey your competitive advantage. If it is done well, your image will be in alignment with your strengths, and you will be positioned for success. If this is done poorly, you will lack credibility, which can then harm, if not destroy, your chances of success.

Sales-Promotion Solutions

Sales promotions provide another set of tools to add to the mix. Various efforts to increase sales volume by specified levels, which either reward purchases or provide discounts, can be effective for both consumer and business-to-business marketing. Sales-promotion solutions do not have to be complex or sophisticated to work. In fact, it is best if they are simple and easily understood. If an incentive program is difficult to figure out, customers may simply not bother to participate, because it won't be worth the trouble. **Exhibit 5-3** identifies some common types of sales-promotion methods.

When to Use Promotional Tools

Promotional tools are best used when the strategy calls for a highly targeted, time-limited boost in response. They can be excellent ways to encourage new-product trials and to raise seasonal performance. They should always be part of the overall marketing strategy and budget. Contests and sweepstakes are a way of securing product engagement and, potentially, repeat sales. Coupons require the customer to actively seek out your product on the shelves or to contact you for the product or service. *Sampling* brings the product or service message to life for the customer through experience. Bonus packs and tie-ins lead to a trial of additional products.

Advertising Specialties

The strategic inclusion of specialty items can be an effective sales-promotion tool. Freebies are always a draw with customers, but do not disappoint them with gifts that look and feel cheap. The best giveaways are those that are useful, such as pens, on which prospective customers will see your business name and contact information. Visit wholesalers, or search online to investigate discount prices on quantities of calculators, watches, pens, or other appropriate items.

Trade Show Exhibits

The use of trade show exhibits is a proven promotional strategy for business-to-business companies and can also succeed for certain types of consumer marketing. This is one of the best forms of experiential

Exhibit 5-3 *Sales-Promotional Tools*	
Consumer	**Business-to-Business**
Coupons	Incentives
Contests and Sweepstakes	Contests
Refunds and Rebates	Refunds and Rebates
Sampling	Sampling
Premiums	Allowances
Tie-ins	Trade Shows
Bonus Packs	

Trade show exhibits for business-to-business promotion.
(© Andrew Holt/Alamy)

marketing, because it lends itself to having prospective customers try out your products, or having services demonstrated. Whereas the cost of trade-show space, a professionally designed booth, transportation, and other related expenses can be relatively high, the opportunity to have impact can make it worthwhile. This is particularly true for business-to-business marketing that can be accomplished at targeted industry and professional conferences, providing an efficient means to reach many potential customers with a consistent message. Tsnn.com reports that there are 15,000 trade shows, exhibitions, public events, and conferences each year. The keys to successful trade show promotion include preparation, booth training for all staff, quality exhibits, careful goal setting, and consistent efforts to reap the benefits of the investment.

Mall Carts or Kiosks

For many seasonal businesses, or businesses that are working to create full-scale retail operations, mall carts or kiosks may prove effective. Signing a multiyear lease for a retail store is not likely to make sense for a seasonal business such as a Christmas or Halloween operation. Sometimes such businesses can find vacant retail spaces to rent for just a season, or they can partner with others to rotate in and out of a store. In other situations, they can create a business model of changing seasonal inventory and focus. However, for many business owners, these options are not practical or desirable, and having a temporary retail location is preferable. Also, if you are working on a retail concept and want to try out the idea—products, prices, and so forth—a temporary location is a good opportunity to "test-drive" your business before investing in longer-term, more costly retail space. Such a trial run may also provide sales and marketing data that will assist you in attracting financing. For an investment of $1,500 to $10,000, plus inventory and rental fees, you could be up and running.

Alternative Marketing

The marketing approaches described thus far have been practiced for many, many years and are considered to be tried-and-true methods. However, marketing has evolved with changing times and technology to include more recent forms. The following is a discussion of some of the alternative types of marketing in use today.

Guerilla Marketing

guerilla marketing
original, unconventional, and inexpensive small-business promotional strategies.

Jay Conrad Levinson coined this term in 1984 with his book of the same name, meaning original, unconventional, and inexpensive small-business strategies. Since then, **guerilla marketing** has expanded to encompass other kinds of unconventional categories, such as viral marketing, buzz marketing, word-of-mouth advertising, and grassroots marketing. The notion is to find creative, surprising ways to get your message to your target market without spending a fortune.

Buzz Marketing

buzz marketing another name for word-of-mouth marketing.

Buzz marketing is another name for word-of-mouth marketing. It can occur naturally (*organic buzz marketing*) or can be jump-started by the organization (*amplified buzz marketing*). It is one of the most effective forms of promotion available, because people are sharing their excitement and enthusiasm about a product or service with others who trust and value the advice. By giving your customers an outstanding experience, you are encouraging organic buzz marketing. If you can create *amplified* buzz marketing, it will boost recognition and marketing still further.

Product Placement/Branded Entertainment

The use of product placement in television, movies, and other scenarios is another good promotional tool. Such positioning reaches consumers on a more subconscious level and does not contain an overt sales pitch. When the movie *E.T.* hit the theaters, Reese's Pieces were included as a product placement, and they continue to be associated with the movie decades later. The duration of in-show brand appearances during an average hour of prime-time network television programming was just short of 8 minutes during the fourth quarter of 2008, with an average of almost 14 minutes during unscripted reality programming, and just about 6 minutes per hour during scripted programs.[7] Today, there are firms that focus on locating and negotiating product placements. Two such companies are Creative Entertainment Services (http://acreativegroup.com) and GameShowPlacements.com (for game and cable shows). Depending on your product, it might be worthwhile to pursue placement possibilities.

Lifestyle Marketing

In order to successfully market their brands, companies are striving to align them with consumer needs, interests, desires, and values and to apply lifestyle marketing with knowledge of consumer behavior. This form of marketing reaches beyond the traditional demographic approaches to engage customers based on how they live.

In-Store Marketing

There are numerous options for carrying out in-store marketing, whether in your own space or in businesses where your product is sold.

---

[7]TNS Media Intelligence press release, May 4, 2009.

Exhibit 5-4 *Other Media Venues*		
Ambient Advertising	**Indoor Advertising**	**Other Advertising**
Parking Lots	Movie Theaters	Carryout Menus
Tunnels	Video Games	Shopping Bags
Escalators	Bathroom Stalls	Advertising on Clothing
Benches (Bus Stops)	Commercial Trucks	Brochure Racks
	Airline In-Flight	

For example, signage, shelf placement, sampling, and "edutainment" can all play roles. Which ones are best will depend on your marketing strategy.

- *Samples or demonstrations.* Offer samples of your product to potential customers who pass by your business. Or take samples to a high-density location, such as a park or town square. If you are selling a service, consider demonstrating it outdoors or in a mall (get permission first). When you open your business, you can give away samples of your product to encourage potential customers to tell their friends about it. Many large businesses, such as BJ's Wholesale Club and Sam's Club, make extensive use of sampling and edutainment to encourage purchases. Edutainment is the combining of education and entertainment to make a more lasting impression on an audience. You might use this method to show the originality of your product and engage the interest of prospective customers.

- *Point-of-purchase and shelf placement.* These opportunities include the complete visual component of your in-store placement, such as packaging, any couponing with shelf placement, and special-display units. By putting products where prospective customers will be drawn to them visually, you are increasing the chances of purchase. Well-designed point-of-purchase materials can make a huge difference in sales.

edutainment a promotion that combines education and entertainment to make a more lasting impression upon an audience.

Other Media Venues

In addition to the methods and media described previously, a number of other venues are worth noting. These options should also be considered in your planning. See **Exhibit 5-4** for examples of other media venues.

E-Active Marketing

Internet advertising has grown with the expansion and adoption of Internet technology. Not only have entrepreneurs and major corporations come to include online advertising and promotion as a regular part of the media mix, entire industry segments have evolved to serve the interactive media field. The number of advertising opportunities is seemingly infinite, ranging from Google to little-known sites. Businesses can elect to use display advertising in the form of banner ads, pay to raise their visibility within search engines, or partner with other online companies to obtain mention and have customers directed to them. They can use social media, blogs, and e-mail. These options continue to expand and evolve at a rapid pace. When the two major components of Internet marketing—e-commerce and interactive marketing—combine, e-active marketing results. You can make the best use of e-active marketing approaches by marrying them with

e-active marketing when the two major components of Internet marketing— e-commerce and interactive marketing—combine.

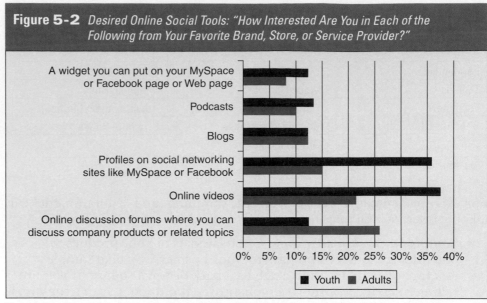

Figure 5-2 *Desired Online Social Tools: "How Interested Are You in Each of the Following from Your Favorite Brand, Store, or Service Provider?"*

Base: U.S. online adults, age 18 and older, and U.S. online youths, ages 12 to 17.
Source: North American Technographics Media and Marketing Online Survey, Q2 2008; North American Technographics Youth Online Survey, Q2 2008; Forrester Research, Inc., *The Social Tools Consumers Want from Their Favorite Brands*, report prepared by Josh Bernoff, April 16, 2009, http://blogs.forrester.com/a/6a00d8341c50bf53ef01156f827e11970c-pi (accessed May 21, 2009).

your offline efforts to create a unified approach to marketing. **Figure 5-2** shows the level of interest in adults and young people in various types of information from businesses.

E-Commerce

The provision of an electronic storefront and/or other forms of electronic commerce is one way of implementing your marketing strategy.

Interactive Marketing

Interactive marketing means addressing customers, absorbing their input, and reaching out to them again to make it clear you have paid attention. Whereas interactive marketing is not necessarily online marketing, the collection of customer information and subsequent communication is facilitated by the Internet. An excellent example of the use of interactive marketing is Amazon.com, which collects user information to make purchase recommendations.

Online Advertising

This typically takes the form of banner advertisements on Web sites. These can be highly targeted, based on the online habits and interests of consumers. Such ads can be purchased directly from the owners of the Web sites on which you wish to advertise, or through brokers who purchase online advertising for specific target markets. For small, local businesses with a Web site, it may be possible to work in partnership with other companies that sell complementary products to create "click-through" opportunities for their customers to visit your site, and vice versa. This type of advertising includes pay-per-click (PPC), wherein firms bid on keywords that they would expect their potential customers to use to search for their type of goods and services, so that they can appear in the search return results as "sponsored ads" and thus become considerably more visible. With this type of advertising, you only pay when someone clicks on your advertisement.

Brand Spiraling

Integrating a company's conventional offline branding strategy with its Internet strategy can be accomplished through **brand spiraling**, which is the term for businesses using conventional approaches through print and broadcast media to drive traffic to their online sites. Once customers are guided to those sites, the companies take advantage of Internet interactivity and learn more about them. This knowledge is used to further refine sales and marketing tactics. They also can use e-mail addresses and other information to reach customers in additional ways. The brand spiral is a continuous learning and changing process for a firm that assists in reaching and influencing customers through both online and offline tactics.

brand spiraling integrating a company's conventional offline branding strategy with its Internet strategy by using conventional approaches to drive traffic to its online sites.

Blogs

A **blog** (short for "Web log") is a journal that appears on the Internet periodically (perhaps daily) and is intended for the public. **Blogosphere** is the collective term used for all the blogs on the Internet. Businesses provide blogs, often written by their owners, to create a personal connection with customers. These are only effective if the information is kept interesting and timely, and customers are led to the sites by other promotions. Some blog-hosting services include:

blog (short for Web log) a journal that appears on the Internet periodically and is intended for the public.

blogosphere the collective term used for all the blogs on the Internet.

Blogger	http://www.blogger.com
Medium	http://www.medium.com
Twitter	http://www.twitter.com (microblogging)
Tumblr	http://www.tumblr.com
TypePad	http://www.typepad.com
WordPress	http://www.wordpress.com

Online Social Networks

The number and variety of online social networks has grown phenomenally in recent years and is expected to continue to do so. Social networks such as Facebook, MySpace, and LinkedIn, as well as those for interest-specific niches (e.g., Flickr, imeem, BlackPlanet, Classmates.com, Goodreads, and MyHeritage), continue to evolve, as new uses emerge. Advertising opportunities on these networks are more complex than those on Web sites with banner ads. For many social networks, advertising and promotion are either banned or taboo. Some users create subtle promotion through what are essentially scripted conversations on the sites. These "undercover," deceptive marketing efforts are intended to appear as if they happened naturally and are referred to as **stealth marketing**.

stealth marketing undercover, or deceptive, marketing efforts that are intended to appear as if they happened naturally.

Recent research by the Internet Advertising Bureau in the United Kingdom addressed the methods for maximizing results from social networking: "The IAB research found that exclusive content, which appeals to 28% of social networkers, and genuine interest in the message, which attracts 37%, are the keys to a positive response from consumers on social networks. And because only 5% say they actively dislike messages from brands, there are big opportunities for marketers who can hit the right notes."[8] In addition to online social networking, the option of **mobile social networking**, the updating of social-network sites via mobile handsets, is increasing. This means that users are accessing the information at all times and at any location.

mobile social networking the updating of social-network sites via mobile handsets.

---

[8]Emma Hall, "How to Get the Most Out of Social Networks and Not Annoy Users," *Advertising Age*, April 27, 2009, p. 30.

Consumer-Generated Advertising

This can include campaigns in which the company solicits advertisements from customers. You can ask them to create videos, stories, print advertisements, and the like—generally through a contest or promotion—to fuel your advertising programs. Such promotion creates authenticity and credibility in a way that company-generated advertising cannot. Consumer-generated media (CGM) also comes in a variety of forms that are not specifically solicited by companies, such as message-board posts, blogs, and forum commentary. Consumer-generated advertising can generate enthusiasm and engagement as well as increased loyalty.

Viral Marketing

viral marketing the process of promoting a brand, product, or service through an existing social network, where a message is passed from one individual to another—much as a virus spreads.

Interactive marketing options have been expanded through technology to include **viral marketing**, a term coined by Tim Draper of Draper Fisher Jurvetson. Viral marketing is defined as the process of promoting a brand, product, or service through an existing social network, typically an online version, such as MySpace or Facebook, in which a message is passed from one individual to another—much as a virus spreads. A viral campaign can be an e-mail or a video that may include hyperlinked promotions, advertisements, games, or online newsletters. There has to be a reason for people to tell others about the message or pass it along, such as entertainment value, uniqueness, or potential financial reward.

In August 2007, with a budget of $150,000, TuitionBids.com's agency, Fanscape, created a viral marketing campaign targeted at 16- to 24-year-old high school and college students and their parents, with the intention of creating buzz and awareness of the company and to drive sales leads.[9] The strategy used was to "surround and deliver [the] target audience with valuable information." Fanscape used a multifaceted approach that "fused online Content and Promotional Integration programs, Social Media techniques, dedicated emails from Fanscape's proprietary database, a pay-per-click (PPC) campaign, and display ad buys to create as many relevant touch points with the target audience as possible." This included an e-mail to 100,000 members of the Fanscape database. The results included "32 million branding impressions with over 40,000 clicks, 150 WOM placements, 26 editorial placements for over 2 million unique views, 8 contests, adding another 3 million unique views, a 25% open rate on the Fanscape email (well above industry averages)." Tuitionbids.com had a 6.4% conversion rate, which is about three times the industry average.

By creatively generating interest in and excitement about your story, or an aspect of your business, you can work to create a viral campaign. Kristen Smith, Executive Director of WOMMA, suggests the following six ways to keep people talking about your company and your products:[10]

1. Listen, speak, listen some more.
2. Be transparent and disclose.
3. Evaluate ROI continually.
4. Spread the word, not the manure.
5. Encourage an enterprise-wide WOMM.
6. Employ online and offline WOMM.

[9]WOMMA Web site http://www.womma.org, accessed May 18, 2009, http://www2.fanscape.com/tuitionbids/womma0808.html.
[10]Kristen Smith, "Six Ways to Leverage Word-of-Mouth," March 1, 2009, accessed May 17, 2009, http://www.womma.org.

Publicity Potential

Generating Publicity

Publicity, sometimes referred to as public relations (PR) is defined by the Institute of Public Relations as "the planned and sustained effort to establish and maintain goodwill and mutual understanding between an organization and its public." Always save any publicity you receive. Frame and display articles prominently in your place of business, and make copies to send or hand out when appropriate. Each item of publicity has enormous value. Consumers give publicity credibility because it is not paid for.

Publicity is important for a small business, which often has a negligible advertising budget. To get publicity, you will need to email or fax a pitch letter and a press release to the magazine, newspaper, TV station, or radio station you hope to interest.

A **pitch letter** sells the story. It tells the person reading it why he or she should be interested in your business. A **press release** is an announcement sent to the media to generate publicity and states the "who, what, when, where, and why" of a story. A pitch letter allows you to explain the story behind the press release and why it would be interesting and relevant to the media outlet's readers, listeners, or viewers.

Before mailing or faxing a pitch letter and press release, call or e-mail the outlet and ask to whom you should direct the material. Say something like, "My name is Jason Hurley, and I'm a young entrepreneur with a downtown delivery/messenger service. I'd like to send WKTU a press release about the commitment we have just made to donate 10 hours of free delivery service per month to Meals on Wheels for seniors. To whom should I direct a press release?" Sometimes you can find this information on the Internet.

Get to know the print, radio, and television journalists pertinent to your business, so you can get publicity. The most effective way to get notice for your venture is to contact the reporters yourself. You might be tempted to hire a professional publicist, but many reporters are bombarded by these people and would rather hear directly from you. Dedicate a block of time to send e-mails and make phone calls pitching your business and explaining why your story is worth covering. Be totally honest and build positive relationships. The type of reporting you want will develop most often because the writer comes to care about your story and sees it as interesting and important. Once you establish rapport and credibility with reporters, they are likely to call you for stories, insights, and comments.

Press releases can generate positive reports and stories about your business in newspapers and magazines and on radio stations. For newspapers, make sure you send the release about a month before the event you are promoting. Follow up with a phone call two weeks later and then one week after that (a week before the occasion). The precise timing will depend on the media outlet and its publication or broadcast schedule.

Telling the Story

Younger entrepreneurs can have an advantage here because relatively few young people start their own businesses. The print, radio, and television journalists in your area may want to hear about you.

Bear in mind, however, that reporters are looking for stories that will interest their readers. It is fine to send out a press release announcing the opening of your business, but be aware that it will not be a story until it

pitch letter correspondence designed to explain the story behind a press release, and why it would be interesting and relevant to the media outlet's readers, listeners, or viewers.

press release an announcement sent to the media to generate publicity that explains the "who, what, when, where, why, and how" of a story.

is up and running. There is no point sending out a pitch letter and press release until you are actually in business and have a story to tell. The fact that your business is open, however, doesn't necessarily translate into a story of interest. You have to make the connection:

- Who are you and what has happened to you or what have you done that would make you and your business an interesting story?
- Did you have to overcome any obstacles to start your business?
- What about your product or service is unique? Is it something your community really needs?
- When is a specific event taking place that is newsworthy or of interest for a story?
- Where are you locating the business, or where is the event or activity occurring?
- How has your business changed you and helped members of your community?

Always answer the basic questions of who, what, when, where, why, and how for reporters. Answers to these questions will help them determine whether your story might be of interest to their readers or viewers. Reporters are busy people, so keep your answers to these questions tight and concise. Try to find one focus or angle for your story. What's the "hook"?

Sample Press Release

As we have said, in order to tell your story in a press release or to a reporter, you will have to answer the six basic questions: who, what, when, where, why, and how. Who are you; what did you do; when, where, why, and how did you do it?

A press release must provide contact information (name, phone, e-mail, and Web site) and answer the six questions (see **Figure 5-3**).

Follow Up a Press Release

Follow up your press releases with phone calls and e-mail. Try to reach the journalists directly. Be polite but persistent. Do not wait for a newspaper or radio station to return your call; call again (but do not make a pest of yourself)—they receive many press releases every day.

We suggest saving all publicity you receive to show potential customers because it has enormous value. Simply put, it can attract more publicity and more customers. Remember, it has greater credibility for consumers than advertising, which you will have paid for.

Public Relations

In addition to publicity, you can build positive public relations for your company through involvement in the local community and in local, national, and international professional and business organizations that pertain to your business. Some ways of doing this are with special events, sponsorship, networking, and public speaking.

Special Events

Hold contests, throw parties, or put together unusual events to attract attention and customers. Contests and sweepstakes can gather valuable names for your mailing list. Or, participate in special events yourself to gain publicity for your business, through effective networking with other participants.

Figure 5-3 *Sample Press Release*

Entrepreneurship Event demonstrates that Springfield Technical Community College students can create their own jobs

EET Contact: Laura MacMinn
Telephone: (800) 930-8021 x705
Cell Phone: (704) 252-1516
Email: laura@iempact.com

FOR IMMEDIATE RELEASE

The Extreme Entrepreneurship Tour features high-energy keynotes and informative workshops designed to provide prospective entrepreneurs with the inspiration they need to follow their dreams, pursue their passions and start their own businesses

Springfield, MA — With the economy continuing to struggle, job hunters - particularly high school and college students and recent college grads - are faced with limited options, often spending weeks or months looking for a job. Yet, what many job seekers don't realize is that creating their own job is within reach.

On Thursday, Sept. 26, the *Extreme Entrepreneurship Tour* will be returning to Springfield for a high-energy event, hosted by Springfield Technical Community College. The event will take place from 9:30 AM to 1:30 PM in the STCC Gymnasium located at One Armory Square in Springfield, MA. Some of the country's top young entrepreneurs, who have developed or sold successful companies before the age of 30, will be the event's keynote speakers.

Since 2006, the *Extreme Entrepreneurship Tour* has hosted more than 500 entrepreneurship events in 35 states, inspiring thousands of young people across the country to become entrepreneurs. Entrepreneur speakers showcase the many faces of entrepreneurship, showing the many opportunities for starting a business beyond the overnight success tech startups we always hear about.

Michael Simmons, co-founder of the Extreme Entrepreneurship Tour and Partner at Empact believes that prospective entrepreneurs should be inspired, not intimidated, by the current economic climate. "More than half the companies on the 2009 Fortune 500 list were launched during a recession or bear market." Simmons said, "Technology and globalization have made it very inexpensive to start a business. Now is the best time to become your own boss."

Laura Mac Minn, Director of Events for the Tour, agrees with Simmons that there is opportunity, and that opportunity can have a significant impact on the job market: "Today's students can be critical forces in the next 10 years to help create the 20 million jobs we need in this decade."

Registration for the Extreme Entrepreneurship Tour at Springfield Technical Community College is available at http://extremetour.org/stcc. On-site registration will begin at 8:30 AM. on Thursday, September 26.

About Empact

Empact's work focuses on facilitating a culture of entrepreneurship in communities across the globe through exposure, celebration and early stage startup support.

Empact has held more than 500 events exposing young people to the many faces of entrepreneurship through its Extreme Entrepreneurship Tour (www.extremetour.org); and annually celebrates the role of young entrepreneurs through the Empact Showcase and Empact100 list of top young entrepreneurs age 30 and under (www.empact100.com).

Each year, Empact brings together the top thought leaders from the entrepreneurship education ecosystem to share and act on the biggest ideas during the Empact Summit. For more information, please visit iempact.com

Source: Empact.

Sponsorships

Sponsoring a local sports team is a great way to involve your business in the community and meet potential customers. Sponsorships are a way of advertising. Just be certain that the audience for the event fits into your target market.

Networking

Networking, as discussed in Chapter 1 with respect to effective selling, is the exchange of information and contacts. When done efficiently and courteously, networking can serve as an excellent promotional vehicle.

Public Speaking

Taking advantage of opportunities to address members of your target audience as a guest speaker or paid professional can build your credibility and attract recognition and customers. In addition, you will have the added weight of the sponsoring organization behind you.

The Fifth P: Philanthropy

Learning Objective 6

Add the fifth P, philanthropy, to your business.

philanthropy a concern for human and social welfare that is expressed by giving money through charities and foundations.

foundation a not-for-profit organization that manages donated funds, which it distributes through grants to individuals or to other non-profit organizations that help people and social causes.

not-for-profit organization an entity formed with the intention of addressing social or other issues, with any profits going back into the organization to support its mission.

There is a long, proud connection in the United States between entrepreneurs and **philanthropy**, a concern for human and social welfare that is expressed by giving money through charities and foundations. A **foundation** is a **not-for-profit organization** that manages donated funds, which it distributes through grants to individuals or to other non-profit organizations that help people and social causes.

Many philanthropic organizations in the United States were established by entrepreneurs. As a business owner, you have a responsibility to help the communities you serve. The people and causes you choose to support should be those that matter to you. Your philanthropy may also generate positive publicity because you can choose to promote your giving. For this reason, marketing experts sometimes consider philanthropy as the fifth marketing P.

The Bill and Melinda Gates Foundation is one of the world's largest charitable organizations, with $36.4 billion in capital. This money comes from the personal wealth they earn from Microsoft and other contributions. As a private foundation, it is required by the federal government to give away a minimum of 5 percent of the fair market value of its assets every year (this is usually less than the earnings on the fund's investments). The Gates Foundation provides a great deal of money annually, $3.4 billion in 2012, to other charities. These in turn use the money for social and community programs that the Gates Foundation supports, such as those relating to education and health care.

You can be philanthropic even if you have very little money to donate. You can give your time in volunteer work for an organization you believe in. If you know how to paint a house, for example, or if you have some carpentry skills, you could contribute your efforts to help build homes for an organization such as Habitat for Humanity, which provides affordable housing for low-income families. If you love animals, volunteer at your local animal shelter, as can your employees.

cause-related marketing promotional efforts inspired by a commitment to a social, environmental, or political cause.

Cause-Related Marketing

Cause-related marketing—marketing inspired by a commitment to a social, environmental, or political cause—is an easy way to work philanthropy into your business. You could donate a fixed percentage of your profits (perhaps 1 or 2 percent) to a particular charity and then publicize that fact in your marketing materials. Or you could donate something from your business. If you own a sporting goods store, you could donate uniforms to the local Little League team.

Encourage your employees to participate in charitable work, too. Volunteerism is a great way to improve morale and make a difference. AT&T pays its employees to devote one day a month to community service.

Gaining Goodwill

Many entrepreneurs try to make a difference in their communities by giving money and time to organizations that help people. Microsoft, for example, made it possible for the National Foundation for Teaching Entrepreneurship (NFTE—now the Network for Teaching Entrepreneurship) to develop an Internet-based entrepreneurial curriculum, BizTech. Microsoft has donated both money and computer-programming expertise to this project. Why would Microsoft do this?

- Bill and Melinda Gates and other Microsoft executives believed in NFTE's mission and wanted to help young people learn about business. The Internet-based program has made it easier to teach entrepreneurship to youth around the world.
- Microsoft gained publicity and goodwill, which is composed of intangible assets, such as reputation, name recognition, and customer relations. Goodwill can give a company an advantage over its competitors.

goodwill an intangible asset generated when a company does something positive that has value.

Not-for-Profit Organizations

Not-for-profit organizations are those whose purpose is to serve a public cause rather than to accrue profits for investors. The Internal Revenue Service classifies nonprofits under section 501(c)(3) in the tax code. These corporations are tax-exempt. This means they do not have to pay federal or state income taxes, and they are neither privately nor publicly owned. Essentially, a board of directors controls the operations of a 501(c)(3) nonprofit.

Such well-known institutions as the Boys and Girls Clubs of America, the YMCA, the Girl Scouts, the Red Cross, and Big Brothers/Big Sisters are all examples of nonprofits. Their founders were social entrepreneurs and, although they did not earn large sums of money personally and could not have sold their organizations at a profit, they received great satisfaction and made a difference. Wendy Kopp of Teach for America and Michael Bronner of Upromise are two examples of social entrepreneurs who founded innovative and successful nonprofit organizations.

Founded in 1990 by Wendy Kopp, Teach for America recruits recent college graduates to become public school teachers. The organization has trained some 28,000 young teachers and placed them in two-year teaching positions in under-resourced schools, where they impact about 750,000 students annually.

Upromise was founded in 2001 by Michael Bronner, a former marketing executive who became a social entrepreneur. Bronner felt strongly that the cost of sending a child to college had become much too expensive for most families. He believed that there needed to be an effective way of helping families save money for higher education.

Bronner developed the idea that a portion of the money families already spent on popular goods and services, such as groceries and toys, could go into a college savings account for their children. Upromise works with thousands of organizations, such as Sprint, Dell, Century 21, and Expedia.com. Every time a member of Upromise makes a qualified purchase from one of these companies, a percentage of the sale automatically goes into a special college account. By 2013, over $700 million has been saved in this way.

What Entrepreneurs Have Built

Many philanthropic organizations in this country were created by entrepreneurs who wanted to do good works with some of the wealth they had earned. Entrepreneurs have financed great museums, libraries, universities, and other important institutions. Some foundations created by famous entrepreneurs (in addition to the Gates Foundation) include the Rockefeller Foundation, the Coleman Foundation, the Charles G. Koch Foundation, the Ford Foundation, and the Goldman Sachs Foundation.

Some of the most aggressive entrepreneurs in American history, such as Andrew Carnegie, have also been the most generous. In 1901, after a long and sometimes ruthless business career, Carnegie sold his steel company to J. P. Morgan for $420 million. Overnight, Carnegie became one of the richest men in the world. On retiring, he spent most of his time giving away his wealth to libraries, colleges, museums, and other worthwhile institutions that still benefit people today. By the time of his death in 1919, Carnegie had given away over $350 million to philanthropic causes.

You Have Something to Contribute

You may not have millions of dollars to give to your community—yet. But there are many ways you can be philanthropic that will help others, get your employees excited, and create goodwill in your community:

- Pledge a percentage of your profits to a nonprofit organization you have researched, believe in, and respect. Send out press releases announcing your pledge.
- Become a mentor to a younger entrepreneur. Help that individual by sharing your contacts and expertise.
- Volunteer for an organization that helps your community. Find out how you can serve on its board of directors or fill another vital role.
- Sell your product to a charity that you support at a discount. The charity can then resell it at full price to raise money.
- After reflection, you will realize that you have a lot to give. Remember, making a contribution does not necessarily mean donating money. You can provide time, advice, and moral support.

These days, customers have access to a lot of information about what companies do with their money. Make sure you are always proud of your business. Choose to support causes that are important to you and that make business sense, too. Philanthropy will strengthen your relationship with your customers because it goes beyond the sale and into what is truly important in people's lives.

Developing a Marketing Plan

Leaning Objective 7

Recognize the importance of a marketing plan.

The marketing plan can be a stand-alone document or the section of a business plan that identifies the organization's marketing strategy and tactics and presents a comprehensive statement of how it will secure and retain its customers. The plan will include a clear discussion of the product or service, price, promotion, and channels of distribution for the company, and a detailed description of the competition and target market. The marketing plan clarifies how you will sell your products or services and where you fit into the competitive landscape. The primary roles of the marketing plan include:

- demonstrating to potential investors that your company can grow and offer returns,
- identifying the most beneficial target markets for the organization,
- evaluating the competitive and industry environments,
- illustrating the pricing strategy, and
- detailing the promotional plan and budget.

Either a stand-alone marketing plan or one incorporated into a business plan will include the same market-analysis information. The stand-alone plan should also include a *situation analysis*; financial projections and information; an implementation time line or outline; and methods for evaluating success and assuring it, as well as any supplemental supporting materials. As with business plans as a whole, marketing plans should be organic documents that are reviewed and revised on a regular basis to keep them timely and useful.

Marketing Analysis

The analysis of the market is the heart of the marketing plan. This brings together the various strategic and tactical components of the marketing efforts into a single comprehensive section. It is essential that the template for the sales plan include the five Ps of marketing. The product, price, promotion, place, and philanthropy are detailed here. Wrapped around the core marketing strategy and selling plan are the descriptions of the overall market and the specific target market for the company, the marketing goals and objectives, and any future and contingency plans. Future plans could include a discussion of planned research and development as well as any growth designs, whether through product line expansion, additional channels of distribution, or other means. Contingency plans show how your organization will react to moves by your competitors or other changes in the marketplace. They will diagram strategies and options you will use to address these changes and demonstrate your understanding of the need to be prepared for change in a competitive landscape.

Marketing as a Fixed Cost

Let's say you want to launch a new software program. You have researched the consumer environment, pinpointed your market segment, and determined your marketing mix. You are now ready to implement a marketing plan that will get your vision out there. There is one more question: Can you afford to carry out your plan?

Marketing is part of your business's fixed costs. Marketing should not be budgeted as a percentage of sales but rather as money that is needed to drive sales. As you remember, fixed costs are those that do not vary with sales; they include utilities, salaries, advertising, insurance, interest, rent, and depreciation. There are also variable costs, such as commissions, that fluctuate with sales. For a business to survive, though, it must be able to cover its fixed costs. Most fixed costs, such as rent, insurance, and utilities, are hard to cut back if your sales are slow.

Marketing costs are more flexible. They fall into the category of advertising, but may also show up under salaries, if you hire a marketing consultant or full-time marketing staff. They will be a critical component in determining your company's breakeven point and its viability.

Calculate Your Breakeven Point

Learning Objective 8

Apply breakeven analysis to evaluate your marketing plan.

The question is this: Can you sell enough units to pay for your marketing plan? The breakeven point, as discussed in Chapter 2, is the moment at which a business has sold enough units to equal its fixed costs. If you estimate that your market is approximately 3 million people, but you have to sell 5 million units just to cover the cost of your marketing, the plan is not viable.

This is why calculating the breakeven point will tell you if your marketing plan can work. It shows whether you will cover your fixed costs with the number of units you plan to sell. If not, the one place you can cut costs is your marketing plan. However, you should do this with care.

Breakeven Analysis for an Artist

Josh is an artist who supports his painting career by creating unique tank tops with airbrushed designs. The shirts are popular with young women in Manhattan's East Village, and Josh sells the shirts each weekend at a flea market on East 4th Street. Let's say he buys eight dozen (96) tank tops for $576. He airbrushes them and sells them all at the weekend flea market for $1,152. Josh considers one tank top his unit of sale. The cost of goods sold (COGS)—without labor—would be calculated as $576/96 = $6, with selling price per unit $1,152/96 = $12.

- How much did each tank top cost Josh? This is his cost of goods sold (COGS).
- How much did he charge for each tank top? This is his selling price per unit.
- Josh's unit of sale is one tank top.
- Josh's cost of goods sold is $6.
- Josh's selling price is $12.

$12 (Selling Price per Unit) − $6 (Cost of Goods Sold per Unit)
= $6 (Gross Profit per Unit)

- Josh's gross profit per unit is $6 per tank top.

Next, Josh needs to take a look at his fixed costs. Let's say he spends $150 a month on renting his space at the flea market and $30 monthly on flyers (advertising). The balance of his marketing is free—on Twitter and Facebook and through word of mouth. His monthly fixed costs are $150 + $30 = $180. How many tank tops does he have to sell to cover his fixed costs each month? Use the following formula:

$$\frac{\text{Fixed Cost}}{\text{Gross Profit per Unit}} = \text{Breakeven Units}$$

$$\frac{\text{Fixed Cost: } \$180}{\text{Gross Profit per Unit: } \$6} = 30 \text{ Breakeven Units}$$

Josh needs to sell 30 tank tops to cover his fixed costs. Josh typically sells about 20 tank tops each weekend, so in one month he can expect to sell

$$20 \text{ Units} \times 4 \text{ Weekends} = 80 \text{ Units}$$

Josh can spend $30 per month on flyers. He could even afford to add another expense to his marketing plan, such as getting business cards printed or setting up a Web site, from which customers could order shirts and also find out where he would be selling on particular a weekend, as his location varies.

We do need to recognize that Josh did not include any labor cost, because he paid himself from the profits. If Josh were to add in $3 per shirt of labor costs, his COGS would rise to $9, and his gross profit per unit would drop to $3. His new breakeven point would be 60 units. Additionally, any payment for the time it took to sell the shirts would come out of the profits.

Breakeven is the point at which fixed costs are recovered by sales, but variable costs are not included and no profit has yet been made. Once you have determined your breakeven point, the next question in the analysis is, "Can my business reach breakeven in its relevant market?" In the previous example, can Mary Ann's reasonably expect to break even and sell 45 buckets of chicken a day? The answer to this question for your business venture will be in the market research you have conducted to get to this, the last step in creating a marketing plan. You should know the answer. If not, you must conduct further research until you can confidently gauge the viability.

Breakeven analysis is a good tool for examining all your costs and should be performed frequently. It is especially important after you have completed your marketing plan and before you open your business, to see if your plan is realistic.

Chapter Summary

Now that you have studied this chapter, you can do the following:

1. Combine the four Ps—product, price, place, and promotion—into a marketing mix.
2. Determine the attributes of your product or service.
3. Price your products for success. Implement strategies and tactics to reach your goals.
   - Value pricing
   - Prestige pricing
   - Cost-plus pricing
   - Markup pricing
   - Penetration pricing
   - Skimming price strategy
   - Meet-or-beat-the competition pricing
   - Follow-the-leader pricing
   - Personalized (dynamic) pricing
   - Variable pricing
   - Price lining strategies

4. Locate and distribute for maximum efficiency and effectiveness.
   * Know and use the key factors for site selection.
5. Choose where and how to advertise your business.
   * Promotion is the use of advertising and publicity to get your marketing message to your potential customers.
   * Publicity is free mention of your business—in newspapers, magazines, and social media or on radio or television.
   * An advertisement is a paid announcement that a product or service is for sale. Examples of advertising include television commercials, billboards, and magazine ads.
6. Decide how your business will help your community philanthropically.
   * Philanthropy is the giving of money, time, or advice to charities in an effort to help solve a social or environmental problem, such as homelessness, pollution, or cruelty to animals.
   * You can be philanthropic even if you have very little or no money to offer. You can donate your time by volunteering for an organization that has aims you want to support.
7. Recognize the importance of a marketing plan:
   * demonstrating to potential investors that your company can grow and offer returns,
   * identifying the most profitable target markets for the organization,
   * evaluating the competitive and industry environments,
   * illustrating the pricing strategy, and
   * detailing the promotional plan and budget.
8. Apply breakeven analysis to evaluate your marketing plan.
   * Breakeven is the point at which a business sells enough units to cover its fixed costs.
   * Breakeven analysis tells you if your marketing plan is viable. It shows whether you can cover your fixed costs with the number of units you plan to sell.

Key Terms

blog	mobile social networking
blogosphere	not-for-profit organization
brand spiraling	penetration pricing
buzz marketing	personalized pricing
cause-related marketing	philanthropy
cost-plus pricing	pitch letter
e-active marketing	press release
edutainment	prestige pricing
follow-the-leader pricing	price lining
foundation	product advertising
goodwill	promotion
guerilla marketing	skimming pricing strategy
institutional advertising	stealth marketing
logo	trademark
markup pricing	value pricing
meet-or-beat-the-competition	variable pricing strategy
pricing	viral marketing

Entrepreneurship Portfolio

Critical Thinking Exercises

5-1. Select a product or service and explain how it will fit into and complement your marketing mix.

5-2. Discuss how pricing tells a story about your product.

5-3. Where do you plan to locate your business? Explain.

5-4. How do you plan to include philanthropy in your marketing mix?

5-5. Use the following chart to illustrate your marketing mix.

	Your Business
Product	
Place	
Price	
Promotion	
Philanthropy	

5-6. Use computer software to create a logo for your business. Do you intend to trademark your logo? Explain.

5-7. If you were to start a home-based business, what would it be? Why? What key factors would you consider before start-up?

5-8. Why is physical location critical for a distribution business?

5-9. What is the role of demographic information in the selection of a retail-location option?

5-10. Identify a well-known public figure and discuss his or her brand. How has this individual enhanced this brand? How has he or she damaged it?

5-11. Why does viral marketing have such success potential? How can a viral marketing campaign work against a company?

5-12. What role should the unique selling proposition play in a company's advertising strategy?

Key Concept Questions

5-13. Define cost-plus pricing. Why is it used so frequently? What are the drawbacks associated with using it?

5-14. What is penetration pricing? Provide an example of a company that has used penetration pricing to introduce a new product. What was the product?

5-15. Brainstorm five creative ways for a small business with a low budget to advertise and promote its products or services using the latest developments in communications and Internet technology.

5-16. Visit Yahoo! Small Business or another provider of online storefronts. List three advantages and three disadvantages of opening a Web site for your business through such a service.

5-17. Summarize why breakeven is a critical concept for any organization.

5-18. What are the types of communications budgets? What is the best method of budgeting?

5-19. List four common marketing objectives. Explain why each is important.

Application Exercises

5-20. What is the role of demographic information in the selection of a retail-location option? Provide an example of a retailer near you and the demographics that are significant for the company.

5-21. Visit a library (public or university) and locate its reference section. What resources can help you to open a business like Honest Tea? Identify at least six.

5-22. Visit three independently owned businesses (in the same industry) in person. Identify the target market for each (demographic, geographic, psychographic, and behavioral). Note the various advertising and promotional methods in use for each location. Search online for company Web sites. Ask the store owner or manager where the business advertises and whether it creates press releases. Report back on the results.

Exploring Online

5-23. Research and report how much it would cost to run a banner ad on three Web sites. What are the pricing options? Are they listed on the companies' Web sites? Where did you find the information?

BizBuilder Business Plan Questions

5.0 Marketing Strategy and Plan

A. Explain how your marketing plan targets your market segment (geography, demographics, psychographics, behaviors). Be specific.

B. What percentage of the market do you need to capture for your business to be profitable? Explain this.

C. Write a positioning statement for your business using the format from Chapter 4.

D. How do you plan to grow the organization (self-generated, franchising, acquisition)?

5.1 Products/Services

A. What products/services do you intend to market?

B. Explain how your product will meet a customer need.

C. Where is your product/service (not the business) in the product life cycle?

D. Describe the features and benefits of the products/services your business will focus on marketing.

E. What copyrights, trademarks, patents, or other intellectual property do you own or expect to own?

F. How will your organization help others? List all the organizations to which you plan to contribute. (Your contribution may be time, money, your product, or something else.)

G. Do you intend to publicize your philanthropy? Why or why not? If you do, explain how you will work your philanthropy into your marketing.

5.2 Pricing

A. Describe your pricing strategy (value, prestige, cost-plus, penetration, skimming, meet-or-beat, follow-the-leader, personalized, variable, or price lining), structure, and the gross margins you expect to generate.

B. What will your discount structure, if any, be? How will it impact your average price?

C. Will you extend credit to customers? On what terms? If engaging in retail sales, what forms of payment will you accept?

5.3 Promotion

A. Identify the ways you plan to promote your product or service, including the message, the media, and the distribution channels. Describe why you have chosen these methods and why you think they will work. Include a table showing the methods and budgets.

B. Show examples of marketing materials you intend to use to sell.

C. What is your business slogan?

D. What is your business logo? How do you intend to protect it?

E. Where do you intend to advertise (be specific, including identifying reach and frequency)?

F. How do you plan to get publicity for your organization?

G. List ways you intend to provide superior customer service.

H. How will you keep your customer database? What essential questions will you ask every customer for your database? What data will you collect through their purchases?

5.4 Place

A. Where do you intend to sell your product (physical and/or virtual locations)? Describe the advantages and disadvantages of your location(s). If you have a specific site, provide detailed information.

B. What are the surrounding businesses? Access routes?

C. If vehicular traffic is important to your organization, what is the traffic count for this location?

D. What is the workforce availability in the area as it pertains to your needs? Use census or workforce data and cite it.

Case Study | Dr. Farrah Gray: Young Millionaire, Entrepreneur, and Philanthropist

Dr. Farrah Gray.
(© Everett Collection Inc./Alamy)

Most 6-year-olds have not begun to dream of entrepreneurship. Most 14-year-olds only dream about being millionaires. Most 21-year-olds are in the early stages of their work lives or in college. None of this was true for Dr. Farrah Gray.

At age 6, young Farrah (who was born in 1984) was selling products door-to-door from his home on the South Side of Chicago, one of the toughest areas of the city. He was a self-made millionaire by age 14. He received an honorary doctorate at the age of 21.

Gray is a master of promotion, inspiration, and entrepreneurship. He achieved more before the age of 29 than most people do in their entire lives. The National Urban League named him one of the most influential black men in America. He has been a syndicated columnist, writing for the National Newspaper Publishers Association, reaching 15 million readers in 200 weekly newspapers. He serves as an AOL money coach and has been featured on the Dream Team of Financial Experts in *O, The Oprah Magazine*. He is a professional speaker on topics that include financial management, creativity, personal development, and leadership. He has been many times in print and on broadcast media.

Dr. Gray has created numerous business ventures, fulfilling his dream of becoming a 21st-century CEO. These include a mail-box franchise, prepaid phone cards, an interactive teen talk show, and Farr-Out Foods. As a 12-year-old, he was the inspirational cohost of Las Vegas-based *Backstage Live*, which was simulcast to 12 million people weekly. He is the author of three books—*Reallionaire: Nine Steps to Becoming Rich from the Inside Out; Get Real, Get Rich: Conquer the 7 Myths Blocking You from Success*; and *The Truth Shall Make You Rich*—and is the CEO of Farrah Gray Publishing. Most recently he partnered with rapper Flavor Flav in creating Flavor Flav's House of Flavor Take Out Restaurant in Las Vegas.

While enjoying this spectacular success, Dr. Gray's commitment to philanthropy also emerged early and continues to flourish. When he was 8, he cofounded the Urban Neighborhood Enterprise Economic Club (U.N.E.E.C.) on Chicago's South Side. He later created New Early Entrepreneur Wonders (NEEW) Student Venture Fund to engage and encourage at-risk young people to find legal sources of entrepreneurial income. This was followed by the establishment of the Farrah Gray Foundation, which supports scholarships for students at historically black colleges and universities (HBCUs) and promotes youth entrepreneurship. He is a spokesman for the National Marrow Donor Program and the National Coalition for the Homeless.

Dr. Farrah Gray is an extraordinary example of a successful young entrepreneur and philanthropist.

Case Study Analysis

5-24. Farrah Gray is a master of integrated promotion. List the promotional methods he has used and why he may have selected each.

5-25. What is the most interesting part of his story for you? Why?

5-26. The Farrah Gray Foundation serves as a vital part of Gray's activities. Explain how it is important.

5-27. If you were going to meet with Farrah Gray, what would you want to discuss and why?

Case Source

Farrah Gray, accessed August 3, 2013, http://www.farrahgray.com.

Malia Mills:
Love Thy Differences

When 25-year-old Malia Mills decided to launch her own swimwear company, she set out to do much more than just sell high-end bathing suits. Mills wanted to inspire a beauty revolution that would fundamentally change the way women felt about themselves. A graduate of Cornell University with a degree in apparel design, with studies at La Chambre Syndicale de la Couture Parisienne in Paris, Mills at first worked in the fashion world as a designer for established apparel companies. But Mills (a native of Hawaii) saved the money for the start-up investment in her own business by working as a waitress in New York City. She started Malia Mills Swimwear in 1991 and began working full time at the company in 1994.

The slogan of Mills's business is "Love Thy Differences," and Mills is serious about encouraging all women, regardless of age, weight, or body type, to feel good about themselves and to celebrate their uniqueness. In Mills's world, if a woman does not like the way she looks in a swimsuit, it is the suit that has to change, not the woman. As she explains, "We are passionate about inspiring women to look in the mirror and see what is right instead of what is wrong."

The Polaroid Project

If you walk past the Malia Mills Swimwear flagship store in New York's SoHo, the first things you will notice are the photographs in the window. Instead of showcasing fashion models, the window display features a collage of Polaroid pictures of actual customers wearing her signature swimwear. These Polaroids draw customers into the store, as it is so unusual to see "real" women wearing a company's swimsuits. This Polaroid project began as an offbeat idea thought up by a summer intern on a particularly slow sales day. Mills liked the idea of using photographs of her customers because it resonated with the core mission of her business.

Place Matters: Setting the Right Tone

To create a comfortable environment for her customers, Mills has constructed her stores to look and feel like cozy lounges. She herself always hated trying on bathing suits in department stores under the glare of unflattering fluorescent lights. In her boutiques, the lighting is soft, and dressing rooms are located in the back so that the customers will not feel exposed to other shoppers. She provides free bottled water so that they can feel relaxed and at home. Sales associates are always on hand to assist with finding the appropriate suits. Mills does not believe in a one-size-fits-all design philosophy. People's bodies do not come in packages of small, medium, and large. Accordingly, her tops are sized like lingerie, and bottoms come in sizes 2 to 16. All pieces are sold as separates, which allows customers to mix and match across different style and fabric options, as well as size. Malia Mills introduced the concept of selling separate tops and bottoms before this was common retail practice.

The Price/Production Connection

Malia Mills's suits are priced at the high end of the swimwear market. A bikini top or bottom will cost somewhere between $145 and $175, and one-piece suits run an average of $325. This pricing scheme reflects some of the choices Mills has made as an entrepreneur about how her suits are

Arnaldo Magnani/Getty Image

produced. For example, she chooses to manufacture in New York City instead of outsourcing production to Asia or elsewhere, where labor costs are lower. According to Mills, "It costs us much more per unit to sew our suits locally but supporting our community is worth it. The women (mostly) who sew our suits do so with extra care—we visit them often and they know how important quality is to us."

Mills chooses to import the fabrics she uses from Europe, and she typically buys them in small quantities, which is more costly, so that her designs stay fresh. Mills also pays a premium to the fabric mills that custom-dye her materials in unique colors, and this also contributes to the bottom line of her manufacturing costs. Her suits are so well made that she sometimes worries about undercutting herself in the marketplace. If the average woman owns two or three bathing suits, and a Malia Mills suit can last several years, it could take a long time for a customer to seek a replacement.

Smart Selling Requires Trial and Error

Early on, Mills sold her suits wholesale to department stores, but she found that this strategy did not fit well with her core mission. Mills's suits got lost on the racks next to other brand-name apparel, and the salespeople did not understand how to answer customers' questions about the unique features of her product, such as how they are sized differently from other swimsuits. Eventually Mills decided to sell directly to the consumer. Maintaining control over the sales process has allowed Mills to stay true to her mission of providing women with an enjoyable and empowering experience, purchasing swimwear that fits in a relaxed environment.

Promotions: Getting the Word Out

Over the years, Mills has been successful in generating PR. Her company has been profiled in major publications such as *The New York Times*, *Sports Illustrated*, and *Harper's Bazaar*. It has helped to have celebrities such as Madonna wearing her suits, especially when they are photographed in public. Recently, Mills began purchasing advertising in local print media. She is doing this as an experiment to see if it has a noticeable impact on generating new customers. In the meantime,

the growth of Malia Mills Swimwear continues to be propelled by word of mouth and customer loyalty. Each day, the business connects with passersby who are lured into the store by the Polaroid photographs of ordinary women wearing her bathing suits. Once these women walk in off the street, there is a pretty good chance that they will walk out as customers.

Case Study Analysis

5-28. List the unique features of Malia Mills's products.

5-29. Malia Mills Swimwear is not inexpensive. Why do you think customers are willing to pay a premium for her suits?

5-30. The case mentions that Malia Mills Swimwear is currently experimenting with paid advertising. If you were in charge of marketing for the company, how would you assess whether it was cost-effective enough to continue purchasing advertising?

5-31. What kind of environment is Malia Mills trying to create in her stores? Why is this important?

5-32. Besides her own boutiques, specialty stores, and the Internet, what might be some additional sales venues for Malia Mills Swimwear to consider exploring?

5-33. Why was the "Polaroid Project" a successful promotional venture?

5-34. Imagine a scenario in which Malia Mills Swimwear hired you as a media consultant. Respond to the following:

- Devise a cause-related marketing strategy for the company.
- Suggest three strategies for the company to pursue in obtaining media coverage.

Case Sources

Malia Mills Web site, accessed July 26, 2013, http://www.maliamills.com.

Pamela Rohland, "Chic to Chic—Turn Style into Sales with a Clothing-Design Company," *Business Start-Ups* magazine, December 1999, http://Entrepreneur.com/article/0,4621,231846,00.html.

6

Smart Selling and Effective Customer Service

Learning Objectives

1. Explain the importance of selling based on benefits.

2. Demonstrate principles of selling to prepare effective sales calls.

3. Plan successful sales calls.

4. Analyze and improve sales calls.

5. Recognize and arrange excellent customer service.

6. Define customer relationship management and interpret its value.

Barry Austin/Thinkstock

"The secret of success is to have a self-seller, and if you do not have one, get one."

—William C. (Billy) Durant, founder of General Motors

Sarah Schupp, University Parent

Sarah Schupp started University Parent Media as a student at the University of Colorado at Boulder and has grown the company through smart selling and effective customer service. (The business plan that she wrote with classmates in 2004 is included in the Appendices). Her original intention was to generate advertising revenue through direct sales. Her team of regional sales forces would sell to businesses near the colleges and universities that would provide the guides for parents of incoming freshmen and transfer students. There could also be salespeople for national accounts. In addition, she would use quarterly direct-mail campaigns targeted to business owners in the respective areas, including a sample issue, cover letter regarding effectiveness and value, and a rate card. However, Sarah soon learned that effective selling meant using a telemarketing team centrally located in Boulder, rather than a direct-sales team in the field.

She also learned that excellent customer service would be critical to the success of University Parent. Because her publications and Web site provide content of general interest to parents of college students, as well as information specific to individual schools, it is important to be able to handle parent questions, serve university admissions and other offices, and manage relationships with the advertisers.

Since its start-up, University Parent Media has grown to a $1.8 million company with some 200 participating colleges and universities, has 17 employees, sends out 100,000 mobile-friendly newsletters per month, and publishes a half-million guides per year.[1]

Selling Skills Are Essential to Business Success

Personal selling is dealing with potential customers face to face and trying to convince them to make a purchase. Salespeople often become successful entrepreneurs because they learn to listen to what the customer needs and wants on a daily and personal basis.

Some great American entrepreneurs (in addition to Billy Durant, whose quote opens the chapter) who started out in sales include:

- Ray Kroc, founder of McDonald's, as we saw in Chapter 1, was selling milkshake machines when he was inspired to turn the McDonald brothers' hamburger restaurant into a national operation.
- Aristotle Onassis was a wholesale tobacco salesman before becoming a multimillionaire in the shipping business.
- King C. Gillette was a traveling salesman when he invented the safety razor.
- W. Clement Stone started out selling newspapers at the age of six before going on to build a great fortune in the insurance industry.
- Mary Kay Ash was in direct sales for 25 years before she cofounded Mary Kay Cosmetics with her son.

---

[1]Judith Ohikuare, "Easing the Stress of Empty Nesters," *Inc.*, July, 2, 2012, accessed August 7, 2013, http://www.inc.com/30under30/judith-ohikuare/sarah-schupp-founder-university-parent-media.html.

Selling Is a Great Source of Market Research

If a customer is dissatisfied, it is often the salesperson who hears the complaint. In that sense, selling is a constant source of valuable market research. Depending on the business you start, you will probably not be able to hire a sales staff immediately. You will be the sales staff.

Even if you have never sold anything in your life, you can make yourself into a fantastic salesperson. In fact, you have already had a lot of practice selling without realizing it. Everyone has tried on occasion to persuade ("sell") others to agree to something or to act a certain way. Being face to face with customers and trying to sell your product may make you uncomfortable, but think of rejections as learning experiences. Personal selling will give you opportunities for ongoing market analysis. You will learn to look forward to sales encounters throughout your entrepreneurial career.

The Essence of Selling Is Teaching

Learning Objective 1

Explain the importance of selling based on benefits.

The creative art of selling is teaching the customer how the *features* of your product or service are *benefits*. Inexperienced salespeople make a common mistake: They think telling the customer about the features of a product will sell it. But remember, a customer who buys a drill does not need a drill; the customer needs to make a hole.

The essence of selling is teaching how and why the outstanding features of your product or service will benefit your customers. William "Billy" Durant succeeded early in his career by showing that a new type of spring (feature) made riding in his buggy carts more comfortable (benefit).

The Principles of Selling

Every entrepreneur has to be able to identify the benefits his or her product can provide and to make an effective sales call. Entrepreneurs sell constantly, not just to customers but to potential investors, bankers, and people they want to hire. Commit the following selling principles to memory and you will lay the groundwork for becoming a successful salesperson. These principles apply to any product or service:

Make a Good Personal Impression

Learning Objective 2

Demonstrate principles of selling to prepare effective sales calls.

When selling your product or service, prepare yourself physically. A salesperson must be clean and well dressed; it is important to dress appropriately for your customer base. If you are selling oil to gas station owners, do not wear $800 suits, but dress professionally. Some suggest that, for sales calls, your business card should not identify you as president or owner, so your prospects can talk with you more easily. This would depend on who you are meeting, so use common sense.

BizFacts

Many salespeople work on *commission*, a percentage earned from each sale they make. A salesperson making a 10 percent commission selling cars, for example, would earn $1,000 after selling a $10,000 car.

$$0.10 \times \$10,000 = \$1,000$$

Entrepreneurs can use commissions to motivate sales staff. When you are starting out and cannot afford to pay sales representatives full-time salaries, you can offer commissions instead, because they get paid as you get paid and earn more as they sell more.

Know Your Product or Service

Understand its features and the benefits they can create. It is your chance to teach the customer about the product or service. Explain the benefits without overselling. Do not try to share everything you know, however, as that is likely to be too much information. You don't want to alienate or bore the customer.

Believe in Your Product or Service

Good salespeople believe in what they are selling and feel good about selling it. If, during this stage, you begin to feel that your product or service does not measure up to your personal standards, reconsider selling it. Your business will likely fail if you do not believe it is of the quality and value that you promise. Always be on the lookout for ways to improve your product or develop a better one.

Know Your Field

Invest in understanding the industry and your competition. Read the trade literature. Learn about your competitors. Buy their products or try their services and compare them with yours. If possible, experience a call from one of your competitor's salespeople. This could be a gold mine of information. Study the strengths and weaknesses of your competitor's product or service; your sales prospects may mention them during your own calls and you should be prepared.

Know Your Customers

Be thorough in the analysis of your customers. What are their needs? How does your product or service address them? Understand what makes them tick. Use resources such as the Internet to get publicly available background information, and access any other resources you can.

Prepare Your Sales Presentation

Know ahead of time how you want to present your product or service. Identify the key points you believe are important to this particular customer. Jot them down on a note card. Study it. Put it away. Practice the sales call. Role-play. Know how to overcome objections.

Think Positively

This will help you deal with the rejections you may experience. Many people do not realize how mentally strong you have to be to conduct sales calls. One entrepreneur went on 400 calls for his import-export firm before he closed a sale of more than $1,000. But this experience made him a much better salesperson.

Keep Good Records

Have your record-keeping system, including invoices and receipts, set up before you go on your first sales call. Use a database system to keep records of your calls and to remind you of appropriate follow-up action. This will be the start of your customer-relationship management process.

Make No Truly "Cold Calls"

Unless you are doing door-to-door or retail sales, your prospect meetings should be "warm" calls. You can send an introductory letter, e-mail, or postcard so that the customer will know why you want to make the visit. Or, better yet, try to get a personal introduction—referral—so that the prospect will feel more comfortable with you from the start.

Make an Appointment

People will be more likely to listen when they have set aside time to speak with you, whether by phone or in person. They will be less than receptive if you interrupt their day unannounced.

Treat Everyone You Sell to Like Gold

Joe Girard is a car salesman who has been dubbed "The World's Greatest Salesman" 12 times by *The Guinness Book of Records*. In his book *How to Sell Anything to Anybody*, Girard states his Law of 250: "Everyone knows 250 people in his or her life important enough to invite to the wedding and to the funeral." He goes on to explain, "This means that if I see 50 people in a week, and only two of them are unhappy with the way I treat them, at the end of the year there will be about 5,000 people influenced by just those two a week."[2] Obviously, if each person you sell to will influence 250 others, you cannot afford to alienate even one sales prospect! (However, this does not mean that you keep trying to sell beyond rejection.)

The Sales Call

A sales call is an appointment with a potential customer to explain or demonstrate your product or service. During the sales call, you will want to do the following:

- make the customer aware of your product or service,
- make the customer want to buy that product or service, and
- make the customer want to buy it from *you*.

Electronic Mail, Blogs, and Social Networks

Learning Objective 3

Plan successful sales calls.

In today's technology-savvy environment, there are multiple methods for communicating with sales prospects. Among these options are e-mail, social networks, and blogs. Which, if any, is best suited to your business will require careful consideration on your part.

Sending e-mail or posting messages to social networks or blogs can help contact sales prospects and keep in touch with the customers you already have, but you must use these methods carefully. In the physical world, you can look for sales prospects by distributing flyers or by calling

Step into the Shoes . . .

Vincent Quigg—TechWorld

Vincent Quigg was a high school student in Southern California when he started TechWorld as part of the NFTE (Network for Teaching Entrepreneurship) program. Vincent's iPhone customization and repair service relied on the simple message of his work being faster and less expensive and of equal quality to that of the original manufacturer. Vincent promoted an $80 service offer, in which work would be completed in 45 minutes for local customers, and within 2 to 3 days for others. He touted a special diagnostic system, a 30-day, "non-accidental" warranty, and a refer-a-friend promotion. Vincent was awarded the $25,000 grand prize as the winner of the 2012 NFTE National Youth Entrepreneurship Challenge.[3]

Vincent Quigg

---

[2]Joe Girard, *How to Sell Anything to Anybody*, New York: Warner Books, 1986, p. 48.

[3]"Vincent Quigg—NFTE New York Final Presentation 2012," October 11, 2012, YouTube, posted November 13, 2012, accessed August 14, 2013, http://www.youtube.com/watch?v=choiZObxCpY.

people from a list. Using e-mail or social networks in a similar fashion can result in your e-mail box being jammed with "flames," or hate mail. Most users do not appreciate receiving unwanted advertisements, called spam, and recipients may respond angrily.

spam unwanted Internet advertisements or e-mails.

If done correctly, becoming active in a social network such as Linked-In or Facebook can lead to *qualified* prospects. Let's say you sell photographic supplies and you hear about an interesting social network for photographers, such as FotoUp. Do not blitz it with ads. Instead, before posting any messages, lurk for a while, meaning that you just read messages and get a feel for the discussions taking place without participating. Once you are comfortable, post a message. It will not be a sales pitch, and no one in the group should take offense, so you may attract potential sales prospects to your Web site.

lurk reading messages and getting a feel for discussions on a Web site, newsgroup, or the like, without participating in the online conversation.

Prequalify Your Sales Calls

Before calling to make an appointment for any sales call, identify and list your prospects, the people and/or organizations that may be receptive to your sales pitch. Include everyone you can imagine, but then go through it carefully and ask:

prospect a person or organization that may be receptive to a sales pitch.

- Is this individual in my market?
- Does he or she need my product?
- Will my product remove a problem or source of "pain" or improve the individual's life?
- Can he or she afford it?

If the answer to any of these questions is "no," making a sales call on that person will probably be a waste of time for both of you. People spend money to buy things they want or need. If your product or service will help, that is great. If not, do not hesitate to move on to consider the next prospect (sometimes called a "suspect" until the call is qualified). Asking such questions is called *prequalifying* a sales call. Invest the time it takes to get your prospect list organized and analyzed. Abe Lincoln's famous saying applies here, "If I had ten hours to chop down a tree, I'd spend nine sharpening my axe." Remember, you can purchase or develop lists of potential customers and conduct research.

Focus on the Customer

During each call, focus on one thought: What does this customer need? Visualize your product or service fulfilling that need. If you believe in your product or service, and there is a good fit, you will be able to see this without any problem. In general, focusing on listening to the potential customer will help you overcome self-consciousness. If you actively listen and probe, the customer will tell you what is personally important, either directly or indirectly. A feature that creates a benefit in your mind may be meaningless to one prospect but extremely important to another. Pay attention.

Mental visualization will help you perform better when you are in the actual situation. Practice the sales call in your mind, visualizing how you want it to go, but be prepared to deviate from that vision. Visualization will enlist your subconscious mind in the sales process, instinctively providing you with subtle verbal and body-language cues that can convince a customer to buy from you. You will be better prepared and more comfortable in your role.

BizFacts

Kay Keenan and Steve Smolinsky are the consummate networkers. They have written a book on the topic highlighting material covered in their *Conversation on Networking*. Following are some of the tips from their book:

- It's a lot more fun to be with upbeat people. Negative stories shove people away. . . . Positive stories bring them closer.
- If you go to an event or meeting with someone, split up. It improves your chances of meeting interesting people.
- Only if you're dead is it okay to say "nothing" when asked, "What's new?"
- Go early (to an event) and study the nametags on the registration table.
- Strong relationships are a two-way street.
- Learn to appreciate silence in a conversation. You can often see people thinking, but you rarely can hear their brains working.
- If you don't ask, you don't get. That means referrals, as well as most other things.
- Being comfortable with yourself leads to being comfortable with others.
- Carry your own nametag with you. Wearing a nametag is a great conversation starter, and your name will always be spelled correctly!
- A wonderful meeting not followed up is like having a winning lottery ticket and not cashing it in.

Source: Kay Keenan and Steven Smolinsky, *Conversation on Networking: Finding, Developing, and Maintaining Relationships for Business and Life,* Birchrunville, PA: Forever Talking Press, 2006.

Conversation on Networking provides insightful information on networking effectiveness. (Conversation on Networking)

All the technological concepts used to identify customers through market research can be instrumental in selling to your segment of the market.

The Eight-Step Sales Call

Whereas each sales call will be as different as the people involved in it, following these eight steps should make your calls more successful.

1. *Preparation.* Prepare yourself mentally and through organization. Think about how the product or service will benefit this specific customer. Have the price, discounts, all technical information, and any other details "on the tip of your tongue" or at your fingertips. Be willing to obtain further information. Visualize the sales call in your mind until it goes successfully. Jot down a few key questions and points that will help. Bring the appropriate materials, samples, and data with you.

2. *Greeting.* Greet the customer politely and graciously. Do not plunge immediately into business talk, unless you know your customer prefers to do so. Take the time to know the prospect's style and be sensitive to it. The first few words you say may be the most important. Keep a two-way conversation going. Maintain eye contact, and keep the customer's attention. Remember that the customer is first and foremost a human being with whom you can make a connection. The more you can learn about his or her family, hobbies, interests—anything to help develop a genuine relationship—the better your chances of eventually securing a sale. Avoid being perceived as overly personal by remaining genuine. The best salespeople keep records on their customers to remind them of

details for future conversations and to follow up over time. Sales may depend on the characteristics and benefits of the product or service, but customers buy from people they know and like when they have a choice. They usually have a choice.

3. ***Showing the product or service.*** Personalize your product or service by pointing out the benefits for this particular customer. Use props and models or the real thing. If possible, meaningfully demonstrate it by showcasing its unique selling proposition.

4. ***Listening to the customer.*** Begin with the customer's needs in mind and be wary of making assumptions about these needs. If you listen actively and probe carefully, you can learn the challenges he or she is facing and tailor your sales pitch. Sit back and let the customer talk about it. This is how you will get your most valuable information. In successful calls the buyer does most of the talking.

5. ***Dealing with objections.*** The best, most effective way to deal with objections is to address likely objections in a positive light before the customer raises them. During the listening phase, you may hear new objections. Always acknowledge objections and handle them. Do not pretend you did not hear, overreact, or be afraid to listen. Do not hesitate to tell the truth about any negative aspect of the prospect or service. Each time you admit a negative, you gain credibility in the customer's mind. However, be careful to not overemphasize a flaw or complain about the product or service yourself.

6. ***Closing the sale.*** Review the benefits of your product or service. If negatives have arisen, point out that the product or service is still an excellent buy. Narrow the choices the customer has to make. Close the sale, if it is time to do so. Do not overstay your welcome. Stop while you are ahead. Remember that the sales cycle for your product or service is a critical factor here. Some sales take months, or even years, to close. A "no" today is not necessarily a "no" forever.

7. ***Follow-up.*** Make regular follow-up calls to assess customer satisfaction. Ask if you can be of any further help. If the customer has a complaint, do not ignore it. Keeping the customer's trust after the sale will be critical to future sales.

    A successful business is built on repeat customers. Plus, every time you talk to a customer, you are deepening your association. Your best sales prospects in the future will be people who have already bought something from you. Keep them posted on the progress of your business.

8. ***Asking for referrals.*** If you did a good job for a customer, ask them for referrals, other potential customers you might contact. Try to set up a system that encourages others to send sales prospects your way. Offer discounts, gift certificates, or other incentives to those who refer people to you. Give customers a few business cards to pass on to their friends.

Three Call Behaviors of Successful Salespeople

Researcher Neil Rackham discovered that successful salespeople exhibit certain "sales-call behaviors."[4] He concluded that these three steps lead to more sales:

1. ***Let the customer talk more than you do.*** According to *SPIN Selling,* "The more your customer talks, the more you will learn about their

---

[4]Neil Rackham, *SPIN Selling*, New York: McGraw Hill, 1996, p. 110.

needs, which puts you in a better position to offer them the most customized and most helpful solutions." Encourage your customers to talk to you about their situations and problems. As they talk, they will begin to understand their own needs better and realize the importance of solving the problem.

2. ***Ask the right questions.*** How do you get customers to talk to you? Rackham notes that you have to ask the right questions. If your sales calls are leaving you with little information and few sales, you are not asking the questions that uncover your customers' needs. Focus on listening to your customers. Try to draw them out. You need to correctly understand the problem *before* suggesting that your product or service can provide a solution.

3. ***Wait to offer products and solutions until later in the call.*** First, let your customer talk. Second, once you have the customer talking, ask the right questions to help uncover the problem. Now you are ready to offer your product or service as a solution to this problem. As Rackham writes, "You cannot know what solution to offer if you do not uncover customer needs and decision criteria first. For example, if you spend your time with the customer talking about how quiet your machine is, and noise is not a factor your customer cares about, you've wasted your time (and theirs)."[5] You cannot offer a valuable solution until you know what problem the customer needs to solve.

Analyze Your Sales Calls to Become a Star Salesperson

Every sales call is an opportunity to improve your selling skills—even if you did not make a sale. The star salesperson analyzes each call by asking:

- Was I able to get the customer to open up to me? Why or why not?
- Did I do or say anything that turned the customer off, or was offensive, or caused her to disbelieve me?
- Which of my questions did the best job of helping the customer focus on her challenges? How can I ask better questions?
- Was I able to make an honest case for my product/service being the one that could solve the customer's problem?
- Did I improve my relationship with this person during the call?

When you analyze your selling at this level of detail, you will discover important opportunities for learning and improving your selling skills.

Turning Objections into Advantages

Learning Objective 4

Analyze and improve sales calls.

Getting the customer to open up may lead to your being told things you may not want to hear about your product or service. These objections, however, can be valuable sources of marketing data. Sales expert Brian Tracy recommends writing down the objections and comments customers make about your product. He classifies objections into six categories and suggests making a list of every objection you have ever heard and then grouping them under the following headings:

1. Price
2. Performance
3. Follow-up service

---

[5]Rackham, *SPIN Selling*, p. 84.

4. Competition
5. Support
6. Warranties and assurances[6]

Once you have put the objections into these categories, take a close look at them. Try to rephrase each set of objections into a single sentence of 25 words or less.

Work on developing objection-proof answers to each of these questions, answers that are backed by proof, testimonials from customers, research, and data comparing your product with the competitions' products. If you make the effort to do this, you will learn to appreciate hearing objections. More importantly, you may be able to head off objections before they arise.

Direct selling experience can be a great foundation for an entrepreneur.
(© Digital Vision/Getty Images)

- You will have well-prepared responses, backed by written documentation.
- If you do hear a new objection for which you have not developed a response, you will be excited about the opportunity to address it.

Use Technology to Sell

Where appropriate and applicable, use the latest advances in technology to sell your product, help your customers understand and use it, and stay in touch with them. Examples include:

- A multimedia demonstration or presentation of your product
- A Web site customers can visit to obtain updates and product facts, to share ideas, and to find technical data
- Use of e-mail, blogs, and social networking to stay in touch with customers
- Webinars and audio conferences to educate and introduce products
- Digital planners and calendars and sales and contact management software to keep prospect lists organized and log sales calls and customer information
- Smart phones, tablets, and other technology to place orders and secure immediate responses to customer inquiries

Global Impact . . .

Keep an Open Mind

Your business may be small, but through the Internet you can participate in an exciting global economy. The more you travel and learn about other cultures, the more effective business leader you will become. The best entrepreneurs are curious about other countries, other cultures, and other ways of life, because these are both interesting in themselves and potential sources of business.

Perhaps you will discover a new product while on a backpacking trip in Europe that you can profitably import into the United States. Perhaps you will find while reading about Panama online a consumer need that you can meet by exporting your product there. Once you realize you are a citizen of the world, the sky is the limit for your career as an entrepreneur.

[6]Brian Tracy, *Be a Sales Superstar: 21 Great Ways to Sell More, Faster, Easier in Tough Markets*, San Francisco: Berrett-Koehler Publishers, 2003, p. 84.

Successful Businesses Need Customers Who Return

Making a sale to a customer is actually only the first step in your relationship with this individual. Your real goal is not the first sale, but to develop repeat business—customers who will buy from you over and over again. Successful companies are built on repeat business. For example, the founder of Home Depot has calculated that one satisfied customer is worth more than $35,000 in sales over a lifetime.

Customer Service Is Keeping Customers Happy

Learning Objective 5

Recognize and arrange excellent customer service.

customer service
everything a business does to keep the customer happy.

Customer service is everything you do to keep your customers happy, especially *after* they've bought something. It includes maintaining and repairing the product or service once it has been sold and dealing with customer complaints. Many businesses do not take the time or effort to provide excellent customer service. Smart entrepreneurs understand, however, that investing in customer service is likely to have a high return, because it retains customers and minimizes their dissatisfaction.

Here are some suggestions that may work for your business:

- Know your customers by name.
- Deliver the product or service on time, every time.
- Help customers carry their purchases to their vehicles.
- Suggest a less expensive product, if it will meet the customer's need, or offer a recommendation to a source of a product that you do not sell, if it is what they want and you cannot offer a substitute.
- Provide a full refund to any customer who is dissatisfied.
- Take time to listen politely and with empathy to complaints.
- Provide a toll-free customer-assistance phone line that is easy to use.
- Offer product or service information of interest to customers in a nonthreatening manner.

Smart entrepreneurs pay close attention to their customers. They constantly ask questions and analyze their needs. They train their employees to look for customer needs that might be going unfulfilled. The most successful entrepreneurs become customer-service experts. Excellent customer service, combined with smart selling and a product that offers a unique competitive advantage, will lead to success.

The Costs of Losing a Customer

Have you heard the expression "The customer is always right"? There will be times when a customer may get angry at you, complain, or make demands that you believe are unreasonable.

In those times, keep in mind four main costs of losing a customer:

1. ***Loss of current dollars.*** The business you currently receive from the customer is terminated immediately.
2. ***Loss of jobs.*** If the customer provided a significant portion of revenue for your firm, you may have to downsize or even close the company; your employees will lose their jobs.
3. ***Loss of reputation.*** Remember Joe Girard's Law of 250. Do you really want to send a person away unhappy? One unhappy customer can keep many people away from your business.
4. ***Loss of future business.*** Once the customer is gone, so is the hope of any future purchases by that customer.

Step into the Shoes . . .

Positively Outrageous Service

T. Scott Gross

T. Scott Gross is a motivational speaker and management training consultant who has operated in both the entrepreneurial and corporate worlds. He was the national director of training for the Church's Chicken chain and became a Church's franchisee in 1985. Gross was fortunate to be able to use his earnings from speaking and consulting to keep the restaurant in business. He and his staff quickly learned that running the restaurant by the book simply was not sufficient. That led to the concept of Positively Outrageous Service (POS).

How much service is enough? How good does it need to be? For Gross and his team, it was not enough just to satisfy customers. Businesses should delight and astound them.[7] He describes POS as, "[T]he story you can't wait to tell . . . unexpected service delivered at random. . . . It is a memorable event and is so unusual that the customer is compelled to tell others."[8]

Gross tells the following story:

In the borderline bizarre category is our now-famous drive-through wind-shield-washing service. It was my response to a suggestion by my brother, Steve, our manager, that we should do 'something outrageous.' Now, while a Church's employee wielding a spray bottle attacks their windshields, I handle the microphone and the other half of the fun: "Good afternoon. Thanks for choosing Church's. As soon as that tubby guy gets out from in front of your car, pull up to the window for the best lunch you've had all day. No, on second thought, when he gets in front of your car, pull on up!" If a woman customer jokes that we should clean the car's interior, too, I might say: "Oh, madam, we aren't going to do insides. But if you come through tomorrow, we're going to try our hand at hair styling, and on Saturday, we're going to take a shot at dentistry!" The result is almost always a customer who is laughing when he or she reaches the pickup window. Doing the unexpected for our customers has earned us a reputation as a fun place to do business, where you can count on getting treated well.[9]

Positively Outrageous Service

- is random and unexpected: the element of surprise is part of its power;
- is out of proportion: it's an extravagant gesture that catches attention;
- involves the customer personally: it's an invitation to play that personalizes the service; and
- creates positive word of mouth: more powerful than advertising, POS generates its own buzz.[10]

Could providing Positively Outrageous Service fit into your business?

Use your self-control to stay polite, even when a customer is getting angry. Do your best to find a solution that will send him or her away satisfied and diffuse any lingering ill will. Your effort will protect your business and may even earn you a customer for life. Often, if you simply ask, "What will it take to make you a satisfied customer?" you will find that the customer will pause and suggest a reasonable solution to the situation.

Customer Complaints Are Valuable

You may not enjoy hearing a customer complain about your product or service, but a complaint is full of valuable information that probably no one else will tell you, and you do not have to pay for it! Listen closely to learn what your customers need and want:

- Always acknowledge complaints and criticism and deal with them. Never pretend that you did not hear a negative comment. If the customer *perceives* a problem, it *is* a problem.

---

[7] T. Scott Gross, *Positively Outrageous Service: How to Delight and Astound Your Customers and Win Them for Life*, 2nd ed., Chicago: Dearborn Trade Publishing, 2004, p.5.

[8] 8 Ibid.

[9] Gross, *Positively Outrageous Service*, p. 6.

[10] T. Scott Gross, accessed August 31, 2010, http://www.tscottgross.com.

Exhibit 6-1 *Words Matter; Smart Customer Service*	
Words to Use	**Words to Avoid**
Please	Cannot
Yes	Never
May I	Do not
Consider this	You have to
Do	Do not tell me no
Let's negotiate	Will not
Will	Not our policy
Thank you	Not my job
You	Profanity
Us	Vulgarity
Appreciate	Problem
Can	Sorry
Use customer's name	Endearments (honey, sweetie, etc.)
Would you like	We'll try
Opportunity	Haven't had time
Challenge	I do not know
Regret	Hang on for a second

Customer service is everything you do to keep the customer happy.
(© redav/Fotolia)

- Do not overreact to negative comments and, above all, do not take them personally.
- Always tell the truth about any negative aspect of your product or service. When you admit a negative, you gain the customer's trust. However, this is different from complaining about your own product, the vendor, or your customers. You need not emphasize any weaknesses, but should acknowledge them when asked and offset them with benefits.

Remember, a successful business is built on repeat customers. When you listen to a customer, you are building a relationship. You are encouraging loyalty to your business.

An angry customer can make you feel angry, too. It is crucial that you and your team members stay calm when dealing with a customer who is upset. Ask the customer to explain the situation, and do not interrupt. This will provide time for him or her to vent and then calm down. If you show you are willing to listen, you will probably defuse much of the irritation.

If the customer is using profanity, however, say something like "I understand your frustration, but I'm not comfortable with the way you are expressing it. Let's find a solution for you."

Exhibit 6-1 offers a list of words to use and words to avoid when dealing with customers.[11]

Customer Relationship Management Systems

Learning Objective 6

Define customer relationship management and interpret its value.

One approach to securing and sustaining customers is to implement a **customer relationship management (CRM)** system, which is the company-wide policies, practices, and processes that a business uses to manage its

---

[11]Elaine Harris, *Customer Service: A Practical Approach*, Upper Saddle River, NJ: Pearson Education, 2003.

interactions with customers to generate maximum customer satisfaction and optimal profitability. CRM is a purposeful program of guidelines to ensure excellence in customer service and relationship management. Carried out properly, the designed positive interactions will encourage repeat purchases and referrals. All of the sales and customer-service skills and best practices introduced in this chapter can be components of a CRM system. Implementation can range from simple, such as methods for greeting and treating customers, to sophisticated, such as using state-of-the-art technology to provide highly targeted customer information and analytics.

CRM affirms that customer service is an aspect of marketing. Marketing brings a customer to your business, but it does not stop there. Once the customer is inside your door or you are speaking to him or her on the phone, the treatment should be consistent with your marketing. If your competitive advantage is speedy service, make sure your employees move quickly. If your advantage is a cozy, easygoing environment, make sure each customer is warmly welcomed and made to feel at home. Your customer service must reinforce your overall marketing plan. Through a well-designed and executed CRM system, you are reinforcing and building marketing effectiveness.

> **customer relationship management (CRM)** company-wide policies, practices, and processes a business uses with its customers to generate maximum customer satisfaction and optimal profitability.

Why Does CRM Matter?

Customer relationship management can be the component of your business that makes it a sustainable entity. The costs of securing new customers are significantly higher than the costs of keeping a repeat customer. According to the Customer Service Institute, 65 percent of a company's business comes from existing customers, and it costs five times as much to attract a new customer as it does to keep an existing one satisfied.[12] *Losing* a customer is even more expensive. TARP Worldwide's (Technical Assistance Research Programs Institute) recent word-of-mouth (WOM) survey found that

> 42% of consumers who hear about a positive product experience will buy that product for the first time and another 21% of those consumers will buy more. The effects of positive WOM mirror those of negative WOM as 42% of consumers who hear of a negative WOM stop buying that product and 14% buy less. However, consumers with negative experiences provide more detailed explanations through more channels than those who have positive experiences.[13]

When you know the purchasing patterns and interests of a customer, you can make informed decisions about the products, services, and promotional offers that will be of interest and result in additional sales. With CRM, you can focus on optimal interactions with customers during all types of transactions (i.e., purchases, returns, ordering, inquiries, and complaints), as well as building on and using data regarding customer behavior to foster positive transactions.

Because customer service is also a valuable source of market research, CRM supports market research for companies that employ it. Market research should not end once you open your business. Each customer can be a valuable source of information. Some easy ways to collect market research as part of your customer service for retail businesses include

- Providing a short survey on a stamped postcard listing every item purchased, or directions to a Web site with a survey and reward printed on every receipt. Or include a survey at the point of purchase that can be redeemed for a discount on the next item bought.

---

[12]Customer Service Institute of America, accessed August 7, 2013, .

[13]"Consumer Word of Mouth Changes Buying Habits 60% of the Time, TARP Worldwide Poll Finds: Men and Senior Citizens Most Likely to Complain," Press release. TARP Worldwide, February 12, 2008, accessed June 23, 2009, http://www.tarp.com/news_wom_poll.html.

- Asking selected customers to fill out a longer survey—again, offering a discount or prize drawing as an incentive.
- Always asking standard questions when completing a sale, such as "Do you have any suggestions on how we could improve our product?" or "Were you satisfied with the service you received today?" or "Were you able to find everything you wanted?"

Components of CRM for the Small Business

CRM has consistent components that may be incorporated across business types and sizes. It encompasses aspects of the marketing, sales, and service functions of a business to create positive customer experiences. **Exhibit 6-2** shows the Solution Map of CRM as described by SAP, the top seller of CRM systems. In the case of businesses that purchase highly sophisticated software, these components are part of the software solution, but for companies with less complex operations and fewer resources, many of these functions can be carried out without software applications beyond basic record keeping with simple databases, contact-management software, and industry-specific systems.

The SBA Web site (http://www.sba.gov) offers a perspective on customer service, and customer relationship management in general, relating it to the axiom inherent in the Golden Rule, "Do unto others as you would have them do unto you," and stating, "Companies of all sizes are realizing that their strongest selling point can sometimes boil down to treating customers as they would like to be treated—or better."[14] The message is getting through. According to John Goodman, president of TARP, "In the past few years, companies began to realize that service was really a competitive factor, and began to view it as an integral part of their product."[15] It is often in the area of service and CRM that a small business can outclass its larger competitors, so that customers may spend more to buy from them because of the service differential. The SBA offers three Golden Rules for small businesses with respect to CRM.

- Golden Rule 1: Put the customer first.
- Golden Rule 2: Stay close to your customers.
- Golden Rule 3: Pay attention to the details.

Exhibit 6-2 *SAP Solution Map for CRM*

Marketing	Sales	Service
Marketing Resource Management	Sales Planning and Forecasting	Service Sales and Marketing
Segmentation and List Management	Sales Performance Management	Service Contracts and Agreements
Campaign Management	Territory Management	Installations and Management
Real-Time Offer Management	Accounts and Contacts	Customer Service Support
Lead Management	Opportunity Management	Field Service Management
Loyalty Management	Quotation and Order Management	Returns and Depot Repair
Communication Promotion	Pricing and Contracts	Warranty and Claims Management
	Incentive and Commission Management	Service Logistics and Finance
	Time and Travel	Service Collaboration, Analytics, Optimization

Source: SAP Web site, http://www.sap.com/solutions/business-suite/CRM/businessmaps.epx, accessed June 20, 2009 (as submitted). SAP Solution Map for CRM courtesy of SAP AG.

---

[14]U.S. Small Business Administration Web site, accessed June 29, 2009, http://www.sba.gov.

[15]Ibid.

The SBA offers further advice on the components of customer care that they translate into five rules. These imperatives are part of the essential components of successful CRM.

1. ***Conduct your own survey.*** Profit from the ideas, suggestions, and complaints of your present and former customers. Talk and meet with your customers. Ask questions. Learn how they feel, what they want, and what they dislike.

2. ***Check employees' telephone manners periodically.*** This link is particularly important for small businesses because bad telephone handling can undermine other constructive efforts to build a profitable enterprise.

3. ***Emphasize the importance of rules such as prompt answering and a cheerful attitude of helpfulness.*** Have someone whose voice is unfamiliar play the role of a customer or prospective customer, preferably a difficult one.

4. ***Make customer service a team effort.*** Use group meetings, memos, posters, and in-house publications to build customer consciousness throughout the organization. Continually drive home the crucial rule that getting and holding customers requires team play, and invite employees' suggestions.

5. ***Extend your efforts after hours.*** It's the friendly feelings people have that draw them to you and your business. Take advantage of the relaxed atmosphere of social occasions, or a neighborly chat over the back fence, to turn friends into customers or to reinforce the loyalty of existing ones.[16]

How Technology Supports CRM

The general conception of CRM is that technology can be used to build and maintain customer relationships. Certainly, as noted, the use of computer technology can have a significant role in CRM, but the system should be inclusive of all forms of relationship management, from greeting a customer on the phone, in-person, or even on the home page of your Web site, to the use of sophisticated software systems. With CRM, customer interactions with all parts of the company are unified and customer information is tracked, analyzed, and used to improve customer satisfaction and business profitability. Specialized CRM software is available to companies large and small. **Exhibit 6-3** shows the top vendors of CRM software.

It truly is not necessary to invest in a sophisticated CRM software system to use technology to benefit your customer relationships. You can purchase a database package to create significant gains. A **database** is a

database a collection of information that is generally stored on a computer and organized for sorting and searching.

Exhibit 6-3 *Worldwide Vendor Revenue Estimates for Total CRM Software (Millions of U.S. Dollars)*		
Company	**2012 Revenue**	**2012 Market Share (%)**
SalesForce.com	$2,525.6	14.0
SAP	$2,327.1	12.9
Oracle	$2,015.2	11.1
Microsoft	$1,135.3	6.3
IBM	$649.1	3.6
Others	$9,437.7	52.1
Total	$18,090.0	100.0

Source: Rob van der Meulen, "Gartner Says Worldwide Customer Relationship Management Software Market Grew 12.5 Percent in 2012," Gartner, Inc., Press Release, accessed August 7, 2013, http://www.gartner.com/newsroom/id/2459015.

---

[16]Ibid.

collection of information that is generally stored on a computer and organized for sorting and searching. Create a database on your computer to collect any information you obtain from customers, either by using a package such as Microsoft Access or with a specialized customer software system for your industry. Your database should include every customer you have ever had, as well as potential ones: friends, family, and other contacts. The database should include contact information (name, e-mail address, phone and fax numbers, and mailing address); any preferences or pertinent personal information (e.g., sizes, birthdays, family, hobbies, memberships); and purchase and payment history. Also, include any contact information, such as when the contact was made, who was involved, what type of contact it was (in person, telephone, text, social network, or e-mail), what was discussed, and when to follow up. Design the database and start collecting this information from the beginning, and you will be ahead of the game when you are ready to make sales calls or send out marketing material.

As your database grows, you can make it more sophisticated by organizing it by region, customer interest, or any number of other variables, so you can send out targeted e-mails. If you sell gourmet sauces, for example, your notes could tell you whether a customer is interested in hot sauces or dessert sauces. When you add a new hot sauce to your product line, you will know whom to target with an e-mail announcement introducing it, possibly with a special offer. Use the resources available to you to maximize your culture of focus on the customer and strong customer relationship management.

Chapter Summary

Now that you have studied this chapter, you can do the following:

1. Explain the importance of selling based on benefits.
   * Features are the qualities of a product or service.
   * Benefits are what the product or service can do to fill customer needs.
   * Customers purchase based on perceived benefits.
2. Demonstrate principles of selling to prepare effective sales calls.
   * Make a good personal impression.
   * Know your product or service.
   * Believe in your product or service.
   * Know your field.
   * Know your customers.
   * Prepare your sales presentation.
   * Think positively.
   * Keep good records.
   * Make an appointment.
   * Treat your customers like gold.
3. Plan successful sales calls.
   * Use technology to assist you.
   * Prequalify your leads, so that you are making the best use of your time and theirs.
   * Focus on the customer, not on the product or service.
   * Incorporate the eight-step sales call.
4. Analyze and improve sales calls.
   * Was I able to get the customer to open up to me? Why, or why not? Did I do or say anything that turned the customer off?
   * Which of my questions did the best job of helping the customer zero in on his or her problem?

- Was I able to make an honest case for my product/service being the one that could solve the customer's problem?
- Did I improve my relationship with this individual during the call?

5. Recognize and arrange excellent customer service.
   - Customer service is everything you do to keep your customers happy, especially after the sale. It includes maintaining and repairing the product or service once it has been sold and dealing with customer complaints.
   - A successful business is built on repeat customers.

6. Define customer relationship management and interpret its value.
   - Identify the key components of CRM.
   - Recognize that CRM can be simple or complex and that you can incorporate technology to obtain higher value.
   - Use CRM to tailor your products, services, and promotions to customers to yield increased profitability.

Key Terms

customer relationship management (CRM)	lurk
	prospect
customer service	spam
database	

Entrepreneurship Portfolio

Critical Thinking Exercises

6-1. Describe the features of each product/service listed below and then create a benefit statement for each that you would use as selling points.
   Product
   a. home pick-up/delivery dry cleaning and laundry service
   b. screen projector cover for smart phones
   c. vegetarian dog food
   d. personal lie detector

6-2. Create a customer profile database for your business containing at least 20 data fields. Which five questions would you ask every customer?

6-3. Describe a business you deal with as a customer. Describe the customer service you receive there. What do you like (or dislike) about it? How could it be improved?

6-4. List five things you intend to do in your business to offer superior customer service.

6-5. Identify five specific sales-call prospects for your business. Prequalify them using these questions: (a) Is the prospect in my market? (b) Does he or she need my product/service? (c) Will my product/service remove a problem or source of "pain" or improve the individual's life? (d) Can he or she afford it?

6-6. Have you created any marketing materials for your business? If so, have three friends and a mentor (someone more experienced whom you respect and who can give you good business advice) look at your materials and give you feedback. Write a memo listing their suggestions and what you plan to do to improve your marketing materials.

Key Concept Questions

6-7. Explain Joe Girard's Law of 250 in your own words, and give examples of it from your own life.

6-8. Why is customer service an extension of marketing?

6-9. Give three reasons why you think it is important to keep collecting market research even after you have opened your business.

6-10. What do you expect your "personal look" to be when you start selling your product/service, and why?

6-11. What sources of information can you use to develop a customer profile?

6-12. List three ways you intend to provide superior customer service.

6-13. Create a company signature for your business e-mail. Keep it under eight words.

Application Exercises

6-14. Develop a brief sales pitch for three items you are wearing. Try out the pitch for each on a partner. Have your partner help you time the pitches to one minute. Do the same for your partner.

6-15. Write a memo to your partner discussing his or her sales calls and how they could be improved. When analyzing your partner's efforts, use the eight steps of a sales call in the text as your guide.

6-16. Arrange to receive a sales pitch from a competitor in the business field you intend to enter. After the presentation, write down your objections to purchasing the product/service. Use Brian Tracy's method to categorize your objections and then phrase them in a single question composed of 25 words or less. Avoid deception in arranging the sales pitch.

Exploring Your Community

6-17. Visit three businesses in your community and take notes on your experience as a shopper. Write a memo comparing the customer service at each. Include such information as the following: Were you greeted when you came in? Did anyone offer to help you? If you bought something, were you given a survey? What differentiates the best of the three from the worst in terms of customer service?

6-18. Interview an entrepreneur about the type of CRM he or she uses. Discuss customer service and complaint handling in particular. Summarize the interview in a short paper.

BizBuilder Business Plan Questions

5.0 Marketing Strategy and Plan

5.1 Products/Services

D. Describe the features and benefits of the product/service your business will focus on selling.

5.3 Promotion

G. List ways you intend to provide superior customer service.

H. How will you keep your customer database? What essential questions will you ask every customer for your database? What data will you collect through their purchases?

Case Study | BNI—Building Businesses through Networking

Dr. Ivan Misner, known as "The Father of Modern Networking," is the ultimate business networking professional. He founded the world's largest business networking organization, Business Networks International, in 1985 and is a *New York Times* best-selling author. His blog (http://www.BusinessNetworking.com) provides insights into building a successful business-referral network.

As of 2013, BNI had over 6,440 chapters throughout every populated continent of the world. BNI reports that it generated 7.1 million referrals resulting in over $3.3 billion worth of business for its members in 2012.[17] According to the organization's Web site, "The mission of BNI is to help members increase their business through a structured, positive, and professional 'word-of-mouth' program that enables them to develop long-term, meaningful relationships with quality business professionals."

BNI members join chapters in their local areas that consist of prescreened individuals with a limit of one member per classification. For example, there can be only one general contractor and one mortgage banker. These groups meet weekly at designated locations to share business opportunities and network with one another. The idea behind BNI is to create "VCP," or *visibility, credibility,* and *profitability* for its members. This is done with the underlying philosophy of Givers Gain®, meaning that, by referring others, the members will build their own businesses.

Members are expected to provide referrals for one another on both a formal and informal basis. For example, they are asked to share information at the regular meetings. They are also expected to carry business cards and distribute them to one another when the opportunity for a referral arises. Webinars for members support creation of effective member profiles and provide guidance on maximizing the benefits of referrals.

Dr. Misner suggests, "You have to be an active, responsible, professional, accountable participant and show your fellow networkers the respect, attention, and support that you want them to give you."[18] BNI is clear that "The most successful chapters of BNI are comprised of participants who are sincerely committed to helping one another through networking. They are a team."

BNI identifies numerous benefits of being a member, including:

- Increased exposure to many other people and businesses
- Building solid business relationships that will last for the rest of your life
- Tools to network more effectively, including educational workshops and mentoring
- Visibility, credibility, and profitability for each member

While members can find participation beneficial, it is important to understand that referral networks work when members trust and respect one another. Joining a networking organization such as BNI is a step toward gaining referrals. However, successful members nurture relationships with other members over time and through their actions. Dr. Misner writes, "Remember, if you start putting together your network when the need arises, you're too late. The better way is to begin developing relationships now with the people whose help you will need in the future."[19]

Case Study Analysis

6-19. How does BNI reinforce the importance of selling based on benefits?

6-20. List three things BNI does that you could adopt to help build business relationships.

[17]BNI, accessed August 15, 2013, http://www.bni.com.

[18]Ivan Misner, "10 Ways to Waste Your Time in a Networking Group," *Professional PerformanceMagazine.com*, July 2013, vol. 21, no. 3, p. 33, accessed August 15, 2013, http://successnet.czcommunity.com/tag/professional-performance magazine/.

[19]Ibid, p. 33.

6-21. What type of referral network might support your proposed venture? Find such a group and write a paragraph about it and why it could be of value.

6-22. Visit the BNI site at http://www.bni .com. and find the chapter closest to your home.

    a. What is the name of the chapter?

    b. When does it meet?

    c. Who is the executive director of the chapter?

    d. How many members are in the chapter?

    e. What are the professional classifications of three of the members?

Case Source

Ivan Misner, "10 Ways to Waste Your Time in a Networking Group," *Professional PerformanceMagazine.com*, July 2013, vol. 21, no. 3, p. 33, accessed August 15, 2013, http://successnet.czcommunity.com/tag/ professional-performance-magazine/.

Case Study | Amazing Customer Service Propels Amazon

During the 2013 holiday season, some of Amazon's deliveries were late. The company's customer promise of two-day delivery was not met. While UPS and FedEx, the delivery companies involved, offered excuses and essentially blamed customers for complaining about the situation, Amazon worked to restore customer satisfaction.[20] Not only did it issue shipping refunds, but it distributed $20 gift cards and apologized profusely and meant it. Customer service is critical for Amazon, and lapses are not tolerated.

A Culture of Service

Founder Jeff Bezos has focused the organization on excellence in customer service since its founding as a pure-play Internet retailer in 1995. Amazon was named the top customer service company by MSN Money/Zogby Analytics four years in a row.[21] As an MSN Money business writer notes, "Amazon's user-friendly website, along with low prices, one-click shopping, no-hassle returns, free-shipping options and even the sense of community it fosters, has welcomed some 180 million happy buyers into the fold. Combined, those contented clickers buy an average of 9.6 million items a day."[22] The National Retail Federation Foundation also ranked Amazon as a top retailer in its Customers' Choice Awards.[23]

Amazon is known for its culture of customer service. Bezos has said, "We see our customers as invited guests to a party, and we are the hosts. It's our job every day to make every important aspect of the customer experience a little bit better."[24] This focus drives the company.

Swimming Against the Current

The company has been innovative and willing to defy the popular wisdom with its customers. When the bookselling industry relied on brick-and-mortar stores, Amazon was created as an Internet-only retailer. Today, many companies have

Jeff Bezos, Amazon.com
(Justin Lane/Newscom)

both online and physical stores. Often, the stores are considered "showrooms" for additional online sales. Greeting and directly serving customers face-to-face is seen as critical. Amazon has steered away from these practices and seen both traditional booksellers and large chains such as Borders go out of business.

Whereas other online retailers tend to specialize in narrow niches for products, Amazon has expanded its offerings to include everything from Kindle books to candy to clothing to cookery. It has become a one-stop shop for millions of consumers, who keep coming back for more.

Using Technology to Sell

The Amazon team is highly skilled in using the available technology to increase sales. Amazon user purchases are tracked and the resulting data is used for multiple purposes. Registered users each have their own custom shopping areas, such as "Caroline's Amazon.com." When they visit, customers are greeted with customized advertising, a visual list of "Related to Items You've Viewed," "More Items to Consider," "New for You," and "Recommendations" to visit. They also have access to account information and wish lists

[20]Jeff Macke, "Amazon proves it's the customer service champ yet again," Yahoo Finance, January 13, 2014, http://finance.yahoo.com/blogs/breakout/amazon-proves-it-s-the-customer-service-champ-yet-again-151657935.html, accessed January 31, 2014.

[21]Karen Aho, "2013 Customer Service Hall of Fame," MSN Money, (n.d.), http://money.msn.com/investing/2013-customer-service-hall-of-fame, accessed January 31, 2014.

[22]Ibid.

[23]National Retail Federation Foundation, Customers' Choice Awards, January 12, 2012, http://www.nrffoundation.com/content/customers-choice-awards, accessed February 2, 2014.

[24]Brainy Quote, http://www.brainyquote.com/quotes/quotes/j/jeffbezos173311.html#8bvMf76imSRezkoa.99, accessed January 31, 2014.

© Alex Segre/Alamy

among multiple other choices. While shopping on the site, they are prompted to add purchases by displays of related products, opportunities to earn free shipping, and advertisements for Amazon Prime. Also, customer reviews and ratings are readily visible to shoppers.

Away from the site itself, customers receive e-mails from Amazon. When they make a purchase, a confirmation e-mail is sent with a thank you. When their orders ship, shipping and tracking information is sent to customers. Customers receive optional promotional e-mails for categories of goods purchased, such as Kindle mysteries, thrillers, and business books. These e-mails are based on purchase data and are tailored to customer groups rather than generic messages.

Actively Seeking Customer Feedback

Customer input is more than just lip service at Amazon. The total experience is wrapped around the customer to build customer satisfaction, sales, and repeat purchases. While some companies seek customer feedback periodically or more subtly, Amazon has multiple points of contact for responses. One direct method is through soliciting feedback on purchases via e-mail. The company sends out e-mails asking for reviews on the products (physical and Kindle) and the packaging. Kindle readers are prompted to provide reviews at the end of each book, and they are offered reviews and ratings on the front end. While on the site, customers can comment on products and indicate their interest in or satisfaction with them.

The Total Customer Experience

With all of the various sophisticated uses of customer tracking data, customer feedback, and other options, Amazon has worked relentlessly to attain its ranking as a leading retailer for customer service and top sales leader.

Case Study Analysis

6-23. Why would Amazon accept responsibility for the shipping problems of its vendors, UPS and FedEx? How would you feel about the company's response if you were among the customers who did not receive two-day shipping as promised?

6-24. List the pros and cons of Amazon's customer relationship management system from the company and customer perspective.

6-25. How has Amazon compensated for the lack of brick-and-mortar stores?

6-26. Go to the Amazon.com site and search for *The Lean Startup* by Eric Ries.
   a. What formats are available?
   b. What other categories of information are provided, and how might they boost sales for the company?
   c. What ordering options are offered? Are any more convenient than others? Why?

Case Sources

Karen Aho, "2013 Customer Service Hall of Fame," MSN Money, (n.d.), http://money.msn .com/investing/2013-customer-service-hall-of-fame, accessed January 31, 2014.

Amazon.com web site, accessed January 31, 2014, https://www.amazon.com.

Jeff Macke, "Amazon proves it's the customer service champ yet again," Yahoo Finance, January 13, 2014, http://finance.yahoo.com/ blogs/breakout/amazon-proves-it-s-the-customer-service-champ-yet-again-151657935.html, accessed January 31, 2014.

National Retail Federation Foundation, Customers' Choice Awards, January 12, 2012, http:// www.nrffoundation.com/content/customers-choice-awards, accessed February 2, 2014.

Kitchen Arts & Letters, Inc.—An Independent Bookstore Defies Industry Odds

During the 1980s independent bookstores could still be found in communities across America. Online megastores such as Amazon.com didn't emerge until the mid-1990s. Barnes & Noble and Borders were beginning to build their big-box chains but hadn't yet reached significant scale. In 1983, Nach (pronounced Nock) Waxman, a former graduate student in anthropology and South Asian studies, wrapped up his 18-year-long career as a book editor and started Kitchen Arts & Letters (KA&L), now a fixture in Manhattan's Upper East Side. Waxman wanted a store that was totally devoted to a single subject—food. He operates from a single location and has no e-commerce site, yet KA&L has become one of the most renowned and beloved of culinary bookstores.

Not Just a Cookbook Store

When Waxman created KA&L, he envisioned a store that was more than just a cookbook outlet. He wanted to provide books on all subjects related to food. As he says, "We are not a cookbook store. . . . We are a place—you could call it a cultural zone—in which one can explore almost every aspect of this everyday feature of all our lives—how and where we get our food, how we distribute it, prepare it, consume it and even how we think about it."[25]

Kitchen Arts & Letters has an inventory of approximately 13,000 titles, quite extensive in depth in the culinary field. In addition to cookbooks, there are books on food chemistry, the restaurant business, ethnographic monographs, and various food-related items, such as stationery and art. Books can be new, used, or "antiquarian" (very old and rare).

Waxman doesn't try to carry every cookbook or food-related volume that has ever been published. In fact, he is selective about what is sold at the store. He is not focused on recipes, rather on looking holistically at the role of food in life. Books are sold through a consultative discussion with a bookseller, and customers often find themselves purchasing books they didn't know existed when they walked into the store.[26]

Serving up Customer Satisfaction

In an online world in which the independent bookstore is becoming increasingly hard to sustain, KA&L continues to thrive through relationships with its clientele. Waxman notes the importance of the variety of food-related topics and of the conversation with customers. More than that, the store is clearly focused on its customers and finding the right books for the right individuals.

KA&L customers are generally either culinary professionals or home cooks. While Waxman treasures the visits from many of the top chefs in the world, he is most interested in the kitchen staff sent by those chefs. Line cooks and others come to Kitchen Arts & Letters to learn more about their craft. When chefs recommend KA&L, they can be confident that its

---

[25]"Kitchen Arts and Letters: Not Your Average Cookbook," *Azure in the Neighborhood* blog posted April 16, 2013, accessed July 25, 2013, http://azureny.com/blog/?p=346.

[26]Craig LaBan. "Nach Waxman Sells Passion for Food at Manhattan Cookbook Store: From Brisket to Culinary Journals, A Food Legend Endures," *The Jewish Daily Forward*, July 22, 2011, accessed July 25, 2013, http://forward.com/articles/140139/nach-waxman-sells-passion-for-food-at-manhattan-co.

employees will be reliably knowledgeable and will share that expertise with their own personnel. Waxman says, "We love the beginners. . . . My favorite kind of thing happens when these kids in jeans come in, some of them rough-looking characters, and say: 'My chef told me I should read Escoffier. What do you recommend?'"[27]

Foodies and home cooks can also find a dazzling array of reading options. However, while the main floor of the store includes an incredible collection of current books in English (as well as many other languages), it doesn't focus on the most popular cookbooks or the most trendy television chefs. If a customer is looking for the most recent cookbook by Rachel Ray or the Hungry Girl, they are likely to do better at Barnes & Noble or on Amazon.com. KA&L may carry a limited supply of some of these books but doesn't get many requests for them. If someone is interested in finding an original Fannie Farmer Cookbook or a something on the culinary history of Vietnam, however, they are likely to find what they want.

Customers are welcome to wander the aisles and peruse books whether or not they intend to purchase them. The store manager and staff are highly trained and passionate about the attention they give the customers. Blog postings on such sites as Yelp and FourSquare reveal KA&L customers raving about how helpful its staff was in finding books tailored to their specific interests.

Not Every Book Is for Sale

Waxman has created a special basement area at KA&L that holds the rare, out-of-print, and "last copies" of books. Some of these are not for sale, but others are only awaiting the right customer.

He has reserved a set of last copies of certain books to serve as a reference library in the bookstore. These may be read by customers in the store, and selected pages may be copied, but they are not for sale. This scenario has created a mystique of its own. Waxman takes a personal interest in finding the right customer for KA&L's rare and out-of-print books.

A Market Divided

Kitchen Arts & Letters is clearly a destination shopping location for its customers. It is a relatively small space on Lexington Avenue that could be passed by without notice; yet it draws thousands of customers per year from around the globe. These customers are not the "mass market" readers who are typically drawn to the larger chains or online behemoths. They are generally either culinary professionals or home cooks. The first category includes chefs, caterers, restaurateurs, cooking instructors, and food writers and editors.

Waxman has noted that the needs of these two groups are basically different, which means the store operates on two levels, literally and figuratively. Store operations and inventory are tailored to both. For the professionals, KA&L stocks the books with photographs of the foods as prepared, restaurant-industry information, culinary history, memoirs, and literature. For the amateur, the focus is more on preparation and cooking techniques (cookbooks) and culinary experiences. Waxman comments, "The customers on each side of the line tend to be pretty firm about their requirements; the professionals invariably identify particular titles as either their kind

---

[27]Alex Whitchel. "At Work With: Nach Waxman; Need a Rain-Forest Recipe? He's the Man to Call, *New York Times*, June 28, 1995, accessed July 26, 2013, http://www.nytimes.com/1995/06/28/garden/at-work-with-nach-waxman-need-a-rain-forest-recipe-he-s-the-man-to-call.html?pagewanted=print&src=pm.

of book or as too 'home-y'; and the home cooks see what they call 'chef-y' books as culinary exercises . . ."[28]

The distinctiveness of the requirements eludes even Waxman: "Certainly in terms of sales, only a handful of books straddle the line successfully. . . . We've found it immensely challenging to try to identify what makes a particular type of book appeal to a particular audience."[29] Nonetheless, it seems that Kitchen Arts & Letters has balanced its market well and succeeded in an industry where it is swimming against the current.

Bookstore Industry Background

The face of the bookselling industry has changed radically over the past two decades. The chains and independent bookstores have seen a shift in focus from the act of selling only books to providing a broader range of products and entertainment. Many stores have online ordering and some, such as Amazon.com, are pure-play e-commerce sites. Both Barnes & Noble and Amazon offer e-readers for electronic books. In essence, the industry has reinvented itself.

The bookstore sector (NAICS code 451211) is dominated by Barnes & Noble, Books-A-Million, and Amazon.com. Barnes & Noble has been in the business since 1973 and started as a used book seller. Today, it has 675 stores in all 50 states, plus 686 college bookstores, as well as its Web site. The company had $6.8 billion in sales in fiscal year 2013.[30] Books-A-Million has more than 250 stores in 31 states and the District of Columbia, a far cry from its origins as an Alabama newsstand in 1917. Books-A-Million has superstores (Books-A-Million, BAM!, Books and Co., 2nd & Charles), traditional stores (Bookland, Books-A-Million, BAM!), Joe Muggs Newsstands, plus wholesale and e-commerce operations.[31] Amazon.com claims to be the world's largest retailer in its pure-play e-commerce business, with over $61 billion in sales and 97,000 employees.[32]

Independent bookstores continue to exist, although many have closed over the last 20 years. Between 1993 and 2004, their numbers dropped by 57 percent, and they were further impacted by the economic downturn, which also lowered sales for the chains.[33] In 2010, there were just over 3,600 such firms (91.4 percent of the total) with under 20 employees in the industry, employing about 16,000 people (13.9 percent of the total), according to the U.S. Census County Business Patterns. In 2007 the Economic Census showed that there were about 1,100 more bookstores, but those with fewer than 20 employees accounted for only about one-third of the almost $17 billion total revenue.

Many independent bookstores have moved to online scenarios rather than maintain bricks-and-mortar retail sites. Others have added services and products—such as cafés and gifts—or featured in-store events like music, author signings and readings, and book clubs. The stores have also become more specialized.

Customer demographics for the bookstore market are primarily defined as:

- College graduates (57 percent of the market, twice the rate of any other group)

---

[28]Nach Waxman. "Nach's Blog," October 2009, accessed July 26, 2013, http://www.kitchenartsandletters.com.

[29]Ibid.

[30]Barnes and Noble, accessed July 26, 2013, http://www.barnesandnobleinc.com/press_releases/6_25_13_2013_FYE_financial_results.html

[31]Books-A-Million, "2013 Annual Report," accessed July 26, 2013, http://www.booksamillioninc.com/annualreport.html, p. 6.

[32]Amazon.com, "2012 Annual Report," accessed July 26, 2013, http://phx.corporate-ir.net/phoenix.zhtml?c=97664&p=irol-reportsAnnual, p. 2.

[33]Veronica G. Rodriguez, "Bookstores," *SDBC Net*, accessed July 25, 2013, http://www.sbdcnet.org/small-business-research-reports/bookstores.

- Adults ages 45 to 64 (spend 28 percent to 33 percent more than average on books)
- Married couples (with or without children)
- Between 18 and 24 and 65 and older (they spend the least)
- High-income buyers
- Residents of the western United States[34]

Both Amazon and Books-A-Million share insights into the factors that are most important to their customers. They each identify *selection, convenience,* and *price* in their annual reports. Books-A-Million adds *customer service* and *ease of access to content* to the list.

Amazon includes a section on the "competition environment" in its annual report to shareholders, which is particularly telling. The portion that pertains to the bookstore industry reads as follows:

> Our businesses are rapidly evolving and intensely competitive. Our current and potential competitors include: (1) physical-world retailers, publishers, vendors, distributors, manufacturers, and producers of our products; (2) other online e-commerce and mobile e-commerce sites . . . (3) media companies, web portals, comparison shopping websites, and web search engines . . .[35]

This is the tough industry environment in which Kitchen Arts & Letters is operating.

Case Study Analysis

U2-1. What opportunity did Nach Waxman identify when founding Kitchen Arts & Letters?

U2-2. What are the business-definition aspects of KA&L (offer, target market, capability, problem solving)?

U2-3. What is the competition, direct and indirect, for the company?

U2-4. Create a qualitative competitor analysis chart for KA&L. Given its target customers, list the top five competitive factors. Select three competitors (name them). This will require some research.

U2-5. Which of the six factors of competitive advantage apply for KA&L? Explain.

U2-6. Describe the segmentation for KA&L in geographic, demographic, psychographic, and behavioral dimensions.

U2-7. Complete the following positioning statement:

Kitchen Arts & Letters, Inc., is the _____ that _____ to _____.

U2-8. Where in the product life cycle are independent bookstores? Where is KA&L? Why is it the same or different from others?

U2-9. Create a three-question survey that would be of value to Nach Waxman and his team. To whom would it be administered? By whom? How would it be administered? Why would it be useful?

U2-10. What secondary research could be of value to KA&L management? Find three specific sources and cite them properly.

---

[34]Best Customers: Demographics of Consumer Demand, 7th edition, Ithaca, New York: New Strategist Publications, Inc., 2010.

[35]Amazon.com, Inc., *2012 Annual Report,* accessed July 26, 2013, http://phx.coporate-ir.net/phoenix.zhtml?c=97664&p=irol-reportsAnnual, p. 3.

SHOW ME THE MONEY: FINDING, SECURING, AND MANAGING IT

Chapter 7
UNDERSTANDING AND MANAGING START-UP, FIXED, AND VARIABLE COSTS

Chapter 8
USING FINANCIAL STATEMENTS TO GUIDE A BUSINESS

Chapter 9
CASH FLOW AND TAXES

Chapter 10
FINANCING STRATEGY & TACTICS

Sergey Nivens/Fotolia

7

Understanding and Managing Start-Up, Fixed, and Variable Costs

Learning Objectives

1. Calculate the investment required for business start-up.

2. Assess the variable costs of starting a business.

3. Analyze fixed operating costs and calculate gross profit.

4. Select financial record keeping for your business.

CHAPTER

Jupiter Images

"All our records had to be hits because we couldn't afford any flops."

—Berry Gordy, founder, Motown Record Company

eeking out optimal medical services has become global, due to advances in technology, ease of travel, and variety of cost structures. Aravind Eye Care System (AECS), a social enterprise, is based in Maduri, India, and claims it is "the largest and most productive eye care facility in the world." Aravind provides eye surgery and outpatient care at each of its five hospitals. AECS was founded in 1976 by Dr. Govindappa Venkataswamy ("Dr. V") with the goal of eliminating blindness. In 2008, Dr. P. Namperumalsamy, Chairman of AECS, was awarded the Ernst & Young Entrepreneur of the Year for Health Care in Mumbai.

In addition to the facilities at its 41 primary, 5 secondary, 5 tertiary, and 6 outpatient eye care centers, AECS provides award-winning telemedicine services in rural areas of the country. It has become an international training center (Lions Aravind Institute of Community Ophthalmology), and AECS treats patients from around the world. The program has focused on creating cost efficiencies in the delivery of care to enable outreach to a broader base of patients. In addition, AECS manufactures optical products (specifically, intraocular lenses for cataract patients) through its Aurolab division for use in its hospitals and for outside sale to raise funds to serve more patients in poverty. Funding for AECS comes from many countries, and a good number of ophthalmology interns are Americans.

The efficiencies achieved by AECS allow it to provide well over half of its surgical care at no cost or reduced fees. By creating what is essentially an assembly-line layout and procedure for cataract surgeries and working in small, specialized teams, AECS minimizes the time necessary for each surgery, and the surgeons complete a maximum number of operations per day. Also, because Indian laws differ from those in the United States, more than one patient can be in an operating room at a time, so that surgeons can rapidly move from one patient to the next with minimal down time.

Between April 2012 and March 2013, some 371,000 people underwent surgeries at one of the Aravind Eye facilities, and 3.1 million obtained care on an outpatient basis. Approximately half of the surgeries were under its free-care programs for the poor.

© Picture Partners/Alamy

What Does It Cost to Operate a Business?

To run a successful business, you will need to keep track of your costs and have more cash coming in than going out. The bedrock principle of business is that it earns a profit by selling products or services for more than they cost.

Learning Objective 1 ▶

Calculate the investment required for business start-up.

A business can make a profit only if the selling price per unit is greater than the cost per unit. A litmus test for profitability is the *economics of one unit* (EOU), as discussed in prior chapters. It tells an entrepreneur if the business is earning a profit on each individual unit. Knowing your EOU will be helpful as you determine your venture's viability.

Many costs are associated with the establishment and growth of a small business. These include start-up purchases, fixed and variable costs, and cash reserves. Each will be discussed in turn. All are components of

Aravind Eye Care System Web site, August 16, 2013, http://www.aravind.org.

your accounting records, the documents that are used to classify, analyze, and interpret the financial transactions of an organization.

Start-Up Investment

Learning Objective 2 ▶

Assess the variable costs of starting a business.

seed capital (start-up investment) the one-time expense of opening a business.

There is another critical cost to discuss before establishing accounting records for your business. We have talked about the costs of operating a business, but what about the money required to *start* the business? Start-up investment, or **seed capital**, is the one-time expense of opening a business. In a restaurant, for example, start-up expenses would include stoves, refrigeration, food processors, tables, chairs, utensils, and other items that would not be replaced very often. Also included might be the one-time cost of buying land and constructing a building or the cost of renovating an existing space. Some entrepreneurs also choose to consider the time they put into getting their businesses off the ground as part of the start-up investment. To do so, place a value on your time per hour and multiply by the number of hours you think you will need to put in to get your business going. You might be shocked at how big that number is.

For a hot dog stand, the start-up investment list might look like this:

Beginning inventory (hot dogs, mustard, buns, etc.)	$50
Business cards and flyers	150
Business licenses (city and state)	200
Hot dog cart	2,500
Cash box and other	100
Total start-up investment without contingency	$3,000
Contingency @ 10% of start-up investment	300
Total start-up investment with contingency	$3,300

prototype a model or pattern that serves as an example of how a product would look and operate if it were produced.

For a more complex business, like a 24-hour franchise fitness center opening in leased space, the summary start-up sheet could be as shown in **Exhibit 7-1**. The items would be broken down into greater detail in order to secure quotations or prices. For example, each piece of equipment would be identified and a quote secured, assuming the franchisor does not have a preset package of equipment that a franchisee must purchase.

For a manufacturing business, developing a prototype for the item being manufactured may be a major start-up cost, perhaps totaling in the millions. A **prototype** is a model or pattern that serves as an example of how a product would look and operate if it were manufactured. Companies that specialize in creating prototypes can be found in the *Thomas Register of American Manufacturers*.

Brainstorm to Avoid Start-Up Surprises

Before starting your business, try to anticipate every possible cost by analyzing all components and possibilities. Talk to others in your industry and ask them what start-up costs they failed to anticipate. Research industry information and obtain quotations from potential suppliers. Use **Exhibit 7-2** to estimate your start-up investment.

Once you have created a list, take it to your advisors and have them review it. They will probably find costs you have overlooked. You might not have realized that the electric company requires a $1,000 deposit to turn on service, for example. Or you

A fitness center is an example of a complex business.
(Jupiterimages/Thinkstock)

Exhibit 7-1 *Seed Capital Estimate for a 24-Hour Fitness Center*		
Item/Category	**Cost**	**Estimate or Quote?**
Start-Up Expenses		
Debt service (interest on $130,000 at 10%)	$2,167	Estimate
Employee wages, salaries, and benefits	$3,100	Estimate
Financing costs and fees (2% of $130,000)	$2,600	Estimate
Franchise fees	$40,000	Quote
Insurance	$1,000	Quote
Licenses and permits	$300	Quote
Memberships (trade associations, chambers of commerce, and the like)	$900	Mixed
Owner time (valued at $25 per hour)*	$5,000	Estimate
Professional services (attorney, accountant, architect, engineers, and the like)	$3,000	Estimate
Promotions and advertising	$1,800	Mixed
Rent on location identified	$2,000	Quote
Supplies	$400	Estimate
Taxes (wage and other)	$500	Estimate
Training, conventions, and seminars	$1,000	Quote
Utilities	$400	Estimate
Total Start-Up Expenses	$64,167	
Start-Up Assets		
Computers and other technology	$5,000	Quote
Deposits on rent and utilities	$5,600	Quote
Equipment, furniture, and fixtures	$105,000	Quote
Installation of equipment and fixtures	$2,800	Quote
Inventory	$200	Estimate
Leasehold improvements	$3,200	Quote
Petty cash	$300	Quote
Total Start-Up Assets	$122,100	
Total Pre-Opening Investment	$186,267	
Contingency Funds (10%)	$18,626	
Start-Up with Contingency**	**$204,893**	

* If no wage or salary is being paid to the owners, this is a "soft" cost and can be considered an optional item on the list. However, including it makes the list more comprehensive and more reflective of the total.

** This figure does not include cash reserves or cash requirements for initial cash shortfall during operations. Both should be added to reflect total financing needed.

may need licenses and insurance you did not expect. Tack on an additional 10 percent to your estimates for contingencies and emergencies.

Keep a Reserve Equal to One-Half the Start-Up Investment

Start-up investment should include one more thing: a **cash reserve**—that is, emergency funds and a pool of cash resources, which should equal at least half your start-up costs. For the previously mentioned hot dog cart example, therefore, the reserve would be half of $3,300, or $1,650, making the total required $4,950.

Entrepreneurs must be prepared for the unexpected; the only good surprise is no surprise. The reserve will provide a moderate cushion of

cash reserve emergency funds and a pool of cash resources.

Exhibit 7-2 *Start-Up Investment Checklist*		
Item/Category	**Cost**	**Explanation/Note**
Land and building (if constructing or purchasing)		
Equipment and machinery		
Furniture and fixtures		
Leasehold improvements (if renting)		
Installation of equipment and fixtures		
Computers and other technology		
Employee wages, salaries, and benefits		
Owner time (valued at $ _____ per hour)*		
Professional services (attorney, accountant, architect, engineers, and the like)		
Promotions and advertising		
Licenses and permits		
Deposits on rent and utilities		
Rent		
Utilities		
Insurance		
Debt service (normally interest only)		
Taxes (wage and other)		
Memberships (trade associations, chambers of commerce, and the like)		
Registration fees		
Training, conventions, and seminars		
Licensing or franchising fees		
Financing costs and fees		
Supplies		
Inventory		
Petty cash		
Total pre-opening investment		
Allowance for contingencies/emergencies (10%)		
Initial Investment**		

*If no wage or salary is paid to the owners, this is a "soft" cost and can be considered an optional item on the list. However, including it is more comprehensive and more reflective of total costs.

**This figure does not include cash reserves, or cash requirements for initial cash shortfall during operations. Both should be added to reflect total financing needed.

protection if you need it. When your computer goes down or an important supplier raises prices, you will be glad you had this money on hand.

Having a cash reserve will also allow you to take advantage of opportunities. Say you own a vintage clothing store and you hear from a friend whose great-aunt died and left him a great deal of authentic vintage clothing and jewelry. He is willing to sell you the whole lot for $500, which you figure you can resell in your shop for at least $2,000. If you have the cash on hand, you can take advantage of this profitable opportunity.

Predict the Payback Period

payback period estimated time required to earn sufficient net cash flow to cover the start-up investment.

When compiling and analyzing start-up costs, one consideration will be how long it will take for you to earn back your start-up investment. The **payback period** is an estimate of how long it will take your business to bring in enough cash to cover the start-up costs. It is measured in months.

$$\text{Payback} = \frac{\text{Start-Up Investment}}{\text{Net Cash Flow per Month}}$$

Example: Ashley's business requires a start-up investment of $1,000. The business is projecting a net cash flow per month of $400. How many months will it take to make back her start-up investment?

$$\text{Payback} = \frac{\$1,000}{\$400} = 2.5 \text{ Months}$$

Knowing the payback period is important for a firm, so that the time horizon is known and timing of funds availability is clear. However, the payback period does not take into consideration future earnings, opportunities for alternative investments, or the overall value of the company. It is based on net cash and is a good indicator of the time needed to earn back initial disbursements.

Estimate Value

Financial managers use several tools to determine the current value of proposed investments, of which *net present value* (NPV) is widely accepted as the most theoretically sound. Entrepreneurs can use such a technique to consider the financial returns on their initial investment. If the NPV calculation yields a positive value, the investment will result in a positive return based on the owner's (and investors') required rate of return.

Ryan McVay/Thinkstock

There are multiple methods of calculating NPV, including using a formula, tables, a spreadsheet program, or a financial calculator. You can calculate NPV with the following information: required rate of return (%), annual net cash flows, initial investment, and number of years of cash flows. **Exhibit 7-3** shows an NPV calculation for a business with an initial investment of $1.5 million.

Exhibit 7-3 *Calculating Net Present Value with Excel*

Description	Data	Notes
Initial investment	$1,500,000	Seed capital needed to start the business
Required rate of return	0.12	Return required by investors (owners)
Net Cash Year 1	$0	First year of operations, yielding no net cash
Net Cash Year 2	$100,000	Second year of operations with earnings
Net Cash Year 3	$200,000	Subsequent year
Net Cash Year 4	$500,000	Subsequent year
Net Cash Year 5	$850,000	Subsequent year
Net Cash Year 6	$1,200,000	Subsequent year
Net Cash Year 7	$600,000	Results show declining market
Net Cash Year 8	$400,000	Further decline
Net Cash Year 9	$0	Company closed
Calculated Present Value	$2,063,067.47	Use NPV formula
Net Present Value	**$563,067.47**	Value above initial investment
NPV > $0?	Yes	NPV is positive, so it is a "go"

Exhibit 7-4 *Manufacturing Business: Unit = 1 Hand-Painted T-Shirt*

Economics of One Unit (EOU) Analysis				
(Define the Unit of Sale)				
Selling Price (per Unit)				$35.00
COGS (Cost of Goods Sold)				
Materials per Unit		$7.00		
Labor per hour	$10.00			
# of Hours per Unit	0.75			
Total Labor per Unit	7.50	7.50		
Total COGS (per Unit)		$14.50	$14.50	14.50
Gross Profit (per Unit)				$20.50
Other Variable Costs				
Commission (10%)		3.50		
Packaging		0.50		
Total Other Variable Costs		$4.00	4.00	4.00
Total Variable Costs (per Unit)			$18.50	
Contribution Margin				$16.50

Fixed and Variable Costs: Essential Building Blocks

variable costs expenses that vary directly with changes in the production or sales volume.

fixed costs expenses that must be paid regardless of whether sales are being generated.

Small business owners divide their costs into two categories. **Variable costs** change based on the volume of units sold or produced. **Fixed costs** are expenses that must be paid regardless of whether sales are being generated.

Variable costs change with production and sales. They fall into two subcategories:

1. Cost of goods sold (COGS) or cost of services sold (COSS). Each is associated specifically with a single unit of sale, including:
   - The cost of materials used to make the product (or deliver the service)
   - The cost of labor used to make the product (or deliver the service)
2. Other variable costs, including:
   - Commissions or other compensation based on sales volume
   - Shipping and handling charges

Fixed costs stay constant over a range of productions, whether you sell many units or very few. Examples of fixed costs include rent, salaries, insurance, equipment, and manufacturing facilities.

Henry Ford spent money on efficient manufacturing equipment (a fixed cost) but saved a fortune on labor (COGS) by doing so. This reduced his total costs because labor was used in each of the millions of cars Ford produced, but he only had to pay for the plant and equipment once.

For any product, you can study its economics of one unit (EOU) to figure out what it cost to make that sale. **Exhibit 7-4** shows an example from a business that sells hand-painted T-shirts.

Calculating Critical Costs

To determine the most important factors with respect to costs in your business, you can calculate *critical* costs. This will help you to determine profitability and the factors that can and cannot be easily changed to impact your profits and cash flow.

Calculating Total Gross Profit (Contribution Margin)

You can use EOU to calculate whether and by how much you will come out ahead on your per-unit costs for each sale. By using the EOU, you can figure the gross profit per unit (**contribution margin** per unit sold, which is the selling price minus all variable costs).

contribution margin gross profit per unit—the selling price minus total variable costs plus other variable costs.

Calculating EOU When You Sell Multiple Products

Most businesses sell more than a single product, and they can also use EOU as a value measure of product profitability. A business selling a variety of products has to create a separate EOU for each item to determine whether each is profitable. When there are many similar products with comparable prices and cost structures, a "typical" EOU can be used.

Example: Jamaal sells four kinds of candy bars at school. He sells each bar for $1, but he pays a different wholesale price for each:

Chocolate Delight	$0.36 each
Almond Euphoria	$0.38 each
Fruit Envy	$0.42 each
Junior Crunch Bar	$0.44 each

Rather than make separate EOUs, Jamaal uses the average cost of his four candy bars (see **Exhibit 7-5**).

Costs of the four candy bars = ($0.36+$0.38+$0.42+$0.44) ÷ 4
Average cost of the four candy bars = $1.60 ÷ 4
Average cost of each bar = $0.40

Using a simple average works as long as Jamaal sells roughly the same number of each brand of bar. If he can no longer get Chocolate Delight and Almond Euphoria at some point, for example, he should then change his EOU to reflect the higher price of the other two bars.

What if each unit of sale is made up of a complex mix of materials and labor? The EOU can still help you figure the COGS, other variable costs, and gross profit for the product, although the process will be more complex.

Example: Denise sells sandwiches from her deli cart downtown on Saturdays. She sells each for $5. The materials and labor that go directly into making one sandwich are the COGS. The costs of the materials and direct labor for production are called **inventory costs** until the product is sold. There will also be some other variable costs, such as napkins, a paper wrapping for each sandwich, and plastic bags.

First, make a list of the COGS and any other variable costs:

inventory costs expenses associated with materials and direct labor for production until the product is sold.

COGS

a. Turkey costs $2.60 per lb. Each sandwich uses 4 ounces of turkey meat (1/4 of a pound).

b. Large rolls cost $1.92 per dozen. One roll is used per sandwich.

c. A 32-ounce jar of mayonnaise costs $1.60. One ounce of mayonnaise is used per sandwich.

Many small businesses have inventory costs.
(Jose Luis Pelaez Inc./Alamy)

Exhibit 7-5 *Retail Business: Unit = 1 Candy Bar*

Economics of One Unit (EOU) Analysis		
One Unit of Sale = One Candy Bar		
Selling Price		**$1.00**
COGS (direct cost of the product or service)		
Average Cost of Candy Bars (COGS)	0.40	
Average Shipping Cost per Unit	0.06	
Total COGS	**0.46**	0.46
Gross Profit		0.54
Other Variable Costs (none)	—	—
Contribution Margin		**$0.54**

   d. Lettuce costs 80 cents per pound. One ounce (1/16 of a pound) is used on each sandwich.

   e. Tomatoes cost $1.16 each. Each sandwich uses one-fourth of a tomato.

   f. Pickles cost 5 cents each. Each sandwich comes with two pickles.

   g. Employees are paid $8 per hour and can make 10 sandwiches per hour (we are assuming no down time and no payroll costs).

Other Variable Costs

   a. Napkins cost $3 per pack of 100. One napkin is included with each sale.

   b. Paper wrapping costs 20 cents per foot (cut from a roll). Each sandwich uses two feet of paper.

   c. Plastic carryout bags cost $7 per roll of 100. Each sandwich sold uses one plastic carryout bag.

The EOU for the turkey sandwich is shown in **Exhibit 7-6**.

Exhibit 7-6 *Retail Business: Unit = 1 Turkey Sandwich*

Selling Price per Unit:					$5.00
Cost of Goods Sold	**Price**	**Units**	**Quantity Used**	**Cost Each**	
Turkey (4 oz.):	$2.60	Per lb.	¼ lb.	$0.65	
Bread (roll):	$1.92	Per dozen	1/12 dozen	$0.16	
Mayonnaise (1 oz.):	$1.60	Per 32-oz. jar	1/32 jar	$0.05	
Lettuce (1 oz.):	$0.80	Per lb.	1/16 lb.	$0.05	
Tomato (¼ lb.):	$1.16	Each	¼ each	$0.29	
Pickles (2):	$0.05	Each	2 each	$0.10	
Direct Labor (6 min.):	$8.00	Per hr.	1/10 hr.	$0.80	
Total Cost of Goods Sold per Unit:				**$2.10**	2.10
Gross Profit					**$2.90**
Other Variable Costs					
Napkin:	$3.00	Per 100-pack	1/100 pack	$0.03	
Paper Wrapping:	$0.20	Per foot	2 feet	$0.40	
Plastic Bag:	$7.00	Per roll (100)	1/100 roll	$0.07	
Total Other Variable Costs per Unit:				**$0.50**	
Total Variable Costs per Unit:					0.50
Contribution Margin per Unit:					**$2.40**

Fixed Operating Costs

Costs that do not vary per unit of production or service, such as rent or the Internet bill, are called fixed operating costs. Total fixed costs do not change based on volume (an advertising cost of $1,000 will be the same whether it generates 50 sales or 500). Fixed cost per unit decreases as the number of units increases ($20 per unit above versus $2).

Fixed operating costs do not change based on sales activity levels; therefore, they are not included in the EOU. A sandwich shop has to pay the same rent each month whether it sells one turkey sandwich or a hundred. However, the owner of the shop can change the cost of the rent by moving or can increase or decrease the advertising budget, for example. These changes are not calculated on a per-unit basis.

It is easier to remember several of the most common categories of fixed expenses by remembering the phrase:

I SAID U R + "Other FXs"

This stands for:

Insurance
Salaries (indirect labor—managers, office staff, sales force)
Advertising
Interest
Depreciation
Utilities (gas, electric, telephone, Internet access)
Rent
Other **F**ixed e**X**penses

Most of these categories are self-explanatory, but *depreciation* may need clarification. Depreciation is the percentage of value of an asset subtracted each year until the value becomes zero—to reflect wear and tear on the asset. It is a method used to *expense* (list as an expense on the income statement) costly pieces of equipment. Fixed costs are expensed during the year the money is spent. When a company pays for advertising, it subtracts that cost from the gross profit for that year. Some items, however, such as a computer server, are expected to last for a number of years. A business could choose to expense the server during the year it was bought, but that would not be accurate. The server that will be used for four years will have been only 25 percent "used up" during the year it was purchased. Expensing the entire cost during that year would make the accounting records and financial statements inaccurate. If more than 25 percent of the server's cost is expensed in the first year, the income statement will show a lower profit than it should. Meanwhile, profits in subsequent years will appear to be higher than they should.

This issue is addressed by depreciation, which spreads the cost of an item purchased by a business over the time during which it will be in use. If the computer server is expected to have a useful life of more than one year, then the full price should be shown as an asset and then expensed according to federal tax law and traditional accounting practice.

Fixed Operating Costs Do Change Over Time

If you pay your restaurant manager $3,600 per month in salary, you will have to pay that amount whether the restaurant sells one meal or a thousand. The cost is fixed.

Fixed operating costs do change over time; at some point you may give your restaurant manager a raise. Or you might hire a new manager at

fixed operating costs expenses that do not vary with changes in the volume of production or sales.

◄ **Learning Objective 3**
Analyze fixed operating costs and calculate gross profit.

depreciation the percentage of value of an asset subtracted periodically to reflect the declining value.

Global Impact . . .

Direct Foreign Investment

Global companies experience opportunities and challenges when determining initial investments in foreign countries. Opportunities arise from such sources as incentives for direct foreign investment (DFI) and lower facilities-construction and fit-out costs. In addition, stocking start-up inventory may be more economical. At the same time, there may be barriers to DFI, such as legal and permitting costs, standards, and other requirements that increase initial investment. Clearly, having a full understanding of the initial start-up investment is crucial and is potentially more complex.

Exchange rates and the economic and political environment in a foreign country can have a significant impact on start-up investment. As is true with domestic start-ups, a realistic estimate of the initial investment is a vital consideration in the go/no go decision.

a higher salary. The word *fixed* does not mean the cost *never* changes, just that it does not change in response to units of production or sales over a relevant range of production. For instance:

- *Advertising.* The cost of advertising will change based on decisions the entrepreneur makes about how much to spend to reach the consumer, not because of current sales (although low sales may provoke an increase in advertising).
- *Heating and cooling costs.* The price of heating and cooling goes up or down based on the weather and utility prices, not on the amount of revenue the business earns.

Allocate Fixed Operating Costs Where Possible

Business owners like to know how much of their revenue will have to be used to cover the cost of goods sold and other variable costs. Whatever is left over after you pay the COGS and other variable costs is your *contribution margin*. You will pay your fixed operating costs from the contribution margin. Whatever is left over after you pay your fixed operating costs (and taxes) is your **net profit**.

net profit the remainder of revenues minus fixed and variable costs and taxes.

Fixed operating costs can be dangerous, because they have to be paid whether or not the business has made a gross profit. The entrepreneur should be careful about taking on fixed costs, but does not have to worry as much about variable costs because, if sales are low, the variable costs will be low as well. Wherever possible, the entrepreneur should seek to allocate or distribute as many costs as possible by making them variable.

Here is an example of how to fully allocate your costs, so that you will know, each time you sell a unit, how much of your fixed and variable costs the sale is covering.

Example: If you sell 300 watches per month at $15 per watch (see **Exhibit 7-7**), your COGS is $2 per watch, and your other variable costs are commissions of $2 per watch and shipping charges of $1 per watch ($5 per watch total variable costs).

Gross profit per unit is $13 ($15 − $2). Contribution margin per unit is $10 ($15 − $5). Some of this gross profit will have to be used to cover the business's fixed operating costs. It is helpful to determine how much profit will be left over after paying the fixed operating costs, assuming your sales are stable. **Exhibit 7-8** shows the calculation of the total cost per unit.

Exhibit 7-7 *Retail Business: Unit = 1 Watch*

Analysis—300 Watches Sold			
Sales (300 watches × $15 per watch):			$4,500
COGS ($2 per watch × 300 watches):		$600	600
Gross Profit (on 300 watches sold)			$3,900
Other Variable Costs			
Commission ($2 per watch)	$600		
Shipping ($1 per watch)	300		
Total Other Variable Costs	$900	900	900
Total Variable Costs (per Unit)		$1,500	
Contribution Margin			$3,000

Exhibit 7-8 *Retail Business: Total Cost Per Unit*

Total Variable Costs (COGS + Other Variable Costs):		$1,500
Fixed Operating Costs (per month):		
Utilities	$50	
Salaries	100	
Advertising	50	
Insurance	50	
Depreciation	50	
Interest	50	
Rent	100	
Total Fixed Operating Costs:	$450	450
Total Costs (Fixed + Variable) =		$1,950
Total Cost per Unit ($1,950 ÷ 300 watches) =		$6.50 per watch

For every watch you sell, your total cost, fixed and variable, is $6.50. If you receive $15 for each watch, therefore, your profit before tax is the following:

$15.00 Selling Price − $6.50 Total Cost per Unit = $8.50 Profit before Tax

The Dangers of Fixed Costs

If a business does not have enough sales to cover its fixed costs, it will lose money. If losses continue and there are not sufficient cash reserves, the business will have to close. As we have discussed, fixed costs are dangerous because they must be paid whether or not the business is making enough sales to cover them.

Using Accounting Records to Track Fixed and Variable Costs

Now you are ready to set up your financial records. Keeping accurate records of the money flowing in and out of your business will be critical to success. The systematic recording, reporting, and analysis of the financial

◀ Learning Objective 4

Select financial record keeping for your business.

Step into the Shoes . . .

Bob's Discount Furniture

Bob Kaufman of Bob's Discount Furniture.
(Richard B. Levine/Newscom)

Bob's Discount Furniture has 49 stores in New England and the Mid-Atlantic States and was named the 2008 Furniture Retailer of the Year.[1] It has come a long way since founder Bob Kaufman

started as a waterbed retailer in 1982. At that time he needed to find creative ways to cut his costs.

Bob found a store to rent for his furniture business, but the landlord wanted him to sign a one-year lease.[2] Bob knew rent was a fixed cost. This meant he would have to pay rent every month, whether he could afford to or not, for a full 12 months. He realized that if sales were low he would get into trouble quickly.

What Bob needed was to change his rent from a fixed to a variable cost. He negotiated with the landlord to pay the rent as a percentage of the monthly sales. That way, if sales were low, Bob's rent would also be low. If sales were high, his rent would go up, but he would be able to pay it. Rent was Bob's largest fixed cost. By changing it into a variable cost, he cut a lot of the risk out of his new business venture.

Bob's Discount Furniture became extremely successful. Today, the company owns many of its locations and pays fixed rent on the rest.

---

[1]Bob's Discount Furniture, accessed August 16, 2013, http://www.mybobs.com.

[2]Original case information provided by John Harris.

---

transactions of a business is called *accounting*. It is the primary language businesspeople use to communicate. When you talk to an investor or a supplier about your business, you will need to use accounting terms. He or she will want to see the financial statements for your business in standardized formats that describe its performance at a glance.

Before you can create financial statements, however, you must be able to keep track of your daily business transactions. If you develop record keeping into a habit, you will be well ahead of many businesspeople who get careless when it comes to keeping good records consistently.

Three Reasons to Keep Good Records Every Day

Accurate financial records will:

1. ***Show you how to make the business more profitable.*** Perhaps your profits are down this month over last. Did your expenses go up? Maybe you need to try lowering your costs. Did your sales drop? Maybe you are not spending enough on advertising. Use accurate records as a base to constantly improve your business.

2. ***Document profitability and cash position.*** If you want people to invest in your business, documenting that it is profitable, or could be, is essential. Keep accurate records to create financial statements and ratios.

3. ***Prove that payments have been made.*** Accurate, up-to-date records help prevent arguments, because they prove you have paid a bill or a customer has paid you. Records can also prove that you have paid your taxes—the fee *levied* (charged) by a government on the income or activity of an individual or legal business entity (corporation). Sometimes the Internal Revenue Service, the federal agency that collects taxes, will visit a business and check its financial records in a process called an **audit**.

audit a review of financial and business records to ascertain integrity and compliance with standards and laws, particularly by the U.S. Internal Revenue Service.

4. ***Take advantage of tax deductions.*** U.S. tax law allows business owners to deduct many expenses from their taxes. These *deductions*, or write-offs, are reductions in the gross amount on which taxes are calculated, and they will save you money. But you must keep receipts and record check payments to show that you actually had the expenses.

Use Accounting Software

There are many excellent computer software programs on the market to help small business owners keep good records and generate financial statements and analytical reports. These include Intuit QuickBooks, Microsoft Office Accounting, and Peachtree Accounting. In addition, companies such as Net Suite offer Web-based accounting for a monthly access fee. There are also programs to help you manage your money. You can use them to pay bills, balance your bank account, and track your income. Some software creates project quotes and invoices. There is specialized software for particular types of businesses and for nonprofit organizations. It may save you time and money to purchase industry-specific software from the start.

The URLs for the major accounting software companies are:

Microsoft, http://www.microsoft.com
QuickBooks, http://www.quickbooks.com
Peachtree Software, http://www.peachtree.com

Some software companies offer free products that you can try for a limited time or that are free but do not have as many features as the for-sale versions. This is a great way to try out accounting and other business software before you buy. The costs of these packages have dropped considerably over time, making them a better value for even the smallest companies. For example, if your business provides services, and potential customers expect estimates, they can be generated and tracked by professional-services software. Take the time to find the software best suited to your needs.

Keep Receipts and Invoices

For a very small business, it is possible to work with a manual system, including a journal and files for storing records of your transactions. As your business grows, you can add organizational tools. However, if you are

Step into the Shoes . . .

Rockefeller's Record Keeping

John D. Rockefeller, who founded Standard Oil (now ExxonMobil) and built one of the most famous family fortunes in history, reportedly kept track of every penny he spent from age 16 until his death in 1937 at the age of 98. His children said he never paid a bill without examining it and being certain that he understood it.

Being up to date with your financial records will give you control over your business and a sense of security.

John D. Rockefeller
(Hulton Archive
Photos/Getty Images)

intending to grow the business beyond a handful of transactions per week, you should use a good computer-based system from the start. Whatever system you elect to use, basic records must be kept.

- A *receipt* is a slip of paper or electronic document with the date and amount of the purchase on it. *Always get a receipt for every purchase you make.* Issue a receipt for all sales, if you have a retail business, whether you create it manually or from your point-of-sales system.
- An *invoice*, or bill or statement, shows the product or service sold and the amount the customer is to pay. Your invoice becomes the customer's receipt. Keep a copy of each invoice in an organized fashion (i.e., numerically, alphabetically, or in order by date), and record all payments promptly.

Keep at Least Two Copies of Your Records

Always keep a copy of your financial records in a location away from your business, preferably in a fire-retardant safe or concrete-lined file cabinet. If you are using software, back up your data and keep the media (CD, jump drive, external hard drive, etc.) in a different location or back up to a cloud storage location. At the end of each day, week, or month, move your new receipts and invoices to this location. How often you do this will depend on your transaction volume and how much data you are willing to risk losing. By having regular off-site backups you will still have your financial records, if anything happens to your journal or your business site. Follow federal records retention rules with these documents.

Use Business Accounts for Business Expenses

Open a checking account to use only for your business. It is inadvisable to comingle your personal and business funds, regardless of your business type or size. Financial institutions routinely require business checks to be deposited into business accounts rather than personal ones, so any customer check payments made out to your business name will have to be deposited into a business account.

Avoid using cash for business. If you must pay in cash, get an itemized receipt, record the expenditure, and file the receipt promptly. It is easy to lose track of cash receipts and miss out on tax deductions for business expenses.

Deposit money from sales right away. When you make a sale, the transaction will not be complete until the cash is deposited, or until the check has cleared, if the payment was made by check. Again, recording every sale is critical to documenting profitability and cash flow. It will also ensure that business receipts and sales match in your transaction records.

Cash versus Accrual Accounting Methods

cash accounting method a system wherein transactions are recorded when cash is paid out or received.

accrual method accounting method wherein transactions are recorded at the time of occurrence, regardless of the transfer of cash.

Financial accounting for businesses is divided between the *cash* and *accrual* methods, and each company may select which one it will use. Small businesses use either method, whereas large firms almost invariably use accrual accounting. It is best to seek professional advice on this issue when starting your business. With the **cash accounting method**, the only time an accounting entry is made is when cash is paid out or received. With the **accrual method**, entries are made according to the occurrence of the transaction, without regard to the date of payment (e.g., for a manufacturer, purchases would be billed when the product is shipped).

Recognizing Categories of Costs

Even if you are using accounting software to record your business transactions, it will be helpful to understand the key categories of accounting data. Brief descriptions follow:

- *Variable costs.* Any cost that changes based on the number of units produced or sold. Includes cost of goods sold (COGS).
- *Fixed costs.* Business expenses that must be paid whether or not sales are made.
- *Capital equipment.* Business equipment that is expected to last a year or more.
- *Investment.* Start-up capital plus any money you or others have invested in the business, but not loans. This is only for money invested in exchange for part ownership (equity).
- *Loans (debt).* Any funds you have borrowed to start or operate the business.
- *Revenue.* Money received from sales.
- *Inventory.* Anything purchased for resale is *inventory*. Includes shipping costs from the supplier.
- *Other costs.* Anything that does not fit into the other expense categories.

Chapter Summary

Now that you have studied this chapter, you can do the following:

1. Calculate the investment required for business start-up.
   - Brainstorming, consulting advisors, and research can be combined to create a comprehensive set of investment requirements.
   - Contingency funds and cash reserves should be added to minimize the impact of unanticipated costs and to permit flexibility to take advantage of opportunities.
   - Payback period is estimation of time required to bring in enough cash to cover the seed funding.
   - Net present value addresses the viability of an investment opportunity that considers investment-return criteria.
2. Assess the variable costs of starting a business.
   - Start-up investment is the one-time expense of starting a business.
   - Cost of goods sold is the direct cost of producing the product or service.
   - Operating costs comprise the funds necessary to run the business, not including the cost of goods sold. There are several main categories of operating costs:

   I SAID U R + "Other FXs"
   - **I**nsurance
   - **S**alaries (indirect labor—managers, office staff, sales force)
   - **A**dvertising
   - **I**nterest
   - **D**epreciation
   - **U**tilities (gas, electric, telephone, Internet access)
   - **R**ent
   - **O**ther **F**ixed e**X**penses

3. Analyze fixed operating costs and calculate gross profit.
   - Variable costs change with sales. They are divided into two subcategories:
     a. Cost of goods sold, which are the costs associated specifically with each unit of sale, including
        - the cost of materials used to make the product (or deliver the service) and
        - the cost of labor used to make the product (or deliver the service).
     b. Other variable costs, including
        - commissions and
        - shipping and handling charges, etc.
   - Fixed costs stay constant whether you sell many units or very few. Examples of fixed costs include rent, salaries, and insurance.
4. Select a financial record keeping system for your business.
   - Recognize the importance of keeping complete, accurate, and timely records.
   - Determine whether to use the cash or accrual accounting method.
   - Categorize the accounting entries properly, whether using a manual or computer-based accounting system.

Key Terms

accrual method	fixed operating costs
audit	inventory costs
cash accounting method	net profit
cash reserve	payback period
contribution margin	prototype
depreciation	seed capital
fixed costs	variable costs

Entrepreneurship Portfolio

Critical Thinking Exercises

7-1. Give an example of a business that you have observed lowering the price of a product. How do you think the business was able to reduce the price?

7-2. Describe the record-keeping system you intend to set up for your business. Why?

7-3. What bank accounts do you intend to open for your business? Which bank will you use? Why?

7-4. Imagine that you have invented a guitar strap that goes over both shoulders, thereby reducing shoulder strain for the guitarist. This item could be a big seller, but, before you can apply for a patent or convince investors to back your production plans, you will need a prototype. Find at least three manufacturers that could create such a prototype for you.

7-5. For a business you would like to start, estimate what you think the fixed and variable costs would be.

Key Concept Questions

7-6. What is the reason to calculate the payback period and the net present value for a business investment? What distinguishes the two?

7-7. Calculate Total Revenue for the items below.

Units Sold	Selling Price	Total Revenue
a. 25	$4.64	$116.00
b. 30	$10.99	_____
c. 12	$1,233.00	_____
d. 75	$545.75	_____
e. 20	$45.03	_____

7-8. Calculate Total Variable Costs for the same items.

Units Sold	Total Variable Costs per Unit	Total Variable Costs
a. 25	$2.00	$50.00
b. 30	$5.50	_____
c. 12	$620.00	_____
d. 75	$280.00	_____
e. 20	$20.00	_____

7-9. Calculate Total Contribution Margin for the same items.

Total Revenue	Total Variable Costs	Total Contribution Margin
a. $116.00	$50.00	$66.00
b.		
c.		
d.		
e.		

7-10. Calculate Total Profit for the same items.

Total Contribution Margin	Total Fixed Operating Costs	Total Profit
a. $66.00	$25.00	$41.00
b.	$60.00	
c.	$425.00	
d.	$12,000.00	
e.	$200.00	

7-11. Calculate Profit per Unit for the same items.

Units Sold	Total Profit	Profit per Unit
a. 25	$41.00	$1.64
b. 30		
c. 12		
d. 75		
e. 20		

7-12. The following business concepts have been developed by your colleagues, and they have asked you to provide feedback on each as a potential investment. Using the data provided, calculate the payback period and NPV of each.

Project	Seed Capital	Rate of Return (%)	Net Cash Flow Year 1	Net Cash Flow Year 2	Net Cash Flow Year 3	Net Cash Flow Year 4	Net Cash Flow Year 5	Other Net Cash Flow	Payback Period	NPV
A	$1,000	5%	$200	$300	$400	$500	$0	$0		
B	$250,000	8%	$2,000	$25,000	$25,000	$1,000,000	$148,000	$200,000 per year for 5 years		
C	$8,000,000	17%	$0	$0	$0	$1,000,000	$5,000,000	$6,000,000 for 3 years		
D	$50,000	25%	$0	$1,000	$29,000	$35,0000	$70,000	$0		
E	$120 million	6%	$0	$0	$20 million	$80 million	$40 million	$20 million in Year 6, $5 million in Year 7		

Application Exercise

7-13. Ariel LeBec, of Ariel's Sandwich Shoppe, sells Po' Boy sandwiches and soda from a sidewalk cart in a popular park near her home in New Orleans. She sets up her rented cart in the summers to raise money for college. Last month, she sold $6,000 worth of product (sandwiches and sodas) to 300 customers. She spent $1,200 on the sandwich ingredients, wrapping materials, and sodas. Her monthly costs are the following: Utilities = $100, Salary = $2,000, Advertising = $150, Insurance = $50, Interest = $0, Rent = $500, Depreciation = $0.

    a. What are Ariel's variable costs? Explain.

    b. What is Ariel's COGS? Explain.

    c. What are her other variable costs? Explain.

    d. What are her fixed costs? Explain.

    e. What is Ariel's EOU?

    f. How much cash reserve should she keep in the bank?

Exploring Your Community

7-14. Ask an entrepreneur in your neighborhood to discuss his or her accounting system. Write a one-page report about the pros and cons of the system and use it to make an oral presentation to the class.

Exploring Online

7-15. Research different accounting software programs online. Choose a program (or programs) for your business and explain your choice in a brief essay.

In Your Opinion

7-16. Would you rather keep your financial records in an accounting ledger or on your computer? Why? In each case, how would you protect your records from being lost in a disaster, such as a fire, or, in the case of the computer, a hard-drive crash?

BizBuilder Business Plan Questions

7.0 Financial Analysis and Projections

A. After an introductory sentence, describe your record-keeping system, including the software you will use and whether it is specific to your industry.

B. List the types of bank accounts you will open for your organization.

7.1 Sources and Uses of Capital

A. How much capital do you need? When? What type and what terms?

B. How will you use the money you raise? Be specific.

C. List the items you will need to buy to start your business and add up the items to get your total start-up capital.

D. What is your payback period? In other words, how long will it take you to earn enough profit to cover start-up capital?

7.2 Cash Flow Projections

A. List and describe your monthly fixed costs.

Case Study | A Cool Business—MooBella, LLC

Freshly made hard-packed ice cream from a vending-machine-sized dispenser—dream or reality? For thousands of customers in New England, this became a reality. MooBella, LLC, founded as Turbo Dynamix in 1992 by Paul Kateman, introduced these innovative machines on a trial basis in 2006 and commercially to universities and medical facilities in 2010.

MooBella's CEO Bruce Ginsberg literally grew up in the ice cream business. He took over International Ice Cream from his father in 1985 and revived it from operating at $1 million in losses on $8.5 million in revenues to earning $50 million in revenues in 1993.

CB2/Newscom

Ginsberg recognized that ice cream can be up to one year old by the time of consumer purchase and that the resulting crystals detract from the taste and texture. He became fascinated by an ice cream-dispensing machine he saw in 1999, which was being developed by Turbo Dynamix. He wanted to create made-to-order hard-pack ice cream that would have excellent flavor and texture because of its freshness. Turbo Dynamix became MooBella, and Ginsberg continued his quest.

This seemingly simple concept was technically complex; it took 18 years and nearly $85 million to bring it to market. The research and development and start-up processes were riddled with challenges. One observer noted, "For all their promise, MooBella's early machines were hideously complex and cost roughly $1 million to make."[3] Ultimately, the MooBella team ended up working with Project Genesis at MIT to bring the dream to reality. It took five years to complete the computer portion of the project, and improvements are ongoing.

Once working it was possible to select any of 96 available flavor combinations for a fresh-made ice cream cup priced at about $3 per 4.5 ounce serving, and have it in about 45 seconds. Commercial customers selected from any combination of 2 base mixes, 3 mix-ins (dry), and 12 flavor mixes. The product was measured, mixed, and flash frozen before being scraped up, formed and dispensed. The specially formulated ingredients required no refrigeration until opened, making them much cheaper and more convenient to store.

In addition to the research and development costs required to create viable technology, MooBella encountered significant marketing expenditures to create the brand and to gain trial and acceptance opportunities. At approximately $40,000 per machine (or $400 per month on a lease), the investment was considerably higher than traditional vending machines and was targeted differently.

The start-up investment for MooBella totaled nearly $85 million since 2000. Investments were critical to keeping the company afloat while the team pursued product development. Some of the start-up funding included:

- Saturn Asset Management: $25 million in equity (2000–2005)
- Inventages: $15 million in 2007 and $18 million in 2009
- Bruce Ginsberg: $1 million[4]
- W. Health L.P.: $9 million in 2009
- Debt: $17.5 million in high-interest loans and convertible notes

Bruce Ginsberg owned almost 5 percent of the company after all the outside investments. Inventages controlled the majority of MooBella.

MooBella demonstrated that it developed a technology that works. Would the investment pay off?

[3]Maureen Farrell, "Big Scoop," *Forbes*, November 22, 2010, p. 122.
[4]Ibid.

Case Study Analysis

7-17. What categories of costs would you expect to see in a list of MooBella start-up costs?

7-18. It took nearly 20 years from idea to market for MooBella. Clearly, this is a long development and start-up period. Reflect on the emotional and other nonmonetary factors that were likely involved for Ginsberg.

7-19. What was the mix of funds—by percentage—used by MooBella to get started?

7-20. What start-up costs would you expect to encounter if you were a college that leased a MooBella machine?

Case Sources

Maureen Farrell, "Big Scoop," *Forbes*, November 22, 2010, p. 122.

MooBella, LLC, accessed August 15, 2013, http://www.moobella.com.

The Problem

The telephone rang. Damon White put on his headset and answered, "Good evening, Seattle Teen Hotline. My name is Damon. How can I help you?" The year was 2009. Damon had been working as a hotline counselor at the Mayor's Youth Committee for three years. Every night, from 6 to 11 p.m., he took calls from teenagers in the Seattle area, advising them on many different issues: relationships, family problems, school, and more. Damon had a natural talent for being a good listener. In fact, he listened so well that over time he started noticing similarities in the types of problems young people were discussing on the hotline. Specifically, Damon observed that younger teens in the Cedar Park and Eastlake neighborhoods did not feel safe going out on the weekends. Parents were also worried about the safety of their children and sometimes called to ask whether the Youth Committee ever sponsored teen parties or other gatherings. Damon always felt bad telling parents that the Committee did not have the funds to organize these types of events. Damon liked helping people, but this was the kind of problem he did not feel he could solve.

Thinkstock/Getty Images

Problems Can Lead to Opportunities

But then, one day in October, Damon came up with an idea:

Everybody was asking, "Is there going to be a Halloween party?" But there was not anyone who was throwing a party, so I said; I'll throw my own party. I did not know how to DJ, but I had friends who worked as professional DJs. I just contacted everyone I knew who could help out and then made it happen.

Damon decided to use all $700 of his personal savings to purchase services and supplies for the party. His intention was to earn this money back and also generate a profit, by charging a $10 admission fee. He thought $10 was a reasonable price, because it was about the same amount that teens would typically spend on a weekend night to go out to a movie or play video games at the arcade. Damon knew he had to be careful about how he allocated his resources, because a $700 start-up investment was not going to get him very far.

Getting Organized

Damon's first step in planning his party was to brainstorm a list of all the things he would need to purchase and arrange. The list he created was as follows:

Item	Cost
Space Rental	
DJ	
Security	
Insurance	
Flyers	
Food	
Party Decorations	

He thought this was a pretty good list; the only problem was that he did not know how much each item would cost. Could he pay for these goods and services with his limited funds? He was not certain. First, he needed to do some research.

Damon Investigates His Costs

Damon called his friend Janae, who worked as a professional DJ, to find out how much she would charge to spin records at the party. Janae normally got $500 as a DJ at Seattle's hottest clubs, but she agreed to reduce her fee to $100, because she saw that Damon was trying to do something positive for the community.

Damon then spoke with another friend, who worked as a security guard, to ask if he could organize a security squad for the event. The friend agreed to find four coworkers who could staff the party for $50 each.

[5]This case is based on a real-life example, but selected details have been fictionalized. Thanks to Stephen Spinelli and Alex Hardy for granting permission to adapt this case from its original version.

Damon needed a large, centrally located venue where he could host the party. He remembered that his friend Quinetta had once rented a dance studio in an old, converted factory. The studio would be perfect because it was located in the heart of downtown Seattle, near the highway. He contacted the studio's owner and negotiated a deal to rent the space for $200 for four hours. This rental fee included insurance, in case there was an accident.

Throughout the planning process, Damon leveraged his personal network to assemble the necessary components for the party. He explained:

> If I had to go out and hire professionals, I wouldn't know them. And the fact that I did not have the money right then to pay full market prices for people's services—but these people trusted me and said, "We believe in what you're doing, so we'll provide our services at a discount."

Damon's final step was to get the word out about the party to teens and parents. He called his friend John, who freelanced as a graphic designer, and offered to pay him $50 to design and print 300 flyers. By this point, Damon had already committed $600 of his savings toward entertainment, space rental, security, and promotional costs. With his remaining $100, he decided to purchase chips, soda, cups, and napkins. He figured that he could recoup his investment by selling these snacks at a modest profit.

After making these arrangements Damon filled in the actual cost of each item on the list.

Item	Cost
Space Rental and Insurance	$200
DJ	100
Security	250
Graphic Design and Flyer Production	50
Food, Decorations, and Misc. Supplies	100
TOTAL	**$700**

Damon felt satisfied that he had managed his limited resources effectively. He was finally ready for the party. All he had left to do was decide on what costume to wear.

The Party

On the night of the party, Damon arrived early to set up. Despite weeks of planning, he still felt nervous. He had never done anything like this before. What if no one showed up and he lost all his money? The doors opened at 9 p.m., and by the end of the first hour only 20 people had arrived. Damon realized that, at $10 apiece, that was only $200. The room looked empty, no one was on the dance floor, and Damon's nerves were on overdrive. Suddenly, at 10:30, the party filled up quickly and, by 11, Damon was amazed to see that a line of kids had formed outside the door. The studio had a fire-hazard limit of 300, and by 11:30 the party was filled to capacity.

Keeping Good Records

In the end, Damon's party was a great success, personal and financial. When he sat down to calculate his revenue, he discovered that the party had generated $3,750. Damon tabulated his receipts and created the chart below, so that he could see how he had accomplished this.

Item	Selling Price per Unit	Number of Units Sold	Revenue Generated
Admission Tickets	$10.00	300	$3,000.00
Chips	$0.50	300	$150.00
Soda	$1.00	600	$600.00
TOTAL SALES REVENUE			$3,750.00

It had taken Damon three long years of careful saving to put away $700 from his part-time job at the hotline, so he was amazed that so much money could be generated in a single evening. As he reflected on the experience, Damon realized:

> Even if not many people had come to the Halloween party, it would have been a success because I put something together, and I profited from it. Not only profited financially, but profited as an individual. It was something deeper than just the money. You've got to go into business because it is something you love to do and you want to create that independence. If you do something that you love, you always do your best.

Future Possibilities

As he drove home after the party, Damon's mind was reeling. He was thinking about the future and what he wanted to accomplish. Maybe he would use some of the profit he earned to throw an even bigger party or perhaps start a party-planning business. He was not sure. After all, organizing the party had caused him a lot of stress. Or maybe he would put the money in his bank account so that he could save up for school. He had several possibilities to consider. Damon drove home and parked his car. As he got ready for bed, he resolved to think further about future plans in the morning.

Case Study Analysis

7-21. Assume that Damon decides to start a party-planning business:

a. Identify two ways he could assess the cost of goods or services sold for this business.

b. Which costs, described in the case, would become part of Damon's operating-cost structure?

c. Make a list of additional items Damon will need to purchase to get his business off the ground. Research the cost of these items.

7-22. One of the reasons why Damon earned a substantial profit is because he convinced his personal contacts to provide their services at a discounted rate. If he decides to grow his party-planning business, do you think he can continue to use this strategy? Why or why not? What would his costs have been if he had paid full price for everything?

7-23. Brainstorm three things Damon might have done differently in planning his party to increase sales revenue.

7-24. At the end of the case, Damon describes how he profited as an individual from the experience of throwing the Halloween party. What did he mean by this? Is it possible to profit from something on a personal level, even if you do not necessarily earn a financial profit? Can you think of an example from your own life where this happened? Explain.

8 CHAPTER

Using Financial Statements to Guide a Business

Learning Objectives

1. Understand an income statement.

2. Examine a balance sheet to determine a business's financing strategy.

3. Use the balance sheet equation for analysis.

4. Perform a financial ratio analysis on an income statement.

5. Calculate return on investment (ROI).

6. Perform "common-sized" (same-size) analysis of an income statement.

7. Use quick, current, and debt ratios to analyze a balance sheet.

Jack Hollingsworth/
Thinkstock/Getty Images

> **"The propensity to truck, barter, and exchange one thing for another is common to all men."**
>
> —Adam Smith, Scottish economist

The allure of an ice cream truck is undeniable, as it travels through a neighborhood where children and adults eagerly gather for frozen treats. For Dylan Bauer, a Temple University entrepreneurship graduate and founder of Chilly Dilly's Ice Cream Company in York, Pennsylvania, the allure was far greater.[1] However, Dylan learned early that it was not enough to have a "cool" business. This young entrepreneur learned the importance of detailed and accurate financial statements early, so that he knew the financial condition of Chilly Dilly's at all times.

Rose Horridge, Lucy Claxton/DK Images Ltd

Each year, Dylan created the next season's cash budget in order to plan major expenditures. The majority of Chilly Dilly's sales occurred between June and September, so Dylan reported, "Each October I am sitting on a ton of cash, but it gets used up over the winter months paying bills and planning for the next season." After five years of operations, he had achieved a 105.7 percent increase in profits—and the fifth year saw a rise of more than 250 percent in revenues over the fourth year. However, as he evaluated future options, Dylan recognized that such growth would likely be unsustainable and financing would be a challenge. Fortunately, Dylan understood his financial circumstances and relied on his financial savvy, marketing expertise, and the input of trusted advisors.

Scorecards for the Entrepreneur: What Do Financial Statements Show?

In this chapter you will learn how to prepare and use the income statement and balance sheet to guide your business and keep it strong. Entrepreneurs use three basic financial documents to track their businesses:

- an income statement
- a balance sheet
- a cash flow statement

Together, they show the health of a business at a glance.

Best practice for entrepreneurs is to use their financial records to prepare monthly income statements and balance sheets and then finalize these at the end of the fiscal year. Cash flow statements (as will be discussed in Chapter 9) should be prepared at least monthly. These statements will provide a concise, easily read and understood company financial picture. Whereas transaction records—such as those kept in a journal or check register—will show the cash balance on hand, the

---

[1]Based on a case prepared by Dr. Jay Azriel and Dr. Andrew Sumutka, of York College of Pennsylvania.

income statement and balance sheet give an overview of the organization. By performing financial-statement analysis, you can gain a comprehensive understanding of how any enterprise is doing.

Income Statements: Showing Profit and Loss Over Time

The income statement shows whether the difference between revenue (sales) and expenses (costs) is a profit or a loss over a given period. If revenues are greater than expenses, the income statement balance will be positive, showing that the business is profitable. If costs are greater than sales, the income statement balance will show that the business is operating at a loss—that it is unprofitable.

The income statement is a scorecard for the entrepreneur. If the business is not making a profit, examining the statement can reveal what may be causing the problem. Steps can then be taken to correct it and prevent insolvency. *Profit* is a reward for making the right business choices. The income statement will enable you to determine whether your decisions have kept you on the right track.

Parts of an Income Statement

Learning Objective 1

Understand an income statement.

The income statement is composed of the following:

1. ***Revenue.*** Income from sales of the company's products or services. For companies using the cash method of accounting, sales are recorded when payment is received.
2. ***COGS (Cost of goods sold)/COSS (Cost of services sold).*** These are the costs of materials used to make the product (or deliver the service) plus the costs of the direct labor used to make the product (or deliver the service). An income statement reports total COGS for a period.
3. ***Gross profit.*** The result of revenues minus COGS.
4. ***Other variable costs.*** Costs that vary with sales and are not included in COGS. (Or, as part of Selling, General and Administrative Expenses.)
5. ***Contribution margin.*** Equals revenues minus COGS and other variable costs, or gross profit minus other variable costs.
6. ***Fixed operating costs.*** Costs of operating a business that do not vary with sales over a relevant range. Common fixed operating costs are rent, salaries, utilities, advertising, insurance, depreciation, and interest. (Often shown as Selling, General and Administrative Expenses—excluding Depreciation.)
7. ***Earnings before interest and taxes (EBIT).*** The result of gross profit minus other variable costs minus fixed costs, except interest and taxes.
8. ***Pre-tax profit.*** EBIT minus interest costs. This is a business's profit after all costs (including Selling, General and Administrative as well as Depreciation) have been deducted, but before taxes have been paid. Pretax profit is used to calculate how much tax the business owes.
9. ***Taxes.*** A business must pay taxes on the income it earns as a separate entity from the owners' personal taxes, depending on its legal form (e.g., a corporation). It may have to make monthly or quarterly estimated tax payments.
10. ***Net profit/(loss).*** This is the business's profit or loss after any taxes.

Entrepreneurial Wisdom . . .

Whenever a number in a financial statement is enclosed in parentheses, it is negative. If you see ($142,938) at the bottom of an income statement, it means the business had a net loss of $142,938.

A Basic Income Statement

The power of the income statement is that it will tell you whether you are fulfilling the formula of buying low, selling high, and meeting customer needs. See **Exhibit 8-1** for an example of an income statement for a relatively simple business. It illustrates how an income statement functions.

Example

Charlene buys 100 handbags at $10 each and sells them all at $25 each at a flea market, producing revenue of $2,500. She gives each customer a petite charm (at a cost of 50 cents) to attach to the handbag. She also spends $25 on flyers to advertise that she will be selling on Saturday at the flea market and $500 to rent the booth. The income statement in **Exhibit 8-2** quickly shows whether she made a profit. The income statement not only shows that Charlene's business is profitable but also illustrates exactly *how* profitable.

The Double Bottom Line

The expression "What's the bottom line?" refers to the last line on an income statement, which shows whether a business has made a profit.

Another bottom line can be considered, though, aside from whether the organization (either for-profit or not-for-profit) is making money. Is your business achieving its mission? If your dream was to have your venture fill a need in the community, is this goal being realized? Are you able

Exhibit 8-1 *Basic Income Statement*

A Basic Company, Inc. Income Statement for the Month Ended June 30, 2014	
Sales/Revenue	$1,025,000
Cost of Goods Sold	325,000
Gross Profit (Gross Income)	$700,000
Selling, General & Administrative Expenses	500,000
Depreciation	80,000
Operating Profit (EBIT)	$120,00
Interest Expense	80,000
Net Profit Before Taxes	$40,000
Taxes (40%)	16,000
Earnings Available to Common Shareholders ($24,000)	
Dividends or Owner Draw	10,000
Net Income	**$6,000**

Exhibit 8-2 *Handbag Store Income Statement*			
David's Income Statement			
Handbag sales at flea market (one time) — for one month			
Sales:	100 handbags × $25/bag		$2,500
Less COGS	100 handbags × $10/bag	$1,000	1,000
Gross Profit			$1,500
Other Variable Costs	100 charms × $0.50/charm	50	50
Total Variable Costs		$1,050	
Contribution Margin			$1,450
Fixed Costs			
Rent ($500 to rent booth)		$500	
Advertising ($25 for flyers)		25	
Total Fixed Costs		$525	525
Pre-Tax Profit			$925
Taxes (25%)			231
Net Profit			$694

to make a profit and operate the business in a way that makes you feel satisfied and fulfilled? Goals that go beyond profit might include:

- being a good citizen by doing business in a way that respects the environment—recycling, minimizing waste, looking for energy sources that do not pollute;
- encouraging local people to invest in the business and become equity owners;
- always dealing honestly with customers and suppliers, and treating everyone you do business with the way you would like to be treated;
- treating employees with respect regarding their health and safety; and
- setting up profit-sharing plans, so that employees can share in the success they help create.

Ideally, you want to have a positive *double* bottom line: You are making a profit so you can stay in business *and* achieve your mission. Not-for-profit organizations all have a double bottom line to measure. They must achieve successful financial results in order to continue operations and work toward their mission. Not-for-profits explicitly strive to attain successful double bottom lines.

An Income Statement for a More Complex Business

The income statement in **Exhibit 8-3** follows the same format as the previous one and its goal is still the same—to show how profitable the business is. However, this statement includes the category of depreciation.

Publicly traded companies have the same essential format as shown in Exhibit 8-3. Their statements are available to shareholders

Working on a financial statement.
(Shutterstock)

Exhibit 8-3 *Income Statement for a Manufacturer*		
Lola's Custom Draperies, Inc. **Income Statement for the Month Ended March 31, 2014**		
Sales:		$85,456
Cost of Goods Sold:		
Materials	$11,550	
Labor	17,810	
Total COGS:		29,360
Gross Profit:		$56,096
Other Variable Costs:		
Sales Commissions	8,000	8,000
Contribution Margin:		$48,096
Fixed Operating Costs:		
Factory Rent and Utilities	$8,000	
Salaries and Administrative	12,000	
Depreciation	2,000	
Total Fixed Operating Costs:		22,000
Profit Before Taxes:		$26,096
Taxes (25%):		6,524
Net Profit/(Loss).		$19,572

and other members of the public through their quarterly and annual filings with the U.S. Securities and Exchange Commission (10Q and 10K reports) and annual reports to shareholders. If you are not familiar with financial statements, it may help to look at the annual report of a large public company in a peer industry. The reports are generally available in the investor- or shareholder-relations section of corporate Web sites.

Global Impact . . .

By the Numbers—Quintiles Transnational Corporation

As the leader in the $20 billion industry of outsourcing clinical trials, with 27,000 employees in some 100 countries, Quintiles Transnational relies on data collection and analysis as its core business. Dennis Gillings, CBE, PhD, a British statistician and former professor at the University of North Carolina at Chapel Hill, is the founder and 24-percent owner of the company that provides clinical, commercial, capital, and consulting solutions in biologic and pharmaceutical services.

However, clinical data is not all that Quintiles tracks. Financial information is essential to guiding company performance. Although privately held until May 2013, the company did report sales of $3.7 billion in 2012. In 2011, Quintiles reported, "$500 million in earnings before interest, taxes, depreciation, and amortization, and $400 million in free cash flow" on revenues of $3.0 billion.[2]

Quintiles recognized the opportunity to improve its financial performance by restructuring its debt financing. In a press release dated March 8, 2011, it announced the start of the refinancing of $2.425 billion in credit facilities to take advantage of better debt terms.[3] Subsequently, its parent holding company has gone public on the New York Stock Exchange.

Understanding and using financial data is critical for this global leader. Financial savvy helped Dennis Gillings grow his entrepreneurial venture from its humble beginnings in a trailer on the UNC campus.

---

[2]Matthew Herper, "Money, Math and Medicine," *Forbes*, November 22, 2010, p. 142.
[3]Quintiles Transnational Corporation, accessed August 18, 2013, http://www.quintiles.com.

The Balance Sheet: A Snapshot of Assets, Liabilities, and Equity at a Point in Time

Learning Objective 2 ▶

Examine a balance sheet to determine a business's financing strategy.

net worth (owner's equity) the difference between assets and liabilities.

owner's equity (net worth) the difference between assets and liabilities.

fiscal year the financial reporting year for a company.

You can quickly see a company's financing strategy by looking at its *balance sheet* (see **Exhibits 8-4** and **8-5**). A balance sheet is a financial statement that shows the assets (what the business owns), liabilities (debts), and net worth of a business. The net worth is the difference between assets and liabilities and is also called owner's equity.

1. **Assets.** Items (tangible and intangible) a company owns that have monetary value.
2. **Liabilities.** Debts a company has that must be paid, including unpaid bills.
3. **Owner's equity.** Also called net worth, the difference between assets and liabilities. It shows the amount of capital in the business. It consists of common equity, preferred equity, paid-in capital, and retained earnings.

The balance sheet for a large business is typically prepared quarterly and at the end of the fiscal year, unlike cash flow and income statements, which are prepared monthly. The fiscal year is the 12-month accounting period chosen by the business. A fiscal year may differ from the calendar year (January 1 through December 31). A business that uses the calendar year as its fiscal year would prepare its balance sheet for the annual time frame ending December 31. Many entrepreneurs, however, also prepare a balance sheet monthly.

Exhibit 8-4 *Balance Sheet (Horizontal)*

A Basic Company, Inc.
Balance Sheet
December 31, 2014

Assets			Liabilities		
Current Assets			**Current Liabilities**		
Cash		$75,000	Accounts payable		$475,000
Accounts receivable		250,000	Notes payable		175,000
Inventory		500,000	Accrued wages payable		75,000
Supplies		80,000	Accrued taxes payable		20,000
Prepaid expenses		15,000	Accrued interest payable		25,000
Total Current Assets		**$920,000**	**Total Current Liabilities**		**$770,000**
Long-Term (Fixed) Assets			**Long-Term Liabilities**		
Land		$500,000	Mortgage		$900,000
Buildings	$700,000		Notes payable		500,000
Less accum. depreciation	70,000	630,000	**Total Long-Term Liabilities**		**$1,400,000**
Vehicles	$200,000				
Less accum. depreciation	60,000	140,000	**Owner's Equity**		
Equipment	$250,000		Prime Owner, paid in capital		$197,500
Less accum. depreciation	12,500	237,500	Retained earnings		100,000
Furniture and fixtures	$50,000		**Total Owner's Equity**		**$297,500**
Less accum. depreciation	10,000	40,000			
Total Fixed Assets		$1,547,500			
Total Assets		**$2,467,500**	**Total Liabilities and Owner's Equity**		**$2,467,500**

Exhibit 8-5 *Balance Sheet (Vertical)*

A Basic Company, Inc.
Balance Sheet
December 31, 2014

Assets

Current Assets

Cash		$75,000
Accounts receivable		250,000
Inventory		500,000
Supplies		80,000
Prepaid expenses		15,000
Total Current Assets		**$920,000**

Long-Term (Fixed) Assets

Land		500,000
Buildings	$700,000	
Less accum. depreciation	70,000	630,000
Vehicles	$200,000	
Less accum. depreciation	60,000	140,000
Equipment	$250,000	
Less accum. depreciation	12,500	237,500
Furniture and fixtures	$50,000	
Less accum. depreciation	10,000	40,000
Total Fixed Assets		**$1,547,500**
Total Assets		**$2,467,500**

Liabilities

Current Liabilities

Accounts payable		$475,000
Notes payable		175,000
Accrued wages payable		75,000
Accrued taxes payable		20,000
Accrued interest payable		25,000
Total Current Liabilities		**$770,000**

Long-Term Liabilities

Mortgage		$900,000
Notes payable		500,000
Total Long-Term Liabilities		**$1,400,000**

Owner's Equity

Prime Owner, paid in capital		$197,500
Retained earnings		100,000
Total Owner's Equity		**$297,500**
Total Liabilities and Owner's Equity		**$2,467,500**

Short- and Long-Term Assets

Assets are all items of worth owned by the business—cash, inventory, buildings, vehicles, furniture, machinery, and the like. Assets are divided into short-term (current) and long-term (fixed).

- **Current assets** are cash itself or items that could be quickly turned into cash *(liquidated)*, or that will be used by the business within one

current assets cash or items that can be quickly converted to cash or will be used within one year.

year. Current assets include accounts receivable, inventory, and supplies.

long-term assets those that will take more than one year to use.

- **Long-term assets** are those that would take more than one year for the business to use, or could not be quickly liquidated. Equipment, furniture, machinery, and real estate are examples of long-term assets.

Current and Long-Term Liabilities

Liabilities are all debts owed by the business, such as bank loans, mortgages, lines of credit, and loans from family or friends.

current liabilities debts that are scheduled for payment within one year.

- **Current liabilities** are debts that are scheduled for payment within one year. These include the portion of long-term debt due within that year.

long-term liabilities debts that are due in over one year.

- **Long-term liabilities** are debts to be paid over a period of more than one year.

The Balance Sheet Equation

Learning Objective 3

Use the balance sheet equation for analysis.

The terms *owner's equity*, *capital*, and *net worth* all mean the same thing: what's left over after liabilities are subtracted from assets. Owner's equity is the value of the business on the balance sheet to the owner. The equation for calculating owner's equity is the *balance sheet equation*. As the name suggests, the balance sheet must always be in balance, with assets equal to the sum of liabilities plus equity. A sure sign of a calculation or record-keeping error is to have an imbalance.

$$\text{Assets} = \text{Liabilities} + \text{Owner's Equity or}$$

$$\text{Assets} - \text{Liabilities} = \text{Owner's Equity or}$$

$$\text{Assets} - \text{Owner's Equity} = \text{Liabilities}$$

- If assets are greater than liabilities, net worth is positive.
- If liabilities are greater than assets, net worth is negative.

For example, if the Dos Compadres Restaurant has $10,000 in cash on hand, owns $8,000 in equipment, and owes $5,000 in long-term liabilities, what is the restaurant owner's equity (net worth)?

$$\$18,000 \text{ (Assets)} - \$5,000 \text{ (Liabilities)} = \$13,000 \text{ (Owner's Equity)}$$

The Balance Sheet Shows Assets and Liabilities Obtained through Financing

Every item a business owns was obtained through either debt or equity. That is why the total of all assets must equal the total of all liabilities and owner's equity.

- If an item was financed with *debt*, the loan is a liability.
- If an item was purchased with the owner's own money (including that of shareholders), it was financed with *equity* (or from the net worth).

The Greasy Spoon Diner owns its tables and chairs (worth $3,000) and its stove (worth $5,000); has $10,000 in cash; and holds $4,000 in

Exhibit 8-6 *Balance Sheet*

	The Greasy Spoon, LLC Balance Sheet December 31, 2013		
Assets		**Liabilities**	
Cash	$10,000	Short-Term Liabilities	$ 0
Inventory	4,000	Long-Term Liabilities	5,000
Capital Equipment	8,000		
Other Assets	0	**Owner's Equity**	17,000
Total Assets	**$22,000**	**Total Liabilities and Owner's Equity**	**$22,000**

inventory. In other words, the business has a capital equipment investment of $3,000 + $5,000 = $8,000, and $4,000 in inventory plus the $10,000 in cash. The restaurant also has a $5,000 long-term loan, which was used to buy the stove. Its total assets are $22,000 ($8,000 + $4,000 + $10,000). It has $5,000 in liabilities (the loan for the stove), which leaves $17,000 in owner's equity.

Assuming the restaurant has no other assets and liabilities, **Exhibit 8-6** shows how its balance sheet would look.

Again, on a balance sheet, assets must equal the total of liabilities and owner's equity.

Total Assets = Total Liabilities + Owners Equity

The OE is $17,000. It is equal to the total of the cash ($10,000); the stove, tables, and chairs ($8,000); plus $4,000 in inventory; minus the $5,000 in liabilities.

The stove is financed with a ($5,000) loan (debt financing). This is a long-term liability. Together, the liabilities and the owner's equity have paid for the assets of the business. When reviewing a side-by-side balance sheet, remember that the assets (what you own) on the left are funded by the liabilities (what you owe), plus equity (your owners' stake) on the right.

The Balance Sheet Shows How a Business Is Financed

The balance sheet is an especially effective tool for looking at how a business is financed. It clearly shows the relationship between debt and equity financing. Sometimes businesses make the mistake of relying too heavily on either debt or equity. The appropriate mix depends on the industry and the individual firm.

- An entrepreneur who relies too much on equity financing from outside owners can lose control of the company. If the other owners control a large percentage of the business, they may insist on making the decisions or may impede decision making and create inefficiency and confusion.
- An entrepreneur who takes on too much debt and is unable to make loan payments can lose the business, and possibly personal assets as well, to banks or other creditors.

All the information you need to analyze a company's financing strategy—total debt, equity, and assets—is in its balance sheet. People who invest in businesses use *ratios* to grasp a company's financial situation quickly. As an entrepreneur, you will want to understand these ratios so you will be able to talk intelligently with investors and analyze costs (vendors) and sales (customers).

Analyzing a Balance Sheet

Comparing balance sheets from two points in time is an excellent way to see whether a business has been financially successful. If it is, the OE will have increased. The ending balance sheets for two consecutive years may be compared to analyze annual progress.

Example

Let's look at The Greasy Spoon Diner example again. This time, several other assets and liabilities have been included (see **Exhibit 8-7**).

The first balance sheet was prepared as of December 31, 2013. The ending balance sheet was compiled a year later, on December 31, 2014. Let's compare the two balance sheets to see how the numbers have changed over the course of a year.

Assets

- *Cash* has decreased from $10,000 to $8,000. Businesses have cash coming in and going out all the time, so this is not necessarily a bad thing as long as the bills are being paid, but it should be monitored carefully.
- *Inventory* has increased from $4,000 to $5,000. If more inventory will help the restaurant put more appealing items on the menu, it could help increase business. If inventory is accumulating without adding value, it can be problematic, because it is effectively cash sitting on the shelf. In any case, inventory is an asset because it has monetary value.
- *Capital equipment* has increased from $8,000 to $9,000. The restaurant bought more equipment during the year. This is another increase in assets.
- *Other assets* have remained constant.
- *Total assets* have not changed. The business is keeping less cash but now has more inventory and capital equipment with which to operate.

There are no more assets at the end of the year than there were at the beginning. Does this mean it did not have a successful year? The rest of this analysis will help you figure that out.

Exhibit 8-7 *Comparative Balance Sheet*

The Greasy Spoon Diner, LLC Balance Sheet		
	Dec. 31, 2014	**Dec. 31, 2013**
Assets		
Current Assets		
Cash	$8,000	$10,000
Inventory	5,000	4,000
Less accum. depreciation	9,000	8,000
Total Assets	**$22,000**	**$22,000**
Liabilities		
Total Current Liabilities	$1,000	$0
Long-Term Liabilities	4,000	5,000
Owner's Equity	17,000	17,000
Total Liabilities and Owner's Equity	**$22,000**	**$22,000**

Unorganized financial records can lead to chaos in a business.
(A. Chederros/ONOKY/Getty Images)

Liabilities

- *Short-term liabilities* have increased from $0 to $1,000. On the surface, this seems to be a negative because it means the restaurant owes more money than it did before. However, it may mean that suppliers have extended trade credit to the company, so that it can add inventory without tying up as much cash.

- *Long-term liabilities* have declined from $5,000 to $4,000 because the restaurant paid off 20 percent of the loan principal. When you make monthly payments on a loan, it is usual for part of the payment to go for interest and the rest to paying off the principal. So, part of the payment is an expense and part is reducing a liability.

- *Owner's equity* has stayed the same. The restaurant has no more value than it had at the beginning of the year, even though its assets and liabilities are distributed differently.

The Greasy Spoon Diner does not have more total assets than it had at the beginning of the year, however, and it has less cash. On the other hand, the business has less debt than it did. The balance sheet equation shows that the owner's equity in the business has not changed because, although the owner paid down some long-term debt, short-term debt was added.

Exhibit 8-8 gives us another look at the balance sheet, with a percentage-change column added. This represents how much change took place over the year. (Note that any value set in parentheses is negative.)

Total assets are unchanged, and the restaurant's liabilities (debts) are the same, which is an unusual set of circumstances. Short-term liabilities are $1,000 greater, and long-term liabilities are less than they had been at the start of the year. Owner's equity is the same.

The restaurant used its cash to increase its inventory and capital equipment, keeping its debt and equity the same. Reallocating your asset mix in such a way can be a smart strategy. The growth of owner's equity is one good way to measure company success.

Exhibit 8-8 *Balance Sheet Variance Analysis*

The Greasy Spoon Diner, LLC Balance Sheet			
	Dec. 31, 2014	Dec. 31, 2013	% Change
Assets			
Current Assets			
Cash	$8,000	$10,000	(20)%
Inventory	5,000	4,000	25%
Capital Equipment	9,000	8,000	13%
Total Assets	**$22,000**	**$22,000**	**0%**
Liabilities			
Short-Term Liabilities	$1,000	$0	N.A.
Long-Term Liabilities	4,000	5,000	(20)%
Owner's Equity	17,000	17,000	0%
Total Liabilities and Owner's Equity	**$22,000**	**$22,000**	**0%**

Depreciation

As we have learned, depreciation is a certain portion of an asset that is subtracted each year until the asset's (book) value reaches zero. Depreciation reflects the wear and tear on an asset over time, or loss of value through obsolescence. A used car or computer, for instance, is almost always worth less money than a new one.

Balance sheets with long-term assets show depreciation as a subtraction from those assets. Because different types of assets depreciate at different rates, based on their classifications, and because assets are purchased at various times, businesses keep depreciation schedules to track the valuation of each asset that is being depreciated. There are multiple methods of depreciation, and it is best to consult with an accounting/tax professional on this topic.

Financial Ratio Analysis: What Is It and What Does It Mean to You?

So far, we have only looked at how an income statement and balance sheet can tell you whether your business is making a profit and whether owner's equity is increasing or decreasing. This is only the tip of the iceberg with respect to what you can learn about a business through financial statement analysis. You can also create financial ratios from your income statement and balance sheet that will help you analyze your business in greater depth. By making comparisons of your company's performance from period to period and against industry norms, you can adapt your operations and strategies to improve results.

Income Statement Ratios

Learning Objective 4

Perform a financial ratio analysis on an income statement.

To create income statement ratios, analysts simply divide sales into each line item and multiply by 100. In this way, line items are expressed as a percentage of sales. Expressing an item on the income statement as a percentage of sales makes it easier to see the relationship between items than when dollar values are used. In the example shown in **Exhibit 8-9**, for every

Exhibit 8-9 *Common-Sized Income Statement*

Excellence, Inc. Income Statement for the Month Ended June 30, 2014			
	Amount (in millions)	**Calculation**	**% of Sales**
Sales	$10	$10/$10 × 100	100%
Less Total COGS	$ 4	$4/$10 × 100	40%
Less Other Variable Costs	$ 0		0%
Contribution Margin	$ 6	$6/$10 × 100	60%
Less Fixed Operating Costs	$ 3	$3/$10 × 100	30%
Profit	$ 3	$3/$10 × 100	30%
Taxes	$ 1	$1/$10 × 100	10%
Net Profit/(Loss)	$ 2	$2/$10 × 100	20%

dollar of sales, 40 cents went to the cost of goods sold. The contribution margin per dollar was 60 cents. The net profit was 20 cents, after 30 cents was spent on operating costs and 10 cents on taxes.

Analyzing a common-sized (or "same size") income statement makes clear how each item is affecting the business's profit. Examining the income statement makes it easy to experiment with ways to improve your business, by changing values to test different financial scenarios.

To increase contribution margin, you could try cutting the cost of goods sold by 10 percent. The next time you analyze your monthly income statement, you will be able to see if this cost-cutting increased the contribution margin, as intended.

Return on Investment

An **investment** is something you put time, energy, or money into because you expect to gain profit or satisfaction in return. When you start your own business, you are investing time and energy into the venture, as well as money. You do this because you believe that someday your business will return more than the value of the time, energy, and money you put into it. One way to express this idea mathematically is to calculate a **return on investment (ROI)**, the net profit of a business divided by the start-up investment, expressed as a percentage of that investment.

Investors think in terms of **wealth**—the value of assets owned minus the value of liabilities owed at a particular point in time, rather than money, per se, because a business may own assets (such as equipment or real estate) that have value but are not actual cash. Return on investment measures how wealth changes over time. To measure ROI, you have to know these three things:

1. **Net profit.** The amount the business has earned beyond what it has spent to cover its costs.
2. **Total investment in the business.** This includes start-up investment (the amount of money that was required to open the business, plus all later additional funding).
3. **The period of time for which you are calculating ROI.** This is typically one month or one year.

$$\text{ROI Formula} = \frac{\text{Net Profit (\$)}}{\text{Investment (\$)}} \times 100 = \text{ROI\%}$$

◀ **Learning Objective 5**
Calculate return on investment.

investment something a person or entity devotes resources to in hopes of future profits or satisfaction.

return on investment (ROI) the net profit of a business divided by its start-up investment (percentage).

wealth the value of assets owned versus the value of liabilities owed.

Entrepreneurial Wisdom . . .

Accounting Differences between Countries

Businesses in different countries prepare and present the income statement differently and even have different names for it. In the United Kingdom, for example, the income statement is called a "group profit and loss account." Topics where global practices can differ widely include inventory measurement methods and ways in which property and equipment are valued. Countries also have varying laws regarding when a sale can be recognized as income and included on an income statement.

In the United States, United Kingdom, Denmark, Norway, Belgium, Brazil, and Japan, for instance, income from a long-term contract can only be included on the income statement as each percentage of the contract is completed. If you have done 10 percent of the work, you can show 10 percent of the income on your statement. In Germany, on the other hand, you cannot include any of the income on your statement until the contract has been 100 percent completed.

Accounting rules differ among countries.
(Michaela Dusíková/ Alamy)

There is an easy way to remember the ROI formula: *What you made over what you paid, times 100.* Normally, ROI is calculated on an annual basis, although it can also be calculated for days, weeks, months, or quarters.

Example

If David wants to figure out what his ROI was for the day at the flea market, he must know the following:

1. *Net profit.* His income statement shows this to be $694.
2. *Investment.* David invested $1,000 in handbags, $25 in flyers, $50 for charms, plus $500 to rent a booth, for a total of $1,575.
3. *Time period.* In this case David is calculating his ROI for one day.

He divides his investment into the net profit.

$$\frac{\text{Net Profit (\$694)}}{\text{Investment (\$1000} + 25 + 50 + \$500)} \times 100 = \frac{\$694}{\$1,575} \times 100$$

$$= .4406 \times 100 = 44\%$$

David's ROI was 44 percent for the day. ROI will tell you what the rate of return was on your investment.

Return on Sales

return on sales (ROS) net income divided by sales for a particular time period (percentage).

Return on sales (ROS) is the percentage created when sales are divided into net income. This is an important measure of the profitability of a business.

$$\text{Return on Sales (ROS)} = \frac{\text{Net Income (\$)}}{\text{Sales (\$)}}$$

profit margin (return on sales) net income divided by sales (percentage).

ROS is also called **profit margin**. To express this ratio as a percentage, multiply it by 100 (as you would to express any ratio as a percentage).

A high ROS ratio can help a company make money more easily; however, the amount of revenue will make a difference. The size of the sale

Exhibit 8-10 *Return on Sales (Profit Margin) Table*

ROS	Margin Range	Typical Product
Very low	2–5%	Very high volume or very high price
Low	6–10%	High volume or high price
Moderate	11–20%	Moderate volume and moderate price
High	20–30%	Low volume or low price
Very high	30% and up	Very low volume or very low price

will also make a difference. Hardware stores sell many inexpensive items, so they have to have a higher profit margin on each to make a profit. Auto dealers sell expensive items, so they can afford a smaller ROS on each car they sell. **Exhibit 8-10** provides a visual description of this concept.

Common-Sized Statement Analysis

Financial ratio analysis will also allow you to compare the income statements from different months or years more easily, even if the sales are different amounts. The percentages let you compare statements as if they were the "same size." For this reason, financial ratio analysis is sometimes called same-size analysis, as well as common-sized analysis.

When the ratio of expenses versus sales is used to express expenses as a percentage of sales, it is called an **operating ratio**. The operating ratio expresses what percentage of sales dollars the expense is using up. You can use operating ratios to compare your expenses with those incurred by other businesses in your industry or for your own company at different times. If your rent is $2,000 per month, and your sales in a given month are $10,000, your operating ratio for rent is 20 percent. Is that high or low for your industry? Check trade association data or statement studies to find comparative values. If it is high, you might want to consider moving to another location (to reduce the expense) or finding a way to increase revenues while holding the expense constant. Remember that industry norms may not be industry ideals; the whole industry may be operating inefficiently, and you can bring efficiency to it. Also, look at whether a ratio is higher or lower than it was a year earlier. This will be particularly helpful for analyzing variable costs within a company, as company performance versus industry performance.

Relating each element of the income statement to sales in this fashion will help you notice changes in your costs from month to month or year to year.

Balance-Sheet Analysis

Taking the time to perform a similar analysis on the balance sheet can also yield valuable historic information and provide perspectives on opportunities for improvement.

Quick and Current Ratios

In addition to what you can learn from an income statement, a balance sheet will tell you about a business's **liquidity**—that is, its ability to convert assets into cash. Businesspeople use quick ratios and **current ratios** to immediately understand what is going on with a business's liquidity. Many business owners prepare a balance sheet monthly and at the end of the fiscal year to keep an eye on liquidity.

◀ Learning Objective 6
Perform "common-sized" (same-size) analysis of an income statement.

operating ratio an expression of a value versus sales.

◀ Learning Objective 7
Use quick, current, and debt ratios to analyze a balance sheet.

liquidity the ability to convert assets into cash.

current ratio liquidity ratio consisting of the total sum of cash plus marketable securities divided by current liabilities.

Some entrepreneurs create fortunes by establishing successful businesses, selling them, and using the resulting wealth to create new enterprises and more wealth. Entrepreneurs also use their wealth to support political, environmental, and social causes. For example, the major philanthropic thrust of the Estée Lauder Company is providing support to the Breast Cancer Research Foundation, which addresses a major health concern of its customer base. What will you do with *your* entrepreneurial wealth?

Marketable securities are investments, such as certificates of deposit or Treasury bills, which can be converted to cash within 24 hours. The **quick ratio** tells you whether you have enough cash to cover your current debt. The quick ratio should be greater than 1. This means you would have enough cash at your disposal to cover all current short-term debt. In other words, if you had to pay all your bills tomorrow (not long-term loans), you would have enough cash to do so.

marketable securities investments that can be converted into cash within 24 hours.

quick ratio indicates adequacy of cash to cover current debt.

$$\text{Quick Ratio:} \frac{\text{Cash and Cash Equivalents} + \text{Marketable Securities} + \text{Accounts Receivable}}{\text{Current Liabilities}}$$

Exercise

Compare the common-sized income statements shown in **Exhibit 8-11**. Rocket Rollerskate did not have as much revenue and did not make as much profit in February as it did in January. The company was able to lower both its COGS and its other variable costs in February, though. Which month was better for Rocket? Explain your thinking.

Exhibit 8-11 *Common-Sized Income Statements*

Rocket Rollerskate Co. Income Statement		For the Month of January 2014	
Revenue	100%		$250,000
COGS	24%	$60,000	60,000
Gross Profit	76%		$190,000
Other Variable Costs	14%	35,000	35,000
Total Variable Costs	38%	$95,000	
Contribution Margin	62%		$155,000
Fixed Costs	34%		85,000
Pre-Tax Profit	28%		$70,000
Taxes (20%)	5.6%		14,000
Net Profit	22.4%		$56,000
Rocket Rollerskate Co. Income Statement		For the Month of February 2014	
Revenue	100%		$225,000
COGS	20%	$45,000	45,000
Gross Profit	80%		$180,000
Other Variable Costs	12%	27,000	27,000
Total Variable Costs	32%	$72,000	
Contribution Margin	68%		$153,000
Fixed Costs	38%		85,000
Pre-Tax Profit	30%		$68,000
Taxes (20%)	6%		13,600
Net Profit	24%		$54,400

Step into the Shoes . . .

Estée Lauder Delivers Beauty

Estée Lauder, born Josephine Esther Mentzer in 1906, parlayed a skin-cream formula developed by her uncle into a company selling products in over 100 countries. Lauder started selling the cream in 1946 and introduced Youth-Dew fragrance in 1953. The company she built with her husband found a niche for women's beauty care and evolved from the single beauty cream into multiple complete lines of makeup, fragrances, skin-care, and hair-care products. Today, the company bearing her name includes numerous brands, such as Clinique, Prescriptives, MAC Cosmetics, Coach, and Aveda. The Lauder family continues to control 70 percent of the company.

Named one of *Time* magazine's 20 most influential business geniuses of the twentieth century, Estée Lauder's name is synonymous with beauty and wealth.

Estée Lauder
(Ron Galella/
Getty Images)

It is also a good idea to maintain a current ratio greater than 1. This indicates that, if you had to, you could sell some assets to pay off all your debts.

$$\text{Current Ratio: } \frac{\text{Current Assets}}{\text{Current Liabilities}}$$

Debt Ratios: Showing the Relationship between Debt and Equity

Most companies are financed by both debt and equity. The financial strategy of a company will be apparent from certain simple financial ratios. If a company has a **debt-to-equity ratio** of one-to-one (expressed as 1:1), for example, it means that for every one dollar of debt, the company has one dollar of assets.

debt-to-equity ratio compares total debt to total equity.

$$\text{Debt-to-Equity Ratio: } \frac{\text{Debt}}{\text{Equity}}$$

A debt-to-equity ratio of 100 percent would mean that for every dollar of debt, the company has a dollar of equity. As noted previously, equity is ownership, which is either kept by the entrepreneur or sold in pieces to investors. If the investors hold a significant enough portion of the equity in a business, they could take over control from the entrepreneur; and this sometimes happens.

All the information you need to analyze a company's financing strategy is in its balance sheet. It is used to create the following ratio.

$$\text{Debt Ratio: } \frac{\text{Total Debt}}{\text{Total Assets}}$$

The **debt ratio** describes how many of the total dollars in the business have been provided by creditors. A debt ratio of 55 percent means you are in debt for 55 percent of your assets. You will not actually own those assets outright until you pay off the debt. On the other hand, if you need to go to a bank to borrow money or to a supplier to establish credit, these creditors will want you to have a moderate debt ratio. You will have to manage your debt based on your objectives, industry norms, and creditor requirements.

debt ratio measures total debt versus total assets.

Exercise

Using the balance sheet for The Greasy Spoon Diner in **Exhibit 8-7**, calculate the quick, debt, and debt-to-equity ratios. What do the ratios tell you about how the restaurant is doing?

Operating-Efficiency Ratios

Once the income statement and balance sheet have been prepared, you can analyze your business's operating efficiency using the following ratios:

1. Collection-period ratio.

$$\frac{\text{Average Accounts Receivable (Balance Sheet)}}{\text{Average Daily Sales (Income Statement)}} = \text{\# of days}$$

This ratio measures the average number of days that it takes for credit sales to be collected. If you extend credit, it is critical to minimize this number to keep cash flowing. It can be compared to industry norms to see how you doing.

2. Receivable turnover ratio.

$$\frac{\text{Total Sales (Income Statement)}}{\text{Average Accounts Receivable (Balance Sheet)}} = \text{\# of times}$$

This also measures the efficiency of your company's efforts to collect receivables.

3. Inventory turnover ratio.

$$\frac{\text{Cost of Goods Sold (Income Statement)}}{\text{Average Inventory (Balance Sheet)}} = \text{\# of times}$$

This is a measure of how quickly inventory is moving. The higher the turnover, the more effectively you are investing in inventory. Inventory that is held too long often becomes obsolete or, in the case of food and other perishable goods, literally spoils. Inventory that is not turning is tying up cash flow. At the same time, the amount of inventory in stock has to be balanced with customer needs and wants.

By using all of these ratios, you can create an internal scorecard for your business, perhaps through a consolidated report on key performance indicators. You will be able to tell at a glance whether you are attaining your goals, where you stand from period to period, and how you compare with your industry. The Appendices in this book include a set of useful formulas and equations to use for such a scorecard.

Chapter Summary

Now that you have studied this chapter, you can do the following:

1. Understand an income statement.
   - An income statement illustrates whether the difference between revenue (sales) and expenses (costs) is a profit or a loss.
   - If sales are greater than costs, the income-statement balance will be positive, showing that the business earned a profit. If costs are greater than sales, the balance will be negative, showing a loss.

- The elements of an income statement are:
  a. *Revenue.* Money a business makes for selling its products or services.
  b. *Cost of goods sold.* The cost of goods sold for one unit times the number of units sold.
  c. *Gross profit.* Revenue less the cost of the product or service.
  d. *Other variable costs.* Costs that vary with sales.
  e. *Contribution margin.* Sales minus variable costs (cost of goods sold + other variable costs).
  f. *Fixed operating costs.* Items that must be paid to operate a business.
  g. *Profit before taxes.* A business's profit after all costs have been deducted but before taxes have been paid.
  h. *Taxes.* Certain businesses, such as corporations, must pay income tax on their profits. (Sales, property, and other taxes are business expenses and are not included on this line.)
  i. *Net Profit/(Loss).* A business's profit or loss after taxes.
2. Examine a balance sheet to determine a business's financing strategy.
   - A balance sheet is a financial statement showing the assets (items the business owns), liabilities (debts), and owner's equity (net worth or value) of a business.
   - Every item a business owns was obtained through either debt (bonds, loans) or equity (stock or other ownership); therefore, the total of all assets must equal the total of all liabilities and owner's equity.
3. Use the balance sheet equation for analysis.

$$\text{Assets} = \text{Liabilities} + \text{Owner's Equity}$$

   - The balance sheet shows the use of debt and equity to support the business.
   - Comparing balance sheets from two points in time can provide insights into the business operations and reveal opportunities for improvement.
   - Depreciation affects the value of assets by reducing them to reflect wear and tear and obsolescence.
4. Perform a financial ratio analysis of an income statement.
   - Expressing each item on the income statement as a percentage of sales makes it easy to see the relationship between items.
   - Financial ratio analysis will also allow you to compare the income statements from different months or years more easily, even if the sales are for varying amounts.
   - The percentages let you compare statements as if they were the same size. For this reason, financial ratio analysis is also sometimes called same-size, or common-sized, analysis.

$$\frac{\text{Net Income}}{\text{Sales}} = \text{Return on Sales (ROS)}$$

5. Calculate return on investment (ROI).
   - ROI is the net profit of a business divided by the start-up costs, which are the original investment in the business.

$$\frac{\text{Net Profit}}{\text{Investment}} \times 100 = \text{Return on Investment (\%ROI)}$$

6. Perform "common-sized" (same-size) analysis of an income statement.
   - Represent expenses as a percentage of sales or operating ratios.
   - Compare with others in the industry.

7. Use quick, current, and debt ratios to analyze a balance sheet.

$$\text{Quick Ratio} = \frac{\text{Cash and Cash Equivalents} + \text{Marketable Securities} + \text{Accounts Receivable}}{\text{Current Liabilities}}$$

$$\text{Current Ratio} = \frac{\text{Current Assets}}{\text{Current Liabilities}}$$

$$\text{Debt Ratio} = \frac{\text{Total Debt}}{\text{Total Assets}}$$

$$\text{Debt-to-Equity Ratio} = \frac{\text{Total Debt}}{\text{Equity}}$$

Key Terms

current assets
current liabilities
current ratio
debt ratio
debt-to-equity ratio
fiscal year
investment
liquidity
long-term assets
long-term liabilities

marketable securities
net worth
operating ratio
owner's equity
profit margin
quick ratio
return on investment (ROI)
return on sales (ROS)
wealth

Entrepreneurship Portfolio

Critical Thinking Exercises

8-1. Repeat the exercise from Key Concept Questions for this chapter using accounting software. Then run the following what-if scenarios and create graphs or other visuals showing how each would affect the business's monthly and yearly financial picture:

- What if the restaurant finds a supplier that is willing to provide paper for only $8,000 in June and $96,000 for the year?
- What if sales for June were $250,000 and sales for the year were $2,000,000? (Do not forget the taxes, assumed at 25 percent.)
- What if the owner of this franchise faced start-up costs of $400,000 instead of $300,000? How would that affect the ROI?

8-2. If you were to open a clothing store, what do you think would be a reasonable operating ratio for the rent, and why?

8-3. Which items in your business would you depreciate, and why?

8-4. Using **Exhibit 8-12**, the balance sheet of Angelina's Jewelry Company at the end of July, which follows, calculate all four financial ratios (quick, current, debt, and debt-to-equity) for the business.

8-5. Write a memo analyzing the financial strengths and weaknesses of Angelina's venture. Use the common-size statement information shown in **Exhibit 8-13**. Would you invest in her business? Why or why not?

8-6. Using The Greasy Spoon Diner balance sheet in **Exhibits 8-7** and **8-8**, answer the following:

a. What are the debt-to-equity ratios at the beginning and end of the 2014 fiscal (business) year? Has it improved? If so, by how much?

b. The restaurant has less cash at the end of the year than it had at the beginning. Is this a bad thing or not? Explain.

c. Does the restaurant have enough cash to pay its expenses going into 2015? Why or why not?

d. If the restaurant grew its owner's equity by 31 percent during the 2014 fiscal year, at that rate, how much will the business have in owner's equity after one more year (on December 31, 2015)?

e. The restaurant added some capital equipment during the year. Did it take out another loan for that equipment, or did it pay cash? Explain your thinking.

Exhibit 8-12 *Balance Sheet for Angelina's Jewelry Company*

Angelina's Jewelry Company
Balance Sheet
As of July 30, 2014

Assets		Liabilities	
Current Assets		**Short-Term Liabilities**	
Cash	$ 1,000	Accounts Payable	$ 1,000
Inventory	1,000	Short-Term Loans	500
Securities	1,000	**Total Short-Term Liabilities**	$ 1,500
Total Current Assets	$ 3,000	**Total Long-Term Liabilities**	1,500
Long-Term Assets	7,000	**Owner's Equity**	$ 7,000
Total Assets	$10,000	**Total Liabilities + Owner's Equity**	$10,000

Exhibit 8-13 *Comparative Balance Sheet for Angelina's Jewelry Company*

Angelina's Jewelry Company Balance Sheet	Aug. 30, 2014	July 30, 2014	% Change
Assets			
Current Assets			
Cash	$ 500	$ 1,000	(50)%
Inventory	2,000	1,000	100%
Securities	1,500	1,000	50%
Total Current Assets	**$ 4,000**	**$ 3,000**	33%
Long-Term Assets	**7,000**	**7,000**	0%
Total Assets	**$11,000**	**$10,000**	10%
Liabilities			
Short-Term Liabilities			
Accounts Payable	$ 1,500	$ 1,000	50%
Short-Term Loans	—	500	(100)%
Total Short-Term Liabilities	**$ 1,500**	**$ 1,500**	0%
Total Long-Term Liabilities	**500**	**1,500**	(67)%
Owner's Equity	**$ 9,000**	**$ 7,000**	29%
Total Liabilities + Owners' Equity	**$11,000**	**$10,000**	10%

8-7. Using spreadsheet software, create a balance sheet for Tropical Aquaculture—a shrimp farm—using the following information. Calculate and analyze the quick, debt, and debt-to-equity ratios.

Cash	$45,000
Accounts receivable	$12,000
Shrimp feed	$8,400
Accounts payable	$9,700
Equipment	$75,000
Bank loan	$20,000
Property and ponds	$124,000

8-8. Use the following balance sheet to answer the subsequent questions:

As you can see, total liabilities and owner's equity equal the total assets.

a. What is the year-to-year percentage change in the value of the following:
   - inventory
   - accounts payable
   - land
   - taxes payable
   - liabilities and owner's equity

b. What is the ratio of the following:
   - Cash equivalent to inventory in 2014? How did it change from 2013?
   - Owner's equity to total assets in 2014? How did it change from 2013?

Jean M's Florida-Style Subs, Inc. Balance Sheet December 31, 2013 and 2014		
	2014	**2013**
Assets		
Current Assets		
Cash and cash equivalents	$10,000	$10,000
Accounts receivable	2,000	7,000
Inventory	20,000	25,000
Total Current Assets	**$32,000**	**$42,000**
Fixed Assets		
Plant and machinery	$5,000	$9,000
Land	9,000	8,000
TOTAL ASSETS	**$46,000**	**$59,000**
Liabilities		
Accounts payable	$10,000	$15,000
Taxes payable	6,000	5,000
Total Liabilities	**$16,000**	**$20,000**
OWNER'S EQUITY	**$30,000**	**$39,000**
LIABILITIES and OWNER'S EQUITY	**$46,000**	**$59,000**

    c. Investors and buyers like to put their money into companies that have a low ratio of liabilities to assets. Has that ratio become more or less appealing from 2013 to 2014?

8-9. Create a projected balance sheet for your business for one year.

    a. Create a pie chart showing your current assets, long-term assets, current liabilities, and long-term liabilities.

    b. What is your debt ratio?

    c. What is your debt-to-equity ratio?

Key Concept Questions

8-10. Given the following data, on a separate sheet of paper create monthly and yearly income statements for this fast-food restaurant in New York City.

    a. Sales for the month of June were $300,000. Sales for the year were $2,600,000.

    b. The sum of $66,000 was spent on food in June ($792,000 for the year). The store spent $9,000 on paper to wrap food items in June and $108,000 for the year.

    c. Taxes for June were $15,000. For the year, they were $233,000.

    d. Fixed operating costs for June were $175,000. For the year, they were $1,000,000.

    e. Use Excel or other software to create a graph showing the monthly and yearly income statements for this business.

8-11. If the owner of this fast-food restaurant invested $300,000 in start-up costs, what was his ROI for the year? (Assume June as average.)

8-12. Calculate the financial ratios (ROI and ROS) for the monthly and yearly income statement. What do the financial ratios tell you about this business?

8-13. What would the profit before taxes be if the owner found a paper supplier who only charged $100,000 for the year?

8-14. What would the profit margin for the year be in that case?

8-15. Suppose the owner wanted to raise profits by $5,000 a month. What would you recommend he do, and why?

8-16. State the financial equation for the balance sheet in three different ways.

8-17. How is depreciation treated on the balance sheet, and what is the logic behind this treatment?

Application Exercise

8-18. The following is a real estate investor's balance sheet (in millions) as of December 31, 2014. All the businesses in her real estate empire were separately incorporated for liability reasons, and many of them were heavily *leveraged*, or debt-financed. Calculate the debt ratios for each of the properties, then answer the questions.

Asset	Estimated Worth	Debt	Net Worth	Debt Ratio
The Pyramids of Gaza	$820	$820	$0	1.0
East Side Yards	450	175	30	_____
Phoenix Casino	640	275	345	_____
Mogul's Lair Casino	600	415	6	_____
Serena's Shuttle	400	400	0	_____
Stefania's Tower	200	100	0	_____
Cash	130	160	−30	_____
Igor's Condos	115	5	45	_____
Marketable Securities	90	75	15	_____
Serena's Palace	80	80	0	_____
Stefania's Plaza	70	50	3	_____
Grand Brand Hotel (50%)	70	30	40	_____
Igor Regency	65	85	−20	_____
Igor Plaza Coops	45	0	25	_____
Mogul Air	40	0	30	_____
Personal Transportation	40	0	30	_____
Personal Housing	30	40	−9	_____
Total (in millions)	$_____	$_____	$_____	_____

a. What was the mogul's highest-priced asset?

b. What was mogul's net worth for the Serena's Shuttle? Why?

    c. On which asset was the mogul's net worth the greatest?

    d. Which asset carried the most debt?

    e. Which properties did the mogul own free of debt?

    f. On which properties did the mogul owe one dollar of debt for each dollar of the asset?

Exploring Online

Use the Internet (try the Edgar site at http://www.sec.gov/edgar/searchedgar/companysearch.html for public companies) to find the balance sheets of two companies with which you are familiar. Use percentages to analyze these balance sheets, and compare how well each is doing compared to The Greasy Spoon Diner example from this chapter. Then compare them to each other. Consider choosing either two similar companies, such as Pfizer Inc. and Johnson & Johnson, or two different industries, such as an airline and a car manufacturer.

  8-19. Create common-size balance sheets for each.

  8-20. Calculate their balance sheet ratios.

  8-21. How do the companies compare in growing owner's equity?

  8-22. How do the companies compare in reducing debt?

  8-23. Describe how you think market conditions (such as gas prices, for example) are affecting each company's growth.

  8-24. How, if at all, do the ratios of these companies relate to that of The Greasy Spoon Diner?

BizBuilder Business Plan Questions

7.0 Financial Analysis and Projections

7.3 Balance Sheet Projections

    A. Create a projected balance sheet for your business for the first four quarters and the second and third years of operation.

    B. Create a pie chart showing your current assets, long-term assets, current liabilities, and long-term liabilities.

7.4 Income Statement Projections

    A. Create a projected income statement for your business for the first four quarters and the second and third years of operation.

    B. Create a bar chart showing your gross revenues, gross profit, and net income.

7.5 Breakeven Analysis

    A. Perform a breakeven analysis and report your breakeven volume.

7.6 Ratio Analysis

    A. Use your projected financial statements to calculate all your key ratios.

    B. Compare these ratios to your industry using publicly available data.

7.7 Risks and Assumptions

    A. List the risks and assumptions that underlie your financial projections.

    B. Identify any external factors that may be substantial risks.

Gentle Rest Slumber, LLC: Using Financials to Build Employee Performance[4]

Sean O'Neal decided he wanted to be his own boss after working for several years making mattresses with a small, custom mattress shop in Santa Fe, New Mexico. He knew that the retail market was dominated by several licensed brands such as Sealy, Serta, Restonic, and Simmons. He also believed he could create products with clear customer value propositions at a profit for himself. When Sean started Gentle Rest Slumber with his meager savings, he promised himself to treat his employees differently from the way he had been treated in the custom shop. Part of this promise was to be honest with his team about the company's financial condition.

© MBI/Alamy

When he brought in employees, Sean took the time to help them understand the company's key performance indicators and to work with them on setting goals. His team consisted of sewers, warehouse staff, truck drivers, and other unskilled and semi-skilled workers. Sean didn't intend to make them all accountants, nor did he wish to become one. However, he was familiar with the critical financial statement ratios for his industry and saw clearly his vision for the company.

At first, the team was uncomfortable with the idea of reviewing financial performance and setting goals for the company. They understood piece-work programs, where they were paid according to the number of quality items they completed per shift, but they weren't so sure about being responsible for more than that. However, by the third year of this "open-book" system, employees were fully engaged and motivated to participate.

Among the key financial data Sean presented to them was the following:

	2014	2013	% Change	Industry 2014
Revenue	$2,200,000	$2,000,000	10%	−5%
Material	14%	10%	4%	11%
Labor	23%	20%	3%	18%
Gross Profit	63%	70%	−7%	72%
ROS	3%	10%	−7%	6%
ROI	6.6%	20%	−13.4%	22%
Current Ratio	0.9	1.1	−18.2%	1.2
Debt-to-Equity	1.5	1.0	50%	1.2
Collection Period	60 days	45 days	−33%	50 days

The employees were excited to see that revenues had increased, but they were concerned about the other results. This led to intense discussions about the concerns and how to best move forward.

Case Study Analysis

8-25. What are the positive aspects the employees could glean from the financial data?

8-26. What concerns should they have?

8-27. What additional information would you want to know?

8-28. What would you recommend if you were an employee? Why?

---

[4]This is a fictional case.

Portland Freelancers' Café: Amy and Steve's Business Idea

In 2003, Amy Chan and Steve Lee formed a partnership to start an Internet café in Portland, Oregon. For many years, Amy and Steve had worked as freelance writers. They enjoyed bringing their laptops to local coffeehouses to complete their writing projects. Having an endless supply of good strong coffee at their disposal helped them to stay focused on their work.

Ryan McVay/Getty Images

Over time, they began to daydream about owning their own café. Although Portland already had many great coffeehouses, Amy and Steve felt that none of them catered well to freelancers like themselves. More and more, people in Portland seemed to be doing their work in informal settings. Everywhere they turned, twenty- and thirty-somethings were sipping lattes while conducting business deals on cell phones. Amy and Steve sometimes wondered if anyone worked in a traditional office anymore.

We Can Do Better

As much as they enjoyed Portland's café culture, they felt that a fatal flaw compromised each of their favorite coffee spots. One was too loud. Another had uncomfortable chairs and tables that weren't well suited for laptop users. Their particular favorite, The Magic Bean, only had three outlets, which meant that only a few laptops could be plugged in at one time. Just a handful of the coffeehouses in downtown Portland offered high-speed Internet access at that time.

Amy and Steve felt they could do a better job of running a café that catered to the needs of freelancers. They made a list of everything they would want in a café and then asked their freelance friends for additional feedback. The two partners resolved that, in their café, customers would be able to enjoy high-speed Internet access; laser printers; a soundproof, quiet room; and comfortable, up to date work stations. To attract their target market, Amy and Steve decided to name their business the Portland Freelancers' Café.

Deluxe Purchases

They spent $10,000 up front installing super-fast T1 Internet lines. They imported a $7,000, top-of-the-line espresso machine from Italy. To make the café look sleek and modern, all of the furniture was custom-designed for the space, as were the curved metallic ceiling and wall panels. Installing the soundproof interior room was more costly than they had anticipated. Their equipment costs totaled $25,000. At $500 per month, they had negotiated a good deal on their rent, so they figured they could afford to splurge on these other features.

Financing

The café's start-up investment totaled $100,000. This included a $10,000 cash reserve. Amy and Steve contributed a combined $20,000 of their personal savings. Steve's brother invested another $20,000, in exchange for a 20-percent equity stake. Amy's mother wrote a check for $10,000, which she gave to the partners as a gift. Also, Amy and Steve received a $50,000 loan from Amy's uncle. The partners agreed to pay back the loan with interest at an annual rate of 12 percent.

Funding Source	Equity	Debt	Gift
Personal Savings (80% equity)	$20,000		
Steve's Brother (20% equity)	$20,000		
Amy's Uncle (12% interest)		$50,000	
Amy's Mother			$10,000
Subtotal	$40,000	$50,000	$10,000
Total Start-Up Investment	$100,000		

[5]Note: This is a fictional case.

Computer Glitch

Because so much money was needed for start-up, Amy and Steve tried to cut costs by hiring a local high school student, who agreed to work 100 hours per month at an hourly wage of $10. It soon became apparent to frustrated customers, however, that none of the staff, including Amy and Steve, knew how to solve the technical problems customers encountered with the computers and printers. Amy and Steve tried to find a permanent technical support person, but computer experts were in high demand at the time, and the partners felt they couldn't afford to pay a competitive salary.

Business Troubles Brew

Before starting their business, Amy and Steve assumed that revenue would come from two primary sources, food and beverage sales and computer/Internet services. Together they had calculated two economics-of-one-unit analyses, one for each of the two sources.

Amy and Steve's EOU

The partners originally assumed that the average customer would spend $6 at the café and that $2 of this revenue would be generated by food and beverage sales. The remaining $4 would come from the sale of computer and Internet services. They believed the business could be very successful if they did well selling computer services. After all, they could charge customers $4 for an hour of service that would only cost them 45 cents to provide. In comparison, food and beverage sales would not be nearly as profitable. For every $2 of lattes and muffins sold, they would pay $1 in direct costs.

Amy and Steve built a 5 percent manager's commission into their EOU, even though they did not yet have the funds to hire a manager. They wanted to account for this cost because they did plan to hire a manager at some point in the future, and the commission would be a real cost of doing business.

The café's EOU based on Amy and Steve's analysis of both revenue streams together follows.

In Hot Water

When the Portland Freelancers' Café first opened, Amy and Steve were encouraged by how busy things seemed. The café was buzzing with customers, and they received some positive reviews in the local papers. They expected to lose money at first but figured that, in a few months' time, the business would become profitable. After three months, they had a major shock when they realized this was not happening. What went wrong?

EOU for Food and Beverage Sales	
Average Sale per Customer	
• Food/Beverage Sales	$2.00
Variable Costs per Unit COGS per Unit	
• Food/Beverage Costs	$1.00
TOTAL COGS per Unit	$1.00
Other Variable Costs per Unit Manager's Commission @ 5%	$0.10
Total Variable Cost per Unit	$1.10
Contribution Margin per Unit	$0.90

EOU for Computer/Internet Services	
Average Sale per Customer • Computer Services	$4.00
Variable Costs per Unit COGS per Unit	
• Paper, Toner	$0.25
TOTAL COGS per Unit	$0.25
Other Variable Costs per Unit Manager's Commission @5%	$0.20
Total Variable Cost per Unit	$0.45
Contribution Margin per Unit	$3.55

Changes in the Environment

Initially, Amy and Steve's customers willingly paid $4 an hour to use the computers and high-speed Internet connection. However, soon after the grand opening, wireless Internet service became available throughout the Portland area. Within two months, the café's customers no longer wanted to pay to go online. They put pressure on Amy and Steve to become a wireless hot spot. This meant that Amy and Steve would have to foot the bill of providing free Internet service.

The partners carried out some research and learned that it would cost $300 to purchase the basic equipment for wireless Internet connectivity, plus an additional $30 per month in service fees. They had counted on charging their customers for Internet access, and now it looked like *they* would have to pick up the tab. They wondered how they could pay for this unexpected cost and also make up the lost revenue they *weren't* selling. On the other hand, they feared that the Portland Freelancers' Café would not be able to compete unless they adapted to changes in the market.

EOU: Average Sale per Customer	
Average Sale per Customer	
• Computer Services	$4.00
• Food and Beverage Sales	$2.00
Variable Costs per Unit	
COGS per Unit	
• Paper, Toner	$0.25
• Food/Beverage Costs	$1.00
TOTAL COGS per Unit	$1.25
Other Variable Costs per Unit	
Manager's Commission—Computer Services @5%	$0.20
Manager's Commission—Food and Beverage @5%	$0.10
TOTAL Commission Costs	$0.30
Total Variable Cost per Unit	$1.55
Contribution Margin per Unit	$3.20

Amy and Steve's EOU Revisited

Three months after they opened the café, Amy and Steve discovered that their monthly unit sales of computer services had been cut by more than half. In their first month, they had sold 1,500 units, but by month three they were only averaging 600. They worried that this number would only continue to decline.

The café was holding steady with its food and beverage sales—in fact, the monthly units sold had climbed steadily from 4,500 units in month one to 5,000 in month three. Customers were enjoying the café's free wireless service. This feature created a situation where people would stay longer and order more coffee. But even with increased sales of cappuccino, the overall finances of the operation were not improving. In looking at their EOU analysis of food and beverage sales, the partners could see that their gross profit per unit for food and beverage sales was only 90 cents. Even if they sold 5,000 food and beverage units per month, they would still only be earning $4,500 in gross profit. In the scheme of things, this was not very much money—not nearly enough to cover the monthly fixed costs of $8,332.

An Uncertain Future

One year into their venture, Amy and Steve began to seriously doubt their decision to start the Portland Freelancers' Café. In hindsight, they realized they knew a lot about being customers, but running a state-of-the-art coffeehouse was a lot harder than they had imagined. By the end of the year, the Portland Freelancers' Café was on the verge of going out of business. Take a look at the café's financial statements in

Exhibits **8-14** through **8-17** and then analyze how this happened.

Case Study Analysis

8-29. Evaluate the economics-of-one-unit analysis that Amy and Steve conducted, and then answer the following:

a. Amy and Steve assumed that, for every $6 in sales, $4 would come from selling computer-related services. Calculate what percentage of their total sales revenue per unit this $4 represents.

b. For every $2 in food and beverage sales, Amy and Steve assumed that their COGS per unit would be $1. Calculate the markup percentage.

c. For every $4 in computer services sales, Amy and Steve assumed that their COGS per unit would be 25 cents. Calculate the markup percentage.

8-30. List three things that Amy and Steve should have considered doing to adapt to the changes in the environment when their customers no longer wanted to pay for Internet services and expected the café to provide free wireless connections.

8-31. Evaluate Amy and Steve's income statement for their first month of operations:

a. Is the café operating at a profit or a loss?

b. How many units above or below breakeven were sold?

8-32. Amy and Steve decided to take on a $50,000 loan to finance their start-up investment. Each month they are paying $1,469 in interest charges. Look at their total monthly fixed costs. What percentage of their total monthly fixed costs does this $1,469 represent?

8-33. What is the debt-to-equity ratio of the Portland Freelancers' Café?

8-34. Look at each section of the café's cash flow statement. Write a memo highlighting three insights you have about why this business is not succeeding, based on what you see in its cash flow statement.

8-35. Review the café's balance sheet. Explain why the net value of the café's property and equipment has decreased from $80,000 in month one to $64,000 at year's end.

Exhibit 8-14 *Start-Up Investment and Economics of One Unit*

Start-Up Investment			
Start-up Costs			
Soundproof Room		$15,000	
Espresso Machine		7,000	
High-Speed Internet Access Setup		10,000	
Workstations		20,000	
Supplies/Equipment		25,000	
Furniture		8,000	
Fixtures		5,000	
Cash Reserves		10,000	
Total Start-up Investments		**$100,000**	

Economics of One Unit (EOU)
Unit of Sale: Computer/Internet Services (Average per Customer)

Average Sale Total (Revenue)			**$4.00**
Less COGS			
Computer time	–		
Printer materials	0.25		
Total COGS	0.25	0.25	0.25
Gross Profit			**$3.75**
Less Other Variable Costs			
Commission 5% to manager	0.20		
Total Other Variable Costs	0.20	0.20	0.20
Total Variable Costs (COGS + Other VC)		0.45	
Contribution Margin			**$3.55**

Economics of One Unit (EOU)
Unit of Sale: Food and Beverage Sales (Average per Customer)

Average Sale Total (Revenue)			**$2.00**
Less COGS			
Food	0.80		
Beverage	0.20		
Total COGS	1.00	1.00	1.00
Gross Profit			**$1.00**
Less Other Variable Costs			
Commission 5% to manager	0.10		
Total Other Variable Costs	0.10	0.10	0.10
Total Variable Costs (COGS + Other VC)		1.10	
Contribution Margin			**$0.90**

Exhibit 8-15 *Income Statement*

The Portland Freelancers' Café INCOME STATEMENT *for the Year Ending 12/31/2003*

		Jan	Feb	Mar	Apr	May	Jun	Jul	Aug	Sep	Oct	Nov	Dec	Year
No. Units Sold—Computer Services		1,500	1,000	600	550	550	500	500	450	450	450	400	400	7,350
No. Units Sold—Food and Beverage		4,500	4,750	5,000	5,100	5,200	5,300	5,400	5,500	5,600	5,700	5,800	6,000	63,850
Revenue														
Computer Service Fees		$ 6,000	$ 4,000	$ 2,400	$ 2,200	$ 2,200	$ 2,000	$ 2,000	$ 1,800	$ 1,800	$ 1,800	$ 1,600	$ 1,600	$ 29,400
Food and Beverage Sales		9,000	9,500	10,000	10,200	10,400	10,600	10,800	11,000	11,200	11,400	11,600	12,000	127,700
Total Revenue		**$15,000**	**$13,500**	**$12,400**	**$12,400**	**$12,600**	**$12,600**	**$12,800**	**$12,800**	**$13,000**	**$13,200**	**$13,200**	**$13,600**	**$157,100**
Less COGS														
Printer Mat'ls (paper, ink)		375	250	150	138	138	125	125	113	113	113	100	100	1,838
Food		3,600	3,800	4,000	4,080	4,160	4,240	4,320	4,400	4,480	4,560	4,640	4,800	51,080
Beverages		900	950	1,000	1,020	1,040	1,060	1,080	1,100	1,120	1,140	1,160	1,200	12,770
Total COGS		$ 4,875	$ 5,000	$ 5,150	$ 5,238	$ 5,338	$ 5,425	$ 5,525	$ 5,613	$ 5,713	$ 5,813	$ 5,900	$ 6,100	$ 65,688
Gross Profit		**$10,125**	**$ 8,500**	**$ 7,250**	**$ 7,163**	**$ 7,263**	**$ 7,175**	**$ 7,275**	**$ 7,188**	**$ 7,288**	**$ 7,388**	**$ 7,300**	**$ 7,500**	**$ 91,413**
Less Other Variable Costs														
Commission, Computer	(5%)	300	200	120	110	110	100	100	90	90	90	80	80	1,470
Commission, Food/Bev.	(5%)	450	475	500	510	520	530	540	550	560	570	580	600	6,385
Total Other Variable Costs		$ 750	$ 675	$ 620	$ 620	$ 630	$ 630	$ 640	$ 640	$ 650	$ 660	$ 660	$ 680	$ 7,855
Total Var. Costs (COGS + Other VC)		5,625	5,675	5,770	5,858	5,968	6,055	6,165	6,253	6,363	6,473	6,560	6,780	73,543
Contribution Margin*		**$ 9,375**	**$ 7,825**	**$ 6,630**	**$ 6,543**	**$ 6,633**	**$ 6,545**	**$ 6,635**	**$ 6,548**	**$ 6,638**	**$ 6,728**	**$ 6,640**	**$ 6,820**	**$ 83,558**

*Remember: Revenue − COGS = Gross Profit − Other Variable Costs = Contribution Margin.

(*continued*)

Exhibit 8-15 *(continued)*

The Portland Freelancers' Café INCOME STATEMENT *for the Year Ending 12/31/2003*

	Jan	Feb	Mar	Apr	May	Jun	Jul	Aug	Sep	Oct	Nov	Dec	Year
Less Fixed Costs													
Utilities													
Electricity	150	150	150	150	150	150	150	150	150	150	150	150	1,800
Gas	250	250	250	250	250	250	250	250	250	250	250	250	3,000
Water	100	100	100	100	100	100	100	100	100	100	100	100	1,200
Telephone	75	75	75	75	75	75	75	75	75	75	75	75	900
High-Speed Internet	425	425	425	425	425	425	425	425	425	425	425	425	5,100
Wireless Internet Service	30	30	30	30	30	30	30	30	30	30	30	30	360
Total Utilities	$ 1,030	$ 1,030	$ 1,030	$ 1,030	$ 1,030	$ 1,030	$ 1,030	$ 1,030	$ 1,030	$ 1,030	$ 1,030	$ 1,030	$ 12,360
Salaries													
Amy & Steve Salary	1,000	1,000	1,000	1,000	1,000	1,000	1,000	1,000	1,000	1,000	1,000	1,000	12,000
Tech Support (Part time)	1,000	1,000	1,000	1,000	1,000	1,000	1,000	1,000	1,000	1,000	1,000	1,000	12,000
Total Salaries	$ 2,000	$ 2,000	$ 2,000	$ 2,000	$ 2,000	$ 2,000	$ 2,000	$ 2,000	$ 2,000	$ 2,000	$ 2,000	$ 2,000	$ 24,000
Advertising	1,000	1,000	1,000	1,000	1,000	1,000	1,000	1,000	1,000	1,000	1,000	1,000	12,000
Insurance	500	500	500	500	500	500	500	500	500	500	500	500	6,000
Interest	1,469	1,469	1,469	1,469	1,469	1,469	1,469	1,469	1,469	1,469	1,469	1,469	17,628
Rent	1,000	1,000	1,000	1,000	1,000	1,000	1,000	1,000	1,000	1,000	1,000	1,000	12,000
Depreciation	1,333	1,333	1,333	1,333	1,333	1,333	1,333	1,333	1,333	1,333	1,333	1,333	15,996
Total Fixed Costs	$ 8,332	$ 8,332	$ 8,332	$ 8,332	$ 8,332	$ 8,332	$ 8,332	$ 8,332	$ 8,332	$ 8,332	$ 8,332	$ 8,332	$ 99,984
Pre-Tax Profit	$ 1,043	($ 507)	($ 1,702)	($ 1,790)	($ 1,700)	($ 1,787)	($ 1,697)	($ 1,785)	($ 1,695)	($ 1,605)	($ 1,692)	($,512)	($ 16,427)
Taxes (20%)	209	($ 07)	—	—	—	—	—	—	—	—	—	—	—
Net Profit	$ 834	($ 07)	($ 1,702)	($ 1,790)	($ 1,700)	($ 1,787)	($ 1,697)	($ 1,785)	($ 1,695)	($ 1,605)	($ 1,692)	($ 1,512)	($ 16,427)

Exhibit 8-16 *Cash Flow Statement*

The Portland Freelancers' Café CASH FLOW STATEMENT *for the Year Ending 12/31/2003*

	Jan	Feb	Mar	Apr	May	Jun	Jul	Aug	Sep	Oct	Nov	Dec	Year
Number of Units—Computer Services	1,500	1,000	600	550	550	500	500	450	450	450	400	400	7,350
Number of Units—Food & Beverage Sales	4,500	4,750	5,000	5,100	5,200	5,300	5,400	5,500	5,600	5,700	5,800	6,000	63,850
Cash Flow from Operating:													
Cash Inflows:													
Computer Usage Fees	$ 6,000	$ 4,000	$ 2,400	$ 2,200	$ 2,200	$ 2,000	$ 2,000	$ 1,800	$ 1,800	$ 1,800	$ 1,600	$ 1,600	$ 29,400
Food and Beverage Sales	9,000	9,500	10,000	10,200	10,400	10,600	10,800	11,000	11,200	11,400	11,600	12,000	127,700
Total Cash Inflows	$ 15,000	$ 13,500	$ 12,400	$ 12,400	$ 12,600	$ 12,600	$ 12,800	$ 12,800	$ 13,000	$ 13,200	$ 13,200	$ 13,600	$157,100
Cash Outflows:													
Variable Costs:													
COGS	$ 4,875	$ 5,000	$ 5,150	$ 5,238	$ 5,338	$ 5,425	$ 5,525	$ 5,613	$ 5,713	$ 5,813	$ 5,900	$ 6,100	$ 65,688
Other Variable Costs	$ 750	$ 675	$ 620	$ 620	$ 630	$ 630	$ 640	$ 640	$ 650	$ 660	$ 660	$ 680	$ 7,855
Utilities													
Electricity, Gas, Water, Telephone	$ 500	$ 500	$ 500	$ 500	$ 500	$ 500	$ 500	$ 500	$ 500	$ 500	$ 500	$ 500	$ 6,000
High-Speed Internet Access	425	425	425	425	425	425	425	425	425	425	425	425	5,100
Wireless Internet	30	30	30	30	30	30	30	30	30	30	30	30	360
Salaries													
Part-Time Tech Support Salary	$ 1,000	$ 1,000	$ 1,000	$ 1,000	$ 1,000	$ 1,000	$ 1,000	$ 1,000	$ 1,000	$ 1,000	$ 1,000	$ 1,000	$ 12,000
Amy and Steve's Salary	$ 1,000	$ 1,000	$ 1,000	$ 1,000	$ 1,000	$ 1,000	$ 1,000	$ 1,000	$ 1,000	$ 1,000	$ 1,000	$ 1,000	$ 12,000
Advertising	$ 1,000	$ 1,000	$ 1,000	$ 1,000	$ 1,000	$ 1,000	$ 1,000	$ 1,000	$ 1,000	$ 1,000	$ 1,000	$ 1,000	$ 12,000
Insurance	$ 500	$ 500	$ 500	$ 500	$ 500	$ 500	$ 500	$ 500	$ 500	$ 500	$ 500	$ 500	$ 6,000
Interest Expense	$ 1,469	$ 1,469	$ 1,469	$ 1,469	$ 1,469	$ 1,469	$ 1,469	$ 1,469	$ 1,469	$ 1,463	$ 1,469	$ 1,469	$ 17,623
Rent	$ 1,000	$ 1,001	$ 1,002	$ 1,003	$ 1,004	$ 1,005	$ 1,006	$ 1,007	$ 1,008	$ 1,009	$ 1,010	$ 1,011	$ 12,000
Total Cash Used in Operating Activities	$ 12,549	$ 12,600	$ 12,696	$ 12,784	$ 12,895	$12,983	$ 13,095	$ 13,183	$ 13,294	$ 13,405	$13,494	$ 13,715	$156,626
Net Cash Flow from Operating	$ 2,451	$ 900	($ 296)	($ 384)	($ 295)	($ 84)	($ 295)	($ 383)	($ 294)	($ 205)	($ 294)	($ 115)	($ 474)

(continued)

Exhibit 8-16 (continued)

The Portland Freelancers' Café CASH FLOW STATEMENT *for the Year Ending 12/31/2003*

	Jan	Feb	Mar	Apr	May	Jun	Jul	Aug	Sep	Oct	Nov	Dec	Year
Cash Flow Out from Investing:													
Soundproof Room	$ 15,000	$ 0	$ 0	$ 0	$0	$ 0	$ 0	$ 0	$ 0	$ 0	$ 0	$ 0	$ 15,000
Espresso Machine	7,000	0	0	0	0	0	0	0	0	0	0	0	7,000
High-Speed Internet Access Setup	10,000	0	0	0	0	0	0	0	0	0	0	0	10,000
Workstations	20,000	0	0	0	0	0	0	0	0	0	0	0	20,000
Supplies/Equipment	25,000	0	0	0	0	0	0	0	0	0	0	0	25,000
Furniture	8,000	0	0	0	0	0	0	0	0	0	0	0	8,000
Fixtures	5,000	0	0	0	0	0	0	0	0	0	0	0	5,000
Net Cash Flow Out from Investing	$ 90,000	$ 0	$ 0	$ 0	$ 0	$ 0	$ 0	$ 0	$ 0	$ 0	$ 0	$ 0	$ 90,000
Financing:													
Cash Received from Uncle (12% APR)	$ 50,000	$ 0	$0	$ 0	$ 0	$ 0	$ 0	$ 0	$ 0	$ 0	$ 0	$ 0	$ 50,000
Cash Received from Brother	20,000	0	0	0	0	0	0	0	0	0	0	0	20,000
Cash Received from Mother	10,000	0	0	0	0	0	0	0	0	0	0	0	10,000
Cash Received from Personal Savings	20,000	0	0	0	0	0	0	0	0	0	0	0	20,000
Net Cash Flow In from Financing	$100,000	$ 0	$ 0	$ 0	$ 0	$ 0	$ 0	$ 0	$ 0	$ 0	$ 0	$ 0	$100,000
Net Increase (Decrease) in Cash	$ 12,451	$ 900	($ 296)	($ 384)	($ 295)	($ 384)	($ 295)	($ 383)	($ 294)	($ 205)	($ 294)	($ 115)	$ 10,474
Cash, Beginning:	$ 10,000	$ 22,451	$ 23,351	$ 22,055	$ 22,671	$ 22,376	$ 21,992	$ 21,697	$ 20,314	$ 20,020	$20,815	$20,521	$ 10,000
Cash, End:	$ 22,451	$ 23,351	$ 22,055	$ 22,671	$ 22,376	$ 21,992	$ 21,697	$ 20,314	$ 20,020	$ 20,815	$20,521	$20,406	$ 20,474

Exhibit 8-17 *Balance Sheet*

Portland Freelancers' Café
BALANCE SHEET
for the Year Ending 12/31/2003

	Opening	Closing
ASSETS		
Current Assets:		
Cash	$110,000	$20,474
Accounts Receivable	0	0
Total Current Assets	**$110,000**	**$20,474**
Fixed Assets (Property and Equipment):		
Soundproof Room	$ 15,000	$15,000
Espresso Machine	2,000	2,000
Workstations	30,000	30,000
Supplies/Equipment	25,000	25,000
Furniture	3,000	3,000
Fixtures	5,000	5,000
Total Property and Equipment	**$ 80,000**	**$80,000**
Less Accumulated Depreciation	**$ 0**	**$15,996**
Total Property and Equipment (Net)	**$ 80,000**	**$64,004**
Total Assets	**$190,000**	**$84,478**
LIABILITIES AND OWNER'S EQUITY		
Current Liabilities:		
Accounts Payable	$ 0	$ 0
Total Current Liabilities	**$ 0**	**$ 0**
Long-Term Liability (Uncle's Loan)	**$ 50,000**	**$32,377**
Total Liabilities	**$ 50,000**	**$32,377**
Owner's Equity	**$140,000**	**$52,101**
Amy	40%	40%
Steve	40%	40%
Steve's Brother	20%	20%
Total Liabilities and Owner's Equity	**$190,000**	**$84,478**

9

CHAPTER

Cash Flow and Taxes

Learning Objectives

1. Understand the importance of cash flow management.

2. Know the difference between cash and profits.

3. Read a cash flow statement.

4. Create a cash budget.

5. Recognize appropriate tax filing information.

UpperCut Images/
Superstock

"Number one, cash is king ... number two, communicate ...
number three, buy or bury the competition."

—Jack Welch, retired Chairman and CEO of General Electric

Jessica Mah and Andy Suh cofounded inDinero Inc. as 19-year-old computer science majors at the University of California at Berkeley. Their company provides a Web-based, real-time financial "dashboard" for small businesses. In addition to receiving seed funding from Y Combinator in 2010, they are backed by angels—including Jeremy Stoppelman (Yelp), Dave McClure (500 Startups), Fritz Lanman (Microsoft), David Wu (Intuit), Jawed Karim (YouTube), and Keith Rabois (Slide).[1] These investors recognize that inDinero fills a need for small businesses in an innovative, compelling, and highly efficient manner.

inDinero users benefit from a simple visual system to keep track of the key financial aspects of their businesses. The dashboard displays such information as revenues, budgets, bank balance, credit card balance, and a cash balance graph. Users enter information from their financial accounts and submit receipts to manage their transactions. For many entrepreneurs, maintaining detailed records is a challenge, and bringing a box of receipts to an accountant at the end of the year can be costly (in the accountant's time) and inaccurate. inDinero is designed to make organizing and understanding simpler, so that companies can avoid cash-flow surprises and perform better.[2]

Andrey_Popov/Shutterstock

Cash Flow: The Lifeblood of a Business

Learning Objective 1

Understand the importance of cash flow management.

Cash is the energy that keeps your business flowing, the way electricity powers a lamp. Run out of cash, and your business will soon go out like a light. Without cash on hand, you will not be able to pay essential expenses, even while the income statement says you are earning a profit. If your phone is cut off, it does not matter what the income statement says. The success of your business will depend on cash from start-up through its entire existence. Cash is essential for the initial investment, ongoing operations, and growth. Managing cash is more critical than managing sales, because sales without cash receipts are a recipe for disaster. Cash truly is the lifeblood of a business.

The income statement shows you sales and profits over a period of time. It tells you how much revenue been recorded and how it relates to the cost of goods sold and operating costs. The balance sheet is a snapshot of your business. It shows your assets and liabilities and net worth at a moment in time. Each of these statements and the associated ratios are important, but without a firm handle on the cash flow, business success is elusive.

---

[1] Rip Empson, "inDinero Now Lets Small Businesses Track Their Financial Transactions and Receipts on One Platform," *TechCrunch*, October 6, 2011, accessed August 26, 2013, http://techcrunch.com/2011/10/06/.

[2] inDinero, accessed August 26, 2013, http://www.inDinero.com.

Step into the Shoes . . .

King C. Gillette Faces a Cash Crunch

Keystone/Getty Images

King Gillette was a traveling salesman for 28 years. In his spare time, he tried to invent a successful consumer product. He invented all kinds of gadgets that did not pan out but, in 1885, when he cut himself shaving with his dull, straight razor, inspiration hit. Gillette thought of a disposable "safety" razor.

Gillette and a partner eventually got financing and launched their business. The future seemed bright, but soon the company was $12,500 in debt. By 1901, even though people were excited about the product, "We were backed up to the wall with our creditors lined up in front waiting for the signal to fire," Gillette wrote later.[3]

Gillette convinced a Boston investor to put money in the company and, by the end of 1904, his company was producing a quarter-million razor sets per year. This is an example of how crucial an infusion of money can be to a business. A temporary cash crunch nearly destroyed a company that is now more than a century old.

[3]Russell B. Adams, *King C. Gillette: The Man and His Wonderful Shaving Device*, New York: Little, Brown, 1978.

The Income Statement Does Not Show Available Cash

For a business using the accrual method (rather than cash method) of accounting, sometimes the income statement shows profitability, but the business has little to no cash. Because of credit terms, there is often a time lag between recording a sale and getting paid. With the accrual method, when a sale is made and the customer promises to pay in a 30 days, the sale is recognized on the income statement immediately—but the cash is not available until the payment is received and available at the bank. Also, there may be a lag between paying for labor and/or materials and receiving payment for the finished goods. Thus, a company may show a profit and have a negative cash flow. *Cash and profit are not the same.*

For all the good information and guidance an income statement provides, daily operations cannot be based on the income statement alone. A business also needs a **cash flow statement** that summarizes the cash coming into and going out of it over a specified time frame.

Calculate a cash balance by subtracting cash disbursements from cash receipts and starting cash. Businesses should never to have a negative cash balance. A negative balance means that they are overdrawn in one or more of their bank accounts. This will reflect poorly in banking relationships, can trigger the accumulation of fees and penalties, and the overdrafts may result in bounced payments to critical vendors. More basically, a negative cash balance means there are cash flow problems.

Because the cash flow statement records inflows and outflows of money as they occur, it is a critical financial control for a business. If a sale is made in June, but the customer does not pay until August, the cash flow statement will not show the inflow until August, when the cash "flows" into the business. With the accrual method, the sale will appear on the income statement in June but not in the cash flow statement until August, so that reported revenue and inflows of cash will be different. When keeping accounting records on a cash basis, the sale appears on the income statement when the payment is received and revenue and cash inflows match.

Learning Objective 2

Know the difference between cash and profits.

cash flow statement
financial report that shows the money coming into and going out of an organization.

Exercise

Name three kinds of businesses that bring in a lot of cash during part of the year and not much the rest of the time.

Rules to Keep Cash Flowing

Cash flow is primarily a factor of accounts receivable, accounts payable, inventory, and the availability of debt or equity. By controlling these factors, a company can control its cash flow. To avoid getting caught with insufficient cash, follow these rules:

1. ***Collect cash as soon as possible.*** When you make a sale, try to get paid immediately. If you must extend credit, make sure you collect the cash as scheduled.

2. ***Pay your bills by the due date, not earlier.*** Do not pay an invoice the day it arrives. Look at the due date and issue your payment so it arrives by that date.

3. ***Check your available cash daily.*** Always know how much cash you have on hand taking into account any checks or bank debits outstanding.

4. ***Lease or finance instead of buying equipment where practical.*** Leasing distributes costs over time. Better yet, acquire functional, used equipment rather than new equipment (if it makes sense to do so).

5. ***Avoid buying inventory you do not need.*** Find the point at which you stock the minimal inventory necessary to satisfy customer demand. Inventory ties up cash: the cash you use to purchase inventory and the cash you spend storing it.

6. ***Plan ahead for seasonal or contractual needs by seeking financing early.*** It takes time to establish a seasonal or contract line of credit, and it is best to plan ahead for requirements so that you have the cash you need for inventory and raw materials and can fulfill your orders or be ready for an influx of customers.

Noncash Expenses Can Distort the Financial Picture

The income statement also is not an accurate reflection of your cash position when it includes **noncash expenses**, or expenses recorded as adjustments to asset values, such as depreciation. When you depreciate an asset, you are deducting a portion of its cost from your income statement. But you aren't actually spending that cash; you are reducing the value of the asset.

noncash expenses adjustments to asset values not involving cash, such as depreciation and amortization.

The Working Capital Cycle

Once a business is operational, an entrepreneur must keep an eye on the **working capital**, the formula for which is current assets minus current liabilities:

working capital the value of current assets minus current liabilities.

> Working Capital = Current Assets − Current Liabilities

Working capital tells you how much cash the company would have if it paid all its short-term debt with the cash it had on hand. What was left over would be cash the company could use to build the business, fund its growth, and produce value for the shareholders.

All other things being equal, a company with positive working capital will always outperform a company with negative working capital. The latter cannot spend the money to bring a new product to market. If a company runs out of working capital, it will still have bills to pay and products to develop; it may not be able to stay afloat.

The Cyclical and Seasonal Nature of Cash Flow

An entrepreneur needs a cash flow statement to determine the cash position of the business at specific points in time. It is crucial to identify and understand any cash flow cycles, because they can make the difference between success and failure. **Figures 9-1** and **9-2** show cash flow cycles for a manufacturer and a residential cleaning company, respectively.

Figure 9-1 *Cash Flow Cycle for a Manufacturer*

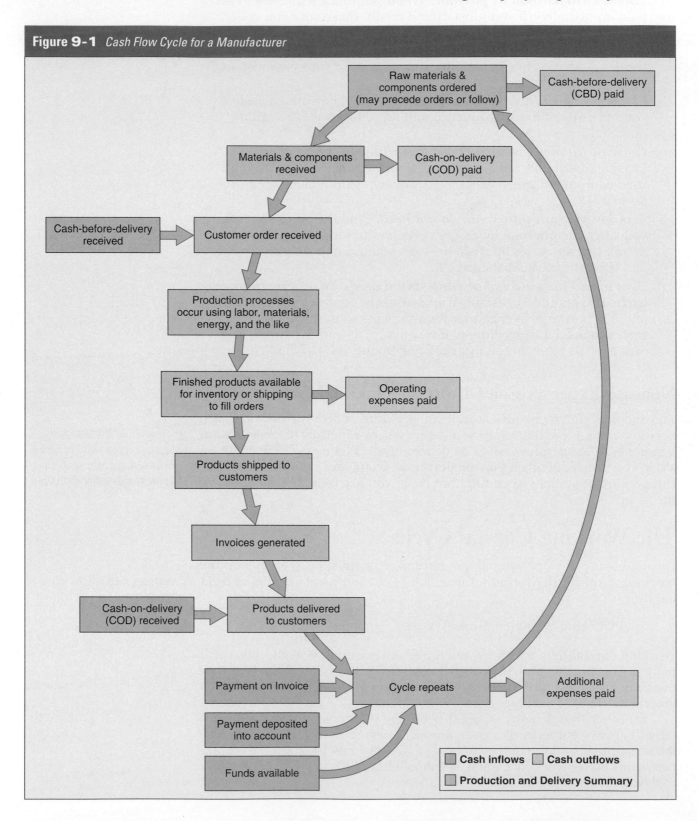

Figure 9-2 *Cash Flow Cycle for a Residential Cleaning Company*

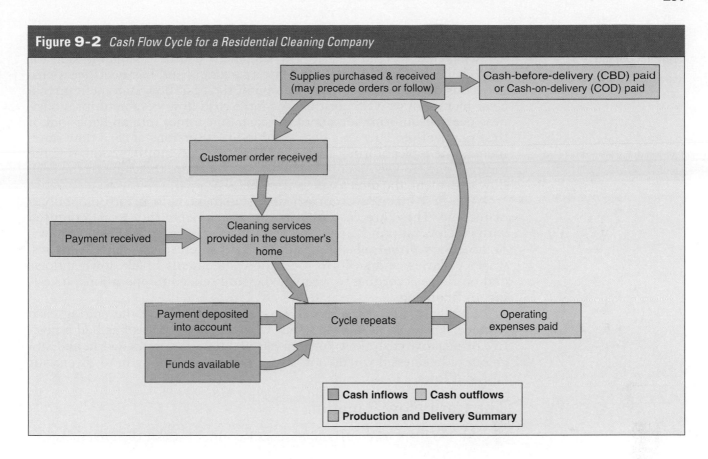

The length of the cycle, amount of cash involved, and up-front cash outlays will differ substantially for these businesses. For example, a manufacturer may have to pay its suppliers and employees before getting paid by a customer. A residential cleaning service, on the other hand, may collect customer payments on the same day the cleaning is provided, so wages can be paid soon after the cash is received. Thus, planning and budgeting will also differ significantly.

In addition to having cash flow cycles relative to specific transactions, cash flow can be seasonal for many businesses, meaning that the amount of cash flowing into a business may depend on where the business is in its fiscal year. A flower store will have a lot of cash coming in around Mother's Day and Valentine's Day, for example, but may have very little during the fall. A college campus bookstore might lay out cash to stock up on books before each semester starts and will then have a lot of cash coming in when students arrive to buy books for their classes.

Charles Orrico/Superstock

This is why keeping an eye on cash flow at all times is crucial to the survival of any business. Utility companies, vendors, and lenders do not care that a company won't have money coming in over the next three months; they want their payments—unless there are special arrangements in advance. When you create your business plan, describe your expectations for seasonal variations in your cash flow and how you will manage your cash to cope with this. Remember, you can ask lenders to create payment schedules based on the seasonal nature of your business. It is often in their best interest to do so, and they appreciate you planning ahead.

Reading a Cash Flow Statement

Learning Objective 3

Read a cash flow statement.

Knowing how to read a cash flow statement will be a valuable skill for any businessperson. Whereas income statements and balance sheets provide considerable insight into a company, the cash flow statement gives a clear picture of its cash position. A simple cash flow statement for a business provides information about the cash that comes into and goes out of the organization. There are direct and indirect versions of cash flow statements. The typical format that is familiar from accounting courses is the indirect one. To keep it simple and to best illustrate the value of the cash flow statement, the direct type is used here.

The first function of a cash flow statement is to record all sources of income. These are cash inflows, or *cash receipts* (not to be confused with receipts for purchases). The next function is reporting cash outflows, or necessary *disbursements*: insurance and interest payments, supplies, wages, salaries, and so forth. Cash flow statements break down inflows and outflows according to whether they are related to operations, investing, or financing.

Finally, it shows the net change in cash flow and the ending cash balance. This tells the entrepreneur whether the business has had a positive or negative cash flow. You can have all the sales in the world and still go out of business if you do not have enough cash flowing in to cover your cash outflows.

The Cash Flow Equation

Cash Flow = Cash on Hand + Cash Receipts − Cash Disbursements

Exhibit 9-1 is an example of a cash flow statement. Inflows and outflows of cash are divided into three categories:

1. *Operations*. Money used to run the business.
2. *Investment*. Money going into (equity) and out of investments in the business, such as equipment, vehicles, or real estate.
3. *Financing*. *Debt* used to finance the business.

Forecasting Cash Flow: The Cash Budget

Learning Objective 4

Create a cash budget.

As you get your business off the ground, and even after it has been operating for many years, you should prepare cash flow projections to make sure there is enough money to pay the bills. In the beginning, monthly—or even weekly—cash flows are in order. There are two steps to forecasting cash flow receipts:

Step 1. Project cash receipts from all possible sources. Remember, orders are not cash receipts, because they may not become cash. Some may be cancelled and some customers may not pay. Cash receipts are cash itself and payments that have cleared the bank. Note the assumptions you are making to arrive at these figures, so that others can understand the logic behind the statements.

Step 2. Subtract expenditures that would need to be deducted to meet this level of cash receipts. Cash expenditures are only those expenses and purchases you will actually have to pay during the projected time period.

Exhibit 9-2 is a sample company budget, and **Exhibit 9-3** shows the assumptions underlying another sample budget.

Exhibit 9-1 *Sample Cash Flow Statement*

Cash Flow Statement for Lola's Custom Draperies Inc. for the Month of March 2014

Cash Flow from Operations		
Cash Inflows		
Sales (Net of Returns)	$65,400	
Total Cash Inflows	**$65,400**	
Cash Outflows:		
Variable Costs		
COGS	($29,360)	
Other VC (Sales Commissions)	(6,540)	
Fixed Costs		
Factory Rent & Utilities	($8,000)	
Sales & Administrative	(12,000)	
Part-Time Tech-Support Salary	(1,000)	
Taxes	(2,875)	($11,500 × 0.25)
Total Cash Outflow in Operating Activities	**($59,775)**	
Net Cash Flow from Operations	**$5,625**	($65,400 − $59,775)
Cash Outflow from Investing		
Purchase of Building	0	
Purchase of Equipment	(6,000)	
Net Cash Flow from Investing	**($6,000)**	
Cash Flow from Financing:		
Loans	$25,000	
Gifts	0	
Equity Investment	0	
Net Cash Flow from Financing	**$25,000**	
Net Increase/(Decrease) in Cash	**$24,625**	($5,625 − $6,000 + $25,000)
Cash, Beginning	**$500**	
Cash, Ending	**$25,125**	($500 + $24,625)

You know that any projections will not be completely accurate, but you should create them to the best of your ability and review and update them routinely. They will be useful for anticipating any shortfalls, so that you can make adjustments to costs, push for increased sales, and/or arrange short-term financing, as needed.

Creating a Healthy Cash Flow

Healthy cash flow management means keeping sufficient cash on hand and available to pay your bills in a timely fashion and in general to have financial resources available to you when you need them. Most entrepreneurs struggle at various times to have sufficient cash to pay for materials, rent, and other expenses. As a business becomes more stable and successful, deciding when and where to invest excess cash to maximize earnings at the appropriate risk level will be an important part of managing the company.

Exhibit 9-2 *Cash Flow Budget for Three Months—Ending June 30, 2014*

	April	May	June
Monthly Sales Net of Returns	$20,000	$22,000	$25,000
Inventory Purchased ($10,000 in March)	11,000	12,500	14,000
Cash Flow from Operations			
Cash Inflows			
In Month of Sales	$10,000	$11,000	$12,500
One Month Later	0	6,000	6,600
Two Months Later	0	0	4,000
Total Cash Receipts from Operations	$10,000	$17,000	$23,100
Cash Outflows			
Inventory Payments			
One Month after Purchase	$8,000	$8,800	$10,000
Two Months after Purchase	0	2,000	2,200
Total Cash for Inventory	$8,000	$10,800	$12,200
Payments for Other Operational Expenses	8,600	8,000	8,000
Interest on Loans	0	100	100
Taxes	0	0	0
Total Cash Payments for Operations	$16,600	$18,900	$20,300
Total Cash Flow from Operations	($6,600)	($1,900)	$2,800
Cash Flow from Investments			
Purchase of Equipment	($20,000)		
Cash Flow from Financing			
Commercial Loan for Equipment	$20,000		
Line of Credit Draw			$10,000
Owner's Personal Investment	35,000		
Total Cash Flow from Financing	$55,000	$0	$10,000
Total Net Cash Flow	$28,400	($1,900)	$12,800
Beginning Cash Balance	$0	$28,400	$26,500
Ending Cash Balance	$28,400	$26,500	$39,300

Global Impact . . .

Cash Flow Statements Are Not Required in Every Country

In the United States, public corporations are required by law to present cash flow statements as part of their compliance reporting. In some countries, however, businesses are not required to present either a statement of cash flow or *statement of fund flow* (another name for it used elsewhere). This is the case in Germany, Italy, and Denmark. In Germany, many large companies voluntarily provide either a cash flow or fund flow statement. The United Kingdom does require cash flow statements but only for large companies. The international trend, however, is moving toward the U.S. practice of requiring cash flow statements from public corporations. Governments are recognizing that income statements do not reveal a company's true cash position, which can be misleading to investors. In light of major corporate scandals of a few years ago, the trend is toward greater transparency and more disclosure.

Exhibit 9-3 *Cash Flow Assumptions*

Category	Assumption
Accounts Receivable	50% in month of sale
	30% one month later
	20% two months later
Inventory (Payable)	0% in month of purchase
	80% one month later
	20% two months later
Utilities	$500 per month
Salaries and Benefits	$6,000 per month
Advertising	$1,000 in April, and $600 per month thereafter
Insurance	$100 per month
Rent	2,000 square feet of space at $6 per square foot per year = $1,000 per month
Depreciation	$0 (depreciation not a cash expenditure)
Taxes	Paid quarterly—none in this period
Interest	Interest only on line of credit and commercial loan for three months
Commercial Loan 1	$20,000 for seven years at 6% for equipment purchase = $100 per month interest only for three months
Line of Credit	$50,000 revolving line of credit, interest only at 12% per year, and no funds drawn until June

Cash inflows and outflows can be handled to control overall cash flow. **Figure 9-3** shows categories of cash flows and the way they affect a company.

Managing Inventory to Manage Cash

Inventory is often one of the largest components of a company's assets, and controlling it is a critical step in managing company cash flow. An entrepreneur takes a risk in spending cash. If you buy inventory, you run the risk that no one will buy it at a price that will give you a profit or even buy it at all. When you invest in inventory, cash is tied up and cannot be

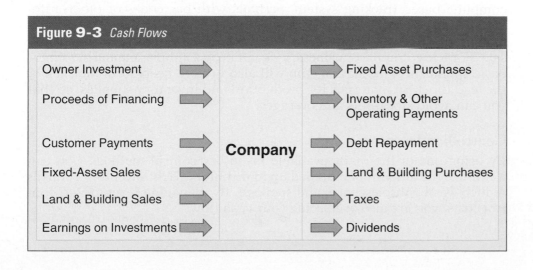

Figure 9-3 *Cash Flows*

Owner Investment →		→ Fixed Asset Purchases
Proceeds of Financing →		→ Inventory & Other Operating Payments
Customer Payments →	**Company**	→ Debt Repayment
Fixed-Asset Sales →		→ Land & Building Purchases
Land & Building Sales →		→ Taxes
Earnings on Investments →		→ Dividends

pilferage theft of inventory.

used for other purposes, such as rent, payroll, and debt service. By managing the level of inventory on hand, you will be dealing with one of the three primary controllable factors in cash availability.

There are two other risks involved with inventory—storage costs and **pilferage**, which is theft of inventory. You will have to be sure you can sell the inventory at a price that will include the cost of storing it and cover pilfering. Barneys, the famous New York clothing store, eventually had a 7 percent pilferage rate, which helped drive the company out of business (although it made a comeback later). Remember to account for these inventory-related costs in your projections.

You should also be cautious about adding inventory based on the expectation of receiving cash from the customers who owe you money. Because a percentage of the receivables owed to you may never be collected, counting on getting all of the cash could cause liquidity problems. You must keep track of your cash flow, or you can get caught in a squeeze between your suppliers, who want you to pay for the inventory you have purchased, and customers who have not yet paid for what they bought. If you cannot pay your creditors, you could lose ownership of your business. That's what happened to Donald Trump and the Taj Mahal in Atlantic City some years ago. He couldn't pay his loans, so he had to turn over 80 percent ownership in the casino to the banks.

Freeing Up Cash by Reducing Inventory

Conceptually, it is clear that reducing inventory releases cash. However, reducing inventory once accumulated is generally easier said than done. If it is finished-goods inventory, it has to be liquidated—sold—if it is to be converted into cash. This often means discounting products in ways that are not in alignment with your overall pricing strategy. If inventory is in the form of work-in-progress, or semi-finished goods, additional materials and labor costs may have to be invested to make it ready to sell. Thus, freeing up cash by reducing inventory is a valid option that can work but should be carefully considered and realistically projected.

Tracking Inventory

Keeping timely and accurate records is vital to controlling inventory costs. Regardless of the methods you select to control your inventory levels and determine your order point(s), the process will only work effectively if you keep accurate records of what inventory you have on hand and on order. Depending on the type of business you operate, you might use a computer-based tracking system, perhaps with bar codes or other automated techniques. More sophisticated methods can tell you where products are located at any given time and what quantities are available for sale. For a less complex business, you can keep a simple manual system or basic spreadsheet tabulation. You will also need to keep accurate track of the lead times on materials for production and inventory supplies, so that you can avoid stock-outs and overages.

Controlling Inventory Levels

By using one of the many available inventory control methods, you can minimize the amount of cash tied up in inventory. Tight inventory controls reduce waste, obsolescence, and spoilage. By managing inventory to control costs, you are also overseeing your cash flow.

Step into the Shoes . . .

Scott Gerber—Serial Entrepreneur

Scott Gerber earned tens of thousands of dollars a month by creating videos while a student at New York University's renowned film school. As he describes his experience, he "got really stupid" and decided that he wanted to be a "new media guru." Rather than continuing to accumulate cash from his thriving video-production business, Scott ended up bankrupt, with only $700 to his name. His mother, a teacher, told him to "get a real job."

However, Scott was not interested in ever getting a real job. He took the $700 and founded Sizzle It! This company creates Sizzle Reels, "3-to-5-minute videos made with fresh visual, audio, and graphics served with a side of creativity and results."[4] These high-impact marketing tools have brought Scott more success. In addition, he authored the book *Never Get a Real Job* and founded the Young Entrepreneur Council.

Scott claims anyone can be an entrepreneur by focusing on simple services. He has learned there is money to be made in such services. He also learned it is critical to keep cash flowing so the business can thrive.

Source: "The Future of Entrepreneurship Summit," Webcast from the University of South Florida, February 20, 2011.
Never Get a Real Job, access April 13, 2011, http://www.nevergetarealjob.com.
Sizzle It, accessed March 15, 2011, http://www.sizzleit.com.

Scott Gerber, serial entrepreneur. (Courtesy of Scott Gerber)

[4]Sizzle It, accessed March 15, 2011, http://www.sizzleit.com.

Managing Receivables to Manage Cash

Managing your accounts receivable to generate prompt payment is another way to conserve cash. In retail trade, payments generally are made immediately (in cash) or with a slight delay (debit or credit card or check). Once you are in a business that extends credit terms to its customers, you will need to manage the timing of payments. The sooner you collect on receivables the better, from a cash flow perspective.

The Cash Effects of Accounts Receivable

Receivables affect cash availability. If you are not actively invoicing and collecting the monies owed, you can rapidly find yourself with too little cash to operate your business. You will be, in effect, lending your precious cash to your customers while they have the use of the products or services they bought.

The Life Cycle of Accounts Receivable

An accounts receivable has a life cycle, which will vary according to your type of business. For most retail businesses, there is no extension of credit and receivables effectively do not exist. Wholesale and manufacturing companies routinely have receivables that depend on their credit policies and collection efforts. One tool that companies employ to manage their receivables is an "aging schedule" for accounts receivable. **Exhibit 9-4** is an example of such a schedule.

By creating and updating an aging schedule on a routine basis, you can keep track of your collections and anticipate your cash flow. You can easily identify problem customers and attempt to work with them to improve payment promptness, or you can decide to discontinue selling to them. Also, aging information can help to establish a forecast of cash flow.

Exhibit 9-4 *Aging Schedule for Accounts Receivable—As of June 30, 2014*

Name	#	Not Due (in disc.)	Not Due (no disc.)	15 Days Past Due	30 Days Past Due	60 Days Past Due	90 Days Past Due	120 Days Past Due
Adams	0123	$120		$240				
Bourdon	0246						$190	$300
Chevaux	3579		$480	$960	$720			
Young	0579					$560	$240	
Zaninga	5811	$480	$1,200					
Total		**$600**	**$1,680**	**$1,200**	**$720**	**$560**	**$430**	**$300**
Percent		**10.9%**	**30.6%**	**21.9%**	**13.1%**	**10.2%**	**7.8%**	**5.5%**

Of course, aging reports are only part of the cash-flow management process. Timely billing and effective collection are critical. If you are extending credit to your customers, a fundamental rule is: *If you don't ask, you won't get*. You have to invoice promptly and collect regularly. Whereas this may seem obvious, one of the most common cash-flow issues for companies is their failure to bill and collect effectively.

One challenge that entrepreneurs face is segregating the collection process from sales and customer relations. A legitimate concern is the potential for losing a customer by asking for—or demanding—payment for previous purchases. A failure to collect on a timely basis can lead to financial disaster for an entrepreneurial venture. Overly aggressive collection attempts, however, can also lead to calamity, through the loss of key customers. Keeping these guidelines in mind will help to maintain a balance:

- Establish clear credit arrangements with customers that reflect acceptable terms for both of you.
- Create comprehensive written credit and collection policies, share them with your team, and implement them.
- Use collection techniques appropriate to the level of delinquency.
- Avoid using salespeople as collectors on their assigned accounts.
- Comply with the Fair Debt Collection Practices Act, and do not use intimidation or deception in collections.
- Recognize that some customers are worth "firing" as credit clientele.

The Financing of Accounts Receivable

factoring receivables financing, or accessing cash for your business in exchange for offering a company the rights to the cash that will be collected from your customers.

Accounts receivable can provide a ready source of cash for your company if you are in a bind. Receivables financing, or **factoring**, provides cash to companies in exchange for the rights to the cash that will be collected from their customers. When you *factor* your receivables, you provide a list of the outstanding amounts and their status in an aging chart to the finance company, and they will offer you a percentage of each category of receivable in exchange for the right to those proceeds when collected. Fresh accounts are worth significantly more than older ones. Sometimes, you can be charged for accounts that do not pay within a specified length of time. Factoring is common in some industries and highly unusual in others. You will need to understand your industry to determine the applicability. The key thing to remember is that you will forgo the opportunity to control the collection process and give up potential profits in exchange for immediate cash. As a general rule, factoring is not the ideal option because it can become the proverbial slippery slope.

Managing Accounts Payable to Manage Cash

Credit is the ability to borrow money. It enables you to buy something without spending cash at the time of purchase. Once you have established a relationship with a supplier, he or she may be willing to extend credit. If you own a store, you might be able to buy Christmas ornaments from a supplier in October and pay for them in 60 days, after your Christmas sales.

credit the ability to borrow money.

If you aren't managing your cash carefully, however, you could get caught in the squeeze between your suppliers and your customers, as described previously. Your suppliers might not extend credit to you in the future. If you get into a position where you cannot pay your suppliers, you will have no further inventory and, thus, no business.

Negotiating Payment

You will have multiple opportunities to negotiate vendor payments, and you should be prepared to take advantage of them when they arise. When you establish a customer-vendor relationship, payment terms will be part of the price negotiation. The leverage you have to negotiate will depend on the balance of power in the relationship. Often, new accounts have less favorable terms with vendors until they establish a solid track record. Other times, a company may offer extended payment terms as part of a new-customer incentive or other promotional program. Once you have been a customer for a while and have demonstrated that you are desirable in terms of purchase volume and timely payment, you can revisit your payment terms to secure additional time. As you become an increasingly significant customer for your vendor, you can renegotiate prices, including payment terms.

You also may be able to negotiate payment terms when you are experiencing difficulty with cash flow. This is not something you should do routinely. However, if you can see that your cash flow will not permit you to pay part or all of the balance due on time, you should notify your supplier, vendor, or creditor and negotiate realistic payment terms. This should be handled deftly, so that they understand you genuinely need their cooperation; they should not become alarmed and retrench on future supplies or credit terms. It can be a delicate transaction.

Timing Payables

Just as you should establish an accounts receivable aging schedule, you should also create an accounts *payable* aging schedule (see **Exhibit 9-5**). In addition to noting where you are in terms of days outstanding, be certain

Exhibit **9-5** *Aging Schedule for Accounts Payable—As of June 30, 2014*						
Name	**Vendor Number**	**Not Due (in discount)**	**Not Due (no disc.)**	**15 Days Past Due**	**30 Days Past Due**	**60 Days Past Due**
Ace Supply	51-09238		$5,000			
Big Guys	62-78749				$1,000	
Champions	10-83297			$4,000		$2,000
Youth Style	23-83940	$7,500				
Zoo Pals	51-10239	$1,000			$2,000	
Total		**$8,500**	**$5,000**	**$4,000**	**$3,000**	**$2,000**
Percent		**37.8%**	**22.2%**	**17.8%**	**13.3%**	**8.9%**

to indicate terms received and variances. Recognize that you may have to start out with prepayment or payment on delivery, which will be difficult for cash flow because you will have to disburse money before you sell anything. Depending on the business you are in, this could be a long interval.

The aging schedule for accounts payable will make your cash requirements clear. You can see what is coming due, where you can benefit from discounts, and where there are problems. This simple approach can be invaluable to your cash management.

Capital Budgeting and Cash Flow

Cash management is not only for operating cash and financing. It also includes the planning for *capital assets* (fixed assets or earning assets). The purchase of machinery, equipment and its installation, and the like requires initial cash outflows for assets and incremental working capital for new projects, the inflow of cash from operations as a result of purchases, and terminal cash flows from liquidation of old, outdated, or replaced equipment.

Capital budgeting will help you understand the cash flow required for investments and the expected impact on operating cash flows. Budgeting will lead you to calculate the depreciation associated with capital investment, so that you can anticipate the tax effects. (Remember, increased depreciation means decreased taxes.) Finally, as you budget for the terminal values, you will see cash flow effects from disposal of assets and the related tax consequences. Making a capital budget can shed considerable light on cash-flow expectations. **Exhibit 9-6** shows a capital budget for

Exhibit 9-6 *NRG Savers, Inc.—Capital Budget 2014*

	Year 1	Year 2	Year 3	Year 4	Year 5
Initial Investment					
Machinery and Equipment	$82,000				
Installation	18,000				
Working Capital	10,000				
Total Initial Investment	**$110,000**				
Operating Cash Flows					
Operating Cash Inflow	$200,000	$300,000	$400,000	$500,000	$550,000
Depreciation	20,000	32,000	19,000	12,000	12,000
Net Change in Income	$180,000	$268,000	$381,000	$488,000	$538,000
Tax Effect (@ 30%)	48,000	80,400	114,300	146,400	161,400
Net Operating Cash Flow	**$132,000**	**$187,600**	**$266,700**	**$341,600**	**$376,600**
Terminal Cash Flow					
Sale of Equipment					$40,000
Tax on Income (sale)					10,500
Net on Sale of Equipment					$29,500
Recovery—Working Capital					10,000
Total Terminal Cash Flow					**$39,500**
Project Cash Flow	**$22,000**	**$187,600**	**$266,700**	**$341,600**	**$416,100**

NRG Savers Inc., as the company considers the purchase and installation of equipment for a new line of environmentally friendly products.

We can see that the components of the capital budget fit into the full cash-flow budget of a company, once the project is accepted or rejected. By creating and analyzing each capital project separately, you can apply your decision criteria and determine which to accept and which to reject. You can plan for your financing needs well in advance and be prepared to justify your repayment plans.

The Burn Rate

When you start your business, it will be normal to have a negative cash flow from operations for at least the first few months. You are likely to spend more than you earn in the beginning stages. Some businesses, such as biotechnology companies that spend a great deal on research and development (R&D), can have a negative cash flow of as much as $1 million per month. You will need to build these initial cash deficits into your business plan so that they can be covered in start-up costs.

Because a new company will probably spend more money than it earns while it is getting off the ground, the question will be: how long can you afford to lose money? The answer will depend on the amount of capital invested and the amount of revenue being earned.

The pace at which your company will need to spend capital to cover overhead costs before generating a positive cash flow is called the **burn rate**. The burn rate is typically expressed in terms of cash spent per month. A burn rate of $10,000 per month means that the company is spending that amount monthly to cover rent and other operating expenses. If the company has $20,000 in cash and is making $2,000 a month in sales, how long could it hold out?

burn rate the pace at which a company must spend capital before generating positive cash flow.

$$\frac{\text{(Cash Available + Revenue)}}{\text{Negative Cash Outflow per Month}} = \text{Number of Months before Cash Runs Out}$$

The Value of Money Changes Over Time

When considering cash and cash flow, it is also important to evaluate the changing value of money over time. A dollar today available for investment is worth more than a dollar tomorrow. Cash goes up or down in terms of buying power depending on several factors. For example, the value of a dollar changes depending on inflation rates and variations in exchange-rate strength relative to foreign currencies. Cash can also grow as the money earned previously gathers interest.

The Future Value of Money

Interest-earning funds grow fastest in investments that offer a *compound* rate of return—that is, those that are calculated on interest that has already accumulated. The younger you are when you start saving for a goal, such as retirement, the more compounding will help your money grow. Suppose you put $100 into an investment that pays 10 percent compounded annually. At the end of a year, you will have $110 ($100, plus $10 interest). At the end of the next year, you will have $121 ($110, plus $11 interest). Your money will grow faster each year because you are earning interest on the interest. The formula for this is

$$FV = PV\,(1 + i)^n$$

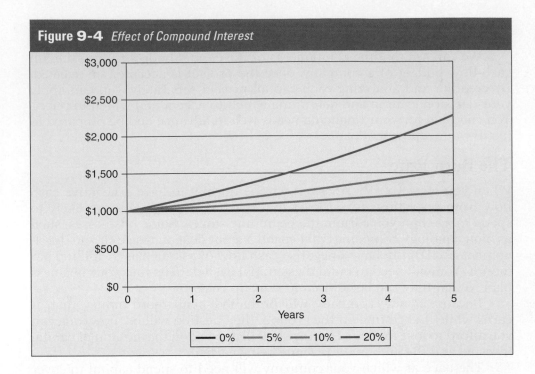

Figure 9-4 *Effect of Compound Interest*

Where **FV** is the future value of the investment; **PV** is the present value, or amount invested today; *i* equals the interest rate per compounding period in decimal form, and *n* equals the number of compounding periods. For example, $1,200 invested at 5 percent per year for 10 years will yield

$$FV = \$\,1{,}200\,(1 + 0.05)^{10} = \$1{,}200 \times 1.63 = \$1{,}956$$

Figure 9-4 shows the effect of compounding $1,000 at 0 percent, 5 percent, 10 percent, and 20 percent for five years.

future value the amount an asset will be worth a number of periods from the present.

The **future value** of money is the amount it will *accrue* (gain) over time through investment. For a single investment at a constant interest rate, you can use the formula provided, or you can determine this easily using a future value chart such as the one in **Exhibit 9-7**. Look up 10 periods at 10 percent on the chart, and you will find that $100 invested at 10 percent will grow to $259 in 10 years. Note that these values can also

Exhibit 9-7 *Future Value of $1 Today in n Periods in the Future*

Periods	1%	3%	5%	8%	10%
1	1.0100	1.0300	1.0500	1.0800	1.1000
2	1.0201	1.0609	1.1025	1.1664	1.2100
3	1.0303	1.0927	1.1576	1.2597	1.3310
4	1.0406	1.1255	1.2155	1.3605	1.4641
5	1.0510	1.1593	1.2763	1.4693	1.6105
6	1.0615	1.1941	1.3401	1.5869	1.7716
7	1.0721	1.2299	1.4071	1.7138	1.9487
8	1.0829	1.2668	1.4775	1.8509	2.1436
9	1.0937	1.3048	1.5513	1.9990	2.3580
10	1.1046	1.3439	1.6209	2.1589	2.5937
15	1.1610	1.5580	2.0789	3.1722	4.1773

be figured on a financial calculator and via spreadsheet software, such as Excel. If there are multiple amounts, variable interest rates, and the like, you can consult a basic financial management book or the Internet for appropriate calculation techniques. Remember, **compound interest**, money making money, is the essence of investment.

The Present Value of Money

Another way to look at investing is illustrated by the old saying, "A bird in the hand is worth two in the bush." You always prefer to have your money *now*. If you cannot have it immediately, you want to be compensated with a return. Your money is worth more to you when it is in your hand for three reasons:

1. *Inflation.* When prices rise, a dollar tomorrow will buy less than a dollar does today.
2. *Risk.* When you put money into an investment, there is always some risk of losing it.
3. *Opportunity.* When you put money into an investment, you are giving up the opportunity to use it for what might be a better investment.

Say a customer promises to pay you $10,000 three years from now for designing a Web site. Your next-best opportunity for investment has an ROI of 10 percent.

Present value is the amount an investment is worth discounted back to the present. Look at the present value chart (see **Exhibit 9-8**) under period three (for three years) and 10 percent. The present value of $1 at three years and 10 percent is $0.751. The present value of the promise of $10,000 in three years, therefore, is $7,510 ($10,000 × 0.751). Your client's promise is worth only $7,510 in the present. If you accept this arrangement, you are essentially providing a loan for three years. Anytime you are asked to wait for payment, you should be compensated, because money in your hand now is worth significantly more than money promised for the future. If you want to calculate this using a mathematical formula, you can use the inverse of the future value formula.

$$PV = FV \left(1/(1 + i)^n \right)$$

compound interest used with interest or rate of return and applied when earnings also accumulate interest or other returns, in addition to earnings on principal.

present value what the future amount of an asset or other investment is worth at face value discounted back to the present.

Exhibit 9-8 *Present Value of $1 to Be Received* n *Periods in the Future*

Periods	1%	3%	5%	8%	10%
1	0.990	0.971	0.952	0.926	0.909
2	0.980	0.943	0.907	0.857	0.826
3	0.971	0.915	0.864	0.794	0.751
4	0.961	0.886	0.823	0.735	0.683
5	0.951	0.863	0.784	0.681	0.621
6	0.942	0.837	0.746	0.630	0.584
7	0.933	0.813	0.711	0.583	0.513
8	0.923	0.789	0.677	0.540	0.467
9	0.914	0.766	0.645	0.500	0.424
10	0.905	0.744	0.614	0.463	0.386
15	0.861	0.642	0.481	0.315	0.239

BizFacts

When you sell a business, the price reflects more than the nuts and bolts of the operation. You are also selling the future stream of income the business will be expected to generate. This income is reflected in the price of the business, which is its *present value*. This is why businesses typically sell for several times their annual net income.

So, the prior example would be

$$PV = \$10,000 \ (1/(1 + 0.10)^3) = \$7,510.$$

Understanding the time value of money permits managers to compare investment options and other opportunities based on their real values so that they can better manage cash flows.

Taxes

Learning Objective 5

Recognize appropriate tax filing information.

Another factor that affects cash flow for a business is taxes. Like other creditors, tax-levying bodies expect payment in a timely fashion. More importantly, tax payments must be kept current, because some delinquencies can result in business closure and substantial personal penalties.

Cash Flow and Taxes

Once your business begins making a profit, you will have to pay taxes on those profits either through your corporation or directly through personal resources, whether or not you have a positive cash flow. In addition, self-employed people such as sole proprietors must pay their own **self-employment tax** on any owner's draws paid to themselves. This is the Social Security tax obligation for those who are self-employed and is the equivalent of the combination of the employee and employer taxes paid for employees. These taxes must be paid quarterly, so cash should be put aside in order to make the payments on the due dates.

self-employment tax federal tax that business owners are assessed on wages paid to themselves.

As an employer, you will collect and pay all employment taxes to the appropriate government entities. These taxes are particularly important to report accurately and pay on time. Federal penalties for tax-code violations with respect to wages are especially harsh. The government may "sweep" your company bank accounts (take out any available funds), assess significant fines, and secure your personal assets. Using withheld wage taxes as a source of cash flow and/or failing to pay these taxes could be a disastrous decision.

sales tax an assessment levied by governments on purchases and collected by merchants.

The federal government is financed largely by personal and corporate income taxes. States usually raise money from **sales taxes** on goods. Most states also levy an income tax. City and other local governments are supported primarily by taxes on property.

Filing Tax Returns

Corporate, partnership, and individual income tax and self-employment tax returns must be filed (mailed or submitted online) to the U.S. Internal Revenue Service (IRS) by specific dates each year. Corporate returns are due earlier than the deadline for individual returns. If you file late, you may have to pay penalties and interest. You can check the IRS Web site at http://www.irs.gov for deadlines, instructions, and forms.

The tax code is extremely complex. Check the aforementioned IRS Web site for information, but if you are still not certain which tax forms to file and when to do so, the IRS also offers booklets and telephone service to help answer questions. Alternatively, you can go to your local IRS office and meet with an agent who will guide you through the forms for free. It can be worth investing the time and money to ensure your own correct tax filings (rates and forms can change from year to year). As soon as you do so, you will probably want to seek the services of a tax professional (an accountant or CPA). Remember, in addition to federal taxes, businesses are subject to state and local taxes. Check with state and local revenue departments for details.

Collecting Sales Tax

If you sell products or services to the public, you will have to charge state sales tax in most states and then turn over the collected money, monthly or quarterly, to the proper agency. Apply to your state's department of taxation for the necessary forms. In New York, for example, entrepreneurs use the New York State and Local Sales and Use form to report quarterly sales taxes. Some states only charge tax on products; some charge tax on products and services, whereas a very few do not have a sales tax.

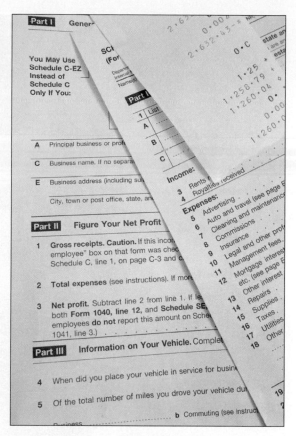

File appropriate tax returns for your business.
(moodboard/Superstock)

Tax Issues for Different Legal Structures

The legal structure best suited to a business depends on a number of variables, which will be discussed later in this text. Each legal structure has tax advantages and disadvantages.

- **Sole proprietorship.** All profit earned by a sole proprietorship belongs to the owner and affects his or her tax liability. The business does not pay taxes on profits separately.
- **Partnership.** The tax issues are basically the same as for the sole proprietorship, except that profits and losses are shared among the partners, who report them on their respective personal income tax returns.
- **Limited partnership.** This is treated the same way as a partnership, except that a limited partner can use losses as a tax shelter without being exposed to personal liability. This can be an incentive for potential investors.
- **C corporation.** A corporation's profits are taxed whether or not a portion of them is distributed to the owners. Owners must also pay personal income tax on any profit distribution they receive. This so-called double taxation is considered a disadvantage of C corporations.
- **S corporation.** Small companies can use this structure to avoid the double taxation mentioned above. The S corporation does not pay tax on profits. Profit is taxed only once, as owner income on personal tax returns. This structure requires all owners to take profits and losses in proportion to their ownership (thus it does not offer the tax-shelter advantages of the limited partnership).
- **Limited liability company (LLC).** This structure separates the members (owners) from personal liability and provides a more flexible allocation of profits and losses.

Organization is critical!
(Thomas Northcut/Thinkstock/
Getty Images)

Finally, note that dividends paid by a business to stockholders are not tax deductible to the business, but interest payments made to creditors are. This can be an incentive to raise capital via borrowing, depending on the tax issues your business faces.

Make Tax Time Easier by Keeping Good Records

You and your tax preparer will have an easier time if you keep accurate records throughout the year. Together, you will determine your net income and many other financial values. If you have kept accurate and timely accounting records, this should not be difficult.

Mistakes on your tax return, or just the luck of the draw, could cause the IRS to *audit* you. The IRS will send an agent (auditor) to your business to examine your books and records to make sure your taxes were filed correctly. An audit can be a time-consuming and stressful process. This is another excellent reason to keep good records and file all invoices and receipts, whether or not you use an accountant for tax preparation.

Do not confuse accounting with taxation. Your accounting software generates financial records, but you will still need tax-preparation assistance and/or tax software, to get your returns ready to file. Some accounting software will allow you to export your financial information into your tax program.

If you prepare your own tax returns on a computer, it will still be a good idea to have a tax professional review them. An accountant will be familiar with changes to the tax code and can offer valuable advice. Accountants often will not charge for questions asked throughout the year, if they have been hired to prepare a business's annual tax return.

One of the best investments you can make is to hire a top-notch small-business tax accountant or attorney as a consultant. Maximize the amount of professional advice and you will minimize the chances of problems with the IRS.

Chapter Summary

Now that you have studied this chapter, you can do the following:

1. Understand the importance of cash flow management.
   - Cash flow is the difference between the money you take in and the money you disburse.
   - Without cash on hand, you can find yourself unable to pay essential bills, even while the income statement says you are earning a profit.
2. Know the difference between cash and profits.
   - Profits are based on accrued revenues and expenses, for most businesses.
   - It is possible to be profitable and to be out of cash.

3. Read a cash flow statement.
   - The first section of the cash flow statement records all sources of cash income that come into the business.
   - The next section reports cash outflows (disbursements).
   - The last section shows the net change in cash flow.
4. Create a cash budget.
   - Project your cash receipts from all possible sources.
   - Subtract the expenses you expect to have from these projected cash receipts.
   - Understand the future value of money.
   - Calculate the present value of money.
5. Calculate working capital.
   - The formula for working capital is: current assets minus current liabilities.
   - It tells you how much cash is left over after paying all your short-term debt.
   - Working capital should be considered when creating cash flow projections.
6. Recognize appropriate tax filing information.
   - Both income tax and self-employment tax returns must be filed by specific dates (corporate returns are due earlier than individual returns).
   - Tax returns must be filed on time and accurately.
   - Collect sales tax. If you sell products or services to the public, in most states, you will have to charge your customers applicable sales tax and then turn it in to the state periodically.
   - Apply to your state's department of taxation for the necessary forms.

Key Terms

burn rate
cash flow statement
compound interest
credit
factoring
future value

noncash expenses
pilferage
present value
sales tax
self-employment tax
working capital

Entrepreneurship Portfolio

Critical Thinking Exercises

9-1. Describe the expected seasonality for one year for each of the businesses listed and explain how cash flow would be affected over the course of the year.

   a. Ski shop in a Mid-Atlantic state
   b. Christmas tree farm
   c. Candy store
   d. Disney World
   e. Car wash in Buffalo, New York
   f. Fitness center

9-2. Imagine you are the owner of an upscale clothing store, like Barneys in Manhattan, which was driven out of business by a 7-percent pilferage rate. What creative solutions could you identify to reduce pilferage?

9-3. State three rules for managing your cash.

9-4. Calculate the projected burn rate for each of the following businesses:

   a. Application developer for iPhones with $550,000 cash on hand, no revenues, and cash outflows of $50,000 per month
   b. Bookstore with $35,000 cash on hand, $3,000 per month in revenues, and cash outflows of $5,000 per month
   c. Restaurant with $1,000 cash on hand, $40,000 per month in revenues, and cash outflows of $42,000 per month

9-5. Figure out how much income tax each of the following individuals owes. The marginal tax rates are structured as follows:

   - $0 to $8,925 = 10% rate
   - $8,926 to $36,250 = 15%
   - $36,251 to $87,850 = 25%
   - $87,851 to $183,250 = 28%
   - $183,251 to $398,350 = 33%
   - $398,351 to $400,000 = 35%
   - $400,001 and above = 39.6%

   The different rates apply to different portions of one's income.

Name	Taxable Income	Tax Due
Jamie	$42,000	_____
Miguel	$98,750	_____
Suzette	$24,000	_____
Kimu	$100,520	_____

Key Concept Questions

9-6. Create a cumulative cash flow graph for a business with the following monthly cash balances:

January	$40,000
February	$25,000
March	$13,000
April	$5,000
May	$12,000
June	$2,000
July	0
August	0
September	$1,500
October	$8,500
November	$12,000
December	$21,000

9-7. Fill in the following table, using the future value chart in this chapter, to show the amounts of one invested dollar's growth at the interest rates and time periods given.

Periods	Interest Rate (%)	Future Value of $10
2	5	$11.03
5	8	_____
10	10	_____
1	1	_____
7	3	_____

9-8. Fill in the following table, using the present value chart, to show the amounts of the net present value of $100 at the interest rates and time periods given.

Periods	Interest Rate (%)	Present Value of $100
2	5	$90.79
5	8	
10	10	
1	1	
7	3	

9-9. Calculate working capital for Angelina's company. Describe how her level of working capital might affect her business decisions.

Angelina's Jewelry Company Balance Sheet July 30, 2014		
ASSETS		
Current Assets		
Cash	$10,000	
Inventory	10,000	
Other Current Assets (Securities)	10,000	
	$30,000	
Total Current Assets		$30,000
Long-Term Assets		70,000
TOTAL ASSETS		$100,000
LIABILITIES		
Short-Term Liabilities		
Accounts Payable (AP)	$10,000	
Short-Term Loans	5,000	
Total Short-Term Liabilities		$15,000
Total Long-Term Liabilities		15,000
OWNER'S EQUITY		70,000
TOTAL LIABILITIES + OWNER'S EQUITY		$100,000

Application Exercise

9-10. Create a projected cash flow statement for your business for one year.

Exploring Online

9-11. Print the tax documents list available at http://www.ideacafe.com/tax_center/ and highlight the forms that a C corporation producing glass bottles would need.

9-12. Visit Business Owners Idea Café online (http://www.businessowners ideacafe.com) and use the tool provided under Financing to figure out how much capital you would need to get your business off the ground.

BizBuilder Business Plan Questions

7.0 Financial Analysis and Projections

7.2 Cash Flow Projections

    A. List and describe your monthly fixed costs.

    B. Create a projected cash flow statement for your business for the first four quarters and the second and third years of operation (using either the direct or indirect method).

    C. Calculate the burn rate for your business.

7.7 Risks and Assumptions

    A. List the risks and assumptions that underlie your financial projections.

    B. Identify any external factors that may be substantial risks.

Case Study | Holterholm Farms—Radical Change for Maximum Impact

Ron Holter is a fifth-generation farmer in Jefferson, Maryland (in the Middletown Valley). He has learned to innovate the management of his farm to create a desirable quality of life for his family, while keeping profits and cash coming in. Holterholm Farms was purchased by William Holter in 1889, and it has been a dairy farm ever since.

Having grown up on this small family farm, Ron saw firsthand the challenges and opportunities inherent in running it. After returning home to the farm to work full time in 1981, Ron realized that the prevalent industrial system of agriculture demanded an incredible amount of labor on his part, for few tangible results. He was not going to be able to spend time with his children as they were growing up. By the 1990s, Ron saw that he would need to make changes for the farm to remain viable. But small producers were barely able to eke out a living. He knew there had to be a way to keep the farm successful and maintain a reliable cash flow.

In 1995, Ron planted the farm's entire 207 acres in permanent vegetative cover (grass) and put the whole herd of cows out to pasture the following year. This grazing system not only provided the animals with a grass-based diet, it also allowed Ron to work fewer hours at a lower intensity to take care of the same acreage and the same number of cows, while simultaneously improving his profitability. Because of the switch to a grazing system, Ron saw a precipitous drop in expenses. Veterinary bills were almost nonexistent, because the grazing animals were healthier on a grass diet than a confinement herd could ever be. Seed purchases ended, because the entire farm was planted in permanent grasses.

Due to the cows' all-grass diet, Holterholm produced nearly a third less milk. But, because of minimized costs, it became one of the most profitable farms in Maryland, netting $1,199.90 per cow in 1996, in comparison to the state average for confinement farms of $471.00 per cow.

Ron took this low-input system of agriculture on Holterholm one step further, by making the decision to operate as a seasonal enterprise. This switch to seasonal production meant a further decline in milk totals. Despite that, Holterholm Farm's profitability stayed roughly the same, and the seasonal system meant less year-round labor to support new calves. Now, all cows born in a given year were about two months' apart in age

Holterholm Farms is a member of the Organic Valley Cooperative.
(© ZUMA Press, Inc./Alamy)

and thus could be fed and cared for together; labor and feeding costs fell even lower.

Starting in 2000, Ron began to operate the farm organically. He did not use drugs or artificial hormones on the cows, nor did he treat the soil with artificial fertilizers or pesticides. When both Horizon and Organic Valley Cooperatives moved into Maryland in 2005, looking for organic producers, Holterholm Farms was able immediately to certify its acreage as "organic"; it took only three months to certify the cows.

In the short term, securing a contract with Organic Valley meant that Ron was paid roughly twice as much for his milk than what he was getting previously. It also meant that Ron had

© Mexrix/Fotolia

to switch to feeding his cows organic grain, to supplement the grass cover. With organic grain prices as high as they were, he soon realized it was not profitable to feed the cows grain. His cash flow was being adversely impacted. He was losing money, despite producing more milk. So, in October 2007, Ron fed the last of the grain to his herd. Milk production dropped, as expected, but the financial results were astounding. In 2008, the farm made $858 per cow—this with no grain feed and less milk production. In 2009, the farm returned to the $1,000 mark, netting $1,004 per cow—again, with no grain-feed expenses.

Holterholm Farms began producing less milk than ever, compared with its days as a confinement operation. In 2009, two years into the no-grain-feed policy, the farm was producing only 22 pounds of milk per cow per day, yet earned as much as in 1996. This was significantly more than could ever have been earned prior to grazing.

Having adapted the dairy portion of Holterholm Farms to become more profitable with fewer inputs, Ron explored and adopted additional sources of revenue. He added beef, eggs, and produce to the mix. These were relatively small revenue generators, but required comparatively few cash outlays and added reliably positive cash flows.

Ron's son, Adam, is making his imprint on the farm's operations by creating a Community Supported Agriculture (CSA) venture that requires an up-front investment in used equipment and marketing that can be recouped quickly. The CSA has the particular benefit of collecting "shares" in advance, to the maximum available, while incurring only the costs of growing and distributing produce from the fertile Holterholm Farms' land. Customers buy shares of the season's produce based on a weekly allocation of the total production. Adam might sell 50 shares in total to collect $25,000 at the beginning of the year and then provide each shareholder with 2 percent of the production each week. The payments are up front, with the expenditures at the back end.

The Holter family is managing the land to sustain it for generations to come.

Case Study Analysis

9-13. Why did switching the cows' feed entirely to grass improve Holterholm Farms' cash flow?

9-14. How could adding beef, eggs, and produce be beneficial from a cash flow perspective?

9-15. Search for Community Supported Agriculture (CSA) on the Internet. Why might it be good for Holterholm Farms to have a CSA? What are the risks involved? Why would consumers be willing to pay for their produce up front?

9-16. What would you ask the Holter family about the cash management of Holterholm Farms?

Case Source
Adam Holter, "A Study in Efficiency: Holterholm Farms," unpublished manuscript, Shepherd University, December 2010.

Managing Cash: CakeLove and Love Café

How does a lawyer with a master's degree in public health from George Washington University become a cake magnate? Warren Brown was a 28-year-old attorney in Washington, D.C., who in 1999 made a New Year's resolution to learn how to bake. This led to his leaving his position at the U.S. Department of Health and Social Services in 2000 to become a full-time baker. Warren opened his first CakeLove bakery in Washington on U Street, N.W., in March 2002 and the Love Café 17 months later.

Warren Brown, CakeLove.
(Cake Love)

He eventually became the owner of five more CakeLove bakeries in the D.C. area, as well as the Love Café. CakeLove pound cakes, brownies, scones, and cookies are available via the Internet for delivery nationwide (http://www.cakelove .com). Warren's first cookbook, *CakeLove*, arrived on bookstore shelves in the spring of 2008, and his second book, *United Cakes of America*, highlights his favorite recipes from every state. To top it off, he hosted the Food Network's *Sugar Rush*. Warren was named U.S. Small Business Administration Entrepreneur of the Year in 2006, and CakeLove was selected top bakery in the *Washington Post Best Bets* readers' poll in 2005 and 2006 and in the *Washington Post Express* in 2009.

This meteoric rise in recognition required a number of essential ingredients. In addition to the all-natural components used in CakeLove's products, the business aspects had to be properly balanced and mixed. Such rapid change demanded a lot of hard work, passion, determination—and cash flow. When Warren stepped away from his secure, full-time government job into full-time entrepreneurship, he had $10,000 of personal resources, including his credit card. In order to open his first storefront, Warren needed $125,000. Fortunately, he was able to secure a commercial loan from his community bank, CityFirst Bank of DC. Commercial lenders at larger, mainstream financial institutions were not convinced that a self-taught baker who had abandoned a promising legal career was a particularly good credit risk. Warren still maintained 100 percent ownership of CakeLove after the acquisition of start-up capital, and he continues as the sole owner after significant growth.

Within a couple of months of opening CakeLove, Warren decided to open Love Café—directly across the street from the bakery. The space popped up as an opportunity, and he wanted to take advantage of it. This required an additional infusion of capital for leasehold improvements, equipment, furnishings, and other start-up costs. There were few expenses from CakeLove that Love Café could leverage for this start-up, to attain economies of scale. Aside from being able to sell bakery-direct to consumers, he had little obvious financial advantage. However, CakeLove was strictly a take-out facility, housing production and sales areas, whereas Love Café would be a full-service establishment with a menu of baked goods, sandwiches, and coffee, in what Warren described as a "laid back, relaxed atmosphere incorporating natural elements and including WiFi, sofas, and large windows." Because CakeLove was new and had little positive cash flow, Warren could not finance the second location with the cash flow of the first. So, he turned again to CityFirst Bank. Ultimately, due to increased rent and competition, Warren closed Love Café in 2012.

Between September 2007 and July 2008, CakeLove opened three additional retail bakeries. Each successive expansion created a need for additional cash. Warren managed to avoid selling shares of the company by leveraging resources and partnering with a community lender. His banking partner, CityFirst, financed each location—to supplement earnings generated from existing operations.

Growth in the number of retail bakery storefronts has carried the business to new heights. Warren continues to serve as the primary manager of cash flow and human resources for his organization. Inventory theft has not been a significant issue because of well-planned store layouts and careful procedures; CakeLove has established cash-handling policies (cash-counting systems) to prevent pilferage from the cash drawers. Because CakeLove sells baked goods and other perishable items, spoilage and unsold product can become significant contributors to cash flow problems. Warren and his team have instituted a waste-tracking system and have been able to keep a "pretty good eye on the way inventory is moving."

The growth of the organization has not been the greatest challenge to cash flow for Cake-Love. Warren notes that diets have been more of a detriment to the business than expansion or an abysmal economy. CakeLove experienced its most significant cash-tightness at the height of popularity of the Atkins Diet, when counting carbohydrates led dieters to cutting out sweets and bakery treats. During times of reduced cash inflow, Warren and his team have to look to cut expenses, particularly by monitoring labor costs more closely than usual. When Warren opened his first CakeLove bakery, he had three employees, including himself. As of July 2008, he had 105. This has meant meeting the cash flow requirements of a large payroll and its associated expenses for the various locations, including being responsible for the support of numerous families.

Warren Brown has the following advice for aspiring entrepreneurs, "Do the homework. Know the industry you want to enter cold, so that you absolutely know how to make or do whatever it is that you want to make or do. Don't rush in. See it well and don't be afraid to get messy and to keep an open mind. There is always a way to improve. Know the product very well and have good confidence in what you are selling. People will always have unsolicited advice for you. If you don't have that confidence, you will get little chinks in your armor that can make your business less enjoyable and even miserable. Confidence is critical." Warren's recipe for growth has produced sweet rewards.

Case Study Analysis

9-17. How has Warren Brown been able to finance the growth of his company?

9-18. What methods has CakeLove used to manage cash flow? What others might it adopt?

9-19. What types of cash flow management issues would you expect CakeLove to encounter if it continues to grow at a rate of three bakeries per year or more?

9-20. How do Warren Brown's recommendations to aspiring entrepreneurs pertain to cash flow?

Case Sources

CakeLove, accessed August 31, 2013, http://www.cakelove.com.

"Lawyer Turned Entrepreneur of the Year, Warren Brown of CakeLove," *The Africana-Connect*, accessed January 12, 2008, http://www.theculturalconnect.com/.

Warren Brown, *CakeLove: How to Bake Cakes from Scratch,* New York: Stewart, Tabori and Chang, 2008.

10

Financing Strategy & Tactics

Learning Objectives

1. Assess your financing preferences.

2. Compare the types of business financing.

3. Evaluate the pros and cons of debt and equity financing.

4. Identify sources of capital for your business.

5. Appraise stocks and bonds as investment alternatives.

CHAPTER

Superstock

> *"You do not get what you deserve, you get what you negotiate."*
>
> —Chester L. Karrass, pioneer of negotiation theory

Etsy, Inc., was founded in 2005 by Robert Kalin, Chris Maguire, and Haim Schoppik in an environment that Kalin describes this way: "Early on it was a little bit like the Wild West where it starts with what you have on hand."[1] Frustrated by his inability to find online distribution for his handcrafted wood products, Kalin created a Web site that connected creators of handmade items and sellers of vintage goods and craft supplies with buyers through e-commerce. With a reported $895.1 million in 2012 in gross merchandise sales of goods and more than 30 million registered users, it has grown from a bootstrap company to one that raised $20 million in its fifth round of seeking venture investment.[2]

Kalin went to people he knew for his earliest financing. He had installed a bar for Spencer Ain and helped restaurateur Sean Meenan with a technology installation before they became his first (2005) and second (2006) round investors.[3] Next, working through his networks, Kalin got Caterina Fake and Stewart Butterfield, founders of Flckr, along with Delicious founder Joshua Schachter, Albert Wenger, and Union Square Ventures to invest $1 million, also in 2006.[4] Union Square Ventures invested again in Series B (January 2007) and C (July 2007) with $3.25 million each round.

The next financing round for Etsy raised $27 million, with the word on the street being that "Etsy was valued at $90 million pre money."[5] Accel Partners was a significant investor in the Series D financing. The fifth, raising $20 million (Series E), round saw Index Ventures as a new lead investor, joined by Accel Partners and Burda Media.[6] Most recently, Etsy raised $40 million from many of the same investors to expand internationally.[7]

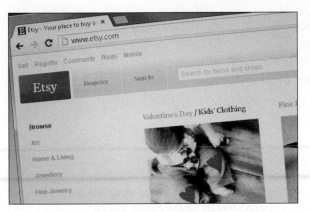

© Web Pix/Alamy

Going It Alone Versus Securing Financing

Learning Objective 1 ▶

Assess your financing preferences.

financing the act of providing or raising funds (capital) for a purpose.

To start or expand a business, entrepreneurs need to have money, either on hand or through **financing**, which is the act of providing or raising funds (capital) for a purpose. For entrepreneurs that means obtaining the money to start and operate a successful business.

There are three ways to finance a business venture, assuming you do not have enough funds in your savings:

1. obtain gifts and grants,
2. borrow money (debt), and
3. exchange a share of the business for money (equity).

[1] Evelyn Ruslie Visits Etsy in New York: Robert Kalin video interview, 2011, accessed April 21, 2011, http://techcrunch.tv/interviews-and-profiles/watch?id=NubDNrMToBvPOXXVnACzktftfSHzFljz.

[2] Etsy, accessed September 1, 2013, http://www.etsy.com.

[3] Op cit.

[4] PrivCo, "Etsy, Inc. Receives $1 Million Series A Investment from Caterina Fake, Stewart Butterfield, Joshua Schachter, and Others," accessed April 21, 2011, http://www.privco.com/private-company/etsy.

[5] Erick Schonfeld, "Etsy Raises $27 Million: Accel's Jim Breyer Joins Board," *TechCrunch*, January 30, 2008, April 11, 2011, http://techcrunch.com/2008/01/30/etsy-raises-27-million-jim-breyer-joins-board/.

[6] Erick Schonfeld, "Index Ventures Buys into Etsy, Triples Valuation to Nearly $300 Million," *TechCrunch*, August 26, 2010, accessed April 21, 2011, http://techcrunch.com/2010/8/26/etsy-300-million-valuation.

[7] Jenna Wortham, "Etsy Raises $40 Million for International Expansion," *New York Times*, May 9, 2012.

Many (or even most) people who want to start a business need financing. Whether that need is for $500 or $50 million, the entrepreneur has to bridge the gap between what he or she has and what the business cash flows and prudent reserves require. Sometimes an entrepreneur can use home equity, credit cards, or funds from friends or family to make up this shortfall. In other cases, these resources are not available, are not sufficient, or would not make sense for the business needs. In those situations, debt or equity financing becomes a necessity.

How Often Do Small Businesses Really Fail?

It is a popular misconception that four out of five small firms fail in the first five years of operation. Well-meaning friends, family, and potential investors all may cite this "fact." According to *recent research*, however, 45 percent—rather than 20 percent—of new small firms survive for five or more years.[8]

creditor person or organization that is owed money.

Business failure is defined by Dun & Bradstreet (D&B), which operates the largest and oldest commercial credit-rating service in the United States, as "business termination with losses to creditors." A **creditor** is an organization or individual that you have borrowed from and must repay. D&B, which followed 814,000 small firms formed in 1977–1978 for eight years, reported that only 20 to 25 percent of those small ventures that were recorded as terminated during their first eight years of operation actually closed because of bankruptcy. The other 75 to 80 percent were reported as terminations, but they were:

- businesses that were sold to new owners;
- businesses that changed—for example, from a flower shop to a general nursery; and
- businesses that were closed when the owners retired or moved on to other businesses.

The article concludes that the survival rate of the small firm, far from being one out of five, is closer to one out of two. More than half of all new small companies can expect to survive for at least eight years.[9]

For many, a small business is considered a high-risk, high-return investment, although in truth entrepreneurs are generally calculated risk takers and only pursue opportunities after they have weighed the chances of success. For the investor willing to accept the risk, a small business can be a great opportunity. The return on investment (ROI) of a successful small business can be thousands of percent, but the possibility of business failure is also relatively high. If a business fails, the founders and investors lose money. The entrepreneur's task, when writing a business plan and doing research, is to demonstrate how the venture will succeed and what level of appropriate returns investors can look forward to for the risk they are assuming.

What Is the Best Type of Financing for You and Your Business?

Financing is not a one-size-fits-all proposition. Each venture has unique requirements and circumstances, along with the structure and challenges of the selected industry. For some businesses, such as restaurants, standard

[8]Entrepreneur Weekly, Small Business Development Center, Bradley University, University of Tennessee Research, January 1, 2014. Accessed at http://www.statisticbrain.com/startup-failure-by-industry/ on May 11, 2014.

[9]E. Lewis Bryan, "Financial Management and Capital Formation in Small Business," *Journal of Small Business Management,* July 1, 1984.

commercial loans may not be an option because commercial lenders see them as too risky and are not willing to make them. For others, such as research-based technology firms, equity will be needed. Regardless of your preferences and the types of financing available, you will invariably have to be the first investor in your business. Lenders and investors alike insist that entrepreneurs have their personal resources involved before they put in additional funding. It is easier to persist and work hard when you have a personal financial stake in success. If putting your personal assets at risk is not something you (or your family) are willing to do, expect to be rejected by investors and lenders.

Your **risk tolerance**, meaning the amount of risk (threat of loss) you are willing to sustain, will also help to define possible financing options. For example, if you own a home and are seeking a commercial loan, you will likely have to put it up as security (collateral), in case you cannot repay the debt. Or, if you are giving up ownership through equity, you may have to give up control of the company you founded to your investors so that you can obtain needed financial resources. Be prepared to face these types of decisions as you seek financing that works.

risk tolerance the amount of risk or threat of loss that an individual is willing to sustain.

There are three ways for a business to raise the capital it needs to grow.

1. ***Finance with earnings.*** If a company is profitable and has positive cash flow, it can use some of its profits to finance expansion. This will help ensure that the company does not take on too much debt or grow more quickly than its finances can handle.

◀ **Learning Objective 2**
Compare the types of business financing.

2. ***Finance with equity.*** If a company is incorporated, it can sell stock privately, or on the stock market, to raise capital. People who purchase shares of stock are getting *equity*. Other types of businesses may also have equity investors.

3. ***Finance with debt.*** Any type of business, depending on its *creditworthiness* and that of its owner(s), can borrow money. An incorporated company can also sell *bonds*, although it is difficult and cost-prohibitive for small businesses to do so. People who purchase bonds will receive interest on the loan they are making to the company, with repayment of principal in a lump sum at maturity.

Both stocks and bonds are heavily regulated by the federal government. Issuing either requires considerable technical guidance and monetary outlay. This is not a do-it-yourself procedure. Rather, the counsel of investment bankers, accountants, and attorneys is required.

Gifts and Grants

The opportunities for gifts and grants to businesses do exist. However, both must be pursued with caution because gifts may come with strings attached and grants generally have requirements. Informal gifts include such items as cash, free use of facilities and equipment, unpaid labor by friends and family, and forgiveness or deferral of debts. Official gifts, furnished primarily by the federal government, may be provided for specific types of investments to stimulate designated geographic areas to support particular populations. These may be in the form of **tax abatements** (legal reductions in taxes) and **tax credits** (direct reduction of taxes). Business grants are primarily made for research and commercialization efforts and are difficult for start-up, low-technology companies to acquire. Because gifts and grants do not require repayment or incur financing costs, they are often at the top of the entrepreneur's list of desired resources. They are also among the hardest to obtain. The most readily available form of gifts for entrepreneurs those found through crowdfunding sites, which are discussed in BizFacts.

tax abatement legal reduction in taxes.

tax credit direct reduction of taxes.

BizFacts

Recently, a number of Internet sites have been created to link entrepreneurs in need of funds with investors. These are often called crowdfunding or person-to-person (P2P) lending sites. Businesses and investors can find sites tailored to their industries and funding requirements. Funds may be gifts or donations, investments, or loans. The sites may screen potential participants and may only offer money to a company after its funding goal is reached. Others may issue partial funding. In some cases, rewards are used to attract repeat investor participation. Some popular crowdfunding sites are shown below.

Crowdfunder Web Sites

Kiva	Microenterprise	www.kiva.org
Profounder	Small business	www.profounder.com
Microfundo	Music	www.microfundo.org
Kickstarter	Creative projects	www.kickstarter.com
Rockethub	Creative arts	www.rockethub.com
Cat Walk Genius	Fashion	www.catwalkgenius.com
IndieGoGo	Creative art	www.indiegogo.com
Grow VC	Mobile & Web 2.0	www.growvc.com

Debt Financing

Many businesses have some combination of debt and equity financing. The variety of loans and investments is quite large and growing. One challenge you may face is determining what type of debt financing to pursue, based on your business type and life-cycle stage, your personal finances, wealth, preferences, and the options available to you. Before pursuing debt for your business, calculate your personal *net worth* by tallying your assets (i.e., cash, investment accounts, personal property, real estate, and intangibles) and subtracting your debts (i.e., credit card balances, vehicle loans, student loans, mortgages, and other loans). Your lenders will want to know what you own, what you owe, and what your business finances are. The percentage of small firms using credit by credit type is shown in **Exhibit 10-1**.

Debt financing comes in many forms, with widely varying repayment and qualification terms. Different types of lenders will have various rates and fees, so it is worthwhile to compare the total package costs. Some debt options are discussed in **Exhibit 10-2**.

Debt Financing: Pros and Cons

Learning Objective 3

Evaluate the pros and cons of debt and equity financing.

promissory note a loan document that is a written promise to pay a specific sum of money on or before a particular date.

principal the amount of debt or loan before interest and fees are added.

To finance through debt, the entrepreneur applies to and contracts with a person or an institution that has money, and borrows it, signing a **promissory note**, a document agreeing to repay a certain sum of money (with interest) by a specified date.

Interest is determined as a percentage (interest rate) of the loan principal. The **principal** is the amount of the loan or outstanding balance on the loan amount, not including interest. If $120,000 is borrowed at 10 percent to be paid back over one year, the interest on the loan is $12,000 ($120,000 × 0.10). Typically, the borrower makes monthly payments until the loan is fully paid. The term, or length, of the loan generally depends on what is being financed, with working capital having the shortest term and real estate the longest.

The lender essentially has no say in the operations of the business, as long as the loan payments are made on time and loan terms are met. The lender will have a say in how the funds are initially disbursed (according to a schedule that you provide) and may set restrictions (protective covenants). The payments are predictable, although they may vary with

Exhibit 10-1 *Percentage of Small Firms Using Credit by Credit Type*

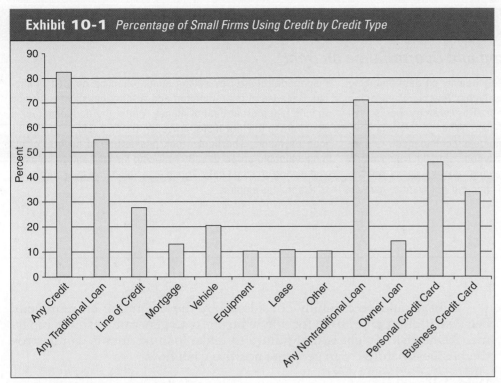

Note: Owner loans for corporations and partnerships only.
Source: U.S. Small Business Administration, Office of Advocacy, "Financing Patterns of Small Firms: Finding from the 1998 Survey of Small Business Finance," September 2003.

Exhibit 10-2 *Selected Sources of Business Financing*

Debt Category	Description	Common Types	Terms
Commercial Loans	Business loans typically provided by a bank or other financial institution.	• Real estate • Equipment and improvements • Working capital • Asset based • Accounts-receivable factoring	Up to 20 years Up to 7 years 1 year or less Depends on the type of asset pledged Often 30 days
Personal Loans	Loans taken out on your personal credit and used for the business. May have a fixed term (length) or "revolving" term.	• *Credit cards* • *Home equity loans* • *Title loan* • *Payday loan*	Revolving Variable terms; some are lines of credit Short-term, fixed repayment Short-term, fixed repayment
Leases	Debts incurred for the rights to use specific property, such as automobiles, trucks, or equipment.	• *Vehicle lease* • *Equipment leases*	Often for 2 or 3 years with a purchase option at the end of the term Varies widely depending on the nature of equipment leased
Bonds	Long-term debt instruments used by corporations to raise large sums of money.	See Bonds section later in the chapter	

changes in key interest-rate measures, if the interest rate is variable rather than fixed. If the loan payments are not made in a timely way, the lender can force the business into liquidation or bankruptcy, even if that loan balance is only a fraction of what the business is worth. Also, the lender can take the home and personal possessions of the owner, depending on the agreement.

Step into the Shoes . . .

Frank Franklin II/AP
Wide World Photos

Donald Trump and Overreliance on Debt

Companies that rely heavily on debt financing are described as highly *leveraged*, meaning financed with debt. This strategy works well when business is good. When business is slow, debt payments can be difficult to meet.

Real estate tycoon Donald Trump made the mistake of relying too heavily on debt in the early 1980s. Trump did not want to give up managerial control by selling stock when he needed financing. Because of his reputation and wealth, banks were willing to lend him a great deal of money. When the economy took a downturn in the late 1980s, however, Trump could not make his loan payments. The banks took possession of several of his most valuable properties. By reducing his real estate holdings and paying off some debt, Trump was able to recover, and go on to expand his empire.

---

leveraged financed by debt, as opposed to equity.

Debt should be carefully considered by the beginning entrepreneur, because it often takes time for a new business to generate cash for repayment. One risk of debt is that failure to make loan payments can destroy the business before it can generate positive cash flow.

Debt Advantages

- The lender has no say in the management or direction of the business, as long as the loan payments are made and contracts are not violated.
- Loan payments are predictable; they do not change with the fortunes of the business.
- Loan payments can be set up so that they are matched with the seasonal sales of the business.
- Lenders do not share in the business's profits.

Debt Disadvantages

default the results of a borrower failing to meet the repayment agreement on a debt.

- If loan payments are not made, the lender can force the business into bankruptcy.
- The lender can take the home and possessions of the owner(s) to settle a debt in case of **default**—when the borrower fails to meet the repayment agreement.
- Debt payments increase a business's fixed costs, thereby lowering profits.
- Repayment reduces available cash.
- Lenders expect regular financial reporting and compliance with the loan contracts.

Equity Financing

Equity means that, in return for money, an investor will receive a percentage of ownership in a company. For the $120,000 investment discussed previously, an equity investor might want 10 percent ownership of the company, which would mean 10 percent of the business's profits. (This would indicate that the business was valued at $1.2 million.) The investor is hoping that 10 percent of the profits will provide a high rate of return, over time, on the initial investment of $120,000.

Step into the Shoes . . .

Apple's Steve Jobs

Relying too heavily on equity can also be the downfall of a founding entrepreneur, as the story of Steve Jobs, cofounder of Apple Computer, illustrates. Because Jobs and his partner, Steve Wozniak, were young men with very little money, debt financing was not an option. To raise money, they sold pieces of the company.

By the late 1980s, Apple had become so successful that Jobs hired a prominent PepsiCo executive, John Sculley, as Apple's chief executive officer. Sculley gradually convinced Apple's board of directors that Jobs was a disruptive influence in the company. Eventually a vote was taken of Apple shareholders, and Jobs did not own enough equity to fend off Sculley's effort to fire him. He was voted out of the highly successful company he started.

Jobs was invited back to lead Apple as interim CEO in 1997, however, and was elected permanent CEO by the shareholders in 2000. He remained a leader of Apple until his death in 2011.

Bloomberg/Getty Images

Equity Financing: Pros and Cons

The equity investor assumes greater risk than the debt lender. If the business does not make a profit, neither does the investor. The equity investor cannot force the business into bankruptcy to get back the investment. If creditors force a business into bankruptcy, equity investors have a claim on whatever is left over after the debt lenders have been paid. However, the potential for return is also higher. The equity investor should make an investment back many times over if the business prospers.

Money raised via equity does not have to be paid back unless the business is successful. Equity investors may offer helpful advice and provide valuable contacts. However, if the entrepreneur gives up more than 50 percent ownership, control of the business may be taken over by the equity holders. Even with less than half the ownership, investors may assert managerial influence.

Equity Advantages

- If the business does not make a profit, the investor does not get paid.
- There are no required regular payments in the form of principal or interest, and dividends for common stockholders are distributed at the discretion of the board of directors.
- The equity investor cannot force the business into bankruptcy in order to recoup the investment.
- The equity investor has an interest in seeing the business succeed and may, therefore, offer helpful advice and provide valuable contacts.

Equity Disadvantages

- Through giving up too much ownership, the entrepreneur could lose control of the business to the equity holders.
- Even with small amounts of equity, investors may interfere with the business via unsolicited advice and/or continuous inquiries.
- Equity financing is riskier for the investor, so she frequently wants both to be able to influence how the company is run and to receive a higher rate of return than a lender.
- The entrepreneur must share profits with other equity investors.

Where and How to Find Capital That Works for You

Learning Objective 4

Identify sources of capital for your business.

The decision of where to seek capital is complex, and the options that are available will depend on both personal and business factors. Your preferences should weigh heavily in the decision. However, it is a rare business owner who wants to pledge all family assets, pay high interest rates and fees, or give up majority ownership. Yet, many start-up and experienced entrepreneurs must do just that to secure the funds they need. Identifying and securing financing often involves exploring multiple potential options and creating a complex, multilayered financing mix. The optimal resources for a business may not be the obvious ones. Therefore, it is valuable to understand the range of sources.

There are many potential sources of capital and it may take you numerous attempts to find what works. Some sources of capital are identified in **Exhibit 10-3**.

Having an Excellent Business Plan Goes a Long Way

When you seek financing for your business, the quality of your business plan could make the difference between success and failure. Lenders and investors alike will need to recover their principal plus interest, or investment plus a rate of return. If your business plan realistically, clearly, and convincingly demonstrates that you can and will achieve your goals, your chances of obtaining financing will greatly increase.

How Capital Sources Read Your Business Plan

People read business plans in different ways, but rarely are they read through from front to back as written. For example, a lender may look at the cash flow projections first. One thing is for certain: you will need to capture the reader's attention in the executive summary or the plan is unlikely to be read.

Family and Friends

Family and friends are obvious sources for loans. But what about offering them equity instead? Explain that if they *loan* you money, they will only earn back the amount of the loan plus interest. If they invest capital in exchange for *equity*, on the other hand, they could get back much more than the original amount. Acknowledge that equity is more risky than debt, but explain that the potential for reward is much higher. Be careful not to take money from friends and family members who could not afford to lose it if the business failed.

Also, be sure that any financial agreements are properly documented and signed, so that there is no misunderstanding later. Online services are available to create formal business agreements between family members, and attorneys will certainly draw up agreements. Nothing ruins a good relationship more quickly than a dispute over money. As Shakespeare's Polonius advises in *Hamlet*, "Neither a borrower nor a lender be; for loan oft loses itself and friends." Whereas borrowing may be unavoidable, the cautionary note on borrowing from friends is well considered.

Financial Institutions and Dimensions of Credit

It can be difficult for new entrepreneurs to get loans from banks and other financial institutions partially because bankers tend to be conservative lenders and start-ups are riskier than established businesses, as performance is

Exhibit 10-3 *Selected Sources of Business Financing*

Financing Source	Category of Financing	Type(s) of Financing	Uses of Funds	Notes
Entrepreneur/Self	Debt or Equity	Loan or Owner's Equity	Any	Debt terms to be established at borrowing. Earnings through dividends and/or sale of company.
Friends or Family	Debt or Equity	Loan or Stock	Any	Negotiable on debt. Earnings through dividends and/or sale of stock.
Small Business Investment Companies (SBICs), Minority Enterprise SBICs (MESBICs), Rural Business Investment Companies (RBICs), New Markets Venture Capital funds (NMVC) *http://www.sba.gov/inv/index.html*	Debt or Equity	Loan or Stock	Varies according to licenses with the SBA and the types of entities served. Funds are to be used as requested by the businesses.	Generally installment loans for debt. Earnings through dividends and/or sale of stock.
Small Business Innovation Research (SBIR) or Small Business Technology Transfer (STTR) *http://www.sba.gov/aboutsba/sbaprograms*	Grant	Research Grant	Specific research as defined in grant application.	Must complete requirements of grant funding.
Community Development Corporations *http://www.opportunityfinance.net*	Linked Deposits and Savings	Gift	According to program guidelines.	Savings and financial literacy requirements.
Venture Capitalists	Equity	Stock	Start-up or growth	IPO, buy-out, dividends, royalties
Community Development Venture Capital Funds *http://www.cdvca.org*	Equity	Stock	Start-up or growth	IPO, buy-out, dividends, royalties
Angel Investors	Equity	Stock	Start-up or growth	IPO, buy-out, dividends, royalties
Investment Banks	Equity	Stock	Private or public placements (IPOs)	Paid in fee income.
Economic Development Agencies *http://www.eda.gov*	Debt	Varies	Varies	Varies broadly from state to state and other localities.
Leasing Companies	Debt	Vehicles or Equipment	To acquire use of vehicles and/or equipment.	Monthly payments of fees. Purchase option generally available at end of term.
Banks/Financial Institutions	Debt	Real Estate Loans	Real estate	Mortgage—long term with installment payments.
		Equipment, Vehicle, or Other Working Capital	Equipment and other capital as specified in the loan request. Supplies, materials, cash flow.	Promissory note—medium term with installment payments. Lines of credit usually with a maximum of 1-year term. Must be paid to $0 annually. Many variations; often a monthly payment.
		Home Equity	Personal loan for any purpose secured against a home.	
		Credit Card	Unsecured loan for business or consumer use.	Revolving credit with minimum monthly payments.

(continued)

Exhibit 10-3 *Selected Sources of Business Financing (continued)*

Financing Source	Category of Financing	Type(s) of Financing	Uses of Funds	Notes
Mortgage Companies	Debt	Real Estate Loans	Real estate	Mortgage—long term with installment payments.
		Home Equity	Personal loan for any purpose secured against a home.	Many variations; often a monthly payment.
Insurance Companies	Debt	Policy Loan	Any	Reduces cash surrender value. Varies.
Community Development Banks http://www.opportunityfinance.net	Debt	Similar to Banks	Capital to rebuild communities through targeted lending.	Terms vary according to mission and community need.
Community Development Credit Unions http://www.natfed.org	Debt	Loans to Members	Per community ownership	Varies depending on type of loan.
Community Development Loan Funds http://www.opportunityfinance.net	Debt	Equipment, Lease-hold, or Other Working Capital	Purchase of essential equipment and improvement for start-up and growth operation.	Primarily term loans. Some lines of credit. Typically for nontraditional credit. May include microloans, lending to not-for-profits, and to developers of affordable housing.
Microenterprise Development Loan Funds http://www.microenterpriseworks.org http://www.opportunityfinance.net	Debt	Primarily Working Capital and Start-Up	Relatively small loans ($35,000 maximum) for purpose detailed in applications and/or business plans.	Installment loans. Designed for nontraditional customers.
Receivable Factors	Debt	Accounts Receivable	Any	Factor is repaid by entrepreneur's customers. Receivables discounted and funds held back until they are paid.
Title Lenders	Debt	Title Loans	Any	Short terms with high interest rates.
Pay Day Lenders	Debt	Pay Day Loans	Any	Short terms with high interest rates.
Vendors	Debt	Trade Credit	Any	Entrepreneur delays payment of invoices.

Figure 10-1 *The Five Cs of Credit*

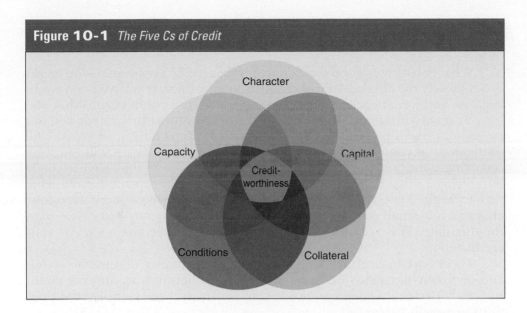

necessarily based on projections rather than historical data. Banks are in the business of lending money they are confident will be repaid with interest. Bankers operate on the principles of the five Cs of credit (see **Figure 10-1**):

1. ***Collateral.*** Property or other assets pledged against the loan that the lender can take and sell if the loan is not repaid. Examples of such assets are business real estate, equipment, inventory, an owner's home, certificates of deposit, money market accounts, stock certificates, and bonds. Commercial lenders do not want to take such assets, but they need collateral so that they can be more confident of debt repayment.

2. ***Character.*** Typically analyzed in the form of the owner's *personal credit* (ability to borrow money) in the small business context. Before a financial services company will lend you money, it will want to know your personal and business **credit history**, which is the record of how reliably and punctually you have repaid past loans. The lender will obtain your credit report from a **credit reporting agency (CRA)**. These companies, primarily TransUnion, Equifax, and Experian, collect and analyze information supplied by financial institutions and others that extend credit.

3. ***Capacity.*** The business cash flow must be sufficient to cover the regular loan payments and expenses. You will have to report your projected cash flow, so the lender can determine whether you will be able to repay the loan. Your **debt service** is the amount you will have to pay over a given period of time, until the loan is repaid.

4. ***Capital.*** Creditors will need to understand how much of your own money you invested in your business and whether your friends or family have invested. A lender needs to see that you are risking your own resources before risking outside funds.

5. ***Conditions.*** This is the state of the industry and economic climate at the time the loan is made and during its anticipated term. If inflation is on the rise, for example, the bank may be concerned that your earnings will not keep pace with it, thus reducing your capacity to repay the loan.

Lenders will expect you to sign a **personal guarantee**, which states that you will be responsible for paying off the loan in the event the business

credit the ability to borrow money.

credit history a record of credit extended and the repayment thereof.

credit reporting agency (CRA) an organization that collects, analyzes, and resells information supplied by financial institutions and others who extend credit.

debt service the amount a borrower is obligated to pay in a given period until a loan is repaid.

personal guarantee the promise to pay issued by an individual.

cannot do so. In other words, in the case of default, the lender will have the right to take business and personal assets even if you are incorporated or have an LLC.

What constitutes good credit may not be readily apparent. Good credit is not merely the absence of bad credit. You may think you have good credit because you have never borrowed money or used a credit card. What you have is *no* credit history. To establish credit, you must prove that you are capable of making regular payments on debts. Typically, most banks will not lend to anyone without a credit history, but many stores will, through revolving **charge accounts**, which are credit accounts that have a single borrowing limit and may be used and repaid on a repeated cycle. One way to begin a good credit history is to open one of these store accounts, charge a few small purchases, and never miss a payment or pay later than the due date. This record of on-time payment will become a part of your credit report.

There have been efforts to encourage the acceptance of regular savings and/or timely payments of rent and utilities in lieu of a traditional credit history.[10] However, when credit markets contract, these flexible credit options are easily discarded.

It will be wise to check your credit reports with the major credit reporting agencies at least once a year, to ensure accuracy. Under the Fair Credit Reporting Act, federal law gives you the right to see and challenge your credit reports from TransUnion, Equifax, and Experian. You can visit http://www.annualcreditreport.com to obtain your reports. Rather than getting the reports all at once, it is better to space them four months apart, so that you can check for errors more frequently. For your business credit reports, you can establish a history at Dun & Bradstreet by self-reporting. Further information about this option is available at http://www.smallbusiness.dnb.com.

Community Development Financial Institutions (CDFIs)[11]

A number of alternate lending institutions can serve a broad range of needs in emerging domestic markets. Although they share the common vision of expanding economic opportunity and improving the quality of life for low-income people and communities, the four CDFI sectors—banks, credit unions, loan funds, and venture capital funds—are characterized by different business models and legal structures:

Community Development Banks

Community development banks (CDBs) provide capital to rebuild economically distressed communities through targeted lending and investing. They are for-profit corporations with community representation on their boards of directors. Depending on the individual charter, such banks are regulated by some combination of the Federal Deposit Insurance Corporation (FDIC), the Federal Reserve, the Office of the Comptroller of the Currency, the Office of Thrift Supervision, and state banking agencies. Their deposits are insured by the FDIC.

Community Development Credit Unions

Community development credit unions (CDCUs) promote ownership of assets and savings and provide affordable credit and retail financial services to low-income individuals, often with special outreach to minority communities. They are nonprofit financial cooperatives owned by their members.

charge account credit extended by a company allowing qualified customers to make purchases up to a specified limit, without paying cash at the time of purchase.

---

[10]C. Glackin and E. Mahoney, "Savings and Credit for U.S. Microenterprises: Integrating Individual Development Accounts and Loans for Microenterprise," *Journal of Microfinance*, Volume 4, Number 2, 2002, pp. 93–125.

[11]Opportunity Finance Network Web site, accessed September 4, 2013, http://www.opportunityfinance.net.

Credit unions are regulated by the National Credit Union Administration (NCUA, an independent federal agency), state agencies, or both. In most institutions, deposits are also insured by the NCUA.

Community Development Loan Funds

Community development loan funds (CDLFs) provide financing and development services to businesses, organizations, and individuals in disadvantaged populations and communities. There are four main types of loan funds: microenterprise, small business, housing, and community service organization. Each is defined by the type of client served, although many loan funds serve more than one type of client in a single institution. CDLFs tend to be nonprofit and governed by boards of directors with community representation.

Community Development Venture Capital Funds

Community development venture capital funds (CDVCs) provide equity and debt-with-equity features for small- and medium-sized businesses in distressed communities. They can be either for-profit or nonprofit and include community representation.

Community Development Financial Institution Resources

Opportunity Finance Network	*http://www.opportunityfinance.net*
Association for Enterprise Opportunity	*http://www.microenterpriseworks.org*
Aspen Institute	*http://www.aspeninstitute.org*
Calvert Foundation	*http://www.calvertfoundation.org*
Coalition of Community Development Financial Institutions (CDFI Coalition)	*http://www.cdfi.org*
Community Development Venture Capital Alliance	*http://www.cdvca.org*
First Nations Oweesta Corporation	*http://www.oweesta.org*
National Community Investment Fund	*http://www.ncif.org*

Venture Capitalists

There are also investors and investment companies whose specialty is financing new, high-potential entrepreneurial companies and second-stage companies. Because they often provide the initial equity investment—venture capital—to start a business venture, they are called **venture capitalists**.

Venture capitalists seek high rates of return. They typically expect to earn 6 to 10 times their money back over a five-year period, or a 45 percent return on investment. Professional venture capitalists will not usually invest in a company unless its business plan shows it is likely to generate sales of at least $25 million within five years. The ideal candidates for venture capital are businesses with financial projections that support revenue expectations of over $50 million within five years, growing at 30 to 50 percent per year, with pretax profit margins over 20 percent.

If your business plan supports those kinds of numbers, you may be able to interest venture capitalists in your idea, but you will need an introduction from one of their trusted colleagues. Venture capitalists generally want equity in return for their capital. They are willing to take the higher risk for higher returns. Venture capitalists sometimes seek a majority

venture capitalist an investor or investment company whose specialty is financing new, high-potential entrepreneurial companies and second-stage companies.

Global Impact . . .

Kiva—Person-to-Person Lending

A relatively new player in the field of socially responsible lending is Kiva. This not-for-profit venture has served as a connector between businesses in need of small amounts of credit and individuals that want to support them. Kiva's mission is "to connect people through lending for the sake of alleviating poverty."[12]

The organization serves as an intermediary between individuals willing to invest at least $25 to a particular microbusiness and the microfinance institutions that will provide direct loans. What makes Kiva noteworthy is the ability to provide person-to-person lending and to have individuals lend without expectation of financial return (no interest is paid to them).

Kiva's microlending field partners made $599,415,450 in loans from October 2005 through August 2014 through 753,769 loans using the person-to-person lending model. The repayment rate was 98.36 percent, and the average loan size was $418.16. The loans were made by 1,803,451 Kiva users through 273 field partners located in 78 countries. Until June 2009, these loans were solely outside the United States.

[12]Kiva, accessed August 18, 2014, http://www.kiva.org.

---

interest in a business so that they will have the final word in management decisions. They can structure deals in a variety of ways.

To finance the Ford Motor Company, Henry Ford gave up 75 percent of the business for $28,000 in badly needed capital. It took Ford many years to regain control of his company. Still, many entrepreneurs turn to venture capital when they want to grow the business and commercial banks are not a good fit.

Venture capitalists typically reap the return on their equity investments in one of two ways:

1. by selling their percentage share of the business to another investor through a private transaction; or
2. by waiting until the company goes public (starts selling stock on the open market) and trading their ownership shares for cash by selling them. The shares can now be traded in the stock market.

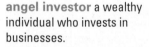

angel investor a wealthy individual who invests in businesses.

Angels

If your business does not meet the high-flying profit picture that would attract venture capitalists, or does not require so much financing, it might still be of interest to **angel investors**—wealthy private individuals (accredited investors) who are interested in investing in entrepreneurial ventures for a variety of reasons, from friendship to a desire to support entrepreneurship in a given field. Bill Gates, for example, has invested in several biotechnology start-ups because of such an interest. Often, successful entrepreneurs want to invest some of their earnings in other ventures that interest them, and they become angel investors to do so. The University of New Hampshire Center for Venture Research reports that, in 2013, active angel investors numbered more than 298,800 and invested in 70,730 companies, for a total of $24.8 billion.[13]

If your business has good management in place and a solid business plan, you might be able to raise angel financing. This type of investment is typically in the $100,000 to $500,000 range. Angels tend to seek a return of 10 times their investment at the end of five years, but their requirements vary widely. Angels may require fees for application and for presentations;

© Jim Thompson/Alamy

[13]Jeffrey Sohl, "The Angel Investor Market in 2013: A Return to Seed Investing," Center for Venture Research, April 30, 2014.

their national association recommends that they be limited to a few hundred dollars for applications and $500 for presentations.[14]

The idea is to get one angel in place and to recruit that individual to find co-investors. Angels can be hard to find. However, several national and regional venture capital networks have been formed to connect entrepreneurs and angels. The regional networks can be helpful because angels tend to invest in businesses they can visit frequently. The Angel Capital Association and *Inc.* magazine compile directories of angel investors, with the Association's list being global. If you search for angel investors, look for people who are interested in or familiar with your markets and field. Angels prefer manufacturing, energy, technology, and some service businesses. They tend to avoid retail ventures.

Insurance Companies

Business owners may obtain a **policy loan**, which is made to a business using a whole-life, variable-life, or universal-life insurance policy based on the policy's cash surrender value. In essence, the owner is borrowing against personal savings.

policy loan a loan made against an insurance policy with cash value.

Vendor Financing

Entrepreneurs frequently benefit from the establishment of trade credit from vendors. By eliminating the need for cash in advance or at the time of purchase, businesses can hold onto the money for a longer period or will have more time to generate cash for payment. In essence, the vendor is providing financing for the business. The **float** is the term for the time between a payment transaction and when the cash is actually in the seller's account. If you receive your phone bill on March 1 and pay it on March 20, you have *floated* the bill for 19 days.

float the time between a payment transaction and when the cash is actually in the payee's account.

Accounts payable is money a business owes its suppliers. You should negotiate the best possible payment terms with your suppliers in advance, so that your business can use float to have as much cash on hand as possible. This is a form of short-term financing from your own company. As you grow and/or establish a record of timely payment, you can ask for better payment terms. If you are not able to pay on time, always call the creditor and discuss the late payment. Never just skip a payment.

Federally Supported Investment Companies

The U.S. government has supported the establishment of a number of privately owned and managed investment funds, primarily licensed and regulated by the SBA, that use their own capital, plus money borrowed with federal guarantees, to make equity and debt investments in qualifying small businesses.[15] They may provide debt or equity for early-stage companies that otherwise could not obtain financing.

The general name for these is Small Business Investment Companies (SBICs). If you are African American, Hispanic, or Asian or belong to another minority group, look into Minority Enterprise Small Business Investment Companies (MESBICs). Also, the SBA and USDA have partnered to create Rural Business Investment Companies (RBICs) to support profit-oriented rural enterprises. In addition, New Markets Venture Capital Companies (NMVCCs) serve smaller enterprises located in low-income geographic areas.

---

[14]Angel Capital Association, accessed May 11, 2014, http://www.angelcapitalassociation.org.

[15]U.S. Small Business Administration, accessed September May 11, 2014, http://www.sba.gov/.

Financing for Rural/Agricultural Businesses

Whereas business owners often think of the SBA in terms of financial support and assistance, the U.S. Department of Agriculture (USDA) also has a long tradition of providing financial and technical assistance to rural/agricultural businesses, through a variety of programs. In addition to the RBICs noted previously, the USDA Web site (http://www.usda.gov) describes additional programs of grants, guarantees, and loans. Some of these programs include: the Farm Service Agency's farm ownership and operating loans, Rural Development's Business and Industry Guaranteed Loan Program (B&I), and the Rural Energy for America Program (REAP) grants and loans. Each program has specific options and limits and can prove invaluable if your business is located in an area served by these USDA grants or loans.

Self-Funding: Bootstrap Financing

bootstrap financing
financing a business by creatively stretching existing capital as far as possible, including extensive use of the entrepreneur's time.

Last but not least, there is always **bootstrap financing**, which is finding creative ways to stretch existing capital resources as far as they can go. If you cannot secure bank, venture, or angel financing, it does not mean that your business model/idea is not good. It may be that it simply does not fit their criteria. It is important to listen to constructive criticism and recommendations from the financing sources that do not fund you. They may provide valuable nuggets of information that will help you find ways to bootstrap more successfully. Many hugely successful businesses have been started for under $10,000 by entrepreneurs who used a variety of techniques to stay afloat, including:

- hiring as few employees as possible by using temporary service agencies for staffing needs, to help cut down on insurance and tax expenditures;
- leasing rather than buying equipment;
- getting suppliers to extend credit terms to take longer to pay bills;
- using personal savings, taking a second mortgage, arranging low-interest loans from friends and relatives;
- floating accounts payable;
- working from home or borrowing office space to save on fixed costs;
- starting on a smaller scale or with more used equipment to establish a track record for traditional financing in the future; and
- putting profits back into the business to keep it going.

Accessing Sources Through Online Networking

The more people who are aware of your product or service and its benefits, the more likely they are to buy it or refer you to someone who will do so. It is also true that the more you explore possibilities in financing options, the more likely you are to find what you need. Networking is the exchange of valuable information and contacts among businesspeople. The Internet is an important extension to your options for networking. You can search for angels and connect with other entrepreneurs online. Use search engines such as Google, Bing, Excite, and Yahoo! to find such Web sites as the Entrepreneurs' Organization at http://www.eonetwork.org.

Be wary of any service that requires upfront payment, will not provide complete references, or in any other way raises a red flag. If a financing

Global Impact . . .

The United States Encourages Other Nations to Become More Entrepreneurial

Entrepreneurship educators encourage you to think globally when it comes to finding customers, researching the competition, and looking for capital. If you live in the United States, you are probably in the best place to find capital for your business. According to a National Venture Capital Association report, venture capitalists made 3,980 deals totaling nearly $29.6 billion in the United States in 2013.[16] In 2012, global venture capital investment (includes the United States, Europe, Israel, China, and India) totaled $41.5 billion with 4,970 investment rounds with the United States and Europe accounting for approximately 85 percent of investment.[17] Europe's share of the venture capital market for 2012 was $5.7 billion or 13.7 percent.

European countries are trying to change that, however. The members of the European Union have set forth an agenda for creating a dynamic, entrepreneurial, knowledge-based economy. Venture capital (called risk capital in Europe) was identified as a key factor in achieving this. Other countries and regions are undertaking a similar effort to become more entrepreneurial, which means more investors in these countries will be looking to finance entrepreneurs.

[16]National Venture Capital Association Yearbook 2014, Thomson Reuters accessed May 11, 2014, http://www.NVCA.org.

[17]Maria Pinelli, Turning the Corner: Global venture capital insights and trends 2013, Ernst and Young, accessed May 11, 2014, http://www.ey.com.

---

source seems to be too good to be true, it probably is. That does not mean you should ignore or reject all online options. On the contrary, explore them—but use good judgment.

Investors Want Their Money to Grow: Can You Make It Happen?

When you ask a banker or friend for money for your business, you are asking for an investment. You should know, therefore, about some of the other options available to your potential investors. After all, they are only going to put money in your venture if you can convince them that it is a more attractive investment than their other options. As your company grows and prospers, you also may become more interested in financial investments. Or, you may already have one and need to decide whether your business idea is the best one.

There are three categories of financial investments that can provide funds:

◀ **Learning Objective 5**
Appraise stocks and bonds as investment alternatives.

1. **Stocks.** Shares of company ownership (equity).
2. **Bonds.** Loans (debt) made to companies or government entities for more than one year.
3. **Cash.** Savings accounts, Treasury bills, or other investments that can be *liquidated* (turned into cash) within 24 hours.

Real estate, land or buildings, is another important investment. All investments involve some risk, which is the possibility that the money could be lost. There is a definite relationship between risk and reward:

The greater the potential reward of an investment, the more risky it probably is.

> High Risk = High Reward

And so, if an investment has little risk, the reward will probably not be great.

> Low Risk = Low Reward

The following sections are a primer on securities investment.

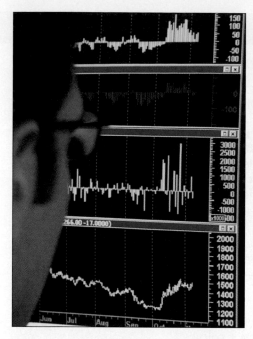

A trader checks stock prices on his computer.
(© Simon Belcher/Alamy)

share a single unit of corporate stock.

How Stocks Work

A corporation, whether privately held or publicly traded, is owned by its stockholders. Each **share** of stock represents a percentage of ownership. A stock certificate indicates how many shares were purchased and how big a piece of the company is owned.

If Street Scooters, Inc., has sold 10 shares of stock, each share to a different individual, it would mean there were 10 stockholders, each owning one-tenth of the company. If Street Scooters sold 100 shares of stock, each share to a different individual, there would be 100 stockholders. Each would own one one-hundredth of the company.

The "stock market" is in more than one location. It is made up of a collection of *exchanges* around the world where stocks are traded. The New York Stock Exchange (http://www.nyse.com) is the most well known in the United States. In recent years it has expanded to become NYSE Euronext, having added a number of European exchanges, and the American Stock Exchange (Amex). The electronic exchange that is home to many new and high-technology stocks is the NASDAQ (http://www.nasdaq.com), which is joined with regional exchanges. Overseas, the London, Tokyo, and Hong Kong exchanges are the most recognized. Stocks may be traded on multiple exchanges, but the companies must meet the criteria for each.

Public corporations sell their stock to the general public to raise *capital*. They use the capital to expand the company or pay off debts. Typically, a corporation sells its stock to an investment banker, who pays an agreed-upon price and then handles the marketing and sales to get the stock into the public market. A public corporation receives the proceeds from the sale before the offering. Once the stock is sold, however, the corporation no longer has control over it. It is traded in the secondary market. The stock can be bought and sold by anyone. Such trading activity occurs continually on the stock market between brokers. A *stockbroker* has a license that confers the right to make trades for customers.

Stocks may be either *preferred* or *common,* with preferred stock having aspects of debt and common stocks being true equity. Preferred stock typically has a fixed dividend that is paid quarterly and takes precedence over common stock in the case of liquidation. Many companies do not issue preferred stock. Common stock represents the true ownership of a company. It is the type of stock that is most often held and can be made available in different classes that define whether it comes with voting rights or not. In case the business is liquidated, common stockholders get repaid after all debt holders and preferred stockholders.

The price of a stock at any given moment reflects investors' opinions about how well that business is going to perform. If the company does well, or its investors expect it to do well, the price of the stock is likely to rise. Investors make their returns by selling stock at a higher price than the one at which they bought it. They also may earn *dividends*, which are the portion of a corporation's earnings distributed to shareholders, typically on a quarterly basis. Dividends are paid at the discretion of a company's board of directors.

The daily record of trading activity appears in tables published in *The Wall Street Journal* and in the business sections of many other publications. They are also available online from numerous services. These tables allow investors to track the changing value of their investments. Information about stocks is available through brokerage firms and services such as ValueLine and Morningstar.

Let's say you own 10 shares of a stock you bought at $10 per share (for a total of $100). You see in the stock table that the price per share has declined to $8.50 that day. Your $100 investment is now worth only $85 (10 shares × $8.50/share = $85). You have three choices:

1. sell the shares before their value declines further;
2. keep them, hoping the decline is temporary and the price will go back up; or
3. buy more shares at the lower price to increase your profit when the price does go back up.

How Bonds Work

Corporations may also use the financial markets to borrow money by issuing *bonds*. Bonds are interest-bearing certificates that corporations offer in order to raise capital. In addition, the federal government, state governments, and even city and town governments use bonds to finance roads, bridges, schools, and other public projects.

Bonds are loans; the original amount borrowed, plus interest, must be paid by the borrower. If you purchase a corporate or government bond, you are loaning your money to the company or government.

Owners of common stock are not certain whether they are going to receive dividends, or if the value of a stock is going to increase. They may make or lose money on the investment. The risks, and therefore the rewards, can be high. Bondholders, on the other hand, are promised a specific return (the coupon interest rate on the bond) and will get the investment back after a given time period. Bonds are rated by several organizations to reflect the levels of respective risk. Bonds and stocks together are referred to as **securities**.

Bonds are different from other loans, because the corporation that issues a bond does not have to pay regular monthly payments on the principal (the amount of a debt before the interest is added). A bond usually pays its yearly interest rate semiannually to the bondholders until **maturity**, when it is redeemed, meaning that the investor gets the face value back on that date.

By financing with bonds instead of a bank loan, a company does not have to make payments on the principal; it only has to make payments on the interest. On the other hand, the company must manage its money carefully, so that it will have the cash available when the bond matures.

If a corporation stops paying interest on a bond, the bondholders can sue the company. A court may force the company to sell assets to pay not only the interest, but the full amount of the bond.

Until maturity, bonds may be traded publicly with their price going above or below their **face value**. The face value of a single bond, also referred to as **par**, is usually $1,000 (with bonds being sold in lots of $10,000). This is the amount to be repaid by the corporation or government at the maturity date of the bond.

When the bond's market value rises above par, it means it is being traded for more than $1,000; perhaps someone purchased it at $1,020. A bond trading above par is trading at a **premium**; in this case, the premium is $20. A bond trading below par is trading at a **discount**. If the bond in this example were trading at $940, the discount would be $60. Prices are quoted with the coupon rate (interest rate) and the price at maturity. For example, a five-year, 12-percent bond might be selling for $899.40 with a par value of $1,000. This means that coupon interest payments will be $120 per year and the investment will yield a 15-percent return based on annual interest payments. Another five-year, 12-percent bond might be

security an investment instrument representing ownership in an entity (stock) or debt (bond) held by an investor.

maturity the date at which a loan must be repaid, including when a bond must be redeemed by the issuer.

face value the amount of a bond, also known as par, to be repaid by the corporation or government at its maturity date.

par the face value of a bond (typically $1,000) and the stated value of a stock.

premium (regarding bonds) the amount above par for which a bond is trading in the market.

discount (referring to bonds) the difference between a bond's trading price and its par value when the trading price is below par.

selling for $1,116.70, for a yield of 9 percent. The price an investor is willing to pay will depend on the return he or she needs to earn on the investment.

When you are buying or selling a bond, the critical determinant of price is the combination of the coupon rate, maturity date, risk, and required return. As an issuer of bonds, you will need to obtain enough financing at a cost that works for you. As an investor, you will have to meet or exceed your required return at a risk level that you can tolerate and on a time horizon that suits your needs.

Chapter Summary

Now that you have studied this chapter, you can do the following:

1. Assess your financing preferences.
   - Understand how much risk you are willing to take when financing your business.
   - Know the success rate in your industry.
   - Determine realistic financing options.
2. Compare the types of business financing.
   - Gifts and grants. Money or in-kind gifts given to support the business without a return required.
   - Debt. Borrowing money and promising to pay it back over a set period of time at a set rate of interest. Large corporations sell debt in the form of bonds.
   - Equity. Owners give up a percentage of ownership in their business for money. The investor receives a percentage of future profits from the business based on the percentage of ownership. Large corporations sell equity in the form of stock. Many businesses can sell equity.
3. Evaluate the pros and cons of debt and equity financing.

   Debt Advantages
   - The lender has no say in the management or direction of the business as long as the loan payments are made.
   - Loan payments are predictable; they do not change with the fortunes of the business.

   Debt Disadvantages
   - Debt can be an expensive way to finance a business if interest rates are high.
   - If loan payments are not made, the lender can force the business into bankruptcy.
   - The lender may be able to take the home and possessions of the owner of a sole proprietorship or of the partners in a partnership to settle a debt.
   - Loan payments increase fixed costs and decrease profits.

   Equity Advantages
   - If the business does not make a profit, investors do not get paid. The equity investor cannot force the business into bankruptcy in order to retrieve the investment.
   - The equity investor has an interest in seeing the business succeed and may offer helpful advice and obtain valuable contacts.

Equity Disadvantages

- Through giving up ownership, the entrepreneur can lose control of the business to the equity holders.
- Equity financing is risky, so the investor frequently wants both to receive a higher rate of return than a lender and to be able to influence how the company is operated.
- The entrepreneur will share profits with other equity investors.

4. Identify sources of capital for your business:
   - entrepreneurs, friends, and family;
   - financial institutions;
   - community development financial institutions;
   - venture capitalists;
   - angels;
   - vendors; and
   - federally supported investment companies.

5. Appraise stocks and bonds as investing alternatives.
   - Public corporations sell their stock to the general public to raise capital.
   - Bonds are interest-bearing certificates that corporations (and governments) issue to raise capital.

Key Terms

angel investor	maturity
bootstrap financing	par
charge account	personal guarantee
credit	policy loan
credit history	premium
credit reporting agency (CRA)	principal
creditor	promissory note
debt service	risk tolerance
default	security
discount	share
face value	tax abatement
financing	tax credit
float	venture capitalist
leveraged	

Entrepreneurship Portfolio

Critical Thinking Exercises

10-1. What type of financing will you seek as start-up capital, and why?

10-2. What steps can individuals take to improve their creditworthiness?

10-3. What is the counter argument for a potential investor who says small businesses fail?

10-4. Identify and describe at least five challenges start-up businesses face.

Key Concept Questions

10-5. Calculate the annual amount of interest (assuming no principal repayment) for each of the following:
   a. Term loan of $122,000 over 15 years at 6.5 percent
   b. Line of credit for $50,000 drawn 50% all year at 10 percent
   c. 15 shares of stock purchased at $12.50 per share
   d. Bonds trading at par for $2,000 with a 7 percent rate

10-6. If the owner of Bright Rays Tanning Salon, Inc., invested $200,000 and had an investor pay in $45,000 for 15 percent of the corporation, what is the valuation of the business for the investor?

Application Exercises

10-7. Imagine A Better Company LLC, which has six members. Five of the shareholders own 7 percent each. Jacinta owns the remaining portion of the company. A Better Company needs $250,000 for equipment, inventory, and working capital to expand into a new market. Jacinta does not want to give up controlling interest in the firm. What percent of her ownership can she sell and retain majority ownership? What would she be valuing the company at if she did so? Name three potential sources (specific types of investors/lenders) that might provide the equity or some form of debt.

10-8. How could accepting an equity investment change your business plans?

Exploring Online

10-9. Visit http://www.privacyrights.org/fs/fs6-crdt.htm to learn about your rights to financial privacy; then answer the following:
   a. Who has access to your credit reports?
   b. What information cannot be legally included in your credit reports?
   c. After how many years is unpaid debt erased from your credit reports?

10-10. Visit the SBA Web site at http://www.sba.gov. Find four possible funding sources (organizations, not types of financing) for a computer rental and repair company. Describe the pros and cons of each and create a proposed financing mix, assuming a need for $58,000 in start-up funds divided as follows:

Equipment	$27,000
Software	$10,000
Supplies	$ 1,000
Marketing	$ 6,000
Utilities/services	$ 4,000
Working capital	$10,000

Exploring Your Community

10-11. Find and list three free and/or paid business networking opportunities in your area. Describe how you could take advantage of them for your business.

10-12. Visit a local bank and ask about its commercial lines of credit. Have the banker explain the terms to you and what a small start-up business would have to show to qualify for a line of credit. Report back to the class. If you cannot visit a bank in person, search the website of a bank and find the same information. Cite your source.

10-13. Are there any angel investors that might be interested in your business? Who are they and how and where did you find them?

BizBuilder Business Plan Questions

8.0 Funding Request and Exit Strategy
8.1 Amount and Type of Funds Requested

A. Clearly state how much money you are requesting in this plan and the terms under which you anticipate obtaining the funds.

B. Do you intend to use debt to finance your business? Explain.

C. If you are asking for equity, how have you determined the value of your company and for what amount?

Sweet Success—Gelato Fiasco Scoops Up Financing

Bentley University graduates Josh Davis and Bruno Tropeano were determined to discover the traditional practices and techniques for making Italian gelato. They researched the products and experimented with innovative flavors, eventually creating recipes for over 1,000 flavors. After submitting 22 applications to banks for loans, they received funding from Camden National Bank to bring their "Italian ice cream" to Brunswick, Maine. They opened a retail shop in 2007 and began to build wholesale distribution at that time.

© apelavi/Fotolia

Four years later, Josh and Bruno had the knowledge, skills, and experience to create delicious gelato treats and to operate their business and were ready to take the business to the next level. They decided to expand into Portland, Maine, and spent eight months searching for the best location. They found that location, but one critical ingredient was needed to bring their dream to reality—money.

The owners of Gelato Fiasco had built a banking relationship, including loans that they repaid with a lender. They went to the bank with their proposal, toured the site, and received encouraging feedback. Josh and Bruno signed the lease and began leasehold improvements only to have the application rejected due to insufficient collateral. They were astonished and greatly disappointed. Over the next eight weeks, they were turned down by five or six other banks, and they reached a point where the funds were needed quickly.

Fortunately, they found Coastal Enterprises, Inc., a Maine-based Community Development Financial Institution that had received loan funds through Create Jobs for USA, a partnership of Starbucks and the Opportunity Finance Network. It took two weeks from application to approval, and Gelato Fiasco had $140,000 in financing that it needed. In addition, Josh and Bruno tapped the Maine Seed Capital Tax Credit Program to acquire some $600,000 in private investments for company growth in 2012.

Gelato Fiasco has been recognized with the Empact 100 Award, the James Beard Foundation, the Associated Press, *Food Network* magazine, *Everyday with Rachael Ray*, and various "Best of" contests. They have two locations in Maine and sell their gelato and sorbetto to customers throughout Connecticut, Maine, Massachusetts, New Hampshire, Rhode Island, and Vermont. They also have a mobile unit for catering.

With the right financing, Gelato Fiasco is experiencing the sweet taste of success.

Case Study Analysis

10-14. Why did Josh and Bruno turn to Coastal Enterprises as a source of capital for their business?

10-15. Did the Maine Seed Capital Tax Credit Program provide 100 percent of the financing? If not, how much did it provide? How do you know?

10-16. What factors made Gelato Fiasco a business that did not qualify for mainstream bank financing (specifically discuss the Cs of credit)?

10-17. When, if ever, would you advise Josh and Bruno to approach mainstream lenders?

Case Sources

Gelato Fiasco, accessed September 1, 2013, http://www.gelatofiasco.com/our-story.

Darren Fishell, "Newsmakers 2011: Josh Davis," *The Times Record*, December 28, 2011, accessed September 1, 2013, http://www.timesrecord.com/news/2011-12-28/Front_Page/Newsmakers_2011_Josh_Davis.html.

James McCarthy, "Seed Capital Tax Credit Program Hits its Cap," *MaineBiz*, March 4, 2013, accessed September 1, 2013, http://www.mainebiz.biz/apps/pbcs.dll/article?AID=/20130304/CURRENTEDITION/302289994/1088.

"Thanks Starbucks! Now I'm Your Competitor," CNN Money interview, n.d., accessed September 1, 2013, http://money.cnn.com/video/smallbusiness/2012/02/16/sbiz_starbucks_loan_gelato.cnnmoney/?fb_ref=fbLike&fb_source=profile_online.

| Chilly Dilly's Ice Cream Company: Financing Growth

Case prepared by Dr. Jay Azriel and Dr. Andrew Sumutka of York College of Pennsylvania.

Dylan sat at his parent's kitchen table going over the season's revenues. He smiled as he checked over his figures for a second time. He could hardly believe that his earnings had increased more than 250 percent over the previous year, despite the tough economic times. His hard work, careful planning, and creative ideas were responsible, at least in part, for a 105.7-percent increase in profits as well. His smile widened as he thought about the role that his entrepreneurship courses and professors at Temple University had played in his success. He had certainly come a long way from that night when he was stranded on the side of a highway with little cash, a dead cell-phone battery, and an ice cream truck that he had used all $5,000 of his savings to buy. However, his smile quickly faded as he got back to work on his strategic plan.

He looked up from the numbers and thought about what he should do next. He knew that growing his business by triple digits the next year would not be as easy as it was during the first two. He had maxed out his line of credit with the only bank in town that would loan his business

Old fashioned ice cream truck.
(© David R. Frazier/Alamy)

money, so it would be a great risk to put even one additional truck on the road. He was glad that he resisted the temptation to pay back his loan early, and instead conserved his cash for investing in the growth of his business. However, his cash balance fell short of what was necessary to finance his business's growth plan. While Dylan had already booked several after-season sales at area companies, these would not generate enough profit to fund his expansion plan for the following year. He knew that putting three additional trucks on the road would extend his operations beyond the area of his hometown of York, Pennsylvania, into some of Maryland's wealthier suburbs that had been overlooked by the few ice cream truck operators still in business. He hoped that he would not have to seriously consider his father's suggestion of inviting a partner into his business. He had heard too many stories of failed partnerships in his entrepreneurship classes. However, what choices did he really have?

Dylan thought hard about what his next steps should be. He knew that his business was at one of those important "crossroads" his professors mentioned. The business he was building was more than just a fleet of ice cream trucks. He wanted to bring back something big, like the ubiquitous "Good Humor Man" of the past. He just needed to figure out how to finance this growth. His family broke his concentration, as they piled into the kitchen to get ready for dinner. He put his paperwork aside and joined his family.

Dylan's Dream

Dylan had always been entrepreneurial. He got his first taste of the world of high finance at the age of nine, when he ran a paper route for five years. While his $2,500 annual earnings were good for a kid of his age, Dylan always dreamed of something bigger. After his paper route, he started a lawn mowing business and, in high school, a concert-promotion company. While Dylan learned a great deal from these ventures, "It was always a dream of mine to start an ice cream business." When he was a senior in high school, Dylan began plans to start his dream business to help pay for college. His first idea was to serve hand-scooped ice cream from a truck. However, this plan was short lived. "After researching this I realized that novelty ice cream is easier and more profitable."

Dylan kept thinking about his ice cream business while studying entrepreneurship at Temple University in Philadelphia. In fact, during his freshman year, Dylan investigated the ice cream industry for one of his courses and recognized an opportunity for starting such a venture in York. He learned that the ice cream vendor industry was fairly fragmented, mostly run by operators who owned one or two trucks. Thus, he would not have to contend with any large players in his market. During winter break in his freshman year of college, he began to seriously investigate purchasing his first ice cream truck. Dylan scoured a number of Web sites and found a truck on eBay that he thought might work. The vehicle he had set his sights on was a Good Humor truck from 1970. Dylan took several train rides to a small community on Long Island, to take a look at the truck. Excited that he would actually be starting a business, he quickly handed over $5000—almost all of his savings—without making more than a cursory inspection of the old GMC P30 Step Van.

On the long drive back to York, an excited Dylan made phone call after phone call on his cell phone to tell people about his newly purchased truck. Then, right outside of Philadelphia his truck just stopped running and coasted to a stop on the side of the interstate—more than two hours from home. Dylan called his local mechanic and had his crippled truck towed back to York. The mechanic's diagnosis was that only the freezer was worth saving. The rest of the truck went to the scrap yard. Dylan lost his truck and the $5,000.

However, Dylan did not let this setback extinguish his dream of becoming York's ice cream king. Armed with more information, he carefully checked out a 1971 Ford Good Humor truck. However, he did not have the $15,000 asking price. "After losing everything, I was forced to ask for money from the bank." Dylan secured a $20,000 loan, which was enough to pay for the truck with an additional $5,000 for start-up costs, including his initial inventory. The loan did not come easily, even with his carefully written business plan; the bank would not make the loan unless he had a qualified cosigner. His father cosigned his loan, and Dylan was in business. His business venture was finally on its way!

Revenue Streams

Food venders often seek out high-pedestrian-traffic areas, such as parks and beaches. Often, special permits are needed to operate in these areas, which cuts down on competition. Dylan knew vendors who made a good living setting up near Temple and selling to the students. However, there were few areas in York that would lend themselves to a one-location setup.

Instead, like most ice cream truck operators, Dylan's Chilly Dilly trucks traveled from neighborhood to neighborhood to sell their products. Chilly Dilly drivers developed their own local routes, which they followed on a weekly cycle. The strategy behind weekly, instead of daily, visits was to create a loyal parental following by not "over-visiting" neighborhoods, while at the same time covering a broader geographic area with the same number of trucks. However, Chilly Dilly's trucks did visit parks and popular recreational areas on a daily basis, to serve the constantly changing clientele.

Dylan also recognized that greater-York-area companies were another outlet for his products and would provide revenues beyond September. Dylan offered these businesses two affordable but profitable group package rates:

Standard: $3.00 per Person

Premium: $4.00 per Person

Both had dozens of delicious choices, including sugar-free and all-natural items. A delivery charge was added to cover the cost of gas.

In his first year of operation, 20 companies hired Dylan to provide their employees with cold treats. This doubled to 45 during his second year. In addition to these corporate outlets, Dylan adapted this "package" model to the catering of private parties, such as barbecues, church picnics, and weddings. Dylan added a third option for these customers: $2.00 for cones and slushies. He made sure he covered his costs by requiring a minimum order of 50.

Business Expansion

In May 2008, Dylan graduated with his degree in Entrepreneurship from Temple. Then he was able to focus on his business full time. He purchased three used trucks at $6,500 each. He financed this expansion with a $25,000 loan from a local bank, at a rate of 6.5 percent (prime plus two). The season was profitable; however, the recession and fuel prices squeezed his margins.

In 2009, Chilly Dilly's, as Dylan named his company, had grown to eight additional employees. The company had six trucks on the road. Two of them sold soft-serve ice cream products—including coffee shakes, which were popular with adults. The first of these he purchased for $36,500, fully outfitted. This truck was on the road seven days per week and was the most profitable of the six, as soft-serve products have a higher profit margin. In addition, Dylan found that making his own high-profit ice cream novelties further boosted the company's bottom line.

Dylan's hard work on developing relationships with local companies had also paid off. Despite route sales being down, his overall sales were up, due to new and repeat business from corporate customers. "My website is paying off, as I am getting more leads from there than from the mailing lists," Dylan noted. However, the recession had put pressure on his business catering, as customers began cancelling bookings as a cost saving measure: "A number of customers who gave me firm bookings cancelled at the last minute due to trying to cut costs. I was quite surprised by this, as we have a package to fit every budget and this just did not happen last year after someone made a commitment."

By the end of the 2009 season, Dylan had grown the business to the point where each truck averaged $30,000 in gross revenue. However, his trucks had been expensive to get into working order and could be expensive to keep on the road. Still, Dylan observed that "We will be spending between $4,000 and $5,000 a year on each truck, since we are now keeping up rather than catching up with maintenance costs."

Dylan's business had started to take off. Grown-ups and kids alike were excited when one of his trucks rolled through the neighborhood. Parents liked to see the Chilly Dilly's trucks, because they did not have to see them every day. The Chilly Dilly's man offered a variety of products at different prices. The coffee-flavored drinks and soft-serve items also proved to be a hit with parents. Dylan's success was due in part to creating Chilly Dilly's as a local brand name, but he needed to figure out a way to expand the business beyond York County.

Funding Chilly Dilly's Growth

Dylan had grown his business from a single truck to eight in less than five years. However, his dream was to create a brand that spanned South Central Pennsylvania and Northern Maryland. Dylan also wanted to expand east, into the wealthier areas of Lancaster, and establish a facility there so that his drivers could save 90 minutes a day in travel time. Dylan knew from his entrepreneurship courses that he would have to carefully plan this expansion. He could only manage so many employees on his own, and he was hesitant to increase his overhead and risk by hiring managers.

Thus, financing the company's growth was a critical issue for the young company. Dylan was able to finance his company's start-up through a local bank loan. However, this bank was not in a position to give him another. The economic conditions were such that banks in general were unwilling to extend loans to small businesses without significant collateral, even with an SBA loan guarantee. Dylan wanted to avoid asking his parents to cosign another loan for him. Thus, he needed to look for other sources to fund Chilly Dilly's growth.

Organic Growth Through Bootstrapping. The first option Dylan looked into was internally funding his business's expansion. He thought about new, higher-margin products that he could manufacture which would provide some additional capital. He had found that his customers were willing to purchase high-margin soft-serve products. But outfitting another truck with this equipment required a higher investment. Then Dylan thought about new ways to increase revenues with the equipment he already owned, or could purchase more cheaply. He also knew that he could grow the demand for his products through low-cost guerilla marketing techniques. He just needed to sit down and think of some new strategies.

Loans from Friends, Family, and Strangers. A second option for Dylan was to approach friends and family for some additional capital. The availability of such funding lay in the liquidity of his family and friends and the level of risk they would be willing to take. In addition, private investors were another potential group he might have been able to tap for growth capital. However, the interest rate could well be higher, and an angel investor might be more interested in owning a piece of his business than lending money. However, an investor with some business savvy might be a smarter move, despite the potential cost. These "smart money" investors are often willing to mentor young entrepreneurs.

Dylan could have also applied for additional credit through a credit card company; however, the interest rate could have exceeded 20 percent. A fairly new option would have been to apply for a loan through a peer-to-peer lending Web site, which would provide between $8,000 and $25,000. Peer-to-peer companies, such as Prosper and Lending Club, act as intermediaries, much like eBay, by matching potential investors with people who are seeking personal or business loans. Generally speaking, these borrowers have problems getting loans from traditional sources, like commercial banks, due to their credit history, debt-to-equity ratio, or a lack of collateral. The lenders seek a higher return than banks do, but interest rates can turn out to be lower than what an entrepreneur could obtain from a local bank, because investors bid against one another and often a loan ends up with a dozen or more individuals who each have a small part of the loan. Thus, the risk is spread.

Equity Investors or Partners. Another option for financing Chilly Dilly's growth would have been to attract either equity investors or business partners. His dad, a chiropractor, was partnered with several other doctors in a professional corporation. This partnership not only allowed the doctors to see more patients and generate higher revenues, but also helped to spread fixed business expenses over a larger patient base. Dylan had given a great deal of thought to finding a partner. However, he did not know anyone with whom he would be willing to share his business. Dylan knew that entering into a partnership was like getting married. His professor, as well as

several guest speakers in his entrepreneurship courses, had related stories of partnerships gone sour. Dylan was thus hesitant to take a partner.

Conclusion

Dylan spoke with his family about his growth plans over dinner. He explained the opportunity to rent space in the local indoor farmers market, which "will not only allow me to sell my products year round, but also give me manufacturing space to produce my novelties and lower my product costs and boost my profits." An earnest Dylan turned to his father and asked, "What should I do to make this happen?"

Case Study Analysis

10-18. What are the advantages and disadvantages for each of Dylan's funding options?

10-19. Are there options to fund Chilly Dilly's growth that Dylan has not considered?

10-20. Which option(s) do you suggest Dylan implement?

Time Line for Each Summer Season					
2004	**2005**	**2006**	**2007**	**2008**	**2009**
Started Chilly Dilly with the purchase of first truck.	First full season	Focused on business catering.	Hired first employee	Graduated from Temple University. Purchased three additional trucks and hired new employees.	Purchased two additional trucks. Started selling coffee drinks.

Lee's Ice Cream

Stephen Wilkes/Getty Images

As the bell rang and the clock struck three, South High School social studies teacher Jimmie Lee raced to the parking lot. It was a sunny afternoon in May, a perfect day to sell ice cream. Four years before, Jimmie had begun selling frozen treats in the spring and summer to children on Cleveland's east side. He had always wanted to be his own boss, and driving an ice cream truck seemed like a great idea because he could operate his business in the afternoons and during the summer months, when school was not in session. It helped that he was one of the most popular teachers at South High. All of Jimmie's students and their parents bypassed the other ice cream trucks and waited for Mr. Lee to drive down the block.

Getting Started: Jimmie Does His Research

To get Lee's Ice Cream off the ground, Jimmie had to learn to be creative, resourceful, and patient. When he first decided to bring his idea to reality, Jimmie called his friend Joy Greaves, who had worked in the ice cream business for over 15 years. He wanted to know how much Joy thought it would cost to start his business. Joy estimated that Jimmie would need about $25,000 to purchase the necessary supplies and equipment, which would include the following list.

Joy's Start-Up Investment Estimates	
Item	**Estimated Cost**
Ice cream truck	$18,000
Freezer	3,000
Soft-serve ice cream machine	2,200
300 portions of soft-serve ice cream, napkins, toppings, and ice cream cones	200
Insurance, first quarterly payment	500
Commercial vendor's permit	100
Electric generator	1,000
Total estimated start-up investment	**$25,000**

Can Jimmie Reduce His Start-Up Investment?

As a public school teacher, Jimmie did not earn a large salary. He had $7,000 in savings but, based on Joy's projections, this was not going to go very far. Initially, Jimmie was discouraged, but then he started to brainstorm. Perhaps he could lower his start-up investment by purchasing used equipment. He wondered whether this would pay off in the long run, if this equipment would need costly repairs or replacement parts that were no longer being manufactured. He scoured the local classifieds for used trucks, generators, and freezers, to see how much he could save. Based on this research, Jimmie calculated a revised start-up investment budget:

Jimmie's Start-Up Investment Estimates	
Item	**Estimated Cost**
Used ice cream truck (including freezer)	$10,000
Used soft-serve ice cream machine	1,500
300 servings of soft-serve ice cream, napkins, toppings, and ice cream cones	200
Insurance, first quarterly payment	500
Commercial vendor's permit	100
Service fees for refurbishing used equipment	1,000
Used electric generator	700
Total estimated start-up investment	**$14,000**
Difference between Joy's total start-up investment estimate and Jimmie's estimate	$11,000

If Jimmie purchased the equipment he researched, he would save $11,000. This was a lot of money. He decided it was worth the risk. He hoped that, if he ever did have to pay for repairs, it would cost less than $11,000, in which case he would still come out ahead.

Financing Strategy

Jimmie felt better knowing that he would only need $14,000 to get his business off the ground. He already had $7,000, which covered half the projected costs. He wondered how he could raise the rest of the money. A friend suggested that he apply for a bank loan, but when he inquired at his bank, he was told that the chances of obtaining a loan were slim. Jimmie had never run a business before and the loan was small, so the bank was hesitant to invest in him. What other options did he have?

Jimmie decided to pitch his idea for Lee's Ice Cream to his friends and family. Perhaps they would be willing to loan him money if he agreed to pay them back with interest. He asked his brothers and sisters, but they turned him down. They did not think Jimmie was truly serious about his business. Then he called his best friend, Greg Allen, who worked as an auto shop teacher at South High, to see if he had any ideas. Greg said he had an old electric generator he would be willing to repair and donate. He even agreed to install it free of charge. Jimmie had planned to pay $700 for a used generator, so this was a great savings. Jimmie was one step closer to achieving his dream.

After hanging up the phone with Greg, Jimmie decided to visit his mother, to see if she would be willing to give him a loan. At first Jimmie's mother was resistant, but he took the time to walk her through the business plan he had created. His mother was not totally convinced, but she liked the fact that Jimmie had thoroughly researched what he would need. She decided to loan him $3,000. Jimmie promised he would pay her back, at 8 percent interest, within a year.

Where Is the Money Coming From?

At this point, Jimmie was close to having his funding in place. He made a chart to get a clearer picture of his start-up progress.

Jimmie was so close to having all his start-up investment capital in place, he could practically taste it. He only needed $3,300. That evening, Greg called to say that he had finished repairing the electric generator and could install it as soon as Jimmie was ready. Jimmie explained that he did not feel comfortable purchasing a truck until he had secured his total start-up investment. "How much do you still have left to raise?" Greg asked. "Only $3,300," Jimmie replied. "Well, if you will sell me an equity stake in your company," Greg said, "I'll write you a check for $3,300."

To Sell or Not to Sell?

Jimmie was not sure how he felt about this. He really liked the idea of owning his business outright. Did he want to share ownership with someone else, even if it was Greg, his best friend? Also, Jimmie was not sure what percentage of his total equity he should offer Greg in exchange for $3,300. How could he figure out what Lee's Ice Cream was worth if his business had not yet earned a dime? Jimmie thanked Greg for his offer and explained that he needed to think about it overnight. He promised to call him back first thing in the morning.

Funding Source	Equity	Debt	Gift
Personal Savings	$7,000		
Relatives		$3,000 loan from his mother (to be paid back at 8% interest within one year)	
Friends			
Grants or Gifts			Electric generator ($700 value)
Other			
Subtotal	$7,000	$3,000	$700
Total Equity + Total Debt + Total Gift = Total Financing: $10,700			
Difference between Total Start-Up Investment and Total Financing = $14,000 − $10,700 = $3,300			

Case Study Analysis

U3-1. If you were in Jimmie's shoes, would you sell Greg an equity stake in Lee's Ice Cream? Explain. If Jimmie does sell equity to Greg for $3,300, what percentage of the business should he offer?

U3-2. Assume that Jimmie rejects Greg's offer. Research three other financing strategies for Jimmie to investigate in greater detail.

U3-3. Jimmie's mother agreed to loan him $3,000 at 8 percent interest. Calculate the total amount Jimmie will owe to his mother.

U3-4. Jimmie will sell his ice cream cones for $2 each. Assume the following about Jimmie's cost of goods sold for one ice cream cone:

Soft-serve ice cream	$0.20
Ice cream cone	$0.05
Napkin	$0.02
Topping	$0.03

- What is the total COGS for one ice cream cone (assuming no direct labor cost)?
- What is Jimmie's gross profit per unit?

U3-5. Jimmie believes he can sell an average of 150 ice cream cones per day at $2 per cone. Jimmie operates his business seven days per week between May and August, for a total of 123 days. Calculate the following:

- How many ice cream cones would Jimmie sell in total?
- What would Jimmie's total revenue be?
- What is Jimmie's total COGS?
- Calculate Jimmie's gross profit for the season.
- Assume that Jimmie's total monthly operating costs are $1,500. His business operates for four months of the year. Calculate his total net profit for one year of business operations.
- Create a projected income statement for the period from May 1 to August 31, 2012. Remember to include the interest to his mother for the four months and taxes at 25 percent. Assume that there is no depreciation or operating costs other than those described above.

U3-6. Examine Jimmie's projected income statement that you developed for the previous question. Assume that Jimmie decides to sell Greg partial ownership in Lee's Ice Cream. Using the projected income statement as a guide, determine what percentage of his total equity Jimmie should offer Greg in exchange for $3,300. Is this a different percentage from the answer you gave in question U3-1? Explain.

OPERATING A SMALL BUSINESS EFFECTIVELY

Chapter 11
ADDRESSING LEGAL ISSUES AND MANAGING RISK

Chapter 12
OPERATING FOR SUCCESS

Chapter 13
MANAGEMENT, LEADERSHIP & ETHICAL PRACTICES

Sergey Nivens/Fotolia

11

Addressing Legal Issues and Managing Risk

CHAPTER

Learning Objectives

1. Choose a legal structure for your business.

2. Discover the importance of contracts.

3. Recognize key components of commercial law.

4. Evaluate ways to protect your intellectual property.

5. Plan to protect your tangible assets and manage risk.

Corbis Images

"Remember that time is money."

— Benjamin Franklin, American statesman, inventor, and author

Dr. John Stith Pemberton
(Corbis Images)

On May 8, 1886, Dr. John Stith Pemberton, an Atlanta pharmacist, produced the syrup for Coca-Cola and brought a jug of it to Jacobs' Pharmacy, where it was mixed and sold as a soda fountain drink. The beverage was proclaimed to be "delicious and refreshing," a theme that Coca-Cola reinforces today.

Dr. Pemberton's partner and bookkeeper, Frank Robinson, thought that "Two C's would look well in advertising," recommended the name *Coca-Cola,* and created the famous trademark in his own script.

Over time, businessman Asa Candler bought into the company and eventually acquired complete control of it. According to the company's Web site, in May 1889 Candler published a full-page advertisement in *The Atlanta Journal* that proclaimed his wholesale and retail drug business as "Sole proprietors of Coca-Cola. . . . Delicious. Refreshing. Exhilarating. Invigorating." By 1892, Candler's flair for marketing had boosted sales of Coca-Cola syrup nearly tenfold. With his brother John, Frank Robinson, and two other associates, Candler formed the Coca-Cola Company as a corporation. The trademark *Coca-Cola*, which had been used since 1886, was registered in the United States Patent Office in 1893, and has been renewed periodically.[1]

Business Legal Structures

Learning Objective 1

Choose a legal structure for your business.

Many businesses, no matter how humble their beginnings, have the potential to grow into much larger ventures, so it is important that founders think through every step of the organization's development as they form it. How the entrepreneur organizes the company—such as the legal structure chosen, the relationships developed with suppliers, the managers hired—will have vital impact on its ability to grow.

After you pick the kind of business and industry you want to be in and you know where you fit in the production-distribution chain, you will also have to choose one of the three basic legal structures:

1. sole proprietorship,
2. partnership, or
3. corporation.

Sole Proprietorship

sole proprietorship
a business owned by one person who has unlimited liability and rights to profits.

A **sole proprietorship** is a business owned by one individual, often with no other employees. This owner earns all the profits from the business and is also responsible for all losses. Most U.S. businesses are sole proprietorships.

The sole proprietor is personally liable for any lawsuits that arise from accidents, faulty merchandise, unpaid bills, or other business

[1]Information from Coca-Cola Web site, http://www.Coke.com.

setbacks. This means a sole proprietor could lose not only business assets in a lawsuit, but could be forced to sell private possessions to satisfy a court judgment. He or she could lose a house or a car, for example.

Advantages of a Sole Proprietorship

- Ease of start. A person becomes a sole proprietor—albeit not a registered, legal one—simply by selling something to someone else.
- Simplicity of registration. Proper registration does not require much paperwork, and it is relatively inexpensive.
- Fewer government regulations. Many regulations exempt sole proprietorships with few employees.
- Rapid decision making. The owner can make quick decisions and act without interference from others.
- Greater rights to profits. A sole proprietor is entitled to all the profits from the business.

Disadvantages of a Sole Proprietorship

- Difficult fund raising. It can be difficult to raise enough money by oneself to start or expand a business, and no investors are permitted.
- Significant time obligations and responsibility. A sole proprietor must often put in long hours, working six or even seven days a week, with no one to share the responsibilities.
- Unlimited personal liability. There is no way to limit personal legal liability from lawsuits related to the business.
- Lack of emotional support. There is often no one to offer encouragement or feedback.
- Taxation of profits. All profits earned are taxed personally, whether or not the funds are withdrawn from the business or cash is left in it.

How to Register a Sole Proprietorship

In most states and localities, it is easy and relatively inexpensive to register a sole proprietorship. When you do, you will have a legal business, which is important for several reasons:

- If you operate a business without registering it, you may be liable to civil or even criminal penalties.
- Registered sole proprietors can use the court system and bring lawsuits.
- Banks want to see legal business ownership the way employers like to see that employees have had previous work experience. If your business is not registered, banks will not even *consider* giving you credit for time in business, although some alternative lenders might do so. The time you operated without registration will be discounted. Lack of registration can be perceived as a lack of integrity.

Steps to Registering

The registration process varies from state to state and by locality, but there will be a few common steps:

- Choose a name for your business.
- Fill out a registration form, which sometimes requires a *doing business as* (DBA) document that will show the name of the business and your name, so the state will know who will be responsible for tax payments.
- An official may then conduct a name search, to make sure the name you have chosen is not already being used in that jurisdiction. You may even be asked to help research the records yourself.

- Once your registration is completed satisfactorily, you will pay the required fee. This fee can range from under $100 to significantly more, depending upon the type of business and state and municipal laws and regulations. Professional firm (e.g., doctor, lawyer) registrations, in particular, can become quite expensive.

- You may be asked to take the form to a **notary**, an individual who has been given the authority by the state to witness the signing of documents, to have it *notarized* and then brought back to the registration office. You will have to show the notary valid identification to prove who is signing the form. There is usually a modest charge for this service.

notary a person who has been authorized by the state to witness the signing of documents.

Partnership

A **partnership** consists of two or more owners, who make the decisions for the business together and share the profits, losses, assets, and liabilities. As in a sole proprietorship, partners face unlimited liability in any lawsuits. This means that *each* partner can be held responsible for paying debts or judgments, even those incurred by other partners without their knowledge or agreement.

partnership a business with two or more owners that make decisions for the business together and share the profits, losses, assets, and liabilities.

The exception to this shared liability is the **limited partnership**. The limited partners have no official say in the daily operation of the business and have, as a result, liability limited to the amount of their respective investments. One or more *general* partners manage the company and assume legal liability. There must be at least one general partner who will be liable for all partnership debts.

limited partnership business partnership wherein there is a general partner with unlimited liability, and one or more limited partners with no official input in daily operations and limited liability.

Ideally, partners bring different strengths and skills to a business. This can help the venture grow and succeed. In addition, partners can support and advise each other. On the other hand, disagreements can become intolerable and destroy the partnership, friendship, and business.

Despite the advantages of partnerships, caution is the watchword. You should be extremely careful and thorough about entering into a partnership, particularly with a good friend or relative. A lawyer should be consulted and a partnership agreement drawn up that carefully defines

PhotoAlto/Superstock

the roles and responsibilities of each partner. A partnership agreement is absolutely critical, regardless of how well or poorly the company ultimately performs.

Corporation

corporation a legal entity composed of stockholders under a common name.

There are several types of **corporations**, but each is considered a "legal person," or *entity*, composed of stockholders under a common name. A corporation has rights and responsibilities under the law, and it can buy and sell property, enter into leases and contracts, and be prosecuted. Corporations issue stock that is divided among the founders and sold to investors. These *shareholders* then elect a board of directors that is responsible for representing their interests in the management of the company. The shareholders who own the stock own the corporation in proportion to the number of their shares.

Advantages of a Corporation

The corporate legal structure offers key advantages:

- Ability to sell ownership shares. Corporations may issue stock to raise money. Essentially, the company sells pieces of itself in the form of equity to stockholders.
- Ease of transfer. Shares of stock may be bought and sold, either privately or on public stock exchanges.
- Limitation of personal liability. The corporation offers limited personal liability to its owners. Unlike sole proprietorships and partnerships, the owners of a corporation are protected from having their personal assets taken to pay business lawsuit settlements or debts. Only the assets of the corporation can be used to pay corporate debts. However, most lenders will not loan money to a small, closely held corporation unless the owners personally guarantee the debt, in which case the owners do become personally liable. In addition, it is possible to "pierce the corporate veil" if the business affairs of the corporation and its shareholders are tightly entwined, so that shareholders may be held personally liable in a lawsuit. This is a strong argument for keeping business and personal finances separate.
- Continued existence. Corporations can exist indefinitely, so they do not cease when an owner dies or otherwise leaves the business.

Disadvantages of a Corporation

- Potential for double taxation. Corporations are often more heavily taxed than sole proprietorships or partnerships. Their profits are often taxed twice: first, as the income of the corporation (except S corporations), and again as personal income, when dividends are distributed to stockholders.
- Loss of founder control. The founder of a corporation may lose control to the stockholders if he or she no longer owns more than half the stock or if the board of directors has voting control.
- Higher start-up costs. It is more expensive to start a corporation than a sole proprietorship.
- Greater government regulation. Corporations are subject to many government regulations although smaller ones may be exempt from certain rules.

As we have noted previously, a disadvantage of corporations is that corporate income is "taxed twice." A corporation must pay corporate income tax on its earnings. Then, the corporation may distribute earnings as dividends to stockholders. The stockholders must include those dividends as personal income on their tax returns. For example, a corporation with taxable income of $100,000 that distributed $10,000 in dividends would have a tax bill of $34,000 (34-percent corporate tax rate), and its shareholders would owe $2,800 (assuming a 28-percent personal tax rate) more, for a total tax of $36,800. The total tax on $100,000 for a sole proprietor could be $28,000 (28-percent personal tax rate), reflecting no dividends—for an $8,800 difference.

If corporate stock is privately held, the shares are typically owned by only a few investors and are not *traded* (bought and sold) publicly, such as on the New York Stock Exchange or that of London or Tokyo. In a public corporation, such as Ford or IBM, the company's stock is offered for sale to the general public; anyone with sufficient resources may purchase it at the market price. Stockholders may be paid dividends when the company's management considers they are warranted by profits, or other considerations. Dividends are part of the stockholders' return on their investment in the company.

There are several types of corporations:

- **C corporation.** Most large companies and many smaller ones are C corporations. They sell ownership as shares of stock. Stockholders have the right to vote on important company decisions at the annual meeting, or to vote by proxy. To raise capital, the C corporation can sell more stock, issue bonds, or secure other types of loans.
- **Subchapter S corporation.** This type of corporation has a limit of 100 stockholders. It offers most of the limited-liability protection of the C corporation, but Subchapter S corporate income is only taxed once, as the personal income of the owners. It is a "pass-through" entity for tax purposes. The net profits of an S corporation are taxed at the personal income-tax rates of the individual shareholders, whether or not the profits are distributed.

Thinkstock

- ***Professional corporation (PC).*** Medical practices, engineering firms, law firms, accounting firms, and certain other professions can form professional corporations. The initials PC after a doctor or lawyer's name mean that the individual has incorporated the practice or belongs to a group of practitioners that has incorporated. Each state designates which professions can form such corporations. Professional corporations are subject to special rules, such as meeting the licensing requirements of bar associations or medical societies. Professional corporations cannot protect individual members from malpractice liability, but the other members of a PC are protected from liability arising from the negligence of one of the group.

- ***Nonprofit corporation.*** A nonprofit corporation is not set up for the purposes of shareholder financial gain, but rather with a specific mission to improve society. Churches, museums, charitable foundations, and trade associations are examples of nonprofit corporations (also called not-for-profits). Nonprofits are tax-exempt. Nonprofits may not sell stock or pay dividends. There are no individual shareholders for a not-for-profit corporation, and any net profits that are earned must go toward the advancement of the mission, so there are no dividends issued and income taxes are not paid. Not-for-profits may have members rather than shareholders. Such organizations must be careful to follow applicable laws, rules, and regulations in order to maintain their tax-exempt status.

- ***Public benefit corporation (B corporation).*** This form of company explicitly includes a civic or environmental benefit in its charter, in addition to including profitability as a goal. The priority level is meant to be the same. B corporations must report on social and environmental impact as well as financial performance.

- ***Limited liability company (LLC).*** The LLC, which combines the best features of partnerships and corporations, can be an excellent choice for small businesses with a small number of owners. In an LLC, profits are taxed only as the personal income of the members, whose personal assets are protected from lawsuits as in a C corporation. In addition, many of the restrictions regarding the number and type of shareholders that apply to the Subchapter S corporation do not apply to LLCs, making them even more attractive. An LLC has a variety of options that make it a flexible type of legal entity. The advice of legal counsel is vital in establishing an LLC, because each state has different laws, and the creation and maintenance of LLC status requires continued compliance.

- ***Series limited liability company (SLLC).*** The SLLC is a form of LLC that provides liability protection across "multiple series" (akin to divisions or subsidiaries) while protecting each from the liability of the others. It is a relatively new form and is available in a few states. The SLLC is like a master corporation with subsidiaries, and may be useful when multiple acquisitions are involved.

To compare these legal structures, see **Exhibit 11-1**.

Tips for Entrepreneurs Who Want to Start a Nonprofit Organization

There are huge needs in society for food, shelter, education, and more, and there are many people who cannot access these fundamental necessities and requirements. In the United States, the 501(c)(3) nonprofit corporation was created to help address this situation (this designation refers to

Exhibit 11-1 *Comparison of Common Legal Structures*

	Sole Proprietorship	General or Limited Partnership	C Corporation	Subchapter S Corporation	Nonprofit Corporation	Limited Liability Company
Ownership	The proprietor	The partners	The stockholders	The stockholders	No one	The members
Liability	Unlimited	Limited in most cases	Limited	Limited	Limited	Limited
Taxation Issues	Individual* (lowest rate)	Individual* (lowest rate)	Corporate rate; "double taxation"	Individual* (lowest rate)	None	Individual* (lowest rate)
How Profits Are Distributed	Proprietor receives all	Partners receive profits according to partnership agreement	Earnings paid to stockholders as dividends in proportion to the number of shares owned	Earnings attributed to stockholders as in proportion to the number of shares owned	Surplus cannot be distributed	Same as partnership
Voting on Policy	Not necessary	The partners	Common voting stockholders	Common voting stockholders	The board of directors/trustees	Per agreed-on operating procedure
Life of Legal Structure	Terminates on death of owner	Terminates on death of partner	Unlimited	Unlimited	Unlimited	Variable
Capitalization	Difficult	Easier than sole proprietorship	Excellent—ownership is sold as shares of stock	Good—same as partnership	Difficult because there is no ownership to sell as stock	Same as partnership

*When the double taxation of corporations is taken into account.

the relevant section in the tax code). A 501(c)(3) is a tax-exempt legal structure that can receive charitable donations from individuals, businesses, the government, and philanthropic foundations. Examples of well-known nonprofit corporations include the Boys and Girls Clubs, the YMCA, and the Sierra Club. People who donate money to not-for-profits benefit from their generosity by knowing that they are making a gift to a cause in which they believe. Also, they may be able to deduct these contributions from their taxable income.

In the United States, close to 1 million organizations were registered with the IRS as public charities in 2012, compared with 600,000 in 1993.[2] Charitable donations rose from $148 billion to $350 billion in the same period, accounting for about 22 percent of total revenues in 2012.[3] Whereas competition for financial resources has increased, more technical and educational resources are now available to support the management and growth of organizations that choose to incorporate as nonprofits.

Like any business, a not-for-profit will need to generate revenue to cover its expenses. Failure to meet cash requirements will mean a failure to survive. A not-for-profit needs to identify a target market (constituency) and determine how it will deliver its products and services. Some key differences and considerations exist, however, and you should be aware of them before you apply to the IRS for approval:

- ***No individual can own a not-for-profit organization.*** A nonprofit cannot be bought and sold like other businesses. You would not be able to dissolve the company and sell it for financial gain. Nor could you issue stock to raise money. These organizations are meant to improve society, not create wealth for the founder, shareholders, or employees.

- ***Nonprofits are mission-driven.*** Before you can operate as a nonprofit, you will need to be crystal clear about your organization's mission. What problem(s) are you trying to solve? The IRS will not grant tax-exempt status without such a stated mission and considerable additional information. Also, ask yourself if there is another organization that is working toward the same goal. Could you work together rather than creating a new entity and duplicating services and costs? Is there a large enough donor base and grant supply to combine with earned income for sustainability? Also, do you expect the organization to accomplish its mission in the foreseeable future and thus cease to need resources?

- ***Define your unit of change.*** In a for-profit business, the return on investment is calculated by looking at the corporation's financial records. Not-for-profit entrepreneurs think about returns a little differently. Not-for-profits do not exist to make money, so the ultimate measure of success will not be financial, although financial goals and measures are part of the equation. Your return on investment will be based on how much it will cost you to provide your services, as compared with the level of change that was brought about as a result of this investment.

- ***Determine how you will evaluate your success.*** As a not-for-profit entrepreneur, you will need to set goals regarding the changes you wish to effect. How many homeless people will you feed? How many students will graduate as a result of your dropout-prevention program? What changes in knowledge, skills, or attitudes will result

---

[2]The Urban Institute, National Center for Charitable Statistics, Business Master File 12/2013, accessed May 13, 2014, http://nccs.urban.org/statistics.

[3]The Urban Institute, National Center for Charitable Statistics, Business Master File 12/2013, accessed May 13, 2014, http://nccs.urban.org/statistics.

from the efforts of your organization? The output and outcome goals you establish must tie back into your financial and human-resource inputs. How much does it cost to provide these services? Given the costs, how many "units of change" did your organization achieve? How can you document that your organization brought about these changes?

- **Analyze your financing strategy.** Nonprofit corporations borrow money as well as earn it. They also have access to a revenue stream that other business structures cannot tap. Nonprofits generate revenue through grants and gifts (donations) from individuals and organizations, but they cannot sell stock to raise equity.

Contracts: The Building Blocks of Business

Regardless of the type of legal entity you elect to establish, you will need to enter into a variety of legal contracts. A contract is a formal agreement between two or more parties to perform or refrain from performing particular actions. When you sign up for mobile telephone service with a provider, such as Verizon or AT&T, you are signing a contract. You agree to pay for the service at a specified price per month, and in return the company agrees to provide you with access to telephone service, voice mail, data services, text messaging, and the like. Remember that rental leases, any promissory notes or mortgages, advertising or partnership agreements, are all contracts. How they are written can often make or break your business.

Contracts are the building blocks of business. The relationships between the links in a production-distribution chain are defined by contracts. For example, if a department store wants to sell your hammered-silver necklaces, you might create a six-month contract specifying how many necklaces you will supply at what price and how and when the store will pay you.

With that contract in hand, you can call your wholesaler. Because you have a large order, you will want to get your supplies in bulk. With the contract as written proof of your relationship with the store, wholesalers may give you credit. You can arrange to buy the silver you need now to fill the order, and pay for it after you sell the necklaces to the store. You can also plan ahead with your advertisers or work out an advertising plan with the store as part of the contract. Or, you may be able to secure bank financing for the contract production.

The power of a contract is that, once the individuals or other entities involved have signed it, they are obligated to comply with its terms and conditions or risk being sued and penalized according to the contract terms, or in a court of law. If the store fails to buy your necklaces as agreed, you can go to court to force payment. Because of the contract, you will be able to honor your contract with your supplier. At the same time, the contract obligates you to produce what you have promised and deliver it when you said you would.

◀ **Learning Objective 2**
Discover the importance of contracts.

contract an agreement between two or more parties that is enforceable by law.

Working with an Attorney

There are certain times in the life of an organization when investing in the expense of professional services is essential, even though the out-of-pocket cost may seem high at the time. Contract drafting and review is one of them.

- Never sign a contract without having an attorney examine it for you.
- Never sign a contract that you have not read completely and carefully, even if your lawyer tells you it is all right. Ultimately, you are responsible for what you sign.

If you are ever taken to court and argue, "I didn't understand that part of the contract," it will not satisfy the judge. Your signature at the bottom tells the court that you read, understood, and agreed to every word.

Attorneys typically charge by the hour, so be as prepared and organized as possible before visiting one. Many issues can be resolved efficiently and effectively through e-mail and telephone calls, so that billable hours are minimized. Always read the contract ahead of time and make a copy of it. Mark sections that you do not agree to or understand. Indicate your suggestions for changes. This will help your attorney advise you effectively.

Drafting a Contract

Consult an attorney if you need to *draft*—write—a first version of a contract or agreement, with the understanding that it will need to be developed and rewritten. Be certain that you identify and make a list of the key points in advance. Attorneys often have standard formats for types of legal agreements, sometimes called **boilerplate language**, which can make the process quicker and less costly.

boilerplate language a standard format for a specific type of legal agreement.

A Successful Contract Should Achieve the Four A's

1. **Avoid** misunderstanding.
2. **Assure** work.
3. **Assure** payment.
4. **Avoid** liability.

Avoid Misunderstanding. When putting together a contract, clearly state everything that will be performed by all parties, even what is obvious. Go into full detail (not just how many shirts you will supply to the store and when, but which types, colors, and sizes). If you do not cover all the details, the person with whom you are contracting may add provisions or find loopholes you will not like. At the same time, leave enough flexibility to accomplish what will need to be done successfully.

Assure Work. For a contract to be legally binding, all parties will be required to do one of the following:

- perform an action or exchange something of value, or
- agree *not* to do something the party was legally entitled to do.

Sometimes $1 is exchanged, as a token payment to legalize a contract. The contract should assure that each party fulfills some kind of obligation. The exact nature of the obligation and the time frame for accomplishing it should be specified fully.

Assure Payment. A good contract specifies how payment will be made, when, and for what. It should leave no room for misinterpretation.

Avoid Liability. Because this world is full of surprises, your contract should spell out **contingencies**, events beyond your control that could cause delay or failure to fulfill contractual responsibilities. The contract should list contingencies for which you would not be liable. Common contingencies are "acts of God" (earthquake, hurricane, etc.) or illness.

contingency a condition that must be met in order for something else to occur.

When you share the draft or a list of key topics of your contract with an attorney, ask these two basic questions:

1. Will this agreement fully protect my interests?
2. What would you add, drop, or change?

Letter of Agreement

Sometimes you will not need a full, formal contract, because the relationship is going to be brief or the work and money involved are relatively minor. In such cases, a **letter of agreement** that puts an oral understanding in writing, in the form of a business letter, may be enough. The other party must respond to it in writing, either approving it or suggesting changes, until an agreement is reached. However, use this option with care and with legal advice.

letter of agreement a document that puts an oral understanding in writing, in the form of a business letter.

Breach of Contract

A contract is broken, or *breached*, when a **signatory** (an individual that signed the contract) fails to fulfill it. The person injured by the signatory's failure to comply with the contract may then sue for **breach of contract**.

For a contract to be breached, it must first be legally binding. Most states require that all signatories be at least 18 years of age and that the contract represent an exchange of value. If a contract is breached, legal action must be brought by the injured party within the state's **statute of limitations**, the time period within which legal action may be taken.

A lawsuit is an attempt to recover a right or claim through legal action. Because attorney's fees are expensive and court cases time-consuming, lawsuits should be avoided whenever possible. Other options are **small claims court** and **arbitration**.

signatory an individual who signs a contract.

breach of contract the failure of a signatory to perform as agreed.

statute of limitations the time period in which legal action may be taken.

small claims court a legal option for solving conflicts involving less than a certain sum of money.

arbitration a method of dispute resolution using an arbitrator to act as the decision maker rather than going to court.

Small Claims Court

Conflicts involving less than a certain sum of money, which varies by state law, can usually be resolved in a small claims court. In Delaware, for example, claims for $15,000 or less (excluding interest) can be settled through civil action in the Justice of the Peace Court. In small claims court, people are allowed to represent themselves before a court official. This individual hears the respective arguments and makes a decision that is legally binding.

Arbitration

Sometimes contracts specify that conflicts may be settled through *arbitration* instead of in court. An *arbitrator*, someone both sides trust, is chosen to act as the decision maker to resolve the conflict. The parties agree to abide by the arbitrator's decision.

A Contract Is No Substitute for Trust

A contract is not a substitute for understanding and communication. If you do not trust someone, having a contract will not improve the relationship, but it will address your concerns in writing. However, entering into a business contract with a party you do not trust could be a poor decision. Avoid signing a contract with someone you do not trust.

A good reason never to sign a contract with such a person is that you might need to renegotiate the terms at some point, and this could be unpleasant and difficult. Running a small business is challenging and unpredictable. In the jewelry example mentioned previously, how would you pay back the silver supplier if the store decided not to buy the necklaces after all? If you had a friendly relationship, you would be able to discuss your situation and possibly renegotiate or cancel the contract.

The Uniform Commercial Code (UCC)

Learning Objective 3

Recognize key components of commercial law.

Contract law varies from state to state, with a common set of standardized practices. The Uniform Commercial Code (UCC) is a collection of business laws adopted by most states that directs a broad spectrum of transactions— such as loans, contracts, and the like. The UCC, first issued in 1952, is a joint project of the American Law Institute and the National Conference of Commissioners on Uniform State Laws. It is not law; rather, it is made up of recommendations for laws that states may adopt as written or with modification. Because so many commercial transactions involve parties located in more than one state, consistency becomes important. For example, if you buy a forklift that is manufactured in Michigan, warehoused in Georgia, sold to you by a company in New Jersey, and delivered to your warehouse in South Carolina, it would be simpler to have uniform laws governing these transactions than four sets of statutes. Note that the UCC is focused on movable property rather than *real* (immovable) property.

The UCC consists of a series of Articles that covers the range of commercial transactions:

Article	Title
1	General Provisions
2	Sales
2A	Leases
3	Negotiable Instruments
4	Bank Deposits
4A	Funds Transfers
5	Letters of Credit
6	Bulk Transfers and Bulk Sales
7	Warehouse Receipts, Bills of Lading and Other Documents of Title
8	Investment Securities
9	Secured Transactions

Source: Copyright © by the American Law Institute and the National Conference of Commissioners on Uniform State Laws. Reproduced with the permission of the Permanent Editorial Board for the Uniform Commercial Code. All rights reserved.

The Law of Agency

The subject of agency law (agent/principal) is a vital area of commercial contract law. An agent (third party) is authorized to act on behalf of a principal (primary party) to create a legal relationship with another individual or business. Common agency relationships include

- employment (employer, employees);
- real estate (real estate agents);
- financial services (stock brokers, insurance agents);
- promotion (modeling, acting, music, publishing, and sports agents).

Agency law is the branch of legal activity that addresses relationships between each party in a situation where one individual or company is authorized to work on behalf of another.

Businesses commonly rely on agents to conduct their affairs, although they are not always perceived as such. Employees are agents of their employers. All individuals carrying out the work of a corporation are agents, because a corporation is a legal entity (person). The principal in an agency relationship (company or person) is contractually bound by any agreement entered into by the agent, as long as the agent is operating within his or her authority.

This is particularly important for you to understand as an entrepreneur. When you authorize others to act for you, you can be legally bound by their actions—for better or worse. Authority can be granted, or perceived to have been granted, by several means:

- contractually, through a written contract;
- words or conduct, if the principals' actions or words would make it so that a reasonable person would assume authority (you say or do something that implies it);
- ostensible authority, if the principal makes it appear to the third party that the agent is authorized, such as putting the agent in a position of authority (manager, supervisor, or sales representative);
- implied—the level of authority, is considered necessary to fulfill the agent's job, such as a partner or senior executive in a business (responsibility and authority are the norm in certain positions).

The area of agency law is quite complex and significant to the entrepreneur. If you are in a partnership, any partner is presumed to have the authority to enter into agreements that bind the other partners (agency power). This could lead to financial disaster. Or, consider a salesperson attempting to close a sale. This individual could commit to giving discounts without your knowledge or approval. As far as the customer is concerned, your company has made the offer. If the offer is not satisfactory to you, as the owner, you are in the awkward position of either doing as promised to keep the customer happy or attempting to renege and alienating the customer, with perhaps further consequences to follow. The law of agency sets parameters for the liability of each party.

Bankruptcy

Although entrepreneurs are an optimistic lot, business sometimes does not progress as planned, and **bankruptcy** may become the best option. Bankruptcy is the legal process in which an individual or business declares the inability or impaired ability to pay debts as they come due. This may be a voluntary petition by the debtor, or it may be forced by creditors (involuntary bankruptcy). Bankruptcy is often used as a way to reorganize finances and secure some breathing room for businesses that are insolvent. The process is meant to ensure the fair treatment of creditors as well as the debtor.

Many companies, large and small, have filed for and emerged from bankruptcy. For example, General Motors, Macy's, and Delta Airlines have all done it. **Figure 11-1** shows the number of business bankruptcy filings from 1985 through 2012. As a business owner, you will not want to file for bankruptcy unless it is your best remaining strategy. As a creditor, you do not want your customers to file for bankruptcy protection because you will have to wait for payment and may lose the money altogether.

The Bankruptcy Reform Acts of 1978 and 2005 govern the eight "chapters" under which bankruptcy may be filed. Chapters 7, 11, and 13 generally apply to small businesses, with Chapters 7 and 11 the most common. Entrepreneurs may be faced with the choice of *liquidation* or *reorganization*.

bankruptcy the legal process in which an individual or business declares the inability or impaired ability to pay debts as they come due.

Chapter 11: Reorganization

This is the form of bankruptcy that can prove to be a lifeline for a company. Businesses can pay off some or all of their debts under court supervision, while continuing to operate. Creditors cannot file legal claims against the

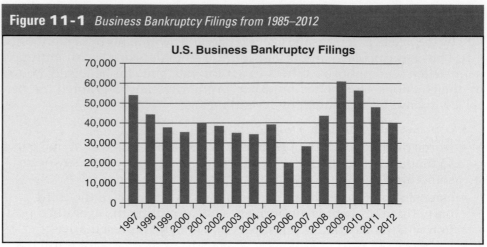

Figure 11-1 *Business Bankruptcy Filings from 1985–2012*

Source: Courtesy of bankruptcydata.com (accessed August 18, 2014).

company while it creates a reorganization plan and schedules debt repayment, or negotiates settlements on the amounts owed. The bankrupt party, known as the *debtor in possession*, gets 120 days to file a reorganization plan with the bankruptcy court. This plan must detail all debts, all categories or classes of creditors (i.e., secured, provisional, and unsecured), amounts each will be paid, and the timing and method of payment. If the debtor fails to file on time, creditors or any other parties involved may submit a plan.

Chapter 7: Liquidation

When this form of bankruptcy protection is sought by individuals or corporations, they must identify all assets and liabilities, turn the assets over to a trustee (court-appointed or elected by the creditors), and allow them to be sold. Creditors receive funds from the proceeds ranging from 0 to 100 percent of their debt claims. Once the funds are paid out, any remaining debts are *discharged* (no longer owed); and the business, if a corporation, is officially dissolved.

It is important to note that debtors cannot avoid the liquidation of assets by transferring ownership to others just ahead of filing for protection. In fact, any transfers of property within the two years prior to filing may be ignored and the assets made a part of the bankruptcy case. Deliberate transfer of assets to avoid debt repayment is a form of fraud, and the entire Chapter 7 bankruptcy petition can be thrown out by the judge, if he or she feels that this has occurred.

On the other side, not all assets are subject to liquidation in a Chapter 7 bankruptcy. The items that are exempt vary by state. Regardless of the asset exemptions, a Chapter 7 bankruptcy filing is financially and emotionally painful and has long-term impacts on credit.

Chapter 13: Individual Debt Reorganization

This is the consumer version of Chapter 11, which is available to individual debtors with secured debts less than $922,975, or unsecured debts below the sum of $307,675. Chapter 13 must be a voluntary filing and the repayment plan can only be filed by the debtor. The plan may include full or partial payment of debts through installments, taking into consideration the debtor's income expectations, and must be approved by a bankruptcy judge. Repayment typically occurs over a three- to five-year period, and the filer can retain individual property. Because a sole proprietorship is essentially an individual, Chapter 13 is of significance to small business.

The bankruptcy of business partnerships, or of major stockholders for privately held corporations, can have other effects on businesses and individuals that are beyond the scope of this text. For additional information, consult appropriate legal and accounting resources.

Protecting Intangible Assets: Intellectual Property

A critical practice for any entrepreneur is to protect his or her ideas, products, inventions, and designs. Federal and state laws are designed to help individuals and organizations protect these kinds of assets from abuse, reputational damage, or theft.

◀ Learning Objective 4

Evaluate ways to protect your intellectual property.

Trademarks and Service Marks

Whether you are advertising your business with flyers at the local laundromat, or through a storefront on the Internet, you will need an easily recognizable logo for your product or business (such as Apple's silhouette of an apple with a bite out of it). This logo should appear on the business's stationery, business cards, flyers, and virtually any other company document or product.

As discussed previously, a trademark is any word, phrase, symbol, design, or combination of words, phrases, symbols, or designs that identifies and distinguishes the source of the goods (products) of one party from those of others.[4] A **service mark** is the equivalent of a trademark, except that it identifies and distinguishes the source of a service rather than a product.

service mark a design that identifies and distinguishes the source of a service rather than a product.

A company uses a trademark so that people will recognize its products instantly, without having to read the company name—or even having to think about it. NutraSweet's red swirl and the Nike swoosh are examples of trademarks most people recognize. Rights to a trademark are reserved exclusively for its owner. To infringe on a trademark is illegal.

---

[4]U.S. Patent and Trademark Office, at http://www.uspto.gov/go/tac/doc/basic/trade_defin.htm.

Global Impact . . .

Vostu—Latin America's Largest Game Developer

Developers of video games face numerous issues in addressing legal issues and managing risk. Vostu, founded in 2007 by a group of four Harvard University students, was no different. The company reported having over 50 million users and released the first 3D farming game for mobile devices, Top Farm, in the fall of 2013 with 40 million early adopters.[5] The game was available in eight languages and was free on Google Play and the iOS Appstore. Vostu's cofounder and CEO Daniel Kafie stated, "Top Farm is the most successful gaming franchise ever in Brazil . . . we are excited to take this game global as part of Vostu's new and exclusive focus on mobile devices."

However, this success was not without controversy and struggle. In June 2011, Vostu was sued by Zynga, publishers of Farmville, Cityville, Words with Friends, and numerous other games, for infringement of its intellectual property (IP). Zynga had a relatively aggressive approach to protecting its IP and sued numerous game developers and publishers. It too, had been involved on the opposite side of infringement claims. In this case, Zynga accused Vostu of copying its games, even going so far as to copy the bugs. Vostu made counter claims

that Zynga had repeatedly copied other games.

The companies settled later that year outside of court. Zynga and Vostu issued the following statement: "Zynga and Vostu have settled the copyright lawsuits and counterclaims

AOL Tech, Inc.

against each other in the United States and Brazil. As part of the settlement, Vostu made a monetary payment to Zynga and made some changes to four of its games."[6]

Such claims and counterclaims became more common as the industry grew globally and games became extremely popular.

---

[5]Daniel Kafie, "Vostu Announces Worldwide Launch of Top Farm, the First 3D Farming Game for Mobile Devices," press release, accessed on May 14, 2014, at http://www.vostu.com.

[6]Leena Rao, "Zynga, Vostu Settle Copyright Lawsuit; Brazilian Gaming Company to Pay Up," TechCrunch, posted December 6, 2011, accessed May 14, 2014, at http://techcrunch.com.

A trademark or service mark does not have to appear on the U.S. Patent and Trademark Office's Principal Register to be legitimate, but there are advantages to being listed on it.

- It is a notice to the public of your ownership claim.
- It displays the legal presumption of your exclusive right to use the mark as registered.
- It allows you the ability to bring an action concerning the mark in federal court.
- It permits the use of the U.S. registration to obtain registration of your mark in other countries.
- It gives you the ability to file this mark with the U.S. Customs Service, so that others cannot import foreign goods with your mark on them.[7]

You do not need to file an application with the USPTO to use ™ (trademark) or ˢᴹ (service mark). However, you cannot use ® until it has been officially registered, and then it can only be used for what is listed in the federal registration. To obtain application information, visit the USPTO Web site at http://www.uspto.gov.

If you plan to do business outside the United States, you will need to make sure your trademark is properly registered and protected. The International Trademark Association (http://www.inta.org) is an excellent resource. It can help you apply for a Community Trade Mark (CTM), which provides trademark protection in the 27 members of the European Union, as shown in **Figure 11-2**. The Office for Harmonization in the Internal Market, based in Spain, administers the CTM.

Figure 11-2 *Map of EU Members*

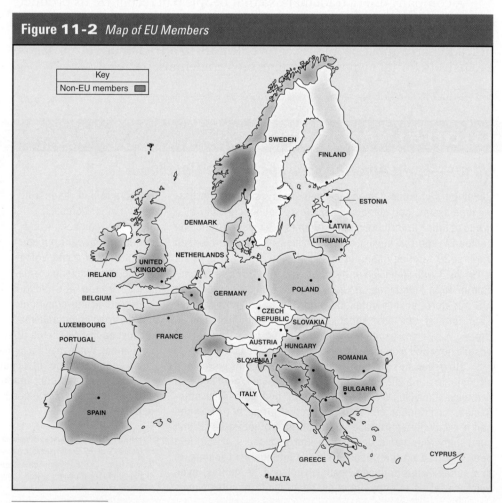

[7]U.S. Patent and Trademark Office.

Copyright

If you are a songwriter, author, or visual artist, you will be creating works that you might sell. If you do not protect your work, however, someone else can appropriate it. A copyright is the form of legal protection offered under U.S. law to the authors of "original works of authorship," including literary, dramatic, musical, and artistic works.[8] Copyright protection is offered for both unpublished and published works. The owner of a copyright has the sole right to print, reprint, sell and distribute, revise, record, and perform the work under copyright. The copyright protects a work for the life of the author/artist plus 70 years. Only the author or someone assigned rights by the author can claim a copyright.

When a work is created, its copyright is automatically secured. According to the Copyright Office, "A work is 'created' when it is fixed in a copy or phono-record for the first time." The use of a notice of copyright is not required, but is recommended, and official registration of the copyright has certain advantages. The elements of notice for visually perceptible copies requires:

- the symbol © (the letter c in a circle) and/or the word "copyright," or the abbreviation "copr." and the current year, and
- the name of the owner of the copyright, or an abbreviation by which the name can be recognized, or a generally known alternative designation of the owner.[9]

Example: *Copyright © 2014 by Janina Joyce*

There are variations for sound recordings. Legal counsel should be sought for any issues that are unclear. To learn how to register a work, visit the U.S. Copyright Office Web site at http://www.copyright.gov.

Electronic Rights

Now that writing, photographs, art, and music can be posted on the Web, entrepreneurs must protect their intellectual property online as well. The right to reproduce someone's work online is called **electronic rights**.

Using artwork without permission, even if it is a song or photo or poem posted online, is Internet piracy. Internet piracy was addressed in 1998 with the Digital Millennium Copyright Act. The act protects copyrighted software, music, and text on the Internet by outlawing the technology used to break copyright-protection devices.

electronic rights the right to reproduce someone's work online.

To protect your electronic rights, beware of contracts that include the following:

- **Work-made-for-hire:** This means you are giving up the rights to your work. Now the buyer can use it anywhere, without paying anything beyond the original negotiated fee.
- **All rights:** This means you are handing over all rights to your work to the buyer.

Here are some strategies for protecting your electronic rights:[10]

- Get the buyer to define exactly what is included in electronic rights. Does it include online publication, CD-ROMs, or anything else?
- Put a limit on how long the buyer can have the electronic rights—one year, for instance.

---

[8]U.S. Copyright Office, http://www.copyright.gov.

[9]U.S. Copyright Office.

[10]Adapted from the *National Writers Union Guide to Negotiating Electronic Rights*. For more information, see http://www.nwu.org.

Step into the Shoes . . .

Haley Hoverter

Sweet Resolve for Sweet dis(Solve)

As a 16-year-old student from East Los Angeles, Haley Hoverter captured the first place prize of $1,500 from NFTE Southern California and a $10,000 NFTE National award, as well as a $5,000 Coleman Foundation Scholarship. She met President Barack Obama at the White House. Haley entered into negotiations with Daymond John, founder of FUBU, for investment and marketing assistance.

What generated all of this interest and financial support was Haley's product and business idea she developed as part of the NFTE program at her high school. Haley was encouraged to match her passion with a business idea, and she did just that. She was passionate about the environment and reducing waste. She also had noticed the large number of sugar wrappers being thrown out at a local coffee shop.

Haley invented Sweet dis(Solve), a sugar packet with a dissolvable, ecofriendly wrapper. She recognized that the product had market potential and filed a preliminary patent to protect her intellectual property. Now, she is turning Sweet dis(Solve) into sweet success.

- Ask for an additional fee for each additional set of rights. A good rule of thumb would be to request 15 percent of the original fee every time your work is used somewhere electronically. If you sell a drawing to a newspaper for $1,000, you could ask for $150 if the paper wants to use it on its Web site.

Patents

patent an exclusive right, granted by the government, to produce, use, and sell an invention or process.

If you have invented a product or process that you want to turn into a business or to license, you may want to obtain a patent from the U.S. Patent and Trademark Office. A **patent** is an exclusive right granted by the government to produce, use, and sell an invention or process. The term of a patent is generally 20 years from its date of filing. A patent grants "the right to exclude others from making, using, offering for sale or selling" the invention in the United States or bringing it into the country via import.[11] Patents come in three forms: *utility* (process or improvement), *design*, and *plant* (varieties of vegetation). A patent cannot be granted unless it is for something that is "useful, novel, and nonobvious."

public domain property rights available to the public rather than held by an individual.

A patent cannot be obtained for a mere idea or suggestion. An invention should be fully developed and actually viable before you can seek patent protection. You will have to prepare detailed drawings showing exactly how it works. If an invention is put into use by the inventor, or discussed publicly for more than one year without obtaining a patent, the invention is considered to be in the **public domain**, which means that a patent will no longer be granted; anyone may use or make it without payment. It is important that you not divulge a proprietary invention or concept in meetings or at events without having received at least preliminary protection.

You do not need to obtain a patent unless you:

- have invented a product that you intend to market yourself or sell to a manufacturer, or
- believe that someone else could successfully sell your invention by copying it.

The average patent takes at least two years to obtain. A patent search has to be undertaken to ensure that the idea is new, and getting a patent is

---

[11]U.S. Patent and Trademark Office, http://www.uspto.gov.

a complex legal process. Before starting it, consult with a registered patent agent or an attorney.

The process of obtaining a patent can be lengthy, time-consuming, and costly. There are many legitimate sources of assistance, including inventors' groups sponsored by state economic development offices, Small Business Development Centers (SBICs), and community development venture capital groups. There are also unscrupulous companies and individuals that promise phenomenal success in commercializing ideas at prices that are inappropriate. Be careful to select reputable advisors, including patent attorneys.

Protecting Tangible Assets: Risk Management

In addition to protecting your intellectual property, you should manage risk by protecting your physical property. Imagine if you lost your business to a fire or flood and did not have the insurance to rebuild and restock. Or, think about an employee being injured and having no insurance for medical care. Risk management goes far beyond insurance. However, understanding business insurance is a good start.

◀ **Learning Objective 5**
Plan to protect your tangible assets and manage risk.

Insurance Protects Your Business from Disaster

Insurance is a system of protection-for-payment provided by insurance companies to reimburse people or businesses whose property or wealth has been damaged or destroyed. There are many kinds of insurance, and almost anything can be insured.

If you owned a restaurant, for example, one type of protection you would need would be fire insurance. Your insurance agent would help you calculate how much money it would take to rebuild and replace everything in it, in case of fire. If you borrowed money from a bank to buy equipment for the restaurant, the bank would require you to carry insurance (with the bank as the named insured) to cover the loan in case the equipment was destroyed.

Assume that rebuilding your restaurant would cost $150,000. You would need an insurance policy that would guarantee you $150,000 in case of fire. You might pay $100 per month for this insurance. This monthly cost of insurance coverage is called a **premium**.

As long as you pay the premiums on your fire insurance policy, you will not have to worry as much about losing your restaurant to a fire. If it does burn down, your insurance company will pay you to rebuild and restart the business. If you carry business interruption insurance, you may get compensation for lost revenue. Insurance helps to prevent random events from destroying you financially.

insurance a system of protection for payment provided by insurance companies to reimburse individuals and organizations when their property or wealth has been damaged, destroyed, or lost.

premium the cost of insurance.

deductible the amount of loss or damage a policyholder covers before the insurer pays on a claim.

Basic Coverage for Small Business

You will not necessarily need insurance if you are selling ties on the street or candy at school, but the moment you move your business into a building or have concerns about people being injured while buying or using your product, you will need it.

A **deductible** is the amount of loss or damage you agree to cover before the insurance pays on a claim. In the restaurant example, the owner might feel confident that he or she could pay $5,000 for damage from a fire. The insurance company would then pay the remaining $145,000. With this

Insurance reduces the risk of losses.
(© 5928/Fotolia)

higher deductible, the premium would be lower, perhaps $90 per month. The policyholder pays a lower premium in exchange for a higher deductible. When buying insurance, choose the policy with the highest deductible you can afford to cover. This will give you the lowest possible premium.

Lower deductible = Higher premium
Higher deductible = Lower premium

Although state laws vary, most require business owners who have people working for them to carry two forms of insurance:

- ***Workers' compensation insurance*** reimburses employees for loss of income and medical expenses due to job-related injuries.
- ***Disability insurance*** compensates employees for loss of income due to a disabling injury or illness.

If you have an automobile or truck that is owned or leased by the business, you must carry the following:

- ***Commercial fleet insurance,*** to cover your liability for personal injuries in an accident, damages to any vehicle involved, and injuries to others.

Other useful types of insurance are:

- ***Property insurance,*** which provides protection against risks to property, such as theft, fire, or weather damage, as specified in the policy. Certain types of "disaster" insurance, such as protection in the event of a flood or earthquake, also fall under this category.
- ***Liability insurance,*** which covers the cost of injuries to a customer or damage to property on a business's premises—for example, a customer slipping and falling in your store.
- ***Product liability insurance,*** which covers the risk of your product harming someone. It is a subset of liability insurance. For example, a caterer may need to be concerned about food-poisoning claims.
- ***Business income insurance,*** which is also known as "business interruption" insurance. It is the equivalent of disability insurance for your business. It provides coverage if you have a temporary shutdown or a significant limitation on your operations. Property insurance may replace your facilities and equipment, but it will not compensate for lost revenue the way this form of insurance does.
- ***Errors and omissions insurance*** is designed to cover you in the event that you have overlooked something and a customer is harmed. It is particularly valuable for service businesses.
- ***Key person life insurance*** covers the life of the owner(s) or other top employees, to assist in the transition and costs of recruitment in case of death.

Still other types of insurance are available that can be tailored to the needs and resources of your business. When you are ready to take this step, ask other businesspeople to refer you to a good insurance agent. Be certain to shop for the best overall value.

How Insurance Companies Make Money

By now you may be wondering, "How can an insurance company afford to pay $150,000 to a restaurant owner whose business has burned down, if that individual has only been paying the insurance company $100 a month?"

The answer is that insurance companies employ experts, known as *actuaries*, who calculate the odds of a particular event actually happening. A company that specializes in fire insurance will have information about

Entrepreneurial Wisdom . . .

Lying about the Risks of Your Product Is Fraud

Failure to inform a customer of potential danger from your product or service, or misrepresenting it in any way for commercial benefit, is a type of fraud. If a customer proves that you knew your product or service was dangerous, but you sold it anyway, you could be directed by a court to pay damages. Your insurance company will not be expected to pay for costs in the case of fraud.

The entrepreneur has a moral duty to inform customers of possible danger. It is best not to sell a product or service that could cause harm when in normal use. Even if you are selling something as "safe" as neckties, make sure they are not made of highly flammable material!

Before you decide to sell a product or offer a service, try to imagine how it might possibly cause injury to someone. If you think it might harm a customer when used according to directions, do not sell it.

fires in restaurants that goes back many years. Analysts at the company study this information and determine how often fires tend to occur and how much damage they cause. Even if some fires do take place, the cost of insurance paid out to a few policyholders has been covered by the premiums paid by many others.

Protect Your Computer and Data

Data are critical to any business. Important business information on your computer might include mailing lists, invoices, letters, and financial records. The risk of the loss of this information is a very real one that you will need to address proactively. Because your computer is an electronic device, you should protect it from the three primary occurrences that can easily wipe out your data:

1. *Power surges or outages:* A power blackout can destroy data. You can purchase an "uninterruptible power supply" (UPS) that will keep your computer running for a certain amount of time after the power goes out. A power surge can damage your computer as well as destroy the data stored on it. Plug all your computer equipment into a multi-outlet surge protector, which can be bought at any hardware store. Or, better yet, invest in a surge protector UPS unit for each computer.

2. *Computer viruses:* Viruses are malicious software that can attach themselves to your software or files and ruin them. Protect your computer with virus-protection software like Norton or McAfee. Remember to set the software to automatically scan your computer frequently.

3. *Disk failure:* Hard drives can crash (fail), destroying valuable data. To prevent this, save everything you do to back-up media, such as external drives, CDs, or jump drives. Periodically back up your entire drive and store it in another location.

Disaster Recovery Plans

What would you do in the case of fire or other catastrophe that would make carrying on your business difficult or impossible? Insurance policies may cover many things, but they do not ensure smooth business operations in times of disaster. Whether you operate a small, home-based business or a large, multinational enterprise, you should have a disaster-recovery plan appropriate to the scale and complexity of your organization. Be sure to write it down and share it with your employees. Practice it once or twice

Maxim Tupikov/Shutterstock

a year with the whole team; the investment of time and money is worthwhile. Include critical information that team members keep securely off-site. Some issues to address are:

- **Communications:** Who will contact each person in the company and critical vendors and customers? How will they reach them? Include names, titles, telephone numbers, e-mail addresses, and street addresses. Update the contact information regularly. Also, know what the message will be.
- **Base of operations:** Where will people go if the normal place of business is inaccessible? This could be someone's home, another company site, or another location entirely.
- **Priority activities:** Which business activities are most essential/time-sensitive? Which activities could be postponed? What is the time frame for reactivation?
- **Return to facilities:** Define a process for regrouping and planning, and designate a leader.

The above is a partial and hypothetical list for a disaster recovery plan. Whereas it may seem to be more than might be needed, a straightforward plan put in place before disaster strikes can make the difference between business failure and survival.

Licenses, Permits, and Certificates

There is more to creating a legal business than naming and registering it. Once registered, you will need to comply with any federal, state, and local regulations that apply to your business. You should research these regulations before deciding to start your business, because they may affect what you can do, how you can do it, where you can operate, and when. Such regulations can completely change your potential business operations.

Zoning regulations often prohibit certain types of businesses from operating in specified areas. There may be other regulations, too, such as restrictions on obtaining a liquor license for a bar or restaurant. If your business involves food, you will need to comply with safety and health regulations, conduct food safety training, and obtain certain permissions and certificates.

Contact local, county, and state government offices, or your chamber of commerce, to find out which licenses and permits will be necessary.

- **Permit** An official document that gives you the right to engage in a specific activity, such as holding an outdoor concert.
- **License** An official document that gives you the right to engage in an activity for as long as the license is valid. A driver's license, until it expires, gives you the right to operate a motor vehicle. A child-care license permits you to operate a particular size and type of child-care facility.
- **Certificate** Official document that verifies something. A certificate of occupancy conveys that a building is safe and ready for use.

permit an official document that gives a party the right to hold a specific event.

license an official document that grants the right to engage in an activity for a specified period of time.

certificate an official document that verifies something.

If you hire people to work for you, your business will need to comply with federal, state, and local regulations regarding employees.

Chapter Summary

Now that you have studied this chapter, you can do the following:

1. Choose a legal structure for your business.
   - A sole proprietorship is owned by one person who also may be the sole employee.
   - A partnership consists of two or more owners who make the decisions for the business together and share the profits and losses.
   - A corporation is a legal entity composed of stockholders under a common name.
   - A Subchapter S corporation limits the number of stockholders to 100. It offers most of the limited liability protection of the more common C corporation, but Subchapter S corporate income is only taxed once—as the personal income of the owners.
   - A nonprofit (or not-for-profit) corporation is set up with a specific mission to improve society. Churches, museums, charitable foundations, and trade associations are examples of nonprofit corporations. Nonprofit corporations are tax-exempt.
   - A limited liability company (LLC) combines the best features of partnerships and corporations and is an excellent choice for many small businesses.
2. Discover the importance of contracts.
   - A contract is a formal agreement between two or more parties.
   - The relationships between the links in a production-distribution chain are defined by contracts.
   - Never sign a contract without having an attorney examine it.
   - Never sign a contract that you have not read yourself from top to bottom.
   - A successful contract should:
     - Avoid misunderstanding.
     - Assure work.
     - Assure payment.
     - Avoid liability.

3. Recognize key components of commercial law.
   - The Uniform Commercial Code is a collection of business laws adopted by most states that covers a broad spectrum of transactions.
   - The law of agency addresses principal-agent relationships.
   - The bankruptcy code concerns the inability or impaired ability to pay debts as they come due.
4. Evaluate ways to protect your intellectual property.
   - Your ideas and creations are your intellectual property.
   - Trademarks and service marks protect your brand identity.
   - Copyrights protect works of authorship.
   - Patents protect invented products and processes.
5. Plan to protect your tangible assets and manage risk.
   - Insurance protects people and businesses from the risk of having property or wealth stolen, lost, or destroyed.
   - When buying insurance, choose the policy with the highest deductible you can afford. This will give you the lowest possible premium.
   - Consider the normal and customary types of business insurance:
     - workers' compensation,
     - disability,
     - commercial fleet,
     - property,
     - liability,
     - business income,
     - errors and omissions, and
     - life.
   - Create and practice a disaster recovery plan.

Key Terms

arbitration
bankruptcy
boilerplate language
breach of contract
certificate
contingency
contract
corporation
deductible
electronic rights
insurance
letter of agreement
license

limited partnership
notary
partnership
patent
permit
premium
public domain
service mark
signatory
small claims court
sole proprietorship
statute of limitations

Entrepreneurship Portfolio

Critical Thinking Exercises

11-1. What can happen to an entrepreneur who is personally liable for the business? How can an entrepreneur protect himself or herself from personal liability? Say your friend wants to start a business making custom skateboards. Write a memo to your friend, explaining the risks involved and offering suggestions for limiting liability.

11-2. With a partner, make a list of the technological tools each of you can personally access. Brainstorm how you might combine your resources to create a successful business. Describe in detail how the partnership would work. For example, would the partner contributing more technology have a larger share of the business, or would profits and expenses be split equally? Draw up a partnership agreement that specifies each partner's duties and how much money and time each will invest.

11-3. Which legal structure will you choose for your business?

a. Why did you choose this structure?

b. Who will the partners or stockholders, if any, of your company be?

c. Describe the steps you will take to register your business. (Find out the process for the place where you would register.)

11-4. If your business will be incorporated, what percentage of the company would be represented by one share of stock? Will your corporation's stock be publicly or privately held? Why?

11-5. Use computer software to create a logo for your business. Do you intend to trademark your logo? Explain.

11-6. Describe any intellectual property you are developing (without improperly disclosing a potential patent).

11-7. How do you plan to protect your intellectual property (e.g., trademark, copyright, patent)? Explain why it would qualify for protection.

11-8. Give an example of a business in your community that you think may be infringing on someone else's intellectual property. Explain why you believe this to be possible?

11-9. What types of insurance will your business need and why? What is the highest deductible you feel you can afford? Pick one type of insurance you want to have for your business and find a company online that sells it. List the premium, deductible, and payout.

Key Concept Questions

11-10. What is the most important contract you will need to operate your business? Why is it so important? Describe any additional contracts you have or plan to secure.

11-11. Negotiate and write a letter of agreement between you and a fellow student. You could agree to become business partners, for example, or to supply a product or service for the other student's business.

11-12. Find a lawyer who might be willing to help you with your business. Ask your parents/guardians who are in business or store owners in your community for referrals. The Small Business Administration or Community Legal Aid Society sometimes offers free or low-cost legal services to entrepreneurs. Describe how you found the attorney and what criteria you used.

11-13. What is the purpose of having a form notarized? What types of documents are commonly notarized?

11-14. What does your signature at the bottom of a contract mean in a court of law? Which two things should you do before signing a contract?

11-15. Suki is buying a van from her father-in-law to start her flower-basket delivery service. She planned to buy auto insurance that would pay all her expenses in case she ever got into an accident. She finds that such insurance would cost $3,000 per year, which, according to her business-plan projections, is more than she can afford. What do you think Suki should do? Why?

11-16. Some businesses sell products and services that can injure customers. List three examples and explain how these companies probably use insurance.

Application Exercise

11-17. Carry out a search online for the name you intend to use for your business. What did you find? Will you still use this name? Why or why not? How do you plan to protect the name of your business?

Exploring Your Community

11-18. For the business you plan to start, research licensing regulations in your area and describe how they will affect your operation.
   a. Have you applied for a sales tax ID number?
   b. What are the zoning laws in your location? Would your business comply?

11-19. What nonprofit business could you start in your community? Answer the following questions to describe it:
   a. What is the name of your nonprofit?
   b. What societal problem(s) are you trying to solve?
   c. Describe the mission of your organization.
   d. Describe the programs and services you plan to create.
   e. How will your organization achieve the changes you intend to bring about?
   f. What is the unit of change (per person, animal, house, etc.)?
   g. How will you measure these changes?
   h. Who are your competitors?
   i. How much will it cost to deliver one unit of service?
   j. What sources of funding will you seek?

11-20. Interview an entrepreneur about insurance policies. Ask how he or she decided what kind of insurance to carry and whether to have high or low deductibles.

BizBuilder Business Plan Questions

3.0 Company Description

E. What is your organization's legal structure (sole proprietorship, partnership, LLC, C corporation, etc.)?

F. Why did you choose this legal structure?

G. In what state are you registered or do you intend to register? Why?

H. Where will you physically operate the organization?

I. What is the geographic reach of the organization?

J. Who will be the owner(s), partners, or stockholders for your company?

K. If applicable, describe what percentage of the company is owned by each shareholder or member.

6.0 Management and Operations

6.2 *Research and Development*

A. What type of product research are you doing? What do you intend to do?

B. What research are others in the industry conducting?

C. How will you legally protect your intellectual property?

6.3 *Physical Location*

A. Describe the actual physical place in greater detail than above. Include a photograph or floor plan in the appendices.

B. What zoning laws apply to your business? Does it comply? Are variances required?

6.5 *Inventory, Production, and Quality Assurance*

J. What methods will you use to ensure that you comply with federal, state, and local tax laws?

K. What laws—such as minimum wage and age requirements, health and safety regulations, or antidiscrimination laws—will affect your business?

Cordia Harrington (known as "The Bun Lady") founded the Tennessee Bun Company in 1996—with the funds from the sale of her McDonald's franchises and her bank savings—to become a supplier for McDonald's. Since then, her company has grown into The Bun Company, including the baking facilities in Dickson and Nashville, Cold Storage of Nashville, and Cornerstone Baking Company. The companies supply fresh and frozen buns, biscuits, and English muffins for chains, including McDonald's, Chili's, and Pepperidge Farm—primarily in the South.

Mandel Ngan/Getty Images

Over the years, Cordia has purchased and sold businesses and worked with numerous suppliers and vendors. From her career in real estate to becoming a McDonald's franchisee and owning a Greyhound bus station to creating the Tennessee Bun Company, Cordia has navigated many legal, regulatory, and risk factors. She added cold storage and delivery capacity to her bakery business when the risk of missed deliveries arose.

In 2011, The Bun Company expanded during a down economy because of customer demand and added biscuit production to its facility in Nashville. This 30,000-square-foot addition is highly efficient, with the capacity to produce 1,800 biscuits per minute.[12] The company used a Decision Matrix (Pugh Matrix) approach for the project and fast-tracked it to meet customer requirements. By using the matrix, company executives evaluated their options and prioritized the factors that would matter most in the process. They also used competitive bids and tested the new equipment multiple times.

Case Study Analysis

11-21. What legal issues has Cordia needed to address?

11-22. What kinds of regulations would you expect her baking, transportation, and storage companies to encounter?

11-23. With whom would you expect Cordia to have contracts? Why?

Case Sources

Laurie Gorton, "Tennessee Bun Company: Revs up Biscuit Line at Nashville," *Baking & Snack*, September 1, 2011, pp. 36–42, accessed September 7, 2013, http://www.nxtbook.com/sosland/bs/2011_09_01/index.php#/36.

Tennessee Bun Company, About, accessed September 7, 2013, http://www.buncompany.com/about-us/.

---

[12]Laurie Gorton, "Tennessee Bun Company: Revs up Biscuit Line at Nashville," *Baking & Snack*, September 1, 2011, pp. 36 – 42, accessed September 7, 2013, http://www.nxtbook.com/.

Airbnb—Navigating the Sharing Economy

Travelers frequently stay with friends and family as they visit various places. Some stay with alumni from their colleges through alumni networking sites; others stay with friends of friends. The concept of "couch surfing" is not new. However, Airbnb has taken the concept global.

Airbnb, founded in 2008 and headquartered in San Francisco, is a pure play Internet business that connects travelers with accommodations in private homes or properties worldwide. The company has offices in San Francisco, London, Paris, Barcelona, Sao Paulo, Copenhagen, Moscow, Hamburg, Berlin, Milan, and Singapore. As of May 2014, Airbnb had accumulated more than 600,000 listings in more than 35,000 cities and 192 countries.[13] This amounted to more than 11 million guests.

Chris Weeks/Getty Images

The Process

Individuals offer rooms in their homes, entire homes or condominiums, or other accommodations or shared spaces on the Airbnb site. They set prices and terms and provide photos and descriptions, as well as house rules to be posted on Airbnb. Their job is to list a site, respond to prospective guest inquiries, accept bookings, and act as a host for the guests.

Guests can visit featured locations or search for places they might like to visit. Through the Airbnb search function, they can find accommodations that match their criteria. They can then view photos, descriptions, rules, available dates, and guest reviews for the situations that interest

them. If they are willing to share a home with a host, they can search for sharing opportunities. If the guest has questions, she can send an inquiry through Airbnb and expect a response directly from the prospective host. The site tracks the speed and frequency of responses for each host, and this is posted for site visitors to see.

Once a guest decides on a place to stay, he or she requests a reservation through the Airbnb site and provides credit card information. Airbnb then requests a booking confirmation from the host. When the host accepts the booking, Airbnb charges the guest's credit card according to its policy. The host is paid one day after the guest checks in at the property.

Legal Guidelines from Airbnb

Airbnb has specific legal language on its Web site defining its role in the transaction and those of the hosts and guests. When hosts register their listing(s) on Airbnb, they agree to certain terms and conditions. Specifically, the site states, "You understand and agree that Airbnb is not a party to any agreements entered into between hosts and guests, nor is Airbnb a real estate broker, agent or insurer. Airbnb has no control over the conduct of hosts, guests and other users of the site, application and services or any accommodations, and disclaims all liability in this regard."[14] It further elucidates:

You acknowledge and agree that you are responsible for any and all Listings you post. Accordingly, you represent and warrant that any Listing you post and the booking of, or Guest stay at, an Accommodation in a Listing you post (i) will not breach any agreements you have entered into with any third parties and (ii) will (a) be in compliance with all applicable laws, Tax requirements, and rules and regulations that may apply to any Accommodation included in a Listing you post, including, but not limited to, zoning laws and laws governing rentals of residential and other properties and (b) not conflict with the rights of third parties. Please note that Airbnb assumes no responsibility for a Host's compliance with

---

[13]Airbnb, accessed May 14, 2014, https://www.airbnb.com/about.

[14]Airbnb, accessed September 14, 2013, http://www.airbnb.com.

any applicable laws, rules and regulations. Airbnb reserves the right, at any time and without prior notice, to remove or disable access to any Listing for any reason. . . .

Airbnb also articulates its limits of liability with respect to guests: "Airbnb cannot and does not control the content contained in any listings and the condition, legality or suitability of any accommodations. Airbnb is not responsible for and disclaims any and all liability related to any and all listings and accommodations. Accordingly, any bookings will be made at the guest's own risk."

Safety and Security

Travelers and hosts alike face risks to their personal safety and property when they connect via Airbnb. To increase safety, Airbnb encourages hosts and guests to take several precautions. They can verify their respective identities through social networks, or by confirming personal details or scanning official IDs. Profiles and confirmed reviews can provide insights into guests and hosts. In addition, guests and hosts can communicate through the Airbnb messaging system. In fact, direct communication is not permitted until the booking is confirmed through Airbnb. The company maintains a customer support team that is available 24 hours a day. Finally, guest payments are handled through a secure server and hosts are paid by Airbnb.

After a 2011 incident, where a host arrived back at her apartment to find it burglarized and heavily damaged by an Airbnb renter, the company added a safety tool, called the Airbnb Guarantee, and created a trust and safety department.[15] According to the company Web site, the $1,000,000 Host Guarantee covers property for guest damages, but doesn't cover cash and securities, rare artwork, collectibles, jewelry, pets, and personal liability. The company encourages hosts to consider carrying homeowner's or renter's insurance, and suggests that they can charge guests a security deposit.

Challenges to Airbnb from Competitors and the Law

Recently, the popularity of sites that provide connections between hosts and guests for short-term stays has triggered challenges on multiple fronts.[16] For organized, registered businesses providing accommodations, such as hotels, motels, and bed and breakfasts, it seems that the homeowners and renters that provide accommodations without legal registration gain an unfair competitive advantage. For landlords and governments, as well as condo, homeowner, and civic associations, the hosts may be violating the culture of the community, lease terms, and zoning regulations and avoiding taxes. This has led to animosity and serious issues for Airbnb and its hosts. In 2012, an Airbnb host returned home after renting out his room to find that his landlord had been charged by New York City authorities for violating the city's transient hotel regulations.[17] This is a scenario in which the "sharing economy" ran afoul of the mainstream economy, with the law on the side of the latter.

With its rapid growth and substantial financial support, Airbnb will face both opportunities and challenges in the future.

Case Study Analysis

11-24. What types of contracts does Airbnb need? With whom?

11-25. How is insurance involved in the Airbnb business model? How would you recommend this be changed, if at all? Why?

11-26. How does Airbnb distribute the liability between itself, hosts, and guests? Provide examples.

11-27. Why would hotels, motels, and bed and breakfasts be unhappy with Airbnb?

11-28. Visit the Airbnb Web site (http://www .airbnb.com) and search for an accommodation for yourself. Describe the legal and risk issues you saw addressed during the process, and those that would be of most concern if you booked a reservation.

---

[15]Lyneka Little, "San Francisco Burglary Inspires Changes at Airbnb: Airbnb User's Home Ransacked," ABC News, August 2, 2011, accessed September 14, 2013, http://abcnews.go.com/Business/airbnb-user-horrified-home-burglarized-vandalized-trashed/print?id=14183840.

[16]Alan Farnham, "Airbnb: Towns Crack Down on Homeowners Who Take Guests," ABC News, September 9, 2013, accessed September 10, 2013, http://abcnews.go.com/Business/users-airbnb-breaking-law-critics-claim/story?id=20148183.

[17]Ron Lieber, "A Warning for Hosts of Airbnb Travelers," *The New York Times*, November 30, 2012, accessed September 14, 2013, http://www.nytimes.com/2012/12/01/your-money/a-warning-for-airbnb-hosts-who-may-be-breaking-the-law.html?pagewanted=all.

Case Sources

Airbnb, accessed September 8, 2013, https://www.airbnb.com/about.

Alan Farnham, "Airbnb: Towns Crack Down on Homeowners Who Take Guests," ABC News, September 9, 2013, accessed September 10, 2013, http://abcnews.go.com/Business/users-airbnb-breaking-law-critics-claim/story?Id=20148183.

Ron Lieber, "A Warning for Hosts of Airbnb Travelers," *The New York Times*, November 30, 2012, accessed September 14, 2013, http://www.nytimes.com/2012/12/01/your-money/a-warning-for-airbnb-hosts-who-may-be-breaking-the-law.html?pagewanted=all.

Lyneka Little, "San Francisco Burglary Inspires Changes At Airbnb: Airbnb User's Home Ransacked," ABC News, August 2, 2011, accessed September 14, 2013, http://abcnews.go.com/Business/airbnb-user-horrified-home-burglarized-vandalized-trashed/print?id=14183840.

12

CHAPTER

Operating for Success

Learning Objectives

1. Examine the significance of operations in a business.

2. Develop a production-distribution chain for your business.

3. Manage suppliers and inventory.

4. Recognize the key factors to consider in the location decision.

5. Explore the design of facilities and their layouts.

6. Evaluate product quality methodologies.

7. Implement technology to benefit your business.

Vasily Smirnov/
Shutterstock

"Excellent firms don't believe in excellence—only in constant improvement and constant change."

—Tom Peters, author and management consultant

Cramer Products Inc. was founded in Kansas in 1918 by Chuck and Frank Cramer. Chuck, a pharmacy student, had created a liniment to treat his own sprained ankle several years earlier. The company was the first devoted to helping athletes prevent injuries and return to action more quickly if hurt.[1] Cramer Products sold primarily to interscholastic sports teams and was an industry leader for over a half a century. That changed in the early 1980s, when athletic programs were disappearing, new products appearing, and competition growing.

Cramer decided on a retail strategy to replace its lost revenues. In 1990, management signed super athlete Bo Jackson to a joint venture for a new brand, called Bo Med, and targeted it to people who engaged in recreational athletics. The line debuted in October. In January, after having been chosen for both the Major League Baseball All-Star Team and the National Football League's Pro Bowl, Jackson suffered an injury that ended his football career. Although he continued playing baseball, his star power suffered.

The Bo Med venture was a failure, and Cramer Products was left deeply in debt, with a great deal of unsalable inventory. The company's position in its primary market was under assault, its viability as a retailer was damaged, and its management team was demoralized.

Cramer Products' president resigned and was replaced by Thomas Rogge. The new president introduced a style that encouraged a free exchange of ideas. He reorganized the management team and gave individual managers more authority. Rogge liquidated the Bo Med line, salvaging as much of the product as possible for repackaging under the Cramer label and selling the rest to a distressed-inventory merchant.

To rebuild the core business, Rogge broadened the audience from coaches and trainers to include school nurses and physical therapists, and he set up a team to develop new products. He put out a new retail line, using the Cramer name. Packaging of both the retail and interscholastic products was consolidated into one format, creating a single inventory.

More than 60 new products were added. In 1994, new products accounted for 12 percent of sales. Rogge reexamined all operational departments, cut the workforce by 25 percent—to 65—and assigned tasks to underused employees, thus improving productivity.

After two years of decline, sales increased 8 percent in 1993 and 12 percent in 1994. Profits set records. Recently, Cramer has grown through acquisitions, including Cosom Sporting Goods (2004), Active Ankle Systems (2008), and Stromgen Athletics (2011).[2] Cramer Products, like so many of the athletes it has helped, recovered from its injuries. Many years later, Cramer is still going strong.

Sean Justice/Corbis

---

[1] Excerpted from Cramer Products: Treating an Injured Company. *Insights and Inspiration: How Businesses Succeed: The 1995 Blue Chip Enterprise Initiative*. Published by *Nation's Business* magazine on behalf of Connecticut Mutual Life Insurance Company and the U.S. Chamber of Commerce, in association with the Blue Chip Enterprise Initiative, 1995, p. 47.

[2] Cramer Sports, accessed September 17, 2013, http://www.cramersportsmed.com.

Operations Permit Businesses to Deliver on Their Promises

Learning Objective 1

Examine the significance of operations in business.

operations a set of actions that produce goods and services.

In order for a company to be successful, it must follow up on promises to customers. Marketing sets the expectations. Finance and accounting ensure that the financial resources are available to produce the expected products and services. Legal structures and staff are in place to support success. Ultimately, the company must deliver the product or service to the customer as promised. **Operations** is the set of actions that produce goods and services, and operational efficiency is critical to business success.

What constitutes operations, and the precise steps involved in carrying them out, will depend on the nature of your industry and the specific conditions of your business. As we have discussed, a manufacturing company is one that makes a tangible product and generally does not sell goods directly to consumers. It typically sells large quantities of product to wholesalers. A wholesale business sells smaller quantities to retailers from warehouses. A retail firm typically sells single items directly to consumers; retailers operate stores (physical or virtual) that are open to the public. The fourth type of business is service. A service company provides intangible benefits, such as time, skills, or expertise, in exchange for a fee. Your business may fit neatly into the above categories or it may be a combination. For example, if you produce jewelry and sell it yourself online and at fairs, you are both manufacturer and retailer. In any case, there is the process of converting inputs to outputs. See **Figure 12-1** for an illustration of this process.

Regardless of what route your business takes, it is important to understand the process of operations.

The Production-Distribution Chain

Learning Objective 2

Develop a production-distribution chain for your business.

The consumer is the final link in a chain that extends from the manufacturer through the wholesaler and retailer to the consumer. When a customer buys a pair of athletic shoes in a sporting goods store, for example, the chain would entail four links:

1. The manufacturer produces a great quantity of a style of athletic shoe.
2. The wholesaler buys a large number of these shoes from the manufacturer.
3. The retailer buys a much smaller number of these shoes to stock a store.
4. The consumer enters the retailer's store and buys one pair of shoes.

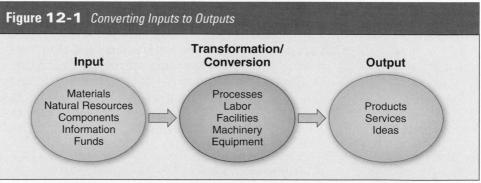

Figure 12-1 *Converting Inputs to Outputs*

Input	Transformation/ Conversion	Output
Materials Natural Resources Components Information Funds	Processes Labor Facilities Machinery Equipment	Products Services Ideas

Source: Adapted from Jae K. Shim and Joel G. Siegel, *Operations Management,* Hauppauge, NY: Barron's Educational Series, Inc., 1999, p. 2.

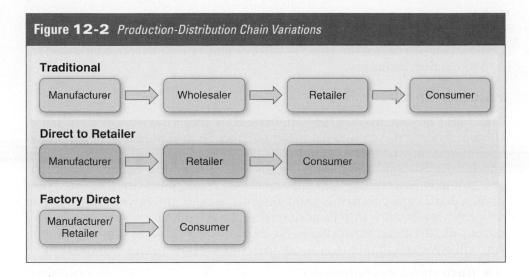

Figure 12-2 *Production-Distribution Chain Variations*

Traditional

Manufacturer ⇒ Wholesaler ⇒ Retailer ⇒ Consumer

Direct to Retailer

Manufacturer ⇒ Retailer ⇒ Consumer

Factory Direct

Manufacturer/ Retailer ⇒ Consumer

At every link in the chain, there are suppliers and customers. For the manufacturer, the suppliers are those who sell the components and raw materials that are needed for production and the customers are the wholesalers. For the wholesaler, the suppliers are the manufacturers and the customers are the retailers or, as in the case of a plumbing wholesaler, the contractors that provide a service using the wholesaler's goods. For the retailer, the suppliers are the wholesalers and the customers are the public—consumers. Consumers are the final customers. Some variations on this chain appear in **Figure 12-2**.

supply chain management (SCM) the management of sourcing, procuring, production, and logistics to go from raw materials to end customers across multiple intermediate steps.

Supply Chain Management

The management of sourcing, procuring, production, and logistics, which go from raw materials to end consumers across multiple intermediate steps, constitutes **supply chain management** (SCM). In order to create and maintain efficient material (supply) flows between supply points, SCM addresses methods and relations. Various partners must work together to use tools and techniques for increased efficiency and to apply their knowledge in making decisions. As you find a place for your company in a supply

◀ **Learning Objective 3**

Manage suppliers and inventory.

Step into the Shoes . . .

Creating Consistency—In-N-Out Burgers

The In-N-Out Burger, founded in 1948 by Harry and Esther Snyder, is a West Coast burger chain that has chosen to stay within a five-state area. It has some 280 stores, all of which are company owned. Now headed by Lynsi Torres, the third generation of the Snyder family, In-N-Out is focusing on product quality and control of the ingredients to ensure it. The menu is limited to burgers, fries, and beverages to stay focused on quality in the product line.[3]

The company sources its ingredients locally, processes them centrally, and distributes them to the In-N-Out stores. The company has its own patty-making facilities in Baldwin Park, California and Dallas, Texas. It produces its own rolls rather than using an outside supplier. The company also cuts its fries

in the individual stores for maximum freshness. Lettuce is hand-torn rather than machine-cut. To ensure freshness at the store level, no microwaves, heat lamps, or freezers are used.

In-N-Out Burger has chosen to keep tight control on both its food and growth—to ensure that the quality of its products will keep loyal customers coming back for more.

© E. J. Baumeister Jr./Alamy

---

[3]In-N-Out, accessed September 21, 2013, http://www.in-n-out.com.

chain, or multiple chains, you can also develop relationships up and down the line to enhance your efficiency and that of your supply-chain partners. Critical components of this process will be identifying and securing suppliers and managing inventory.

Finding Suppliers

The world is your market for suppliers. Raw materials, component parts, subassemblies, and completed products may be available to you from anywhere. You may be growing and packaging your own fruits and vegetables and have seed, fertilizer, packaging, and machinery and equipment suppliers. You may be creating Web sites where your suppliers are software companies, hardware companies, and Internet service providers. Or, you may own a retail gift store with hundreds of suppliers, who themselves each have dozens of suppliers. Regardless of the complexity of your supply partners, you will have to find them and work with them. Some places to look include:

- trade shows or conferences,
- trade catalogs or journals,
- the *Yellow Pages*,
- Internet search engines,
- wholesale supply houses and brokers,
- newspapers and magazines,
- competitors,
- firms like yours that are outside of your trading area,
- sales representatives, and
- customers.

visual control inventory-management method in which an individual assesses the stock level on hand by visual inspection and reorders when the supply appears low.

Your suppliers will become "partners" in your business. Your success will depend on their capacity to deliver what you need, when you need it, and at a price you are willing to pay. Their success depends on you delivering your product or service and getting paid for it, so they can get paid and be successful, too.

Flying Colours Ltd./Getty Images

Managing Inventory

Managing inventory is vital to marketing success and to cash flow and there will be an ongoing tension between them. If inventory is kept at a maximum, customer satisfaction may be high, but costs can become prohibitive. If inventory is maintained at very low levels, customers may become dissatisfied (even leaving entirely), but cash tied up in inventory is minimized. To balance service and cost management, factors such as demand, cost, sales price, carrying costs, order and setup costs, and lead times must be known. In reality, demand projections, lead times, and other variables are often estimated—with varying degrees of accuracy. Business owners can use the best available information and established techniques and tools to make inventory-management decisions.

Visual Control

A common approach to inventory management in small companies is **visual control**, which simply means that you look at the inventory on hand, and when the stock level of an item appears to be low, you reorder. This unscientific method of choosing when to order depends on your knowledge of the product-selling rate and delivery times. It is most effective when you sell relatively few items and are actively involved in the business.

Safety Stock and Reorder Points

To avoid running out of materials, businesses frequently establish **safety stock** levels, which are the amounts of inventory or raw materials and work-in-progress that are kept to ensure satisfying customer demand. The inventory **reorder point (ROP)** is the level at which materials should be ordered again. A challenge for any business is to find the optimal safety stock levels and reorder points for all inventory items. If too much inventory is on hand, the costs of storage and tying up money may be great. If too little inventory is available, the costs associated with lost sales and loss of goodwill may be significant. In addition to the holding and stock-out costs, the expenses associated with last-minute ordering may be substantial.

There are a variety of methods for calculating safety stock and reorder points. The calculation of the ROP requires a knowledge or projection of demand, lead time, and safety stock level, and is calculated as

safety stock the amount of inventory or raw materials or work-in-progress that is kept to guarantee service levels

reorder point (ROP) the level at which materials need to be ordered again.

> ROP = (Average Demand per Unit of Lead Time × Lead Time) + Safety Stock

For example, if the lead time for showerheads is two weeks, and you sell 25 showerheads per week, so that you always want at least 10 showerheads in stock, the calculation is

> ROP = (25 × 2) + 10 = 60

Whenever inventory falls to 60 showerheads, it is time to reorder. **Figure 12-3** shows this in graph form.

Economic Order Quantity

The **economic order quantity (EOQ)** is the amount of inventory that will equal the minimum total ordering and holding costs, calculated as

economic order quantity (EOQ) the amount of inventory to order that will equal the minimum total ordering and holding costs.

$$EOQ = \sqrt{\frac{2DO}{C}}$$

Figure 12-3 *Reorder Cycle*

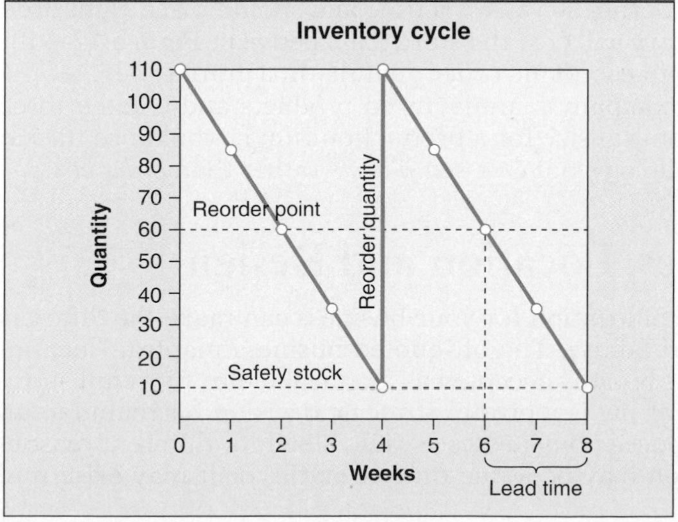

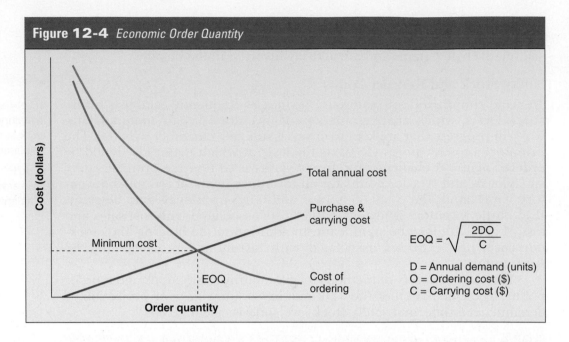

Figure 12-4 *Economic Order Quantity*

EOQ = $\sqrt{\dfrac{2DO}{C}}$

D = Annual demand (units)
O = Ordering cost ($)
C = Carrying cost ($)

in which D equals annual demand for the item in units (not dollars), O equals the ordering cost per order in dollars or other currency (not units), and C equals the carrying cost per unit in dollars or other currency. For example, Dominique's Bridal Shop buys bridal veils at $80 per unit from its supplier. Dominique's sells 640 veils annually, distributed evenly over the months. The holding cost (also known as carrying cost) is 5 percent of the total, or $4 per veil per year. The ordering cost is $20 per order. So,

$$EOQ = \sqrt{\frac{2\,(640)\,(\$20)}{\$4}} = \sqrt{6400} = \textbf{80 veils}$$

The total number of orders to place per year = D/EOQ = 640/80 = **8 orders**.

Total Inventory Costs = Carrying Cost + Ordering Cost
= (C × EOQ/2) + (O × D/EOQ)
= ($4) (80/2) + ($20) (500/80) = **$285 per year**

From this example, Dominique's Bridal Shop should have an inventory policy of ordering 80 veils at a time and should place eight orders per year. This inventory will cost the store $285 per year. **Figure 12-4** illustrates the calculation of economic order quantity in a graph.

If the company manufactured products and wanted to calculate the most economical size for a production run, it would use the same calculation methodology, but *O = setup costs* rather than *order costs*.

Facilities, Location and Design

The choice of location for your business can make the difference between success and failure. The oft-quoted business mantra, "location, location, location," is broadly accepted as a crucial factor for retail stores. However, the choice of site is a pivotal strategic decision for manufacturing, wholesale, and Internet businesses as well, albeit for different reasons. The location decision may be a one-time scenario, or it may arise multiple times

Global Impact . . .

Paper Wealth

Zhang Yin (Cheung Yan) of Nine Dragons Paper (Holdings) Limited, in China, is the richest self-made woman in the world. Her personal wealth is estimated at $4.7 billion.[4] Her company recycles scrap paper, often from the United States, and produces cardboard. The cardboard is used to make boxes for Chinese goods, many of which find their way back to the United States.

Zhang Yin, originally an accountant from Guangdong Province, has moved between China and the United States, first opening a paper company in Hong Kong (1985) with $3,800 in cash, and then a paper-export company in the United States (1990). American Chung Namp Inc. became the largest exporter of waste paper from U.S. sources. Working with her Taiwanese-born and Brazilian-raised husband and her brother, she cofounded Nine Dragons in Hong Kong in 1995. The company raised almost $500 million through its initial public offering on the Hong Kong Stock Exchange in 2006.

American Chung Namp and Nine Dragons are able to maintain low overhead by hauling away unwanted scrap and by creatively exploiting shipping opportunities.[5] Rates to China are particularly attractive because of excess capacity on ships returning to China from the United States.

As of 2007, Nine Dragons had 5,300 employees, 11 huge papermaking machines, and reported profits of $175 million on $1 billion in annual revenues.[6] It expanded into a third manufacturing plant, located near Shanghai, in August 2008 and a fourth facility opened in Tianjin in September 2009.[7] By using the latest in machinery and less costly labor and fuel, the company has significant production advantages. Nine Dragons met ISO (International Organization for Standardization, discussed later in this chapter) quality and

Zhang Yin, Nine Dragons Paper. (Mike Clarke/Getty Images)

environmental standards and obtained Occupational Health and Safety management system certification to support its continuous improvement. In addition to paper production, according to its Web site, the company has facilities to provide "power, steam, water treatment and excellent logistical support. The integration of these facilities provides and increases the Group's operational flexibility and control, while enabling the Group to facilitate best practices in terms of environmental protection."

The Nine Dragons Web site clearly states the company's goal: "The Group aims to become the world's leading containerboard product manufacturer in capacity, profitability and efficiency."

[4]Allen Cheng, "Cardboard Puts Woman at Top of China's Rich List," *The Standard*, January 17, 2007, accessed November 14, 2009, http://www.thestandard.com.hk/.

[5]Ibid.

[6]David Barboza, "Blazing a Paper Trail in China," *New York Times*, January 16, 2007, accessed November 13, 2009, http://nytimes.com/2007/01/16/business/.

[7]Nine Dragons Paper (Holdings) Limited, accessed November 13, 2009, http://www.ndpaper.com.

during the life of a business. Location strategy impacts revenues, customer satisfaction, costs, and overall levels of risk and profitability.

Your business may need to generate customer floor traffic, to provide conveniently located services, or to have ready access to highways, a port, a railroad line, or an airport, or it may be able to operate virtually anywhere. In any case, the location decision will affect your access to markets and essential aspects of your cost structure. For a brick-and-mortar retailer, the marketing expenditures required to generate potential customers in a low-traffic location will probably be significantly higher than in a high-traffic area. For businesses with high transportation costs, a poor location choice can translate into prohibitive expenses. On the other hand, distribution-cost efficiencies can save money and offer a competitive advantage.

Key Factors in Deciding on a Location

The important factors in deciding on a location will depend on the nature of the business and its customers. Common considerations include

- access for customers
- access to suppliers
- climate and geography
- convenience
- cost of facilities (rent, construction, and the like)
- demographics

◀ Learning Objective 4

Recognize the key factors to consider in the location decision.

- economic conditions and business incentives
- governmental regulations and laws, including environmental impact
- labor pool
- proximity to competitors
- visibility

Figure 12-5 shows the factors affecting location decisions at the country, regional/community, and site levels.

Each business has a unique set of location criteria and priorities. Trade publications and industry research will provide insight into industry-specific location issues. What's important to a specialty retailer at a brick-and-mortar location might be meaningless for a service business. The challenge is to identify the critical success factors for your business, tempered by the realities of budget and other constraints, to find your best available option.

The selection of a location—a critical business success factor—is often a one-time event and is generally expensive to change. Therefore,

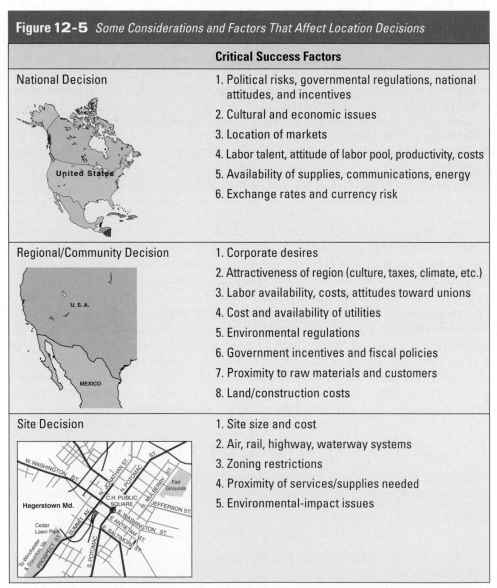

Figure 12-5 *Some Considerations and Factors That Affect Location Decisions*

	Critical Success Factors
National Decision	1. Political risks, governmental regulations, national attitudes, and incentives
	2. Cultural and economic issues
	3. Location of markets
	4. Labor talent, attitude of labor pool, productivity, costs
	5. Availability of supplies, communications, energy
	6. Exchange rates and currency risk
Regional/Community Decision	1. Corporate desires
	2. Attractiveness of region (culture, taxes, climate, etc.)
	3. Labor availability, costs, attitudes toward unions
	4. Cost and availability of utilities
	5. Environmental regulations
	6. Government incentives and fiscal policies
	7. Proximity to raw materials and customers
	8. Land/construction costs
Site Decision	1. Site size and cost
	2. Air, rail, highway, waterway systems
	3. Zoning restrictions
	4. Proximity of services/supplies needed
	5. Environmental-impact issues

Source: Jay Heizer and Barry Render, *Operations Management,* 8th ed. (Upper Saddle River, NJ: Pearson Prentice Hall, 2007), p. 249.

Global Impact . . .

Disney Selects a European Site[8]

Site selection can create magic when done well. It can also ruin dreams when done poorly. Walt Disney planned to add a European property in looking to the future of his company. In the 1980s, Disney began a search with approximately 1,200 potential locations for its proposed Euro Disney Resort. Ultimately the list was reduced to two sites in Spain and two in France. The governments offered incentives for locating in each, and Disney executives decided on one in France. The Euro Disney Resort opened to much fanfare in 1992 in a location about 20 miles from Paris in Marne-la-Vallée.

The initial reception for the French location was disappointing for Disney, which expected a resounding success from the opening day. However, some Europeans thought of Disneyland as an American cultural intrusion, and the term "euro" is associated primarily with money and business. Yet, in the years since EuroDisney was renamed Disneyland Paris Resort and repositioned, it has gained considerable ground.

© Photoshot Holdings Ltd/ Alamy

---

[8]Adapted from Andrew Lainsbury, *Once Upon an American Dream: The Story of Euro Disneyland*, University Press of Kansas, 2000.

---

familiarizing yourself with some of the methods for evaluating location alternatives is good practice. These methods range from simple and inexpensive to highly sophisticated and costly. The expense of selecting the profit-maximizing location for your business is an investment in its future success.

New business owners commonly opt for the simplest method of site selection: go with the one you know. Although this is a more intuitive method than the others, it can be effective. For a lifestyle business, one that draws from a limited local area or one where physical location is less critical, such an approach may produce solid results. When you live and/or work in an area, you become familiar with the demographics, traffic patterns, and existing businesses through daily observation. However, it is risky to assume that your perceptions will be entirely accurate. This method is best used as a preliminary filter, to be followed up with objective research.

Another common technique for location analysis is the **factor-rating method**, whereby decision criteria are prioritized and weighted to eliminate subjective features. This method incorporates quantitative and qualitative considerations. The factor-rating method can be employed for any type of business and can include as many or as few factors as desired, in six basic steps:

factor-rating method
location-decision criteria that are prioritized and weighted to eliminate subjective considerations.

1. Develop a list of critical success factors.
2. Determine the weight of each factor according to its relative importance.
3. Create a measurement scale for the factors.
4. Score each proposed location for each factor (best if done by a team) according to the scale.
5. Multiply the factor weight by the factor score for each factor in each location.
6. Use the sum of these weighted factors for the locations, to compare them and make a location recommendation/decision.[9]

---

[9]Jay Heizer and Barry Render, *Operations Management*, 10e, Upper Saddle River, NJ: Prentice Hall, 2011, p. 253.

Exhibit 12-1 *Factor Ratings for a Hybrid Automobile Manufacturing Plant*

Critical Success Factors	Weight	Scores (out of 10)		Weighted Scores	
		Michigan	Delaware	Michigan	Delaware
Labor (United Auto Workers Union)/Management Relations	0.25	5	10	1.25	2.50
Readiness of Facility	0.20	7	9	1.40	1.80
Proximity to Customers	0.20	7	7	1.40	1.40
Tax and Financial Incentives	0.20	10	6	2.00	1.20
Proximity to an Atlantic Port	0.15	3	10	0.45	1.50
Total	1.00			6.50	**8.40**

Exhibit 12-1 shows factor rating for a proposed electric car manufacturing plant. In 2009, an innovative, federally funded, and venture-backed company faced a location decision that included the entire country. After management decided to consider only locations where automotive plants had recently closed, the decision alternatives rapidly narrowed. Although the factor-rating criteria shown are highly speculative, the firm made a commitment to a location in Delaware rather than in the heart of car country in the Midwest.

One tool that is available to entrepreneurs at all stages is geographic information systems (GIS). These include demographic data; extensive maps and topographic information; and major transportation routes, health care facilities, and the like. After you have identified the factors that are important to your business, you can use a GIS system to discover potential profit-maximizing locations.

Larger companies often develop customized GIS systems tailored to their particular location requirements. Franchisors such as Dunkin' Donuts can use GIS to target areas for new stores. For entrepreneurs with fewer resources, Microsoft MapPoint software may be well suited. MapPoint includes demographics and maps that can be combined with firm-specific or industry data. **Figure 12-6** shows a GIS map for Prince William County, Virginia.

A decidedly more low-tech approach to assessing locations is to gather demographic, psychographic, and geographic data and information on competitors to create lists of location options. The U.S. Census Bureau can provide substantial data to inform your decision. Maps and traffic data can be added to the mix, as can trade association information. For example, if the jewelers' trade association reports that customers will travel two miles to purchase jewelry, you can identify possible locations with sufficient people to sustain your business. Then, you can narrow your choice by assessing the competitive environment (both **clustering** in "jewelers' row" and stand-alone should be considered), weighing personal preferences, site availability in the potential location, traffic counts, and other factors that would contribute to success.

clustering the strategy of similar businesses locating near each other.

Facilities Design and Layout

The geographic location and suitability of business facilities matter greatly. You may have seen signs from real estate companies stating, "Will build to suit." This means that they will put up a structure for your particular business. A purpose-built edifice is necessary for certain businesses, such as

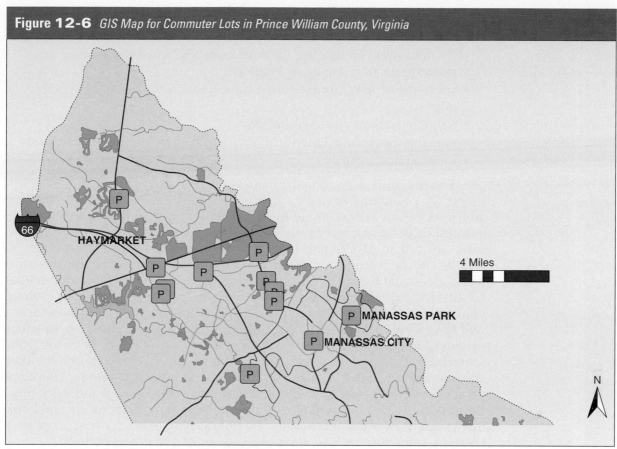

Figure 12-6 *GIS Map for Commuter Lots in Prince William County, Virginia*

Source: Adapted from © 2014 Prince William County. The information contained on this page is not to be construed or used as a legal description. Map information is believed to be accurate but accuracy is not guaranteed. Any errors or omissions should be reported to the Prince William County Geographic Information Systems Division of the Department of Information Technology. In no even will Prince William County be liable for any damages, including loss of data, lost profits, business interruption, loss of business information or other pecuniary loss that might arise from the use of this map or the information it contains.

restaurants or hotels. Other buildings may be constructed for general purposes and outfitted for a specific business through supplemental work. If a building is leased, these changes to adapt an existing structure are called **leasehold improvements**.

The type and size of facility, as well as other physical requirements, will depend on the type of business you are operating. For manufacturing, warehousing, and distribution firms, key considerations include

- capacity for efficient movement of materials, equipment, and people (floor space and ceiling height will matter);
- flexibility to adapt to changing business requirements;
- loading docks and vehicle access for deliveries and outbound shipments;
- an environment conducive to work requirements (natural light, appearance, and the like);
- the ability to include requisite controls, such as regulation of temperature and humidity and cleaning rooms;
- parking for commercial and employee vehicles, as well as spaces for visitors (including those with special accessibility needs);
- adequate utility services to the building (including power, water, and telecommunications); and
- security and safety.

leasehold improvements changes made to adapt a rented property for a particular business.

◄ **Learning Objective 5**
Explore the design of facilities and their layouts.

Retail facilities must meet such business requirements as

- appropriate selling area and configuration of that space;
- permission to complete necessary leasehold improvements or improvements to be made by landlord;
- space for offices, storage, restrooms, deliveries, and other special needs;
- suitable signage rules/regulations;
- parking that is adequate for the anticipated customer volume; and
- lighting and security.

Service and professional businesses have unique facilities requirements. A plumbing-service company may need space for parts storage and parking for service vehicles. A physician's office may need the same amount of floor space but require waiting areas, examination rooms, and safe, convenient patient parking.

Whatever business and facility you decide on, you will need to create a work space that is suited to the company's operations. If you have a home-based venture, you will have to create an area in your living space where your business can operate. With a retail store, floor design and storage will be critical to successful operation. For a factory, repair shop, or other production facility, the layout of the machinery, equipment, inventory, raw material, and component sections will be of crucial importance. Another consideration will be the access to loading and unloading areas. There are professionals who specialize in floor planning, space design, and work flow. Some of these may be employed by the equipment manufacturers and landlords who want you as a customer. Do not hesitate to ask for free services in these matters. **Figure 12-7** shows the layout of a mattress factory.

Store layout is a particularly important part of a retail business's marketing and revenue-generation operations. The exterior of the store, including window displays and signage, can attract or repel customers. Even the cleanliness of the windows sends a message.

In-store layout should be designed to entice customers to make purchases, preferably spending more than they had initially planned. Retail stores often place new items or signature products at the front, with sale goods toward the rear or against the walls, thereby compelling customers to pass by a variety of potentially enticing items. "End-caps" and other prominent display areas throughout the store can be used to promote merchandise. Also, well-designed stores rarely place their check-out registers near the entrance doors, thereby avoiding reminders to the customers of the money they will be spending.

Furniture store interior.
(JG Photography/Alamy Images)

Figure 12-7 *Factory Layout, Mattress Factory*

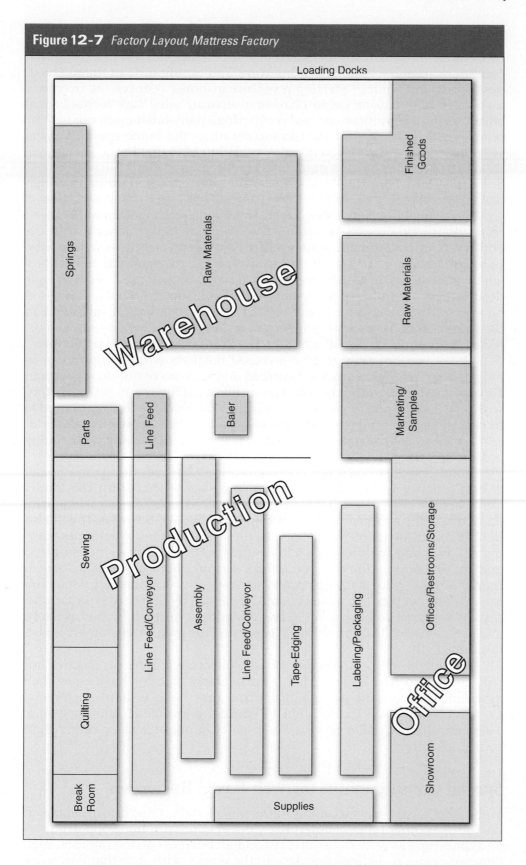

Special Considerations for Home-Based Businesses

Entrepreneurs starting home-based businesses face numerous exceptional conditions, ranging from allocating work and family time to unique business space and zoning. Starting a venture at home reduces the overhead associated with leasing or purchasing a separate site. With technological advances in communications and computing, many businesses can now be home-based. However, the decision to set up in the home should be part of an overall strategy. The National Association of Home Based Businesses (NAHBB) provides links to numerous resources, and D&B Small Business Solutions (http://smallbusiness.dnb.com) has articles pertaining to home-based enterprises.

Also, you will need to thoroughly investigate zoning ordinances, deed restrictions, and civic association rules. You may have to check with several levels of government zoning offices for requirements—such as city, borough, township, or county. If you live in a deed-restricted community where there is a civic association or if you rent, you will need to check your deed restrictions or lease. Some places forbid the operation of home-based businesses, whereas others may restrict the type or size of operation in the neighborhood—such as number of cars, foot traffic, or commercial vehicles. Sometimes hours of operation are limited and signage proscribed.

Often, you can operate a home-based business without a problem as long as your neighbors are not disturbed and have no reason to report you. However, it is far better to be fully cognizant of zoning requirements before writing your business plan and investing funds. The last thing you need is to run afoul of zoning regulations and have to make costly changes, relocate, or close your business. Of course, if you are not happy with zoning ordinances, you can work to get them changed.

Another issue to consider is the allocation of space within your home. A best practice is to clearly delineate your work area from the family living area. This is a practical matter as well as one of professionalism, particularly if customers will be visiting your place of business. It will also be difficult to focus on your work in the midst of family activities. Crying children and barking dogs will distract both you and your customers, and give the impression that you are not serious about business. Establish family ground rules with respect to the way you will interact while you are working, so that there aren't conflicts caused by differing expectations. Also, if you elect to have a home-based business, furnish it appropriately, and get a separate telephone line. A separate entrance for customers is also desirable.

A home-based business may be viable from a zoning perspective but still not be the best choice. This is particularly true for businesses such as retail, service, and professional firms that have walk-in customers. Customers will need the location to be safe, convenient, and appealing. They may simply prefer to visit an office building or a store rather than someone's home.

Special Considerations for Web-Based Businesses

Web-based businesses face many of the same location, facilities, and layout decisions as other types of enterprises, but encounter unique opportunities and challenges as well. Because they conduct business on the Internet, such companies can be located anyplace in the world, with staff that may work remotely from anywhere. The physical space needed could be a one-room office if (1) orders are taken only online and merchandise is drop-shipped directly from suppliers, (2) delivery of goods or services is provided online,

Step into the Shoes . . .

Small Parts Manufacturing

Small Parts Manufacturing Company Inc. (SPM) is a custom-fabricated metal parts manufacturing firm founded in 1946 by Merton Rockney in Portland, Oregon. SPM is a contract manufacturer, a job shop that makes metal machine parts for companies that either use them as components for larger assemblies or resell them.[10] SPM has a state-of-the-art facility to create the parts.

As a job shop, SPM has a variety of equipment for the machining of parts, and a staff of skilled tool makers, machinists, and computer technicians. They start with "extruded bar stock" in various shapes to make the parts. Materials include low-carbon alloy, or stainless steel, brass, aluminum, plastics, and exotic metals. The company uses traditional machinery, such as screw machines, bench grinders, drill presses,

and turret lathes. SPM also employs computer-controlled (CNC) machines and computer-aided design and manufacturing (CAD/CAM).

The layout of SPM is primarily fixed, with the products moved from machine to machine as needed for production. By using its cutting-edge technology, SPM delivers on its promise to provide high-quality parts to its customers.

---

[10]Small Parts Manufacturing, accessed October 3, 2013,

© imagebroker/Alamy

---

or (3) offered services are to be performed in the client's home or office. For completely online businesses and those using drop shipments, location is more a function of personal preference, cost, or proximity of vendors.

Location, facility, and layout decisions for Web-based businesses should aim to minimize distribution costs. While Amazon.com can have its call centers, computer processing, and the like almost anywhere, its distribution centers require considerable location analysis.

Defining Quality: It Is a Matter of Market Positioning

The concept of **quality** is used broadly and has multiple definitions, including how to determine degrees of excellence and conformance to specifications or standards. As a business owner, quality products or services will be largely defined by your market-positioning strategy. For example, a meal at a five-star restaurant will be vastly different from one at a local diner. In either case, excellence is a matter of consistently performing to the standards that have been established to meet or exceed customer expectations. However you position your organization, your quality and the viability of the business will depend on the match between the expectations you create through market positioning and the experience of your customers.

◀ **Learning Objective 6**

Evaluate product quality methodologies.

quality degrees of excellence; conformance to specifications or standards.

Profits Follow Quality

For many years, American companies had focused less on quality than on short-term profits. In the early 1950s, however, American economist W. Edwards Deming argued that business should focus on making quality products instead of on maximizing profits and that profit would follow from that focus. His revolutionary concept was ignored by American corporations, so he went to Japan, which was rebuilding its economy after the devastation of World War II.

In those days, Japan was notorious for the poor quality of its manufactured goods. The phrase "Made in Japan" was jokingly used to refer to anything poorly fabricated. Deming gave a series of lectures in Japan,

Step into the Shoes . . .

Positioning Stone Hill Winery through Quality

Stone Hill Winery (Lucinda Huskey/ Stone Hill Winery)

Jim and Betty Held took over the Stone Hill Winery in 1965 with four young children and a vision of restoring the historic Hermann, Missouri winery to its pre-Prohibition glory days.[11] They succeeded until the 1970s, when high interest rates combined with escalating costs. The winery grew slowly during the 1980s and into the 1990s, and then more rapidly from the later years of that decade.

Sweet and semi-sweet wines have always been the most popular items that Stone Hill Winery produced. Jon Held states, "We have provided a wide spectrum of wine styles to satisfy all consumers rather than only the tastes of a select few wine elite. Most importantly, we have listened to our customers rather than to the wine pundits." The Helds analyzed consumer loyalty to wine brands and discovered that one significant factor was first-time consumption of the product, specifically the atmosphere in which it was consumed. They changed their advertising message accordingly, inviting the public to, "Come out to the winery and have a great time."

The Helds knew that if they could invest in new vineyards and equipment, they could attain economies of scale.[12] As recently as 2008, the winery expanded through the addition of new fermentation and storage capacity, totaling 99,000 gallons. They needed to apply the latest grape-and-wine production technology so that the winery could consistently produce a range of wine styles of high quality and value. To raise money for this technology, they had to grow significantly. The marketing approach with the application of technology worked.

Stone Hill Winery is a three-location tourist destination. It now produces more than 260,000 gallons of wine annually with gross revenues exceeding $9 million per year, while employing the Helds, two of their adult children, and more than 100 other people. Stone Hill has 190 acres of vineyards under cultivation and uses grapes from other Missouri vineyards to supplement production.

Jim and Betty Held and their family combined market research, determination, state-of-the-art production equipment and techniques, and quality assurance to create an award-winning enterprise.

[11]Stone Hill Winery, accessed September 21, 2013, http://www.stonehillwinery.com/ourWinery/.

[12]"Stone Hill Winery: New Tastes, New Approach," *Insights and Inspiration: How Businesses Succeed, The 1995 Blue Chip Enterprise Initiative*®. Published by *Nation's Business* magazine on behalf of Connecticut Mutual Life Insurance Company and the U.S. Chamber of Commerce, in association with the Blue Chip Enterprise Initiative, 1995, p. 27. Courtesy of Stone Hill Winery.

though, that the Japanese took to heart. They began focusing on quality and soon proved that Deming's theory—profits follow quality—was correct. The subsequent quality of Japanese cars and stereos, among other products, became famous and won customers worldwide.

American entrepreneurs and corporate executives traveled to Japan to study why the Japanese had become so successful. They brought Deming's ideas back home, where they finally began to be adopted.

As you develop your business, it will be the consistent quality of your product or service that will lead to profits. If you can develop a way to deliver quality consistently, you will have a business model that can be profitable, with the potential for generating even greater revenues in the future.

Organization-Wide Quality Initiatives

Quality management and quality assurance is not solely the job of the production team. As organizations have evolved in our rapidly changing technology- and service-driven environment, quality has come to require the active involvement of the entire company. A number of initiatives and methods have been formed to help businesses ensure quality. Among these are lean manufacturing, *benchmarking, ISO 9000, Six Sigma, Total Quality Management*, and *The Malcolm Baldrige Award*. Each of these can assist your company in providing the quality that your customers should expect.

Benchmarking

benchmarking the comparison of a company's performance against that of companies in the same industry, or against best practices, standards, or certification criteria.

One of the most basic organization-wide approaches you can pursue is the use of **benchmarking**, which is the comparison of your company's

Exhibit 12-2 *Quality Measures for the Country Diner*					
Measure of Quality	**Rating (1 Is Poor, 5 Is Excellent—Based on Industry and Customer Data)**				
Customers per labor hour	1	2	3	④	5
Average customer wait time for seating	1	2	3	4	⑤
Satisfactory inspection ratings	1	②	3	4	5
Number of meals returned to the kitchen	1	2	③	4	5
Customer satisfaction ratings	1	2	3	④	5
Amount of food wasted	1	2	3	④	5
Return on sales	①	2	3	4	5

performance against that of other companies in your industry—or against best practices, standards, or certification criteria. Benchmarking is what you are doing when you create a competitive comparison for marketing purposes or when you compare your projected or actual financial ratios to industry levels. In addition to standard performance measures, such as return on investment, profitability, market share, and the like, individual industries have benchmarks. For example, retail stores measure sales per square foot, and restaurants evaluate by number of customers per labor hour. By using benchmarking, you can identify opportunities for improvement.

A simple method of benchmarking is to create a list of measures that are important to your customers (using primary market research) or to customers in your industry (using secondary research, such as trade-journal reports) and then to compare outcomes. You can then compare other statistics, if it is helpful. **Exhibit 12-2** illustrates a portion of such a table for a restaurant.

ISO 9000

The family of standards for quality management systems established by the International Organization for Standardization (ISO) is ISO 9000. These standards are certified by independent companies to document that consistent business procedures are being used and that the organization has been independently audited for compliance. Initially, ISO standards were applied solely to manufacturing. However, service firms have become the predominant recipients of certificates. Organizations will sometimes market their ISO certification as a mark of excellence, although it is rather a guarantee of compliance with standards.

Numerous standards have been employed under varying numbers. Beginning with the ISO 9001:2000 version, **process management** (measuring, monitoring, and optimizing tasks), upper management involvement, continuous improvement, recording customer satisfaction, and using numeric measures of effectiveness all became critical to the process. Industry-specific variations may apply to your business. There are eight quality-management principles for organizational improvement:

process management the measurement, monitoring, and optimization of tasks.

1. customer focus
2. leadership
3. involvement of people
4. process approach
5. system approach to management

6. continual improvement
7. factual approach to decision making
8. mutually beneficial supplier relationships

Regardless of the size of your firm, you can find considerable information on the ISO standards and build them into your organization from the start. Assistance is available through the American Society for Quality (ASQ) at http://www.asq.org, the American National Standards Institute at http://www.ansi.org, and ISO at http://www.iso.org.

Six Sigma

Six Sigma is a measurement of quality that was originated in the 1980s by Motorola engineers. It is the use of statistical methods to eliminate defects to a failure rate of 3.4 defects per 1 million opportunities, or a 99.9997-percent success rate. This is a rigorous process-improvement program that aims to achieve near-perfection. The two sub-methodologies employed are DMAIC and DMADV.[13] The DMAIC (define, measure, analyze, improve, and control) system is intended to enhance existing production. The DMADV (define, measure, analyze, design, and verify) process is meant to support new procedures and products.

For most enterprises, this is an intense program, maybe more so than is practical in the early stages of a business. However, it may be worthwhile to learn about it and consider whether you can include such methods as you start your business. Further information is available at:

SSA & Company	*http://ssaandco.com*
The Quality Portal	*http://www.thequalityportal.com*
iSixSigma LLC	*http://www.isixsigma.com*
Motorola	*http://www.motorola.com/motorolauniversity.jsp*

Total Quality Management

total quality management (TQM) the quality-assurance methodology of striving for strategic advantage through quality.

continuous improvement always identifying and implementing changes throughout an organization to focus on the requirements of internal and external customers.

The quality-assurance methodology of striving for strategic advantage through quality concepts inspired by Deming is called **total quality management (TQM)**. Developed in the 1950s, as described earlier, many of the principles of TQM are still valid and valued. **Continuous improvement**, or always identifying and implementing changes throughout the organization to focus on requirements of internal and external customers, is valid for any business. TQM involves constant improvement of processes, typically using specific measures of quality, such as compliance with product specifications and operating standards, volume of production, on-time delivery, and repeat rates.

TQM's success depends on the commitment of all employees to treat one another as customers and to work together to ensure that standards are met at all stages. Each employee accepts responsibility for a role in the production of the products and services.

Malcolm Baldrige Award

Whereas the previous concepts have focused on quality-management methodologies, the Malcolm Baldrige Award is a competitive process established by the United States Congress in 1987 to recognize quality management. The Baldrige Award is given to businesses and educational and nonprofit organizations by the president of the United States and is administered by

---

[13]Available at http://www.isixsigma.com.

the National Institute of Standards and Technology (NIST).[14] Organizations apply for the award and are judged in the areas of:

- leadership: organizational leadership and social responsibility;
- strategic planning: strategy development and deployment;
- customer and market focus: market and customer knowledge and customer relationships and satisfaction;
- measurement, analysis, and knowledge management: measurement and analysis of organizational performance and management of information and knowledge;
- human resources focus: work systems, employee learning and motivation, and employee well-being and satisfaction;
- process management: value-creation and support processes;
- business results, including customer focus, product and service, financial and market, human resources, organizational effectiveness, governance, and social responsibility.

Thousands of organizations use the Baldrige criteria for self-assessment, training, and the creation of business processes. You can obtain a list of these Baldrige standards and incorporate them into your business at any time. They are more comprehensive than many of the specific production and process measures identified previously in this chapter.

Using Technology to Your Advantage

Regardless of the size or nature of your business, technology can work to your advantage. Even if your business is not technological, you can apply technology to make your operations more efficient and effective. The technology could be as simple and common as a telephone or as complex as a specialized piece of medical equipment. What *is* important is that you are aware of the technology available to you and how it might benefit your business. At the same time, you should be wary of adopting new technology just for the "wow" factor. A cost/benefit analysis for technology implementation is as important as for any other substantial investment.

◀ Learning Objective 7

Implement technology to benefit your business.

hyperlink word(s) that, when clicked on, transfer the computer user to another Web page.

Computer Access Is Essential

Advances in technology that ordinary people can use have been an important part of the entrepreneurial scenario for at least 15 years. With this in mind:

- Every entrepreneur should have access to a computer.
- Every business should have a Web site and electronic mail access.
- Every business should hire employees who are conversant and comfortable with technology.
- Every entrepreneur should be aware of the specialized computer software and equipment that is designed for his or her industry.

The Internet came into being in 1989, when an English man named Tim Berners-Lee invented **hyperlinks**, words that, when clicked on, transferred the reader to

Cultura/Corbis Images

---

[14]Available at http://www.nist.gov/public_affairs/factsheet/.

uniform resource locator (URL) a Web-page address.

hypertext Web-based documents that combine text and graphics.

a new document page somewhere else on the Internet. Today, pictures, or even video, can be links as well. Every Web page has an "address," called a **URL (uniform resource locator)**, and you can surf from one URL to another using hyperlinks. Web pages are **hypertext** documents, meaning they combine text with graphics, video, or sound.

One of the best early investments you can make for your business is a computer. You do not need to have the latest model or even a new one; refurbished computers can be purchased quite inexpensively. Even the most basic model can be used to

- access the Internet;
- create stationery and business cards (although professional designs are preferable);
- produce professional letters and check spelling, grammar, and syntax;
- keep financial records; and
- maintain an updated mailing list of customers and printed mailing labels.

Capture the Potential of the Telephone

Do not forget, however, that technology does not have to be new to be useful. The telephone is still one of the businessperson's most important technological tools. You can turn your phone into an answering service for your business by using a voice-mail system, or you can hire an answering service to provide a more personal touch. Either approach is acceptable until you have the staff to answer customer inquiries—although some companies use automated telephone-answering systems, even if they have hundreds, or thousands, of employees.

Whether you use voice mail or an answering service, make sure the message that callers hear represents your desired business image and is clear and professional. Change your message periodically to advertise specials and sales and to keep customers listening. Use mobile phones to stay in touch with customers, employees, and suppliers.

A separate telephone line for your business will provide a number of advantages. Business telephones can be listed under your business name in directories, and you will know to always answer with your business name when that phone rings. Also, if you have a home-based business and children, it will be easier to have them resist answering the phone when it is clearly the business line. With text messaging and e-mail sent over mobile phones, the versatility and importance of telephones to today's businesses cannot be overstated.

Identify Market-Specific Software and Technology

To increase efficiency and effectiveness in operations, businesses use software and technology designed for their industry or type of business. For example, retail stores often use point-of-sales (POS) systems that are tailored to their products, and restaurants use ordering systems customized to their menus. Not-for-profits have specialized fund-raising and accounting software. Sports stadiums, concert venues, and movie theaters have ticketing systems. Manufacturing plants have materials-planning and inventory systems.

Typically, trade journals feature advertisements for software specific to an industry. Software companies commonly exhibit at trade shows and conferences. Evaluations and comparisons of hardware and software solutions can be found in trade publications and on the Internet.

An investment in industry-specific technology is often many times greater than in generic business equipment and software. However, the up-front investment may lead to both considerable efficiency and savings over the short and/or long term.

Electronic Storefront (Web Site)

No matter what type of business you have, opening an **electronic storefront** will make it more accessible to local customers and can introduce it to potential customers all over the world. An electronic storefront is an online site that customers can visit to view your catalog, price lists, and other information. Today, it is relatively easy to add the option of purchasing your products online, either directly, through a credit-card merchant account, or through a service such as PayPal, Bill Me Later or BitCoin.

You will need to decide if you want to put your store up with an online service or by yourself. An online service would typically build your storefront for you and include promotion and advertisements as part of the deal to help make its subscribers aware of your store. On the other hand, if you put a site up yourself, you would have more control over what it looked like and where it was located; and your potential customers would not be limited to the subscribers to a particular online service. One of the most cost-efficient ways to set up an electronic storefront is to hire a competent consultant to help you design it and choose which server to use.

electronic storefront an online site that customers can visit to view a company's catalog, price lists, and documentation.

Chapter Summary

Now that you have studied this chapter, you can do the following:

1. Examine the significance of operations in a business.
   - Operations is delivering on promises.
   - What is required depends on the specific industry and business.
   - Inputs are transformed or converted into outputs through operations.
2. Develop a production-distribution chain for your business.
   - Manufacturers make products in large quantities.
   - Wholesalers buy smaller quantities in bulk from manufacturers.
   - Retailers buy from wholesalers (and sometimes manufacturers).
   - Consumers buy from retailers.
3. Manage suppliers and inventory.
   - Supply-chain management is used to create and maintain efficient flow of materials between supply partners.
   - Suppliers may be found in a variety of ways and may be located worldwide.
   - Inventory can be managed to minimize cost and maximize customer satisfaction.
4. Know the key factors to consider in the location decision.
   - The most important factors will be governed by the nature of the business.
   - Key factors for most organizations include:
     - access for customers and to suppliers,
     - climate and geography,
     - cost of facilities,
     - demographics,
     - economic conditions and business incentives,

- laws and regulations,
- workforce readiness,
- competitive environment.

5. Explore the design of facilities and their layouts.
    - Manufacturing, warehousing, and distribution facilities must provide the space to operate cost effectively.
    - Retail facilities must draw maximum revenue from design and layout.

6. Evaluate product quality methodologies.
    - Quality is determined by meeting and exceeding standards, including customer satisfaction.
    - Profits follow quality.
    - Organization-wide approaches to quality include
      - ISO 9000 certification,
      - Six Sigma certification,
      - total quality management (TQM), and
      - Malcolm Baldrige Awards.

7. Implement technology to benefit your business.
    - Technology can provide competitive advantage.
    - Computers are a necessity in today's business world.
    - The telephone continues to be a major asset.
    - Industry-specific software and equipment are frequently beneficial.
    - Electronic storefronts (Web sites) provide additional distribution opportunities.

Key Terms

benchmarking
clustering
continuous improvement
economic order quantity (EOQ)
electronic storefront
factor-rating method
hyperlink
hypertext
leasehold improvements

operations
process management
quality
reorder point (ROP)
safety stock
supply chain management (SCM)
total quality management (TQM)
uniform resource locator (URL)
visual control

Entrepreneurship Portfolio

Critical Thinking Exercises

12-1. Answer the following questions about the production-distribution chain:

a. How do you plan to distribute your product to your target market?

b. What is the estimated delivery time between when you place an order with your supplier and when the product will be available for your customers?

12-2. Give an example of a business that is known internationally for the quality of its products. What defines quality for this company?

12-3. How does the design of a facility affect product quality and production efficiency?

12-4. Choose a partner in class and make a list of the technology each of you can personally access. Brainstorm how you might combine your technological resources to create a successful business. Describe in detail how the partnership would work. For example, would the person contributing more technology have a larger share of the business, or would profits and expenses be split equally? Draw up a partnership agreement that specifies each partner's duties and how much money and time each will invest in the business.

12-5. Examine a label on either the shoes or a piece of clothing you are wearing today. Which items were made in foreign countries? How many dollars per hour do you think the people earned who made these articles of clothing? Why do you think the company that manufactured these items had them made abroad?

12-6. Identify two sets of business clusters in your area. Explain why they may have formed.

12-7. Where would you locate your business and why?

12-8. If you were to start a home-based business, what might it be? Why? What key factors would you consider before start-up (specific to the topics in this chapter)?

12-9. What is the customary role of demographic information in the selection of a retail location?

Key Concept Questions

12-10. Use your local telephone company's business-to-business directory, *The American Wholesalers and Distributors Directory,* or an online wholesaler directory to locate wholesalers you could visit or from whom you could order products for resale. Where did you find them? What did you observe about the availability of contact information?

12-11. Choose one of the quality-assurance methodologies described in this chapter and explain how it might apply to your educational institution.

12-12. What factors are most critical to the location decision for a manufacturer?

12-13. How can zoning affect the location for a home-based business?

Application Exercises

12-14. What might the supply chain look like for one of the following?
   a. manufacturer of custom tire rims for automobiles
   b. car dealership
   c. building materials wholesaler
   d. video game publisher
   e. medical device distributor

12-15. Suggest at least three quality-assurance measures for the following businesses:
   a. bank
   b. residential cleaning service
   c. commercial HVAC (heating, ventilation, and air conditioning) contractor
   d. computer manufacturer
   e. pure play Internet shoe retailer

12-16. Xavier Zumsteg is selecting a location for his upscale urban fashion boutique. He has selected three cities to consider and needs to make a choice. Using the factor-rating method, identify the five key factors to consider and their weights. Then, rate each of the cities on a scale of 0 to 100. Calculate the most preferable option.

Factor	Factor Weight	Detroit Rating	Atlanta Rating	Boston Rating	Detroit Weight	Atlanta Weight	Boston Weight
Total	1.00	xxxxxx	xxxxxx	xxxxxx			

Exploring Your Community

12-17. Identify two businesses in your community with which you are familiar. Suggest four measures of quality for each. Rate each business on these quality dimensions. Then, answer the questions below.

Measure of Quality	Rating (1 is poor, 5 is excellent)				
Company Number 1					
Measure 1	1	2	3	4	5
Measure 2	1	2	3	4	5
Measure 3	1	2	3	4	5
Measure 4	1	2	3	4	5
Company Number 2					
Measure 1	1	2	3	4	5
Measure 2	1	2	3	4	5
Measure 3	1	2	3	4	5
Measure 4	1	2	3	4	5

a. What do these measures tell you about the respective businesses?

b. How might they improve on one of the indicators?

c. Does each business have a customer feedback mechanism? If so, what is it? If not, what would you recommend?

12-18. Visit the Web site of a business you know has at least three locations in your area (preferably not a franchise or chain).

a. Obtain the addresses of the locations nearest to your home (up to 10).

b. Map these locations on an ordinary street map.

c. Plot them on a census map.

d. What geographic pattern, if any, emerges?

e. Is there a common set of demographic data? If so, what?

f. Name a couple competitors and map up to 10 of their locations.

g. Does the pattern that emerges show clustering?

12-19. Visit the U.S. Census Bureau Web site at http://www.census.gov. Pull up the census tract data both for your home address and for your campus address. If the tracts are the same, pick another college or university. Compare and contrast the two locations as potential sites for each of the following. Use a street map, too, if it will help.

a. A bookstore

b. A store specializing in golfing-related goods

c. A children's day-care center

d. A distribution center for cleaning supplies

BizBuilder Business Plan Questions

5.0 Marketing Strategy and Plan
5.4 Place

A. Where do you intend to sell your product (physical and/or virtual locations)? Describe the advantages and disadvantages of your location(s). If you have a specific site, provide detailed information about it.

B. What are the surrounding businesses? Access routes?

C. If vehicular traffic is important to your organization, what is the traffic count for this location? Who provided the data?

D. What is the workforce availability in the area as it pertains to your needs? Use census or workforce data and cite it.

6.0 Management and Operations
6.3 Physical Location

A. Describe the actual physical place in greater detail than above.

B. What are the zoning laws in your area? Does your business comply?

6.5 Inventory, Production, and Quality Assurance

A. From what companies or individuals will you purchase the products you plan to sell or the parts you will use to manufacture those products? Illustrate your supply chain.

B. Do you intend to manufacture your product? If so, describe the manufacturing processes you will use. If not, describe how your product is manufactured.

C. Are there any economies of scale to be attained for your business? If so, what are they and at what point do you anticipate attaining them?

D. Have you developed and/or adopted any innovations in production, inventory management, or distribution that are significant? What are they and why are they meaningful?

E. How do you plan to distribute your product to your target market?

F. Illustrate the production-distribution channel for your business and the markups along the chain.

G. What is the estimated delivery time between when you place an order with your supplier and when you will have the product available for your customers?

H. What method(s) will you use to define and ensure the quality of your products/services?

Producing Quality American-Made Furniture: Gat Creek Furniture

In 1996, Gat Caperton decided that his future lay in purchasing and operating a manufacturing venture. At the time, he was a graduate student in Chicago and a full-time consultant specializing in manufacturing. Caperton envisioned that he would benefit from increasing production efficiency and revenues in an existing business rather than through starting his own venture.

During his acquisition search, Caperton found Tom Seely Furniture in Berkeley Springs, West Virginia, saw value in the acquisition, and purchased the company. Tom Seely created the company to produce reproductions of antique furniture some 40 years earlier after his experience as an antiques dealer taught him that he could manufacture and sell reproductions for greater profit and have more satisfied customers.

Caperton recognized the market value of hand-made Appalachian cherry wood antique reproductions and worked to create a production facility that would create the products for his target market. After some years of operating as Tom Seely Furniture, the company became Gat Creek Furniture and Caperton Furniture Works for its wholesale and private label markets respectively. Each furniture piece is hand-crafted and signed by one of Caperton's 120-plus employees or made by a local subcontractor (often individual craftspeople) using the company's specifications.

The skilled craftspeople at Gat Creek do not use assembly lines; rather they build and complete pieces at their stations. Materials are sourced locally with 95 percent of raw materials originating within 350 miles of the factory.

While the furniture is assembled by the local workforce in a traditional way, the company makes use of modern technology to ensure quality and minimal environmental impact. For example, Gat Creek monitors all materials entering and leaving its facility to reduce waste, pollution, and emissions. Gat Creek uses a state-of-the-art renewable biomass boiler system so that scrap materials become fuel for heating. The company has an innovative storm water management system and has received recognition for its efforts.

A core value for Caperton is sustainability, and he has implemented a manufacturing process that emphasizes care for the environment throughout its processes. As Caperton states, "Over the past five years we have won a number of design, environmental, and workplace safety awards. The award we cherish most is our customers' trust. We hold home sacred and hope to have the opportunity to share some of our craft with you and your home."[15]

---

[15]Gat Creek Furniture, accessed September 19, 2013, http://www.gatcreek.com/index.php/about-us/our-story.

Gat Creek Furniture

Case Study Analysis

12-20. How has Gat Creek brought modern technology to the traditional processes of building furniture?

12-21. What is the source of production inputs for Gat Creek?

12-22. How might Gat Creek assure quality? Why?

12-23. What types of regulations are particularly important to Gat Creek and its employees, given the nature of the business?

12-24. How are the company's core values exhibited?

Case Sources

Gat Creek Furniture, accessed September 20, 2013, http://www.gatcreek.com.

"Gat Creek Takes Sage Environmental Award," *Home Furnishings Business*, October 15, 2012, accessed September 24, 2013, http://furniturecore .com/Default.aspx?tabid=732&articleid= 5484&gat-creek-takes-sage-environmental- award.

Case Study | Sewing Up Business in New Ways—Sew What? Inc.

Question: What do Maroon 5, Slip Knot, Green Day, Rod Stewart, Elton John, Madonna, and schools near you have in common?

Answer: They are customers of Sew What? Inc., a manufacturer of custom draperies and curtains for theaters, concert tours, exhibitions, and special events.

Sew What? founder Megan Duckett has been passionate about theater and concert production since high school. She started her career as a part-time employee at the Arts Centre in Melbourne, Australia, before she graduated from a Church of England girls' grammar school (high school). The Arts Centre, the heart of theater in Melbourne, provided an opportunity to apprentice as a lighting technician with a master theater electrician, Jim Paine. There, Megan was exposed to the businesses that serve the theater industry; she discovered that working in this industry was what she was born to do.

Not long after that, 18-year-old Megan moved into the rock-and-roll marketplace and continued to work as a lighting technician and on other backstage aspects of the business. A critical turning point in her life came unexpectedly one year later. She was assigned to drive Billy Joel's band around while they were in Melbourne. They had an instant rapport, and the crew invited her to visit the United States. Much to their surprise, Megan showed up on their doorstep shortly thereafter—and soon got a job at a staging company for rock concerts. Megan knew she needed to find her niche and stand out from everyone else. As she has noted, "I needed to be invaluable and irreplaceable." Little did she know that sewing would be her ticket to success.

The opportunity to make her mark through sewing essentially came out of nowhere. However, Megan quickly realized it was the opportunity she sought. Her first sewing job was to reupholster 10 coffins for a Haunted Halloween show. She had neither the equipment nor the materials to do the job when she accepted it. Undeterred, Megan rented a sewing machine and went to a local fabric store, where she bought the necessary supplies (at full retail price) and did the work at her kitchen table. The customer could see that it was wonderfully done and called two weeks later with more work. That customer referred others and the business took off. That was

Megan Duckett
(Sew What Inc.)

in 1992. For five years, Megan says, "The phone kept ringing with orders."

As Megan was preparing her tax return in 1997, she realized that the earnings from the custom projects sewn at her kitchen table matched the pay from her 40-hour-a-week job. She and her husband, Adam, had just purchased a home and transformed the garage into a sewing room. After considerable discussion, Megan left her steady, full-time employment, incorporated Sew What? a few weeks later, and rented an 800-square-foot space a few miles from their house. She had no formal advisors and no written plan, but she did have a strong customer base, determination, and an understanding of the business. Just six weeks later, Megan landed a contract big enough so that she had to hire her first employee—a stitcher named Maria—who continues as part of the Sew What? family to this day. In 2002, Adam quit his own job and joined Sew What?

Megan relates, "The soft-goods industry is traditionally very much a cottage industry and is not known for embracing technology. We didn't like the way that felt." From the beginning, the Ducketts incorporated technology into the

413

business. The company team recognized that, as the quality of the clientele and the size of the contracts increased, customers would expect excellence. Sew What? began deliberately streamlining and fine-tuning the product and service aspects of the business.

Advances in technology were instituted throughout the operation. The office equipment was upgraded to include a network setup, faster computers, and multiple servers to increase speed, in order to function in real time with customers. Sew What? is currently on its third inventory-management system. The first was an Excel-based configuration developed in house. The second method was part of the automated accounting program. The most recent arrangement is a sophisticated manufacturing system called VISTA, from Epicor. Sew What? has moved into lean manufacturing procedures, and every function is timed, scanned, and measured to reduce waste and maximize use of resources. In addition, some patterns are cut using computer-guided tools, although many are still cut by hand—because runs of fabric can be so long and the tolerances so tight that hand cutting makes the most sense.

The company's Web site is a particularly important sales tool. Megan lost a substantial job early on because, without one, her business lacked credibility with the prospective customer. Megan resisted the idea of putting up a Web site, but she came to realize that she needed it, so she built one over a weekend using clip art—a far cry from the professional site Sew What? has today. Megan notes, "Generation Y will be the purchasing agents of the future. They expect a Web site. They need the visual communication." A Web site is particularly helpful for Sew What?, which has clients across the country and around the world (the company is headquartered in Rancho Dominguez, California). The site includes e-swatches, so that visitors can look at fabric samples online.

The sales force and production team also benefit from the use of technology, through a custom software program. By means of a series of drop-down menus, such variables as fabric, color, and production method can be selected. To that can be added dimensions and other specifications. The system calculates a "bid window" of the high and low price that can be offered. It determines the minutes of labor and the yards of materials. Once the job is sold and a contract secured, the file is digitally editable, and the Sew What? team can make final adjustments. It is then sent to a report generator (Crystal Reports) and translated into Spanish for the team of stitchers. This system permits Sew What? to sell more effectively, quote more accurately, replicate the work more easily, and make fewer mistakes. Sew What? has used its technological infrastructure to maximize productivity.

The company won the Dell/NFIB (National Federation of Independent Business) 2006 Small Business Excellence Award and was featured on the Dell Web site for the Integration of Technology into a business. With a 15,000-square-foot building and a staff of more than 30, finding ways to maximize technology is essential.

The Sew What? team
(Sew What Inc.)

The sales and order cycles for Sew What? are largely dependent on the type of customer. For example, rock-and-roll touring curtains might take anywhere from three days to four weeks from inquiry to order. These customers may also recycle or replace their curtains after a tour. (They may even donate them to charity.) Often, quick delivery is important for the touring customers, and because Sew What? generally uses only U.S.-milled products, the production cycle can be relatively quick after the order is placed.

For a school or church group buying or replacing stage curtains, the cycle is often three to six months. The process generally includes multiple steps, such as when a group realizes the drapes don't open/close properly or it needs new ones. A student or PTA parent researches available vendors and calls Sew What? The sales team helps by focusing first on making sure the individual knows what is needed and what will be provided. The customer is directed to samples and possible solutions, often through the Web site. Sew What? submits a price, the gatherer compares prices, and the school or church group raises funds. With money in hand, they finalize the order, and Megan's team speaks with the person who will install the drapes. Sew What? makes and ships the drapes, the customer receives and installs them, and Megan reaches out to see that they are satisfied.

In July 2008, Megan Duckett launched a second company, Rent What? Inc. with partner Marce Forrester. Offering rental stage curtains (manufactured by Sew What?) and theatrical equipment to the concert and special event market, Rent What? gives customers the means to rent the same high-quality products that are available through Sew What? Rent What? has provided rental drapery and equipment to diverse clients, including Journey, Lady Antebellum, and the television show *Glee*. In the summer of 2010, Rent What? began its third year of operation with the launch of a new customer-focused redesign of its Web site (http://www.rentwhatinc.com).

Megan was thrilled to have her products on the cover of the 1,000th issue of *Rolling Stone*. She won a 2007 Stevie Award for Most Innovative Company of the Year (up to 100 employees) and was a finalist for the 2008 Enterprising Woman of the Year. Sew What? was named to DiversityBusiness.com's 2008 list of the top 500 small businesses in the United States. In her feature as a young millionaire in *Entrepreneur* magazine, Megan stated, "The secret [to success] is hard work, dedication, and being able to take a blow and get up and move forward again. Be willing to accept criticism and comments, find mentors and learn from others. Try to be inspired by other people's success." With sales of about $5 million annually, the answer to Sew What? is "sewing up business." Or, as the company's Web site declares: *Sew What? Inc. It's not a question, it's the answer.*

Case Study Analysis

12-25. How did technology sustain Megan Duckett's business?

12-26. Why did Megan credit computer technology and the Web for a significant portion of her company's growth?

12-27. What were some critical steps in the growth of the company? Why were they so important?

12-28. Describe and illustrate the sales cycle(s) for Sew What?

12-29. What channels of distribution would you expect the company to use? Why?

12-30. Visit the company website at http://www.sewwhatinc.com. What new process, quality and/or production changes do they report?

Case Sources

Dell Case Studies, at http://www.dell.com/html/us/segments/bsd/case_studies/sew/index.html.

Sew What? Inc., accessed November 15, 2009, http://www.sewwhatinc.com.

"Young Millionaires Say More," http://www.entrepreneur.com/slideshow/184476.html.

Management, Leadership, & Ethical Practices

Learning Objectives

1. Identify leadership styles.
2. Describe the tasks handled by managers.
3. Develop your organizational culture.
4. Determine your organizational structure.
5. Understand the functions of human resources management.
6. Pursue ethical leadership to build an ethical organization.
7. Incorporate social responsibility into your company.

Pressmaster/Shutterstock

"Give a man a fish and you feed him for a day. Teach a man to fish and you feed him for a lifetime."

— Lao Tzu, founder of Taoism

Madam C. J. Walker, born to an impoverished couple in Louisiana in 1867, was reared in poverty by her married sister. Having overcome incredible difficulties, she became the first self-made American female millionaire and one of the first African-American millionaires in her 40s.

She worked for many years in cotton fields and as a laundress, moving to St. Louis, Denver, and Indianapolis, before inventing and marketing hair-care products for African-American women. Madam Walker quickly became successful enough to build a factory to manufacture her line of products. At first she sold her shampoos and hair-growth merchandise door to door, but soon organized and trained a group of agent-operators.

At the peak of her career, Walker employed 2,000 African-American agents. One of her successful marketing strategies was to organize the agents into clubs that promoted social and charitable causes in their communities. She offered cash prizes to those clubs that accomplished the most. She also encouraged her agents to open beauty salons and other corollary businesses. Madam Walker's methods foreshadowed the emphasis we see on socially responsible entrepreneurship and created a rich legacy of black female entrepreneurial leadership.

Madam C. J. Walker
(Library of Congress)

The Entrepreneur as Leader

No matter who you hire to manage your company, *you* will set the tone for how the business operates. Are you disorganized and chaotic? Chances are your company will be, too. Are you honest and straightforward? Your managers and employees are likely to behave similarly.

leader a person who gets things done through influence, by guiding or inspiring others to voluntarily participate in a cause or project.

A **leader** is someone who gets things done through influence, by guiding or inspiring others to voluntarily participate in a cause or project. *Leadership* comes from self-esteem applied to knowledge, skills, and abilities. If you believe in yourself and know what you are doing, you can accomplish things confidently and inspire others. Develop a positive attitude, and you can become a leader. Great leaders are optimists; they have trained themselves to think positively. Running a successful business requires leadership.

Leadership Styles That Work

Learning Objective 1

Identify leadership styles.

As your business grows, the type of leader you are will be reflected throughout your company. Some leadership styles are more conducive to internal competition, whereas others foster teamwork and a collaborative environment. You may find that you have to blend leadership styles or shift from one to another to some extent, as circumstances change.

Companies like Wal-Mart and Home Depot invest significant sums to create a work environment that inspires and motivates their employees.

Iromaya/Thinkstock/Getty Images

You may not have the sort of funds they do, but you can model a positive leadership style. How you or your managers treat one another and the employees will determine the company culture. Adopt the best leadership style for your company, maintain it consistently, and learn to adapt it as needed. According to researcher Daniel Goleman, the principal styles and their advantages and drawbacks are[1]

- **Coercive.** To *coerce* means to pressure someone into doing what you want. This commanding approach can be effective in a disaster scenario or with problem employees who need a forceful manager. In most situations, however, a coercive leadership style damages employee morale and diminishes the flexibility and effectiveness of the company. Employees stop thinking and acting for themselves.

- **Authoritative.** An authoritative leader takes a "come with me" approach, stating the overall goals but giving employees freedom to figure out how best to achieve them. This can work well if the leader is an expert, but may not be so effective if the scenario is one of a nominal leader heading up a group of individuals who have more expertise in the field than he or she does (a team of scientists, for example).

- **Affiliative.** This "people come first" method is effective when the business is in the team-building stage. It can fail when employees are lost and need direction.

- **Democratic.** This style gives employees a strong voice in how the company is run. It can build morale and work if employees are prepared to handle responsibility, but it could result in endless meetings and a sense of leaderlessness and drifting.

- **Pacesetting.** This type of leader sets high personal performance standards and challenges employees to meet them, too. This can be very good when employees are also self-motivated and devoted, but can overwhelm those who are not so committed.

- **Coaching.** This style focuses on helping each employee to grow, through training and support. This can be a good approach for starting and growing a business, but may not work with employees who have been with the company for a while and are resistant to change.

How Entrepreneurs Pay Themselves

Before you hire employees, figure out how to pay your first employee—yourself. Once your business is breaking even, decide how you will distribute the profit on a cash-available basis. The decision you make will affect your financial record keeping and your taxes, so think it through. But remember, you can change it to fit circumstances, too. The choices are

- **Commission.** A set percentage of every sale. It is treated as a variable operating cost because it fluctuates with sales.

- **Salary.** A fixed amount of money paid at set intervals. You could choose to receive your salary once a week or once a month. A salary is a fixed operating cost because it is not connected to fluctuating sales.

---

[1]Daniel Goleman, "Leadership That Gets Results," *Harvard Business Review*, March–April 2000.

- *Wages.* If you have a service or manufacturing business, you could pay yourself an hourly wage. Wages are frequently a cost of goods sold, because they are factored into the cost of the product or service.
- *Dividend.* Usually a share of a company's profits issued to shareholders, based on what remains after investments. As a small business owner, you could use this method to pay yourself; your compensation would depend on how the business is doing.

Entrepreneurs who do not pay themselves regularly tend to overstate their return on investment; they have not taken their compensation as a cost of the business. Recognize that you can only pay yourself (or anyone else) when you have sufficient cash to do so.

Another reason to pay yourself is that it enables you to be honest about whether the business is really worth your time. Could you be making more money in a different business or working for someone else? What are your opportunity costs? Is the best choice to keep working for yourself? Thinking entrepreneurially includes a realistic consideration of whether you would be happier *not* running a business, at least for a while.

Manage Your Time Wisely

Leaders learn how to manage their time, so that they can accomplish more with less. One of the most important things you can do is to learn how to manage your time efficiently. Getting more done in less time can contribute to success.

Even if you do not have employees to manage, you could probably use your own time better. **Exhibit 13-1** is an example of a valuable tool called a Gantt chart that you can use to organize the many things you need to do. This one is related to business start-up tasks. As your venture grows, you can use the Gantt concept to manage more complex operations. You can also create charts using software, such as Microsoft Project, and share them among team members. The best method to select is the one that you will actually use.

Exhibit 13-1 *Sample Gantt Chart*

Task	Week 1	Week 2	Week 3	Week 4	Week 5	Week 6
Build banking relationship						
Order letterhead						
Select location						
Register business						
Obtain bulk mail permit						
Select ad agency						
Meet with attorney						
Meet with accountant						
Create vendor statement						
Pay utility deposits						
Order marketing material						
Install phone system						
Have Web site designed						
Set up database						
Network computers						

Leaders perpetually have more tasks to complete than time to complete them, even when using project-management tools. It is easy to get sucked into unexpected meetings and conversations. For founders, this is compounded by being the locus of more company and product expertise than others, because of being a "one-person band"—or at least a high percentage of a small founding team. This means being called in as the "fire-fighter," or problem solver. The balancing act between being accessible—and creating a positive environment—and being inaccessible can be intricate. Time-management issues are also more difficult for leaders who cannot let go of decision making and involvement in every aspect of the company, even when they should delegate responsibilities.

There is a seemingly endless variety of books and articles on time management and on managerial and organizational effectiveness. Some tips that can assist in increasing such effectiveness include:

- Prioritize. Know what is important.
- Set realistic daily goals, allowing for customer contact, meetings, and some flexibility for surprises.
- Don't spend too much time on e-mail. It is easy to become distracted by nonessential correspondence. If you check at the beginning, middle, and end of the day, you will be able to focus better on other tasks.
- Avoid letting your attention get caught up in portable electronic devices. Whereas multitasking and constant availability may seem to increase efficiency, each interruption is a diversion from the work in progress and may cause you to lose your train of thought. These disruptions may also distract your coworkers, decreasing productivity even more.
- Schedule sit-down meetings only when they will be more efficient than other less time-consuming methods of communication. Try stand-up meetings. Also, consider going to other staff members' offices, so that you can end the meetings more easily.
- Only accept meeting invitations where your presence is required in order for progress to occur. As the firm grows, many of the operational meetings should disappear from your schedule. If you don't know why you have been invited to a meeting, don't attend it.
- Delegate responsibility and authority and trust your team; hire the best people for the job and support them in their success. There is little that is more wasteful and counterproductive than a manager who does not delegate or who nominally delegates and then undermines the team's work.
- Remember to allow yourself downtime, play time, and creative-thinking time. One of the reasons people become entrepreneurs is to gain control over their time And one positive characteristic of entrepreneurs is their creativity. By allowing time to think and relax, your company will benefit.

Business Management: Building a Team

As a business grows, it reaches a point where the entrepreneur and a few employees can no longer handle operations efficiently. At that stage, the company will need professional management.

Many successful entrepreneurs are creative individuals who get bored with the everyday details of running a business. Or, they simply dislike managing employees or recognize that their strengths lie elsewhere. Wise entrepreneurs recognize these characteristics, if they have them, and hire managers to run the business. This will free the entrepreneurs to spend more time thinking up new ideas, pitching product, or doing whatever they do best.

What Do Managers Do?

There are numerous descriptions, conceptions, and misconceptions about what managers do and do not do with their time. Their four primary functions are planning, organizing, leading, and controlling.

◀ **Learning Objective 2**
Describe the tasks handled by managers.

1. *Planning.* Managers perform three types of planning: strategic, tactical, and operational.
   - **Strategic plans** are typically three- to five-year overall strategies for achieving long-term growth, sales, and positioning goals.
   - **Tactical plans** provide the short-term implementation to accomplish strategic goals. Tactical plans are for one year or less and have limited, specific objectives.
   - **Operational plans** are short-term procedures for achieving tactical goals. These include budgets, regulations, and schedules for day-to-day operation of the business.
2. *Organizing.* This function includes everything from finding resources to hiring employees to buying/leasing equipment. It includes setting up an organizational chart and defining each staff member's responsibilities.
3. *Leading.* This function is about the style in which managers direct the company. For example, achievement-oriented managers encourage employee input, share authority and responsibility, and focus on achieving long-term goals. Managers need to understand their employees' skills, knowledge, and work styles to be effective. Good managers recognize that employees are not all the same and need to be handled individually. Effective managers can adapt to the employee or situation. Decisions managers make may affect employee motivation and morale—positively or negatively.
4. *Controlling.* This step involves measuring the business's performance and determining how to improve it. Is the business adhering to its budget? Are products achieving the level of sales and quality goals that were set? How about customer service? If there are variances between what was planned and what the company actually achieved, controlling will require corrective action to align plans and actions.

strategic plan typically a three- to five-year overall design to achieve long-term growth, sales, and positioning goals for a business.

tactical plan a short-term (one year or less) implementation that has limited, specific objectives.

operational plan the stated short-term methods for achieving tactical goals.

recruitment the act of finding and hiring employees.

Businesswomen conferring. (Color Day Production/ Getty Images)

Adding Employees to Your Business

One of the most important things a business owner does is to bring in capable, motivated people. It is a major decision to become responsible for the wages and salaries of others. For many entrepreneurs, the decision to hire is an agonizing one because they fear having to let the individual go at a later date or are not comfortable giving up some control. Businesses may bring in employees too soon and not be able to afford them—or too late and face overwhelming challenges. With a carefully developed and updated operational plan for your business, you should know when to add employees to the mix. This process of finding and hiring employees is called **recruitment**.

In *Good to Great,* management expert Jim Collins writes that great leaders "get the right people on the bus—sometimes even before a company decides exactly what business it will be in."[2] Louise Hay, founder of Hay House, Inc., a publisher, once said, "In the early days, I didn't have the money to pay decent salaries, so I didn't get good people. I got nice people, but I didn't get good employees." Some possible ways to bring good employees into your business are

- Bring them in as partners. Partners share the risks and rewards of the venture and will co-own the business. They will have the incentive to work diligently for the company's success.

- Hire experts to accomplish specific tasks on a contractual or hourly basis. You may not need full-time, or even part-time, employees for professional staff positions, but some expertise will be needed on a limited basis. For example, you might hire a professional accountant to work one day per month to review your record keeping.

- Hire someone as a part-time or full-time regular employee. Invest the time and money required to recruit and hire the best-qualified person you can afford.

There are specific steps in the recruiting process:

1. ***Defining the job.*** First, think about what you need this employee to do and what kinds of skills are needed to create a job profile, and then develop a position description. The **job profile** identifies the knowledge, skills, and abilities required to perform the specific tasks of the job. The **position description** includes the knowledge, skills, and abilities from the job profile, as well as what the reporting and working relationships and goals and objectives of the position will be. It should also contain a description of the physical requirements and special working conditions of the position (for example: lifting, bending, walking, etc.). Prioritize the list of key requirements you will develop with those who will work with the new hire. Be certain to designate specific experience, qualifications, characteristics, and traits that will be required. Also, decide on the wage or salary range that fits your budget before recruiting.

2. ***Posting and advertising the job.*** Determine how people will find out about the position. Are there potential internal candidates? Will you place an ad in a newspaper, run online ads, or solicit employee referrals? Finding good employees has become much easier with the advent of online job-listing services such as Indeed (http://www .indeed.com) and Monster.com (http://www.monster.com), as well as industry-specific sites, which are often managed by trade and professional associations.

3. ***Screening resumes and/or applications.*** A resume is a summary of an individual's education and work experience. Ask interested parties to send their resumes. Some online services permit you to screen resumes using keywords that are important to your search. Other times, you might have an individual or committee review applicants against basic requirements. You may have a secondary review to narrow the search to the top three to five candidates, whom you will then interview.

4. ***Assessing skills.*** Identify pertinent skills and determine ways to assess them. For example, if a new employee is supposed to write

job profile identification of the knowledge, skills, and abilities required to perform the specific tasks of an employment position.

position description the explanation of the knowledge, skills, and abilities of a job profile, as well as the position's reporting and working relationships, plus its goals and objectives.

Managers conducting a panel interview.
(Cathy Yeulet/Thinkstock/Getty Images)

grants, create a brief scenario and ask the applicant to create a document according to your specifications. For an administrative staff member, typing proficiency and skills in written communications and editing may be required and can be tested. If a job requires measurement and math skills, both can be evaluated easily. It is far better to eliminate unqualified applicants early in the process rather than waste their time and yours. The time to find out if a candidate is capable is before hiring.

It is critical to use the same process (such as a typing test) at the same stage in the interview for all applicants to guard against discrimination, especially involving "protected classes." For example, if a typing test is given to administrative job applicants, it should be given to all applicants at the same point in the process (usually prior to the job interview). It is also important to ensure that the assessment-instrument design could not be perceived as discriminatory. It is best to use instruments that have already been validated. Instruments that are not already tested are potentially dangerous because a protected-class applicant who is not hired because of a test score might have a legitimate case for legal action.

5. *Interviewing candidates.* Based on the resumes you receive, select several individuals to interview. Prepare an **interview guide**, a document to assist in developing questions regarding an applicant's knowledge, skills, abilities, and interests. Determine who will interview the candidates and whether the interviews will be performed one-on-one or by a panel. Many books, articles, and online resources can guide you in creating a **behavioral interview**, which is designed to determine the fit of a prospective employee with the requirements of the position, using prior-experience examples. Remember, the candidate should be provided with the interview schedule in advance. **Exhibit 13-2** suggests the topics to cover in an interview. **Exhibit 13-3** provides some sample interview questions.

interview guide a document to assist in question development regarding an individual's knowledge, skills, abilities, and interests.

behavioral interview dialogue designed to determine the fit of a prospective employee with the requirements of a position, using prior-experience examples.

> **Exhibit 13-2** *Examples of Competencies That May Be Included in Job Interviews*
>
> - General questions on skills and interests
> - Teamwork
> - Problem solving
> - Communications
> - Productivity/time management
> - Customer service (internal or external customers)
> - Interpersonal

6. ***Checking references.*** Ask the candidates who interest you to provide at least three references from previous employers or others who could tell you about their character and work performance. Check the references. Create a few questions that are pertinent to the job being filled and related career paths. Include questions about how the candidate and his or her references know each other. One question that often provides critical insight from former coworkers, managers/supervisors, and others is, "Would you rehire this person?" Some employers will only provide confirmation of former employees' dates of employment, so you might need to request additional references. Reference-check forms should be consistent and ask the same questions for each candidate being considered for a position.

   Some search firms and employers request an extensive list of references. For example, Diversified Search, a top executive search firm in Philadelphia, routinely requests 10 references and completes 30-minute or longer interviews with each of them. By the time the recruiter completes the reference-checking process, a comprehensive picture of the candidate has emerged. Such an extensive process is reserved for the finalists in top-executive-level quests, but could be applied to whatever level you might deem it helpful. Requesting so many references offers information in and of itself. Some candidates can send the complete list virtually immediately, whereas others simply vanish at that point. One human resources professional tells the story of calling several references provided by a candidate, who looked excellent on paper and interviewed like a dream. Each and every reference directly told her to avoid hiring him at all costs. This reinforces the importance of checking references.

   You also may want to call previous employers and interview each supervisor (be sure to have a release signed by the applicant). By the time this process is complete, you will have a better picture of the candidate. This vetting process is time-consuming, but it can prevent considerable issues later. Consider the case of a small business that had found an ideal marketing manager, until it made reference checks and was repeatedly told to stay away from that individual for both legal and ethical reasons.

   Whether you request a few or many references, be sure to contact them and ask sound, well-thought-out questions.

7. ***Negotiating compensation.*** You and the candidate you choose will negotiate how much you will pay as well as any benefits the job includes, such as paid vacation, sick leave, and health insurance. You should have a clearly defined pay range for each position and stay within it. Don't fall in love with a candidate you just cannot afford.

Exhibit 13-3 *Sample Interview Questions*

General

- Could you share with us a recent accomplishment of which you are proud?
- What are your qualifications in this area of expertise; i.e., what skills do you have that make you the best candidate for this position? Discuss any special training you have had (on-the-job, at college, continuing education, seminars, reading, etc.) and related work experience.
- Tell us about a personal or career goal that you have accomplished and why it was important to you.
- Why should we hire you?
- If you were offered this position, when would you be available to start?
- Tell us anything else you would like us to know about you that will aid us in making our decision.
- What questions would you like to ask us?

Teamwork

- How do you think the people you work with would describe you?
- Tell us about the most effective contribution you have made as part of a task group or special-project team.
- When groups work together, conflicts often emerge. Tell us about a time that conflict occurred in one of your work groups and what you did about it.

Problem Solving

- What was one of the toughest problems you ever solved? What steps did you take to solve it?
- How do you analyze the different options to determine which is the best alternative? Give an example of when you have done this.

Communications

- Describe a time when you were able to overcome a communication barrier.
- Give an example of how you consider your audience prior to communicating. What factors influence your communication style?

Productivity/Time Management

- When you have a lot of work to do, how do you get it all done? Give us an example.
- Describe a time you identified a barrier to your (and/or others') productivity and what you did about it.
- How do you determine what amount of time is reasonable to complete a task? Please give an example.

Customer Service

- We all have customers or clients. Who are your clients and how do you identify them?
- Tell us about a time when you went out of your way to give great service to a customer.
- Tell us about a time when you had trouble dealing with a difficult or demanding customer. How did you handle this?

Interpersonal

- Describe what you see as your strengths related to this job/position. Describe what you see as your weaknesses related to this job/position.
- Describe how you prefer to be managed. What is the best relationship you've had with a previous boss/supervisor?
- What kind of people do you find most difficult to work with? Give an example of a situation where you had difficulties dealing with someone different from yourself. How did you handle it?
- What do you do when you know you are right and your manager disagrees with you? Give an example of this happening in your career.
- Describe a difficult time you have had dealing with an employee, customer, client, or coworker. Why was it difficult? How did you handle it? What was the outcome?
- Describe a situation you wish that you had handled differently, based on the outcome. What would you change if faced with a similar situation?

Source: Adapted from the Society for Human Resource Management, http://www.shrm.org (accessed January 2, 2010).

However, you also should be realistic about the compensation package you are offering. Benchmark your total package against that of other potential employers.

Recently, an executive found himself in an untenable position. He had begun a search to fill a critical leadership role, formed a search committee, advertised in professional journals and at conferences, had extensive two-day interview schedules for five finalists, received two recommendations from the committee, and threw out the search. He decided he needed a more experienced candidate and insisted on a second search. Committee members were outraged. They had found fully qualified candidates based on the position description, the charge given to them, and the salary available. Some of the committee members participated in a second-round search, eventually making an offer to a candidate satisfactory to their manager. The candidate declined the offer. Again, the committee members conducted a search, with particular weight placed on meeting individuals at an annual professional conference. Round three also fell flat because the salary to be offered was $25,000 to $35,000, too low to attract ideal candidates. The position remained vacant for almost two years while the search dragged on; the compensation issue stood in the way, the search committee was frustrated, and the responsibilities of the job went unfulfilled.

8. ***Hiring.*** After negotiating compensation, you will have additional work to complete before the new employee's start date. These undertakings include background checks, drug testing, offer letters, and physicals. The **job offer letter** is a formal, written invitation extended by an employer to a candidate that states basic employment terms—the position offered, the start date, the salary, the benefits start date, and other pertinent information. Employers typically have the candidate sign and return the letter to indicate acceptance and an understanding of what is being offered. A physical examination may be required; this must be performed after the offer has been accepted but prior to the start date.

The nature and extent of a background check (including reference checking) will depend on the specific position. A basic background check, a criminal background check, and drug testing is good practice. The $50 or so investment in a criminal background check could save thousands of dollars. Don't be guilty of negligent hiring because you ignore this precaution. A rural taxi service recently went out of business after the bad publicity generated by the arrest of one of its drivers on charges of assaulting an elderly passenger. The driver had a history of assaulting older women, and the company was held liable for putting him in a position in which he had the opportunity to commit another crime. In addition to criminal background checks, you may also want to examine official copies of college transcripts or high school diplomas, and be sure to check previous employment history—the positions held and dates of employment. If the job requires driving, a check with the Department of Motor Vehicles will also be appropriate.

Comply with all employment laws in carrying out these checks and investigations, getting signed release forms as required. Drug-test authorization and background-check release forms are typically provided as part of an employment-application package and should be completed prior to interviewing the candidate. Once you decide to hire someone, you will also have to complete an I-9 and tax and

job offer letter a formal written invitation extended by an employer to a candidate selected for hiring that states basic employment terms, such as the position offered, starting date, and salary.

payroll forms. The I-9 form must be completed on the first day of hire, to ensure that the employee is legally authorized to work in the United States.

9. ***Orientation.*** This is the process of introducing the employee into the company, including its mission and its culture, and teaching him or her about the position. An employee manual that has passed legal review can save you a great deal of money and heartache. Orientation should be more than a brief talk about employee benefits, instructions to complete necessary forms, and a review of the employee handbook. Ideally, orientation is an extensive process of helping a new employee understand the structure of the organization and its mission, getting to know other employees, and even circulating through various departments. Some companies require that all new hires spend some time in customer service as part of orientation. Retail organizations may have all employees work on the floor for a while, or as a cashier, to experience customer contact.

Growing Your Team

Once you decide to add employees to your company, it could take considerable time and effort to identify and hire the right talent. Even in times when the economy is weak and unemployment is high, qualified candidate pools may be thin. You may have to find individuals to bring into your organization, rather than waiting for them to come to you. The less known your company is or the more remote its location, the more likely will be the need to actively recruit candidates.

Companies plan and hire according to staffing requirements and budgets and typically use a combination of internal recruiters (employees), outside recruiters (retained search firms or contingency search firms), and Internet job-board postings. Certainly, advertising and online postings may uncover a strong candidate pool and eliminate the need for internal or external recruiters. However, from time to time, you may need to use either or both of them. If you are growing rapidly and are looking for a skilled, educated workforce or if you are hiring executives, recruitment may be the key to successful hiring. Some ways to find the employees that will fit your company include the following:

- ***Campus recruiting.*** Established companies visit college campuses to meet and scout students who are about to graduate. Firms in banking, consulting, accounting, consumer products, technology, health care, and other segments of the economy are major recruiters on campuses. Smaller employers may participate in job fairs and other recruitment events. Contact the career service offices of the colleges and universities to find out about recruitment and internship possibilities.

- ***Executive or retained searches.*** When companies need to hire a senior executive, they often engage in an executive, or retained, search. These top job openings are commonly not advertised; the process is frequently managed by a retained search firm (sometimes called a "headhunter"). Executive search firms perform a full range of recruitment, screening, interviewing, and reference services. They work with clients to develop a detailed job profile and position description and then to create a profile of the ideal candidate. In the end, though, companies will decide which candidates to hire. Retained search firms are paid for searches regardless of whether they fill the position. Contingency searches are much like retained searches, but compensation is based on finding a successful applicant.

Creating and Managing Organizational Culture

Learning Objective 3

Develop your organizational culture.

A primary role of the founding entrepreneur is to convey the vision for the company and to foster its culture. The *culture* of an organization is the shared beliefs, values, and attitudes—informally referred to as "how things are done around here." The culture of an entrepreneurial firm can be its competitive advantage. As a company grows and adds employees, one challenge for an entrepreneur is to maintain the culture or to guide its evolution strategically. When culture is explicit and strategic, it is more readily shared through orientation and storytelling. Hewlett-Packard was famously recognized for stories told about its cofounder, David Packard, that reinforced "the Hewlett-Packard way."

The culture you create for your business should be a strategic translation of your vision and mission into norms, values, and behaviors. It should combine the best practices in business with the type of work environment you want. Your business will reflect the messages you send. Consciously or not, employees take their cues from their managers. What you say and do (or don't say or do) telegraphs messages to your team.

Culture is not an isolated aspect of your business, rather a combination of its parts. Company culture incorporates qualities of integrity; diversity; concern for society, community, employees, and customers; quality of products and/or services; and mission. For many companies today, this includes a focus on a balance between work and family life and the need for a positive, enjoyable environment.

Organizational culture is sometimes located in the continuum between the entrepreneurial and the administrative. Firms of most any size can be placed somewhere within these parameters, although it becomes increasingly difficult to operate effectively in an informal, entrepreneurial style as a firm adds employees. A company's culture is made clear through a multitude of words and actions. The type of culture you create is a choice you make, reinforce, and revise on a continuous basis. **Exhibit 13-4** identifies cultural clues, large and small. Consider the messages they send, and which of them you would want to incorporate into your business's culture.

Determining Organizational Structure

Learning Objective 4

Determine your organizational structure.

As you create and grow your company, you will change its organizational structure for your evolving requirements. Initially, you may be a one-person band, handling all responsibilities yourself. Or you may have a founding team that is a centralized locus of control, with team members serving in multiple roles. With growth will come a need for specialization, delegation, supervision, and management. A relatively "flat" organization may work with few employees and ready communications; as the number of employees changes, so must the organizational structure. One of the most difficult transitions for founding entrepreneurs is often from entrepreneur to entrepreneurial manager—a critical success factor for company growth.

A number of organizational structures may be viable for emerging firms. The evolutionary process for a business involves moving from one stage of maturity and structure to another. This process is not defined by time. It is not strictly defined by the number of employees, either. However, communications, control, and coordination are primary drivers. With emerging structural changes, companies often evolve from simple **line organizations**, in which each person reports to one supervisor, to **line and staff organizations** that also include specialists such as attorneys who assist in the management. Managerial **spans of control**, or the number of direct reports, become more defined, and the **chain of command**, or hierarchy of reporting and communications, is more distinct. A management

line organization a business structure in which each person reports to a single supervisor.

line and staff organization a business structure that includes the line organization, plus staff specialists (such as attorneys) who assist management.

span of control the number of direct reports for a manager or supervisor.

chain of command hierarchy of reporting and communications.

Exhibit 13-4 *Selected Aspects of Organizational Culture Communications*

Internal Communication	
Positive, upbeat, affirming	Doom-and-gloom, mean-spirited, sarcastic, teasing, cursing
Information-sharing, including financial performance	Information held closely, with sharing on a need-to-know basis
Employees contribute ideas and input, which is valued	Employees may be heard but not listened to
Employees address one another as peers	Hierarchy reinforced through the use of formal titles and forms of address (i.e., Mr., Mrs., Dr.), or formal address for managers and informal address for others
Customers spoken about with respect and value	Customers ridiculed or spoken about as an inconvenience
Storytelling used as a way to share history and culture	History and culture communicated through orientation and indoctrination
Telephones answered promptly and in a polite and friendly manner	Telephones answered slowly or not at all and in a grudging or unfriendly manner
Face-to-face communication valued highly	Formal written communications valued and face-to-face communications avoided or discounted

Structure and Hierarchy	
Flat organization with few levels of supervision	Hierarchical organization with multiple layers and clear distinctions between them (i.e., everyone communicates with only those one level above or below, and their peers)
Individual and communal	Paternalistic
Quick discussion and task-focused decisions	Meetings, meetings, meetings
Empowerment	Single locus of control
Flexible work schedules	Punching a time clock or closely observed comings and goings
Telecommuting	Anchored to the office/plant
No offices or little distinction in work environments	Office or workspace laid out by rank
Common eating area/cafeteria	Executive dining room
Shared parking area—first come, first served	Reserved parking for select individuals
All employees initially trained in a common customer-contact role, such as customer service or point of sales	No common training experience
Employee input in performance review and goal setting	Manager or supervisor prepares performance reviews and sets goals
Shared dress code, as appropriate to work conditions	Executives, the "suits," dress distinctly differently from others

Other	
Egalitarian	Elitist
Equal treatment	Preferential treatment with respect to such things as punctuality, extended meals, family
Individual and team recognition	Individual performance valued most highly
Environmental concerns practiced (e.g., reducing carbon footprint, recycling, energy efficiency)	Lack of environmental concern, or active damage to the environment
Community involvement encouraged (e.g., paid volunteer time, United Way corporate campaign, charitable contributions, or product tie-ins)	Community involvement discouraged (i.e., charitable contributions and work-time volunteerism avoided)
Ethics, or the focus on doing the right things	Focus on profitability over ethics
Quality, or the focus on doing things right; meeting and exceeding standards	Focus on profitability over quality
Personal space, if any, reflects the employee	Sterile personal space
Fun, playful, positive work environment	Dour, dull, negative environment
Opportunities to fail as a positive	Failure is not an option
Trust	Distrust
Shared glory	Blame game
Clean, well-maintained physical environment	Poor maintenance and dirty physical environment
Family friendly—such as photos in offices, child care on site, maternity and parental leave, referral services for child and/or eldercare, children welcome at work in emergencies, telecommuting, sick days available for child illness	Unfriendly to families; parents act as if their families don't exist during working hours

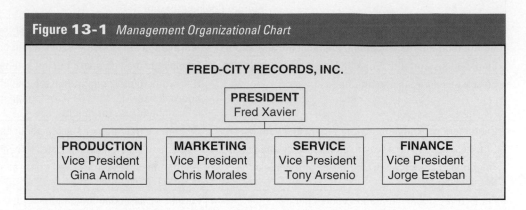

Figure 13-1 *Management Organizational Chart*

FRED-CITY RECORDS, INC.

PRESIDENT
Fred Xavier

PRODUCTION	MARKETING	SERVICE	FINANCE
Vice President	Vice President	Vice President	Vice President
Gina Arnold	Chris Morales	Tony Arsenio	Jorge Esteban

organizational chart for a typical small business might look like the example in **Figure 13-1**.

Whatever organizational structure you choose for your company at each stage of growth, it should be a strategic decision. Be careful not to create a hodgepodge of positions in a convoluted structure in order to keep people who do not fit.

Getting the Best Out of Your Employees

When you hire people, treat them fairly and with respect. Respect for individuals, diversity, and a balance of work and family will create a culture that affirms the value of employees. Employees who are valued are likely to want to go the extra mile for their employers. In addition to creating a strong, positive culture, many companies make their employees owners by giving them shares of corporate stock, thereby entitling them to a portion of the company profits, or offer them various incentives for positive performance.

Follow these basic guidelines to be a good to excellent employer:

- Get the right people. Taking the time and effort to fill positions with personnel who fit is at least half the battle. Know each employee's knowledge, skills, abilities, interests, and character traits.
- Provide a competitive salary and superior working conditions.
- Share your vision for the company and create an environment that encourages buy-in to your goals.
- Give employees incentives to work effectively. Ensure that the incentives match the company's goals and objectives and do not skew results.
- Empower employees by giving them control over their work.
- Provide career opportunities and training and development.
- Communicate expectations and goals clearly, and provide ongoing feedback and recognition.

Human Resources Fundamentals

human resources the segment of a business that hires, trains, and develops a company's employees.

Human resources is the branch of a company that is responsible for staffing, training and development, compensation and benefits, employee relations, and organizational development. Human resources is commonly referred to as HR, human capital, casting (Disney's term), or personnel.

For a business just starting out, it may not be practical to have a director of human resources, and the founding entrepreneur will handle these tasks. A company will probably not need a full-time human resources professional until it has 20 or more employees.

Regardless of how many, once you have any employees, there will be human resources functions to be managed. For companies of sufficient

Step into the Shoes . . .

Matching Employers and Employees—Indeed

With over 100 million unique visitors per month, Indeed, a subsidiary of Recruit Holdings Co., Ltd., claims the top spot among job sites on the Internet.[3] Founded in 2004 by Rony Kahan and Paul Forster, Indeed has offices in four U.S. cities and London and Dublin. The service covers some 50 nations and a multitude of languages.

Indeed is a pay-for-performance recruitment advertising network that provides free access to jobs from company Web sites and job boards. It consolidates available openings into a single meta-search for job seekers. Employers pay for the service when job seekers click on job openings.

Prior to founding Indeed, Kahan and Forster were successful cofounders of jobs inthemoney.com, a site for financial professionals. They sold it to Financial News in 2003 and founded Indeed a year later.

[3]Indeed.com, accessed October 4, 2013, http://www .indeed.com/intl/en/ourcompany.html.

Creatas/Thinkstock/ Getty Images

---

size, each of the following areas might represent one or more full-time jobs in the HR department.

- ***Compensation and payroll.*** This addresses such issues as the level of wages and base salary, bonuses, sales commissions, stock grants, stock options, other forms of compensation, and the issuance of payroll and associated taxes (although payroll is often a finance department function).

- ***Benefits.*** Full-time employees expect to be provided an array of paid benefits—and opportunities to purchase discounted benefits—as part of their compensation package. Basics may include health insurance (including the employee's family), life and accidental death and dismemberment insurance, paid holidays, vacation and sick time, and retirement savings plans. Other options may offer tuition reimbursement, disability, and insurance discounts such as automobile, long-term care, and even pet health insurance. HR usually leads the process of selecting the benefits programs the company will make available.

- ***Organizational development.*** The HR team plays a pivotal role in organizational development particularly with respect to organizational structure, employee retention, and succession planning.

- ***Education and development.*** Even senior executives require professional-development education from time to time. Human resources managers develop employee training in-house and may use outside training providers for specific situations.

- ***Labor law and HR compliance.*** The United States has well-developed laws to protect the rights of employees. Everyone involved in hiring, firing, and managing people needs to be aware of the letter and spirit of these laws, which are typically translated into policies by a company's HR and legal teams. As the business grows and you hire employees, you will have to become familiar with the laws and tax issues affecting employment. Among the laws and tax issues of concern:
  - **Payroll taxes** are a series of wage taxes based on earnings that are deducted from employees' pay.
  - The **Equal Pay Act of 1963** requires employers to pay men and women the same amount for substantially equal work.

> **◀ Learning Objective 5**
> Understand the functions of human resources management.

> **payroll tax** a deduction employers must make from their employees' pay and forward to the appropriate governmental entity.

BizFacts

Many companies staff their human resources units using a ratio of one HR executive per 50 to 200 employees.

- The **Fair Labor Standards Act**, passed in 1938, requires that employees receive at least the federally mandated minimum wage. It also prohibits hiring anyone under the age of 16 full time. Also, minimum-wage information must be posted in a visible location.
- **Title VII of the Civil Rights Act of 1964** prohibits discrimination against applicants and employees on the basis of race or color, religion, sex, pregnancy, or national origin, including membership in a Native American tribe. It also prohibits harassment based on any of these protected characteristics and employer retaliation against those who assert their rights under the Act. This Act is enforced by the U.S. Equal Employment Opportunity Commission (EEOC).
- The **Age Discrimination in Employment Act (ADEA)** prohibits discrimination against and harassment of employees aged 40 or older. Employers may not retaliate against those who assert their rights under the Act. This Act is also enforced by the EEOC.
- The **Americans with Disabilities Act (ADA)** prohibits employers from discriminating against a person who has a disability or who is perceived to have a disability in any aspect of employment. It also prohibits refusal to hire or discrimination against someone related to or an associate of someone with a disability. ADA prohibits harassment and retaliation in these cases. This Act is enforced by the EEOC and the U.S. Department of Justice.
- The **Immigration Reform and Control Act of 1986 (IRCA)** prohibits employers from discriminating against applicants or employees on the basis of their citizenship or national origin. In addition, it affirms that it is illegal for employers to knowingly hire or retain in employment individuals who are not authorized to work in the United States. Employers must keep records that verify that all employees are authorized to work here.

Performance Management

performance appraisal
the formal process used to evaluate and support employees' work performance.

You can maintain and build your team through appraisal and thorough follow-up. Although often dreaded, a **performance appraisal**, the formal process used to evaluate and support employee performance, can be valuable for both employees and employers. It is an opportunity to set goals, assess progress, identify opportunities for improvement, plan for individual growth and development, and provide performance feedback. Done poorly, the process is a waste of time and energy at best, and counterproductive at worst.

The keys to valuable performance appraisals are planning and consistency. Be clear about the purpose of appraisal and create a system for it. Nothing in the appraisal process should come as a surprise for anyone involved, if performance feedback is discussed routinely and course corrections are made throughout the year. Good channels of communication make the performance-appraisal process work more fluidly.

Performance appraisal is an opportunity to communicate goals, establish training and development needs, and provide feedback to increase productivity and employee retention. An effective process will also link performance to pay, which will help create a high-accomplishment culture in which superior performers earn higher pay increases than inferior ones. It also can help to protect a company against lawsuits by employees who have been fired, demoted, or not given a pay raise. Appraisals provide formal documentation for discussions on performance.

There are multiple methods of implementing performance appraisal, and these often vary according to the size and culture of an organization. A condensed version of the supervisor/manager portion of a performance review form appears in **Exhibit 13-5**. There are numerous variations on

Exhibit 13-5 *Sample Performance Review Form—Supervisor/Manager Portion*

Name: _____

Period Under Review: _____

Date of Review: _____

Department: _____

Part A. Success Factors

Factors	Rating					Comments
I. KEY RESPONSIBILITIES FOR THIS POSITION						
Performs key responsibilities as articulated in the job description. *(insert each essential function from the position description)*	1	2	3	4	5	
II. CORE COMPETENCIES						
1. Inclusiveness (defined in greater detail)	1	2	3	4	5	
2. Problem solving / decision making	1	2	3	4	5	
3. Planning and organizing	1	2	3	4	5	
4. Communication	1	2	3	4	5	
5. Quality focus	1	2	3	4	5	
6. Leadership	1	2	3	4	5	
7. Teamwork	1	2	3	4	5	
8. Department-specific competency	1	2	3	4	5	

Part B. Last Period's Goals

Rate the progress made on each of the goals established at the beginning of the period and any new goals. Note any modifications to the original goals.

Goal	Rating					Comments
1. (specify as many goals as are appropriate for the employee)	1	2	3	4	5	
2.	1	2	3	4	5	
3.	1	2	3	4	5	

OVERALL RATING (based on Parts A and B)	1	2	3	4	5	

Part C. Next Period's Goals

Enter the performance goals for the next period to be evaluated.

1. Measure of success:
2. Measure of success:
3. Measure of success:

Progress toward meeting these goals will be reviewed at the time of the next evaluation.

Part D. Professional Development Plan

Signatures:

Employee: _____ Date: _____

My signature indicates that I have received a copy of this evaluation.

_____ I would like to include comments from my self-assessment.

Manager/Supervisor Name:_____

Signature: _____ Date: _____

Department Manager Name: _____

Signature: _____ Date: _____

Global Impact . . .

Human Resources Service Firms

Many companies, large and small, are dedicated to providing human resources services to corporate clients around the globe. Here is how some leading firms got started: Adecco was founded in 1957, when Henri-Ferdinand Lavanchy, an accountant at the time, was asked by a client to help him fill a position. Today, Adecco provides staffing services to 250,000 clients around the world. In 1969, Lester Korn and Richard Ferry started a recruitment firm with a $10,000 investment. Today, with over $650 million in revenue, Korn/Ferry International specializes in helping clients hire top executives, including CEOs. When companies have thousands of employees, the task of getting paychecks out twice a month can be daunting. Payroll provider Automatic Data Processing Inc. (ADP) cuts checks for more than 50 million employees on behalf of its clients. ADP was started by Henry Taub in 1949, when he was 22. The company had eight clients and $2,000 in revenue in its first year.

the forms used and the style of presentation. Consulting any of the many books on human resources or visiting the Society for Human Resource Management (http://www.shrm.org) should provide ample information.

Firing and Laying Off Employees

Sometimes you hire someone and it just does not work out, even after repeated attempts to fix the problems. If you have to let someone go, you should document the reasons as they occur. You can be sued for wrongful termination, or breach of contract, if an employee believes he or she was fired for no good reason. The rules for termination vary from state to state, so it is essential to know your state's laws.

- Protect your company from wrongful-termination claims by conducting regular employee-performance reviews. Use performance-improvement or development plans to give the employee an opportunity to fix those aspects of performance that are subpar.
- If an employee is violating rules, give notification in writing (and keep a copy for your records) and work on corrections as the problems arise, rather than waiting for a performance review. If performance continues to be unsatisfactory, and you have to let the employee go, you will have documentation that there were problems with his or her performance. Be very careful to document the problem, not to editorialize or speculate about the employee.

Sometimes you might have to lay off employees. They may have performed their jobs well, but you either no longer need their skills or cannot afford to continue employing them. To minimize complications, if you can do so, offer employees **severance**, pay that is continued for a limited time as compensation for being let go, and make serious efforts to help them find new employment.

severance pay that is continued for a limited time to an employee who has left a company.

Ethical Leadership and Ethical Organizations

> **Learning Objective 6**
>
> Pursue ethical leadership to build an ethical organization.
>
> **ethics** a system of moral conduct and judgment that helps determine right and wrong.

True leadership comprises all of the actions and attributes that have been noted, plus the personal values underlying them. **Ethics** are a system of principles that define a code of behavior to distinguish between good and bad or right and wrong. The Golden Rule, "Do unto others as you would have others do unto you," is a well-known and widely accepted ethic. A behavior may be legal and still not be ethical.

Ethical business behavior is not only moral but makes good business sense. Have you ever bought something from a store and felt you were

Step into the Shoes . . .

Charles Schwab Does Well by Doing Good

Charles "Chuck" Schwab opened his own brokerage firm in the early 1970s when he was 34. Like Jacoby & Meyers with legal services, Schwab uncovered a market niche when he began offering discount pricing for informed investors who were tired of paying sizable commissions to stockbrokers. These investors did not need anyone else to do their research and make their decisions, and they flocked to take advantage of the lower rates.

By 1981, Charles Schwab & Company's earnings were $5 million. In 1983, Bank of America bought the company for $55 million but left Schwab in place as CEO.[4] Just four years later, management repurchased the company and took it public as Charles Schwab Corporation. In the 1990s, Schwab became the leading online discount broker and the fastest-growing American company of the decade.

Chuck Schwab expressed his attitude toward employees as, "I have yet to find the man, however exalted his station, who did not do better work and put forth greater effort under a spirit of approval than criticism." As of the end of the third quarter of 2013, Schwab had $2.08 trillion in assets under management, 9 million active brokerage accounts, 1.3 million corporate retirement plans, and 926,000 banking accounts.[5]

Charles Schwab (John Todd/ AP Images)

[4]Charles Schwab Corporation, accessed October 5, 2013, http://www.aboutschab.com.
[5]Schwab Corporation, accessed October 5, 2013, http://www.schwab.com/investor_relations.

cheated? How did you react? Did you want to go back? Probably not. You may have even told your friends about the experience. The store lost more than just one customer.

An Ethical Perspective

For a business, ethics are individual and organizational moral principles applied to actions and issues within the company context. To create an ethical organization, the values and standards of conduct must be clearly and broadly understood and accepted. Each substantive decision has an ethical component, although sometimes the right thing to do is so evident that many choices are virtually automatic.

However, the right thing to do is not always easy to determine. Often the choice is not between right and wrong, but rather between partially right and partially wrong, so that making a choice is difficult at best. There is sometimes a gray area in a scenario that cannot be clarified by relying on individuals to simply "know what's right."

Establishing Ethical Standards

One of the best ways to create an ethical business is to codify the fundamental rules of the game. Underlying values provide a basis for ethical behavior; clear, written guidelines can create a firmer foundation and more consistent implementation. Many companies create a code of ethics, a code of business conduct, or a combined code of ethics and business conduct. A **code of ethics** is the statement of the values of a company. A **code of conduct** is a set of official standards of employee behavior. A **code of ethics and business conduct** combines the two. By creating, disseminating, and establishing employee buy-in, a business will *empower* employees, meaning they will be free to make decisions and take action on their own, around a core set of ethical norms and rules for action.

A code of conduct can help to eliminate the problem of **ethical relativism**, which arises when ethical standards are believed to be subject to interpretation. It can also help to prevent or resolve **ethical dilemmas**, which are situations in which employees do not have a clear choice. By clarifying which actions should and should not be taken, many of the gray

code of ethics a statement of the values of a company.

code of conduct a set of official standards of employee behavior for a company.

code of ethics and business conduct a combination of a written statement of values with official standards of employee behavior.

ethical relativism situation where ethical standards are believed to be subject to interpretation.

ethical dilemma a circumstance in which there is a conflict of ethical values, which thus muddies decision making.

Exhibit **13-6** *Six Pillars of Character: Ethical Values*	
Value	**Actualized Form**
Trustworthiness	Honesty, integrity, reliability (promise-keeping), loyalty
Respect	Civility, courtesy, decency, dignity, autonomy, tolerance, acceptance
Responsibility	Accountability, pursuit of excellence, self-restraint
Caring	Concern for others, compassion, benevolence, altruism
Fairness	Process (open), impartiality, equity
Citizenship	Law abiding, volunteerism, environmental awareness, action

Source: Six Pillars of Character® adapted from the Josephson Institute of Ethics, http://josephsoninstitute.org (accessed January 25, 2010). Six Pillars of Character is a registered trademark of the Josephson Institute. Used by permission.

areas that invite confusion are eliminated. One general recommendation is that organizations put into place a procedural guide for dealing with ethical challenges. This document will contain a basic method, with a multistep process of asking key questions, to get at the best answer with regard to an ethical consideration. A company will include in the guide actual scenarios that have arisen or that could be expected to occur.

A comprehensive list of potential ethical values would be quite long, but they are neatly summarized in the Six Pillars of Character, as described in **Exhibit 13-6**.

By selecting 6 to 10 of these actualized concepts, you can develop a core value set and create a code of conduct that specifies the actions that are in alignment with those values. For example, if *impartiality* is critical, the code of ethics might require that employees refrain from accepting personal gifts from stakeholders, such as vendors.

As with any standards, a code of ethics and business conduct is only as good as its practice. Appropriate rewards for compliance and consequences for breaches of ethics are needed to have a viable code of ethics. What will happen to an employee who takes company funds? What if an employee consistently takes extra-long lunches, comes in later than scheduled, or leaves early? What if he takes home pens and paper? What if she goes on Facebook or eHarmony during working hours?

Corporate Ethical Scandals

The issue of business ethics exploded in 2002 when several large corporations were found to have published inaccurate financial statements. These fictitious numbers made the companies look so good that they were some of the most highly recommended stock picks on Wall Street.

Top executives at Enron, WorldCom-MCI, Tyco, Global Crossing, and other well-known firms had inflated corporate earnings so that they would receive huge bonuses, while misleading shareholders and employees. When the truth came out, public confidence in the stock market plummeted along with stock prices. Investors lost millions.

One of the companies, the energy giant Enron, had strongly encouraged its own employees to invest their retirement funds in company stock, even while top executives knew the worth of that stock was based on false numbers. These employees had their life savings wiped out by the unethical behavior of the executives.

Enron collapsed and thousands of employees lost their jobs and saw their pensions reduced to nothing; Tyco was split into four different companies. Tyco's CEO was forced to resign because he used company money to buy an $18 million apartment in Manhattan and furnish it with expensive artwork—among other egregious abuses.

An advisory board can provide valuable guidance.
(Nick White/Thinkstock/Getty Images)

The scandals of 2002 were a failure of **corporate governance**, meaning that these companies did not have rules and safeguards in place to ensure that executives behaved legally and ethically. Even early in developing your business, think about how you will guarantee that your company remains both ethical and legal as it grows.

corporate governance rules and safeguards to ensure that executives behave legally and ethically.

- ***Do not treat company profits as personal funds.*** Haphazardly taking business profits for your own use is a bad habit. Decide on a wage or salary you will pay yourself and always document this, as well as your business expenses. You should enjoy the rewards of a successful venture, but be careful to do it ethically and legally. In particular, **tax evasion**, which is trying to avoid paying taxes through illegal or deceptive means, is to be avoided.

tax evasion the deliberate avoidance of an obligation to pay taxes; may lead to penalties or imprisonment.

- ***Keep accurate records.*** Have your business records checked once a year by a professional accountant. By the time your company becomes a multimillion-dollar corporation, you will have established a reputation for honest financial reporting.

- ***Use financial controls.*** This will help to eliminate the potential for embezzlement, which is the crime of stealing money from a company. Once you have employees, use such simple financial controls as
  - Always have two people open the mail, so no one is tempted to take company checks.
  - Arrange for yourself and one other person to be required to sign all checks sent out by the business. Using a double signature will assure that no one can use the company money for personal expenses.
  - Implement a cash-counting and control system, if employees will be handling cash.

- ***Create an advisory board.*** Ask selected businesspeople and other community leaders you respect to be on your **advisory board** or **advisory council**. This group of people will provide you with sound, ethical business advice without having the responsibilities of a board of directors. Choose the members carefully, and listen to what they have to say.

advisory board or council a group that provides advice and counsel, but does not have the responsibilities of a board of directors.

Doing the Right Thing in Addition to Doing Things Right

As a business, ethical practices involve doing the right things and doing them ethically. There is a potential conflict between strategic priorities and ethical behavior. Profit maximization is one of the most common challenges to ethical behavior. By harming the environment, using substandard components, or cutting corners, a company can maximize its short-term profitability. A clearly defined and commonly shared code of ethics and business conduct can go a long way toward incorporating ethical decision making into strategic priorities. This will facilitate incorporating "doing the right thing" into company strategy from the start, thereby avoiding ethical conflicts.

Balancing the Needs of Owners, Customers, and Employees

Although it may seem simple and straightforward to retain your integrity, it can become more complex as you add partners, customers, and employees to the equation. People's moral compasses do not always point in the same direction. What seems just, right, and fair to one person may seem unjust, unfair, and wrong to another. Often, this is caused by the conflicting needs of owners, customers, and employees.

Owners face multiple pressures, such as the need to have their businesses survive, the repayment of debts, and the welfare of employees. Customers need products and services that meet expectations. Employees need to earn a living wage and experience job satisfaction. On the surface, fulfilling these aims should not pose ethical challenges.

However, as each constituency strives to meet its needs, ethical dilemmas may arise. As a business owner, for example, you may have to make a choice between paying a vendor in accordance with the credit terms, or as otherwise promised, and having sufficient cash to cover the employee payroll. Or, you might have to choose between paying a vendor for critical production materials and paying withholding taxes to the federal government. Making a choice between the two would certainly be an ethical dilemma. Who would you make wait for the money? Or, imagine yourself as an employee that has to make a choice between reporting illegal pollution by your employer, which could close down the company and result in your unemployment, or turning a blind eye to the situation to keep your family housed and fed. The short-term interest of both the company and the employee in these examples would be to act unethically.

Or, envision the customer that benefits from a company's mistake and has to decide what to do. Have you ever been given too much change for a purchase or had an item left off a bill? You gain and the business loses. On the flip side, a company may overcharge, double-bill, or somehow provide less than promised. Then you lose and the company gains. The relationship between a company and its customers is fraught with potential ethical challenges.

corporate social responsibility the ethical obligation of a company to its community.

social entrepreneurship the sale of products or services on a for-profit basis to benefit a social purpose.

Learning Objective 7

Incorporate social responsibility into your company.

Social Responsibility and Ethics

Ethics, corporate social responsibility, and social entrepreneurship are three related topics that are often conflated. **Corporate social responsibility** is the ethical obligation of a company to its community. **Social entrepreneurship** is the sale of products and/or services on a for-profit basis to benefit a social purpose. Both have ethical components and can be of value to entrepreneurial firms.

Companies exhibit their commitment to the communities they serve through a variety of means and with varying motivations. Some examples are financial contributions to not-for-profit community organizations, supporting volunteerism, and in-kind donations. An **in-kind donation** is a contribution of products or services, including employee time, rather than cash. Companies also show this commitment through paying livable wages and providing safe and sanitary working conditions. Another aspect of corporate social responsibility is to make any financial investment in only ethical and legal ventures, and in countries with human rights values in alignment with the company's ethics. Environmental friendliness is another way of demonstrating community care. For example, Peninsula Regional Medical Center, on the Eastern Shore of Maryland, is working toward becoming eco-friendly and energy efficient.

in-kind donation a contribution of products or services that may include time or goods, rather than cash.

Leading with Integrity and Examples

Leading by example is the best way to command the attention and respect of others. If you refuse to accept inferior goods, your employees will, too. If you give voice and form to company values and demonstrate integrity, the workplace will become and remain a community of stakeholders that values integrity, honesty, and open communication. Modeling the behavior you desire is an excellent route to attaining the desired results.

Encourage Your Employees to Be Socially Responsible

As you have read, early in the twentieth century, Madam C. J. Walker motivated her employees by encouraging them to get involved in helping their communities, and in the process she became the first African-American millionaire. Entrepreneurs can use their businesses to contribute to society in many ways. By being an entrepreneur, you have already made an important contribution by providing goods or services to consumers in your area who need them. You can also use your business to support social issues that are important to you. By running your company in a way that

Global Impact . . .

Mohammad Yunus and Grameen Bank: Banker to the Poor

Mohammad Yunus, Nobel Peace Prize winner, social entrepreneur, and "banker to the poor," has used his enterprising spirit to foster entrepreneurship and lift literally millions of people out of poverty. He describes his activities: "I did something that challenged the banking world. Conventional banks look for the rich; we look for the absolutely poor. All people are entrepreneurs, but many don't have the opportunity to find out."

Grameen Bank, founded in Bangladesh in 1976, is largely owned by its borrowers. As of December 2012, Grameen Bank had disbursed $1,437 billion (cumulative) and had $997 million in loans outstanding, from 6.71 million active borrowers, served by 2,914 branches, with a staff of 22,610. Over 96 percent of the borrowers are women.[6]

The basis of Grameen Bank's relationship with its borrowers is a core set of values explicitly stated in its Sixteen Decisions. Grameen has found a way to flip conventional banking knowledge on its head. For Grameen Bank, credit is perceived as a

human right, not a benefit for the wealthy. Its branches are distributed across rural areas, bringing the bank to the people.

In 2002, Grameen created its Struggling Members Programme, targeted at beggars. This initiative has encouraged people to give up begging and make a living as door-to-door salespeople. As of 2012, 19,678 of the 111,296 who joined the program had left begging. About 10 percent of the program members became members of mainstream Grameen groups, and 80 percent of the funds disbursed have been repaid.

Mohammad Yunus (Vittorio Zunino Celotto/Getty Images)

Source: Grameen Bank Web, accessed October 5, 2013, http://www.grameen-info.org/.

[6]Grameen Bank, accessed October 6, 2013, http://www.grameen-info.org.

is consistent with your ethics and core values, you will develop a socially responsible business.

Ways to make your business socially responsible include

- recycling paper, glass, and plastic;
- donating a portion of your profits to a charity;
- refusing to use animal testing on products;
- offering employees incentives to volunteer in the community; and
- establishing a safe and healthy workplace.

sustainable referring to a scenario in which current needs are met while preserving future resources.

You can also emphasize being a **sustainable** business, as you ensure meeting the Earth's current needs while preserving resources for future generations.

Chapter Summary

Now that you have studied this chapter, you can do the following:

1. Identify leadership styles.
   - A leader is someone who has the confidence and energy to do things on his or her own.
   - Leadership comes from self-esteem. If you believe in yourself, you can do things with confidence and inspire confidence in others.
   - Leaders learn how to manage their time so they can get more done.
2. Describe the tasks handled by managers.
   - Planning: strategic, tactical, and operational
   - Organizing
   - Leading
   - Controlling
3. Develop your organizational culture.
   - The culture of a company is the shared beliefs, values, and attitudes among employees.
   - The entrepreneur can strategically determine the culture.
   - Cultures vary, from entrepreneurial to administrative.
   - A multitude of cultural components are conveyed through words, actions, and structures.
4. Determine your organizational structure.
   - Structure evolves as the company grows and changes.
   - The transition from entrepreneur to entrepreneurial manager is often difficult.
   - Different organizational stages are related to the maturation of the company.
5. Understand the functions of human resources management.
   - Compensation and payroll
   - Benefits administration
   - Organizational development
   - Education and development
   - Labor law and HR compliance
   - Performance of appraisal and review
   - Human resources strategy
   - Firing and laying off employees

6. Pursue ethical leadership to build an ethical organization.
   - View decisions through an ethical lens.
   - Establish ethical standards.
   - Build ethical employer/employee relationships.
7. Incorporate social responsibility into your company.
   - Encourage environmentalism.
   - Support charitable efforts.
   - Maintain a safe and healthy workplace.
   - Consider sustainability throughout the organization.

Key Terms

advisory board or council
behavioral interview
chain of command
code of conduct
code of ethics
code of ethics and business
   conduct
corporate governance
corporate social responsibility
ethical dilemma
ethical relativism
ethics
human resources
in-kind donation
interview guide
job offer letter

job profile
leader
line organization
line and staff organization
operational plan
payroll tax
performance appraisal
position description
recruitment
severance
social entrepreneurship
span of control
strategic plan
sustainable
tactical plan
tax evasion

Entrepreneurship Portfolio

Critical Thinking Exercises

13-1. Will you be hiring employees during your first year of operations? If so, name their positions and describe the required qualifications, anticipated compensation, and their role in helping your business.

13-2. How can managers make a business a positive and rewarding place to work?

13-3. Why is establishing job profiles and position descriptions before recruiting important?

13-4. What are the benefits of a well-executed performance-appraisal process?

13-5. Describe the components of an organizational culture you would find appealing.

13-6. What are the characteristics of an organizational culture you would find unappealing?

13-7. Describe three leaders you admire. What characteristics do you most admire about them and why?

13-8. Consider ways that you could find 10 additional hours in your weekly schedule to manage your business. Create a weekly time-management schedule for yourself that includes this additional activity.

13-9. Design a Gantt chart for your business or one that you can imagine, or use Microsoft Project or other project software to do the same thing.

13-10. Thinnow Corporation, an entrepreneurial venture, has developed a weight-loss drug, Fatgo. After an intense FDA review and approval process, Thinnow has received permission to bring Fatgo to market. Testing showed that there may serious (even deadly) side effects to the consumers of Fatgo. A warning label is being provided by Thinnow. Identify any legal and ethical issues with this situation.

Key Concept Questions

13-11. How old does someone have to be before he or she can work full time in the United States?

13-12. What is one kind of tax employers have to pay for employees?

13-13. Can you legally fire an employee if you have an argument about religion? Justify your answer.

13-14. What is an interview guide? What are the critical components of an interview guide?

13-15. What are the functions of management? Describe each briefly.

13-16. What are antidiscrimination laws? What protections do they include? Name at least two of them.

13-17. Compare and contrast two leadership styles as identified in this chapter.

13-18. What is a code of conduct? What are its potential benefits?

13-19. What is the relationship between social responsibility and ethics?

Application Exercises

13-20. What qualities and qualifications would you look for in employees for your business? List five and explain why they are the most important to you.

13-21. What would push you to fire an employee? List five reasons you believe would justify termination. Describe how you would expect to handle the firing.

13-22. Visit a local bricks-and-mortar business (not a Web site) where you buy products or services. Go through your shopping experience as you normally would. Once you have left the place of business, describe its culture. Use the information in **Exhibit 13-4** to assist you.

13-23. Identify a business leader, preferably an entrepreneur. Describe his or her leadership style based on at least two public sources (excluding any *wikis*, such as Wikipedia) and give examples to support your conclusion.

13-24. Keep track of the direct opportunities to decide whether to act ethically/unethically and/or legally/illegally that arise during a 48-hour period. What, if anything, surprises you about the list?

13-25. Choose three things you would plan to do to run a socially responsible business. Explain why you made the selections you did.

Exploring Online

13-26. Visit the Web site for a U.S. state, or use another reliable source, to identify the antidiscrimination laws in that state. What form(s) of discrimination do they prohibit? When were they enacted? To which organizations (type and size) do they apply?

13-27. Search the Internet for two position descriptions from different businesses. Make a chart identifying which of the following are included: job title, job summary, duties to be performed, nature of supervision, and the job's relation to others in the company. How might each description be improved?

13-28. Using an online search engine, find a company that practices corporate social responsibility and answer the following:

a. Which values are important?

b. How are these values translated into action?

c. Are the values shared broadly within the company, or are they primarily those of the president/CEO?

In Your Opinion

13-29. Discuss with a group: Should an employer be able to fire an employee if the latter is often ill? Before the discussion, prepare by searching the Internet to determine the legal issues that may be involved. Be ready to identify your sources.

BizBuilder Business Plan Questions

6.0 Management and Operations

6.1 Management Team

    A. Create an organizational chart for your business, if it will have more employees than you at any point. You may want to create one for the start-up period and one for a future time period, such as year 3.

    B. Will you be hiring employees? If so, describe what their qualifications should be, what you intend to pay them, and how they will help your business. Detailed position descriptions can be placed in the appendices.

    C. Do you intend to pay yourself a salary, wage, dividend, or commission? Explain the method and the decision criteria regarding the level of compensation.

    D. What will your most important policies toward employees be? How will you make your organization a positive and rewarding place to work?

    E. Describe the corporate governance plan for your organization. It should include five policies (rules) that will be the backbone of your organization's ethics.

    F. Provide information for each of your mentors or advisors. If there is a board of advisors, list each member and describe his/her commitment to the board.

Appendices

Resumes and Position Descriptions

    A. Include a resume for each key team member.

    B. Add position descriptions for any vital start-up positions that are not yet filled.

AYZH Inc.—Seeing Opportunities to Improve Women's Health

"We exist as a commitment to save lives and change lives, one product at a time, making one happy woman at a time."

—Zubaida Bai

Zubaida Bai is an accomplished professional woman who has chosen a path that incorporates her skills and passions. She is a leading entrepreneur in the delivery of health care to impoverished women. Her role reflects the confluence of a number of facets of her life.

Tim Gainey/Alamy

Zubaida grew up in India and completed her initial education there, earning a degree from Madras University. She studied development of modular products at Sweden's Darlana University en route to a master's degree in engineering. She later moved to the United States and earned an MBA in social sustainability enterprise at Colorado State University.

This entrepreneur and engineer gained several years of work experience in the social development space. One role was as a Project Officer at the Lemelson Foundation Initiative, collaborating with Impoverished Innovations Network and the Indian Institute of Technology Madras. She also knows five languages: English, Hindi, Tamil, Gujarati, and Teluga. Among the terms she uses to describe herself are: "brainstormer, business mentor, change agent . . . social entrepreneur."[7]

Zubaida has earned a number of awards and fellowships, including:

- Echoing Green Fellow—Echoing Green, 2012
- One of 60 Designs to Improve Life Globally—INDEX Awards, 2011
- Affordable Health Innovation Award—World Health Care Congress, 2011
- Young Champion of Maternal Health—Ashoka and Engender Health, 2010
- Outstanding Commitment Award—Clinton Global Initiative University, 2010
- TEDIndia Fellow—TED Ideas Worth Spreading, 2009
- International Presidential Fellow—Colorado State University, 2008[8]

Addressing Social Issues

As a child and young woman in India, Zubaida saw her own mother, and numerous other women, burdened by health and financial struggles. She wanted to find a way to relieve these problems. This purpose became even more personal when Zubaida's first child was born. She contracted an infection at childbirth that left her suffering. Her doctors said more children were out of the question. Zubaida was determined to take action and moved to the United States to add business skills to her engineering know-how.

She founded AYZH Inc. in 2010, with Habib Anwar and Kellen McMartin. Today, Zubaida is a recognized leader in engineering design of economical health products for developing areas.

---

[7]Zubaida Bai, "TED Community: Zubaida Bai," accessed October 6, 2013, http://www.ted.com/profiles/254505.

[8]Changemakers, "About Zubaida Bai: AYZH, Founder and Chief Executive," accessed October 6, 2013, http://www.changemakers.com/users/zubaida-bai.

As Zubaida states, "AYZH aims to be the leading global provider of life-saving, life-changing health products for underprivileged women worldwide. Our goals are to reduce maternal and infant mortality through improved quality of care at time of birth."[9]

Operating as a For-Profit Business with a Social Mission

AYZH's first product is the JANMA (Sanskrit for "birth") Clean Birth Kit. It consists of a biodegradable "purse" with six items that are used to reduce maternal and infant infections and mortality in underprivileged areas of the world. The tools can ensure safe and sterile conditions. The "purse" can be used after the delivery. As of August 2013, AYZH sold 38,000 Clean Birth Kits, primarily in India and Africa.[10] In India, the kits are assembled by local women.

Additional types of kits are planned to meet other needs in related health problems. In addition, the company plans to extend its reach to disadvantaged populations on a global scale. AYZH is focused on connecting its products to the Safe Birth Checklist Initiative of the World Health Organization.

AYZH launched an Indiegogo campaign in August 2013, which raised $14,711 from 114 funders (on a $50,000 goal). The company planned to use the funds for "impact" research and to train healthcare workers.

As a relatively new company, AYZH has a small core team, as well as interns and contract employees. Zubaida serves as Chief Executive. One of her cofounders, Habib Anwar, is responsible for operations and finance. Other team members are responsible for communications and public relations, fundraising, social media, and sales and partnership building. The third cofounder, Kellen McMartin, serves as an advisor. As noted above, assembly of the JANMA Clean Birth Kits is done by contracted women in India.

Growing the Organization's Outreach through Partnerships

AYZH relies on both for-profit and not-for-profit customers and partners to distribute its products to developing areas and for support. For-profit institutions, such as clinics and rural health centers, sell the kits. JANMA Clean Birth Kits are also distributed by nongovernmental aid organizations. Scholars at Harvard University are working to conduct an analysis of Clean Birth Kits' effectiveness in improving health outcomes. In addition, AYZH is partnering with the Rural Technology Business Incubator in India. Rural healthcare workers will receive pertinent information via voice messages through the groundbreaking Mobile Phone Training Program.

If Zubaida Bai has her way, women's health will improve around the world.

Case Study Analysis

13-30. What type of leader do you think Zubaida is, according to Goleman's typology?

13-31. What motivates Zubaida in her company?

13-32. How do her education and experience relate to her role as founder and CEO of AYZH?

13-33. What is the role of ethics at AYZH? How might the company's integrity be challenged?

13-34. What human resource issues would you anticipate for this organization?

Case Sources

Akosha Changemakers, "About Zubaida Bai: AYZH, Founder and Chief Executive," accessed October 6, 2013, http://www.changemakers.com/users/zubaida-bai.

Karen Eng, "Women and Children First: Fellow Friday with Zubaida Bai, who creates lifesaving kits for maternal health," *TED Blog*, August 16, 2013, accessed October 6, 2013, http://blog.ted.com/2013/08/16/women-and-children-first-fellows-friday-with-zubaida-bai-who-creates-lifesaving-kits-for-maternal-health/.

Zubaida Bai, "Small purse BIG CHANGE," Indiegogo.com., August 21, 2013, accessed October 6, 2013, http://www.indiegogo.com/projects/small-purse-big-change.

Zubaida Bai, "TED Community: Zubaida Bai," accessed October 6, 2013, http://www.ted.com/profiles/254505.

---

[9]Karen Eng, "Women and Children First: Fellow Friday with Zubaida Bai, who creates lifesaving kits for maternal health," *TED Blog*, August 16, 2013, accessed October 6, 2013, http://blog.ted.com/2013/08/16/women-and-children-first-fellows-friday-with-zubaida-bai-who-creates-lifesaving-kits-for-maternal-health/.

[10]Zubaida Bai, "Small purse BIG CHANGE," Indiegogo.com, August 21, 2013, accessed October 6, 2013, http://www.indiegogo.com/projects/small-purse-big-change.

Case Study | Crisis at Agritechno Hybrid*

Agritechno geneticist Dr. Lev Andropov is working in his laboratory with his colleague, Dr. Tamika Brown (also a geneticist), and his two lab assistants, André and Bonita. As the four are conducting their work, Donna Holbrook from Marketing, Stefan Girard from Accounting, and Jaylen Castillo from Product Development enter the lab with some discouraging news. They have been getting early reports from growers in the South that some of the caterpillar-resistant transgenic corn developed by Agritechno and planted this year is failing in areas that are having higher than normal rainfall. The group must decide how, if at all, they should report the information to growers and investors.

© Blend Images/Alamy

Dr. Andropov led the team that developed the caterpillar-resistant transgenic corn, in addition to having come up with numerous other strains of insect- and disease-resistant hybrids and varieties of this plant. Dr. Brown has worked alongside Dr. Andropov for many years and is hoping to be promoted to head her own lab for the development of transgenic fruits. The success of the caterpillar-resistant corn would be essential to her being promoted this year. Doctors Andropov and Brown are disappointed to hear of the crop failures and would like to investigate the cause. They do not want to commit to time lines or solutions without proper scientific inquiry.

Stefan Girard is focused on shareholder value and the potential damage to stock prices if these problems leak out to investors. He wants to send a letter to shareholders immediately, stating that the few incidents of crop failure are flukes. At the same time, Donna Holbrook insists on sending a letter to the growers, alerting them to an overwatering problem. Donna, Stefan, and Jaylen Castillo all agree that the letters have to be sent right away because heavy rains are expected in Nebraska, where 40 percent of the seeds have been sold.

Dr. Andropov is frustrated and nearing anger at these suggestions. He asks, "How can we do this? We don't even know that our product is flawed. We cannot send out conflicting messages." Also, he asks, what they should tell people who are both growers *and* investors? Dr. Brown adds that they do not know that the problem is in the seeds, and they cannot say with certainty when an analysis will be completed and a solution found. She does not want to promise what the company cannot deliver.

Jaylen is more anxious about getting a letter out to investors immediately. She suggests telling them that Agritechno's scientists have figured out the problem and found a solution. The scientists bristle at the suggestion.

Donna then attempts to find a satisfactory approach for all participants by reframing the situation to focus on yields for the coming year. Dr. Andropov is not satisfied with this option, noting that Agritechno won't know how many bushels of the transgenic corn have been produced for another four or five months, and they won't be able to fully identify the problem until then. He suggests sending out a letter stating that a few crops have failed and Agritechno is investigating.

Stefan grumbles that he hates to report problems to investors because it scares them away.

---

*This is a fictional case study developed to illustrate topics covered in this chapter.

Case Study Analysis

13-35. Why are Drs. Andropov and Brown frustrated and angry about the suggestions from Holbrook, Girard, and Castillo?

13-36. What are the arguments for and against notifying Agritechno's investors? What is the basis for each argument?

13-37. What are the arguments for and against notifying Agritechno's growers? What is the basis for each argument?

13-38. What method of communication, if any, would you recommend for investors? Growers?

13-39. What should Agritechno tell its investors and growers, if anything, about the crop failures and proposed solutions?

Case Study | Casino Grande[11]

In the early afternoon of June 20, 1992, as Roger Parks, the reservation manager of Casino Grande, was packing his briefcase to go out of town to a hospitality association conference, Randolph Jackson, the general manager, called him into his office and the following conversation ensued.

Don Hammond/Alamy Images

Jackson: Damn it, Roger, didn't I tell you to talk to those two girls about getting to work on time? All they do around here is drink coffee. I guess I'm going to have to install martial law around here. They both recently got raises, too; who do they think they are, anyhow? You tell them in no uncertain terms that if they don't shape up, we'll give them the sack. We can still hire people who follow the rules.

Parks: Whoa, back! What's going on? What in the heck are you talking about?

Jackson: Don't pretend with me. You know just what I'm talking about. It's those two girls, Kane and Palumbo. I saw them come into the employee cafeteria this morning at 8:00 and they were still there when I left at 8:20 to come upstairs. They couldn't have gotten to their desks until 8:30 or later! Then, at 10:30 they were back down there for coffee; I saw them with my own eyes! They're just going to have to shape up. Other people have noticed as well. Why, Cooperider (housekeeping assistant manager) mentioned it just the other day. Why on earth didn't you talk with them like I told you to do?

Parks: Cool it, Randy. I did talk the whole thing over with Marshall, and she talked with the two women. She told me later that she had, and said the women had agreed to do better from then on.

Jackson: Posh, they aren't doing it! We just gave them salary increases, too. We gave them increases, and that's how they're showing their appreciation. I say, if they don't shape up we fire their butts. That Kane's a pain. She says she wants more responsibility, we give it to her, and a raise; and then she comes in late every morning and drinks coffee all day long.

Parks: Simmer down, Randy. You'll have to admit we don't set much of an example. It seems there is always a gang of supervisors in the coffee line at all times, and your secretary and her friend stand around the cigarette machine way after 8:00 A.M.

Jackson: That's not relevant. You can't get cigarettes unless you stand in that line. Cripes, we can't go clear out to the lobby stand, can we? Oh, it's all right to grab a cup of coffee on occasion, but those two girls are always out together. They're abusing the privileges. They drive to work together every day; I've seen them, and then they go into the cafeteria at 8:00 and have breakfast. It's got to end.

Parks: Okay, okay. We'll have another chat with them. The offices and the whole back-of-the-house are pretty lax in regard to timeliness. I agree we don't want reservations standing out as the worst offenders. Part of it is that they go out together, and that makes it conspicuous alright. I'm leaving town this afternoon, but I'll talk with them personally today and let you know before I take off.

Jackson: Okay. Just make it good. We've got to stop abuses, or we'll just have to crack down on everyone. It's always a few who make it hard on everyone.

On the way back to his own office, Mr. Parks detoured into reservations and found Ms. Jean Marshall, talking on the telephone. When she hung up, Mr. Parks related his conversations with

[11]Craig C. Lundberg and Cheri A. Young, *The Hospitality Case Manual: Developing Competencies in Critical Thinking and Practical Action*, Upper Saddle River, N.J.: Pearson Education, Inc., 2009, pp. 152–156.

Mr. Jackson. This was the second time in two months that Mr. Jackson had called the behavior of Kane and Palumbo to his attention. After a brief discussion, they decided that the proper thing to do was to call the two women into the departmental conference room and talk with them. When Mr. Parks, Ms. Marshall, Mrs. Kane, and Mrs. Palumbo had assembled, the following conversation took place.

Parks: While I sure don't like to bring up a complaint a few hours before I go out of town, I've just come from Mr. Jackson's office. He has complained again about you two getting to work late and about you taking so much time away from your desks for coffee. He rather emphatically stated that he has seen you in the cafeteria after 8:00 several times and that you both seem to be there having coffee together every time he stops by. I believe Jean spoke with you about this several weeks ago. What do you think we ought to do about it?

Kane: Yes, Ms. Marshall talked to us before about it. We've been trying to watch it since then. I believe we've been doing a lot better. You know how hard it is to get to work winter mornings, and we do go down once in a while for a cup of coffee. The new cafeteria is so nice now. Everybody is using it more. Why shouldn't we?

Parks: Yes, you're right, of course. More people are using the cafeteria. You'll agree with me, I'm sure, that this property has a pretty relaxed attitude about getting to work on time occasionally and about getting out of the office for coffee or Coke or a smoke. But let's face it. Mr. Jackson is riled. If we abuse the privileges we have, it will be necessary for Jackson to create some rules that constrict us. We'll all suffer then. There must be some way you can work it out so you'll not be so conspicuous when you take a break once in a while? Isn't it possible for you two to get to work on time so when you take a break it won't be so objectionable?

Kane: All the other reservations women do it. All the office force does it. The smokers go out all the time. Most use the lavs, but it's always so crowded there we prefer to go down to the cafeteria.

Parks: Part of the problem, of course, is that you two are always seen together. That makes you stand out. Why can't you split up, or go some other place? Mrs. Kane, you've indicated more than once that you want more responsibility in reservations. Let's face it; we can't get it for you if the GM thinks you're abusing the situation.

Kane: Of course that makes sense. What do you want us to do? Stop taking breaks altogether?

Parks: Mrs. Palumbo, what do you think you should do?

Palumbo: Gee, I don't know. We don't do anything that the others don't do. But we don't want to get into trouble. The Casino has been generous enough.

Parks: The way things stand now, well, you can see how things are. Both Mr. Jackson and Cooperider have commented on you. Jackson's the GM, remember, he approves all job changes and all recommendations for raises. It's just not smart to have him on your case.

Kane: We want to do what's right, of course. I sure wouldn't want to do anything that would hinder my next promotion. I suppose we could go somewhere else and maybe not take so many breaks—at least not together. Suppose we lay low for a while until the top brass forgets about it?

Parks: And, get to work a little more promptly in the morning. Sure, all of us are a touch lax sometimes about getting in on time, but the finger is pointing at you, so how about doing a bit better than you've been doing of late?

Kane: Okay, but as you know, I've three kids to get off to school every day. What with car problems, the storms tying traffic up, it's awfully hard to get here on time.

Parks: I'll leave it up to you. I know you're both good workers, and I know you're both trying to get ahead here. You must realize that if old Jackson doesn't see an immediate turnaround, well, I'm not sure what he'll do. You've been talked to twice now. We wouldn't want our GM to do something that would hurt all of the staff, now, would we? (Pause) Jean, what do you think is the best thing to do?

Marshall: You've outlined the situation very well, Mr. Parks. I think these women are attracting undue attention by going out together all the time. The whole staff has been lax about starting promptly. I'll certainly work with reservations to see that we put a drive on to get us to work on time. I think they shouldn't take quite so many breaks, and not together. That way they won't cause so many negative comments.

Parks: Well, it's up to these women. I'm about to leave for a conference, tonight, in fact. I'll be away, so I won't hear anything. If Jackson gets in a twit, he'll no doubt call you down, Jean, and I know you'll do whatever he says. See if you two ladies can't stay out of trouble, please. I'll be back in five days. Good luck.

Roger Parks returned to his own office and telephoned Mr. Jackson. He told Jackson that he and Ms. Marshall had talked to Kane and Palumbo and that he believed that Jackson would see an immediate improvement. Parks asked Jackson to call Ms. Marshall if there are any further complaints. Jackson replied, "You're darn right I will."

About Casino Grande

Casino Grande was an older, mid-sized casino hotel, employing approximately 2,000 people, on the boardwalk section of a mid-Atlantic city. Mr. Randolph Jackson was the general manager of Casino Grande and, as such, had the ultimate authority over all departments and functions at the property. He took unusual interest in the human resource activities of the casino/hotel, establishing both personnel policies and office procedure personally. The ordinary interpretation of these policies and procedures, however, was handled by the department managers and section supervisors with consultation available from the employee relations department.

Roger Parks was the manager of Casino Grande's reservations department. He had begun his employment with the casino in 1982 as a night programmer in the accounting department, while he was finishing his B.S. in hotel administration from a prominent eastern university. After graduation, Roger continued to work in accounting for two years; then he requested a transfer to the newly established computer system group, where he worked for another two years before he replaced a section head and, thus, acquired his first truly supervisory experience. In late 1987,

Roger obtained an interview for a section manager's position in the front desk department, and for which he was hired. In 1990, Casino Grande significantly upgraded its computer facilities, including a sophisticated reservations system. Roger was transferred to the reservations unit to take charge of it. When he began to organize this function, he hired Ms. Marshall and two clerks. About a year later, when an opening occurred, Mrs. Kane was hired. In Mr. Parks's opinion, Ms. Marshall was a technical whiz who got along fairly well with her people. She had a reputation within the reservations group of sometimes being impatient; she kidded her workers a lot and usually got a lot of high-quality work from them, but was considered somewhat lax in enforcing discipline.

Mrs. Kane, about 39 years old, had three children of ages 11, 8, and 6. Her husband was a sales trainer with a major manufacturing company and was away from home for extended periods. Mrs. Kane's mother lived with them, taking care of the children so that Mrs. Kane could work. She was made senior reservations clerk on January 1, 1992, receiving a substantial raise. At that time, Mrs. Kane was told she was doing excellent work but had a quick temper that sometimes disturbed her fellow employees. She was also told that she often disrupted the office by talking too loudly and too often. The position of senior reservationist provided a wage differential over the others and required her coworkers to bring their questions about procedures and assignments to her. All other matters, such as salary and training questions as well as performance appraisals, were handled by Ms. Marshall. Mrs. Kane took her work seriously and expressed resentment toward the indifferent attitude of the younger reservation clerks. She was trying to get ahead financially. She did not like housekeeping or childcare and planned to continue working as long as her mother could look after her children.

Mrs. Palumbo was about 28 years old and a college graduate. Her husband was in the Army and had been in the Middle East for two tours after Operation Desert Storm. Mrs. Palumbo lived alone in a small apartment and planned on working only until her husband was posted in the United States. Mrs. Palumbo did a good job as a reservation clerk and got along well with everyone in the department. She also got a raise on January 1, 1992.

The office rules at Casino Grande did not permit smoking on the job but allowed personnel to leave the office to do so, although there were no designated smoking spaces.

On Monday, August 15, 1992, the following notice was posted on the bulletin board just inside the employees' entrance to the property:

TO: All Casino Grande Office Personnel

Some employees have been taking advantage of our company's coffee break privilege. In order to be fair to those who are being reasonable about going to the cafeteria for coffee, we do not wish to rescind this privilege altogether. We do expect all office employees to start work at 8:00 in the morning, meaning come ready to work, already having had breakfast. There is no excuse for having coffee, therefore, after 8:00 A.M.

From now on the following rules will apply to coffee breaks:

1. No one should visit the cafeteria for coffee before 9:30 A.M.
2. Groups from the same department should not take breaks together, since this would disrupt the service provided.
3. No one should stay away from his/her workstation for longer than 15 minutes.
4. It is unnecessary to leave one's office for coffee or any other beverage more than once a day.

These simple rules should be clear to everyone. If, in the future, these rules are ignored, the coffee break privilege will be canceled altogether. Your wholehearted cooperation is expected.

R. L. Jackson
General Manager

Case Study Analysis

13-40. List the pros and cons of Mr. Jackson's decision to post the coffee-break notice. Was it a good management decision? Why or why not?

13-41. Imagine a scenario where you are Mr. Parks. What do you think you would have done after the conversation with Mr. Jackson? Write a paragraph describing your action plan.

13-42. Write a paragraph describing Mr. Jackson's philosophy of human-resources management.

13-43. List some examples of why the ladies might see the reprimands as unfair or unjust.

13-44. What is Jackson's leadership style?

ONLC Training Centers—
Virtual IT Training in a Classroom

ONLC Training Centers has used its many locations to drive significant sales growth and become one of the leaders in the information technology (IT) training industry, an industry that was in rapid decline from 2000 through 2009. Today, ONLC has some 300 locations from coast to coast; but as recently as 2004 it only had offices in Philadelphia; Wilmington, Delaware; and Princeton, New Jersey. In 2009, ONLC Training Centers was named the eighth fastest-growing education company on *Inc.* magazine's list of fastest-growing companies. How did it achieve such remarkable growth in a declining industry during the worst economic downturn in 70 years?

Riding the Tide and Battling the Currents

Bucking industry and economic trends, ONLC realized multiple new revenue streams by rapidly expanding its geographic distribution of classroom training. In 2009, approximately 50 percent of ONLC's revenues came from sites that had not been open a year earlier. Two of the key drivers to the success were the strategic use of locations to accelerate sales and the redefinition of classroom training.

Jim Palic and Andy Williamson, ONLC
(ONLC Training Centers)

Andy Williamson and Jim Palic left the DuPont Company to cofound ONLC in 1983, and they were at the leading edge of the PC revolution when they began offering classroom training to individuals using personal computers in the workplace. Throughout the rest of the 1980s and the 1990s, their original facilities were IT classrooms designed for face-to-face instruction. However, as corporate training and travel funds dried up after 2000, the demand for these services dropped precipitously and the industry consolidated rapidly. Many companies with large computer-training facilities closed or switched to other lines of business, such as IT consulting.

Pivoting the Business

Andy and Jim recognized that, although the demand for training had significantly declined, it had not disappeared. To serve the small market demand for public IT training (classes not held by companies on their own sites), they needed to transform their business model.

They considered offering virtual training, where people would join ONLC's classes from their homes or offices, which would certainly reduce costs. However, their years of industry experience taught them that people preferred formal classroom training for many good reasons. A classroom provides an interruption-free environment in which to learn. There are fewer technical issues when training is conducted in a classroom. And last, but not least important, going to an offsite location elevates the importance of the event and helps people focus on the job of learning.

The founders thought they could design a training offering that would include the classroom as an important part of the mix. Adding an actual classroom to virtual training would significantly increase ONLC costs but provide a better learning experience. In addition, they saw that their competitors were beginning to offer virtual training. If hundreds of other companies started to offer training virtually, how would ONLC be able to differentiate itself?

Differentiation through Remote Classroom Instruction

Instead of abandoning bricks-and-mortar classroom-based training, Andy and Jim decided to go deeper into that strategy. They designed a virtual training solution that keeps the classroom as part of the solution and called it "remote classroom instruction" (RCI). Their clients obtain a higher-quality learning solution, and ONLC achieves a more defensible market position.

Challenges Facing Classroom IT Training after 2000.
(Courtesy of ONLC Training Centers)

Their solution was this: a single national training schedule is promoted on the ONLC Web site (http://www.onlc.com). If people see a class that they want to take that is running on January 15, for example, they can register for that class in any one of over 250 locations around the country. These locations contain small classrooms that can seat two to four people at a time. The class running on January 15 might be taught in a traditional classroom in Philadelphia, with an instructor teaching three students face-to-face in that room. In addition, as many as nine other people could be joining the class from up to nine other physical locations around the country.

"It is our ability to easily aggregate low demand for public training that makes our model successful," Andy explains. By combining the enrollments from hundreds of locations, they are able to have fewer classes cancelled because of low enrollments. In any given city, there might only be one or two people interested in an event. Whereas competitors who needed a large number of students in a room with an instructor would have had to cancel the class, ONLC is able to run it with one attendee.

Systematic Site Selection

ONLC management has carefully studied potential opportunities and identified strategic roll-out priorities by looking at U.S. Census data by metropolitan statistical areas (MSAs). Unlike its old business model, in which leases were secured for multiple years and each site had to be staffed, the new model relies on a network of executive-suite locations. The company can sign short-term, six-month leases for only the needed space. It can start by renting a single classroom in any city. If demand becomes strong enough, it can rent additional rooms; if demand is low, it can cancel the lease at the end of the term and redeploy its computer hardware to a new, more productive location.

Training sites in areas with greater population densities have survived because there were more people. However, some rural areas are also successful. While those areas have lower demand, there are typically no direct

ONLC Training Sites—2013.
(Courtesy of ONLC Training Centers)

competitors. Whereas the total demand in the area might be relatively low, the demand facing the firm is higher, because ONLC can capture a larger share of the market. In addition, the small-site strategy is more cost effective.

ONLC estimates that over 80 percent of the U.S. population is within an hour's drive from one of its training sites. Andy explains how ONLC has overcome the tyranny of geography that author Chris Anderson defines as an audience being spread so thinly that it is the same as no audience at all.[12] Andy observes, "People wanting training in remote locations have been suffering from the tyranny of geography where no classroom training is available to them because demand is so low. When demand for a particular class drops below a certain point, a traditional face-to-face class is taken off the schedule of the local training company. When demand for IT training in general drops below a certain point, the traditional training company closes its doors."

The Business of ONLC Is Logistics

By creating hundreds of small, efficient training facilities and aggregating the demand for training across the country through its remote-classroom-instruction model, ONLC cost-effectively captures the demand for public IT classes. The staff schedules more than 100 events and registers more than 700 students weekly. Then, they ensure that each class has an instructor and that books are shipped to hundreds of locations each week. Student and instructor connections are established for each class and phone bridges are managed. In fact, ONLC is a logistics company that delivers training.

Through rapidly expanding the number of training facilities to provide nationwide coverage and by redefining classroom training with its RCI model, ONLC cost-effectively delivers classroom training where its competitors can't. As Andy says, "Lowering the cost of delivery has radically changed the economics of providing training and has democratized distribution. It has also positioned ONLC for a successful future delivering virtual training in a classroom."

Case Study Analysis

U4-1. What does ONLC do to determine where to offer training? What are the critical location factors?

U4-2. How does this business model democratize distribution?

U4-3. How can ONLC have over 300 locations and maintain an efficient cost structure at low volumes in each?

U4-4. What is the level of importance of the location of the ONLC headquarters? Why?

U4-5. What were the main differentiating characteristics of ONLC's remote-classroom-instruction offering, compared to its competitors who were also offering virtual training?

U4-6. What is the ONLC business model?

Case Source

Courtesy of ONLC Inc.

---

[12]Chris Anderson, *The Long Tail: Why the Future of Business Is Selling Less of More*, New York: Hyperion, 2006.

CASHING IN THE BRAND

Phasinphoto/Fotolia

14

CHAPTER

Franchising, Licensing, and Harvesting: Cashing in Your Brand

Learning Objectives

1. Assess how you want to grow your business and eventually exit from it.

2. Describe how businesses use licensing to profit from their brands.

3. Explain how a business can be franchised.

4. Use methods of valuing a business.

5. Compare five ways to harvest a business.

Evan Agostini/
Getty Images

*"All businesses were launched by entrepreneurs
and all were once small."*

—Nat Shulman, family business owner and columnist

Paula Jagemann

Some entrepreneurs have experienced more than one way to exit from a business. Paula Jagemann is a serial entrepreneur who has taken one company public, sold another one, and then retired. Paula was the Vice President of Investor and Public Relations at UUNET Technologies Inc., which was the largest Internet service provider in the world when it went public on the NASDAQ in 1995. She was there when it was acquired by Metropolitan Fiber Systems (MFS) for $2 billion in 1996, and when WorldCom acquired MFS for $12.4 billion later that year, and she stayed on through the merger of MCI and WorldCom.

In her early 30s and not ready to retire, Paula formed OnLineOfficeSupplies.com as the first online office-supply retail company, and it reached $18 million in sales in 18 months. She and her co-founders sold it in 2001 to First Call Office Products. She also cofounded eCommerce Industries, Inc. (ECI^2) to support the business systems needed for OnLineOfficeSupplies and recognized that the greater potential was in ECI^2. The company was awarded Microsoft's Ecommerce Solution of the Year in 2000 and continues to thrive. Paula sold the company for $95 million in 2005 and retired, vowing to avoid start-ups.

In 2010, Paula was serving on the board of trustees of her local hospital when she discovered a need for convenient, accessible, and reliable sources for products that served people who had breast cancer. She was lured out of retirement to create Someone With, LLC, which was launched in 2011. She quickly learned that there also was a need for a funding mechanism to support the high cost of products that were required but not covered by private health insurance or Medicare. More recently, she led the formation of the Someone With Group, which created a debit-based solution for health care systems. Whether Someone With will eventually be acquired or go public, it is not likely that Paula will exit via retirement anytime soon.

What Do You Want from Your Business?

Learning Objective 1

Assess how you want to grow your business and eventually exit from it.

Just as people start businesses for a variety of reasons and have different goals and objectives, they also have different reasons for leaving them—and different ways of doing so. Some entrepreneurs enjoy the stability and earnings associated with carrying on a successful business they have established. Others want to "grow and go." Still others are serial entrepreneurs, who create new ventures repeatedly. What do you want? **Exhibit 14-1** identifies some of the options available.

Regardless of which route you choose, your business plan should clearly state your intentions. If you are asking people to invest, you should tell them how they will realize the return on their investment. If it will take several years to grow the business, that should also be spelled out.

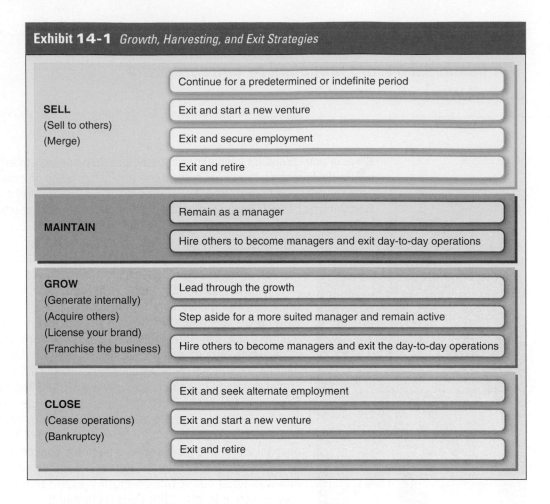

Exhibit 14-1 *Growth, Harvesting, and Exit Strategies*

SELL
(Sell to others)
(Merge)

- Continue for a predetermined or indefinite period
- Exit and start a new venture
- Exit and secure employment
- Exit and retire

MAINTAIN

- Remain as a manager
- Hire others to become managers and exit day-to-day operations

GROW
(Generate internally)
(Acquire others)
(License your brand)
(Franchise the business)

- Lead through the growth
- Step aside for a more suited manager and remain active
- Hire others to become managers and exit the day-to-day operations

CLOSE
(Cease operations)
(Bankruptcy)

- Exit and seek alternate employment
- Exit and start a new venture
- Exit and retire

Continuing the Business for the Family

The multigenerational family-owned-and-operated business best exemplifies the company that provides continued employment and wealth to an entrepreneur and his relatives. Malden Mills, a company located in Lawrence, Massachusetts, that continued to pay its employees while rebuilding following a fire, was an example of a firm that was operated as a closely held private company for three generations and had a clear interest in maintaining employment in its community. For this type of business, sufficient cash flow for wages and continued operations is primary. If such a venture is your goal, create a growth plan that will permit you to buy back investments from outsiders, so that the business will be truly family-owned.

Growth through Diversification

diversification the addition of product or service offerings beyond a business's core product or service.

One way to grow your business is to use **diversification**, which is the addition of offerings beyond your core product or service. By diversifying your operations, you will be increasing the potential for sales. To a budding entrepreneur or a seasoned executive, diversification can be the way to get more market share. On the flip side, author and marketing expert Al Ries argues that diversification comes at a price: "It unfocuses the company and leads to loss of power."[1] Focusing, in contrast, attracts the right employees to a company and reinforces its strength in the marketplace.

---

[1]Al Ries, *Focus: The Future of Your Company Depends on It*, New York: Harper Business, 1996, p. 273.

Growth through Licensing and Franchising

One way to grow without considerable direct investment in physical and human capital is through **licensing**, or renting your brand or other intellectual property to sell products. Another way to replicate a successful business formula is through franchising.

It is important that you are aware of the possibilities offered by franchising and licensing from the moment you start your business. Stay organized and try to develop a foolproof operational system. Someday hundreds, or even thousands, of entrepreneurs might be eager to buy or rent that system from you.

Franchising and licensing are called **replication strategies**, because they are ways to obtain money from a business you created by letting others copy (*replicate*) it.

licensing renting your brand or other intellectual property to increase sales.

replication strategy a way for a business to obtain money by letting others copy its success formula for a fee.

Focus Your Brand

As noted in Unit 3, a *brand* identifies the products or services of a company and differentiates them from those of competitors—representing the company's promise to deliver consistently a specific set of benefits to its customers. Customers who buy Liz Claiborne clothes, for example, expect classic styling suitable for the workplace. They have come to trust that brand to meet their needs.

Businesses do better when customers know what to expect from their brands, according to Ries.[2] He argues that, in industry after industry, the narrowly focused companies are the big winners. He contends that too many managers are hooked on growth for its own sake and develop misguided expansion that dilutes the strength of a company's brand.

Many companies known for one type of merchandise, such as Adidas with its athletic shoes, have applied their brand with disastrous results—such as Adidas cologne. Sneakers and cologne were not a good association. Bic, known for its pens, branched into panty hose and had a similar failure.

Using an established brand to promote different kinds of products is called **line extension**. It can work if the brand is strong and the new product is not completely dissimilar to the original. For example, the Jell-O brand name was successfully applied to a line of puddings, after it had been established as the preeminent gelatin dessert.

< Learning Objective 2
Describe how businesses use licensing to profit from their brands.

line extension using an established brand to promote different kinds of products.

When Licensing Can Be Effective

A company can profitably license its brand when it has a core group of loyal customers. Licensing is effective when the licensor is confident that the company name will be enhanced by the licensee's use of it. If Coca-Cola licensed its name to a T-shirt manufacturer that wanted to print its logo on T-shirts, Coca-Cola would get free advertising as well as royalties.

However, licensing, if not handled carefully, can damage your brand. For example, if the T-shirt maker used the Coca-Cola logo on T-shirts that contained obscene messages, the company's reputation would be tarnished. Coca-Cola would

The Hard Rock Hotel and Casino, Las Vegas; a clearly focused brand can go a long way.
(© Dave Stamboulis/Alamy)

[2]*Ibid.*

A Pizza Hut franchise in Los Angeles.
(Bill Aron/PhotoEdit Inc.)

not license its name to a soft-drink manufacturer because it would be creating a direct competitor. Licensing your brand is one potential way to increase brand recognition and extend your product line without investing in entry into additional markets or producing new product lines.

Franchising Revisited from the Franchisor Perspective

As discussed in Chapter 1, a franchise is a business that markets a product or service in the manner prescribed by the parent business. One way for you to start a business would be to secure a franchise; you also could develop a concept and a business operation that could be reproduced and licensed to other entrepreneurs. They would buy the right to run the business in the way you prescribed and pay you a franchise fee and royalties.

There are both benefits and drawbacks to being a franchisor. The benefits include:

- growth with minimal capital investment;
- lower marketing and promotional costs; and
- royalties.

The drawbacks to the franchisor include:

- the potential for a tarnished franchise reputation if a franchisee disregards the training and fails to operate the business properly;
- difficulty securing qualified franchisees;
- payment issues and lawsuits from franchisees that do not experience success; and
- costs and challenges due to the many federal and state regulations regarding franchising.

How a McDonald's Franchise Works

Let's look at how franchising can grow a business. McDonald's is a classic example of a franchise operation. McDonald's was developed by Ray Kroc, who had persuaded the McDonald brothers to let him become the franchising agent for their highly successful hamburger restaurant in San Bernardino, California, in 1955. Kroc's great insight was to realize that the people who bought McDonald's franchises would need extensive training and support in order to make the food taste like that of the original restaurant. Kroc timed and measured everything exactly. McDonald's franchisees are taught precisely how many minutes to fry potatoes and when to turn a burger, among a host of other details. They are even taught how to greet customers.

A McDonald's franchisee owns the restaurant, but agrees to market the food under the McDonald's name and trademark following the precise methods developed by the company. This is spelled out in the franchise agreement. In return, the franchisee knows that he or she is investing in a proven, successful business concept. The franchisee also benefits from use of the McDonald's trademark and from the management training, marketing, national advertising, and promotional assistance provided by the parent company. McDonald's, as franchisor, receives a franchise fee and royalties.

Although franchising has existed in the United States since the Singer Sewing Machine Company first developed it in the 1850s, its popularity has exploded over the last several decades. The number of individual franchises has grown to approximately 750,000, with thousands of franchisors in the market space.[3]

Do Your Research before You Franchise

Before you get involved in franchising your business, consult with a franchise attorney and carry out extensive research. The International Franchise Association (http://www.franchise.org) provides considerable information for franchisors, including a prospective franchise forum. Use available resources to understand what is expected of a franchisor and how the relationship works, before speaking with an entrepreneur who is interested in a franchise. Recognize that your franchisees will expect significant support and attention for the fees they pay you. To better understand the franchisee perspective, you can visit the American Association of Franchisees and Dealers at http://www.aafd.org. You must offer products or services that are sufficiently original and create unique marketing strategies to justify the cost of the franchise.

Part of the process of franchising a business will be to create a franchise agreement, which is the contract between the franchisor and franchisee. This contract establishes the standards that assure uniformity of product (or service) throughout the franchise chain.

> **◀ Learning Objective 3**
> Explain how a business can be franchised.

Harvesting and Exiting Options

Licensing and franchising are possible growth strategies for entrepreneurs who want to stay in a business. For those who do not wish to continue their businesses, harvesting and exiting are options.

When to Harvest Your Business

There may come a time in the life of your firm when you will want to close or leave it. **Harvesting** your business means you sell it, take it public, or merge with another company. Unlike replication, the entrepreneur is usually no longer involved once the business is harvested; he or she walks away with cash, stock, or a combination of the two. The founding entrepreneur may also work in the reorganized company for a specified time period.

In William Petty's article on harvesting,[4] he quotes Steven Covey, author of *The Seven Habits of Highly Effective People*, who writes that a key to being effective in life is "beginning with the end in mind." To that, Petty adds, "If the entrepreneur's goal with the venture is only to provide a living, then the exit or harvest strategy is of no concern. But if the goal is to create value for the owners and the other stakeholders in the company, a harvest strategy is absolutely mandatory."

It usually requires at least 10 years to build a company of sufficient value to harvest. Make the timing of harvesting part of the plans for your business. The harvest strategy is important to the investors because it lets them know up front how their investment will eventually be turned into cash or stock.

> **harvesting** the act of selling, taking public, or merging a company to yield proceeds for the owner(s).

---

[3]International Franchise Association, "2013 Franchise Business Outlook," accessed October 7, 2013, http://emarket.franchise.org/UpdateEconomicOutlookInfographic_March2013.pdf

[4]William Petty, "Harvesting," in *The Portable MBA in Entrepreneurship*, 2nd ed., William D. Bygrave, ed., New York: Wiley, 1997, p. 103.

Global Impact . . .

Photodisc/Thinkstock/Getty Images

VISTA Staffing Solutions: Global Physician Staffing Founders Acquired

VISTA Staffing Solutions is a leading provider of permanent-physician search services and *locum tenens*, or temporary physician staffing. The business was founded in 1990 as an employee-owned company, with medical practices, hospitals, and governments as its primary clients. VISTA provides short- and long-term placements in the United States and internationally (Australia and New Zealand). The founders of VISTA are Mark Brouse, Katie Abby, and Clarke Shaw.

VISTA Staffing Solutions was acquired by On Assignment, Inc., a NASDAQ-traded leader in the professional staffing industry, in 2007. The sale included $41 million in cash and an earn-out provision. VISTA shareholders and option holders could receive an additional $8 million, depending on the firm's performance. At the time of its acquisition, VISTA had a pool of more than 1,300 physicians and had anticipated revenues in excess of $60 million.

Mark Brouse stated, "The two companies have remarkably similar cultures, putting people first and providing the best professional for each assignment. With the VISTA management team staying in place following the completion of the transaction, we believe the combined organization will be well positioned to maximize growth opportunities and achieve operating efficiencies." Two years after the acquisition, all three founders continued to manage VISTA Staffing Solutions.

Source: On Assignment, Inc. Web site, http://www.onassignment.com, press release dated December 21, 2006, and VISTA Staffing Solutions, accessed October 7, 2013, http://www.vistastaff.com.

Not every business can be harvested. Some are loaded with debt or have not created a product or service of lasting value. The entrepreneur can only leave such a business via **liquidation** (selling all the assets), closure, or bankruptcy.

liquidation the sale of all assets of a business concurrent with its being closed.

How to Value a Business

Learning Objective 4

Use methods of valuing a business.

Business valuation is both an art and a science. A business that is profitable and likely to be so in the future can be sold for a sum that represents its *net present value* today. This is net present value in action. (Most wealth is created by buying and selling assets that will have a *future* value.) Ultimately, a business is worth what others are willing to pay for it and what the owners will accept.

There are many ways to estimate the net present value of a business. Value, after all, is *subjective*, meaning it is based on individual opinion or preference. One person might be willing to pay a higher price than another would. The first buyer feels more optimistic about the business's future (and may have some personal insight in that regard) or may simply want it more than another potential buyer does.

Here are some methods entrepreneurs use to estimate the value of a business:

- Compare it with similar businesses. If you are looking to sell your dry-cleaning company, check out, if possible, how much other dry-cleaning stores in your area are bringing in when they are sold.
- Use industry benchmarks. In most industries, there are one or two key benchmarks that will help to value a business. For gas stations, it might be the amount of gasoline sold per week; for a dry cleaner, it might be the number of shirts laundered per week.
- Look at a multiple of net earnings. One rule of thumb says a business can be sold for about three to five times its annual net earnings. If the business earns $100,000 net profit per year, for example, it could be expected to sell for at least $300,000.

The ultimate goal of company valuation is to arrive at a **fair market value**, which, according to the IRS, is "The price at which property would change hands between a willing buyer and willing seller, neither under any compulsion to buy or sell and both having reasonable knowledge of the relevant facts."[5]

fair market value the price at which a property or business is valued by the marketplace; the price it would fetch on the open market.

The Science of Valuation

There are three primary methods that buyers and sellers use: book value, future earnings, and market-based value. These three approaches are often used concurrently, and all provide helpful perspectives on a company's value. Furthermore, there are variations on each. The SBA Web site provides assistance in valuation, and accountants and other professional business advisors can provide assistance as well.

- **Book value (net worth = assets − liabilities).** One of the most common methods for computing a company's valuation, the **book value** technique, looks at a company as assets minus liabilities. This is the most common way to value companies, and also the simplest. Note, book value does not take into account the fact that assets are estimated at their depreciated level rather than at market value.

book value valuation of a company as assets minus liabilities.

- **Future earnings.** This system uses a company's estimated future earnings as the main determinant of its value. It is most useful for companies that are growing quickly. In these cases, past earnings are not accurate reflections of future performance. This method of valuation must take into account the time value of money, as well as the rate of return.

- **Market-based (value = P/E ratio × estimated future net earnings).** In the market-based approach, the value of the company is compiled from the price/earnings (P/E) ratio of comparable public companies. The P/E ratio is determined by dividing a company's stock price by its earnings per share. This method is effective because of its simplicity, but may be lacking when there are no similar public companies with which to compare the business.

Despite the sophistication of these three techniques, all of them are ultimately only estimates. Each business will have particular characteristics and special circumstances. In the end, it will be the entrepreneur's job to get the highest price possible through negotiation.

Once you decide to sell your business or pursue some other exit strategy, use the Internet to maximize your prospects. You can list your business with such databases as http://www.BizBuySell.com or http://www.BizQuest.com, which sends registered users who might want to buy your business e-mails alerting them to your offer.

Creating Wealth by Selling a Profitable Business

As noted previously, a successful small business can usually be sold for between three and five times its yearly net profit, because the buyer expects the business to continue to keep generating income. If your net profit for one year is $10,000, you should be able to get at least $30,000 (3 × $10,000). From the buyer's perspective, this represents a 33 1/3 percent annual

---

[5]Available at http://www.irs.gov.

return on the investment required to buy the business ($10,000/$30,000 = 33 1/3%), which is a very attractive return.

If you are in business for three years, however, and increase your net profit each year, your business will be worth even more. If your company earns $10,000 in year one, $25,000 in year two, and $60,000 in year three, it could be valued at $180,000 by applying the three-times rule of thumb. How a business grows will affect its value. A business with increasing yearly net profit will be considered more valuable than a business with static earnings.

Entrepreneurs establish successful businesses, sell them, and use the resulting wealth to create new enterprises and more wealth. Entrepreneurs also use their wealth to support political, environmental, and social causes. What will you do with your wealth?

Harvesting Options

Learning Objective 5

Compare five ways to harvest a business.

> An overview of harvesting strategies should help you plan the final stage of your relationship with the company you are starting to create now. Harvesting options for exiting a business fall into five categories:

1. ***Increase the free cash flow.*** For the first 7 to 10 years of operation, you will want to reinvest as much profit as possible into the company in order to grow. Once you are ready to exit, however, you can begin reducing investment and taking cash out. This strategy will require investing only the amount of cash needed to keep the business effective in its current target markets, without attempting to move into new ones.

   Advantages
   - You can retain ownership of the firm with this strategy.
   - You do not have to seek a buyer.

Step into the Shoes . . .

Flickr Turns Online Photo Sharing into Opportunities for Its Founders

Caterina Fake
(Larry Busacca/Getty Images)

Stewart Butterfield and Caterina Fake launched Flickr in early 2004 and sold it just over one year later to Yahoo!. The sale price was $35 million in cash. It would appear that the couple harvested their company very quickly, but the story begins several years earlier.

Flickr is an online site that hosts images and videos, is an online community, and provides Web services. It is most widely known and used for its photo-sharing capacity. However, Flickr was actually created by Vancouver-based Ludicorp (founded in 2002 by Butterfield and Fake) using tools for an online game, *Game Neverending,* that was never launched. Fake recognized that the photo-sharing technology was more marketable than the game, and Ludicorp pursued Flickr.

The couple remained at Yahoo! for the requisite three years after the sale but departed soon afterwards. Fake left Yahoo! in June 2008, and her husband announced his resignation in the same month. Then Fake, a 1991 graduate of Vassar College, founded and became Chief Product Officer at Hunch, an Internet start-up that provided recommendations on a multitude of user-generated topics. She is a board member and investor in Etsy, has written a book about start-ups, and continues blogging on Caterina.net. In addition, Fake has invested in 20 × 200, Small Batch, Flowgram, Maya's Mom, and Daily-Booth. Butterfield, a graduate of the University of Victoria and the University of Cambridge, has cofounded Tiny Speck and invested in Flowgram, Etsy, and Rouxbe.

This couple found a way to translate a business idea into wealth and to use that wealth to found and invest in other start-up companies.

Source: Jefferson Graham, "Flickr of Idea on a Gaming Project Led to Photo Website," *USA Today,* February 27, 2007, http://www.usatoday.com. Crunchbase at http://www.crunchbase.com. Ludicorp Web site, accessed January 13, 2010, http://www.ludicorp.com.

Disadvantages

- You will need a solid financial strategy to minimize taxes.
- You have to be patient, as it can take a long time.

2. *Management buyout (MBO).* In this strategy, the entrepreneur sells the firm to its managers, who raise the money via personal investments and debt.

Advantages

- Managers often want to buy the business.
- You get emotional satisfaction of selling to people you know and have trained.

Disadvantages

- If the managers buy with debt, they may never finish paying off the purchase.
- Managers may have incentives to lower the profits, if the payout to you depends on company earnings.

3. *Employee stock ownership plan (ESOP).* This strategy both provides an employee retirement plan and allows the owners to sell their stock and exit the company. The firm establishes a plan that allows employees to buy company stock as part of their retirement; when the owners are ready to exit, the ESOP borrows money and uses the cash to buy their stock. As the loan is paid off, the stock is added to the employee benefit fund.

Advantages

- The ESOP has some special tax advantages; for example, the company can deduct both the principal and interest payments on the loan, and the dividends paid on any stock held in the ESOP are considered a tax-deductible expense.
- Employees will be more committed to the company's success.

Disadvantages

- This is not a good strategy if the entrepreneur does not want the employees to have control of the company. The ESOP must extend to all employees and requires the entrepreneur to open up the company's books.

4. *Merging or being acquired.* Selling the company to another company can be an exit strategy for an entrepreneur who would like his or her creation to have an opportunity to grow significantly by using another company's funds.

Advantages

- The acquiring company can realize growth that was not possible for you.
- You can exit the company at the time of the **merger** or acquisition or be part of the growth and exit later.

merger the joining of two companies in order to share their respective strengths.

Disadvantages

- This can be an emotionally draining strategy, with a lot of ups and downs during negotiations; a sale can take over a year to finalize.

5. *Initial public offering (IPO).* An initial public offering (IPO), or "going public," will mean selling shares of your company in the stock market. It will require choosing an investment banker to develop the IPO, making sales presentations ("the road show") to brokers and institutional investors, and offering stock on the market and holding your breath as you watch its price go up—or not.

Advantages
- An IPO can be a very profitable way to harvest your company. The market may place a large premium on your company's value.
- Very few entrepreneurial firms ever complete an IPO, but, if successful, it can bring significant financial rewards.

Disadvantages
- An IPO is a very exciting, but stressful, all-consuming, and very expensive way to harvest a company.
- It requires a lot of work from the entrepreneur.
- Ultimately, the market determines the outcome.

This overview of harvesting strategies should help you plan the final stage of your relationship with the company you are starting to create now.

Exit Strategy Options

Simply claiming that your business will go public one day will get a skeptical reaction from potential investors. They understand that you cannot *guarantee* how they will recoup their investment or predict your exact exit strategy, but you can show you are aware that, for the vast majority of small businesses, going public is a fantasy. Demonstrate your understanding of exit strategies by thinking through the following four basic possibilities. Which one do you think best describes what you intend to make happen for your business?

1. *Acquisition.* Do you believe you could create a business that someone would want to buy one day? Your exit strategy could be to create a company that would be valuable for one of your suppliers or a major competitor. The purchase price would pay you and your equity investors a return on investment. As we have said, a common rule of thumb states that a small business should be worth at least three times its annual net profit.

2. *Earn-out.* To use an earn-out strategy, you will need projected cash flow statements that show the business eventually generating a strong positive cash flow. At that point, you can start offering to buy out your investors' shares at a price greater than they paid for them. The purchase price will usually rise over time.

3. *Debt/equity exchange.* If your investors will be lending you money, eventually you can offer to trade equity for portions of the debt. This will slowly reduce the interest due over time (as the face value of the loan decreases). In this way, you can decide at what pace and at what price to reduce your debt.

4. *Merge.* This strategy is similar to that of acquisition but, in a merger, two companies join together to share their strengths. One company might have an extensive customer base, whereas the other might possess a distribution channel the first company needs. Or perhaps each company is doing well in different geographical areas, and a merger would open up these respective markets to the other's products. Regardless, cash will change hands, and the original investors can make their shares available for sale to complete the merger.

Investors Will Care about Your Exit Strategy

We have emphasized that your exit strategy will be important to your investors. Your business plan should spell out in how many years you expect them to be able to cash out and the financial data in your plan must show this. Again, it will not be enough to mention that someday the company will go public and their share of the business will be worth "a lot" of money. Of the thousands of new ventures launched every year in the United States, only a small percentage will ever be listed on a stock exchange. Yet, according to David Newton, on Entrepreneur.com (January 15, 2001), over 70 percent of formal business plans presented to angel investors and venture capitalists cite going public as the primary exit strategy. Most estimate that going public will happen within just four years from the business's launch date. Be more realistic.

Chapter Summary

Now that you have studied this chapter, you can do the following:

1. Assess how you want to grow your business and then exit from it.
   - Decide what your ultimate goals and objectives are.
   - Consider creating a business that will provide employment and wealth for your family.
   - Identify options to broaden product and service offerings through diversification.
   - Evaluate replication strategies.
2. Describe how businesses use licensing to profit from their brands.
   - A brand is a name, term, sign, logo, design, or combination of these that identifies the products or services of a company and differentiates them from those of competitors.
   - The licensee pays a fee for the license and will probably also pay the licensor a royalty (share of the profits).
   - Licensing is only effective when the licensor is confident that his or her company name will not be tarnished by how the licensee uses it.
3. Explain how a business can be franchised.
   - A franchise is a business that markets a product or service in the exact manner prescribed by the founder or successors of the parent company.
   - As an entrepreneur, you could develop a concept and business operation that can be reproduced and sold to other entrepreneurs. They would pay you a fee for the right to run the business exactly the way you direct and pay you a royalty as well.
4. Use methods of valuing a business.
   - Book value (net worth = assets − liabilities)
   - Future earnings
   - Market-based (value = P/E × estimated future net earnings)
5. Compare five ways to harvest a business.
   - Increase the free cash flows. Once you are ready to exit, you can begin reducing reinvestment and collecting revenue as cash.

- Management buyout. The entrepreneur sells the firm to the managers, who raise the money to buy it via personal savings and debt.
- Employee stock ownership plan (ESOP). This provides an employee retirement plan and allows the entrepreneur and partners, as they exit the company, to sell their stock to the employees.
- Merging or being acquired. Joining together with another company or being bought by one.
- Initial public offering (IPO). Going public is getting your company listed on the stock exchange to be traded on the open market.

Key Terms

book value	line extension
diversification	liquidation
fair market value	merger
harvesting	replication strategy
licensing	

Entrepreneurship Portfolio

Critical Thinking Exercises

14-1. Compare and contrast licensing and franchising agreements.

14-2. Provide an example of a business that could lead to licensing agreements and a business that could be franchised.

14-3. Do you plan to franchise your business or license any of your products? Explain.

14-4. Describe the exit strategy you plan to use to harvest your business. Why do you think this exit strategy will be attractive to potential investors?

Key Concept Questions

14-5. Analyze two companies that merged during the past three years. Describe the structure of the merger and what has happened to the resulting organization since then.

14-6. Select one of the harvesting strategies described in the chapter and research it in depth. Write a report per instructor guidelines.

Application Exercises

14-7. Look around your local community and evaluate a popular business that is an independent company—not a franchise or part of a major corporation. Propose the possible harvesting strategies that the owners(s) could employ. What would you recommend and why?

14-8. Select five companies that are profiled in this text from the Step into the Shoes and Global Impact features. Research whether each has been harvested (you may need to do an Internet search). If so, what strategy did the owner(s) employ? If not, what would you recommend?

Exploring Online

The American Association of Franchisees and Dealers (AAFD) is a national trade association that represents the rights and interests of franchisees and independent dealers across the country. Visit this association online at http://www.aafd.org to learn more about franchises and the resources available. As a potential franchisor, you should know what your prospective customers are reading.

14-9. Search the site for the article, "AAFD Road Map to Selecting a Franchise." Read the section called "8 Things to Look for in a Franchise." For each of the tips in the article, write a one-sentence summary and note how it might apply to your business as a franchisor. If you cannot access this article, find another article on franchise selection criteria and follow the instructions here. Include a citation.

14-10. Identify a franchise through an online search that is similar to one you might want to create. Answer the following:

a. What is the franchise? What does it sell?

b. Why are you interested in it?

      c. What is the franchise fee?

      d. What are the start-up costs?

      e. What is the royalty fee?

      f. Describe the training the franchisor offers to franchisees.

      g. Describe the marketing the franchisor provides for franchisees.

14-11. Find a company online that is similar to the type of business you would like to launch. Assume you would want to sell it. Using financial data on the company, calculate your desired selling price and explain your valuation method(s).

BizBuilder Business Plan Questions

8.0 Funding Request and Exit Strategy

8.2 Exit Plan

      A. How will investors get paid back/out? Public offering? Employee buyout? Merger or acquisition? Liquidation? Stock buyback?

      B. When will this happen?

      C. Do you plan to franchise your business or license any of your products? Explain.

8.3 Milestones

      A. Create a Gantt chart for your organization to make your plans clear to potential investors.

Anago Cleaning Systems— Growth through Franchising

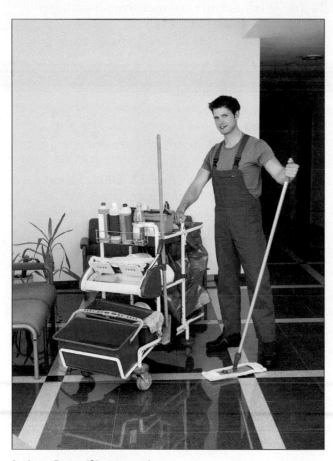

Andrey_Popov/Shutterstock

Anago Cleaning Systems, based in Pompano Beach, Florida, is a company created for growth through franchising. As a 15-year veteran of owning a cleaning business, David R. Povlitz exited his Florida retirement to start Anago. His original cleaning business, Imperial Professional Building Maintenance, was in Michigan, and he owned it with his three brothers. When they sold the company, Povlitz retired and relocated. A short while later, he took a job at leading janitorial franchisor Jani-King and learned more about its franchising system. Anago was born in 1989 and started franchising in 1991.

Anago Cleaning Services focuses on commercial rather than residential cleaning. It takes advantage of the cost-cutting methods developed over years of experience and knowledge of competitors.

Franchising from the Start

Growth has been through increasing the number of franchises. According to Anago's Web site, the number of "unit" franchises is 2012 was 2,427, compared with 732 in 2005 and 73 in the 1990s. The number of "master" franchises has reached 30 and continues to grow. The company was ranked as *Entrepreneur* magazine's 10th fastest growing franchise in 2013 and was 5th in 2010 and 2011.

Master Franchises

The company focuses largely on the acquisition of master franchises to grow. Anago master franchises, called Regional Franchises, have the exclusive rights to the company's system in their contractual territories. Each contractual region has a population base of at least 500,000 people and at least 5,000 businesses. It is the master franchise's job to recruit unit franchises within its territories. As the Anago site explains, "As a Master Franchise Owner, you are not in the cleaning business, you are in the franchising business."

Master franchises pay for assistance in site selection, live and computer training, computer software, and various support options. Fees are about $39,000 for the regional franchise rights with an additional $75,000 to $100,000 in working capital. Plovitz reduced the price from the usual $150,000 to $250,000 in 2011 and challenged other top franchise companies to reduce their fees.

Unit Franchises

Anago's unit franchises, or Janitorial Franchises, are responsible for cleaning the commercial properties that master franchises get under contract. The bulk of marketing and administrative tasks are handled by master franchises through regional offices. Unit franchises do not have to identify clients, prepare estimates, or set up cleaning contracts. They also are not responsible for billing and collections. The regional office provides them with orientation and ongoing support.

Unit franchises pay a franchise fee of $4,590 to $32,348 with an investment of $11,185 to $66,853.

There is a 10 percent discount for veterans. The ongoing royalty fees are 10 percent of gross revenues, and franchise contracts are for 10 years and are renewable. Franchisees do not need prior business or janitorial experience and are expected to be owner-operators.

Continued Opportunities for Growth

The company continues to actively recruit master franchises with a list of 66 available territories. Povlitz has successfully leveraged his knowledge, experience, and resources to grow Anago Cleaning Systems.

Case Study Analysis

14-12. What benefits did Anago Cleaning Systems gain from franchising?

14-13. What benefits do Anago's master franchises get from the company that they would not have independently?

14-14. What are the demographic requirements for selecting a master franchise region?

14-15. Who is most likely to be interested in an Anago unit franchise? Why?

Visit the Anago Cleaning Systems Web site at http://www.anagousa.com and find information about obtaining a master franchise.

14-16. What are the competitive advantages that Anago identifies?

14-17. What proprietary systems and services are noted?

14-18. How are master franchisees incorporated into the site?

Case Sources

Anago Cleaning Systems, http://www.anagousa.com.

Dennis Romero, December 22, 2008, "Anago Cleaning Systems: Meet a franchisor with a willingness to get his hands dirty," *Entrepreneur*, accessed November 11, 2013 at http://www.entrepreneur.com/article/199294.

Tracy Stapp Herold, "2013 Franchise 500: #39 Anago Cleaning Systems," *Entrepreneur*, December 12, 2012, accessed November 12, 2013 at http://www.entrepreneur.com/franchise500/index.html.

When iContact cofounders Ryan Allis and Aaron Houghton decided to exit from their company, they sold it to Vocus Inc. for $169 million. They founded the company in Raleigh, North Carolina, in 2003 and sold it in February 2012.[6] At the time of the sale, iContact had some 300 employees, $50 million in annual sales, and 70,000 customers.[7]

iContact

The company offers e-mail marketing software for small and medium-sized businesses and not-for-profits. The iContact products automate the creation, delivery, and tracking of e-mail communications. The software permits its users to determine the effectiveness of e-mail marketing campaigns through the analysis of critical data, such as number of e-mails opened, customer "likes," follows, click-throughs, and so forth. One feature that provides a competitive advantage for iContact is the ability to integrate with Facebook and Twitter for campaigns that will use social networks to build word-of-mouth support. According to the iContact website, the platform has some one million registered users.

iContact, as operated by its founders, describes itself in press releases as "a purpose driven company that makes social media and email marketing easy, so that small and midsized companies and causes can grow and succeed . . . the company maintains B Corporation status, a certification awarded to companies meeting comprehensive and transparent social and environmental performance standards. As part of its ongoing social mission, iContact applies the 4-1s Corporate Social Responsibility Model, donating one percent from each of its payroll, equity, product, and employee time to local and global communities."

Vocus Inc.

Vocus, based in Beltsville, Maryland, is a publicly traded company (NASDAQ: VOCS) that already had search marketing, social marketing, and publicity applications in its operations. According to the Vocus Web site, "our software sends real-time marketing opportunities directly to marketers in the form of leads, prospects, social media conversations, curated content and inbound media inquiries. With our marketing consulting and services team ready to help, our software solution delivers marketing success." As a provider of cloud-based public relations and marketing software, the addition of e-mail marketing capabilities will broaden its range of products and strengthen its marketing suite.

Vocus was founded in 1992 by Rick Rudman and Bob Lentz, primarily as a political public relations firm. The firm expanded and went public in 2005, raising $45 million in its initial public offering. Starting in 2006, the company acquired PRWeb, Help a Reporter Out (HARO), and North Social. Vocus reported revenues of $170.8 million in 2012, with customers that included British Airways, Farmers Insurance, Make-A-Wish Foundation, and Wyndham Worldwide.

iContact's Founders

Both Ryan Allis and Aaron Houghton are serial entrepreneurs. Ryan was born in Pittsburgh in 1984. He created Virante, a Web-design business, while in high school. He received his undergraduate degree in economics from the University of North Carolina at Chapel Hill and then completed the EO/MIT Entrepreneurial Masters Program. After a year in the Harvard MBA program, Ryan went to San Francisco to start Connect.

Ryan has many interests and talents. He has authored *Zero to One Million* (McGraw-Hill, 2008) and *The Startup Guide: Building a Better World Through Entrepreneurship* (http://www.startupguide.com). He is a philanthropist and agent of social change through his roles as a member of the United Nations Foundation Global Entrepreneur Council, Board Chairman of Nourish International, and Founder of the Humanity Fund. He has invested in such companies as EvoApp, Ark, and Close and served as the National Co-Chairperson for Technology for President Obama. Ryan is the recipient of numerous awards for his humanitarian work.

Aaron Houghton is currently running his 15th start-up, the Raleigh-Durham-based Boost-Suite, where he is a cofounder and the CEO. He received his undergraduate degree in computer

---

[6]Leena Rao, "Vocus Acquires iContact for $169 Million," *TechCrunch*, February 28, 2012, accessed October 7, 2013, http://techcrunch.com/2012/02/28/vocus-buys-email-marketing-company-icontact-for-169-million.

[7]"Ryan Allis," CrunchBase profile, accessed October 13, 2013, http://www.crunchbase.com/person/ryan-allis.

science from the University of North Carolina at Chapel Hill (2003), where he and Ryan met. He also completed the Entrepreneurial Masters Program at MIT (2012).

Aaron was the President and CEO of Preation, both before and during his tenure as Chairman of the iContact Board of Directors. Prior to that, he was the CEO of College-United, CollegeDirect, and CTO MainBrain. He is also a cofounder of StartUpWithMe.com and DowntownDurhamStartups.com, both of which support emerging businesses. His business investments include SimpleRelevance, Idea Fund Partners, Argyle Social, and Eden Platform. Aaron enjoys wakeboarding, playing the acoustic guitar, and participating in outdoor activities.[8] He, too, has received numerous awards.

Ryan and Aaron are involved in many business and philanthropic activities and continue their phenomenal success as young entrepreneurs.

Case Study Analysis

14-19. What options did iContact's founders have for harvesting their investment?

14-20. Why did a sale to Vocus make strategic sense, if at all?

14-21. What opportunities did selling the company open up for Ryan and Aaron?

14-22. As young, serial entrepreneurs, how might the founders plan for their respective futures? What have they done since selling iContact?

Case Sources

"Aaron Houghton, Co-founder and CEO, BoostSuite," *Techpreneur*, November 19, 2012, accessed October 13, 2013, http://www.techpreneurspotlight.com/aaron-houghton-co-founder-and-ceo-boostsuite/.

Jeff Clabaugh, "Vocus Raises $45M in Stock Offering," *Baltimore Business Journal*, December 7, 2005, accessed October 13, 2013, http://www.bizjournals.com/baltimore/stories/2005/12/05/daily18.html.

iContact, accessed October 13, 2013, http://www.icontact.com.

Leena Rao, "Vocus Acquires iContact for $169 Million," *TechCrunch*, February 28, 2012, accessed October 7, 2013, http://techcrunch.com/2012/02/28/vocus-buys-email-marketing-company-icontact-for-169-million.

"Ryan Allis," *CrunchBase* profile, accessed October 13, 2013, http://www.crunchbase.com/person/ryan-allis.

Vocus, accessed October 13, 2013, http://www.vocus.com.

---

[8]"Aaron Houghton, Co-founder and CEO, BoostSuite," *Techpreneur*, November 19, 2012, accessed October 13, 2013, http://www.techpreneurspotlight.com/aaron-houghton-co-founder-and-ceo-boostsuite/.

Honest Tea—From Start-Up to Harvest

Mission Statement
Honest Tea creates and promotes delicious, truly healthy, organic beverages. We strive to grow with the same honesty we use to craft our products, with sustainability and great taste for all.

Seth Goldman likes to say that Honest Tea got started because he was thirsty. Apparently, so were a lot of other people! Honest Tea grew from an operation with 3 employees and revenues of $250,000 in 1998 to 98 employees and $47 million in sales in 2009. Along the way, exit strategies described in the 1999 Honest Tea Business Plan have been executed. Seth and his cofounder, Barry Nalebuff, identified "investment by a strategic partner" and "complete acquisition" as potential exit strategies for investors. Honest Tea honestly followed these strategies in 2008 and 2011, respectively, when the company concluded an installment sale to the Coca-Cola Company. This is a clear case of entrepreneurs planning for the harvest from the start and doing what they set out to do.

The Honest Tea Story

During one of Seth's classes at the Yale School of Management, he and his professor, Barry Nalebuff, found they shared a passion for a less sweet but flavorful beverage while discussing a Coke-vs.-Pepsi case study. While he liked the idea of creating the perfect beverage, Seth decided to follow his passion for social change and work for the Calvert Group, managing marketing and sales for this socially responsible investment firm. While doing so, he expanded his already keen interest in social enterprise.

The entrepreneurial drive that began early in Seth's life became even stronger after a long run in Central Park, when he couldn't find any drinks to quench his thirst. Thinking back to the Coke-vs.-Pepsi case study discussion, Seth e-mailed Barry, who had just returned from India, where he had been studying the tea industry. Barry had learned that most U.S. beverage

Seth Goldman, Co-Founder and TeaEO, Honest Tea.
(Courtesy of Seth Goldman and Honest Tea)

companies do not use whole tea leaves to make their bottled tea. Instead, they take whatever is left after the quality leaves have been packaged for "better" products, such as tea bags—leftover bits of tea described as "dust" or "fannings." Seth and Barry had a sense that they were honing in on an opportunity. Even better, Barry had already come up with a name for a company that would make beverages using top-of-the-line tea leaves. The company would be called Honest Tea.

Seth decided to leave the Calvert Group to pursue the idea, brewed batches of tea in his kitchen and launched Honest Tea in February 1998. During their first meeting with the Whole Foods Regional Office, the buyer sampled teas that Seth brought with him in borrowed thermoses and placed an order for 15,000 bottles. Honest Tea made its first deliveries in June 1998, offering five varieties of tea. Today, the product lines have expanded into Honest Tea (21 varieties) in glass or PETE-1 (plastic) bottles, Honest Ade (4 varieties), Honest Kids (5 varieties in pouches), Honest Fizz (5 varieties), Honest Splash (3 varieties), and a zero-calorie line made with organic Stevia (2 varieties). For most of the company's history, its products were distributed through independent beverage distributors, with the greatest success coming from natural foods outlets.

The following chart shows the growth of Honest Tea's revenues from 1998 through 2009 when they sold a portion of the company to Coca Cola. The remarkable upswing in revenues between 2004 and 2005 is due in part to the company's teas becoming USDA Certified Organic. These exceptional revenue increases did not initially translate into profitability, according to Seth's blog. This is where financing options became critical.

Honest Tea's Competitive Advantages

The team at Honest Tea has worked hard to define the brand around the features that make its products stand out from the competition. In Seth's own words, "Given that this is a highly competitive market, the most important factor in our favor is that we offer a differentiated product. What we are offering is a very strong brand that is consistent with what is in the package and very meaningful to customers."

For example, Honest Tea was the first brand to make an organic certified bottled tea. What does this mean, and why does it matter? When an item is labeled USDA Certified Organic, it confirms that chemical pesticides and fertilizers have not been used in growing or producing the ingredients

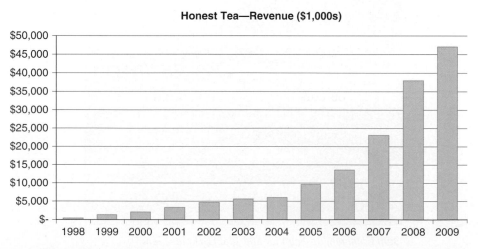

Honest Tea Revenues 1998–2009

Courtesy of Seth Goldman and Honest Tea

in the product. Increasingly, consumers, particularly the health-conscious, are seeking out organic goods in the marketplace.

Honest Tea also uses up to two-thirds less sugar in its teas compared with its competitors, such as Snapple and Arizona. Most varieties include the phrase "Just A Tad Sweet" on the label. This feature appeals to consumers who care about their health and diet.

Socially Responsible Business

Honest Tea's mission extends beyond using organic ingredients, whole tea leaves, and less sugar than most other beverages. The company goes to great lengths to educate consumers about the its ethical and socially responsible business practices. It wants customers to know that when they buy Honest Tea, they are also doing something good for the community. As Seth puts it, "A commitment to social responsibility is central to Honest Tea's identity and purpose. The company strives for authenticity, integrity, and purity in our products and in the way we do business."

Staying in the Game

The beverage market is highly competitive, but Honest Tea appears to be thriving because it is delivering a differentiated product, using organic ingredients that customers feel good about buying. However, this does not happen magically. The Honest Tea team has had to expend considerable effort to secure the financial resources needed to fulfill their dream.

Initially, Seth and Barry invested their own funds and those of friends and family to seed the company. This first round of investors put in approximately $500,000 to get the business started. The money was primarily used to pay for the first production run. It was rapidly apparent that additional funding was going to be needed to pay for more production and a sales staff to support additional growth. Barry created an innovative financing structure, using warrants to protect the interests of the founders.

The 1999 Business Plan that appears in this text is the one that was developed to secure additional funding. By the end of 1999, Honest Tea had raised in excess of $1.7 million in capital investment, primarily from small, private investors. Rather than going out into the venture capital community, as he had expected to do, Seth was able to secure commitments from a number of individuals who had expressed interest in investing in the company.[9] He writes, "The hardest money to raise was the $1.2 million in 1999, when we took in money from people we didn't know."[10] In the same year, Honest Tea jointly purchased ownership in Three Rivers Bottling, LLC, to have greater control over production and to eliminate potential problems of production shortfalls. The following year, the company secured additional funding from earlier investors. Over the following years the enterprise continued to grow, fueled in part by sales growth and additional equity raises.

Honest Tea and Coca-Cola— A Marriage Made in Beverage Heaven?

In February 2008, Honest Tea celebrated its 10th anniversary and announced another milestone. The company had accepted a 40-percent investment from the Coca-Cola Company that could help expand production and distribution, just as the founders had suggested in the 1999 Business Plan. At the time, Seth stated, "We started Honest Tea ten years ago with five thermoses and an ambitious vision for offering a new type of beverage—a delicious healthier drink produced with a consciousness about the way the ingredients are grown. As more consumers become aware of how their decisions impact the health of the planet and themselves, we are thrilled to receive this investment from the world's largest beverage company to help take our brand and our mission to a larger scale and wider audience."[11] At part of the investment, Coca-Cola North America's Venturing and Emerging Brands (VEB) Business Unit retained an option to purchase the remaining ownership in 2011.

There was considerable angst among loyal Honest Tea customers as they became aware of the investment by Coca-Cola. Many were unhappy that this mission-driven company with a focus on health and organics would be subsumed by a large, multinational corporation with a different agenda. At the time, Gary Hirshberg, President and "CE-Yo" of Stonyfield Farm, and mentor and advisor to Seth, responded with the following: "The knowledge and access that Coca-Cola North America and its distribution system can provide comes at a perfect time as Honest Tea is at an exciting inflection point. I look forward to helping Seth and the team continue to build the business the right way in the years ahead."[12] Barry Nalebuff added, "This is our chance to bring organic beverages to the mainstream."[13]

In his February 5, 2008, blog, Seth addresses the customer questions head on: "So how do we move from the ideal to the real without screwing up what we've created? The world of mission-driven business is littered with entrepreneurs whose companies lost their soul or at least lost their leadership. . . . I am determined to make sure that never happens with Honest Tea. Our challenge is to find a partner who wants to 'buy in' to our mission, rather than one who wants us to 'sell out.' Any partner that we consider must understand that the 'Honest' brand stands for great-tasting,

[9]Paul Gompers, "Honest Tea," Harvard Business School Case Study, 2001.

[10]Seth Goldman, "Seth's Blog," Honest Tea Web site, April 28, 2009, accessed April 20, 2011, http://www.honesttea.com.

[11]Samme Menke, "The Coca-Cola Company Signs Agreement for 40% Stake in Honest Tea," Press Release, Honest Tea, Bethesda, Maryland, February 5, 2008.

[12]Ibid.

[13]Op cit.

Courtesy of Seth Goldman and Honest Tea

healthier beverages that are produced in a more sustainable manner. As long as that partner buys into our approach, we welcome the opportunity to expand the scale and reach of Honest Tea." From the initial investment in 2008 until early in 2011, the number of distributors of Honest Tea grew, as did the number of outlets selling Honest Tea.

In 2010, Honest Tea worked with Coca-Cola to create a tea-brewing system inside a Coca-Cola bottling plant. Seth wrote, in an April 2010 blog posting, "There's no more visible way to communicate the level of commitment Coke is making in our brand's future than to show a picture . . . of the Big Brewer—not only because it is a financially significant investment (more than $1 million) but because it takes up such a large piece of real estate in the middle of a production plant where space is limited and quite expensive. . . . The payback on such an expensive system is at least three years, far beyond the investment timeframe that Honest Tea could make on its own—we're rarely in a position to make capital investments beyond the next two months."

The company had been growing, but still had not become profitable. It needed to expand distribution and reach more people to fulfill its mission. As Seth noted in his blog posting on March 1, 2011, "even with our aggressive pace of growth, we kept losing money. Our margins were thin because our buying power was weak compared to the big brands, and we needed to hire more people to keep building the brand up and down the street. In order to stretch our limited funds, we've always been very frugal."

In the same blog entry, he added, "More importantly, we were fortunate to develop a group of angel investors who helped us stay in business by continuing to support us financially with equity and debt investments." Honest Tea needed to give back to its patient investors, Seth suggested: "The only way we were able to stay in business was because our investors believed they would gain a return for the investments. Given our margins, dividends weren't going to be an option, so an exit would have to come either via acquisition or IPO." Although the team at Honest Tea briefly thought that an IPO would be an option, it reconsidered in 2007. Recognizing that "distribution is the key to winning in the beverage industry" and that the current network of independent distributors could not yield the necessary reach, it was determined that discussions with Coca-Cola made sense.

Honest Tea continues to operate as a separate division within Coca-Cola. Seth elected to reinvest the majority of his proceeds from the sale back into Honest Tea. The company has the opportunity to help fulfill the dream of bringing organics into the mainstream. In fact, in one of Seth's most recent blog posts, he wrote: "I can't imagine walking away from the business now that we finally have a national footprint in place and the chance to democratize organics in a way that's never been done. This tea party is just getting started."

Case Study Analysis

U5-1. What are Honest Tea's competitive advantages?

U5-2. Look at the list you generated. Which is most important to you as a consumer and why?

U5-3. Given what you already know about Honest Tea's business philosophy and practices, if you were Seth's business advisor, what additional competitive advantages would you encourage him to develop?

U5-4. What does it mean for a company to engage in "socially responsible business practices"?

U5-5. What methods of capital acquisition did Honest Tea employ? Why?

U5-6. How did the sale to Coca-Cola impact Honest Tea's investors?

U5-7. What are the arguments for and against selling equity to Coca-Cola?

Case Sources

Honest Tea, accessed April 18, 2011, http://www.honesttea.com.

Seth Goldman, "Seth's Blog," accessed April 18, 2011, http://www.honesttea.com.

Paul Gompers, *Honest Tea*, Harvard Business School Case Study, 2001.

Samme Menke, "The Coca-Cola Company Signs Agreement for 40% Stake in Honest Tea," Press Release, Honest Tea, Bethesda, Maryland, February 5, 2008.

Appendix 1

Sample Student Business Plan

University Parent, Inc.

Fesehaye Abrhaley
Michelle Dorenkamp
Kara Grinnell
Ryan Roth
Sarah Schupp

University Parent, Inc.

Table of Contents

Executive Summary 3

Product/Service Description 5

Industry and Marketplace Analysis 7

Marketing Strategy 8

Operations Strategy 10

Development Strategy 12

Roll-Out Plan 13

Management Team 15

Risk Analysis 16

Financial Plan 17

Offering 19

Appendix

Income Statement .... A

Balance Sheet .... B

Cash Flow Statement C

Monthly and Quarterly Cash Flow Statements .... D

Break-Even Analysis .... E

Capital Expenditure Detail .... F

Financial Assumptions .... G

Development Timeline .... H

Summary of Customer Surveys I

Management Team Resumes .... J

2890 Shadow Creek – Boulder, Colorado – 303.579.9871 – info@upi.com

University Parent, Inc.

Executive Summary

University Parent, Inc.
University Parent (UPI) produces institution-specific guides and comprehensive websites for parents of college students. Revenues are generated through the sale of advertising in the local guides and on the websites.

Today, there are 32 million parents of college students
According to surveys and interviews conducted by UPI, parents do not receive the information they need from colleges. They want to know where to have a nice dinner in their student's college town, where to stay, and fun activities to do while visiting. They also want to know how to parent their college student and need to understand the issues their child is facing such as managing money, avoiding credit card debt, and balancing school, a part-time job, and extra-curricular activities.

UPI can help
UPI will produce three free guides per year for each college that will be distributed during summer orientation and August move-in, Fall Parent's Weekend, and in the Spring to prospective parents through the Admissions Office and Campus Tour Office. At the University of Colorado, over 25,000 prospective parents tour the campus. The magazines will be distributed through the university, hotels, and restaurants. The magazine content will include: restaurant reviews, a lodging directory, a shopping guide, calendar of events, graduation requirement Information, map of the city, and a Q&A section.

Proven track record
The first issue of the *Parent's Guide to Boulder* was published in October 2003 and immediately profited from advertising sales. The second edition will be published June 2004, and due to advance advertising sales, will also be profitable. Demand for these first guides have proved that advertisers are committed to purchasing space in the guide and that parents are interested in reading the guide.

Experienced, enthusiastic management team
Sarah Schupp is the founder, CEO, and Chairman of the UPI Board of Directors. She published the initial *Parent's Guide to Boulder* in 2003. A graduate of the University of Colorado with degrees in Business Administration and English Literature, Sarah is capable of expanding the vision of UPI to Colorado and Texas. In Year 3, UPI plans to hire a CEO with national rollout experience.

Other UPI employees include VP Marketing Michelle Dorenkamp, CFO Kara Grinnell, and CTO Ryan Roth. In addition to an excellent management team,

3

University Parent, Inc.

UPI is in the process of developing a board of twelve directors that bring experience in advertising, magazine writing, start-ups, and venture capital.

Plan for expansion
Because of the initial success of the *Parent's Guide to Boulder*, UPI is currently expanding its marketing base to Colorado State University and the University of Denver. A regional office in Boulder will handle advertising sales for the three guides. UPI plans to broaden its base beginning in Year 2, with a goal of being in 44 schools by Year 5.

The offering
UPI is offering 35% of the company for $500,000. This will provide investors with a 60% rate of return, translating to $4.3 million in Year 5 when UPI plans to sell to Hearst Publishing or Conde Nast Publishing. UPI breaks-even in Year 2, generating revenues of $1.8 million. In Year 5, UPI will have revenues of $12 million and a net profit of $4.1 million.

Company Overview

With two successful publications for the University of Colorado and established relationships with over 35 advertisers, UPI is positioned for nation-wide expansion. In October of 2004, UPI plans to produce a total of 9 publications and 3 websites for the University of Colorado, the University of Denver, and Colorado State University. We project UPI will produce 132 publications and high-traffic websites for 44 colleges and universities by Year 5. This will result in net revenues of $12.3 million, net profits of $4.1 million, and a valuation of $70 million. Also in Year 5, UPI plans to market the company to suitable buyers such as Hearst Publishing or Conde Nast Publishing.

2890 Shadow Creek – Boulder, Colorado – 303.579.9871 – info@upi.com

University Parent, Inc.

Product/Service Description

Introduction

You arrive on campus to drop off your freshman student. This is always one of the hardest times of the year for you. Leaving your child miles from home, millions of questions are running through your head. How do they register for classes? How many credits will they need to graduate? What issues will they face being away from home? As you are signing in for orientation, you receive a magazine that specifically answers these questions. Not only does it answer campus life questions, it also offers restaurant reviews, lodging suggestions, and a detailed map of the city. The magazine directs you to a website where you can talk to other parents who have your same concerns. Suddenly you have a sense of relief. Now you have a source of information at your fingertips.

As a Boulder business, you have always wondered how you can directly advertise to CU parents who visit often and spend thousands of dollars while visiting. One day a packet arrives at your business with the first *Parent's Guide to Boulder* from the 2003 Parent's Weekend and a rate card. You are excited that there is now a reasonably priced and direct way to contact CU parents and inform them of your business. You know that purchasing advertising will be well worth every dollar. (Boulder, Colorado served as UPI's test market.)

Description

University Parent produces a comprehensive local guide as well as a website for parents of college students. Through its compilation of articles, pictures, maps, current events, and advertisements, it provides a convenient, thorough source of information for CU parents.

Parent

Guide Feature	Benefit
Distribution through the university, hotels, and restaurants	Convenience
Provides useful information about their student's environment and community	Comfort, Sense of Security
Makes navigating Boulder easier and allows for advance planning	Saves Time
Free! Gives information and coupons for good values in: lodging, eating, shopping, and having a good time	Saves Money

5

University Parent, Inc.

Advertiser

Guide Feature	Benefit
Targets specific niche	Targeted ROI
Mid-ranged priced advertising	Saves Money
Effective distribution channels	Reaches Target Market, Generates Revenue

Market Comparison

Unlike other publications in college towns, UPI offers its readers focused, relevant information that is unavailable through local newspapers and magazines. It also offers advertisers a targeted, identifiable market.

Stage of Development

UPI produced its first guide in Boulder for Parent's Weekend '03. The profitability of the first guide demonstrated UPI's ability to sell advertising and to produce a useful product. UPI is currently marketing and creating articles for its Summer '04 publication. Our CTO, Ryan Roth, launched the Guide to Boulder's website in April of '04, http://www.guidetoboulder.com. Advertising sales for the website are scheduled to begin in May '04.

Client Base

UPI currently has over 35 clients for the *Parent's Guide to Boulder.* These advertisers include: Wells Fargo, Walnut Realty, McGuckin Hardware, the CU Book Store, the CU Foundation, Greenbriar Inn, Boulder Broker Inn, Boulder Outlook Hotel & Suites, Boulder Express Shuttle, and many more. Of the initial advertisers in the Fall '03 guide, 100% of advertisers solicited purchased advertising for the Summer '04 guide.

Potential Readership Base

Demographic

> 32 million U.S. parents of college students, growing at an annual rate of 6%
> We expect 20% of each college's parent population to read our magazines

Family Income

> Most families sending children to college have a combined household income ranging from $80,000 to $150,000

Cost of Education

> A college education is likely the biggest investment they will make in their student
> A college education costs anywhere from $30,000 to $200,000
> Parents typically provide for their children while in college, paying for expenses such as transportation (car, bike), car insurance, textbooks, clothing, computers and software, food, rent, etc.

6

University Parent, Inc.

These expenses average between $800–$1,500 per month.

Potential Advertisers
Independent marketing firms that handle national accounts
Local business owners and/or Marketing Managers representing
hotels, restaurants, retail stores, travel agencies that must make
buying decisions based on distribution and cost.

Industry and Marketplace Analysis

The publication industry has over 17,000 magazines that gross $24 billion
in revenue each year. Historically, this industry has grown at a rate of 7
percent, and is expected to grow 6 percent in the future. There is little demand
for new titles with the exception of demand for specialty, niche magazines that
enable advertisers to reach a well-defined market. Our primary, unexplored
niche consists of parents of college students. According to surveys, virtually all
CU parents (95%) are uninformed about campus activities, news, and pertinent
issues. Currently no other publications are addressing these needs and
concerns of CU parents.

In recent years, there has been an increase in online magazines and online
versions of print magazines. Major threats in the periodical industry include other
advertising mediums such as television, radio, and print. The most competition
for publications is in print advertising, which ranges from daily newspapers to
monthly magazines. Another threat to the publication industry is the rising cost of
paper, which is driving down profits. Some of the internal market changes
revolve around a concern over rising paper costs because of deforestation.

Leading advertisers in the magazine industry include: automobile manufacturers,
consumer goods companies, entertainment conglomerates, and tobacco firms.
Some of the internal market changes revolve around a concern over rising paper
costs because of deforestation.

Leading advertisers in the magazine industry include: automobile manufacturers,
consumer goods companies, entertainment conglomerates, and tobacco firms.
The publication industry is affected by changes in economic conditions since
revenue is advertising-dependant.

University Parent, Inc.

Marketing Strategy

Introduction
UPI's target readership market will include students, parents of present and future students, university faculty and staff, and high school counselors. Aggressive distribution will insure that all sectors of our target market will receive our free guide as well as website information. Our target market for advertising is businesses that want to make parents of college students aware of their products and/or services. We provide these businesses an opportunity to reach a specific, identifiable market at a reasonable cost.

Target Market Advertising Strategy
We will position ourselves as the only publication offering information specifically for parents of CU students and as the only publication offering businesses the opportunity to advertise to these parents.

In Boulder, the primary advertising media are the *Colorado Daily*, *Daily Camera*, *The Onion*, and *Boulder Magazine*. UPI's targeted, niche market strategy offers businesses a superior, more cost-effective media product at a lower cost than these publications. UPI will produce a quarterly mailing to businesses in Boulder that offer a product/service that CU parents may be interested in purchasing. The mailing will be directed to the "businesses' owners" and will include a previous *Parent's Guide to Boulder*, a cover letter specifying why advertising with UPI is effective, testimonials from current advertisers, and a rate card.

As UPI moves into additional markets, this strategy will be replicated and customized as needed.

Pricing Strategy
University Parent will generate revenue from two sources: print advertising in our guides and online advertising on our website.

Print advertising prices (per guide):

Size	Full Color
Eighth Page	$250
Quarter Page	$400
Half Page	$600
Full Page	$800
Back Cover, Inside Cover, Back Inside	$1000

2890 Shadow Creek – Boulder, Colorado – 303.579.9871 – info@upi.com

University Parent, Inc.

Website advertising prices (per month):

Size	Full Color
2" x 1"	$400
2" x 2"	$500
Banner, 1" x 7"	$700
Pop Up	$1000
Ad in email newsletter	$500

Businesses can purchase yearlong magazine and website advertising at a10% discount. The website advertising prices are likely to change based on our website's traffic. The higher the traffic, the higher the price we can charge.

Distribution Strategy

UPI will distribute guides to parents through the university admissions office, parent relations office, and campus tour office. The guide will also be distributed in hotels, restaurants, businesses, and through the Chamber of Commerce. There will be an option on the website to download the guide or have it mailed for a small fee (postage).

Advertising, Sales & Promotion Strategy

UPI will be promoted to advertisers through local networking at Boulder Chamber of Commerce events, press releases in local papers, direct mailings, and referral incentives for current clients. In addition, the website will serve as an effective tool to inform both businesses and parents of our services.

Marketing & Sales Forecasts

UPI's revenue is generated through print and website advertising sales. We project revenues from print advertising at 54% and website advertising sales at 46% of total revenues.

Advertising revenues are calculated by using the print advertising rates multiplied by expected sales for three guides. UPI projects sales of 25 print advertisements per issue at an average cost of $1,000 and 72 website sales per year per institution at an average cost of $750.

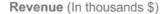

Revenue (In thousands $)

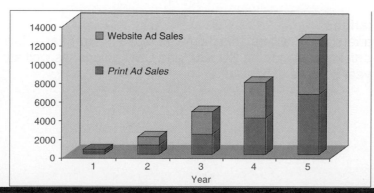

University Parent, Inc.

Revenue Projections

	Year 1	Year 2	Year 3	Year 4	Year 5
Product A—Magazine					
Number of Schools	3	9	22	32	44
Total Issues/Year	9	36	66	96	132
Magazines Printed/Year	90,000	360,000	660,000	960,000	1,320,000
Printing Cost/Per Magazine	0.25	0.23	0.21	0.19	0.17
Number of Units/Ad	225	900	1,800	2,925	4,425
Avg. Price/Ad Page	$1,000	$1,100	$1,210	$1,331	$1,464
Print Adv Total	$225,000	$990,000	$2,178,000	$3,893,175	$6,478,643
Product B—Website					
Advertisements Sold/Yr	360	1,080	2,640	3,840	5,280
Price per unit	$750	$825	$908	$998	$1,098
Web Adv Total	$270,000	$891,000	$2,395,800	$3,833,280	$5,797,836
Net Revenue	$495,000	$1,881,000	$4,573,800	$7,726,455	$12,276,479

Operations Plan

Operations Strategy

Our strategy is to establish a reputation with readers and advertisers that UPI consistently delivers well-received, well-designed, informative magazines and websites. We will develop this reputation by providing products that are professionally designed, error-free, and exceed the expectations of both our readers and our advertisers. We will measure our success through in-person as well as online surveys of our customers.

Our goal is to have highly satisfied customers—our parent readers and our advertisers. To that end, UPI will provide training for all employees that stresses the necessity of exceeding the expectations of our customers in ways such as delivering advertising proofs early or following up with a parent's question promptly and thoroughly.

Scope of Operations

At UPI headquarters, there will be 15 full-time employees. In Year 1, this office will handle advertising sales for the CU, DU, and CSU guides, as well as negotiate next year's Texas expansion.

2890 Shadow Creek – Boulder, Colorado – 303.579.9871 – info@upi.com

University Parent, Inc.

Headquarters Office Personnel
Boulder, Colorado

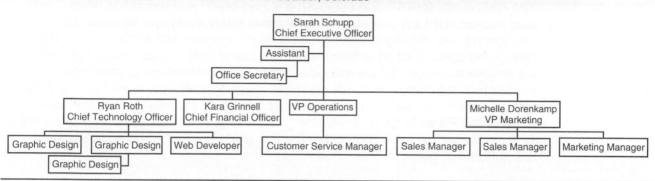

Regional Office Personnel
Locations: Dallas, Atlanta, Boston, Kansas City

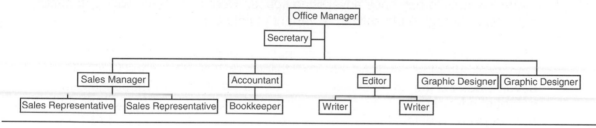

Ongoing Operations

UPI headquarters will coordinate with the regional offices to produce a website and three magazines annually for each college. Issues will be published every summer, fall, and spring. The website will be updated as needed, daily if necessary. Advertising sales as well as contact with parents and university faculty and staff will be continuous throughout the year

Operating Expenses

	Year 1	Year 2	Year 3	Year 4	Year 5
Total Operating Expenses	$854,967	$1,547,676	$2,588,328	$3,611,938	$5,083,166
% of Revenue	172.7%	82.3%	56.6%	46.7%	41.4%

11

University Parent, Inc.

Development Plan

Development Strategy

The first priority for UPI is to establish a strong brand and reputation within each new market. UPI will publish a guide approximately every four months. Our relationship with advertisers will become much stronger with each issue as they realize the value from advertising in our magazine. After three issues (one year), we believe our relationships with advertisers will significantly increase revenues. In year two, returning clients will purchase more advertisements and clients who watched their competitors gain revenue from advertising with us. For the second issue of the *Parent's Guide to Boulder,* advertising sales doubled and every client who purchased an advertisement in the Fall guide purchased an advertisement in the Summer guide.

During the publication cycle for each issue, the first order of business is to brainstorm new ideas and themes. Once the themes are decided, we make those themes available to the advertisers. We then give advertisers a three-month window to purchase advertising space. Contact is made with potential advertiser through "cold-selling," a variant of cold calling.

The "cold-selling" begins with a mass mailing, which is followed up with an e-mail. One week after the e-mailing, our staff follows up with a telephone call. The next seven weeks in the ad purchasing "window" are reserved for meetings with potential advertisers. Through our past experience, we have found that such meetings are vital for closing most deals.

The artwork acceptance window is open from the moment an advertising contract is signed until the artwork acceptance deadline, one week after the close of advertising sales. The first payment for the advertisement is due on the last day of advertisement sales. The second payment is due one week before we send the magazine to the printer.

While ad sales are in full swing, the design of the magazine is developed. Concurrently, article research and story writing for the magazine are performed. Immediately after the design and story writing are finalized, we finalize the layout and update the website; both of these occur over a two-week period.

As soon as the layout is finished, the final copy is sent to the printer. Within 5 days, the printer overnights a digital proof for UPI's approval. Once approved, printing takes approximately one week. Once the copies are received, the magazine is ready for distribution. Distribution takes place over a two-week period. Most magazines are mailed directly from the printer to the distribution point. These distribution points include: the university, hotels, restaurants, and other local businesses.

2890 Shadow Creek – Boulder, Colorado – 303.579.9871 – info@upi.com

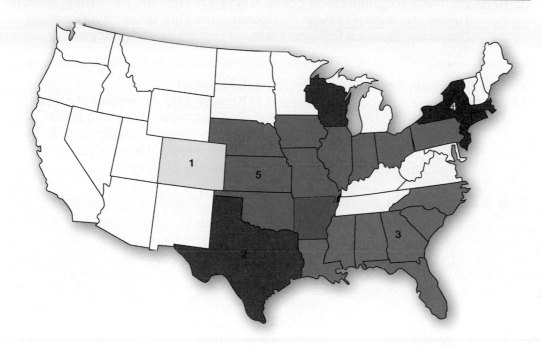

University Parent, Inc.

Roll-Out Plan

Year 1: Colorado
3 Schools: CU, University of Denver, and Colorado State University

Year 2: Colorado and Texas
9 Schools: *New Regional Office opens in **Dallas**: Southern Methodist University, University of Texas at Austin, A&M, Trinity University, Baylor University, Rice University

Year 3: Colorado, Texas, South
22 Schools: *New Regional Office opens in **Atlanta**: University of Georgia, University of the South, University of North Carolina, University of South Carolina, Duke University, University of Florida, Rollins College, University of Virginia, University of Richmond, University of Louisiana, Louisiana State University

13

University Parent, Inc.

Year 4: Colorado, Texas, South, Northeast
32 Schools: *New Regional Office opens in **Boston**: Harvard, MIT, Tufts, Boston University, Boston College, Princeton, New York University, Columbia University, Barnard College, Villanova University, University of Connecticut

Year 5: Colorado, Texas, South, Northeast, Midwest
44 Schools: *New Regional Office opens in **Kansas City**: University of Kansas, Kansas State University, University of Oklahoma, Oklahoma State University, University of Missouri, Missouri State University, University of Ohio, Ohio State University, Purdue University, University of Michigan, University of Wisconsin, University of Illinois

Year 6: *Continued Expansion*: Northeast, Midwest, West

2890 Shadow Creek – Boulder, Colorado – 303.579.9871 – info@upi.com

University Parent, Inc.

Management

Sarah Schupp, Chief Executive Officer

Sarah founded *The Parent's Guide to Boulder* in June of 2003. A graduate of the University of Colorado with degrees in Business Administration and English Literature, Sarah is capable of expanding the vision of UPI across the U.S. In addition, she has developed relationships with the University of Colorado through her 2004 position as the Senior Class President and member of the President's Leadership Class.

Ryan Roth, Chief Technology Officer

Ryan comes to UPI with an extensive background in high-level web technology and information system deployment strategies. As team leader of numerous successful system development projects, Ryan is a valuable addition to UPI as Chief Technology Officer. He joined our team in early 2004 to provide in-depth, focused research on technology issues and solutions to provide University Parent with customized solutions unmatched by any other magazine publisher today. Ryan graduated from the Leeds School of Business at the University of Colorado with a B.S. in Business Administration and an emphasis in Information Systems.

Kara Grinnell, Chief Financial Officer

Kara is equipped with the financial knowledge needed to accomplish all the tasks included in the job of Chief Financial Officer. With a degree in Finance from the University of Colorado, Kara has the appropriate background to help UPI meet its financial goals. Kara has firsthand field experience with financial measurements and is prepared to help UPI become a $100 million venture.

Michelle Dorenkamp, VP Marketing

Michelle will graduate with a Bachelor of Science Degree in Business from the University of Colorado in May 2004. For the past three summers, she has worked in marketing and advertising for a real estate company. She has successfully worked with companies doing a direct mail campaign similar to the one that will be used to attract advertisers for the local guides.

University Parent, Inc.

Business Risks

Another company will copy our idea.

Because of a magazine's low start-up costs, it is likely that people will copy our concept. However, we can mitigate this risk by negotiating with national advertisers for annual contracts and with universities for distribution rights. Another way we can mitigate this risk is through strategic growth. By identifying the best regions for expansion, we will capture a new region each year. We are targeting geographically central locations with a high concentration of colleges and universities.

Universities will not cooperate to help us distribute the guide.

When selling advertisements to businesses, our greatest strength is that universities allow us to distribute the guide on campus. This distribution point makes advertisers believe their ROI will be greater because parents pay close attention to materials given to them by the university. However, our guide is an effective public relations tool for universities to give to parents and by maintaining appropriate content, we eliminate this obstacle.

Businesses will not buy advertising.

Our revenue projections are based on selling 25 or more print advertisements per issue and 10 Web ads per month per location. If businesses do not believe that our magazine will serve as an effective marketing tool, they will not purchase advertising. We must prove to advertisers that parents do and will read our magazine and will make buying decisions based on our information.

Each university has a different environment with different demographics.

Because we are producing guides with location-specific information, we must insure that the information we publish is accurate and appropriate for the area. If we miss the target demographic or culture of the area, parents will not read the guide and advertisers will not purchase advertising. To make sure we understand the area, representatives from our regional office will be familiar with every location in their region and will have student interns at each school that will help UPI understand the area and its parent population. In addition, we will use our website to collect marketing data. Weblogs, an online parent chat room, will allow us to track parents' comments and their geographic location, which will enable us to understand the issues at each university.

University Parent, Inc.

Financial Plan

Financial Summary

Revenue for UPI is derived from magazine and website advertising sales. UPI plans to sell advertising to both national and local advertisers. As more people read our magazine and visit our website, the prices we can charge advertisers will increase.

The following table summarizes five years of pro forma financial statements. Assumptions for the financial statements are located in Section G of the Appendix.

	Year 1	Year 2	Year 3	Year 4	Year 5
Operating Revenue	$495,000	$1,881,000	$4,573,800	$7,726,455	$12,276,479
Operating Expenses					
Salaries, Wages, & Benefits	$323,000	$692,230	$1,152,524	$1,526,238	$1,907,539
Depreciation	$6,667	$20,000	$40,000	$60,000	$80,000
Rent & Utilities	$40,000	$85,600	$131,592	$180,803	$233,460
Total Operating Expenses	$854,967	$1,547,676	$2,588,328	$3,611,938	$5,083,166
Income Taxes	$0	$0	-$550,989	-$1,542,198	-$2,749,048
Net Income (Loss)	($401,329)	$197,583	$1,227,012	$2,313,297	$4,123,572

17

University Parent, Inc.

Balance Sheet
Years 0–5 ($)

	Begin	Year 1	Year 2	Year 3	Year 4	Year 5
ASSETS						
CURRENT ASSETS						
Cash	530,000	117,763	281,640	1,616,578	4,006,443	8,252,410
Accounts Receivable		0	0	0	0	0
Inventories		0	0	0	0	0
Other Current Assets		113	3,947	50,228	63,484	75,729
Total Current Assets	530,000	117,875	285,588	1,666,806	4,069,927	8,328,139
PROPERTY & EQUIPMENT	0	16,533	50,133	81,733	109,333	136,133
TOTAL ASSETS	530,000	134,409	335,721	1,748,539	4,179,261	8,464,272
LIABILITIES & SHAREHOLDERS' EQUITY						
CURRENT LIABILITIES						
Short-Term Debt	0	0	0	0	0	0
Accounts Payable & Accrued Expen		5,625	9,281	191,445	306,567	464,840
Other Current Liabilities		113	186	3,829	6,131	9,297
Current Portion of Long-term Debt	0	0	0	0	0	0
Total Current Liabilities	0	5,738	9,467	195,274	312,698	474,137
LONG-TERM DEBT (less current portion)	0	0	0	0	0	0
STOCKHOLDERS' EQUITY						
Common Stock	30,000	30,000	30,000	30,000	30,000	30,000
Preferred Stock	500,000	500,000	500,000	500,000	500,000	500,000
Retained Earnings		(401,329)	(203,746)	1,023,266	3,336,563	7,460,135
Total Equity	530,000	128,671	326,254	1,553,266	3,866,563	7,990,135
TOTAL LIABILITIES & EQUITY	530,000	134,409	335,721	1,748,539	4,179,261	8,464,272

18

University Parent, Inc.

Offering

Investment Requirements
UPI initially requires $500,000 in seed funding for the first year of operations. This amount will fund the expansion to the University of Denver and Colorado State University as well as funding new employee salaries and the opening of a Colorado regional office in Boulder. Investors will own 35% of the venture.

Valuation
Using the venture capital method, in Year 5, assuming net earnings of $4.1 million, and an industry P/E ratio of 17.3, UPI will have a market value of $70 million.

Financing
UPI seeks $500,000 in seed funding in Year 0. This round will provide the investor with a 35% stake in the venture at a 60% annual rate of return.

Exit Strategy
In Year 5, UPI we be marketed to Hearst Publishing and Condé Nast Publishing. These are logical acquirers because both companies own over 30 niche magazines.

University Parent, Inc.

Appendices

Income Statement...A

Balance Sheet ....B

Cash Flow Statement...C

Monthly and Quarterly Cash Flow Statements.......................................D

Break-Even Analysis..E

Capital Expenditure Detail..F

Financial Assumptions ....G

Development Timeline ....H

Summary of Customer Surveys...I

Management Team Resumes ....J

    Sarah Schupp, CEO

    Kara Grinnell, CFO

    Ryan Roth, CTO

    Michelle Dorenkamp, VP Marketing

20

2890 Shadow Creek – Boulder, Colorado – 303.579.9871 – info@upi.com

University Parent, Inc.

Appendix A, Income Statement, Years 1–5 ($)

	Year 1	Year 2	Year 3	Year 4	Year 5
NET REVENUES	495,000	1,881,000	4,573,800	7,726,455	12,276,479
COST OF REVENUE	26,362	90,741	152,471	204,023	255,692
% of Revenues	5.3%	4.8%	3.3%	2.6%	2.1%
GROSS PROFIT	468,638	1,790,259	4,421,329	7,522,432	12,020,787
% of Revenues	94.7%	95.2%	96.7%	97.4%	97.9%
OPERATING EXPENSES					
Sales & Marketing	240,750	364,610	674,953	1,023,764	1,734,098
Research & Development	219,800	291,186	360,569	434,809	514,245
General and Administration	394,417	891,880	1,552,806	2,153,364	2,834,823
Total Operating Expenses	854,967	1,547,676	2,588,328	3,611,938	5,083,166
% of Revenues	173%	82%	57%	47%	41%
EARNINGS FROM OPERATIONS	(386,329)	242,583	1,833,001	3,910,495	6,937,620
EXTRAORDINARY INCOME/ (EXPENSE)	(15,000)	(45,000)	(55,000)	(55,000)	(65,000)
EARNINGS BEFORE INTEREST & TAXES	(401,329)	197,583	1,778,001	3,855,495	6,872,620
INTEREST INCOME/(EXPENSE)	0	0	0	0	0
NET EARNINGS BEFORE TAXES	(401,329)	197,583	1,778,001	3,855,495	6,872,620
TAXES	0	0	(550,989)	(1,542,198)	(2,749,048)
NET EARNINGS	(401,329)	197,583	1,227,012	2,313,297	4,123,572
% of Revenues	-81.1%	10.5%	26.8%	29.9%	33.6%

University Parent, Inc.

Appendix B, Balance Sheet, Years 0–5 ($)

	Begin	Year 1	Year 2	Year 3	Year 4	Year 5
ASSETS						
CURRENT ASSETS						
Cash	530,000	117,763	281,640	1,616,578	4,006,443	8,252,410
Accounts Receivable		0	0	0	0	0
Inventories		0	0	0	0	0
Other Current Assets		113	3,947	50,228	63,484	75,729
Total Current Assets	530,000	117,875	285,588	1,666,806	4,069,927	8,328,139
PROPERTY & EQUIPMENT	0	16,533	50,133	81,733	109,333	136,133
TOTAL ASSETS	530,000	134,409	335,721	1,748,539	4,179,261	8,464,272
LIABILITIES & SHAREHOLDERS' EQUITY						
CURRENT LIABILITIES						
Short-Term Debt	0	0	0	0	0	0
Accounts Payable & Accrued Expen		5,625	9,281	191,445	306,567	464,840
Other Current Liabilities		113	186	3,829	6,131	9,297
Current Portion of Long-Term Debt	0	0	0	0	0	0
Total Current Liabilities	0	5,738	9,467	195,274	312,698	474,137
LONG-TERM DEBT (less current portion)	0	0	0	0	0	0
STOCKHOLDERS' EQUITY						
Common Stock	30,000	30,000	30,000	30,000	30,000	30,000
Preferred Stock	500,000	500,000	500,000	500,000	500,000	500,000
Retained Earnings		(401,329)	(203,746)	1,023,266	3,336,563	7,460,135
Total Equity	530,000	128,671	326,254	1,553,266	3,866,563	7,990,135
TOTAL LIABILITIES & EQUITY	530,000	134,409	335,721	1,748,539	4,179,261	8,464,272

2890 Shadow Creek – Boulder, Colorado – 303.579.9871 – info@upi.com

University Parent, Inc.

Appendix C, Cash Flow Statement, Years 1–5 ($)

	Year 1	Year 2	Year 3	Year 4	Year 5
OPERATING ACTIVITIES					
Net Earnings	(401,329)	197,583	1,227,012	2,313,297	4,123,572
Depreciation	7,467	24,400	48,400	72,400	97,200
Working Capital Changes					
(Inc.)/Dec. Accts. Rec.	0	0	0	0	0
(Inc.)/Dec. Inventories	0	0	0	0	0
(Inc.)/Dec. Other CA	(113)	(3,835)	(46,281)	(13,256)	(12,245)
(Inc.)/Dec. Accts Pay Expenses	5,625	3,656	182,163	115,122	158,274
(Inc.)/Dec. Other CL	113	73	3,643	2,302	3,165
Net Cash Provided/(Used) Operating Activities	(388,237)	221,878	1,414,937	2,489,865	4,369,967
INVESTING ACTIVITIES					
Property & Equipment	(24,000)	(58,000)	(80,000)	(100,000)	(124,000)
Other					
Net Cash Used in Investing	(24,000)	(58,000)	(80,000)	(100,000)	(124,000)
FINANCING ACTIVITIES					
(Inc.)/Dec. Short-Term Debt	0	0	0	0	0
(Inc.)/Dec. Curr. Portion LTD	0	0	0	0	0
(Inc.)/Dec. Long-Term Debt	0	0	0	0	0
(Inc.)/Dec. Common Stock	0	0	0	0	0
(Inc.)/Dec. Preferred Stock	0	0	0	0	0
Dividends Declared	0	0	0	0	0
Net Cash Provided/ (Used) by Financing	0	0	0	0	0
INCREASE/(DECREASE) IN CASH	(412,237)	163,878	1,334,937	2,389,865	4,245,967
CASH AT BEGINNING OF YEAR		530,000	117,763	281,640	1,616,578	4,006,443
CASH AT END OF YEAR	530,000	117,763	281,640	1,616,578	4,006,443	8,252,410

23

University Parent, Inc.

Appendix D, Monthly and Quarterly Cash Flow Statements, Years 1–5 ($)

	Year 1	Year 2	Year 3	Year 4	Year 5
OPERATING ACTIVITIES					
Net Earnings	(401,329)	197,583	1,227,012	2,313,297	4,123,572
Depreciation	7,467	24,400	48,400	72,400	97,200
Working Capital Changes					
(Inc.)/Dec. Accts. Rec.	0	0	0	0	0
(Inc.)/Dec. Inventories	0	0	0	0	0
(Inc.)/Dec. Other CA	(113)	(3,835)	(46,281)	(13,256)	(12,245)
(Inc.)/Dec. Accts Pay Expenses	5,625	3,656	182,163	115,122	158,274
(Inc.)/Dec. Other CL	113	73	3,643	2,302	3,165
Net Cash Provided/(Used) Operating Activities	(388,237)	221,878	1,414,937	2,489,865	4,369,967
INVESTING ACTIVITIES					
Property & Equipment	(24,000)	(58,000)	(80,000)	(100,000)	(124,000)
Other					
Net Cash Used in Investing	(24,000)	(58,000)	(80,000)	(100,000)	(124,000)
FINANCING ACTIVITIES					
(Inc.)/Dec. Short-Term Debt	0	0	0	0	0
(Inc.)/Dec. Curr. Portion LTD	0	0	0	0	0
(Inc.)/Dec. Long-Term Debt	0	0	0	0	0
(Inc.)/Dec. Common Stock	0	0	0	0	0
(Inc.)/Dec. Preferred Stock	0	0	0	0	0
Dividends Declared	0	0	0	0	0
Net Cash Provided/ (Used) by Financing	0	0	0	0	0
INCREASE/(DECREASE) IN CASH	(412,237)	163,878	1,334,937	2,389,865	4,245,967
CASH AT BEGINNING OF YEAR	530,000	117,763	281,640	1,616,578	4,006,443
CASH AT END OF YEAR	530,000	117,763	281,640	1,616,578	4,006,443	8,252,410

2890 Shadow Creek – Boulder, Colorado – 303.579.9871 – info@upi.com

University Parent, Inc.

Appendix E, Break-Even Analysis, Years 1–5 ($)

	Year 1	Year 2	Year 3	Year 4	Year 5
Revenue	495,000	1,881,000	4,573,800	7,726,455	12,276,479
Cost of Revenue					
Variable	24,562	85,341	141,671	186,023	228,692
Fixed	1,800	5,400	10,800	18,000	27,000
Total	26,362	90,741	152,471	204,023	255,692
Operating Expenses					
Variable	49,500	188,100	457,380	772,646	1,227,648
Fixed	805,467	1,359,576	2,130,948	2,839,292	3,855,519
Total	854,967	1,547,676	2,588,328	3,611,938	5,083,166
Total Costs & Expenses					
Variable	74,062	273,441	599,051	958,668	1,456,340
Fixed	807,267	1,364,976	2,141,748	2,857,292	3,882,519
Total	881,329	1,638,417	2,740,799	3,815,960	5,338,858
Variable Costs/Revenue Ratio	0.15	0.15	0.13	0.12	0.12
Break-Even Point Revenues	949,301	1,597,154	2,464,540	3,262,032	4,405,087

Appendix F, Capital Expenditure Detail

	Year 1	Year 2	Year 3	Year 4	Year 5
Net Revenues	495,000	1,881,000	4,573,800	7,726,455	12,276,479
Capital Expenditures					
Computers, Software, & Office Equipment	20,000	40,000	60,000	80,000	100,000
Plant & Equipment	0	0	0	0	0
Other	4,000	18,000	20,000	20,000	24,000
Total Capital Expenditures	24,000	58,000	80,000	100,000	124,000

25

University Parent, Inc.

Appendix G, Financial Assumptions

General Assumptions

First Month of Operations	June 2004
Estimated Inflation	2.5%
Corporate Tax Rate	38%

Annual Projections

	Year 1	Year 2	Year 3	Year 4	Year 5
Product A—Magazine					
Number of Schools	3	9	22	32	44
Total Issues/Year	9	36	66	96	132
Number of Units/Ad	225	900	1,800	2,925	4,425
Avg. Price/Ad Page	$1,000	$1,100	$1,210	$1,331	$1,464
Print Advertising Sales	$225,000	$990,000	$2,178,000	$3,893,175	$6,478,643
Product B—Website					
Advertisements Sold/Year	360	1,080	2,640	3,840	5,280
Price per Unit	$750	$825	$908	$998	$1,098
Web Advertising Sales	$270,000	$891,000	$2,395,800	$3,833,280	$5,797,836

Printing Costs

	Year 1	Year 2	Year 3	Year 4	Year 5
Magazines Printed/Year	90,000	360,000	660,000	960,000	1,320,000
Printing Cost/Magazine	0.25	0.23	0.21	0.19	0.17
Total Costs	22,500	82,800	138,600	182,400	224,400

Funding

Total Shares Outstanding	2,000,000
Preferred Shares (Investors)	700,000 (35%)
Common Shares (Founders/Employees)	130,000 (65%)
Expected Investor IRR	60%
Total Funding Required	$500,000
Founders' Contribution	$30,000

2890 Shadow Creek – Boulder, Colorado – 303.579.9871 – info@upi.com

University Parent, Inc.

Appendix H, Development Timeline, Year 1

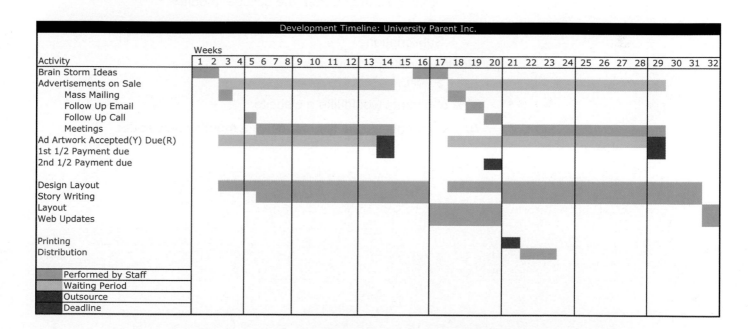

2890 Shadow Creek – Boulder, Colorado – 303.579.9871 – info@upi.com

University Parent, Inc.

Appendix I, Customer Survey Results

40 Parents were interviewed about the UPI concept.

- Parents currently purchase:
  - ✓ Newsweek, Time, Weekly Standard, Economist, Forbes, Money, Sports Illustrated, AAE Journal, Martha Stewart Living, Real Simple, Family Circle, People, Young Riders, Redbook, Budget Traveler, Business Week, Kiplingers, Smithsonian, Business World, Outside, New Yorker, More, Good Housekeeping, In Style, Cosmopolitan, Allure, Fast Company, Inc, Prevention, Readers Digest, Sunset, Tennis, Golf, Consumer Reports, Veranda, Scientific American

- Currently purchase magazines:
  - ✓ Subscription, Airport, Grocery Store

- 90% percent of parents surveyed would purchase the magazine

- Parents want information about:
  - ✓ Grades, Scholarships, Travel Opportunities, Housing Expenses, Activities in College Town, Time Management, Social Life, Programs, Internships, Job Placements, Curriculum, Student Safety, Speakers, Career Guidance, Graduation Requirements, Student Groups, Transportation

- Currently receive information:
  - ✓ From the student, from the college, media

- Would like to purchase UP:
  - ✓ Subscription

- Would be willing to pay:
  - ✓ $1–$5

- 60% of parents would like a website

- 70% of parents would like to receive a monthly newsletter

28

Appendix 2

BizBuilder Business Plan

Congratulations! Since you have made it this far, you've given yourself a comprehensive, basic education in entrepreneurship, and you may have made progress toward creating a business model and/or a business plan that will guide your success in many ways. At this point, you may want to expand and enhance your business plan. A sample comprehensive outline follows. With the exception of the Cover Page and Table of Contents, each question should be answered in clear, concise and complete sentences and paragraphs without the lettered lists (A, B, C and the like). Some sections will require very few sentences and others will be considerably longer.

BizBuilder Business Plan Outline Questions/Notes

Cover Page

A. Full legal name of your organization.

B. Contact information for the organization, including the names of majority owners.

C. Confidentiality/nondisclosure language.

D. Date of the plan.

Table of Contents (Can Be Placed Before or After the Executive Summary)

A. List the key sections of the plan and the page numbers.

1.0 Executive Summary

A. Name of your organization.

B. Description of your business idea and the nature of the target market.

C. Type of organization (e.g., C corporation, LLC, sole proprietorship) and location.

D. Brief description of the products and/or services you will offer.

E. Description of your marketing and sales strategy. Explain how your business idea will satisfy a customer need.

F. Key success factors.

G. Short-term business goals (less than one year).

H. Long-term business goals (from one to five years).

I. Resources and skills that you and other owners and managers have that will help make your organization successful, plus other skills needed and how they will be obtained.

J. Plan to share ownership (if there will be more than one owner).

K. Sources and uses of funds.

L. Summary of financial projections.

M. Growth and exit strategy.

2.0 Mission, Vision, and Culture

A. Write a mission statement for your organization in 21 to 40 words that clearly states your competitive advantage, strategy, and tactics.

B. Create a vision statement for your organization.

C. Describe the core beliefs you will use to run your organization and how they will be reflected in its culture.

D. Identify the ways you plan to run a socially responsible organization.

3.0 Company Description

A. What industry are you in?

B. What type of organization is it (manufacturing, wholesale, service)?

C. What needs will this business satisfy?

D. What is your strategic advantage?

E. What is your organization's legal structure (sole proprietorship, partnership, LLC, C corporation, etc.)?

F. Why did you choose this legal structure?

G. In what state are you registered or do you intend to register?

H. Where will you physically operate the organization?

I. What is the geographic reach of the organization?

J. Who will be the owner(s), partners, or stockholders for your company?

K. Identify what percentage of the company is owned by owner.

4.0 Opportunity Analysis and Research

A. Describe your target customer along as many dimensions as you have defined (demographic, geographic, needs, trends, and decision-making process).

B. Describe the research methods you used to develop this section (surveys, focus groups, general research, and statistical research).

4.1 Industry Analysis (Remember to correctly cite any sources)

A. What is the industry or set of industries in which your organization operates (include the NAICS codes and/or SIC codes)?

B. How large is your industry (historic, current, projected size)?

C. What are the current and anticipated characteristics and trends in the industry?

D. What are the major customer groups for the industry (consumers, governments, businesses)? Describe them in detail.

E. How large is your target market (number of customers, size of purchases, frequency of purchases, trends)? Quantify it. Describe the entire potential market and the portion that you will address or target.

F. What factors influence the demand for your product or service?

G. What factors influence the supply for your product or service?

4.2 Environmental Analysis

A. Perform a SWOT (strengths, weaknesses, opportunities, and threats) analysis of your organization. Remember that strengths and weaknesses are internal to your organization, and opportunities and threats are external.

B. What external/environmental factors are likely to impact your business? How likely are they?

C. Are there customers for your business in other countries? How do you plan to reach them?

4.3 Competitive Analysis

A. Define/describe your competition, both direct and indirect.

B. Describe your competitive advantage(s) along the dimensions of quality, price, location, selection, service, and speed/turnaround as they apply.

C. Find three competitors and describe them. Use the comparative analysis tables in Chapter 3 to perform a qualitative and/or quantitative analysis.

D. Describe any international competitors who may be able to access your customers. How do you intend to compete against them?

E. Describe your strategy for outperforming the competition.

F. What tactics will you use to carry out this strategy?

G. What barriers to entry can you create to block out competitors? How will you do so?

5.0 Marketing Strategy and Plan

A. Explain how your marketing plan targets your market segment (geography, demographics, psychographics, behaviors). Be specific.

B. What percentage of the market do you need to capture for your business to be profitable? Explain this.

C. Write a positioning statement for your business using the format from Chapter 4.

D. How do you plan to grow the organization (self-generated, franchising, acquisition)?

5.1 Products/Services

A. What products/services do you intend to market?

B. Explain how your product will meet a customer need.

C. Where is your product/service (not your business) in the product life cycle?

D. Describe the features and benefits of the product/service your business will focus on selling.

E. What copyrights, trademarks, patents, or other intellectual property do you own or expect to own?

F. How will your organization help others? List all the organizations to which you plan to contribute. (Your contribution may be time, money, your product, or something else.)

G. Do you intend to publicize your philanthropy? Why or why not? If you do, explain how you will work your philanthropy into your marketing.

5.2 Pricing

A. Describe your pricing strategy (value, prestige, cost-plus, penetration, skimming, meet-or-beat, follow-the-leader, personalized, variable, or price lining), structure, and the gross margins you expect to generate.

B. What will your discount structure, if any, be? How will it impact your average price (your pocket price)?

C. Will you extend credit to customers? On what terms? If doing retail sales, what forms of payment will you accept?

5.3 Promotion

A. Identify the ways you plan to promote your product or service, including the message, the media, and the distribution channels. Describe why you have chosen these methods and why you think they will work. Include a table showing the methods and budgets.

B. Show examples of marketing materials you intend to use to sell.

C. What is your business slogan?

D. What is your business logo? How do you intend to protect it?

E. Where do you intend to advertise (be specific, including identifying reach and frequency)?

F. How do you plan to get publicity for your organization?

G. List ways you intend to provide superior customer service.

H. How will you keep your customer database? What essential questions will you ask every customer for your database? What data will you collect through customer purchases?

5.4 Place

A. Where do you intend to sell your product (physical and/or virtual locations)? Describe the advantages and disadvantages of your location(s). If you have a specific site, provide detailed information.

B. What are the surrounding businesses? Access routes?

C. If vehicular traffic is important to your organization, what is the traffic count for this location?

D. What is the workforce availability in the area as it pertains to your needs? Use census or workforce data and cite it.

6.0 Management and Operations

6.1 Management Team

A. Create an organizational chart for your business, if it will have more employees than you at any point. You may want to create one for the start-up period and one for a future time period, such as year 3.

B. Will you be hiring employees? If so, describe what their qualifications should be, what you intend to pay them, and how they will help your business. Detailed position descriptions can be placed in the appendices.

C. Do you intend to pay yourself a salary, wage, dividend, or commission? Explain the method and the decision criteria regarding the level of compensation.

D. What will your most important policies toward employees be? How will you make your organization a positive and rewarding place to work?

E. Describe the corporate governance plan for your organization. It should include five policies (rules) that will be the backbone of your organization's ethics.

F. Provide information on each of your mentors or advisors. If there is a board of advisors, list each member and describe his/her commitment to the board.

G. Provide contact information for your accountant, attorney, banker, and insurance agent.

6.2 Research and Development

A. What type of research are you doing? What do you intend to do?

B. What are others in the industry doing?

C. How will you protect your intellectual property?

6.3 Physical Location

A. Describe the actual physical place in greater detail than above.

B. What zoning laws apply to your business? Does it comply? Are variances required?

6.4 Facilities

A. What type of building and equipment will you have?

B. Identify which technological tools you plan to use for your organization, and explain why.

C. How do you plan to get access to the technology you need?

6.5 Inventory, Production, and Quality Assurance

A. From what companies or individuals will you purchase the products you plan to sell or the parts you will use to manufacture those products? Illustrate your supply chain.

B. Do you intend to manufacture your product? If so, describe the manufacturing processes you will use. If not, describe how your product is manufactured.

C. Are there any economies of scale to be attained for your business? If so, what are they and at what point do you anticipate attaining them?

D. Have you developed and/or adopted any innovations in production, inventory management, or distribution that are significant? What are they and why are they meaningful?

E. How do you plan to distribute your product to your target market?

F. Illustrate the production-distribution channel for your business and the markups along the chain.

G. What is the estimated delivery time between when you place an order with your supplier and when you will have the product available for your customers?

H. What method(s) will you use to define and ensure the quality of your products/services?

I. What types of insurance will your business need, and why?

J. What methods will you use to ensure that you comply with federal, state, and local tax laws?

K. What laws—such as minimum wage and age requirements, health and safety regulations, or antidiscrimination laws—will affect your business?

7.0 Financial Analysis and Projections

A. Describe your recordkeeping system, including the software you will use and whether it is specific to your industry.

B. List the types of bank accounts you will open for your organization.

7.1 Sources and Uses of Capital

A. How much capital do you need? When? What type and on what terms?

B. How will you use the money you raise? Be specific.

C. List the items you will need to buy to start your business and add up the items to get your total start-up capital.

D. List the sources of financing for your start-up capital. Identify each source as equity, debt, or gift. Indicate the amount, type, and desired terms for each source.

E. What is your payback period? In other words, how long will it take you to earn enough profit to cover start-up capital?

F. Describe financing sources that might be willing to invest in your business in exchange for equity.

G. Describe any debt financing you intend to pursue. What is your debt ratio? What is your debt-to-equity ratio?

H. Do you plan to use bootstrap financing? Explain.

I. Do you plan to pursue venture capital? Why or why not? List potential sources of venture capital.

7.2 Cash Flow Projections

A. List and describe your monthly fixed costs.

B. Create a projected cash flow statement for your business for the first four quarters and the second and third years of operation.

C. Calculate the burn rate for your business.

7.3 Balance Sheet Projections

A. Create a projected balance sheet for your business for the first four quarters and the second and third years of operation.

B. Create a pie chart showing your current assets, long-term assets, current liabilities, and long-term liabilities.

7.4 Income Statement Projections

A. Create a projected income statement for your business for the first four quarters and the second and third years of operation.

B. Create a bar chart showing your gross revenues, gross profit, and net income.

7.5 Breakeven Analysis

A. Perform a breakeven analysis and report your breakeven volume.

7.6 Ratio Analysis

A. Use your projected financial statements to calculate all of your key ratios.

B. Compare these ratios to your industry using publicly available data.

7.7 Risks and Assumptions

A. List the risks and assumptions that underlie your financial projections.

B. Identify any external factors that may be substantial risks.

8.0 Funding Request and Exit Strategy

8.1 Amount and Type of Funds Requested

A. Clearly state how much money you are requesting and the terms under which you anticipate obtaining the funds.

B. Do you intend to use debt to finance your business? Explain.

C. If you are asking for equity, how have you valued your company?

8.2 Exit Plan

A. How will investors get paid back/out? Public offering? Employee buyout? Merger or acquisition? Liquidation? Stock buyback?

B. When will this happen?

C. Do you plan to franchise your business or license any of your products? Explain.

8.3 Milestones

A. Create a GANTT chart for your organization to make your plans clear to potential investors.

Appendices

Resumes and Position Descriptions

A. Include a resume for each key team member.

B. Add position descriptions for any vital start-up positions that are not yet filled.

Sample Promotional Materials

A. Include any sample logos, letterhead, advertisements, brochures, or other items that can be inserted into the plan.

B. Add photos of any promotional items, signage, or larger materials to provide examples.

Product Illustrations/Diagrams

A. If you have nonproprietary drawings or properly authorized proprietary drawings, illustrations, or diagrams of your product or service concept, insert them here.

B. Any floor plans, assembly layouts, or the like should be included.

Detailed Financial Projections

A. Financial projections that are in greater detail than the main business plan document might be provided here.

B. Include detailed assumptions and notes underlying the projections.

C. Include information about significant contracts.

If You Are Starting a Not-for-Profit Organization, Also Consider

1. What is the name of your organization?
2. What problem(s) are you trying to reduce or eliminate?
3. What is the mission of your organization?
4. What programs and services will you create?
5. How will your organization achieve the intended changes?
6. What is the unit of change (per person, animal, house, etc.)?
7. How will you measure these changes?
8. Who are your competitors?
9. How much will it cost you to deliver a unit of service?
10. What are your proposed sources of funding (earned income and grants/gifts)?

Appendix 3

Resources for Entrepreneurs[1]

Books

On Starting a Business—and Succeeding

The $100 Startup: Reinvent the Way You Make a Living, Do What You Love, and Create a New Future, Chris Guillebeau (Random House, 2012).

The Art of the Start: The Time-Tested, Battle-Hardened Guide for Anyone Starting Anything, Guy Kawasaki (Portfolio, 2004).

Crush It: Why Now Is the Time to Cash In on Your Passion, Gary Vaynerchuk (Harper Studio, 2009).

Do More Faster: Tech Stars Lessons to Accelerate Your Startup, David Cohen and Brad Feld (Wiley, 2010).

The 4-Hour Workweek, Timothy Ferriss (Crown Archetype, 2009).

The Four Steps to the Epiphany: Successful Strategies for Products That Win, Steve Blank (K&S Ranch Publishing, 2013).

Good to Great: Why Some Companies Make the Leap . . . and Others Do Not, Jim Collins (Harper-Business, 2001).

In Search of Excellence: Lessons from America's Best-Run Companies, Thomas J. Peters and Robert H. Waterman (Harper, 2004).

The Innovator's Solution: Creating and Sustaining Successful Growth, Clayton M. Christensen and Michael E. Raynor (Harvard Business School Press, 2003).

The Lean Startup: How Today's Entrepreneurs Use Continuous Innovation to Create Radically Successful Businesses, Eric Ries (Crown Business, 2011).

Online Success Tactics: 101 Ways to Build Your Small Business, Jeanette S. Cates (Twin Towers Press, 2002).

Reality Check: The Irreverent Guide to Outsmarting, Outmanaging, and Out-marketing Your Competition, Guy Kawasaki (Portfolio Trade, 2011).

Resourcing the Start-Up Business, Oswald Jones, Allan MacPherson, and Dilani Jayawarna (Routledge, 2014).

Screw Business as Usual, Richard Branson (Portfolio, 2011).

Social Entrepreneurship: What Everyone Needs to Know, David Bornstein and Susan Davis (Oxford University Press USA, 2010).

Start Your Own Business, 5th ed., Rieva Lesonsky (Entrepreneur Press, 2010).

The Startup Owner's Manual, Steve Blank and Bob Dorf (K & S Ranch, 2012).

What No One Ever Tells You About Starting Your Own Business: Real-Life Start-Up Advice from 101 Successful Entrepreneurs, 2nd ed., Jan Norman (Kaplan Business, 2004).

The Young Entrepreneur's Guide to Starting and Running a Business: Find Out Where the Money Is . . . and How to Get It, Steve Mariotti (Crown Business, 2014).

---

[1]Please note that the publisher cannot guarantee that listed URLs will remain active and is not responsible for future changes to the content of the Web sites.

On Thinking Like an Entrepreneur

The 7 Habits of Highly Effective People, anniv. ed., Stephen Covey (Simon & Schuster, 2013).

Awakening the Entrepreneur Within: How Ordinary People Can Create Extraordinary Companies, Michael Gerber (Harper, 2009).

Delivering Happiness: A Path to Profits, Passion, and Purpose, Tony Hsieh (Business Plus, 2010).

Escape from Cubicle Nation: From Corporate Prisoner to Thriving Entrepreneur, Pamela Slim (Berkley Trade, 2010).

The Entrepreneurial Mindset: Strategies for Continuously Creating Opportunity in an Age of Uncertainty, Rita Gunther McGrath and Ian MacMillan (Harvard Business School Press, 2000).

Focus: The Future of Your Company Depends on It, Al Ries (Harper, 2005).

Heart, Smarts, Guts, and Luck: What It Takes to Be an Entrepreneur and Build a Great Business, Anthony K. Tjan, Richard J. Harrington, and Tsun-Yan Hsieh (Harvard Business Review Press, 2012).

The Innovator's DNA: Mastering the Five Skills of Disruptive Innovators, Clayton M. Christensen, Jeff Dyer, and Hal Gregersen (Harvard Business Review Press, 2011).

Never Get a "Real" Job: How to Dump Your Boss, Build a Business, and Not Go Broke, Scott Gerber (Wiley, 2010).

Oh, the Places You'll Go! Dr. Seuss (Random House, 1990).

Secrets of the Young & Successful: How to Get Everything You Want Without Waiting a Lifetime, 2nd ed., Jennifer Kushell and Scott M. Kaufman (Ys Media Corp., 2006).

The Student Success Manifesto: How to Create a Life of Passion, Purpose, and Prosperity, Michael Simmons (Extreme Entrepreneurship Education Co., 2003).

Think and Grow Rich: The Secret to Wealth Updated for the 21st Century, Napoleon Hill (CreateSpace, 2010).

A Whack on the Side of the Head: How You Can Be More Creative, 25th anniv. rev. ed., Roger Von Oech (Business Plus, 2008).

On How Other Entrepreneurs Succeeded

The Accidental Entrepreneur: The 50 Things I Wish Someone Had Told Me About Starting a Business, Susan Urquhart-Brown (AMACOM, 2008).

Brewing Up a Business: Adventures in Beer from the Founder of Dogfish Head Craft Brewery, 2nd ed., Sam Calagione (Wiley, 2011).

Built from Scratch: How a Couple of Regular Guys Grew The Home Depot from Nothing to $30 Billion, Arthur Blank and Bernie Marcus (Crown Business, 2001).

By Invitation Only: How We Built Gilt Groupe and Changed the Way Millions Shop, Alexis Maybank and Alexandra Wilkis Wilson (Penguin Group, 2012).

Display of Power: How FUBU Changed a World of Fashion, Branding and Lifestyle, Daymond John (Thomas Nelson Publishers, 2007).

Entrepreneurs in Profile: How 20 of the World's Greatest Entrepreneurs Built Their Business Empires . . . and How You Can Too, Steve Mariotti and Michael Caslin with Debra DeSalvo (The Career Press, Inc., 2002).

The Everything Store: Jeff Bezos and the Age of Amazon, Brad Stone (Little, Brown and Company, 2013).

Founders at Work: Stories of Startups' Early Days, Jessica Livingston (Apress, 2007).

The Idea Man, Paul Allen (Penguin Group, 2011).

Kitchen Table Entrepreneurs: How Eleven Women Escaped Poverty and Became Their Own Bosses, Martha Shirk, Anna Wadia, Marie Wilson, and Sara Gould (Westview Press, 2004).

Losing My Virginity: How I Survived, Had Fun, and Made a Fortune Doing Business My Way, Richard Branson (Crown Business, 2011).

The Men Behind Def Jam: The Radical Rise of Russell Simmons and Rick Rubin, Alex Ogg (Omnibus Press, 2009).

The Midas Touch: Why Some Entrepreneurs Get Rich—And Why Most Don't, Donald Trump and Robert Kiyosaki (Plata Publishing, 2011).

Shark Tales: How I Turned $1000 into a Billion Dollar Business, Barbara Corcoran with Bruce Littlefield (Penguin Group, 2011).

Start Something That Matters, Blake Mycoskie (Spiegel & Grau, 2011).

Steve Jobs, Walter Isaccson (Simon & Schuster, 2011).

Student Entrepreneurs: 14 Undergraduate All-Stars Tell Their Stories, Michael McMyne and Nicole Amare (Premium Press America, 2003).

Trump: The Way to the Top: The Best Business Advice I Ever Received, Donald Trump (Crown Business, 2004).

Wild Company: The Untold Story of Banana Republic, Mcl and Patricia Ziegler (Simon & Schuster, 2012).

You Need to Be a Little Bit Crazy: The Truth About Starting and Growing Your Business, Barry J. Moltz (Authorhouse, 2008).

On Negotiating

The Art of Woo: Using Strategic Persuasion to Sell Your Idea, G. Richard Shell and Mario Moussa (Penguin Group, 2007).

Bargaining for Advantage: Negotiation Strategies for Reasonable People, G. Richard Shell (Penguin Group, 2006).

Getting to Yes: Negotiating Agreement Without Giving In, Roger Fisher, William L. Ury, and Bruce Patton (Penguin, 2011).

Winning, Jack Welch (HarperCollins, 2005).

On Accounting

The Accounting Game: Basic Accounting Fresh from the Lemonade Stand, 2nd ed., Judith Orloff and Darrell Millis (Sourcebooks, Inc., updated rev. ed., 2008).

Accounting Made Simple: Accounting Explained in 100 Pages or Less, Mike Piper (Simple Subjects, LLC, 2013).

Barron's Accounting Handbook, 5th ed., Joel G. Siegel and Jae K. Shim (Barron's Educational Series, 2010).

E-Z Accounting, 5th ed., Peter J. Eisen (Barron's Educational Series, 2009).

Financial Statements: A Step-by-Step Guide to Creating and Understanding Financial Reports, Thomas R. Ittelson (Career Press Inc., 2009).

On Investing, Money Management, and Personal Finance

The Entrepreneur's Guide to Finance and Business: Wealth Creation Techniques for Growing a Business, Steven Rogers (McGraw-Hill, 2002).

Irrational Exuberance, 2nd ed., Robert J. Shiller (Broadway Business, 2006).

The Laws of Money, The Lessons of Life: Keep What You Have and Create What You Deserve, Suze Orman (The Free Press, 2003).

Rich Dad, Poor Dad: What the Rich Teach Their Kids About Money—That the Poor and Middle Class Do Not! Robert T. Kiyosaki and Sharon L. Lechter (BusinessPlus, 2010).

Understanding Wall Street, 5th ed., Jeffrey B. Little (McGraw-Hill, 2009).

On Marketing

Anatomy of Buzz: How to Create Word of Mouth Marketing, Emanuel Rosen (Crown Business, 2002).

The Art of the Pitch: Persuasion and Presentation Skills That Win Business, Peter Coughter (Palgrave MacMillan, 2012).

Blue Ocean Strategy: How to Create Uncontested Market Space and Make Competition Irrelevant, W. Chan Kim and Renée Mauborgne (Harvard Business School Press, 2005).

Brand Sense, Martin Lindstrom (Free Press, 2010).

Buy-o-logy: Truth and Lies About Why We Buy, Martin Lindstrom (Crown Business, 2008).

Contagious: Why Things Catch On, Jonah Berger (Simon & Schuster, 2013).

Conversation on Networking: Finding, Developing, and Maintaining Relationships for Business and Life, Steven Smolinsky and Kay Keenan (Forever Talking Press, 2006).

Crossing the Chasm: Marketing and Selling High-Tech Products to Mainstream Customers, Geoffrey A. Moore (Harper Business, 2006).

The Dragonfly Effect: Quick, Effective, and Powerful Ways to Use Social Media to Drive Social Change, Jennifer Aker, Andy Smith, Dan Ariely, and Chip Heath (Jossey-Bass, 2010).

Duct Tape Marketing: The World's Most Practical Small Business Selling Guide, John Jantsch (Thomas Nelson, 2008).

Guerilla Marketing: Easy and Inexpensive Strategies for Making Big Profits from Your Small Business, 4th ed., Jay Conrad Levinson (Houghton Mifflin Harcourt, 2007).

Influence: The Psychology of Persuasion, Robert B. Cialdini (Harper Collins, 2009).

The Long Tail: Why the Future of Business Is Selling Less of More, Chris Anderson (Hyperion, 2006).

Made to Stick: Why Some Ideas Survive and Others Die, Chip Heath and Dan Heath (Random House, 2007).

Permission Marketing: Turning Strangers into Friends, and Friends into Customers, Seth Godin (Simon & Schuster, 1999).

Poke the Box, Seth Godin (The Domino Project, 2011).

Positioning: The Battle for Your Mind, 3rd ed., Al Ries and Jack Trout (McGraw Hill, 2000).

Purple Cow: Transform Your Business by Being Remarkable, Seth Godin (Portfolio, 2003).

The Sales Bible: The Ultimate Sales Resource, New Edition, Jeffrey Gitomer (HarperCollins, 2008).

Selling the Invisible: A Field Guide to Modern Marketing, Harry Beckwith (Business Plus, 1999).

Setting the Table: The Transforming Power of Hospitality in Business, Danny Meyer (Harper Paperbacks, 2008).

Smarter, Faster, Cheaper: Non-Boring, Fluff-Free Strategies for Marketing and Promoting Your Business, David Siteman Garland (Wiley, 2010).

The Tipping Point: How Little Things Can Make a Big Difference, Malcolm Gladwell (Back Bay Books, 2002).

Web Analytics 2.0: The Art of Online Accountability and Science of Customer Centricity, Avinash Kaushik (Sybex, 2009).

Web Sites

Association Directory: http://www.asaecenter.org/Communities/Directories/associationsearch.cfm, from the American Society of Association Executives.

BizBuySell: http://www.bizbuysell.com—sends registered users who might want to buy your business e-mails, alerting them that you want to sell.

Business Owners Idea Café: http://www.businessownersideacafe.com/—a tool for figuring out how much capital you will need to get your business off the ground.

Census Data: http://www.census.gov.

Copyright Office: http://www.copyright.gov.

Currency Converter: http://finance.yahoo.com/currency-converter/.

Internal Revenue Service: http://www.irs.gov.

Internet Public Library: http://www.ipl.org—a good source for industry and market statistics.

InterNIC: http://www.internic.net—register the name of your Web site through the U.S. Department of Commerce.

Practical Money Skills: http://www.practicalmoneyskills.com.

Standards of Corporate Responsibility: http://www.svn.org/initiatives/standards .html—provides ideas on how to make your business socially responsible.

Surveys can be created using *http://www.surveymonkey.com.*

Additional Resources

The **Small Business Administration (SBA)** is a federal agency created to support and promote entrepreneurs. The SBA offers free and inexpensive pamphlets on a variety of business subjects. Some local offices offer counseling to small business owners.

Contact the SBA at: Small Business Administration, 409 Third Street, SW, Washington, DC 20416, (800) 827–5722, or visit *http://www.sba.gov.*

The **Minority Business Development Agency (MBDA)** is a federal bureau created to foster the establishment and growth of minority-owned businesses. MBDA provides funding for a network of Minority Business Development Centers (MBDCs), Native American Business Development Centers (NABDCs), and Business Resource Centers (BRCs). The centers provide minority entrepreneurs with one-on-one assistance in writing business plans, marketing, management and technical assistance, and financial planning to assure adequate financing for business ventures.

To find a Minority Business Development Center in your area, visit *http://www.mbda.gov.*

The **Service Corps of Retired Executives (SCORE)** is a group of retired businesspeople who volunteer as counselors and mentors to entrepreneurs. To locate an office near you, contact SCORE Association, 409 3rd Street, SW, 6th Floor, Washington, DC 20024, (800) 634-0245, *http://www.score.org.*

The **National Association of Women Business Owners** helps female entrepreneurs network. You can join a local chapter of female entrepreneurs in your area.

National Association of Women Business Owners, 601 Pennsylvania Avenue, NW, South Building, Suite 900, Washington, DC 20004, (800) 55-NAWBO, *http://www.nawbo.org.*

The **United States Department of Agriculture (USDA)** is a federal agency that provides financial and business support in rural communities through its Business and Community Development Programs. It also offers Cooperative Services Programs to promote the use of co-ops to distribute and market agricultural products. Much like the SBA-supported Small Business Development Centers, there are Rural Business Entrepreneurship Centers nationwide.

USDA, 1400 Independence Avenue, SW, Washington, DC 20250, (202) 720-2791, *http://www.usda.gov.*

The **Kauffman Foundation** is a private foundation dedicated to creating economic independence through education and entrepreneurship. It offers a variety of resources for entrepreneurs, including training, research, and videos.

The Kauffman Foundation, 4801 Rockhill Road, Kansas City, MO 64110, (816) 932-1000, http://www.kauffman.org and http://www.entrepreneurship.org.

Awards for Entrepreneurs

If you are an entrepreneur under age 25, you may qualify for awards that promote youth entrepreneurship and education. Check the Internet for new programs.

Ernst & Young Entrepreneur of the Year Award

http://www.ey.com

To qualify for the Ernst & Young award, you must be an owner/manager primarily responsible for the recent performance of a privately held or public company that is at least two years old.

National Association for the Self-Employed Future Entrepreneur of the Year Award

http://www.nase.org/Membership/Benefits/NASE_Scholarships_Program.aspx

This scholarship is given to a young man or woman who is a micro-business owner and demonstrates leadership and academic excellence, ingenuity, and entrepreneurial spirit.

NFIB Young Entrepreneur Award

http://www.nfib.com/page/nfibYoungEntrepreneurAward.html

The NFIB Young Entrepreneur Foundation grants NFIB Young Entrepreneur Awards to high school seniors nationwide.

NFTE Global Young Entrepreneur of the Year

http://www.nfte.com

NFTE graduates can win an all-expenses-paid trip to New York City for NFTE's annual "Dare to Dream" Awards Dinner and a grant to be used in the awardee's business or applied toward college.

SBA Young Entrepreneur of the Year Award

http://www.sba.gov

At National Small Business Week, one outstanding entrepreneur is named to represent each state, the District of Columbia, Puerto Rico, and Guam as the state Small Business Person of the Year. From this group, the National Small Business Person of the Year is chosen.

Staples Youth Social Entrepreneurship Competition

http://www.changemakers.com/competition/staplesyv

For young people from 12 to 24 inclusive who are operating a youth-led social venture and are able to demonstrate impact. Hosted by Ashoka and Staples, Inc.

Appendix 4

Useful Formulas and Equations

Liquidity Ratios

$$\text{Current Ratio} = \frac{\text{Current Assets}}{\text{Current Liabilities}}$$

$$\text{Quick Ratio} = \frac{\text{Current Assets} - (\text{Inventory} + \text{Prepayments})}{\text{Current Liabilities}}$$

Activity Ratios (Efficiency Ratios)

$$\text{Accounts Receivable Turnover} = \frac{\text{Annual Net Credit Sales}}{\text{Average Accounts Receivable}}$$

$$\text{Average Collection Period} = \frac{\text{Accounts Receivable}}{\text{Average Daily Credit Sales}}$$

$$\text{Inventory Turnover} = \frac{\text{Cost of Goods Sold}}{\text{Average Inventory}}$$

$$\text{Days' Sales in Inventory} = \frac{\text{Ending Inventory}}{\text{Daily Cost of Goods Sold}}$$

Profitability Ratios

$$\text{Gross Profit Margin} = \frac{\text{Gross Profit}}{\text{Net Sales}}$$

$$\text{Return on Sales} = \frac{\text{Net Income}}{\text{Sales}}$$

$$\text{Return on Assets (ROA)} = \frac{\text{Net Income} + \text{Interest} + \text{Income Taxes}}{\text{Average Total Assets}}$$

$$\text{Return on Common Equity (ROE)} = \frac{\text{Net Income} - \text{Preferred Stock Dividends}}{\text{Average Common Stockholders' Equity}}$$

Market Ratios

$$\text{Earnings per Share (EPS)} = \frac{\text{Net Income} - \text{Preferred Stock Dividends}}{\text{Common Shares Outstanding}}$$

$$\text{Return on Investment (ROI)} = \frac{\text{Net Income}}{\text{Average Owners' Equity}}$$

Debt Ratios (Leverage Ratios)

$$\text{Debt Ratio} = \frac{\text{Total Liabilities}}{\text{Total Assets}}$$

$$\text{Debt-to-Equity Ratio} = \frac{\text{Total Debt} + \text{Value of Leases}}{\text{Total Equity}}$$

$$\text{Times Interest Earned or Interest Coverage} = \frac{\text{EBIT}}{\text{Interest Expense}}$$

Glossary

accrual method accounting method wherein transactions are recorded at the time of occurrence, regardless of the transfer of cash.

acquisition a business purchase.

advertising paid promotion through media outlets.

advisory board or council a group that provides advice and counsel, but does not have the responsibilities of a board of directors.

angel investor a wealthy individual who invests in businesses.

arbitration a method of dispute resolution using an arbitrator to act as the decision maker rather than going to court.

asset any item of value.

asset valuation a method that analyzes the underlying value of a business's assets as a basis for negotiating a price.

audit a review of financial and business records to ascertain integrity and compliance with standards and laws, particularly by the U.S. Internal Revenue Service.

balance sheet a financial statement summarizing the assets, liabilities, and net worth of a business.

bankruptcy the legal process in which an individual or business declares the inability or impaired ability to pay debts as they come due.

barriers to entry the factors that contribute to the ease or difficulty of a new competitor joining an established market.

behavioral interview dialogue designed to determine the fit of a prospective employee with the requirements of a position, using prior-experience examples.

benchmarking the comparison of a company's performance against that of companies in the same industry, or against best practices, standards, or certification criteria.

blog (short for Web log) a journal that appears on the Internet periodically (perhaps daily) and is intended for the public.

blogosphere the collective term used for all the blogs on the Internet.

boilerplate language a standard format for a specific type of legal agreement.

book value valuation of a company as assets minus liabilities.

bootstrap financing financing a business by creatively stretching existing capital as far as possible, including extensive use of the entrepreneur's time.

brand a type of product or service from a particular company under a specific name.

brand spiraling integrating a company's conventional offline branding strategy with its Internet strategy by using conventional approaches to drive traffic to its online sites.

breach of contract the failure of a signatory to perform as agreed.

breakeven point when the volume of sales exactly covers the fixed costs.

burn rate the pace at which a company must spend capital before generating positive cash flow.

business model a company's plan to generate revenue and make a profit from operations.

business plan a document that thoroughly explains a business idea and how it will be carried out.

buzz marketing another name for word-of-mouth marketing.

capital money or property owned or used in business.

capitalism the free-market system, characterized by individuals and companies competing for economic gains, ownership of private property and wealth, and price determination through free-market forces.

cash accounting method a system wherein transactions are recorded when cash is paid out or received.

cash flow statement a financial statement showing cash receipts less cash disbursements for a business over a period of time.

cash flow statement financial report that shows the money coming into and going out of an organization.

cash flow valuation a method of calculating the worth of a business by using projected future cash flows and the time value of money.

cash reserve emergency funds and a pool of cash resources.

cause-related marketing promotional efforts inspired by a commitment to a social, environmental, or political cause.

certificate an official document that verifies something.

chain of command hierarchy of reporting and communications.

charge account credit extended by a company allowing qualified customers to make purchases up to a specified limit, without paying cash at the time of purchase.

clustering the strategy of similar businesses locating near each other.

code of conduct a set of official standards of employee behavior for a company.

code of ethics a statement of the values of a company.

code of ethics and business conduct a combination of a written statement of values with official standards of employee behavior.

commission   a percentage of a sale paid to a salesperson.

competitive analysis   research that compares an organization with several direct and indirect competitors by name in a manner that is meaningful to targeted customers.

competitive strategy   the combination of the business definition with its competitive advantage.

compound interest   used with interest or rate of return and applied when earnings also accumulate interest or other returns, in addition to earnings on principal.

contingency   a condition that must be met in order for something else to occur.

continuous improvement   always identifying and implementing changes throughout an organization to focus on the requirements of internal and external customers.

contract   an agreement between two or more parties that is enforceable by law.

contribution margin   gross profit per unit—the selling price minus total variable costs plus other variable costs.

core values   the fundamental ethical and moral philosophy and beliefs that form the foundation of the organization and provide broad guidance for all decision making.

corporate governance   rules and safeguards to ensure that executives behave legally and ethically.

corporate social responsibility   the ethical obligation of a company to its community.

corporation   a legal entity composed of stockholders under a common name.

cost of goods sold (COGS)   the cost of selling one additional unit of a tangible item.

cost of services sold (COSS)   the cost of selling one additional unit of a service.

cost/benefit analysis   a decision-making process in which the costs of taking an action are compared to the benefits.

cost-plus pricing   takes the organization's product cost and adds a desired markup.

credit history   a record of credit extended and the repayment thereof.

credit reporting agency (CRA)   an organization that collects, analyzes, and resells information supplied by financial institutions and others who extend credit.

credit   the ability to borrow money.

creditor   person or organization that is owed money.

culture   the beliefs, values, and behavioral norms of an organization.

currency   a term for money when it is exchanged internationally.

current assets   cash or items that can be quickly converted to cash or will be used within one year.

current liabilities   debts that are scheduled for payment within one year.

current ratio   liquidity ratio consisting of the total sum of cash plus marketable securities divided by current liabilities.

customer relationship management (CRM)   company-wide policies, practices, and processes a business uses with its customers to generate maximum customer satisfaction and optimal profitability.

customer service   everything a business does to keep the customer happy.

database   a collection of information that is generally stored on a computer and organized for sorting and searching.

debt ratio   measures total debt versus total assets.

debt service   the amount a borrower is obligated to pay in a given period until a loan is repaid.

debt-to-equity ratio   compares total debt to total equity.

deductible   the amount of loss or damage a policyholder covers before the insurer pays on a claim.

default   the results of a borrower failing to meet the repayment agreement on a debt.

demographics   population statistics.

depreciation   the percentage of value of an asset subtracted periodically to reflect the declining value.

direct labor   employees that actively produce or deliver a product or service.

direct marketing   includes telemarketing, direct mail, in-person selling, and other personalized promotional efforts.

discount   (referring to bonds) the difference between a bond's trading price and its par value when the trading price is below par.

diversification   the addition of product or service offerings beyond a business's core product or service.

dividend   each stockholder's portion of the profit-per-share paid out by a corporation.

due diligence   the exercise of reasonable care in the evaluation of a business opportunity.

e-active marketing   when the two major components of Internet marketing—e-commerce and interactive marketing—combine.

earnings valuation   a method that assesses the value of a business based on a stream of earning that is multiplied either by an agreed-upon factor (the capitalization factor) or by the price/earnings ratio (for a publicly traded company).

economic order quantity (EOQ)   the amount of inventory to order that will equal the minimum total ordering and holding costs.

economics of one unit of sale (EOU)   the amount of gross profit that is earned on each unit of the product or service a business sells.

edutainment   a promotion that combines education and entertainment to make a more lasting impression upon an audience.

electronic rights   the right to reproduce someone's work online.

electronic storefront   an online site that customers can visit to view a company's catalog, price lists, and documentation.

elevator pitch   a 30-second to 2-minute presentation that conveys in an engaging way what a business is proposing and why the listener should be interested.

entrepreneur   a person who recognizes an opportunity and organizes and manages a business, assuming the risk for the sake of potential return.

environmental analysis   a review that addresses the roles of the community, region, nation, or the rest of the world, as they relate to a business.

ethical dilemma   a circumstance in which there is a conflict of ethical values, which thus muddies decision making.

ethical relativism   situation where ethical standards are believed to be subject to interpretation.

ethics   a system of moral conduct and judgment that helps determine right and wrong.

face value   the amount of a bond, also known as par, to be repaid by the corporation or government at its maturity date.

factoring   receivables financing, or accessing cash for your business in exchange for offering a company the rights to the cash that will be collected from your customers.

factor-rating method   location-decision criteria that are prioritized and weighted to eliminate subjective considerations.

fair market value   the price at which a property or business is valued by the marketplace; the price it would fetch on the open market.

feasibility analysis   a study to assist in making the go/no go decision based on a close examination of product/service, market, industry, and financial data in a sufficient degree of detail to ensure confidence in the results.

financing   the act of providing or raising funds (capital) for a purpose.

fiscal year   the financial reporting year for a company.

fixed costs   expenses that must be paid regardless of whether sales are being generated.

fixed operating costs   expenses that do not vary with changes in the volume of production or sales.

float   the time between a payment transaction and when the cash is actually in the payee's account.

follow-the-leader pricing   a pricing strategy that is similar to a meet-or-beat-the-competition method, but uses a particular competitor as the model for pricing.

foreign exchange (FX) rate   the relative value of one currency to another.

foundation   a not-for-profit organization that manages donated funds, which it distributes through grants to individuals or to other nonprofit organizations that help people and social causes.

franchise   a business that markets a product or service developed by a franchisor, typically in the manner specified by that franchisor.

free-enterprise system   economic system in which businesses are privately owned and operate relatively free of government interference.

future value   the amount an asset will gain over time.

gazelle   a company that achieves an annual growth rate of 20 percent or greater, typically measured by the increase of sales revenue.

goodwill   an intangible asset generated when a company does something positive that has value.

green entrepreneurship   business activities that avoid harm to the environment or help to protect it in some way.

gross profit   total sales revenue minus total cost of goods sold.

guerilla marketing   original, unconventional, and inexpensive small-business promotional strategies.

harvesting   the act of selling, taking public, or merging a company to yield proceeds for the owner(s).

human resources   the segment of a business that hires, trains, and develops a company's employees.

hyperlink   word(s) that, when clicked on, transfer the computer user to another Web page.

hypertext   web-based documents that combine text and graphics.

income statement   a financial document that summarizes income and expense activity over a specified period and shows net profit or loss.

industry analysis   a critical view of industry definition, industry size and growth (or decline), product and industry life cycle, and any current or anticipated legal or regulatory concerns.

initial public offering (IPO)   first offering of corporate stock to investors on the open (public) market.

in-kind donation   a contribution of products or services that may include time or goods, rather than cash.

institutional advertising   provides information about an organization, rather than a specific product, and is intended to create awareness about a firm and enhance its image.

insurance   a system of protection for payment provided by insurance companies to reimburse individuals and organizations when their property or wealth has been damaged, destroyed, or lost.

interview guide   a document to assist in question development regarding an individual's knowledge, skills, abilities, and interests.

inventory costs   expenses associated with materials and direct labor for production until the product is sold.

investment   something a person or entity devotes resources to in hopes of future profits or satisfaction.

job offer letter   a formal written invitation extended by an employer to a candidate selected for hiring that states basic employment terms, such as the position offered, starting date, and salary.

job profile   identification of the knowledge, skills, and abilities required to perform the specific tasks of an employment position.

leader a person who gets things done through influence, by guiding or inspiring others to voluntarily participate in a cause or project.

leasehold improvements changes made to adapt a rented property for a particular business.

letter of agreement a document that puts an oral understanding in writing, in the form of a business letter.

leveraged financed by debt, as opposed to equity.

liability a business debt.

license an official document that grants the right to engage in an activity for a specified period of time.

licensing renting your brand or other intellectual property to increase sales.

lifestyle business a microenterprise that permits its owners to follow a desired pattern of living, such as supporting college costs or taking vacations.

limited partnership business partnership wherein there is a general partner with unlimited liability, and one or more limited partners with no official input in daily operations, and limited liability.

line and staff organization a business structure that includes the line organization, plus staff specialists (such as attorneys) who assist management.

line extension using an established brand to promote different kinds of products.

line organization a business structure in which each person reports to a single supervisor.

liquidation the sale of all assets of a business concurrent with its being closed.

liquidity the ability to convert assets into cash.

logo short for logotype, a company trademark or sign.

long-term assets those that will take more than one year to use.

long-term liabilities debts that are due in over one year.

lurk reading messages and getting a feel for discussions on a Web site, newsgroup, or the like, without participating in the online conversation.

market a group of people or organizations that may be interested in buying a given product or service, has the resources to purchase it, and is permitted by law and regulation to do so.

market research the collection and analysis of data regarding target markets, industries, and competitors.

market segment a group of consumers or businesses that have a similar response to a particular type of product or service.

marketable securities investments that can be converted into cash within 24 hours.

marketing the development and use of strategies for getting a product or service to customers and generating interest in it.

marketing mix the combination of the four factors—product, price, place, and promotion—that communicates a marketing vision.

marketing plan a statement of the marketing goals and objectives for a business and the intended strategies and tactics to attain them.

markup pricing a cost-plus pricing strategy in which a predetermined percentage is applied to a product's cost to obtain its selling price.

maturity the date at which a loan must be repaid, including when a bond must be redeemed by the issuer.

meet-or-beat-the-competition pricing constantly matching or undercutting the prices of the competition.

mentor a trusted advisor with whom a person forms a developmental partnership through which information, insight, skills, and knowledge are shared to promote personal and/or professional growth.

merger the joining of two companies in order to share their respective strengths.

microenterprise a firm with five or fewer employees, initial capitalization requirements of under $35,000, and the regular operational involvement of the owner.

mission a concise communication of strategy, including a business definition and explanation of competitive advantage.

mission statement a brief, written statement that informs customers and employees what an organization's goal is and describes the strategy and tactics to meet it.

mobile social networking the updating of social-network sites via mobile handsets.

net profit the remainder of revenues minus fixed and variable costs and taxes.

net worth (owner's equity) the difference between assets and liabilities.

net worth the difference between assets and liabilities.

noncash expenses adjustments to asset values not involving cash, such as depreciation.

notary a person who has been authorized by the state to witness the signing of documents.

not-for-profit organization an entity formed with the intention of addressing social or other issues, with any profits going back into the organization to support its mission.

operating ratio an expression of a value versus sales.

operational plan the stated short-term methods for achieving tactical goals.

operations a set of actions that produce goods and services.

opportunity cost the value of what must be given up in order to obtain something else.

owner's equity (net worth) the difference between assets and liabilities.

owner's equity net worth.

par the face value of a bond (typically $1,000) and the stated value of a stock.

partnership a business with two or more owners that make decisions for the business together and share the profits, losses, assets, and liabilities.

patent an exclusive right, granted by the government, to produce, use, and sell an invention or process.

payback period estimated time required to earn sufficient net cash flow to cover the start-up investment.

payroll tax a deduction employers must make from their employees' pay and forward to the appropriate governmental entity.

penetration pricing a pricing strategy that uses a low price during the early stages of a product's life cycle to gain market share.

performance appraisal the formal process used to evaluate and support employees' work performance.

permit an official document that gives a party the right to hold a specific event.

personal guarantee the promise to pay issued by an individual.

personalized pricing a dynamic pricing strategy in which the company charges a premium above the standard price for a product or service to certain customers, who will pay the extra cost.

philanthropy a concern for human and social welfare that is expressed by giving money through charities and foundations.

pilferage theft of inventory.

pitch letter correspondence designed to explain the story behind a press release, and why it would be interesting and relevant to the media outlet's readers, listeners, or viewers.

policy loan a loan made against an insurance policy with cash value.

position description the explanation of the knowledge, skills, and abilities of a job profile, as well as the position's reporting and working relationships, plus its goals and objectives.

positioning distinguishing a product or service from similar products or services being offered to the same market.

premium (regarding bonds) the amount above par for which a bond is trading in the market.

premium the cost of insurance.

present value what the future amount of an asset or other investment is worth at face value discounted back to the present.

press release an announcement sent to the media to generate publicity that explains the "who, what, when, where, why, and how" of a story.

prestige pricing the pricing strategy in which a firm sets high prices on its products or services to send a message of uniqueness or premium quality.

price lining the process of creating distinctive pricing levels.

primary research conducted directly on a subject or subjects.

principal the amount of debt or loan before interest and fees are added.

process management the measurement, monitoring, and optimization of tasks.

product advertising is designed to create awareness, interest, purchasing behavior, and post-purchase satisfaction for specific products and services.

product life cycle (PLC) the four stages that a product or service goes through as it matures in the market—introduction, growth, maturity, and decline.

product something tangible that exists in nature or is made by people.

profit amount of money-remaining after all costs are deducted from the income of a business.

profit and loss statement (P&L) an income statement.

profit margin (return on sales) net income divided by sales (percentage).

promissory note a loan document that is a written promise to pay a specific sum of money on or before a particular date.

promotion the use of advertising and publicity to get a marketing message to customers.

proof of market an investigation that provides evidence of a market opportunity.

prospect a person or organization that may be receptive to a sales pitch.

prototype a model or pattern that serves as an example of how a product would look and operate if it were produced.

public domain property rights available to the public rather than held by an individual.

public relations community activities that are designed to enhance an organization's image.

publicity free promotion.

quality degrees of excellence; conformance to specifications or standards.

quick ratio indicates adequacy of cash to cover current debt.

recruitment the act of finding and hiring employees.

reorder point (ROP) the level at which materials need to be ordered again.

replication strategy a way for a business to obtain money by letting others copy its success formula for a fee.

return on investment (ROI) the net profit of a business divided by its start-up investment (percentage).

return on sales (ROS) net income divided by sales for a particular time period (percentage).

risk tolerance the amount of risk or threat of loss that an individual is willing to sustain.

safety stock the amount of inventory or raw materials or work-in-progress that is kept to guarantee service levels.

salary fixed amount of money paid to an employee at regular intervals.

sales tax an assessment levied by governments on purchases and collected by merchants.

secondary research carried out indirectly through existing resources.

security an investment instrument representing ownership in an entity (stock) or debt (bond) held by an investor.

seed capital (start-up investment) the one-time expense of opening a business.

self-employment tax federal tax that business owners are assessed on wages paid to themselves.

service   intangible work that provides time, skills, or expertise in exchange for money.

service mark   a design that identifies and distinguishes the source of a service rather than a product.

severance   pay that is continued for a limited time to an employee who has left a company.

share   a single unit of corporate stock.

signatory   an individual who signs a contract.

skimming pricing strategy   seeks to charge high prices during a product's introductory stage, to take early profits when the product is novel and has few competitors, and then to reduce prices to more competitive levels.

small claims court   a legal option for solving conflicts involving less than a certain sum of money.

social business   a company created to achieve a social objective while generating a modest profit to expand its reach, improve the product or service, and subsidize the social mission.

social entrepreneurship   a for-profit enterprise with the dual goals of achieving profitability and attaining social returns.

social entrepreneurship   the sale of products or services on a for-profit basis to benefit a social purpose.

sole proprietorship   a business owned by one person who has unlimited liability and unlimited rights to profits.

spam   unwanted Internet advertisements or e-mails.

span of control   the number of direct reports for a manager or supervisor.

statute of limitations   the time period in which legal action may be taken.

stealth marketing   undercover, or deceptive, marketing efforts that are intended to appear as if they happened naturally.

strategic plan   typically a three- to five-year overall design to achieve long-term growth, sales, and positioning goals for a business.

strategy   a plan for how an organization or individual plans to proceed with business operations and outperform that of its competitors.

supply chain management (SCM)   the management of sourcing, procuring, production, and logistics to go from raw materials to end customers across multiple intermediate steps.

sustainable   referring to a scenario in which current needs are met while preserving future resources.

SWOT analysis   a review conducted by an organization to identify its internal strengths and weaknesses and its external opportunities and threats.

tactical plan   a short-term (one year or less) implementation that has limited, specific objectives.

tactics   the specific ways in which a business carries out its strategy.

target market   groups defined by common factors such as demographics, psychographics, age, or geography that are of primary interest to a business.

tax abatement   legal reduction in taxes.

tax credit   direct reduction of taxes.

tax evasion   the deliberate avoidance of an obligation to pay taxes; may lead to penalties or imprisonment.

total quality management (TQM)   the quality-assurance methodology of striving for strategic advantage through quality.

trademark   any word, name, symbol, or device used by an organization to distinguish its product.

trade-off   the act of giving up one thing for another.

uniform resource locator (URL)   a Web-page address.

unique selling proposition (USP)   the distinctive feature and benefit that set a company apart from its competition.

unit of sale   the basic unit of the product or service sold by the business.

value pricing   "more for less" strategy that balances quality and price.

variable costs   expenses that vary directly with changes in the production or sales volume.

variable pricing strategy   provides different prices for a single product or service.

venture capitalist   an investor or investment company whose specialty is financing new, high-potential entrepreneurial companies and second-stage companies.

venture philanthropy   a subset or segment of social entrepreneurship wherein financial and human capital is invested in not-for-profits by individuals and for-profit enterprises, with the intention of generating social rather than financial returns on their investments.

viral marketing   the process of promoting a brand, product, or service through an existing social network, where a message is passed from one individual to another—much as a virus spreads.

vision   a broader and more comprehensive perspective on an organization than its mission; built on the core values and belief systems of the organization.

visual control   inventory-management method in which an individual assesses the stock level on hand by visual inspection and reorders when the supply appears low.

voluntary exchange   a transaction between two parties who agree to trade money for a product or service.

wage   fixed payment per hour for work performed.

wealth   the value of assets owned versus the value of liabilities owed.

working capital   the value of current assets minus current liabilities.

Index

Abrhaley, Fesehaye, 483
Accel Partners, 317
Access to Capital for Entrepreneurs
  (ACE Capital), 119
Accounting
  accrual method, 238
  cash method, 238
  defined, 235–236
  differences between countries on, 264
  taxation vs., 306
Accounting records, 235–238
Accounts payable
  aging schedule for, 299–300
  vendor financing and, 331
Accounts receivable
  cash effects of, 297
  financing of, 298
  life cycle of, 297–298
Accrual accounting method, 238, 288
ACE Capital, 119
Acquisition
  defined, 21
  as exit strategy, 468
  as path to ownership, 21
Activity ratios, 525
Actuaries, 372
Adjusted book value, 113
Advertising. See also Promotion
  in business plan, 49
  consumer-generated, 178
  customer awareness and, 139
  fixed costs and, 234
  institutional, 170
  objectives of, 169–170
  online, 175–178
  product, 171
  promotion and, 165
  pros and cons of different types of, 171
  types of, 170
Advisors, 11, 13
Advisory boards, 437
Advisory councils, 437
Affiliative leaders, 418
Agarwal, Shrada, 162
Age Discrimination in Employment Act
  (ADEA), 432
Agency law, 364–365
Aging schedule for accounts payable, 299–300
Aging schedule for accounts receivable, 297–298
Agritechno Hybrid, 447
Ain, Spencer, 317
Airbnb, 381–382
Allen, Greg, 347
Allen, Paul, 15
Allis, Ryan, 475, 476
Alternative marketing, 174–175
Amazon.com, 93, 97, 176, 217–218, 221, 222
American Electrical, Inc., 153
American Law Institute, 364
American Military University, 139
American Society of Association
  Executives, 138
American Stock Exchange (Amex), 334
Americans with Disabilities Act (ADA), 432
Amplified buzz marketing, 174
Anago Cleaning Systems, 473–474

Analysis
  of balance sheets, 260–262, 265–268
  of competitive advantage, 100–101
  cost/benefit, 10–11
  financial, in business plan, 51–55
  financial ratio, 262–268
  industry, 37–39, 48
  SWOT, 18, 55
  of targeted market, 37–39
Angel investors, 330–331
Annual reports, 133
Appendices, business plan, 56
Apple Computer, 93–94, 106–107, 158, 323
Appointments, for sales call, 200
Arbitration, 363
Arm & Hammer, 139
Ash, Mary Kay, 197
Asian Garden Mall, California, 35
Assets, 53
  in balance sheet, 256, 257–258, 260
  defined, 53
  in financial section of business plan, 53
  long-term, 258
  protecting intangible, 367–371
  protecting tangible, 371–374
Asset valuation method, 113
Association for Enterprise Opportunity
  (AEO), 22
Attorneys, contracts and, 361–362
Audience, business plan, 56–57
Audits, 236
Authoritative leadership style, 418
Awards, for entrepreneurs, 524
AYZH Inc., 445–446
Azriel, Jay, 342

Background checks, 426
Bai, Zubaida, 445–446
Balance sheet equation, 258
Balance sheets, 53, 251, 287
  analyzing, 260–262
  assets in, 257–258, 260
  defined, 53, 256
  depreciation and, 262
  examples, 54, 256–257, 285
  financial ratio analysis of, 265–268
  in financial section of business plan, 53
  frequency of preparing, 256
  liabilities in, 258, 261
  showing assets and liabilities obtained
    through financing, 258–259
  showing how a business is financed, 259–260
Baldridge Award, 402–403
Bank of America, 170
Bankruptcy, 318, 323, 327–328, 365–367
Bankruptcy Reform Acts (1978) (2005), 365
Banks
  community development, 328
  financing through, 324
Banner advertisements (online), 176
Barnes & Noble, 219, 221
Barriers to entry, 38, 101
Bauer, Dylan, 251
B corporations, 358
Behavioral interviews, 423
Behavioral market segmentation, 14

Beijing Redstone Industries Co. Ltd., 95
Benchmarking, 400–401
Bezos, Jeff, 217
Big Brothers/Big Sisters, 183
Big Green Egg, 119
Bill and Melinda Gates Foundation, 182, 183
Bimbo Bakeries USA, 97
BizBuilder Business Plan, 511–518
  template, 43, 44
BizMiner, 137, 138
Biz Plan Builder (software), 44
BizPlan.com (software), 44
Black, Bruce, 21
Blakely, Sara, 123–126
Blank, Steve, 131
Blog-hosting services, 177
Blogosphere, 177
Blogs, 177, 200
BNI (Business Networks International), 215
Bob's Discount Furniture, 236
Body Shop International, 16, 142
Boilerplate language, 362
Bonds, 319, 333, 335–336
Books, as research source, 133, 138
Books-A-Million, 221, 222
Bookstore industry
  changes in, 221
  customer demographics for, 221–222
  Kitchen Arts & Letters (KA&L), 219–221
Book value, 113, 465
Bootstrap funding, 332
Bosack, Leonard, 30
Boys and Girls Clubs of America, 183
Brain, building your, 24
Brand
  building your, 160–161
  defined, 130
  focusing your, 158–160
  licensing to profit from, 461
  successful advertising and, 170
Brand spiraling, 177
Branded entertainment, 174
Branson, Sir Richard, 9, 101, 125, 164
Breach of contract, 363
Breakeven point, 54–55
  calculating, 186–187
Brick-and-mortar retailers, 391, 392
Bridgecreek, 35
Broken contract, 363
Bronner, Michael, 183–184
Brouse, Mark, 464
Brown, Warren, 313–314
Budget
  capital, 300–301
  cash, 292, 294, 295
  promotional, 167–168
Bulk, selling in, 108
Bun Company, The, 380
Burda Media, 317
Burger King, 140, 146
Burn rate, 301
Burrell, Thomas, 143, 157
Burrell Advertising, 143
Business(es)
  closing a, 23
  competitive advantage of, 99–103

Business(es) (*Continued*)
core values of, 95, 96
costs of operating, 225–226
culture of, 97–98
definition, 94
determining the value of, 113–114
exiting, 463–469
exit strategy options for, 468–469
failure of, 318
growth, harvesting and exit strategies
for, 459–460
growth of, 460–463
harvesting, 463–464
marketing by (*See* Marketing)
mission statement of, 96–97
profit and, 23–24
rules for building a successful, 24
selling, 466–468
start-up investments, 226–230
team approach to, 24–25
valuing, 464–466
vision of, 97
Business definition
competitive strategy and, 105
elements of, 94
Business format franchise, 21
Business ideas
creating, 16
evaluated through SWOT analysis, 18
feasibility analysis of, 36–39
as not always being an opportunity, 17
Business income insurance, 372
Business legal structures, 353–361
comparison of, 359
corporations, 356–361
partnerships, 355–356
sole proprietorships, 353–355
Business management, 421–422
Business Model Canvas, 40–43
Business Model Generation site, 42
Business models, 40–43
Business Networks International (BNI), 215
Business PlanMaker Professional (software), 44
Business Plan Pro® (software), 44, 55
Business plans, 36–91
BizBuilder (sample), 511–518
Business Models Canvas for, 40–43
components of, 45–56
contents and components of, 45–56
contents of, 43
defined, 43
examples of, 43, 65–91
feasibility analysis and, 36–40
financing and, 324
guidelines and suggestions for writing,
56–57
Honest Tea, 65–91
loan packages and, 35
outline of, 46
presentation of, 44–45, 57–59
purposes of, 44–45
reasons for writing, 44–45
software for, 44
template for, 43
University Parent, Inc., 483–510
venture competitions and, 59–60
Business Resource Centers (BRCs), 523
Butterfield, Stewart, 317
Buyer power, 39
Buzz marketing, 174

CakeLove, 313–314
Campus recruitment, 427
Candler, Asa, 353

Capital
business plan as key to raising, 45
defined, 5
seed, 226
sources and uses of, in business plan, 51, 52
sources of, for financing, 324–332
working, 289
Capital assets, 300
Capital budgeting, cash flow and, 300–301
Capital equipment costs, 239
Capital funds, community development, 329
Capitalism, 4–5
Carnegie, Andrew, 184
Carroll, Lewis, 35
Case studies
on cash and cash flow, 311–315
on costs, 245–249
on entrepreneurial opportunities, 30–33
on exit strategy, 475–476
on financing, 340–350
on franchising, 473–474
on legal issues, 380–383
on marketing, 153–155
on marketing mix and plan, 192–195
on operations, 411–415
on opportunity, 119–126
on selling and customer service, 215–218
Cash
avoiding use of, 238
importance of, 287
investments, 333
Cash accounting method, 238
Cash budget, 292, 294, 295
Cash flow
accounts payable management and, 299–300
accounts receivables management and,
297–298
capital budgeting and, 300–301
case studies, 311–315
changing value of money and, 301–304
creating a healthy, 293
cyclical and seasonal nature of, 290–291
forecasting, 292–293
harvesting and, 466–467
importance of managing, 287
rules for having, 289
taxes and, 304
Cash flow assumptions, 295
Cash flow budget, 292, 294
Cash flow statements, 53, 251
as critical financial control, 288
defined, 288
equation, 292
examples of, 283–284, 293
functions of, 292
not required in all countries, 294
reading, 292
Cash flow valuation, 114
Cash receipts, in cash flow statements, 292
Cash reserve, 227–228
Casino Grande case study, 449–452
Cause-related marketing, 182–183
C corporations, 305, 357, 359
Census data/research, 137. *See also*
U.S. Census research
Certificates, 375
Chain of command, 428
Chambers of commerce, research through,
133, 138
Chan, Amy, 277–280
Channels (CN), in business plan, 42, 43
Chapter 7 bankruptcy, 365, 366
Chapter 11 bankruptcy, 365–366
Chapter 13 bankruptcy, 366–367

Charge accounts, 328
Charles G. Koch Foundation, 184
Chilly Dilly's Ice Cream Company, 251, 342–345
Chung Namp Inc., 391
Cisco Systems, 30
Clustering, 394
Coaching leadership style, 418
Coastal Enterprises, Inc., 340
Coca-Cola Company, 353, 461–462, 477, 480–481
Code of conduct, 435
Code of ethics, 435–436
Code of ethics and business conduct, 435–436
Coercive leadership style, 418
Cold calls, avoiding, 199
Coleman Foundation, 184
Collins, Jim, 422
Commercial fleet insurance, 372
Commission, 9, 198, 418
Common stock, 334
Communication
employee, 432
marketing, 165–167, 185–187
Community development banks, 328
Community development credit unions, 328–329
Community development financial institutions
(CDFIs), 328–329
Community development loan funds (CDLFs), 329
Community development venture capital funds
(CDVCs), 329
Community Trade Mark (CTM), 368
Company culture, 428
Compensation
for employees, 424, 426
for entrepreneurs, 417–418
Competition
learning about your, 102–103
venture, 59–60
Competitive advantage, 99–103
analyzing your, 100–101
competitive strategy and, 105–106
definition of, 99–100
Honest Tea, 478–479
marketing materials reinforcing your, 171–172
market position and, 146–147
six factors of, 101
strength of, 101–102
Competitive analysis
in business plan, 48–49
defined, 48
Competitive rivalry, evaluating, 38
Competitive spending, used for promotional
budget, 168–169
Competitive strategy, 105–106
Complaints, customer, 207–208
Compound interest, 303
Computers. *See also* Internet
importance of access to, 403
protecting, 373
Consumer-generated advertising, 178
ContextMedia, Inc., 162
Contingencies, 362
Contingency (employee) searches, 427
Continuous improvement, 402
Contracts, 361–363
Contribution margin, 231, 252
Conversation on Networking (Keenan/
Smolinsky), 202
Cooling and heating costs, 234
Copyright, 369
Core values, 95, 96
Corporate governance, 437
Corporate social responsibility, 438–440
Corporation for Enterprise Development
(CFED), 14–15

Corporations
  advantages of, 356
  compared with other business legal
    structures, 359
  defined, 356
  disadvantages of, 356–357
  nonprofit, 358, 360
  types of, 357–358
Cosmetic industry, 141, 142
Cost/benefit analysis, 10–11
Cost-leadership strategy, 19–20
Cost of goods sold (COGS), 107, 230,
  231–232, 252
Cost of services sold (COSS), 230, 252
Cost-plus pricing, 163
Costs
  calculating critical, 230–238
  categories of, 239
  fixed, 230
  fixed operating, 233–235
  operating, 225–226
  start-up investment, 226–230
  variable, 230
Cost structure, competition and, 103
Coupons, 172
Cover page, business plan, 46
Covey, Steven, 463
Cramer, Chuck, 385
Cramer, Frank, 385
Cramer Products, Inc., 385
Create Jobs for USA, 119
Creating a World without Poverty (Yunus), 14
Creative Entertainment Services, 174
Creativity
  entrepreneurship and, 8
  recognizing business opportunities and, 16
Credit
  accounts payable management and, 299
  defined, 299, 327
  establishing, 328
  five Cs of, 327
  good, 328
Credit history, 327
Creditor
  business failure and, 318
  defined, 318
Credit reporting agency (CRA), 327
Credit reports, 328
Credit unions, community development, 328–329
Critical costs, calculating, 230–239
CRM (customer relationship management),
  208–212
Crowley, Dennis, 31–33
Culture
  company, 97–98, 428, 429
  defined, 47
  leadership and, 97–98
  of your business, in business plan, 47
Currency, 112
Current assets, 257–258
Current liabilities, 258
Current ratio, 265
Customer relationship management (CRM),
  208–212
Customer Relationships (CR), in business plan,
  42, 43
Customers. *See also* Customer service; Target
  market
  balancing needs of owners, employees
    and, 438
  costs of losing, 206
  focus on, for sales call, 201–202
  owning a perception in mind of, 140
  purchasing practices of, 139–140

researching your, 135–137
selling and knowing your, 199
successful salespeople behaviors with, 203–204
teaching, 141
Customer Segments (CS), in business plan,
  40–41, 43
Customer service
  by Amazon.com, 217–218
  complaints and, 207–208
  customer relationship management (CRM)
    as part of, 208–212
  defined, 206
  by Kitchen Arts & Letters, 219–220
  Positively Outrageous, 207
  suggestions for, 206
  as a team effort, 211
  words to avoid and use for, 208

Data, protecting, 373
Database
  creating a, 212
  defined, 211
Database searches, 133
Davis, Josh, 340
Debt/equity exchange strategy, 468
Debt financing, 319, 320–322
Debtor in possession, 366
Debt ratios, 267, 525
Debt service, 327
Debt-to-equity ratio, 267
Deductibles, 371–372
Dees, Gregory, 13–14
Default, defined, 322
Def Jam Records, 19, 24, 154–155
De Garis, Hugo, 24
Deming, W. Edwards, 399
Democratic leadership style, 418
Demographic market segmentation, 142
Demographics, 137
Demonstrations, marketing through, 175
Dennis Publishing, 106
Depreciation, 233
  in balance sheets, 262
  in income statements, 254
Differentiation strategies, 19, 20
Direct foreign investment, 234
Direct labor, 107, 108, 110
Direct marketing, 49
Directory of Associations, 138
Direct version of cash flow statements, 292
Disability insurance, 372
Disaster recovery plans, 373–374
Disbursements, in cash flow statement, 292
Discounts, in bond trading, 335
Disney, 393
Distribution firms, facilities design and layout
  considerations for, 395
Diversification, 460
Diversified Search, 424
Dividends, 334
  benefits of entrepreneurship and, 9
  defined, 9
  as form of self-payment, 419
DMADV process (define, measure, analyze,
  design, and verify), 402
DMAIC process (define, measure, analyze,
  improve, and control), 402
Dodgeball, 31
Dolan, Kerry A., 95
Domino's Pizza, 140
Dorenkamp, Michelle, 483
Dorsey, Jack, 168
Dow AgroSciences, 96
Draft, of a contract, 362

Draper, Tim, 178
Draper Fisher Jurveston, 178
Drell, Lauren, 51
Drucker, Peter, 15, 16
Duckett, Megan, 413
Due diligence, 21
Dun & Bradstreet, 137, 328
DuPont Company, 96, 97
Durant, William C., 197, 198
Dyer, Wayne, 124

E active marketing, 175–178
Earnings before interest and taxes (EBIT), 252
Earnings valuation, 113–114
Earn-out exit strategy, 468
EBay, 8
E-commerce, 176
ECommerce Industries, Inc., 459
Economic order quantity (EOQ), 389–390
Economics of one unit of sale (EOU), 107,
  108–112, 225, 230, 231–232, 233
Economy, defined, 4
Edutainment, defined, 175
Efficiency (activity) ratios, 525
Eight-step sales call, 202–203
Electronic rights, 369–370
Electronic storefront, 405
Elevator pitch, 58
E-mail, for sales calls, 200–201
Emerson, Rip, 287n1
Empact (Extreme Entrepreneurship
  Education), 120–121
Empact Showcase, 121
Empact Summit, 121
Employees, 3
  background checks of, 426
  balancing needs of owners, customers,
    and, 438
  checking references of, 424
  compensation for, 424, 426
  finding and hiring, 421–422
  firing, 434
  guidelines for treatment of, 430
  interviewing potential, 423, 424, 425
  labor laws for, 431–432
  laying off, 434
  orientation for, 427
  performance appraisal of, 432–434
  recruiting, 422–423, 427
  socially responsible, 439
Employee stock ownership plan (ESOP), 467
Enron, 436
Entrepreneurs
  awards for, 524
  defined, 3–4
  "Do You Have What It Takes" quiz for,
    12–13
  entrepreneurship tour for, 120–121
  as leaders, 417–418
  mentors of, 11, 13
  payment methods for, 418–419
  resources for, 519–524
  taking the long view, 7
Entrepreneurship
  defined, 15
  green, 14–15
  many faces of, 22–23
  options for, 13–15
  potential benefits of, 8–9
  potential costs of, 9–10
  social, 13–14
Environmental analysis, 48
Equal Pay Act of 1963, 431
Equations, 525

Equity, financing with, 319
Equity financing, 322–323, 333
Ernst & Young Entrepreneur of the Year
    Award, 524
Errors and omissions insurance, 372
Estée Lauder Company, 266, 267
Ethical dilemmas, 435
Ethical relativism, 435
Ethical values, 436
Ethics, 434–440
    corporate scandals involving, 436–437
    defined, 434
    establishing standards for, 435–436
    Six Pillars of Character, 436
    social responsibility and, 438–440
Etsy, Inc., 317
Etter, James P., 139
Euro Disney Resort, 393
European Union (EU), 368
Excel, calculating net present value with, 229
Excess funds, used for promotional budget, 169
Executive (employee) searches, 427
Executive summary, in business plans, 46–47
Exit strategies, 468–469
    in business plan, 55–56
    case study, 475–476
    harvesting, 463–464
Expenses, noncash, 289
External opportunities, 18–19
Extreme Entrepreneurship Tour (EET), 120–121

Facebook, 177
Face value, 335
Facilities
    described in business plan, 50
    design and layout of, 394–397
    location of, 390–394
Factoring, 298
Factor-rating method, 393–394
Factory layout, 397
Fad products, 145
Fair Credit Reporting Act, 328
Fair Labor Standards Act (1938), 432
Fair market value, 465
Fake, Caterina, 317, 466
Family, as source of financing, 323
Family-owned-and-operated businesses, 460
Fanscape, 178
Farrah Gray Publishing, 192
Feasibility analysis
    defined, 36
    financial, 39–40
    industry, 37–39
    market, 37–39
    product, 36–37
    service, 36–37
    using economics of one unit of scale,
        106–112
Federal Express, 102
Federally supported investment companies, 331
Ferris, Matt, 21
Fields, Debbie, 4, 23
Financial analysis, in business plan, 51–55
Financial controls, 437
Financial feasibility, analysis of, 39–40
Financial ratio analysis, 262–268
Financial records, 235–238
Financial statements, 251–252. *See also*
    Balance sheets; Cash flow statements;
    Income statements
Financing
    bootstrap, 332
    case studies, 340–350
    choosing best type for your business,
        318–319

with debt, 319, 320–322
defined, 317
with earnings, 319
equity, 319, 322–323
with equity, 319
gifts and grants, 319, 320
investments, 333–336
by nonprofit corporations, 361
online networking and, 332–333
risk tolerance and, 319
for rural/agricultural businesses, 332
sources of capital for, 324–332
three methods for, 317–318
Firing employees, 434
First Call Office Products, 459
Fiscal year, defined, 256
Fixed costs (FC), 185, 239
    accounting records for tracking, 235–238
    dangers of, 235
    defined, 230
    in income statement, 252
Fixed operating costs, 233–235, 252
Flavor Flav's House of Flavor Take Out
    Restaurant, 192
Fleiss, Jennifer, 10
Flickr, 466
Float, defined, 331
Flying Tigers, 102
Focus
    on brand, 158–160
    on customer, during sales call, 201–202
Focus groups, 36, 132
Focus strategy, 20
Following-up, after sales call, 203
Follow-the-leader pricing, 164
Ford, Henry, 102, 230
Ford Foundation, 184
Ford Motor Company, 3, 102, 159–160, 330
Foreign exchange (FX) rate, 112
Forrester, Marce, 415
Foundations, 182, 184
Foursquare, 31–33
Franchises, 462–463
    business format, 21
    defined, 21
    as path to ownership, 20, 21
    securing rights to, 21
Franchising
    case study on, 473–474
    product/trade name, 21
Franklin, Benjamin, 353
Fraud, 373
Freebies, as sales promotional tool, 172
Free-enterprise system, 4–5
    benefits of, 5
    disadvantages, 6
    voluntary exchange and, 5
Freelancers Cafe (Portland, Oregon),
    277–285
Free trade, 5
Friends, as source of financing, 323
Future earnings, earnings valuation
    method and, 113
Future value, 301–303

Gale Publishing, 138
GameShowPlacements, 174
GANTT charts, 56, 419
Gap Inc., 142
Gates, Bill, 8, 15, 330
GATT (General Agreement on Tariffs
    and Trade), 5
Gazelles, 22
Gelato Fiasco, 340

General Agreement on Tariffs and Trade
    (GATT), 5
General Motors, 97
Gentle Rest Slumber, LLC, 276
Geographic information systems (GIS), 394
Geographic market segmentation, 142
Gerber, Scott, 297
Gifts, financing with, 320
Gillette, King C., 197, 288
Ginsberg, Bruce, 245
Girard, Joe, 200
Girl Scouts, 183
GIS (geographic information systems), 394
Global Crossing, 436
Global venture capital investments, 333
Golden Rules of CRM, for small
    businesses, 210
Goldman, Laurie Ann, 124, 125
Goldman, Seth, 43, 477–481
Goldman Sachs Foundation, 184
Good credit, 328
Good to Great (Collins), 422
Goodwill, concept of, 183
Gordy, Berry, 225
Gore, Bill, 8
Grameen Bank, 439
Grants, financing with, 320
Gray, Farrah, 192–193
Greaves, Joy, 346
Green, Sarah, 120
Green entrepreneurship, 14–15
Greeting, for sales call, 202–203
Grinnell, Kara, 483
Gross, T. Scott, 207
Gross profit, 107, 108, 252
Growth of business
    family businesses, 460
    through diversification, 460
    through franchising, 462
    through licensing, 461–462
Guerilla marketing, 174

Hall, Dawn, 119
Hall, Terry, 119
Happy Belly Curbside Kitchen, 119
Harrington, Cordia, 380
Harvesting, 463–469, 466–468
Hattikudur, Mangesh, 106
Hay, Louise, 422
Heating and cooling costs, 234
Held, Betty, 400
Held, Jim, 400
Herper, Michael, 255
Hewlett-Packard, 93, 97–98, 428
High risk investments, 333
Hiring employees, 426–427
Historical earnings, 113
Holter, Ron, 311–312
Holterholm Farms, 311–312
Home-based businesses, 396, 398
Homebrew Club, 93
Home Depot, 141, 206
Honest Tea, 477–482
Honest Tea Business Plan, 43, 65–91
Houghton, Aaron, 475–476
Hoverter, Haley, 370
How to Be a No-Limits Person (Dyer), 124
Hsieh, Tony, 92, 121
Human resources, 430–434
    areas of, 430–431
    defined, 430
    labor law compliance by, 431–432
Hyman, Jennifer, 10
Hyperlinks, 403
Hypertext, 404

I-9 form, 426–427
IBISWorld, 137
IBM, 93
Ice cream businesses, 340–349
iContact, 475–476
Ideas, business. *See* Business ideas
Imagination, use of, 17
Immigration Reform and Control Act
    of 1986 (IRCA), 432
Impressions, personal selling and, 198
Income statements, 53–54, 251, 287
    analyzing, 263
    bottom line on, 253–254
    in business plan, 53
    for complex businesses, 254–255
    defined, 53
    examples of, 253, 281–282
    financial ratio analysis and, 262–265
    not showing available cash, 288
    parts of, 252
    showing profit and loss over time, 252
Indeed.com, 422
Index Ventures, 317
InDinero, Inc., 287
Indirect version of cash flow statements, 292
Individual debt reorganization, 366–367
Industry analysis, 37–39, 48
Industry associations, research through, 133
Industry research, 137–138
Industry Surveys (Standard and Poor's), 137
Information technology (IT) training
    industry, 453
Initial public offering (IPO), 55–56, 467–468
In-kind donations, 439
In-N-Out Burger, 387
Institutional advertising, 170
In-store marketing, 174–175
Insurance, 371–373
Insurance companies, policy loan from, 331
Intangible assets, protecting, 367–371
Intellectual property, 367–371
Interactive marketing, 176
Internal opportunities, 18–19
Internal Revenue Service (IRS). *See* IRS
    (Internal Revenue Service)
International Organization for Standardization
    (ISO), 401
International trade, 5
International Trademark Association, 368
Internet
    accessing financing sources through
        networking on, 332–333
    advertising on, 175–178
    electronic storefronts on, 405
    importance of access to, 403–404
    industry research on, 138
    online businesses on, 164–165
    posting jobs on, 422
    pros and cons of advertising through, 171
    secondary research on, 133
    websites for entrepreneurs on, 522–523
Internet Advertising Bureau, 177
Interview guide, 423
Interviews
    for industry research, 138
    job, 423, 424, 425
    market segmentation and, 143
    as primary research method, 131–132
Intuit QuickBooks, 237
Inventory control, 50
Inventory costs, 231, 239
Inventory management, 295–296, 388–390
Investment
    defined, 263
    direct foreign, 234

equity financing, 322–323
    return on investment (ROI) and, 263
Investment costs, 239
Investments
    federally supported companies for, 331
    high-risk, 333
    low-risk, 333
    start-up, 226–230
    by venture capitalists, 329–330
Investors
    angel, 330–331
    venture capitalists, 329–330
IRS (Internal Revenue Service), 304–305, 306, 360
Isenberg, Daniel, 15
ISO 9000 standards, 401–402

Jackson, Bo, 385
JackThreads, 51
Jagemann, Paula, 459
Jao, Frank, 35
Jao, Kathy, 35
Japan, 399–400
Job interviews, 423, 424
Job offer letter, 426
Job profile, 422
Jobs, Steve, 93–94, 106–107, 112, 158, 323
John, Daymond, 370

Kafie, Daniel, 367
Kaiser, Henry J., 93
Kalin, Robert, 317
Kauffman Foundation, 523–524
Kaufman, Bob, 236
Keenan, Kay, 202
Key Activities (KA), in business plan, 42, 43
Key Partnerships (KP), in business plan, 42, 43
Key person life insurance, 372
Key Resources (KR), in business plan, 42, 43
Kidder, David S., 123n5
KidSmart Vocal Smoke Detector, 21
Kiosks, 173
Kitchen Arts & Letters (KA&L), 219–221
Kiva, 97, 330
Koplovitz, Kay, 121
Kopp, Wendy, 183
Krispy Kreme Doughnuts, 97
Kroc, Ray, 129, 197, 462
Kroll, Luisa, 95

Labor
    direct, 107, 108, 110
    economics of one unit and, 110
Labor laws, 431–432
Landrum, Gene, 121
Law of 250 (Girard), 200
Law of agency, 364–365
Laying off employees, 434
Leadership. *See also* Management
    ethical, 434–440
    styles of, 417–418
    time management and, 419–420
Lean Launch Pad, 131
The Lean Startup (Ries), 131
Lean Start Up process, 98
Leasehold improvements, 395
Lee, Jimmie, 346–348
Lee, Steve, 277–280
Lee's Ice Cream, 346–349
Legal issues
    agency law, 364–365
    bankruptcy, 365–367
    case studies, 380–383
    contracts, 361–363
    human resource compliance to labor law,
        431–432

intellectual property, 367–371
    licenses, permits, and certificates, 374–375
    risk management, 371–374
    Uniform Commercial Code (UCC), 364
Legal structures. *See* Business legal structures
Lerner, Ben, 51
Lerner, Sandy, 30
Letters of agreement, 363
Leveraged companies, 322
Leverage (debt) ratios, 525
Levied fee, 236
Liabilities
    in balance sheet, 256, 258, 261
    defined, 53
    in financial section of business plan, 53
Liability insurance, 372
Libraries, research at, 133
Licenses, 375
    as path to ownership, 20
Licensing
    growth through, 461–462
    to profit from brand, 461
Licensing technology, 20, 21–22
Lifestyle businesses, 22
Lifestyle marketing, 174
Limited liability company (LLC)
    compared with other business legal
        structures, 359
    explained, 358
    tax issues with, 305
Limited partnership, 305, 355, 359
Lindahl, Sheena, 120–121
Line and staff organization, 428
Line extension, 462
Line organization, 428
LinkedIn, 177
Liquidation, 366, 464
Liquidation value, 113
Liquidity, 265
Liz Claiborne, 461
Loan funds, community development, 329
Loans
    bonds, 333, 335–336
    policy, 331
    as source of financing, 239, 324, 327–328
Location
    in business plan, 50
    as factor of competitive advantage, 101
    factors affecting, 166
    home-based businesses and, 398
    importance of, 390–391
    key factors in deciding on a, 165–166,
        391–394
    as part of marketing mix, 158, 164–165
Logos, 367
    brand personality and, 161
    consistency of marketing materials
        and, 171
    creating, 160
    defined, 160
Long-term assets, 258
Long-term liabilities, 258
Love Café, 313, 314
Low risk investments, 333
Lurking, defined, 201

Magazines, advertising through, 171
Maguire, Chris, 317
Mah, Jessica, 287
Main Seed Capital Tax Credit Program, 340
Mainstream small firms, 23
Malcolm Baldrige Award, 402–403
Malden Mills, 460
Malia Mills Swimwear, 194–195
Mall carts, 173

Management. *See also* Leadership
  advertising, 169
  in business plan, 50
  human resources, 430–434
  organizational structure for, 428, 430
  performance, 432–434
Management buyout (MBO), 467
Managers, 420–421
Manufacturing businesses
  defined, 386
  economic order quantity (EOQ) and, 390
  economics of one unit (EOU), 109
  facilities design and layout considerations
    for, 395
  production-distribution chain and, 386–387
  unit of sale and, 107
Manufacturing companies, 386
MapPoint software, 394
Market
  analysis of, 37–39, 185
  defined, 93, 130
  saturated, 146
Marketable securities, 266
Marketing
  alternative types of, 174–175
  amplified buzz, 174
  case studies, 153–155
  cause-related, 182–183
  defined, 130
  direct, 49
  e-active, 175–178
  as a fixed cost, 185–187
  guerilla, 174
  in-store, 174–175
  interactive, 176
  research for, 130–131
  stealth, 177
  viral, 178
  word-of-mouth, 174
Marketing communications
  as a fixed cost, 185–187
  promotion and, 165–166
  unique selling proposition and, 166–167
Marketing mix. *See also* Promotion
  in business plan, 49
  case studies, 192–195
  creating a total product/service concept,
    158–159
  defined, 49
  four factors of, 157–158
  place (location) in, 158, 164–165
  price in, 158, 162–164
  product in, 157, 158–161
  promotion in, 158, 165–182
Marketing plan, 147
  analysis of market for, 185
  in business plan, 49
  defined, 49
  developing, 184–185
  philanthropy, 182–184
  primary roles of, 185
  stand-alone plan, 185
Market ratios, 525
Market research
  collecting data from market segment, 144
  competitive advantage and, 101
  customer, 135–137
  customer relationship management and,
    209–210
  defined, 134
  industry, 137–138
  questioning market segment, 143–144
  selling and, 198
Market segment/segmentation, 141–146
  applying methods of, 142–143
  Body Shop and, 142

  data collection from, 144
  defined, 141
  methods, 142–144
  targeting specific, 142
Markkula, Mike, 94, 107
Markup pricing, 163
Maturity, defined, 335
McCormick, Tom, 153
McDonald, Maurice, 129
McDonald, Richard, 129
McDonald's, 21, 129, 140, 197, 462
Media, publicity and, 180
Meenan, Sean, 317
Meet-or-beat-the-competition pricing, 163–164
Mental Floss (magazine), 106
Mentors, 11, 13
Mentzer, Josephine Esther, 267
Mercedes-Benz, 157
Mergers, 468
Metropolitan Fiber Systems (MFS), 459
Microenterprises, 22
Microsoft, 8, 182, 183, 237
Microsoft MapPoint software, 394
Microsoft Office Accounting, 237
Military, college degrees for, 139
Millennial Generation, 6
Mills, Malia, 194–195
Minimum viable products (MVP), 98
Minority Business Development Agency
  (MBDA), 523
Minority Business Development Centers
  (MBDCs), 523
Minority Enterprise Small Business Investment
  Companies (MESBICs), 331
Minority-owned businesses, 16, 141
Misner, Ivan, 215
Mission, of a business, 47
Mission statements, 47, 96–97
Mobile social networking, 177
Monetary reasons for starting a business, 6–7
Money
  future value of, 301–303
  present value of, 303–304
Monster.com, 422
MooBella, LLC, 245–246
MOOT Corp., 56
Morgan, J.P., 184
Morningstar, 334
Most Chocolate Cake Company, 96–97,
  103–105, 111
Mrs. Fields Cookies, 4
Multigenerational family-owned-and-operated
  businesses, 460
Mycoskie, Blake, 160
MySpace, 177

NAFTA (North American Free Trade
  Agreement), 5
NAICS (North American Industry Classification
  System), 137
Nalebuff, Barry, 43, 477–478, 480
National Association for the Self-Employed
  Future Entrepreneur of the Year
  Award, 524
National Association of Women Business
  Owners (NAWBO), 523
National Conference of Commissioners on
  Uniform State Laws, 364
National Credit Union Administration
  (NCAU), 329
National Institute of Standards and Technology
  (NIST), 403
National Minority Supplier Development
  Council, 141
National Venture Capital Association (NVCA),
  333

Native American Business Development Centers
  (NABDCs), 523
Negative cash balance, on income
  statement, 288
Negotiation
  for determining value of a business, 113
  of payment, 299
  of salary, 424, 426
Net present value (NPV), 229
Net profit, 234, 263
Net profit/(loss), in income statement, 252
Network for Teaching Entrepreneurship
  (NFTE), 183, 200, 370
Networking, 182
Net worth, 53, 256
New Early Entrepreneur Wonders (NEEW)
  Student Venture Fund, 192
New Market Venture Capital Companies
  (NMVCCs), 331
Newspapers, advertising through, 171
Newton, David, 469
New Venture Creation, 101
New York Stock Exchange, 334, 357
NFIB Young Entrepreneur Award, 524
NFTE (Network for Teaching
  Entrepreneurship), 183, 200, 370
NFTE Global Young Entrepreneur of the
  Year, 524
Nike, 130
Nine Dragons Paper (Holdings)
  Limited, 391
Nitti, Alejo, 160
Nokia, 146
Noncash expenses, 289
Nonprofit corporations. *See* Not-for-profit
  organizations
North American Free Trade Agreement
  (NAFTA), 5
*North American Industrial Classification System:
  United States, 2007*, 137
North American Industry Classification System
  (NAICS), 137
Notary, 355
Not-for-profit organizations, 182, 183–184, 358,
  359, 360
NYSE Euronext, 334

Objections, sales call, 204–205
Observation
  industry research through, 138
  primary research through, 132
Offer, in business definition, 94
Office for Harmonization in the Internal
  Market, 368
Onassis, Aristotle, 197
O'Neal, Sean, 276
One unit, economics of, 108–112
ONLC Training Centers, 453–456
Online businesses, 164–165
Online marketing, 175–178
Online networking, for financing,
  332–333
Online searches, 133
Online social networks, 177
Operating-efficiency ratios, 268
Operating ratio, 265
Operational plans, 421
Operations. *See also* Location; Quality
  in business plan, 50
  case studies, 411–415
  defined, 386
  home-based businesses, 398
  production-distribution chain, 386–387
  supply chain management, 387–390
  technology for, 403–405
  for web-based businesses, 398–399

Opportunities
  of business ideas, 18
  case studies, 119–126
  characteristics of, 17
  decision processes, 98, 99
  external, 18–19
  five roots of, 18
  identification of, 15–18, 98
  internal, 18–19
  as situational, 18
  SPANX case study in, 123–126
Opportunity costs, 11
Oprah Winfrey Leadership Academy
  Foundation, 125
Organic buzz marketing, 174
Organizational chart, 50
Organizational culture, 428, 429
Organizational development, in human
  resources, 431
Orientation, employee, 427
Osterwalder, Alexander, 40
Osterwald-Pigneur canvas, 40, 41
Outdoor media, advertising through, 171
Owner's equity, 53, 256. *See also* Net worth
Owner's equity (OE), in balance sheet, 256
Ownership, paths to small business,
  20–23

Pacesetting leadership style, 418
Packard, David, 428
Palic, Jim, 453, 454–456
Pan Shiyi, 95
Par (bond), 335
Partnerships
  caution with, 355–356
  compared with other business legal
    structures, 359
  defined, 355
  taxes issues with, 305
Patents, 370–371
Payback period, 228–229
Payment, negotiating, 299
Pay-per-click (PPC) advertising, 176, 178
Payroll, in human resources department, 431
Payroll taxes, 431
Peachtree Accounting, 237
Peachtree Software, 237
Pearson, Will, 106
Pemberton, John Stith, 353
Penetration pricing, 163
Percentage of sales, used for promotional
  budget, 168-169
Performance appraisal, 432–434
Permits, 375
Personal guarantees, 327–328
Personal interviews, 131–132
Personalized (dynamic) pricing, 164
Personal selling, 197. *See also* Selling
PERT charts, 56
Peters, Tom, 385
Pet Rock, 145
Petty, William, 463
Philanthropy, 182–184, 192
Pigneur, Yves, 40
Pilferage, 296
Pitch letter, 179, 180
P'Kolino, 56
Place, as part of marketing mix, 158, 164–165.
  See also Location
Point-of-purchase promotion, 175
Point-of-sales (POS) systems, 404
Policy loans, 331
Porter, Michael, 19, 20, 37, 39
Position description, 422
Positioning, 146–147, 174
Positively Outrageous Service (POS), 207

Povlitz, David R., 473–474
Preferred stock, 334
Premium(s), 335, 371–372
Prequalifying a sales call, 201
Presentation
  of business plan, 44
  sales, 199
Present value, 303–304
Press releases, 179, 180, 181
Prestige pricing, 163
Pre-tax profit, on income statement, 252
Price
  as part of marketing mix, 158, 162–164
  sales objections and, 204
Price lining strategy, 164
Pricing
  in business plan, 49
  cost-plus, 163
  follow-the-leader, 164
  markup, 163
  meet-or-beat-the-competition, 163–164
  penetration, 163
  personalized (dynamic), 164
  prestige, 163
  skimming, 163
  strategies for effective, 162–164
  value, 163
  variable, 164
Primary research, 131–132
Principal (debt financing), 320
Process management, 401–402
Product(s)
  analyzing feasibility of, 36–37
  belief in, and selling, 199
  benefit of, in business plan, 49
  benefits *vs.* features of, 140
  defined, 3
  as part of marketing mix, 157, 158–161
  quality, 399–400
  refining your total, 158–159
  selling and knowing your, 199
  service *vs.*, 158
Product advertising, 170
Production, defining your, 94
Production-distribution chain, 386–387
Product liability insurance, 372
Product life cycle (PLC)
  defined, 144
  illustration of, 145
  stages of, 144–145
  understanding where product/service
    is in the, 145–146
Product placement, 174
Product/trade name franchising, 21
Product-uniqueness strategies, 19
Professional corporation (PC), 358
Professional development, in human resources
  department, 431
Profit
  defined, 23
  entrepreneur's choices and, 23–24
  gross, 107, 108, 252
  in income statements, 252, 253–254
  necessity of, 23
  negative cash flow with, 288
  quality and, 399–400
  as signal to entrepreneur, 23
Profitability, calculating, 108–109
Profitability ratios, 525
Profit and loss statement (P&L), 53
Profit margin (return on sales),
  264–265
Promissory notes, 320
Promotion. *See also* Advertising
  advertising and, 165
  budget for, 167–169

  in business plan, 49
  integrated marketing communications
    and, 165–167, 185–187
  as part of marketing mix, 158, 165
  planning, 167–169
  publicity and, 165
  reinforcing competitive advantage,
    171–172
  sales promotion methods, 172–173
Promotional planning, 167–169
Proof of market, 48
Property insurance, 372
Prospects, sales call, 201
Prototype, 36, 226
Psychographic market segmentation, 142
Public agencies, research through, 133
Public benefit corporations, 358
Public domain, 370
Publicity
  in business plan, 49
  community involvement and, 180–182
  generating, 179
  pitch letters, 179
  press releases, 179, 180, 181
  promotion and, 165
  story of interest for, 179–180
Publicly traded companies, 254–255
Public relations, 49, 179
Public speaking, 182
Purchasing
  customer practices, 139–140

Quality
  benchmarking and, 400–401
  competitive advantage and, 101, 103, 105
  defined, 399
  ISO standards for, 401–402
  Malcolm Baldridge Award for, 402–403
  profits following, 399–400
  Six Sigma, 402
  total quality management, 402
Questionnaires, market research, 143–144
Questions, interview, 425
QuickBooks, 237
Quick ratio, 266
Quigg, Vincent, 200
Quintiles Transnational Corporation, 255

Radio advertising, 171
Rainert, Alex, 31
Ratio analysis, 55, 262–268
Ratios
  formulas and equations for, 525
  income statement, 262–265
  operating-efficiency, 268
The Rebel Billionaire (TV reality show), 125
Record-keeping, 199, 235–238
Recruitment, 421–427
Red Cross, 183
References
  asking for, 203
  checking for employee, 424
Registration, for sole proprietorship,
  354–355
Regulations, complying with, 374–375
Rent the Runway, 10
Rent What? Inc., 415
Reorder point (ROP), 389
Reorganization, 365–366
Replacement value, 113
Replication strategies, 461–462
Research. *See also* Market research
  levels of, 130
  methods, 131–133, 138
  as ongoing part of business, 138–139
  before opening your business, 130–131

Research (*Continued*)
primary, 131–132
secondary, 133–134
Research reports, 136–137
Resources
scarce, 4
value added to, 4
Resumes, 422
Retail businesses, 386
economics of one unit (EOU), 109
facilities for, 396
location and, 390–391, 396
online, 164–165
point-of-sales systems used by, 404
production-distribution chain and, 386, 387
unit of sale and, 107
Retained (employee) searches, 427
Return on investment (ROI), 263, 318
Return on sales (ROS), 264–265
Revenue
defined, 239
as part of income statement, 252
Revenue Streams (R$), in business plan, 42, 43
Revson, Charles, 129
Rich, Adam, 51
Ries, Al, 460
Ries, Eric, 131
Risk management, 371–374
Risk Management Association (RMA), 55, 133, 138
Risks and assumptions, in business plan, 55
Risk tolerance, 319
Rivalry, evaluating, 38
Rockefeller, John D., 237
Rockefeller Foundation, 184
Rocket Rollerskate Co., 266
Roddick, Anita, 16, 142
Ross, Jason, 51
Roth, Ryan, 483
Royalties, 20
Rubin, Rick, 19, 24, 154
RunTunes, 31
Rural businesses, 331, 332
Rural Business Investment Companies (RBICs), 331
Rural Entrepreneurship Center, 47
Rush Communications, 154, 155

Safety stock, 389
Salary
benefits of entrepreneurship and, 9
defined, 8
negotiating, 424, 426
self-payment through, 418
Sales calls
analyzing your, 204
appointment for, 200
eight-step, 202–203
electronic methods of, 200–201
focusing on customer during, 201–202
objections during, 204–205
objectives for, 200
prequalifying, 201
prospects for, 201
salesperson's behaviors for successful, 203–204
technology used for, 205
"warm" calls for, 199
Sales presentations, 199
Sales promotions, 172–173
Sales taxes, 304, 305
Samples (product), 175
Sampling, as sales promotional tool, 172
Sara Blakely Foundation, 125

Saturated market, 146
Say, Jean-Baptiste, 4
SBA Young Entrepreneur of the Year, 524
Scandals, corporate ethical, 436–437
Scarce resources, 4
Schachter, Joshua, 317
Schneider, J.B., 56
Schoppik, Haim, 317
Schumpter, Joseph, 15
Schupp, Sara, 43, 197, 483
S corporations, 305, 359
Sculley, John, 323
Secondary research, 131, 133–134
Securities, 335
Securities and Exchange Commission (SEC), 133
Seed capital, 226. *See also* Start-up costs
Self-employment tax, 304
Self-funding, 332
Selling
business success and, 197
commission and, 198
customer service and, 206
market research and, 198
principles of, 198–200
teaching as essence of, 198
Selvadurai, Naveen, 31–33
Series limited liability company (SLLC), 358
Service(s)
analyzing feasibility of, 36–37
belief in, and selling, 199
benefit of, in business plan, 49
defined, 3
economics of one unit (EOU), 109
online, 165
product *vs.*, 158
refining your total, 158–159
selling and knowing your, 199
unit of sale and, 107
Service companies, 386
ISO certification and, 401
Service Corps of Retired Executives (SCORE), 523
Service marks, 367–368
The Seven Habits of Highly Effective People (Covey), 463
Severance, 434
Sew What?, Inc., 413–415
Shah, Rishi, 162
Share (stock), 334
Shelf placement promotion, 175
ShoeSite.com, 93
Shulman, Nat, 459
Signal One Vocal Smoke Alarm, 21
Signatory, 363
Simmons, Michael, 120–121
Simmons, Russell, 19, 24, 154–155
Singer Sewing Machine Company, 463
Situational opportunities, 18
Situation analysis, 185
Six Pillars of Character, 436
Six Sigma, 402
Sizzle It!, 297
Skimming pricing strategy, 163
Small Business Administration (SBA), 523
Small Business Administration, Office of Advocacy, 6
Small Business Development Center (SBDC), 57
Small businesses
customer relationship management (CRM) and, 210
defined, 6
facts on, 6

failure of, 318
mainstream, 23
microenterprises, 22
paths to ownership of, 20–23
Small Business Investment Companies (SBICs), 331
Small claims court, 363
Small Parts Manufacturing Inc. (SPM), 399
Smith, Adam, 250, 251
Smith, Kristen, 178
SMI Ventures, 51
Smolinsky, Steve, 202
Snyder, Esther, 387
Snyder, Harry, 387
Social business, 14
Social entrepreneurship, 13–14, 438
Social media, advertising opportunities through, 177
Social networks, for sales calls, 200–201
Social responsibility, 438–440, 479
Software
accounting, 237
for assessing location, 394
business plan, 44
customer relationship management (CRM), 210–211
SOHO China, 95
Sole proprietorship, 305, 353–355, 359
Spam, 201
Span of control, 428
SPANX, 123–126
Spiraling, brand, 177
Sponsorships, 182
Standard and Poor's *Industry Surveys*, 137
Standards, quality management, 401–402
Staples Youth Social Entrepreneurship Competition, 524
Starbucks, 157
Start-up costs
in business plan, 51, 52
cash reserve equal to one-half of, 227–228
checklist for, 228
explained, 226
payback period and, 228–229
preventing surprises in, 226–227
for 24-hour fitness center, 2327
Start-up Digest website, 15
Statement of fund flow (cash flow statement), 294
Statistics
government, 137
industry research and, 138
population data, 137
research companies providing, 136–137
Statute of limitations, 363
Stealth marketing, 177
Stockbroker, 334
Stocks, 319, 333, 334–335
Stone, Biz, 168
Stone, W. Clement, 197
Stone Hill Winery, 400
Store layout, 396
Strategic plans, 421
Strategy(ies)
defined, 19, 106
establishing, 19–20
tactics *vs.*, 106
Strengths, of business idea, 18
The Student Success Manifesto (Simmons), 120
Subchapter S corporations, 357
Substitutes, threat of, 38
Success, definitions of, 6–7

Suh, Andy, 287
Sumutka, Andrew, 342
SunRocks, 132
Suppliers
    finding, 388
    location decisions and, 391
    power of, 38–39
    production-distribution chain and, 387
Supply chain management, 387–390
Surveys
    for customer research, 136
    market research, 144, 243–244
    telephone, 132
    written, 132
Sustainable businesses, 440
Sustainable competitive advantage, 99, 102, 105
Sweet dis(Solve), 370
Swinmurn, Nick, 93
SWOT analysis, 18, 55
Sydney, Robin, 132
Szaky, Tom, 3, 47

Table of contents, for business plan, 46
Tactical plans, 421
Tactics, 106
Tandy, 93
Tangible assets, protecting, 367–371
Target market
    analysis of, 37–39
    in business plan, 48
    defined, 48
    defining your, 94
    resources for learning more about, 167
    understanding media habits in, 170–171
TARP (Technical Assistance Research Programs Institute), 209
Tax abatement, 319
Tax credit, 319
Tax deductions, 237
Taxes
    cash flow and, 304
    corporations and, 356–357
    I-9 form, 426–427
    in income statement, 252
    legal structure and, 305–306
    payroll, 431
    sales, 304, 305
    self-employment, 304
Tax evasion, 437
Tax returns, filing, 304–305
Teach for America, 183
Team approach, 24–25
TechCrunch website, 15
Technology. *See also* Internet
    Amazon.com's use of, 217–218
    computer access and, 403–404
    customer relationship management (CRM) and, 211
    electronic storefront, 405
    exploiting changes in, 15
    market-specific software and technology, 404–405
    during sales call, 205
    telephone and, 404
TechWorld, 200
Telephone, potential of, 404
Telephone manners, 211
Telephone surveys, 132
Television, advertising through, 171
Tennessee Bun Company, 380
TerraCycle Inc., 3, 14, 47
Threats, in business ideas, 18
Thrillist.com site, 51

Time, having control over, 8
Time management, 419–420
Timmons, Jeffry A., 4, 101
Title VII of the Civil Rights Act of 1964, 432
TOMS Shoes, 160
Total quality management, 402
Toyota, 163
Tracking, as research method, 133, 138
Trade associations, 138
Trade barriers, 5
Trademarks, 367–368
Trade offs, 23, 24
Trade show exhibits, 172–173
Training, for franchisors, 462
Tropeano, Bruno, 340
Trump, Donald, 296, 322
TuitionBids.com, 178
Turbo Dynamix, 245
Turco-Rivas, Antonio, 56
Twitter, 168
Tyco, 436

Ultimate Business Planner (software), 44
Uniform Commercial Code (UCC), 364
Uniform resource locators (URLs), 404
Union Square Ventures, 317
Unique selling proposition (USP), 102–103, 166–167
United States Department of Agriculture (USDA), 523
Unit of sale, 107, 108
University of New Hampshire Center for Venture Research, 330
University Parent
    Business Model Canvas for, 42, 43
    business plan, 43
University Parent, Inc. Business Plan, 483–510
University Parent Media, 197
Upromise, 183–184
UPS (United Parcel Service), 102
Urban Decay, 30
Urban Neighborhood Enterprise Economic Club (U.N.E.E.C.), 192
URLs (uniform resource locators), 404
U.S. Census Bureau, 394
U.S. Department of Labor, 136
U.S. Internal Revenue Service (IRS), 304–305, 306, 360
U.S. Patent and Trademark, Principle Register Office, 368
U.S. Postal Service, 102
U.S. Securities and Exchange Commission, 255
U.S. Small Business Administration, 22
UUNET Technologies Inc., 439

Valuation methods of, 113–114
ValueLine, 334
Value of a business, determining, 113–114, 464–465
Value pricing strategy, 163
Value Proposition (VP), in business plan, 41–42, 43
Variable costs (VC), 230, 231–232, 235–238, 239, 252
Variable pricing strategy, 164
Venture capitalists, 329–330
    global, 333
Venture Frog Incubators, 93
Venture-funding competitions, 59–60
Venture philanthropy, 14
Verner, Adam, 119
Viral marketing, 178

Virgin Airlines, 9
Virgin Atlantic Airways, 101, 164
Virgin Corporation, 101
Virgin Galactic, 9
Virgin Group, 9
Virgin Megastores, 101
Virgin Mobile, 101
Virgin Records, 9
Viruses, computer, 373
Vision
    as broad perspective, 97
    in business plan, 47
    examples of, 97
VISTA Staffing Solutions, 464
Visual control, 388–389
Vocus Inc., 475
Voice-mail system, 404
Volume, selling in, 111
Voluntary exchange, 5
Volunteerism, 182, 183, 184
Volvo, 141, 142
Vostu, 367

Wages. *See also* Salary
    benefits of entrepreneurship and, 9
    defined, 9
    as form of self-payment, 419
Walker, Madam C. J., 417, 439
The Wall Street Journal, 133, 334
Wal-Mart, 164, 165
Warehousing firms, facilities design and layout considerations for, 395
Waxman, Nach, 219
Wealth
    defined, 263
    return on investment and, 263
Web-based businesses, 398–399
Web sites, for entrepreneurs, 522–523
Welch, Jack, 97, 287
Wenger, Albert, 317
Wetfeet.com, 137
Wholesale businesses, 386
    economics of one unit (EOU), 109
    production-distribution chain and, 386, 387
    unit of sale and, 107
Wikipedia, 133
Williams, Evan, 168
Williamson, Andy, 453, 454–456
Winfrey, Oprah, 124, 125, 159
Women-owned businesses, 16
Word-of-mouth advertising, 174
Word-of-mouth marketing, 174
Word-of-mouth survey, TARP, 210
Workers' compensation insurance, 372
Working capital, 289
Work-made-for-hire, electronic rights and, 369
WorldCom-MCI, 436, 459
World Trade Organization, 5
Wozniak, Stephen, 93, 106–107, 112, 158, 323
Written surveys, as research method, 132

YMCA, 183
Young Entrepreneur Council, 297
Yunus, Mohammad, 14, 439

Zappos.com, 93, 96
Zhang Xin, 95
Zhang Yin, 391
Zimmerman, Paul, 2
Zomnir, Wende, 30
Zoning regulations, 374
Zorbitz, Inc., 132
Zynga, 367